Second Edition

CyberLaw
Text and Cases

Gerald R. Ferrera
Bentley College

Stephen D. Lichtenstein
Bentley College

Margo E. K. Reder
Boston College

Robert C. Bird
Seton Hall University

William T. Schiano
Bentley College

THOMSON
™
SOUTH-WESTERN
WEST

Australia · Canada · Mexico · Singapore · Spain · United Kingdom · United States

THOMSON

SOUTH-WESTERN

WEST

CyberLaw: Text and Cases, 2e
Gerald R. Ferrera, Stephen D. Lichtenstein,
Margo E. K. Reder, Robert C. Bird, and William T. Schiano

VP/Editorial Director:
Jack W. Calhoun

VP/Editor-in-Chief:
George Werthman

Senior Acquisitions Editor:
Rob Dewey

**Senior Developmental
Editor:**
Jan Lamar

Marketing Manager:
Steven Silverstein

Production Editor:
Chris Hudson

**Media Developmental
Editor:**
Christine Wittmer

Media Production Editor:
Amy Wilson

Manufacturing Coordinator:
Rhonda Utley

Production House:
Trejo Production

Printer:
Phoenix Color,
Hagerstown, Maryland

Internal and Cover Design:
Bethany Casey

Internal Image:
Digital Vision, Ltd.

Cover Image:
Oliver Burston, Getty Images

In loving memory of Susan and Raymond Ferrera and Karna and Lawrence McCabe

—GRF

For my wife, Cindy, our children Jeff and Julie, and my parents, Max and Frances

—SDL

For my family, with gratitude for your encouragement throughout this project

—MEKR

For my father, Dennis, and my mother, Lois

—RCB

About the Authors

GERALD R. FERRERA received a B.S. from Boston College, an M.S. in taxation from Bentley College, and a J.D. from New England School of Law. He has co-authored texts in business law and legal environment and has written numerous law review articles. He was granted the Gregory H. Adamian Law Professorship, the first endowed chair of the law department at Bentley College. In 2002 he was awarded the Senior Faculty Award of Excellence from the Academy of Legal Studies in Business.

Publication awards include the Ralph C. Hoeber Award given by the Academy of Legal Studies in Business, numerous Bentley College publication awards, and the Bentley College Scholar of the Year Award. Teaching awards include the Charles M. Hewitt Excellence in Teaching Award granted from the Academy of Legal Studies in Business, and from Bentley College, the Gregory H. Adamian Teaching Award and the Innovative Teaching Award. He is the founder and executive director of the Bentley College CyberLaw Center. He was president of the North Atlantic Regional Business Law Association and currently serves on the Executive Committee and the board of editors of the *Business Law Review.* He was chair of the Bentley College Law department and is presently a research fellow at the Center for Business Ethics at Bentley College. He is also a member of the Massachusetts and federal bars.

STEPHEN D. LICHTENSTEIN has a B.S. from Boston College, a J.D. from Suffolk University Law School, and a Certificate in Mediation. He has authored and co-authored numerous law review articles on many business law–related topics. Publication awards include a Ralph C. Hoeber Award given by the Academy of Legal Studies in Business. He is the founder of the Bentley Consumer Action Line, a community-service learning program under the auspices of the Massachusetts attorney general's office, where students mediate actual consumer complaints against businesses. He is also co-director of the Bentley College CyberLaw Center. In 2000 he received the prestigious Bentley College Adamian Award for Excellence in Teaching. Professor Lichtenstein is past president of the North Atlantic Business Law Association, and he currently serves on the Executive Committee and the board of editors of the *Business Law Review.* He is a legal consultant to business and individuals and a member of the Massachusetts and federal bars. Currently, he is the chair of the Bentley College Law Department.

MARGO E. K. REDER is a Lecturer in Law at the Carroll School of Management, Boston College. Her courses in the M.B.A. program focus on e-commerce and cyberspace law. She has previously served as a prosecutor and counsel for a start-up. She is past president of the North Atlantic Regional Business Law Association and currently serves on both its executive and editorial boards. Ms. Reder has contributed to a number of legal texts and authored over twenty law review articles. She is widely cited for her work in securities regulation, arbitration, employment, international transactions, and most recently in the cyberlaw field. Ms. Reder graduated from the

University of Massachusetts, London School of Economics and Political Science, and Suffolk University Law School. She is a member of the state and federal bars.

ROBERT C. BIRD received his B.S. in information systems from Fairfield University, a J.D. from Boston University School of Law, and an M.B.A. from Boston University Graduate School of Management. He is currently an assistant professor of legal studies at Seton Hall University and has taught as an adjunct professor at Fairfield University and Sacred Heart University. Mr. Bird teaches undergraduate and graduate legal courses to business students. He presently serves as a staff editor to the *Journal of Legal Studies* and the *American Business Law Journal*. Also, he is a member of the Academy of Legal Studies in Business, the North Atlantic Regional Business Law Association, and the Northeast Academy of Legal Studies in Business. His research interests include contract law, employment law, and, of course, cyberlaw.

Mr. Bird's articles have appeared in the *Kentucky Law Review,* the *American Business Law Journal,* and the *William & Mary Journal of Women & the Law*. Besides being a two-time finalist in the Academy of Legal Studies in Business/Master Teacher Competition, he has won the Seton Hall University's Excellence in Teaching Award for his first year in full-time teaching, spring 2001. Mr. Bird is licensed to practice law in Connecticut and New York. He has also served as a law clerk to a number of courts including the Connecticut Appeals Court, the U.S. Bankruptcy Court, and the Massachusetts Superior Court. Mr. Bird also acts as an appellate adviser on civil legal matters, authoring a victorious legal brief for the plaintiffs in *Pequonnock Yacht Club v. City of Bridgeport,* 259 Conn. 592 (2002).

WILLIAM T. SCHIANO is an assistant professor and chair of the MIS department at Bentley College. He developed and taught two graduate MIS courses, "Information Technology Management and Policy" and "Electronic Commerce in the Global Economy," and he has written numerous articles, papers, and Harvard Business School cases. He is a VanDuyne Scholar from the Williams College Department of Economics, with other honors and awards that include participant in the 1995 Ernst & Young Foundation ICIS Doctoral Consortium and a Harvard University Fellowship.

Brief Contents

Contents

Part 2 Intellectual Property Issues in Cyberspace

3 Trademarks, 47

Part 3   Business and Financial Issues in Cyberspace

6   Online Contracting, 151

Part 4   Special Issues in Cyberspace

9   Privacy, 257

Preface

"Clicks and bricks" is a vital business model in today's competitive e-commerce environment. Managing in this milieu necessitates a basic understanding of cyberlaw as online business transactions develop at an exponential pace. Courts, legislatures, administrative agencies, and international directives all contribute to the e-commerce legal landscape of the 21st century. As digital technology continues to permeate every facet of business, the latest laws relevant to this phenomenon are explained and discussed in this second edition.

Since the first edition of *CyberLaw: Text and Cases,* we have witnessed the dot com demise, a languishing economy, an aggressive attitude by content providers to protect all of their intellectual property interests, a challenge to the U.S. Supreme Court on the duration of a copyright, an awareness of a loss of online privacy, and other dramatic new legal developments that we address in this second edition. The authors' predominant concern continues to be producing a textbook that will be useful to instructors in preparing business students to manage in the high-tech legal environment. Because the potential liability exposure of a contemporary business is so vast, understanding the legal consequences of e-commerce transactions is not a luxury for the business manager. This textbook explains and discusses the "corpus juris" of cyberlaw from a business and social perspective. The values of the U.S. Constitution and ethical dilemmas are addressed throughout the textbook. Global issues as they relate to each chapter are explained as an essential component of the online environment.

The authors hope that instructors and students enjoy this business journey through cyberspace as each chapter reveals the legal consequences of transactions in the online environment. We are striving to educate managers to understand the legal, social, and ethical consequences of their business decisions.

SUBJECT MATTER AND BASIC ORGANIZATION OF THE TEXT

The subjects covered follow a logical application of the legal issues surrounding e-commerce. The book's focus is on the needs of business managers working, in some fashion, in the online environment. The authors are convinced that this includes the needs of almost every business school graduate about to enter the work force.

ACCREDITATION

The subject matter of the textbook covers ethical, political, and international issues as well as a main focus on technology as it relates to the world of business. This makes a course in cyberlaw suitable for American Assembly of Collegiate Schools of Business (AACSB) accreditation.

OUTLINE OF THE TEXT

Part 1—Introduction to Cyberspace

Chapter 1—Technology and Cyberlaw. A revision of the chapter in the first edition, the authors discuss the technological infrastructure of the Internet and World Wide Web in the context of cyberlaw. The chapter offers a brief history of the Internet and outlines technologies such as firewalls, encryption, HTML, and cookies for nontechnical readers. The chapter broadens the focus on electronic commerce and updates the technology coverage to include filtering software and peer-to-peer technologies such as instant messaging and file sharing.

Chapter 2—Jurisdiction. Because e-commerce is global in nature, this chapter reviews the laws relevant to a court in a foreign state or country having personal jurisdiction over an e-business. This chapter reviews the laws relevant to a court's personal jurisdiction over a nonresident e-business, including the principles of national enforcement that define a country's power beyond its borders. The famous *Yahoo!/France* case is discussed along with *Pavlovich*, *Verizon Online Services*, and *America Online*.

Part 2—Intellectual Property Issues in Cyberspace

Chapter 3—Trademarks. Online liability exposure continues to focus on domain name arbitration and litigation. The laws of trademarks are explained with a discussion of the Anticybersquatting Consumer Protection Act, the Uniform Domain Name Dispute Resolution Policy, trademark infringement, and trademark dilution. Cases include a WIPO arbitration decision involving Julia Roberts and other cases such as *Checkpoint Systems*, *A.B.C. Carpet Company*, *E&J Gallo Winery*, and the leading meta-tag case of *Playboy Enterprises v. Welles*.

Chapter 4—Copyrights. The use of digital content in e-commerce continues to challenge conventional copyright laws regarding fair use. This chapter provides a general overview of copyright law as it applies to the online environment. The Digital Millennium Copyright Act is discussed along with leading cases, including the U.S. Supreme Court decision of *Eldred v. Ashcroft* on the duration of a copyright, and *Napster* and the *Religious Technology Center* cases.

Chapter 5—Business Methods Patents and Trade Secrets. An entirely new chapter, this material covers all aspects of managing these forms of intellectual property. We discuss legal and businesses strategies, as well as how to manage challenges relating to claims, inventorship, and infringement. Often overlooked as an alternative, we provide ample discussion of trade secrets, along with recent cases. These cases cover disputes involving: Amazon, Barnes & Noble, Pepsi, Priceline.com, State Street Bank & Trust Company, and Signature Financial Group.

Part 3—Business and Financial Issues in Cyberspace

Chapter 6—Online Contracting. A revision of the previous chapter, this material covers critical legal aspects of forming, performing, and enforcing online contracts.

This chapter examines the requirements for creating a contract, online warranties, and other terms of use provisions common in cyberspace. The Uniform Computer Information Transactions Act and the Uniform Electronic Transactions Act are also reviewed, with up-to-date commentary on interpretations of these important acts. After a discussion of electronic signatures and software licensing, the chapter discusses recent issues arising from shrinkwrap agreements, e-commerce insurance policies, and international matters.

Chapter 7—Sales Tax in E-Commerce. An e-business must consider the potential obligation of collecting sales tax on behalf of the state where it has a tax nexus. This chapter reviews the U.S. Constitution's limitation on tax jurisdiction, the Internet Tax Freedom Act, sales tax and the dormant commerce clause, the latest development of the Streamline Sales Tax Project, along with the leading cases in this area, including National Bellas Hess and the leading U.S. Supreme Court case of *Quill Corp. v. North Dakota.*

Chapter 8—Online Securities Offerings and Transactions. A revision of the previous chapter, this material condenses coverage of the laws governing online offerings and expands coverage of online transactions. The chapter focuses on why capital is needed, where to find capital, and the offering process. We have selected entirely new cases, and we cover disputes involving such issues as selling stock in virtual companies, Internet offerings of nonexistent shares, investors suing after enormous price declines in the stock, and financial publishers duped into publishing false press releases in which share prices are consequently affected. The cases cover disputes involving SG, Ltd., Abacus International Holdings, Max Internet Communications, Internet Wire, and Bloomberg News.

Part 4—Special Issues in Cyberspace

Chapter 9—Privacy. This chapter has been revised and updated. It retains discussions of the sources of the right to privacy but expands the discussion of privileged communications under state law. Major emphasis is placed on recent federal legislation including the collection and use of personal information contained in medical (Gramm-Leach-Bliley Act of 1999) and financial records (Health Insurance Portability and Accountability Act of 1996). New materials are presented regarding children's privacy, identity theft, pretexting, Carnivore—the FBI's surveillance tool, and spam. The *DoubleClick* case has been added to the discussion of the Electronic Communications Privacy Act (ECPA) as well as a new section regarding the Pen Register Act (Title III of the ECPA). Workplace privacy has been expanded to include new cases as well as suggestions for a computer usage and monitoring policy. The chapter concludes with a focus on the major global privacy issues with emphasis on the European Privacy Directive.

Chapter 10—Obscenity. The Internet allows the publication of pornography and obscene material. This chapter has updated discussions of the relevant cases and legislation regarding the ongoing, albeit ineffective, efforts of Congress to protect children from pornography and the issues posed to these efforts by the First Amendment. Two new cases are presented. *U.S. v. Playboy Entertainment Group* involves the issues surrounding blocking children's access to adult cable programming, and *Ashcroft v. American Civil Liberties Union* involves the issue of whether or not community standards can be used to determine if material is obscene and therefore not suitable for children. The sections on employee access to adult Web sites and global obscenity issues have also been updated.

Chapter 11—Defamation. Cyberspace is a forum for defamatory speech. This chapter focuses on the major issues of defamation in cyberspace. There are revisions, updated discussions, cases, and materials related to the issues of jurisdiction and defamation, and the liability and immunity for service providers under the Communications Decency Act of 1996. A new section on anonymous speech has been added, including a discussion of the so-called *John Doe* cases in which a plaintiff in a suit for defamation attempts to obtain a subpoena to determine the identity of the alleged defamer. One such recent case is *Dendrite International, Inc. v. John Doe*. There is also a new section on SLAPP suits (Strategic Lawsuits Against Public Participants) in which corporations, government officials, and others attempt to use defamation suits against plaintiffs who express their opinions, criticisms, and comments online. The chapter concludes with revised discussions of the international issues of defamation. *Ellis v. Time, Inc.,* is presented to illustrate a case where a plaintiff attempted to convince a U.S. court to apply English libel law to allegedly defamatory statements and an e-mail message posted online in England.

Chapter 12—Internet and Information Security. A revision of the first edition chapter, we first discuss the purposes of information security and how this is achieved—a complex effort due to the open architecture of the Internet. Major emphasis is on transactional security systems, especially those involving cryptography. We outline the major challenges to the use of cryptography. Finally, we review government efforts to promote information security. Focus is on how these efforts—such as the USA Patriot Act, Carnivore/DCS-1000 and Magic Lantern/Key Logger Systems—impact our constitutional rights. There are five new cases in this chapter, and just one case from the first edition: *Corley, Junger, Bernstein, Scarfo, Kyllo,* and *Karn*.

Chapter 13—Internet and Computer Crime. A revision of the first edition chapter, we discuss the various crimes being perpetrated over the Internet and how the Internet's architecture and relatively lax security procedures produce the perfect environment for Internet crime. We cite those laws that address cybercrime. Emphasis is on the business environment as well as on government functions. Finally, we discuss cyberterrorism and the government response to it. There are three new cases, and two cases from the first edition: *Sample, Free Speech Coalition, Czubinski, Morris,* and *Rothberg*.

FEATURES

Manager's Checklist. Each chapter provides a Manager's Checklist that offers suggestions useful to business managers working in online environments in an effort to reduce their companies' liability exposure. Also included in this section are ethical issues that relate to the chapter topic. These checklists help blend the practical with the necessary theoretical legal analysis found in the case decisions.

Web sites. Throughout the textbook Web sites are noted that apply to the subject matter. They can be used for additional reading, legal resources, and topics of interest. The majority of these sites are called out in "http://" boxes integrated throughout the text.

End-of-chapter short cases. Five cases are included at the end of each chapter for classroom testing or discussion of the material.

Appendices. Brief annotations from selected statutes relevant to the material covered in the text are found in the appendix at the end of the text. When available, we also provide the URL where the entire statute can be found.

SUPPLEMENTS

An **Instructor's Manual**, prepared by the text authors, is available. For each chapter, the manual includes a chapter summary, a chapter outline, a suggested lecture outline, answers to the case questions, a suggested student assignment, and answers to the end-of-chapter case problems.

A **Test Bank**, prepared by John Hayward, Bentley College, is available to adopters. It includes approximately 35 to 40 multiple-choice questions and 2 to 3 short essay questions per chapter.

A set of **PowerPoint slides** designed to enhance lectures is available to adopters.

A **Text Web Site** at *http://ferrera.westbuslaw.com* is available for both instructors and students. It contains links to Web sites referenced in the text and case updates. Both students and instructors can download the PowerPoint slides from this Web site. Also, instructors can download the Instructor's Manual and the Test Bank (both are also available in print form).

Westlaw. Ten complimentary hours of Westlaw are available to qualified adopters from West's premier legal research system.

West's Video Library. Qualified adopters may choose from West's vast video library including Court TV® and Drama of the Law videos. For a complete listing of videos that are available, go to *http://www.westbuslaw.com*.

ACKNOWLEDGMENTS

We would like to thank the following reviewers of this book for taking time from their demanding schedules and providing their helpful suggestions:

Jason Ashford
Macon State College

Jeanne Calderon
New York University

Mark Conrad
Fordham University

Lori K. Harris-Ransom
Caldwell College

John C. Lautsch
California State University, Fullerton

Owen McWhorter, Jr.
Texas Tech University

Pamela Samuelson
University of California at Berkeley

Diana Walsh
New Jersey Institute of Technology

We are thankful for the excellent work and advice of the West/Thomson Learning publishing team—Rob Dewey, Steve Silverstein, Chris Hudson—and especially Jan Lamar, whose guidance and counsel have been most appreciated and invaluable.

The Bentley College authors wish to thank President Joseph Morone, and former vice president and dean of faculty, H. Lee Schlorff, for their continued support and enthusiasm for this project, and chancellor and former president of Bentley College, Gregory H. Adamian, for his support and encouragement over the years; Roseann Cotoni, administrative assistant of the Law Department, for her assistance; and graduate student assistants Maria Pere-Perez and Li Zhu for their work on the Bentley College CyberLaw Center that provides valuable links to material relevant to the chapters in this textbook. In particular, Gerald Ferrera would like to thank his graduate assistant Li Zhu for her research on portions of his manuscript.

The Boston College author, Margo E. K. Reder, wishes to recognize the entire faculty and staff at the Carroll School of Management for encouraging this project and for its Celebration of Scholarship. Particular thanks are due to Christine Neylon O'Brien, chair of the Business Law Department. She has cheered me on for fifteen years, and through her example, showed me how to excel—always with kindness and humor. Finally, I wish to thank Dave Twomey, past chair of the Business Law Department, for his interest in faculty development, and as an example to me in achieving high teaching standards.

Gerald R. Ferrera
Stephen D. Lichtenstein
Margo E. K. Reder
Robert C. Bird
William T. Schiano

List of Cases

Note: The principal cases are in **bold** type. Cases cited or discussed in the text are in roman type.

Part 1

Introduction to Cyberlaw

TECHNOLOGY AND CYBERLAW

I honestly believe, without hyperbole, that the people in this room are doing things which will change the world more than anything since the capture of fire.

—John Perry Barlow, Electronic Frontier Foundation co-founder, USENIX Conference Keynote Address, January 1994

LEARNING OBJECTIVES

After you have read this chapter, you should be able to:

1. Briefly explain how the Internet and World Wide Web evolved and how they work.
2. Understand some of the terminology and technology of the Internet.
3. Explain how businesses and consumers connect to and use the Internet.
4. Understand security risks and remedies of the Internet.
5. Understand the challenges of regulating Internet traffic and commerce.
6. Understand the impact of globalization on the Internet.
7. Describe some of the legal issues related to the use of the Internet.

INTRODUCTION

The Internet has dramatically changed commerce. Hundreds of millions of people, most large businesses, and a growing number of small businesses throughout the world routinely use the Internet for purchasing, information, research, finance, and correspondence. The most often discussed facet of such electronic commerce, or e-commerce, is business to consumer (B2C), that is, the sale of goods and services to consumers over the World Wide Web. Estimates of retail e-commerce sales in 2002 ranged from $50 billion to $100 billion, and projections call for continued 20 to 40 percent annual growth. Although this represents a significant market, for perspective, Wal-Mart's 2002 sales, predominantly in traditional brick-and-mortar stores, were over $225 billion. Most B2C commerce has been conducted in more developed nations, particularly the United States. In contrast, business to business (B2B) commerce is expected to top $1 trillion in 2003, and the Internet, and especially the World Wide Web, have become a crucial infrastructure for transactions among businesses worldwide.

In the past, business managers had to know the basics of our legal system to understand the fundamentals of face-to-face business transactions. Now they must also understand the legal functioning of e-commerce as creative online business models radically change the legal environment of business.

Before we discuss and explain the new legal ramifications of Internet transactions, it will be helpful for you to understand the material in this introductory chapter. As you read the chapter, try to visualize how technology has changed traditional ways of doing business. Our courts and legislators are crafting a distinct body of laws, discussed in this textbook, which will assist you in understanding the online business environment.

Cyberlaw—law governing the use of computers and the Internet—focuses on a combination of state and federal statutory, decisional, and administrative laws arising out of the use of the Internet. These new laws often build on traditional laws that apply to brick-and-mortar companies and apply technology to e-commerce.

To discuss cyberlaw meaningfully, it is necessary to understand the potential and limits of the technology in question. This chapter establishes a brief background for the discussion of cyberlaw, from the history of the Internet to its current global use, and places this technology in a business context. To a great extent the material discussed in this chapter governs behavior and business transactions. Keep in mind that software and hardware can affect important cyberlaw issues such as privacy, contracts, and intellectual property rights.

HISTORY OF THE INTERNET

Most people think of the Internet as synonymous with the World Wide Web, but it is not. The Internet is a network of computer networks. The very name *Internet* comes from the concept of internetworking, where multiple computer networks are joined together. In the business arena, electronic mail (e-mail), file transfer, and chat rooms take place through the Internet; commerce and considerable information dissemination take place through the World Wide Web. Together they comprise a world of cyberspace where important legal issues are often raised.

The Internet began in 1969 as ARPANET, an effort by the U.S. Department of Defense to enable defense researchers at various sites across the country to communicate and collaborate. Many of these sites were large universities, and academics at those schools began using the Internet, especially e-mail, to communicate about non-defense matters. Other features included discussion groups, access to databases, and file transfers. In 1973, ARPANET became connected to more networks, including networks in other countries, and it evolved into the Internet. In the late 1980s, the National Science Foundation built its own network, and by 1990, ARPANET ceased to exist, although its functions lived on. Its history shows the Internet was never intended to be a commercial network, and until 1991, when the World Wide Web was developed, users were held to an acceptable use policy that expressly prohibited commercial applications.

HISTORY OF THE WORLD WIDE WEB

The World Wide Web began in 1991 at CERN (public.www.cern.ch/public), the European Laboratory for Particle Physics, as a way for physicists to exchange formatted academic and technical papers. Every researcher had access to the Internet by the 1980s, but there was no easy way to use it to display complex documents. In 1990, Tim Berners-Lee at CERN developed and named the World Wide Web, which became available for universal use on the Internet a year later. It was not until the early 1990s that e-commerce was taken seriously by the business world. Keep in mind that Amazon and Yahoo!, now household words, did not exist prior to this time.

How the Internet Works

To connect to the Internet, individuals and firms use **Internet service providers (ISPs)**, such as Sprint or EarthLink, for local and international connections. All users, whether commercial or individual, connect to their ISPs via communication lines—typically telephone lines, although increasingly other means such as satellite dishes and cable television lines are being used. The capacity, called the *bandwidth*, of the lines is determined by the needs of the business or individual. Slower connections use modems; while faster connections use other types of connectors, such as network interfaces.

Large ISPs are typically connected directly to the high-speed backbone of the Internet, and they often establish their own international networks to improve security and reliability for their customers. Smaller ISPs connect to the Internet by connecting to larger ISPs. Some services, such as America Online, serve as an ISP while also providing services not on the World Wide Web, such as member-only chat rooms, reference materials, and other content.

Internet Addresses

Every computer on the Internet has a unique **Internet protocol (IP)** address that consists of four series of three numbers ranging from 0 to 256, separated by periods. These numbers are important because they are required for communication from one computer to another. However, a string of up to twelve digits would be a cumbersome way to access sites, so the **domain name system (DNS)** was implemented in 1984. The DNS matches the numerical IP addresses of computers with text names in a manner similar to a telephone directory, which matches names with phone numbers. Each domain name is associated with a unique IP number. When a text address is typed into a browser (such as Internet Explorer) or sent as an e-mail message, the name is looked up (resolved) on a domain name server and the connection is made.

A domain name consists of a top-level domain name and a subdomain name. When the DNS was established, each country was assigned a country code as its top-level domain name. As an example, a site in England would have the top-level domain name ".uk" and the subdomain would be the specific site in the United Kingdom, such as "amazon.co.uk." In the United States, other top-level domains include .com for commercial sites, .gov for government sites, .net for networks, and .org for organizations. For example, *http://www.ustreas.gov* is the Web site on the Internet of the U.S. Treasury, and *http://www.ustreas.gov* is the Web site of the United Nations. In Great Britain, the top-level commercial domain name is .co (as in amazon.co.uk, or dmgt.co.uk, for the London newspaper the *Evening Standard*).

Domain names have a significant application in cyberlaw because conflicts often emerge between trademarks and domain names used by a competing company. Chapter 3, "Trademarks," discusses this in detail.

The Language of the Internet

Because many scientists used mainframe and UNIX workstation computers, file format compatibility was a major challenge for collaborative work. **Hypertext markup language (HTML)** was developed as a standard document format, and **hypertext transfer protocol (http)**, the http:// you see at the beginning of a Web address, as the way of exchanging such files. This means that HTML can be viewed on any type of computer, using any operating system, as long as it is equipped with an appropriate viewer, called a Web browser.

Accessing a Web Site

Within a given domain, there may be many different Web pages, each identified by a unique address called a **uniform resource locator (URL)**. A URL is simply the name of a file stored on a Web server. Accessing a Web page involves transferring files from a server computer to a client, or browser. Within a given Web page there may be many files, including pictures, sound, and video, for which the codes used to create them can be seen. This makes protecting the design of Web pages very difficult. For companies trying to protect their brand, the inability to control how these pages are found or the context in which they are displayed can be frustrating.

Transmitting Information

The Internet, like all computer networks, operates exclusively with digital transmissions, represented by zeroes and ones. All data on the Internet travels in small bundles called **packets**, and each packet includes a *header* with address information. A

http://web.dotster.com

single e-mail message might be sent as several packets. Figure 1.1 shows the contents of an Internet packet.

The packets travel to the addressee by passing through many other computers, and each computer examines the address information in the packet header and sends it to the next node in the network. Not every packet necessarily travels the same route; thus each packet is numbered so the sequence can be reestablished at the other end. The multiple connections were a deliberate effort to provide redundancy; if one connection fails, the others can be used to keep traffic moving despite congestion.

Packets allow many users to use the same connection and to reduce the amount of data that must be resent in the event of a network error. Figure 1.2 shows the route a test packet traveled from telestra.net in Australia to Bentley College in Waltham, Massachusetts. (Note the IP addresses in parentheses.) One packet traveling through eighteen connections gives us an idea of the sheer volume of data flowing through the Internet each day. This volume and the multiple connections make regulation of the Internet difficult.

Netiquette

The Internet's academic origins and prohibitions on commercial use created a strong culture on the Internet that survives today. Using intrusive or overly aggressive advertising, ignoring site or group policies, and asking questions for which answers are available in frequently asked questions (FAQs) documents are all considered breaches of *netiquette*. Such breaches are met with a variety of responses, from tolerance to vitriol.

REGULATION OF CYBERSPACE

Because the Internet is a coalition of networks throughout the world, no one organization owns the Internet. The Internet Society oversees boards and task forces that

FIGURE 1.1   Contents of an Internet Packet (Annotated)

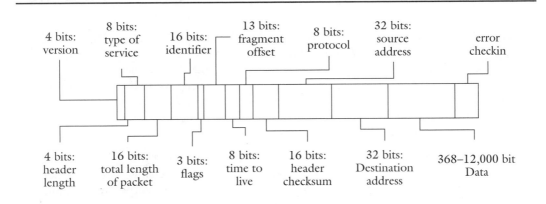

FIGURE 1.2   Trace of the Route from Bentley College to Australia

traceroute to athena.bentley.edu (141.133.239.248), 30 hops max, 40 byte packets

1 Ethernet0.dickson.Canberra.telstra.net (203.50.0.1) 1.439 ms 1.704 ms 1.371 ms
2 Serial6-5.civ2.Canberra.telstra.net (139.130.235.1) 3.188 ms 3.179 ms 2.54 ms
3 Fddi0-0.civ-core1.Canberra.telstra.net (139.130.235.226) 3.26 ms 3.48 ms 2.058 ms
4 Hssi0-1-0.pad-core3.Sydney.telstra.net (139.130.249.33) 33.954 ms 171.456 ms 63.008 ms
5 139.130.249.235 (139.130.249.235) 25.87 ms 20.75 ms 122.246 ms
6 205.174.74.33 (205.174.74.33) 221.518 ms 230.233 ms 225.299 ms
7 199.37.127.67 (199.37.127.67) 220.604 ms 323.975 ms 222.63 ms
8 s2-0-0.paloalto-cr18.bbnplanet.net (4.1.142.253) 227.638 ms 227.733 ms 325.946 ms
9 p3-2.paloalto-nbr2.bbnplanet.net (4.0.3.85) 236.601 ms 223.836 ms 226.26 ms
10 p4-0.sanjose1-nbr1.bbnplanet.net (4.0.1.2) 303.175 ms 231.028 ms 223.42 ms
11 p1-0.sanjose1-nbr2.bbnplanet.net (4.0.5.86) 225.687 ms 226.534 ms 238.566 ms
12 p4-0.nyc4-nbr2.bbnplanet.net (4.0.5.98) 289.694 ms 296.001 ms 292.647 ms
13 p1-0.nyc4-nbr3.bbnplanet.net (4.0.5.26) 326.089 ms 296.495 ms 292.014 ms
14 p2-3.cambridge1-nbr2.bbnplanet.net (4.0.2.173) 396.145 ms 301.188 ms 296.95 ms
15 p3-0.cambridge1-nbr1.bbnplanet.net (4.0.5.17) 299.059 ms 296.572 ms 295.969 ms
16 p0-0-0.cambridge1-cr18.bbnplanet.net (4.0.5.74) 299.101 ms 296.297 ms 313.018 ms
17 s1.bentley.bbnplanet.net (4.1.130.214) 307.736 ms 326.592 ms 331.458 ms
18 athena.bentley.edu (141.133.239.248) 343.785 ms 302.765 ms 307.842 ms

deal with network policy issues. Among these are the Internet Engineering Steering Group, which is responsible for final approval of Internet Standards, and the Internet Engineering Task Force, the protocol engineering and development group. The Internet Corporation for Assigned Names and Numbers (ICANN) oversees the domain name system (DNS). The World Wide Web Consortium (W3C) develops Web technologies. The Internet is largely self-policing—networks that do not conform to the norms of the Internet are cut off from the rest.

The Internet was designed as a collaborative environment and therefore was not a high-security environment. Founded by academics, the open exchange of information became a basic tenet of the Internet. This is in direct contrast to corporate computer network environments, where the assumption is that all access is denied without explicit authorization and measures are taken to ensure security. In addition, the sudden expansion of World Wide Web commercial usage has raised numerous legal issues regarding privacy, security, and copyright and trademark infringement. This textbook explains the relationship of these legal issues to e-commerce. It will be helpful as you read the text to keep in mind the technology used in e-commerce transactions.

http://

For more on the governing bodies of the Internet and World Wide Web, see

- **http://www.isoc.org/**
- **http://www.ietf.org/**
- **http://www.icann.org**
- **http://www.w3.org/**

Business and Individual Users

Security and privacy concerns on the Internet extend to both the individual user and the business user. The most straightforward way in which businesses obtain information from individual users is through a form completed and submitted by a user. However, many users fear more insidious, invisible data-gathering methods.

Currently, if a company wants to track a user's behavior over time without asking the user for data, the only way to do so is with **cookies**, small text files that a server can store *on the user's machine*. When a user visits a site, the server may store up to twenty cookies on the user's machine, and when the user returns to the site, the server can request any cookies previously stored *by that server only* to see information from previous visits. Cookies can store information on which pages were viewed and when, or any information the user entered, such as username, password, age, sex, and so on, or simply contain an identification code that can be used to match the user to records stored in a database. Based on the information stored in the cookies or in its databases, the site may then deliver a page customized to the user.

http://

- For more about how cookies work and how to manage them, see **http://www.cookiecentral.com/**

Even with cookies, HTML is not sophisticated enough for a Web site to execute programs on a user's computer, so a common language, **Java**, was developed to offer greater power and flexibility. The Java language is run by a special program built into most Web browsers called the *Java virtual machine (JVM)*. When a Java program is executed on a user's machine, the JVM is designed to protect the computer from harmful or malicious programs. However, hackers have found ways to permeate the protection of the JVM, and Java can be used to capture additional information about a user and transmit it to a server. Users can protect themselves by disabling Java. Chapter 9, "Privacy," and Chapter 12, "Internet and Information Security," explain how this technology applies to e-commerce.

When a Web page is viewed, a copy is held in a temporary storage space on the user's hard drive called the **cache**. The browser overwrites the oldest file in the cache each time a new page is loaded, but because users return to the same pages often, those pages are kept in the cache and not routinely deleted. This allows anyone with access to the user's computer a robust view of the recent browsing patterns of the user. Users can protect themselves by cleaning out their caches periodically.

Information Security

Like users worried about the capture of sensitive data, companies hosting Web sites often want their sites to integrate with some systems in the organization while protecting other systems from unauthorized access from the Internet. To control access to these systems, **firewalls** are used: computer programs that limit the access to other computers based on a variety of rules and techniques, including IP address, passwords, time of day, and type of request.

Some Internet access is limited by filtering technology that prevents access of inappropriate material for minors or employees. Such filters use several methods to screen material. Some block access to sites based on keywords contained in the documents, but such filters may restrict access to legitimate sites, particularly for health information, such as breast cancer. Other filters categorize sites and senders by maintaining a list of ratings developed by filter software providers, users, or the content providers themselves. The W3C developed the Platform for Internet Content Selection (PICS), a specification for how to insert labels into documents, to facilitate the labeling of sites based on rating criteria developed by others.

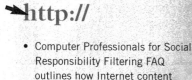

- Computer Professionals for Social Responsibility Filtering FAQ outlines how Internet content filtering works: **http://www.cpsr.org/ filters/faq.html**

Commercial filtering products include Websense and Surfcontrol, and products for home use include Net Nanny, CyberSitter, and Cyber Patrol. Internet Explorer, with its Content Advisor, may be used to enable filtering based on PICS. Because all transmissions pass through the filter, many filtering software products may also be used to monitor what users are viewing and when.

Security risks come not only from exposure of the computer itself, but also during transmission. Because packets pass through myriad sites during transmission, they can be intercepted; therefore, encryption is used to prevent unauthorized access to the contents of sensitive packets. There are two types of encryption schemes commonly used: private key and public key. **Private key** is the simpler scheme: messages are encrypted using a key known only to the communicating parties. Assuming the key is kept secure, the message is known to be authentic, because only someone with the key could have locked up the message.

Public key encryption avoids the cumbersome problems of private key encryption. With public key encryption, each party creates a pair of keys, one public and one private. The private key is never released, but the public key is distributed to anyone with a need for it. A good analogy is a night deposit slot at a bank. The bank builds a safe at the bottom of a chute. At the top of the chute is a locked door. Customers needing to make after-hours deposits are given a *public* key to the chute so they can securely deposit money, because only the bank has the *private* key to the safe. On the Web, public/private keys underlie the Secure Socket Layer (SSL) that protects browser communications. See Chapter 12, "Internet and Information Security," for a discussion of how this technology applies to cyberlaw.

The FBI's Carnivore system is capable of monitoring Internet transmissions by intercepting the transmissions at the ISP level. But strong encryption has complicated such monitoring, because the intercepted streams are undecipherable. To address this, the FBI has begun to use **key logging systems (KLS)**, which is software installed on a user's computer to capture keystrokes. This software captures the passwords needed to decrypt the transmissions. Magic Lantern is a planned enhancement that would enable the KLS to be installed from a remote location onto a user's computer.

Public/private key pairs can also be used for authentication, through the creation of **digital signatures**. To ensure that a message or file is from a specific sender, the sender may encrypt it in his or her *private* key. The only way the file may be decrypted is with the matching *public* key, which the recipient has. If the public key decrypts the file, then it was sent by someone who had the private key. Assuming the sender has kept the private key secure, the file is authentic. Authentication prevents **spoofing**, where sites are set up to appear similar to other sites. One common method of spoofing is using common misspellings. For instance, Amazon.com is such a popular site that www.*amazom*.com receives many hits due to misspelling.

There are a number of vulnerabilities throughout the Internet, in addition to the interception of transmissions and rogue Java programs. **Denial of service attacks** involve overloading a server to keep other users from gaining access. Viruses can be transmitted as attachments to e-mail or embedded in files. Passwords can be stolen or guessed at, allowing unauthorized access. Once hackers have entered a system, they may simply "look around," or vandalize the server, or make subtle changes in programs on the server that may not be detected by system administrators. The changes could be for amusement or financial gain.

Ping of Death

The Internet Communications Management Protocol (ICMP) was developed to ease the diagnosis of network problems. ICMP provides a command called *Ping* to determine the speed of a connection to another machine on the Internet. A small packet is sent from one machine to another and then returned. The time of the travel is calculated. One way service was denied to machines was by sending much larger packets, called a *Ping of Death*.

BUSINESS USES OF INTERNET TECHNOLOGIES

The Internet can be used within an organization, such as a corporation, government agency, or university, in which case it is called an **intranet**. Sometimes companies open up their systems to a limited number of customers, suppliers, or other business partners. This limited access system is called an **extranet**. *Virtual Private Networks* use the public Internet, but secure it so it behaves like a private network. **File transfer protocol (FTP)** is used to move files from one computer to another. FTP sites are often used for the transfer and exchange of pirated software or other electronic content (video, audio, etc.) on sites called *warez* (pronounced "wares"). These sites are shut down by the hosting ISPs when they are located, and they often last only a few hours. *Peer-to-peer* networks such as Kazaa and Gnutella connect individual machines on the Internet for the purpose of sharing files without the need for a third-party server. *Instant messaging* is a means of communicating via the Internet in real time. *Videoconferencing* is becoming increasingly popular on the Internet, requiring a camera and some additional software.

The predominant use of the Internet remains electronic mail. There are many potential pitfalls for e-mail. E-mail addresses can be spoofed or made to look similar to more formal addresses. One pitfall is unsolicited commercial e-mail, often referred to as *spam*. Such messages clog e-mail systems and individual e-mailboxes; e-mail servers can also be overloaded by the sheer volume of messages, a process known as *flooding*.

E-mail addresses are harvested from a number of sources, including mailing lists and bulletin board systems. E-mail has been used to send vitriolic messages to individuals and firms, called *flames*.

Because businesses have begun to rely on e-mail as a way to conduct business, e-mail messages are routinely stored as a backup measure. This allows the company to easily retrieve all messages to or from a specific e-mail account.

GLOBALIZATION

Much of the growth of the Internet in the late 1990s was outside the United States, and by 2002 most estimates showed that more than two-thirds of all Internet users were outside the United States. Although Web sites remain predominantly in English, sites in other languages are rapidly increasing in number. The world does grow smaller as the global use of the Internet and World Wide Web increases.

The legal concerns that affect us domestically are the same concerns that affect our use of the Internet internationally. Issues regarding privacy, security, jurisdiction, trademarks, and commerce are all affected by our expanding use of computers to communicate, collaborate, and trade.

LAW AND CYBERSPACE

Some issues of privacy and security have been mentioned, but there are many other issues with which individuals and businesses must be familiar when using the Internet and the World Wide Web. Many potential legal issues may arise while doing commerce on the Internet. For example, do users approve of the insertion of anything into their computers without their knowledge and consent? Are cookies legal? Can sales made on the Internet be taxed? What constitutes defamation on the Internet? Is Web content protected by copyright laws, or can it be considered public domain information? How can laws related to the Internet be enforced? This text answers some of these questions and others, and possibly raises even more.

Chapter 1 provides this introduction to cyberlaw, and then Chapter 2 moves on to jurisdiction. Because the legal environment of electronic commerce has no geographical boundaries, it must be determined who will have legal authority to hear cases in the event of a legal dispute.

Chapters 3, 4, and 5 cover the intellectual property issues of trademarks, copyrights, and business method patents. Copyrights protect the creative content of Web pages. Trademark disputes are among the most common types of litigation involving the online environment and business method patents extend protection to novel ways of doing business, often encapsulated in software.

Chapters 6, 7, and 8 discuss legal issues dealing with doing commerce on the Internet: online contracting and licensing, taxation, and online securities offerings. Laws that govern the making and enforcement of contracts and the legal remedies that are available in the event of a breach are covered, especially those aspects that most affect e-commerce. Sales and use tax on e-commerce is considered the most critical tax controversy confronting a Web-based business as vendor companies face sales tax liability for failure to collect and remit sales tax on out-of-state sales. Finally, online securities are covered. These transactions traditionally conducted by investment banks and brokerage firms are now also conducted electronically. Although the same laws govern Internet transactions, adjustments to the traditional regulatory framework have had to be made.

Chapters 9, 10, 11, 12, and 13 discuss the social side of legal issues relating to the Internet. Topics include privacy, obscenity, defamation, Internet and information security, and computer crime. Laws exist currently that cover these issues, but adjustments must be made to these regulations in the unique environment of the Internet.

Summary

This chapter reviews the history of the Internet as it applies to its current structure. The Internet's open, consensus-driven, academic roots clearly influenced the current configuration, creating challenges for commerce and law. The technology of the Internet and the Web are explained to clarify the basis of legal issues discussed throughout the book. The nature and extent of security issues are described, establishing that security is possible on the Internet, but not the default. Finally, the scope of business use on the Internet is described to establish the context for the myriad legal issues raised.

Key Terms

cyberlaw, *4*
Internet service providers
  (ISPs), *5*
Internet protocol (IP), *5*
domain name system
  (DNS), *5*

hypertext markup language
  (HTML), *6*
hypertext transfer protocol
  (http), *6*
uniform resource locator
  (URL), *6*

packets, *6*
cookies, *9*
Java, *9*
cache, *9*
firewalls, *10*
private key, *10*

Manager's Checklist

√ Determine what transmissions need to be protected from interception and alteration, and implement appropriate security measures.

√ Weigh the benefits of customization using cookies and other technologies against possible perceptions of invasion of privacy.

√ Balance the use of advanced technologies with security risks.

√ Monitor the Internet to see if anyone is spoofing your site. This will require searching for your company on search engines and examining the results for impostors.

√ Once you implement a Web site, your company becomes accessible globally. Determine the extent to which you will serve customers outside your country and prepare for the required compliance.

√ Ethical Considerations

• Software and hardware needed to administer the networks and servers that comprise the Internet may be used to monitor and even disrupt transmissions for ethical and unethical reasons.

• Outline the ethical responsibilities of the designers and distributors of system administration products.

• Describe the extent to which designers and distributors should ensure that their products are used appropriately.

JURISDICTION

The French court's order is but one example of the sort of judgment that this and other American courts can expect to see with interesting frequency as Internet use expands throughout the world. It is a predictable consequence of the global character of the Internet. . . . The court below recognized that enforcement of the French Order would be inconsistent with basic First Amendment principles and refused to permit the seeds of foreign censorship to be planted on U.S. soil.

—**Yahoo!, Inc. v. La Ligue Contre Le Racisme et L'Antisemitisme,** *169 F. Supp. 2d 1181 (N.D. Cal. 2001), Brief of Amici Curiae*

LEARNING OBJECTIVES

After you have read this chapter, you should be able to:

1. Understand the traditional common law principles for analyzing a court's personal jurisdiction over a nonresident defendant. An e-business is online 24/7 in every state and in most countries. Explain when a court in another state or foreign country has the authority to hear and dispose of an aggrieved end user's case.
2. Explain how personal jurisdiction applies to an e-business doing business in a foreign state. Understand when an electronic presence in a state or foreign country is sufficient to create personal jurisdiction over an e-business.
3. Explain the distinction between a passive and an interactive Web site and why that distinction is relevant to Internet jurisdiction. Explain why just posting information (for example, advertising a business on a Web site) is not sufficient to create jurisdiction in a foreign state or country.
4. Explain what is meant by a Web site that is "purposefully availing itself" to doing business in a foreign state. Explain how an e-business can control where it can be sued and what law will apply.
5. Distinguish general jurisdiction from specific jurisdiction and understand their relevance to online transactions.
6. Explain the basic principles of national enforcement that define a country's power beyond its borders.
7. Understand the legal and cultural conflicts involved with asserting one's national jurisdiction into a cyberspace forum.

http://

- Additional material relevant to this chapter may be found at the Bentley College CyberLaw Center Web site (**http://ecampus.bentley. edu/dept/cyberlaw**) under Jurisdiction.

INTRODUCTION

Cyberspace has no geographical boundaries and neither does an e-business. Because a Web presence is national and global at the same time, it has potential liability exposure anywhere the site can be accessed and cause a legal grievance. Hence the e-commerce manager has a new standard of diligence regarding where the company is doing business, the manner in which it transacts business, the content on its Web site, and certain statements in its Terms of Use regarding jurisdiction that are discussed in this chapter.

Your e-commerce business is no longer just where you think it is. For instance, an e-business located in Kansas is subject not only to its state laws; it is possible that the laws of other jurisdictions may govern the company's transactions.

Online jurisdiction raises a number of relevant questions. For example, do courts in other countries have jurisdiction over a U.S. e-business in ways that threaten its ability to distribute content on the Internet? To what extent are free expressions on the Internet, however offensive, protected under the First Amendment, even though they may violate another country's laws? The Yahoo! case cited here (discussed in the international jurisdiction section of this chapter) startled the e-commerce community when a French court ordered Yahoo!, Inc., a U.S. corporation, "to take all necessary measures to dissuade and make impossible any access via Yahoo.com to the auction services for Nazi merchandise as well as to any other site or service that may be construed as an apology for Nazism or contesting the reality of Nazi crimes." The U.S. court ruled the display and sale of Nazi memorabilia, although illegal in France, is protected speech under the First Amendment of the U.S. Constitution.

The global implications of e-commerce will continue to present novel legal questions that will be litigated. The resulting new laws regarding jurisdiction will become an integral part of cyberlaw. This chapter discusses the jurisdictional laws that are essential knowledge for a manager of an e-business in order to assist him or her in understanding the legal consequences of doing business online.

A national or foreign company may bring lawsuits against an e-business based on alleged legal grievances. Such potential liability exposure may occur when there is an alleged claim against (1) a traditional business that launches a new Web site, (2) a traditional business with a Web site that decides to upgrade its content, or (3) a start-up business that goes online (see Figure 2.1).

FIGURE 2.1   Maintaining or Creating a New E-Business with Potential Global Liability Exposure

Traditional offline business with an existing Web site ⟶ upgrade the Web site

Traditional offline business ⟶ create a new Web site

Start-up e-business ⟶ exclusive e-business

In each of the instances in Figure 2.1 there are consequential jurisdictional issues that may determine the place, other than the e-company's location, where it can be sued. In subsequent chapters we discuss potential liability exposure when doing business online. This chapter explains where the e-company can be sued (i.e., in what state, court, or country) and the protective steps the business may take to control the place of trial and the law to be applied. As you read this textbook, notice how cyberlaw often builds on traditional legal principles and is sometimes forced to create new rules to accommodate the unique online legal environment.

Jurisdiction is the authority of a court to hear a case and resolve a dispute. Because the legal environment of e-commerce has no geographical boundaries, it establishes immediate long-distance communications with anyone who can access the Web site.

Usually an online e-merchant has no way of knowing exactly where the information on its site is being accessed. Hence jurisdiction issues are of primary importance in cyberspace. Engaging in e-commerce on the World Wide Web may expose the company to the risk of being sued in any state or foreign country where an Internet user can establish a legal claim. Legal counsel and insurance underwriters should carefully review this potential risk and its accompanying cost to the business. In each case, they must determine whether an online presence will subject the e-business to jurisdiction in a distant state or a foreign company.

CATEGORIES OF JURISDICTION

The several categories of jurisdiction are generally based on the relationship of the state where the court is located and the defendant or the defendant's property. **Personal (in personam) jurisdiction** over an out-of-state defendant that had personal contacts with the state, either contractual or tortious, is generally required for a court to have personal jurisdiction over the defendant. Because an e-business has at least an electronic presence in every state, personal jurisdiction is discussed in depth in this chapter.

Once a nonresident e-business is found liable by the court and a judgment issued, it becomes a "judgment debtor" and, under the Full Faith and Credit Clause of the U.S. Constitution, the judgment may be collected in any state where the defendant company has property.

Qualified

Subject matter jurisdiction is determined once the court has the power and authority to hear the case under personal jurisdiction. The court must have the competence to hear the claim based on the nature of the plaintiff's case. For instance, there are courts, often called superior courts, that hear civil matters, lower courts called municipal or district courts with limited jurisdiction based on the amount of money in controversy, and groups of specialized courts such as family, land, and probate courts. Federal courts have subject matter jurisdiction when the case arises under the laws of the United States, such as a patent or trademark case, or where there is diversity of jurisdiction because the plaintiff is a resident of one state and the defendant is from another state and the amount of money in litigation exceeds $75,000.

In a diversity of citizenship case, the federal court generally applies the state law where the court is located. There are specialty federal courts wherein only they can hear a case, such as in bankruptcy, admiralty, and patents.

In rem jurisdiction claims (jurisdiction over the thing) are generally found in probate and land title cases. The only relief the court may grant in an in rem jurisdiction case is to order the defendant to sell the property and pay the proceeds from the sale to the plaintiff up to the amount of damages found by the court. For example, a plaintiff from Massachusetts may have a claim against an e-business from Texas for inventory warehoused in Colorado. The Colorado court has in rem jurisdiction over the property and could hear the case and render a judgment against the property (see Figure 2.2).

When trial lawyers represent online clients who are being sued in a foreign court, they always consider having the case litigated in the jurisdiction where their client's primary business is located rather than the plaintiff's state or country.

Although the case could be litigated in a state court, it is more commonly a federal court because cyberspace issues often involve federal statutes (e.g., copyright and/or trademark law) or diversity jurisdiction (i.e., a plaintiff from one state suing an e-business defendant from another state with damages of $75,000 or more). This *home court advantage* is important for several reasons:

1. Local law will apply. This may be state law and/or the federal law of that particular judicial circuit (see Figure 2.3).
2. A local law firm's attorneys will not have to travel to another jurisdiction for depositions and other kinds of pretrial discovery given by its client.
3. It will not be necessary to hire attorneys from another state to file pleadings and so on.
4. If the case is tried in the client's home region, the jury may be familiar with and sympathetic to the e-business.
5. The trial lawyer will be familiar with the local judges and their decisions. We could say there is a legal comfort zone in trying a case in a local court.

FIGURE 2.2   Categories of Jurisdiction

Subject matter jurisdiction: The case must be entered in the proper court based on the nature of the claim (e.g., probate, land court, bankruptcy court, etc.).

Personal (in personam) jurisdiction: The out-of-state defendant must have had personal contacts in the state where the plaintiff is bringing the lawsuit.

Jurisdiction over property (in rem): The defendant's property must be in the state where the court resides.

FIGURE 2.3   **The Federal Judicial Circuits**

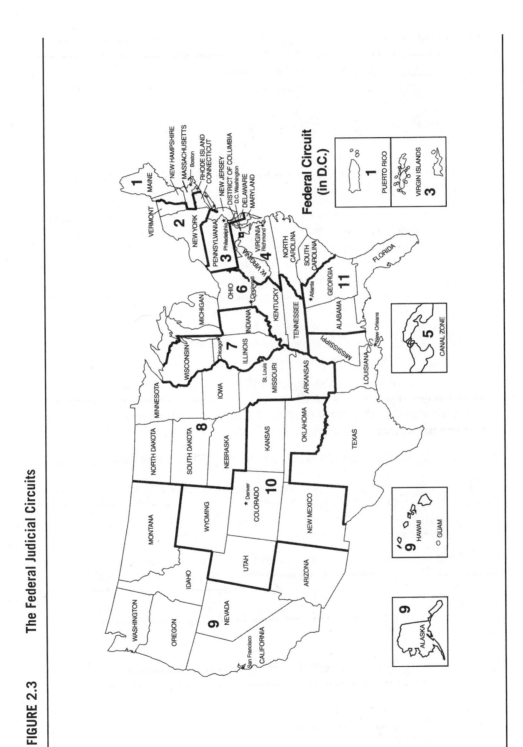

Keep in mind that jurisdiction does *not* resolve the issue of liability but only the issue of the court where the case will be tried. The issues addressed by personal jurisdiction over a nonresident e-business defendant are discussed in this chapter. In succeeding chapters we illustrate the vast liability exposure of electronic commerce in general.

TRADITIONAL PRINCIPLES OF JURISDICTION

Common law principles of personal jurisdiction evolved from judges' opinions in their case decisions long before the online world existed. The cases that created our traditional principles of personal jurisdiction are applied to e-commerce.

When a nonresident e-business defendant raises the issues of lack of personal jurisdiction by a motion to dismiss, the plaintiffs must generally prove satisfaction of *both* the local state's long-arm statute and the due process clause of the U.S. Constitution (see Figure 2.4). Because e-commerce on the Internet reaches unknown marketplaces, the aggrieved end user may file a lawsuit in any state (or country) where the court has personal jurisdiction over the nonresident defendant. Keep in mind that the term *personal jurisdiction* includes a "person" doing business as a sole proprietor, corporation, partnership, or other form of business organization. Most e-businesses are corporations, so a foreign court must have personal jurisdiction over it if challenged by a motion to dismiss.

Later in this chapter we discuss suggested legal safeguards to protect against lawsuits in a foreign jurisdiction. Included among them should be a forum selection and choice of law clause in every e-business's Terms of Use, which commonly appears at the end of the Web site's home page.

State Long-Arm Statutes and Personal Jurisdiction over a Nonresident Defendant

Jurisdiction over a nonresident e-business is based on the local state **long-arm statute**. The metaphor of a *long arm* is useful if you think of a local state with a long arm reaching out to grab a nonresident e-business and bring it into the state to account to the plaintiff for its illegal acts.

State long-arm statutes authorize the courts to claim personal jurisdiction over a nonresident defendant whose principal business is outside the state. Although long-arm statutes differ from state to state, all have one thing in common: they establish personal jurisdiction over a nonresident defendant based on business transactions or torts committed *within* the state.

FIGURE 2.4   Plaintiff's Burden of Proof for Personal Jurisdiction

Personal jurisdiction over a nonresident e-business =
state long-arm statute + due process clause

Always keep in mind that the statutory requirements of the long-arm statutes vary. Some state long-arm statutes assert jurisdiction over nonresident defendants who transact business, commit torts, or own or use property within the state. Other states (e.g., California, Oklahoma, Rhode Island, and Wyoming) simply assert jurisdiction if it is reasonable to do so, consistent with the due process clause of either the Fourteenth Amendment (if a state claim) or the Fifth Amendment (if a federal claim), as we discuss later. Once the court is satisfied that the facts of the case apply to the long-arm statute over the nonresident e-business defendant, it must then determine if the facts comply with the requisites of the due process clause.

A 1985 U.S. Supreme Court case, *Burger King Corp. v. Rudzewicz*, 471 U.S. 462, stated that when nonresident defendants reach out beyond one state and create continuing relationships with the citizens of other states, they are subject to regulations in that state and sanctions for the consequences of their actions. Through some business transaction the out-of-state defendant must purposefully avail itself of the privilege of conducting activities with the forum state, thereby invoking the benefits and protections of its laws. This case, and others discussed in this chapter, laid the groundwork for personal jurisdiction over a nonresident e-business resulting from electronic transactions that create continuing business relationships with citizens of other states.

Think of driving an automobile through different states. Imagine telling a traffic cop that stopped you for speeding, "That's not the speed limit where I live!" An online company doing business in foreign states (e.g., eBay) could be subject to the laws where the customers reside. An e-business doing extensive business could be accountable to its customers under the laws in all fifty states and numerous countries.

Application of the Due Process Clause over a Nonresident Defendant

A court is limited in exercising its powers over a nonresident defendant by the due process clause of the Fifth and Fourteenth Amendments to the U.S. Constitution. The due process clause of the Fifth Amendment to the U.S. Constitution, which applies to the federal government, provides in part that "no person shall be deprived of life, liberty, or property, without due process of law." The due process clause of the Fourteenth Amendment provides that "no state shall . . . deprive any person of life, liberty, or property, without due process of the law."

For a court to render a judgment (i.e., monetary damages) against a nonresident e-business defendant and thereby deprive that company of a property interest, it must do so within traditional notions of due process. This property interest is the amount of money stated in the judgment issued by the court that an e-business owes the plaintiff. However, due process is not defined in the U.S. Constitution. Its meaning has been shaped by U.S. Supreme Court decisions.

In 1980, the U.S. Supreme Court in *World Wide Volkswagen Corp. v. Woodson*, 444 U.S. 286, stated, "The due process clause of the Fourteenth Amendment limits the power of a state court to render a valid personal judgment against a nonresident defendant. . . . We have never accepted the proposition that state lines are irrelevant for jurisdiction purposes. . . . The states retain sovereign power to try cases in their courts." An e-business, without geographical boundaries, remains subject to this pre-Internet constitutional principle of limiting a court's ability to reach across state lines. Remember, the nonresident e-business defendant has the constitutional right to due process before another court can assume personal jurisdiction over its company.

Think of due process as a federal constitutional right that an e-business has before it is subject to a foreign court's jurisdiction. **Due process** as it relates to personal jurisdiction is a constitutional requirement based on two criteria:

1. The nonresident e-business defendant had sufficient *minimum contacts* in the forum state where the case is being tried.
2. Jurisdiction in that court will not offend *traditional notions of fair play and substantial justice*

Due process requires the out-of-state e-business to have certain minimum contacts with the forum state. Minimum contacts are evidenced by facts demonstrating either general or specific jurisdiction.

General jurisdiction is the authority of a court to hear any case involving a defendant that had "continuous and systematic" contacts with the forum state. Because there are usually sporadic purchases from a state, the courts generally do not assert general jurisdiction based on the existence of an Internet Web site. (*Millennium Enterprises, Inc., v. Millennium Music LP*, 33 F. Supp. 2d 907 [D. Or. 1999]).

Specific jurisdiction comports with due process when the out-of-state defendant performed an act or a transaction (e.g., a contract) within the forum state by "purposefully availing" itself of the privilege of doing business in the state and enjoys its benefits and protections. The claim must arise out of the defendant's activities in the state, and the court's jurisdiction must be reasonable and fair.

These federal constitutional principles are discussed throughout this chapter. However, it is useful to further explain minimum contacts before we look at the cases.

A nonresident defendant must purposely avail itself of the benefits of the state's economic market to establish **minimum contacts**. The court may exercise personal jurisdiction under the due process clause when the business transaction was such that a defendant's conduct and connection with a forum state are such that he or she should reasonably anticipate being hauled into court. This makes personal jurisdiction reasonably foreseeable by the defendant who elected to do business in the foreign state.

In *Burger King Corporation v. Rudzewicz*, 471 U.S. 462 (1985), the U.S. Supreme Court has stated,

> If a foreign corporation purposely avails itself of the benefits of an economic market in the forum state, it may subject itself to the state's in personam jurisdiction even if it has no physical presence in the state. The substantial connection between the foreign defendant and the court necessary for a finding of minimum contacts must come about by an action *purposely directed* toward the forum state. The mere act of using interstate commerce does not of itself constitute a purposely directed act.

Keep this rule in mind as you think about e-business in cyberspace. Although a physical presence is not necessary for the court to find personal jurisdiction over a nonresident company, simply going online and "using interstate commerce" may be insufficient to establish personal jurisdiction.

Motion to Dismiss for Lack of Personal Jurisdiction over a Nonresident Defendant

The nonresident e-business defendant's lawyer generally brings a pretrial **motion to dismiss** the case for lack of personal jurisdiction and attempts to have the case tried in the state where the e-business is headquartered and not necessarily where the company is incorporated. The lawyer may argue that the local state's long-arm statute does not apply to the facts of the case and the due process clause will be violated if the case is tried in a foreign court (see Figure 2.5).

JUDICIAL HISTORY OF PERSONAL JURISDICTION

Constitutional Framework for Due Process under the *International Shoe Company* Case

The judicial pre-online history of personal jurisdiction over a nonresident defendant has its origin in an 1878 U.S. Supreme Court case, *Pennoyer v. Neff,* 95 U.S. 714. The Court, in order to establish personal jurisdiction over the nonresident defendant, required the defendant's physical presence in the state where the court was located. Before a court had personal jurisdiction over a nonresident defendant, the defendant had to be served a summons and complaint by a sheriff while physically present in that state. So after 1878, a nonresident defendant just remained out of the state to avoid being sued.

FIGURE 2.5   **Motion to Dismiss for Lack of Personal Jurisdiction over a Nonresident Defendant**

PLAINTIFF'S BURDEN OF PROOF WHEN DEFENDANT FILES A
PRETRIAL MOTION TO DISMISS FOR LACK OF PERSONAL
JURISDICTION OVER A NONRESIDENT DEFENDANT

(P) End User	*v.*	(D) E-Business
P must prove: (1) The local state "long-arm statute" applies *and* (2) There is no violation of D's due process rights under the Constitution.		D files and argues a motion to dismiss for lack of personal jurisdiction.

Of course we can easily see the impracticality of that rule as interstate commerce and communications developed. In 1945, the U.S. Supreme Court decided the landmark case *International Shoe Company v. Washington State,* 326 U.S. 310. The defendant, International Shoe Company, had its principal office in Missouri but transacted business in the state of Washington, where it took orders for shoes. It did not own an office, warehouse, or any property in Washington; its employees merely took orders on shoes where only one shoe was displayed—hence the argument of no inventory in the state of Washington. The purchase orders were accepted in Missouri, where the shoes were shipped to customers in Washington.

When the state of Washington sought to collect unemployment taxes from the corporation, International Shoe argued the Washington court had no personal jurisdiction over it because it had no physical presence in the state. The court found that the business activities in the state of Washington established "sufficient contacts or ties with the state of the form to make it reasonable and just according to our traditional concepts of fair play and substantial justice to permit the state to enforce the obligations that incurred there." Note that the court found personal jurisdiction even though the defendant had no physical presence in the state of Washington. This concept of doing business in a state without a physical presence became important as the courts began to analyze e-commerce engaging in electronic interstate activity without a physical presence.

At the time this case was decided, there were no state long-arm statutes. Hence the U.S. Supreme Court in the *International Shoe Company* case had to build its legal argument of finding personal jurisdiction over the nonresident defendant on constitutional fairness under the due process clause of the Fourteenth Amendment because the case involved the state's claim for taxation.

Two-Pronged Analysis for Finding Personal Jurisdiction in the *International Shoe Company* Case

The Supreme Court in the *International Shoe Company* case in finding due process considered the many business minimum contacts the shoe company had in the state of Washington. In deciding for the state of Washington, it found no violation of traditional notions of fair play and substantial justice. To prove minimum contacts, the plaintiff must persuade the court that the nonresident defendant purposefully availed itself of the privilege of doing business in the marketplace of the forum state. Both minimum contacts and traditional notions of fair play and substantial justice must be satisfied to find personal jurisdiction.

In cyberspace this would require more than a casual online presence. The defendant's e-business must have actively solicited business in the plaintiff's state. In addition, the exercise of personal jurisdiction over a nonresident defendant must be reasonable and not unfairly inconvenient to the defendant to travel to the foreign state where the case will be tried.

Because International Shoe used the state of Washington to sell shoes and developed substantial income from those transactions, it met the minimum contacts requirement.

The traditional notions of fairness and substantial justice were not violated within that context so long as jurisdiction in the state of Washington was reasonable.

After the *International Shoe Company* decision allowing states to tax nonresident businesses that carried on substantial business within the state, various state legislatures seeking taxes from out-of-state businesses passed long-arm statutes that subjected out-of-state defendants to its jurisdiction whenever they do business within their state.

PERSONAL JURISDICTION IN THE ONLINE ENVIRONMENT

We have discussed personal jurisdiction as it applies to a traditional brick-and-mortar business, but the rules are also relevant to the online environment. When an e-business establishes and maintains a Web site and engages in electronic commerce, it is entitled to the protection of the U.S. Constitution, the state constitution, and the local law where the company is located. Any person, including a distant user, who accesses the company's Web site is entitled to the same legal protection.

In *World Wide Volkswagen v. Woodson*, 444 U.S. 286, the U.S. Supreme Court held that merely placing a product in interstate commerce does not of itself "purposefully avail oneself" to a forum state's jurisdiction. What is required is "additional conduct," defined as an intent to serve the market in the forum state.

In a leading online trademark infringement case, *Digital Equipment Corporation v. AltaVista Technology, Inc.*, 960 F. Supp. 456 (D. Mass. 1997), a Massachusetts company (Digital) sued a California corporation (AltaVista Technology) in the federal district court in Massachusetts. The court denied defendant's motion to dismiss for lack of personal jurisdiction due to Alta Vista Technology's contacts in Massachusetts and stated, "Massachusetts has an interest in protecting its citizens from . . . trademark infringement." There is a chance that an out-of-state Web site "may be hauled into court in any state where their Web site causes harm or transacts business."

Passive Web Sites versus Interactive Web Sites

National or worldwide personal jurisdiction over a nonresident e-business does not automatically follow developing a Web site and going online with a service or product. A **passive Web site** that merely transmits information and does not solicit business generally does not incur personal jurisdiction in a foreign state or country. Consider the number of professional Web sites that merely advertise an accounting or legal service. Students often have a passive Web site that displays a résumé and other information and does not solicit business. An **interactive Web site** *does* solicit business. Figure 2.6 highlights the differences between nonactive and interactive Web sites.

The following case involved a Web site that was essentially informational. Although it did solicit some business in its own state of Missouri, it was not soliciting business in New York, and hence the court refused to find personal jurisdiction. Maintaining a passive Web site that posted information about its business was not enough to confer out-of-state personal jurisdiction.

FIGURE 2.6   **Personal Jurisdiction Analysis Based on Nature of the Web Site**

Passive Web site

- Provides only information
- Does not solicit business
- Is not usually subject to personal jurisdiction in a foreign country

Interactive Web site

- Provides information for users to make make purchasing decisions
- Actively solicits business
- May be subject to personal jurisdiction in a foreign country or state

"Effects" Test of Jurisdiction

The court had to decide whether a state may find jurisdiction over a nonresident defendant who operated a Web site in another state and posted on the Web site information that may have violated the trade secrets of California residents. Note that the court decided the case based on whether the defendant purposefully availed himself of forum benefits under the "effect" test as applied in the U.S. Supreme Court case of *Calder v. Jones*, 465 U.S. 783 (1984). The court in the following case stated, "In *Calder*, a reporter in Florida wrote an article for the National Enquirer about Shirley Jones, a well-known actress who lived and worked in California. The president and editor of the National Enquirer reviewed and approved the article, and the National Enquirer published the article. The U.S. Supreme Court held that California could exercise jurisdiction over the individual defendants based on the effects of their Florida conduct in California. The court found jurisdiction proper because California was the focal point both of the story and of the harm suffered."

Pavlovich v. The Superior Court of Santa Clara County and DVD Copy Control Assn., Inc.
58 F.3d 2 (2002)

Facts

On December 27, 1999, Pavlovich was a computer-engineering student at Purdue University in Indiana, a leader of the "open source" movement, and founder of the LiVid video project that promoted the development of an unlicensed system of DVD playback and copying. Pavlovich also owned and operated a Web site where he posted the DeCSS code containing the keys to unlock the "Content Scramble System" used by the motion picture industry to prevent the unauthorized copying of DVD movies. The opinion credits Pavlovich with the development, in conjunction with other individuals, of the DeCSS program. Subsequent to the filing of the complaint, Pavlovich moved to the state of Texas. Pavlovich "knew that California is commonly known as the center of the motion picture industry, and that the computer industry holds a commanding presence in the state." In his deposition, Pavlovich stated, "Yeah, they make a lot of movies in California, Hollywood, yeah." He also added, "Hollywood is the big area in California where they make a lot of movies and a lot of movie stars and whatnot." Pavlovich also testified that he had heard of Silicon Valley. He stated, "That's an area where there is a lot of technology-related companies, software writers, hardware manufacturers, programmers."

Pavlovich never obtained a license to use DVD technology for his LiVid project. He knew that obtaining a license was required for using certain aspects of DVD technology, that is, access to the trade secret CSS technology. Pavlovich, acting in concert with others, distributed the decryption program for the CSS technology.

The issue is whether the state of California may exercise jurisdiction under its long-arm statute consistent with due process over a nonresident individual who operates a Web site located in another state and posts on that Web site information that may violate the trademark secret rights of some California corporate residents when that nonresident individual has never set foot in California, contacted any person in California, or earned any money from any activity there.

Because Pavlovich knew that posting DeCSS on the LiVid Web site would harm the movie and computer industries in California, the Court of Appeals found he purposefully availed himself of forum benefits under the *Calder* effects test. The court also concluded that the exercise of jurisdiction over Pavlovich was reasonable.

Judicial Opinion *(Judge Brown)*

We now consider whether Pavlovich's contacts with California meet the effects test. We conclude that the evidence in the record fails to show that Pavlovich expressly aimed his tortious conduct at or intentionally targeted California.

In this case, Pavlovich's sole contact with California is LiVid's posting of the DeCSS source code containing DVD CCA's proprietary information on an Internet Web site accessible to any person with Internet access. Pavlovich never worked in California. He owned no property in California, maintained no bank accounts in California, and had no telephone listings in California. Neither Pavlovich nor his company solicited or transacted any business in California. The record also contains no evidence of any LiVid contacts with California.

Here, LiVid's Web site merely posts information and has no interactive features. There is no evidence in the record suggesting that the site targeted much less downloaded the DeCSS source code from, the LiVid Web site. Thus, Pavlovich's alleged conduct in posting a passive Web site on the Internet is not, by itself, sufficient to subject him to jurisdiction in California.

Nonetheless, DVD CCA contends posting the misappropriated source code on an Internet Web site is sufficient to establish purposeful availment in this case because Pavlovich knew the posting would harm not only a licensing entity but also the motion picture, computer, and consumer electronics industries centered in California. According to DVD CCA, this knowledge establishes that Pavlovich intentionally targeted California and is sufficient to confer jurisdiction under the *Calder* effects test.

The only question in this case is whether Pavlovich's knowledge that his tortuous conduct may harm certain industries centered in California is sufficient to establish express aiming at California. We concluded that his knowledge, by itself, cannot establish purposeful availment under the effects test.

Pavlovich may still face the music—just not in California.

Judgment of the Court of Appeals is reversed.

Case Questions

1. What is the "effect" test for jurisdiction?
2. Why did the court refuse to find the "effect" test applied in this case?
3. Is it ethical to decrypt DVD movies?

A federal court may find jurisdiction under the due process clause if the facts of the case satisfy general or specific jurisdiction.

General Jurisdiction

General jurisdiction (see Figure 2.7) exists over a nonresident defendant in cases where the contract activity in the forum state is obvious. The test applied by the courts to determine if general jurisdiction is present is whether or not the defendant's activities in the forum state were "systematic and continuous," extensive, and persuasive, including activities unrelated to the forum [*Helikopteros Nacionales de Colombia, S.A. v. Hall*, 466 U.S. 408 (1984)]. General jurisdiction is seldom found in Internet cases. One court ruled, "To hold that the possibility of ordering products from a Web site establishes general jurisdiction would effectively hold that any corporation with such a Web site is subject to general jurisdiction in every state. The court is not willing to take such a step" [*La Salle Nat'Bank v. Viro*, 85 F. Supp. 2d 857, 862 (N.D. Ill. 2000)].

Specific Jurisdiction

Specific jurisdiction (see Figure 2.8) does not require systematic and continuous business activity in the forum state. The courts find specific jurisdiction when an online

FIGURE 2.7   General Jurisdiction

The out-of-state defendant had a

- substantial,
- continuous, and
- systematic presence in the foreign state.

FIGURE 2.8   Specific Jurisdiction

Minimum contacts:

- Defendant purposefully availed itself to conduct business in the foreign state.
- Litigation arises directly out of defendant's activities in the foreign state.
- Foreign jurisdiction was reasonably foreseeable.

defendant purposefully avails itself of the privileges of doing business in the forum state, the claim in court arose out of the forum-related activity, and it is reasonable to impose specific jurisdiction over the defendant [*CompuServe, Inc. v. Patterson*, 89 F.3d 1257 (6th Cir. 1996)]. Courts have found specific jurisdiction in Internet cases involving copyright and trademark jurisdiction and breach of contract. A court noted, "The vast majority of Internet-based personal jurisdiction cases involve specific jurisdiction" [*Coastal Video Comm. Corp. v. Staywell Corp.*, 59 F. Supp. 2d 562, 570 n.6 (E.D. Va. 1999)].

In the following case, the court analyzed the sending of spam through a privately owned ISP based on defendant's motion to dismiss for lack of personal jurisdiction in the Virginia court. Spamming is discussed in greater detail in Chapter 8. Notice how and why the court found specific jurisdiction over the nonresident defendant.

Verizon Online Services, Inc. v. Ralsky
Eastern District Ct. of Virginia,
Civil Action No. 01-432-A (2002)

Facts

The plaintiff, Verizon Online Services, Inc. ("Verizon"), is an ISP that is a Delaware corporation with its principal place of business in Reston, Virginia. It provides a content-based online service to its customers that includes the use of e-mail and access to the Internet. Verizon operates a computer network throughout the United States that includes seven e-mail servers in Reston, Virginia. Every e-mail addressed to a Verizon subscriber who uses the domain name @bellatlantic.net is processed by Verizon's e-mail servers in Reston, Virginia.

Defendants Alan Ralsky and Lance McDonald are residents of Michigan. Defendants alleged to have acted in concert with four to a hundred as-of-yet unidentified John Does to send spam to and through Verizon's servers in Virginia.

Verizon alleges that from at least November 2000 through December 2000, defendants transmitted, or facilitated, the transmission of millions of spam messages addressed to Verizon subscribers through Verizon's computer network. Verizon has policies prohibiting the transmission of spam over its network. These policies are available at various Verizon Web sites. The messages allegedly transmitted by defendants contained hypertext links to

Web sites advertising goods and services including credit repair tools, new car buying services, computer programs, diet pills, and online gambling. According to Verizon, defendants used a number of fraudulent and deceptive methods to cloak their identities and remain anonymous.

According to Verizon, the spam allegedly transmitted by defendants harmed Verizon on several levels. The spam imposed burdens on Verizon's computer system by consuming the network services needed to deliver e-mail to Verizon subscribers. Verizon's servers have a finite capacity that is designed to accommodate the demands of its subscribers.

Defendants moved for dismissal of the case for lack of personal jurisdiction.

Judicial Opinion *(Memorandum Opinion, District Judge, Gerald Bruce Lee)*

The issue presented is whether Defendants' transmission of millions of spam to Verizon's subscribers through Verizon's servers in Virginia constitutes sufficient minimum contacts to satisfy the demands of the due process clause of the Fourteenth Amendment of the Constitution.

Spam is defined as "an unsolicited, often commercial, message transmitted through the Internet as a mass mailing to a large number of recipients." Anyone who has ever operated an e-mail account is familiar with spam. Spam is the twenty-first century version of junkmail and over the last few years has quickly become one of the most popular forms of advertising over the internet, as well as one of the most bothersome. To determine whether personal jurisdiction exists over a nonresident defendant, courts engage in a two-step inquiry. First, the court looks to the law of the forum state, in this case the Virginia long-arm statute, to assess whether the plaintiff's cause of action against the defendant and the nature of the defendant's contacts with Virginia fall within the law's scope. The court must then determine whether the reach of the long-arm statute's grasp under the circumstances comports with the Due Process Clause of the Fourteenth Amendment of the United States Constitution.

To extend long-arm jurisdiction under §8.01-328.1(A)(4), in addition to alleging that the defendant causes a tort in Virginia, the complaint must allege that a defendant regularly conducted or solicited business, or engaged in any other persistent course of conduct, or derived substantial revenue from goods used or consumed or services rendered in Virginia. The Due Process Clause requires "that no defendant shall be hauled into court unless the defendant has 'certain minimum contacts [with the state] . . . such that the maintenance of the suit does not offend traditional notions of fair play and substantial justice.'" There are two types of personal jurisdiction a federal court may exercise over a nonresident defendant—general or specific. In this case, as Verizon concedes, Defendants have not subjected themselves to general jurisdiction, which concerns the exercise of jurisdiction over the Defendant in a suit unrelated to the Defendant's contacts with the forum. Rather, the inquiry in this case is whether defendants' contacts flowing from Verizon's claims are sufficient to establish specific jurisdiction. In determining minimum contacts for specific personal jurisdiction, "a court properly focuses on the 'relationship among the Defendant, the forum, and the litigation."

Defendants should have reasonably expected to be hauled into a court in any state where they violated Verizon's public anti-"spam" policy and compromised its servers. Any other result would grant spammers like defendants carte blanche to spam with impunity.

By allegedly transmitting millions of e-mails to make money at Verizon's expense, knowing or reasonably knowing that such conduct would harm Verizon's e-mail servers, Defendants should have expected to get dragged into court where their actions caused the greatest injury.

Applying these factors, the exercise of personal jurisdiction over defendants in this case is constitutionally reasonable. Although it may be somewhat burdensome for Defendants to defend a suit in Virginia, defendants should have been aware of the possibility of being sued where their "spam" inflicted the greatest injury to Verizon. Virginia has a strong interest in resolving this dispute because it involves a Virginia resident and Virginia law.

Motion to dismiss for lack of personal jurisdiction denied.

Case Questions

1. Explain why there was no general jurisdiction over the defendant in this case.
2. Explain why the defendants should have reasonably expected to be sued in Virginia.
3. What is the two-step inquiry a court must engage in to determine whether personal jurisdiction exists over a nonresident defendant?

Sliding Scale Analysis of Personal Jurisdiction over a Nonresident E-Business

A clear analysis of online jurisdiction appears in the trial court's decision of *Zippo Mfg. Co. v. Zippo Dot Com, Inc.*, 952 F. Supp. 1119 (1997). Zippo is the Pennsylvania-based manufacturer of Zippo lighters. It sued a California Internet news service for trademark infringement based on the defendant's use of the domain name "zippo.com." In finding jurisdiction over the nonresident California defendant, the court articulated a sliding-scale standard used in deciding subsequent e-business decisions that relates jurisdiction to the amount and type of online commercial activity.

The court stated,

> The likelihood that personal jurisdiction can be constitutionally exercised is directly proportionate to the nature and quality of commercial activity that an entity conducts over the Internet. . . .

> At one end of the spectrum are situations where a defendant clearly does business over the Internet. If the defendant enters into contracts with residents of a foreign jurisdiction that involve the knowing and repeated transmissions of computer files over the Internet, personal jurisdiction is proper (e.g., *Compuserve, Inc. v. Patterson*, 89 F.2d 1257, 6th Cir. 1996). At the opposite end are situations where a defendant has simply posted information on an Internet Web site that is accessible to users in foreign jurisdictions. A passive Web site that does little more than make information available to those who are interested in it is not grounds for the exercise of personal jurisdiction (e.g., *Bensusan Restaurant Corp., v. King*, 937 F. Supp. 296 [S.D.N.Y. 1996]). The middle ground is occupied by interactive Web sites where a user can exchange information with the

host computer. In these cases, the exercise of jurisdiction is determined by examining the level of interactivity and commercial nature of the exchange of information that occurs on the Web site.

This sliding-scale standard is useful in illustrating that having only an electronic presence in a foreign state is insufficient to establish personal jurisdiction over an e-business (see Figure 2.9).

For instance, an online consulting company's informational site that posts a newsletter free of charge and does not solicit business is not commercial activity and does not subject the owner to out-of-state jurisdiction. Remember that if grounds for a lawsuit exist, and there is no personal jurisdiction over the nonresident e-business, the case could be tried in the company's state. Lack of jurisdiction does not mean there is no liability.

A nonresident interactive e-business that solicits online business in a foreign state will be subject to its jurisdiction. Online cases that appear to fall between passive and interactive transactions are based on a perceived level of commercial activity. As the courts attempt to quantify the amount of Internet business, they appear to assert jurisdiction over a nonresident online defendant when the amount of commercial activity is high.

Each case is "fact sensitive" and requires a careful analysis to determine jurisdiction. Some of the uncertainty over jurisdiction can be resolved by the appropriate use of forum selection clauses.

Forum Selection and Choice of Law Clause

Most Web sites include at the bottom of their home pages their *Terms of Use*, which include a **forum selection clause** and **choice of law clause** in the event that a lawsuit is brought against the online company.

http://

- For an example of a forum selection clause, click on Terms of Use at **http://www.aol.com**

Note that not all courts automatically follow the forum selection and choice of law clause that requests to have the case litigated in a particular state and court and a certain law applied to the case.

Because the forum selection clause is a unilateral, non-negotiable jurisdiction clause, it is legally referred to as an

FIGURE 2.9   **Sliding-Scale Analysis of Personal Jurisdiction**

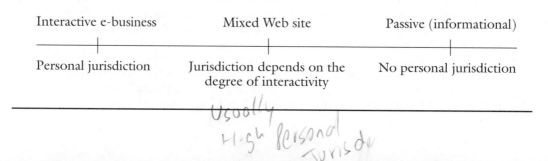

Interactive e-business	Mixed Web site	Passive (informational)
Personal jurisdiction	Jurisdiction depends on the degree of interactivity	No personal jurisdiction

adhesion contract. Such contracts are legal providing they are "reasonable" and "fair." The U.S. Supreme Court in *Burger King v. Rudzewicz,* 471 U.S. 462, 472 n. 14 (1985), has stated that because a person can consent to personal jurisdiction, such clauses are in general valid and enforceable. However, in *The Bremen v. Zapata Off-Shore Co.,* 407 U.S. 1 (1972), the Supreme Court stated that these clauses must be "freely negotiated" and not "unreasonably unjust." We could question whether an electronic click to a Web site, with its Terms of Use buried at the end of the home page, satisfies that requirement.

In the following case, notice how the California court refused to follow the forum selection and choice of law clause in the America Online contract with its subscriber because it conflicted with the state's consumer protection law and thereby violated public policy.

Am. Online, Inc. v. Superior Court (Mendoza)
90 Cal. App. 4th 1, 108 Cal. Rptr. 2d 699 (2001)

Facts

A class action was filed by Mendoza for himself and others against AOL seeking compensatory and punitive damages, injunctive relief, and restitution. The complaint alleges that the parties are former subscribers to AOL's Internet service who, over the past four years, paid about $22 each month for the service. Monthly payments were made by allowing AOL, to debit automatically the credit cards of class members. The class members terminated their subscriptions to AOL, but, without authorization, AOL continued to debit their credit cards for monthly service fees. Mendoza individually alleged that he gave AOL notice of the cancellation of his subscription in October 1999, but AOL continued to charge monthly fees against his credit card at least through February 2000, at which time Mendoza cancelled his credit card in order to stop the debits.

The complaint alleged separate causes of action including violations of California's Unfair Business Practices Act, violations of California's Consumer Legal Remedies Act, common law conversion/trespass, and common law fraud.

Shortly thereafter, AOL filed a motion to dismiss the action on the ground of inconvenient forum. As noted, the motion was based on the forum selection clause contained in the Terms of Service (TOS) agreement entered into between Mendoza and AOL at the time he subscribed to AOL's proprietary Internet. The TOS states in part the following: "You expressly agree that exclusive jurisdiction for any claim or dispute with AOL or relating in any way to your membership or your use of AOL resides in the courts of Virginia and you further agree and expressly consent to the exercise of personal jurisdiction in the courts of Virginia in connection with any such dispute including any claim involving AOL or its affiliates, subsidiaries, employees, contractors, officers, directors, telecommunications providers and content providers. . . ." Additionally, paragraph 8 contained a choice of law provision designating Virginia law as being applicable to any dispute between the parties: "The laws of the Commonwealth of Virginia govern this Agreement and your membership."

Mendoza objected, claiming the document did not accurately reflect what was displayed to him when he commenced service with AOL. Instead, he described seeing displayed on his home computer monitor a "densely worded, small-size text that was hard to read on the computer screen." This objection formed the leitmotif for Mendoza's claim that the TOS was an unconscionable adhesion contract, and that under applicable rules of contract construction, the forum selection clause was unenforceable. In addition, Mendoza contended the TOS was unreasonable and unenforceable because it necessarily required him and the putative class members to relinquish legal rights in derogation of California public policy.

Judicial Opinion *(Judge Haerle)*

Our law favors forum selection agreements only so long as they are procured freely and voluntarily, with the place chosen having some logical nexus to one of the parties or the dispute, and so long as California consumers will not find their substantial legal rights significantly impaired by their enforcement. Therefore, to be enforceable, the selected jurisdiction must be "suitable," "available," and able to "accomplish substantial justice." The trial court determined that the circumstances of contract formation did not reflect Mendoza exercised free will, and that the effect of enforcing the forum selection clause here would violate California public policy by eviscerating important legal rights afforded to this state's consumers. [We] must determine if the substantive law of the selected forum is in conflict with a fundamental public policy of California. If so, the choice of law provision is not to be enforced if California has an interest in having its own law applied to the dispute.

JUDGMENT FOR MENDOZA AFFIRMED.

In so holding we reject Mendoza's contention that the clause should not be enforced simply because it would be patently unreasonable to require him or other AOL customers who form the putative class to travel to Virginia to litigate the relatively nominal individual sums at issue.

But the additional cost or inconvenience necessitated by litigation in the selected forum is not part of the calculus when considering whether a forum selection clause should be enforced. Our Supreme Court has put this matter to rest in *Smith Valentino* when it quoted: "Mere inconvenience or additional expense is not the test of unreasonableness since it may be assumed that the plaintiff received under the contract consideration for these things." (*Smith Valentino, supra,* 17 Cal. 3d at p. 496; see also *Furda v. Superior Court* 161 Cal. App. 3d 418, 426–427 [Cal. App. 4 Dist. 1984].)

The choice of law provision is not to be enforced [because] California has an interest in having its own law applied to the dispute.

Case Questions

1. Explain what the court meant by stating that a mere inconvenience or additional expense in having to travel to a foreign state is not enough to invalidate a forum selection clause.

2. How can an e-business know if a forum selection and choice of law clause will be enforced by a foreign court?

3. Is it ethical for an e-business to force a customer into its jurisdiction as a condition of using the site?

The national trend follows a Massachusetts case, *Jacobson v. Mailboxes, Etc. U.S.A., Inc.*, 419 Mass. 572 (1995). The court found that the unilateral and nonbargaining nature of a forum selection clause, accompanied by its undue inconvenience over the plaintiff litigating the claim in the defendant's state, argues in favor of the clause being unenforceable as an unfair and unreasonable adhesion contract.

Terms of use generally appear in small print at the end of the Web merchant's home page and consist of boilerplate (i.e., standard legalese) provisions. A typical clause may state *"[T]he parties agree that a condition of using this site is that any and all claims arising out of use of this site will be tried in Massachusetts and Massachusetts law will apply."* The court in *Jacobson* held the "overreaching must be based on something more than the mere fact that the forum selection clause was a boilerplate provision on the back of the form." Because most major online companies are using forum selection clauses on their Web sites and it has become a trade practice to do so, it appears the clauses will be enforced if they are drafted in a way that is fair and reasonable.

INTERNATIONAL JURISDICTION IN CYBERSPACE

Who Governs the Online World?

Just as the Internet offers unprecedented opportunities for international communication and commerce, so the Internet presents unique and difficult jurisdictional questions. The question of who exactly has jurisdiction to resolve a cyberspace issue is far from certain. For example, in 1998, members of the American Bar Association completed a report addressing the problems of jurisdiction in cyberspace. The report affirmed that "a critical element of the predictability necessary for electronic commerce to evolve profitably and efficiently is businesses' and consumers' knowledge of what regulatory regimes will apply to the businesses in which they engage and with which they interact." Businesses must know what law applies to their dealings so they may comply with these laws. In other words, businesses must know the court's choice of law in a cyber-dispute. Businesses must also be aware of the appropriate forum for resolving international legal disputes in cyberspace. Whether a dispute will be resolved in the United States or Germany may have significant impact on the business decisions of a global cyber firm.

Nearly all commentators agree that it is simply not possible for a single entity or group to control the Internet and thus have jurisdiction over its boundaries. Making matters more difficult, data is so easily converted and packaged as it moves from one computer to the other that the origin of the offending data may be easily masked by the author. Distance no longer matters, as a transmission from California to Nevada is as easy as one from California to India. Fundamentally, Internet users place themselves in a number of "virtual places" when they make a statement, purchase, or sale online. The users and their data are "present" in the location of the originating computer, the locations of the routing networks of cyberspace, and the destination of the transmission. Thus jurisdiction may be asserted in one of many places, such as the location of the following:

1. Internet user
2. Internet service provider
3. various communications conduits through which the data flows
4. content provider
5. server that hosts the content provider's information

The question remains: Whose national laws apply in a truly global online world? It is virtually impossible for a global online firm to comply with every applicable law in every nation when doing business around the world. Some law must apply, but whose national law that should be in a particular circumstance remains undecided.

PRINCIPLES OF NATIONAL ENFORCEMENT

A number of principles establish the power of countries over their national boundaries. These perceptions of sovereignty have been well settled for hundreds of years. With the advent of cyberspace, they present significantly differing views on the sources of international authority for regulating cyberspace. The following three principles are the most relevant to jurisdictional issues in cyberspace.

The **territoriality principle** states that a nation is sovereign over its physical territory to the exclusion of other states. Nations have the power to sanction and control conduct within the bounds of their own physical boundaries. The territoriality principle allows nations to regulate Internet content and services offered from within its boundaries. However, this principle cannot easily encompass cyberspace because cyberspace does not have a concrete location. Cyberspace is a network so large and so distributed that removing one, ten, or even a hundred computers would not damage the entire network.

The **nationality principle** affirms that a nation may control its citizens. This principle also defines the rights and responsibilities of citizens both inside and outside the territory of the nation. This principle has been used to establish that a court has criminal jurisdiction if the defendant is a national of the forum state and that a state may tax the worldwide income of its nationals. The nationality principle would guide Internet jurisdiction by establishing the nationality of the parties as the key factor determining jurisdiction, not their physical location.

The **effects principle** holds that a country may protect its interests by criminalizing an act that it deems harmful to its national security. If a nation deems a practice particularly harmful, it may ban this act both within and outside its national borders. For example, U.S. courts have been willing to apply market-based regulations abroad, even when they conflict with foreign law. No doubt the effects principle has already manifested itself through national regulations of the Internet. For example, in September 2002, China blocked its citizens from access to Google, a popular search engine, because it allowed access to subjects that the Chinese government deemed harmful to its national and security interests. Other nations have attempted to impose regulation on Internet casinos that operate outside its borders. These and other disputes have generated significant discussion as nations assert their own values across their physical boundaries into cyberspace.

Although these examples are notable, they pale in controversy compared to one of the most widely examined Internet jurisdictional disputes in the world. This clash pits the commercial and speech interests of a leading multinational Internet corporation against the values and laws of a single nation. The following case highlights this exciting controversy and provides an American judicial view of the problem of international online jurisdiction.

Yahoo!, Inc. v. La Ligue Contre Le Racisme et L'Antisemitisme
169 F. Supp. 2d 1181 (N.D. Cal. 2001)

Facts

Yahoo!, the world's most popular search engine and Web directory, permitted Nazi memorabilia to be sold on its auction site. This practice conflicted with French law, which prohibits the sale or exhibition of objects that incite racial hatred, like Nazi memorabilia. Two human rights organizations filed a lawsuit in France against Yahoo! alleging that its auction practices violated French law. The French court ruled that Yahoo! was violating French law by failing to block French users from accessing the prohibited material. The judge stayed the execution of the judgment until a panel of experts could decide whether it was technically possible for a U.S.-based Internet company to identify and exclude French users.

The panel concluded, by inspecting the Internet service provider addresses of users, that a filtering system could be implemented to block most French users. The judge then confirmed his ruling and gave Yahoo! 90 days to comply. If Yahoo! failed to do so, it would be fined $13,000 a day until it complied with the order. Yahoo! responded by removing the offending material from its French portal and placing warning messages on its U.S. site informing French users that they could be breaking the law in their country if they observed certain offensive material.

Yahoo! responded by filing this lawsuit in California, seeking a declaration that the French court's order was unenforceable in the United States.

Judicial Opinion *(Judge Fogel)*

As this Court and others have observed, the instant case presents novel and important issues arising from the global reach of the Internet. Indeed, the specific facts of this case implicate issues of policy, politics, and culture that are beyond the purview of one nation's judiciary. Thus it is critical that the Court define at the outset what is and is not at stake in the present proceeding.

This case is *not* about the moral acceptability of promoting the symbols or propaganda of Nazism. Most would agree that such acts are profoundly offensive. By any reasonable standard of morality, the Nazis were responsible for one of the worst displays of inhumanity in recorded history. This Court is acutely mindful of the emotional pain reminders of the Nazi era cause to Holocaust survivors and deeply respectful of the motivations of the French Republic in enacting the underlying statutes and of the defendant organizations in seeking relief under those statutes. Vigilance is the key to preventing atrocities such as the Holocaust from occurring again.

Nor is this case about the right of France or any other nation to determine its own law and social policies. A basic function of a sovereign state is to determine by law what forms of speech and conduct are acceptable within its borders. In this instance, as a nation whose citizens suffered the effects of Nazism in ways that are incomprehensible to most Americans, France clearly has the right to enact and enforce laws such as those relied upon by the French Court here. . . . In particular, there is no doubt that France may and will continue to ban the purchase and possession within its borders of Nazi and Third Reich related matter and to seek criminal sanctions against those who violate the law.

What *is* at issue here is whether it is consistent with the Constitution and laws of the United States for another nation to regulate speech by a United States resident within the United States on the basis that such speech can be accessed by Internet users in that nation. In a world in which ideas and information transcend borders and the Internet in particular renders the physical distance between speaker and audience virtually meaningless, the implications of this question go far beyond the facts of this case. The modern world is home to widely varied cultures with radically divergent value systems. . . . If the government or another party in one of these sovereign nations were to seek enforcement of such laws against Yahoo! or another U.S.-based Internet service provider, what principles should guide the court's analysis?

The Court has stated that it must and will decide this case in accordance with the Constitution and laws of the United States. It recognizes that in so doing, it necessarily adopts certain value judgments embedded in those enactments, including the fundamental judgment expressed in the First Amendment that it is preferable to permit the non-violent expression of offensive viewpoints rather than to impose viewpoint-based governmental regulation upon speech. The government and people of France have made a different judgment based upon their own experience. In undertaking its inquiry as to the proper application of the laws of the United States, the Court intends no disrespect for that judgment or for the experience that has informed it. . . .

Comity

No legal judgment has any effect, of its own force, beyond the limits of the sovereignty from which its authority is derived. 28 U.S.C. § 1738. However, the United States Constitution and implementing legislation require that full faith and credit be given to judgments of sister states, territories, and possessions of the United States. U.S. CONST. art. IV, §§ 1, cl. 1. The extent to which the United States, or any state, honors the judicial decrees of foreign nations is a matter of choice, governed by "the comity of nations." *Hilton v. Guyot, 159 U.S. 113, 163, 16 S.Ct. 139, 40 L.Ed. 95 (1895).* Comity "is neither a matter of absolute obligation, on the one hand, nor of mere courtesy and good will, upon the other." *Hilton, 159 U.S. at 163–64, 16 S.Ct. 139 (1895).* United States courts generally recognize foreign judgments and decrees unless enforcement would be prejudicial or contrary to the country's interests. . . .   *Authoritivly order*

As discussed previously, the French order's content and viewpoint-based regulation of the Web pages and auction site on Yahoo.com, while entitled to great deference as an articulation of French law, clearly would be inconsistent with the First Amendment if mandated by a court in the United States. What makes this case uniquely challenging is that the Internet in effect allows one to speak in more than one place at the same time. Although France has the sovereign right to regulate what speech is permissible in France, this Court may not enforce a foreign order that violates the protections of the United States Constitution by chilling protected speech that occurs simultaneously within our borders. . . .

The reason for limiting comity in this area is sound. The protection to free speech and the press embodied in the First Amendment would be seriously jeopardized by the entry of foreign judgments granted pursuant to standards deemed appropriate in another country but considered antithetical to the protections afforded the press by the U.S. Constitution. Absent a body of law that establishes international standards with respect to speech on the Internet and an appropriate treaty or legislation addressing enforcement of such standards to speech originating within the United States, the principle of comity is outweighed by the Court's obligation to uphold the First Amendment. . . .

Accordingly, [Yahoo!'s] motion for summary judgment will be granted. The Clerk shall enter judgment and close the file.

IT IS SO ORDERED.

Case Questions

1. This case was widely discussed by commentators as a watershed decision. How does this case highlight the development of how the courts, government, and society think about the Internet?
2. Would the French court decision or American court decision be different if Yahoo! could block access by French users with a minimum of cost and effort? Why or why not?
3. How does this decision enlighten lawmakers about the power of individual governments to regulate global cyberspace?

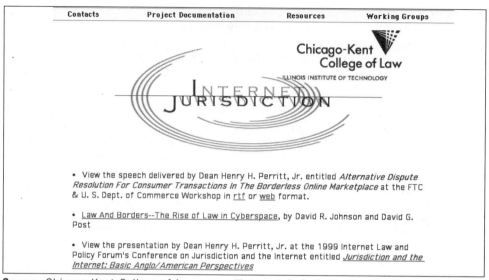

Source: Chicago-Kent College of Law page, "Internet Jurisdiction" as found on *http://www. kentlaw.edu/cyberlaw/*. Reprinted with permission.

Summary

It should be comforting to the owners of both e-business start-ups and legacy companies with an e-business to know they have constitutional rights that will protect them from a foreign court's jurisdiction. Under the *due process clause,* before an out-of-state court has jurisdiction over an e-business, the company must have purposefully directed its sales to the marketplace of the foreign state.

Pre-Internet cases have established the ground rules for personal jurisdiction in cyberspace. The U.S. Supreme Court as early as 1945 in the *International Shoe Company* case held that a *physical presence* was *not* required for a nonresident defendant to be subject to the court's jurisdiction so long as the due process clause was satisfied.

This decision, and subsequent cases that require compliance with *both* the state's long-arm statute and the due process clause, created a legal foundation for personal jurisdiction over a nonresident e-business with only an *electronic presence* in a state to be accountable to a foreign court. Potentially, every e-business is subject to jurisdiction all over the country.

As long as the state's long-arm statute and the due process clause of the U.S. Constitution are satisfied, the nonresident e-business must have the case tried in the foreign state.

An e-business manager should be aware of this global jurisdictional exposure and discuss with its lawyer the drafting of a *forum selection and choice of law clause* on the e-business's home page in its Terms of Use. Federal courts have ruled that choice of law contacts are generally enforced. [See *AMF, Inc. v. Computer Automation, Inc.*, 573 F. Supp. 924, 926 (S.D. Ohio 1983).] The company should also consider limiting the product or services on the Web site to certain states and countries. Failure to take these precautions could lead to costly litigation in distant jurisdictions. An e-business manager should also consider the international jurisdictional implications of doing business online. Each nation has its own concepts of jurisdiction and may enforce its laws beyond its own borders when it sees fit. As the Yahoo! case reveals, managers may be faced with the tough decision of controlling content based on one country's objections or facing legal action in that country and paying damages.

Key Terms

jurisdiction, *17*
personal (in personam)
   jurisdiction, *17*
subject matter
   jurisdiction, *17*
in rem jurisdiction, *18*
long-arm statute, *20*

due process, *22*
general jurisdiction, *22*
specific jurisdiction, *22*
minimum contacts, *22*
motion to dismiss, *23*
passive Web site, *25*
interactive Web site, *25*

forum selection clause, *32*
choice of law clause, *32*
adhesion contract, *33*
territoriality principle, *36*
nationality principle, *36*
effects principle, *36*

Manager's Checklist

√ Be aware that an interactive Web site that solicits business worldwide may subject the company to personal jurisdiction in any state or country.

√ Consider the use of technology that counts the Web site hits and have it audited by a CPA firm to document the number of sales in the foreign state or country. This may be useful in proving the site does little or no business in the state where the plaintiff is bringing the lawsuit.

√ Consider using a technological filter that prevents the Web site from being seen in certain states or countries where you do not want to do business. This will limit your liability exposure to those states and countries where you are soliciting business. If appropriate, let users know you are restricting the sale of your product or service to certain states and countries.

√ Include a forum selection and choice of law clause in the Web site's Terms of Use as a condition of doing business with the company. The clause states, "In the event of a dispute, the laws of the state of . . . will govern and the case will be tried in that state." Be aware that not all state or federal courts will be obliged to follow that requirement.

√ Review insurance contracts to ensure that you can cover the additional costs of defending lawsuits in remote jurisdictions.

√ Consider disclaimers in the Web site's Terms of Use regarding not doing business in selected states and/or countries.

√ Consider incorporating the Web site that sells the product or service as a separate business entity from a related existing business it supports to protect it from liability based on a claim against the e-business.

√ In a B2C (business-to-consumer) transaction, an ethical issue for managers is requiring a consumer/user to bring a claim against the e-business in its own forum when it would cause a financial hardship to the consumer.

√ Ethical Considerations

Consider the ethics of an e-business that includes a forum selection and choice of law clause in its Terms of Use. An aggrieved consumer may be forced to travel to a foreign state and at great expense bring the lawsuit in the foreign state or have the case dismissed. For instance, Amazon's "Conditions of Use" (see *http://www.amazon.com*) state, "By visiting Amazon.com, you agree that the laws of the state of Washington, without regard to principles of conflict of laws, will govern these Conditions of Use and any dispute of any sort that might arise between you and Amazon.com or its affiliates." An East Coast consumer that sues Amazon may have to bring the suit in the state of Washington. This is hardly a "balanced playing field" for the consumer.

Case Problems

1. Plaintiff Music Millennium Enterprises, Inc., an Oregon music retailer, sells CDs from its two in-state stores, via telephone, mail order, and from its Web site. Defendants, Millennium Music LP and Millennium Music, Inc., are in the same business of retail music stores and employ similar distribution channels. One small supplier, Allegro Corporation in Portland, Oregon, mailed a credit document on July 7, 1998, to plaintiff, which was intended for defendant. In August, plaintiff structured an Internet purchase of CD from defendants and sued defendants a week after for violating plaintiff's state and common law trademark rights. The defendants moved to dismiss the case for lack of personal jurisdiction. Decide, and state your reasons why there is or is not personal jurisdiction in Oregon. [*Millennium Enterprises, Inc., d/b/a Music Millennium, et al. v. Millennium Music, et al.* 33 F. Supp. 2d 907 (1999)]

2. Plaintiffs, AOL and its subsidiary, ICQ, Inc. (Delaware corporations with principal place of business in Dulles, Virginia), offer a variety of online services. The ICQ service, shorthand for "I Seek You," offers two users real-time "chat"/Internet communication and interaction via e-mail. Defendant eAsia, Inc. (California corporation with its principal place of business in Taiwan), "through its subsidiaries, develops Internet related software and provides Internet related service for customers in Taiwan and other parts of Asia." It offers a communications protocol named "ICQ" and registered <cicq.net> and <picq.net> as domain names with Network Solutions Incorporated (NSI), at the cost of approximately $35 per year. Plaintiffs sued eAsia in Virginia for, among others, violating trademark infringement under the Lanham Act. Defendant moved to dismiss the case. Decide, and state your reasons why

there is or is not personal jurisdiction in Virginia. [*America Online, Inc., et al. v. Chih-Hsien Huang, et al.*, 106 F. Supp. 2d 848 (2000)]

3. Plaintiffs, Nissan Motor Co. (a large Japanese automaker) and Nissan North America Inc. (located in California, marketing and distributing Nissan vehicles in the United States) are the owners of various registered trademarks using the word *Nissan* in connection with automobiles and other vehicles. Defendant, Nissan Computer Corporation (a North Carolina company in the business of providing computer sales and services), registered a trademark for its Nissan Computer logo with the state of North Carolina. It also registered two Internet domain names: "Nissan.com" and "Nissan.net," using its president Mr. Uzi Nissan's surname. In August 1999, defendant altered the content of its "Nissan.com" Web site, displaying banner advertisements and Web links to various Internet search engines and merchandising companies, including links to automobile merchandisers (some are California automobile companies). The plaintiffs filed a complaint alleging "(1) trademark dilution in violation of federal and state law; (2) trademark infringement; (3) domain name piracy. . . ." Defendant responded with a motion to dismiss the case for want of personal jurisdiction. Do the plaintiffs have personal jurisdiction over the defendant? [*Nissan Motor Co., Ltd. V. Nissan Computer Corporation*, 89 F. Supp. 2d 1154 (C.D. Cal. 2000)]

4. Plaintiffs, Porsche cars North America, Inc. and dr. Ing. H.c.F. Porsche AG, market cars, goods, accessories, and services under "Porsche" and "Boxster" through their registered "PORSCHE.COM" and "PORSCHE-USA.COM" as the domain names for their Web site. Plaintiffs discovered that some 128 other sites using similar names, such as "PORSCHE.NET", "PORSCHECLUB. NET", either in use or dormant, channels no consumers to Porsche's Web site. Rather than filing an in personam action against those who registered the allegedly offending domain names, Porsche filed an in rem proceeding against the domain names themselves, including the two names cited here. "PORSCHE.NET" and "PORSCHECLUB.NET" have appeared through counsel and move to dismiss for lack of jurisdiction. Decide, and state your reasons why there is or is not personal jurisdiction over the plaintiffs. [*Porsche Cars North America, Inc., et al. v. Porsche.com, et al.*, 51 F. Supp. 2d 707 (1999)]

5. An American business magazine published an article accusing two prominent Russian citizens of being involved in organized crime in Russia. The article was published in North America, where the magazine had a circulation of over 785,000; Russia, where only 13 copies were distributed; and England, where the magazine had a circulation of just under 2,000 and a total readership of about 6,000. An online version of the magazine was also available to UK residents. The plaintiffs, who both claimed to have significant connections with

England, chose to bring libel actions against the publisher and editor of the magazine in England, rather than in the United States or Russia. Does the UK court have jurisdiction? [*Berezovsky v. Forbes, Inc.* (1999), E.M.L.R. 278, 1999 WL 1043805, *aff'd sub nom*, Berezovsky v. Michaels, 2 All E.R. 986, 2000 WL 544123 (House of Lords, May 11, 2000)]

Additional Readings

- August, Ray. "International Cyber-Jurisdiction: A Comparative Analysis." *American Business Law Journal* 39 (Summer 2002): 531.

- Kalow, Gwenn M. "From the Internet to Court: Exercising Jurisdiction over World Wide Web Communications." *Fordham Law Review* 65 (1997): 2241.

- Kurland, Philip B. "The Supreme Court, the Due Process Clause and the In Personam Jurisdiction of State Courts—From Pennoyer to Dencla: A Review." *University of Chicago Law Review* 25 (1958): 569.

- Lessig, Lawrence. *Code and Other Laws of Cyberspace*, Chapter 14, "Sovereignty." New York: Basic Books, 1999.

- Perchbacher, Rex R. "Minimum Contacts Reapplied: Mr. Justice Brennan Has It His Way" in *Burger King Corp. v Rudzewicz*, 1986. *Arizona State Law Journal* (1986): 585.

- Wilske, Stephan, and Schiller, Teresa. "International Jurisdiction in Cyberspace: Which States May Regulate the Internet?" *Federal Communications Law Journal* 50 (1997): 117.

Part 2

Intellectual Property Issues in Cyberspace

TRADEMARKS

When a domain name is used only to indicate an address on the Internet and not to identify the source of specific goods, the name is not functioning as a trademark.

—**Data Concepts, Inc. v. Digital Consulting, Inc.,**
150 F.3d 620, 627 (6th Cir. 1998) (Judge Merritt)

LEARNING OBJECTIVES

After you have read this chapter you should be able to:

1. Explain and define a trademark under the Lanham Act.
2. Understand, define, and explain the meaning of a trademark dilution and its application to e-commerce.
3. Understand and explain surface linking and deep linking as they may relate to trademark infringement.
4. Understand, define, and explain "metatags" as a possible trademark infringement, trademark dilution, or unfair competition.
5. Explain framing as a possible trademark infringement and/or a trademark dilution.
6. Understand and explain the difference between trademark infringement and trademark dilution and how they may apply to the online environment.
7. Understand and explain the Anticybersquatting Consumer Protection Act of 1999 and its use in protecting trademark owners against a domain name holder.
8. Explain key international treaties related to trademark law.
9. Understand current international disputes over the application of trademark law to Internet domain names.
10. Explain the meaning of "meta-tagging" and its relation to international trademark infringement.

http://

- Additional material on trademarks is found under Intellectual Property in the Bentley College CyberLaw Center Web site (**http://ecampus. bentley.edu/dept/cyberlaw**).

INTRODUCTION

After a great deal of thought in selecting a domain name for your e-business, an accredited registrar has informed you of its "availability." (For a listing of accredited domain name agencies, see *http://www.internic.net/alpha.html.*) In order to save time and money, you have decided against a comprehensive trademark search. That selection of an "available" domain name may be illegal. A trademark owner of the same or a confusingly similar name, but not registered as a domain name, may sue your e-business on the basis of a "bad faith" registration.

The selection process is discussed in this chapter, but first we present an overview of trademark law to provide a framework for analyzing current trademark practices. Keep in mind as you read this chapter that online trademarks disputes are a common basis of litigation and arbitration.

INTELLECTUAL PROPERTY

Trademarks are only one part of a company's proprietary rights comprising intellectual property. Historically, they consist of *trademarks* or *service marks, copyrights, patents*, and *trade secrets.* This chapter discusses trademarks that, in general, are used to distinguish a company's goods or services from others. Copyrights are original works of authorship that are used in protecting content on Web sites (see Chapter 4). Patents and trade secrets are discussed in Chapter 5. Patents are new and useful processes used in e-commerce, and trade secrets consist of information that provides the owner with a competitive advantage in the marketplace and are maintained in a way to prevent competitors from discovering them.

TRADEMARKS

Trademark disputes are among the most common types of litigation involving the online environment. A **trademark** is defined under the **Lanham Act** of 1976 as a "word, name, symbol, device or other designation, or a combination of such designations, that is distinctive of a person's goods or services and that is used in a manner that identifies and distinguishes them from the goods or services of others" [(15 U.S.C., Sec. 1127 (2000)]. To be granted federal registration, the mark must be used, or promise a "good faith" intent to be used, in commerce (see Figure 3.1). Merely displaying the e-business trademark online does not generally automatically

FIGURE 3.1   Business Objective for Trademarks and Legal Strategy to Protect the Trademarks

Business Objective	Legal Strategy
Secure the e-business brand equity	Federal registration of trademarks
Do not infringe or dilute another trademark	Constant vigilance to assure there is no trademark infringement

establish use in interstate commerce unless it is used to distinguish the goods or services of the e-business from others.

It is important that an online company register its distinctive domain name as a trademark with the **U.S. Patent & Trademark Office (USPTO)**. Keep in mind that different companies can use the same trademark for different classes of goods and services (e.g., Delta Airlines and Delta Dental), but only *one* company can register a particular domain name. Federal registration of a trademark with the USPTO establishes the applicant as the owner of the trademark and allows the owner to sue for trademark infringement and, if the trademark is "famous," (discussed later) to sue for dilution in the federal court system.

The distinctive domain name must be used to identify the product or service produced by the company to qualify for federal trademark registration. The selection of an inappropriate domain name, discussed later, is often the basis of a trademark infringement suit by the trademark owner against the domain name registrant. Great care should be taken in the registration of a domain name, even though it may be available by an accredited registrar. This chapter also discusses the various remedies that a trademark owner may pursue to protect its federally registered trade name.

Trademarks are classified into five categories (see Figure 3.2):

1. *Generic marks* do not receive protection because they do not distinguish a business's mark from other products or services (e.g., "Instant Message" and "You Have Mail.")
2. *Descriptive marks* do not receive protection unless the applicant can prove the mark is either inherently distinctive or has acquired a secondary meaning in the marketplace. As brick-and-mortar companies mutate into e-businesses and start-ups establish an online Web presence, they will select numerous domain names. A **domain name** (e.g., www.ford.com) is merely a business address on the Internet, and without use in commerce to identify the service or product sold is not a trademark. A secondary meaning does not require that the trademark be inherently distinctive, as long as there is a change in the public perspective about the meaning of the trademark (e.g., Kentucky Fried Chicken).
3. *Suggestive marks* suggest some quality of the product or service (e.g., "Coopertone").
4. *Arbitrary marks* exist without any inherent relationship to the product. They are words used in an unusual way to help the public remember the trademark owner (e.g., Amazon and Banana Republic).
5. *Fanciful marks* also have no inherent relationship to the product (e.g., the board game's trademark Candyland and Kodak).

The last three categories, suggestive, arbitrary, and fanciful, generally receive trademark protection because they are automatically inherently distinctive (see Figure 3.2). We will discuss this in more detail in the next section.

FIGURE 3.2   Trademark Classifications: A Specific Example

Generic. Apple Produce Mart cannot register *apple* as its trademark. It is too general.

Descriptive. Apple, a company that sells computers, *can* register *apple* as a trademark because it is an *inherently distinctive* trademark for a computer.

Suggestive. Apple may register the *apple logo* (an apple with a bite taken out) because it is suggesting its product is as easy to use as eating an apple.

Arbitrary. Because there is no relationship between a computer and an apple, this is a trademark that can be registered, as it is inherently distinctive.

Fanciful. The trademarks *apple* and *macintosh* in relationship to a computer have no significance from a name perspective and are inherently distinctive.

Apple Computer, Inc., can thus register the trademarks Apple, the Apple logo, and Macintosh. By applying a general word to an unrelated product, Apple Computer creates a distinctive image.

Service Marks

Service marks are words, phrases, logos, or other graphic symbols that identify and distinguish the services of a company. Service marks are also granted ordinary legal protection. Service marks can be registered in the USPTO and are protected under the Lanham Act. Although it is not legally necessary to do so, it is a good practice to place an "sm" next to the service mark to confer ownership.

Trade Dress as a Trademark

Trademarks have been expanded to now include a **trade dress** that may be a colored design or shape associated with a product. Trade dress is the overall "look and feel" of the product and its package. Most franchises are known by their trade dress because the general public associates the color scheme and ambiance of a business with the franchise (e.g., the McDonald's restaurant is red and yellow). A color design and graphics on a Web site's home page associated with a product or service may be federally registered as a trade dress if the colors, graphics, and icons function as trademarks. The trade dress then becomes part of the goodwill of the e-business and a valuable asset of the online company.

In 2000, the U.S. Supreme Court in *Wal-Mart Stores, Inc. v. Samara Brothers, Inc.* decided a leading trade dress case involving Samara Brothers, Inc., designers and manufacturers of children's clothing, that sued Wal-Mart for infringement of unregistered trade dress under sec. 43 (a) of the Trademark Act of 1946 (Lanham Act). Wal-Mart contracted with a supplier to manufacture children's clothing based on photographs of Samara's garments and sold them as "knockoffs." The court ruled that the design and color of the dresses were not inherently distinctive. It distinguished *Two Pesos, Inc. v. Taco Cabana, Inc.* on the theory that the trade dress there was a restaurant decor, which does not constitute product design, but rather product packaging. The Court held in an action for infringement of an unregistered trade dress that a product's design is protected only upon showing of a secondary meaning. This case may make it more difficult to federally register the trade dress of a Web site that has not acquired a secondary meaning based merely on a distinctive color and design. Making the service or product as illustrated on a Web site more appealing does not in itself identify the source and will not be registered by the USPTO unless it has acquired a secondary meaning in the minds of the consuming public.

Registering a Trademark, Trade Dress, or Service Mark with the USPTO

To register a trademark, trade dress, or service mark in the USPTO, an applicant e-business must be capable of *distinguishing the applicant's goods and/or services* from those of others. It no longer has to be first used to be registered, as long as no one else is currently using the trademark in business.

An appropriate trademark registration in the USPTO will be allowed because of actual use or a good-faith intent to later use the mark in commerce. This "later use" provision is useful in building a Web site and business plan for a start-up e-business that may apply for federal registration before using the trademark in commerce. The trademark may then be used on the Web site and business plan before the e-business is actually launched.

A search will be made by the USPTO to determine if another party is using the trademark in the same or a similar business. If not, a distinctive trademark will generally be registered. Once registered, there is *constructive notice* to all businesses that a particular company now owns the mark. The owner should display the circled (®) and/or (SM) on its Web site home page to give *actual notice* of federal registration and its claim of ownership.

This is a valuable designation in an infringement lawsuit where the plaintiff must first prove *ownership* of the trademark. Federal registration with the USPTO is prime facie evidence of trademark ownership. At the court's discretion, the plaintiff may be awarded up to three times the damages proved, court costs, and, in certain cases, reasonable attorney's fees.

Duration of a Trademark

The initial registration is for a term of ten years. This may be renewed indefinitely. The mark will be automatically canceled at the end of the sixth year if the registrant does not file in the fifth year an affidavit indicating its continuing use of the trademark in interstate commerce. If the trademark is not used, there must be specific reasons, and the registrant must state there is no intent to abandon the mark (see Figure 3.3).

http://

- Home page of USPTO: **http://www.uspto.gov** Courtesy of the U.S. Patent & Trademark Office.

The renewal process is rather involved, and the e-business and its legal counsel must carefully follow the Lanham Act procedures to assure trademark renewal (see 15 U.S.C. Sec. 1058 and 1059).

FIGURE 3.3   **Duration of a Trademark**

Date of federal registration—5 years: renew affidavit—10 years: renew

TRADEMARKS AS DISTINCTIVE: EITHER INHERENTLY OR THROUGH A SECONDARY MEANING

A trademark is deemed distinctive when it is either **inherently distinctive** or has an acquired distinctiveness through a **secondary meaning**. As previously mentioned, suggestive, arbitrary, and fanciful trademarks are inherently distinctive.

Trademarks made up of common or ordinary words are not distinctive. People's names, geographic terms, and descriptive names are generally not distinctive and cannot be registered. However, a person's name that has acquired a "secondary meaning" (e.g., Michael Jordan) may be protected by registration, as he has acquired great public recognition beyond the world of basketball. "Calvin Klein" was once a nondistinctive trade name that has acquired a valuable secondary meaning.

If a trademark is not distinctive and has not yet acquired a secondary meaning, it may be placed on the **Supplemental Register** in the USPTO that provides constructive notice of ownership to companies in all fifty states. If the trademark remains on the Supplemental Register for five years with continuous use in commerce, it may then be placed on the **Principal Register** in the PTO under the *secondary meaning rule* and secondary meaning is presumed.

This process of filing the trademark in the Supplemental Register is especially useful for an e-company that has a nondistinctive trademark and seeks national protection. Because domain names can be federally registered, the owner should consider the benefits of its registration in the Principal Register, or, if necessary, the Supplemental Register.

Common use of a circled ® indicates it has been registered with the Patent and Trademark Office. This should appear on the Web site's home page to indicate actual notice of ownership along with other intellectual property claims that have federal registration, such as the circled © for a copyright and "SM" for a service mark.

Domain names, discussed later, were designed for entirely different purposes than trademarks. This chapter explains that difference and its consequent legal problems and how domain names and trademarks have acquired business value in cyberspace.

Most companies whose distinctive corporate trade name is a federally registered trademark with the USPTO in Washington, D.C., try to register the same name as their domain name with **Network Solutions, Inc. (NSI)**, its successor, the **Internet Corporation for Assigned Names and Numbers (ICANN)**, or other certified domain name registrars. NSI has been registering domain names since 1992 under an agreement with the National Science Foundation and the Department of Commerce. Prior to the creation of ICANN, it enjoyed a monopoly status and had registered more than 6 million Internet addresses. By agreement with the Department of Commerce, NSI has opened the registration of domain names to more than eighty international companies.

ICANN is a nonprofit public-benefit nongovernmental organization with an international board of directors. In 1998, ICANN was selected by the U.S. government to manage the domain name system. Its accredited registrars must agree to rules developed by ICANN such as the Uniform Domain Name Dispute Resolution Policy. In 1999, ICANN assumed management of the domain name system from Network Solutions Inc.

ICANN approved seven new TLDs, namely .biz for businesses; .names for registration by individuals; .pro for accountants, lawyers, and physicians; .info for an unrestrictive use including any organization; .aero for the commercial air industry; .museum for museums; and .coop for cooperatives.

ICANN grew out of the U.S. government's decision to privatize the domain name system. ICANN and its accredited registrars are responsible for the registration of second-level Internet domain names that appear with the top-level names (*amazon* is an example of a second-level well-known domain name). They register the second-level name on a first-come, first-served basis and do not evaluate whether the second-level name infringes on the rights of a trade name owner. Hence it is quite possible for a second-level domain name to be the same as, or deceptively similar to, a federally registered or common law trademarks.

The following two trademark-infringement cases were brought against NSI for allowing registration of domain names that were previously used by the plaintiffs who had similar federally registered trademarks with the USPTO. In both cases the court found no trademark infringement by NSI because it was only the registering agent for the domain names and not the user of the names.

In *Lockheed Martin Corp. v. Network Solutions, Inc.,* 985 F. Supp. 949 (Cal. 1997), the court held that NSI did not "use" the plaintiff's trademark as required for direct infringer liability merely by registering the mark as a domain name. Because NSI had no unequivocal knowledge that the domain name was being used to infringe on the plaintiff's trademark, there was no contributory trademark infringement liability. The same federal court in *Motion Picture Arts and Sciences v. Network Solutions, Inc.,* 989 F. Supp. 1276 (C. D. Cal. 1997) found no contributory infringement on the basis of NSI registering domain names containing the terms *oscar* and *theoscars* because NSI could exercise no control over the *use* of those domain names by the registrant.

http://

- http://www.icann.org/registrars/accreditation.htm
- ICANN's Articles of Incorporation and bylaws are available at **http://www.icann.org/general/articles.htm** and **http://www.icann.org/general/bylaws.htm**

ICANN's domain name dispute resolution policy between a trademark owner and the holder of the same or a confusingly similar registered domain name has been established to resolve these conflicts, if possible, out of court. It accredited the National Arbitration Forum and Disputes.org to join the World Intellectual Property Organization (WIPO) as the dispute resolution service providers. (See Appendix D, Uniform Domain Name Dispute Resolution Policy, page 470.)

The following WIPO arbitration decision under ICANN's Uniform Domain Name Dispute Resolution Policy ruled that the federal trademark registration of Julia Roberts's name is not required because it has acquired common law trademark rights.

ADMINISTRATIVE PANEL DECISION
Julia Fiona Roberts v. Russell Boyd
Case No. D2000-0210

The Parties

Claimant is Julia Fiona Roberts, a United States citizen, with a principal place of business c/o Armstrong Hirsch Jackoway Tyerman & Wertheimer, 1888 Century Park East 18th Floor, Los Angeles, California 90067 USA.

Respondent is Russell Boyd, a United States citizen with a mailing address 189 Carter Road, Princeton, New Jersey 08540 USA.

The Domain Name and Registrar

The domain name at issue is <juliaroberts.com >. The registrar is Network Solutions, Inc. (the "Registrar") 505 Huntmar Park Dr., Herndon, Virginia 20170 USA.

Procedural History

The WIPO Arbitration and Mediation Center (the "Center") received the Complaint of Complainant on March 25, 2000 by email and on March 29, 2000 in hardcopy. The Complainant paid the required fee. On March 29, 2000, the Center sent an Acknowledgement of Receipt of the Complaint to the Complainant.

On March 27, 2000, the Center sent to the Registrar a request for verification of registration data. On March 28, 2000, the Registrar confirmed, *inter alia*, that it is the registrar of the domain name in dispute and that <juliaroberts.com> is registered in the Respondent's name.

Having verified that the Complaint satisfies the formal requirements of the ICANN Uniform Domain Name Dispute Resolution Policy (the "Policy"), the Rules for Uniform Domain Name Dispute Resolution Policy (the "Rules"), and the Supplemental Rules for Uniform Domain Name Dispute Resolution Policy (the "Supplemental Rules"), the Center on March 29, 2000 sent to the Respondent, with a copy to the Complainant, a notification of the administrative proceeding together with copies of the Complaint. This notification was sent by the methods required under paragraph 2(a) of the Rules. The formal date of the commencement of this administrative proceeding is March 29, 2000.

In a series of correspondence with the Center, Respondent requested and was granted an extension of time to file his Response. On May 8, 2000, the Center received Respondent's Response. On May 18, 2000, after receiving their completed and signed Statements of Acceptance and Declarations of Impartiality and Independence, the Center notified the parties of the appointment of a three member Administrative Panel consisting of Mr. Richard W. Page as the Presiding Panelist, Ms. Sally M. Abel as Complainant's party-appointed panelist and Mr. James Bridgeman, as Respondent's party-appointed panelist.

On May 8 and 9, 2000, Complainant tendered a Reply by fax and email. The acceptance of a Reply is subject to the discretion of the Panel.

The Panel met by telephone conference call on May 25, 2000. During the telephone conference call the Panel decided not to accept or consider Complainant's Reply.

Factual Background

The Complainant, Julia Fiona Roberts, is a famous motion picture actress. She has appeared in such movies as Erin Brockovich, Notting Hill, Runaway Bride, Stepmom, My Best Friend's Wedding, Conspiracy Theory, Everyone Says I Love You, Mary Reilly, Michael Collins, Something to Talk About, I Love Trouble, Ready to Wear, The Pelican Brief, The Player, Dying Young, Hook, Sleeping With the Enemy, Flatliners, Pretty Woman, and more. A partial filmography for the Complainant is found at Yahoo! Movies. The Complainant is widely featured in celebrity publications, movie reviews, and entertainment publications and television shows, and she has earned two Academy Award nominations. Her latest film, Erin Brockovich (released nationwide on March 16, 2000), is currently ranked #1 at the box office.

Respondent registered the subject domain name on November 9, 1998. As of March 24, 2000, the website www.juliaroberts.com featured a photograph of a woman named "Sari Locker." The Respondent has placed the domain name up for auction on the commercial auction website, "eBay," specifically at *http://cgi.ebay.com/aw-cgi/eBayISAPI. dll?ViewItem&item=285891617*.

The Respondent has also registered over fifty (50) other domain names, including names incorporating other movie stars names within <madeleinestowe.com> and <alpacino.com> and a famous Russian gymnast's name within <elenaprodunova.com>. Respondent lists his email address as mickjagger@home.com. Respondent was offered US$2,550 in the eBay auction for the domain name registration.

Parties' Contentions

A. Complainant contends that the domain name <juliaroberts.com> is identical to and confusingly similar with the name "Julia Roberts" and the common law trademark rights which she asserts in her name pursuant to the Policy paragraph 4(a)(i).

Complainant contends that Respondent has no rights or legitimate interest in the domain name <juliaroberts.com> pursuant to the Policy paragraph 4(a)(ii).

Complainant contends that Respondent registered and is using the domain name <juliaroberts.com> in bad faith in violation of the Policy paragraph 4(a)(iii).

B. Respondent does not contest that the domain name <juliaroberts.com> is identical with and confusingly similar to Complainant's name. Respondent does contest whether Complainant has common law trademark rights in her name. Respondent admits that he selected the domain name <juliaroberts.com> because of the well-known actress.

Respondent contends that he has rights and legitimate interest in <juliaroberts.com> because of his registration and use of the domain name.

Respondent contends that his registration and use of <juliaroberts.com> is in good faith.

Discussion and Findings

Identity or Confusing Similarity

The initial consideration of the Panel was whether Complainant had sufficiently alleged the existence of common law trademark rights in her Complaint. On page 5 of her Complaint, Complainant alleges that "The Respondent's use of www.juliaroberts.com infringes upon the name and trademark of Complainant and clearly causes a likelihood of confusion as defined by Section 2(d) of the United States Lanham Act, Section 2(d), 15 U.S.C. Section 1052(d)." From this allegation, the Panel understood that Complainant asserted common law trademark rights in her name. The Panel further decided that registration of her name as a registered trademark or service mark was not necessary and that the name "Julia Roberts" has sufficient secondary association with Complainant that common law trademark rights do exist under United States trademark law.

A recent decision citing English law found that common law trademark rights exist in an author's name. The Policy does not require that the Complainant should have rights in a registered trademark or service mark. It is sufficient that the Complainant should satisfy the Administrative Panel that she has rights in common law trademark or sufficient rights to ground an action for passing off. See Jeanette Winterson v. Mark Hogarth, WIPO Case No. D2000-0235, May 22, 2000.

Having decided that Complainant has common law trademark rights in her name, the next consideration was whether the domain name <juliaroberts.com> was identical to or confusingly similar with Complainant's name. The second level domain name in <julia roberts.com> is identical to the Complainant's name. Therefore, the Panel finds that the requirement of the Policy paragraph 4(a)(i) is satisfied.

Rights or Legitimate Interest

Respondent has no relationship with or permission from Complainant for the use of her name or mark. The domain name was registered with the Registrar on November 9, 1998. At this time Complainant has already been featured in a number of motion pictures and had acquired common law trademark rights in her name. Respondent admits at page 13 of his Response that "I registered JuliaRoberts.com because, after seeing several of her movies, I had a sincere interest in the actor . . ."

In the conclusion of the Response on page 16, the Respondent elaborates that "If Julia Roberts had picked up a phone and said, 'Hi Russ, can we talk about the domain name juliaroberts.com?' she would own it by now." Then Respondent concludes "But as I mentioned at the beginning of this response, I still think Julia is nifty crazy wacko cool."

The original content posted on the website www.juliaroberts.com had little if anything to do with Julia Roberts. It was not until this dispute arose that her likeness was posted.

In addition, Respondent admits that he has registered other domain names including including other well-known movie and sports stars and having placed the disputed domain name <juliaroberts.com> for auction on eBay.

The Complainant has established a prima facie case that the Respondent has no rights or legitimate interest in the domain name and the Respondent has not provided any evidence to rebut this. It is clear from the submissions and evidence provided to this Administrative Panel that Respondent has failed to show (a) use of the domain name in connection with the offering of any goods or services, (b) common knowledge that he is known by the domain name, (c) legitimate noncommercial or fair use of the domain name, or (d) any other basis upon which he can assert rights or a legitimate interest.

Therefore, the Panel finds that Respondent has no rights or legitimate interest in the domain name <juliaroberts.com> and that the requirement of the Policy paragraph 4(a)(ii) is satisfied.

Bad Faith

Paragraph 4 of the Policy provides that evidence of bad faith registration and use includes circumstances showing:

(ii) you have registered the domain name in order to prevent the owner of the trademark or service mark from reflecting the mark in a corresponding domain name, provided that you have engaged in a pattern of such conduct.

The Respondent admits that he has registered other domain names including several famous movie and sports stars. Such actions necessarily prevent Complainant from using the disputed domain name and demonstrate a pattern of such conduct.

Therefore, the Panel finds that Respondent has registered and used the domain name <juliaroberts.com> in bad faith and that the requirement of the Policy paragraph 4(a)(iii) is satisfied.

In addition, the Respondent has placed the domain name up for auction on the commercial website eBay. When considered in conjunction with the pattern of registrations described above, the Panel finds that such action constitutes additional evidence of bad faith.

Decision

The Panel concludes (a) that the domain name <juliaroberts.com> is identical to Complainant's common law trademark in her name "Julia Roberts," (b) that Respondent has no rights or legitimate interest in the domain name and (c) that Respondent registered and used the domain name in bad faith. Therefore, pursuant to paragraphs 4(i) of the

Policy and 15 of the Rules, the Panel orders that the domain name <juliaroberts.com> be transferred to Complainant Julia Fiona Roberts.

Case Questions

1. Why did the arbitrators decide Julia Roberts has common law trademark rights in her unregistered name?
2. What were the reasons the arbitrators found that constituted a "bad faith" registration on the domain name <juliaroberts.com>?
3. Why did the arbitrators find that the respondent had no legitimate interest in the domain name <juliaroberts.com>?

A computer user who knows the domain name will key in the URL (Universal Resource Locator) and view the company's Web site home page. (See Chapter 1 for a technical explanation of the URL.) If the domain name is not known, the end user may use a search engine and type in a name or keyword that will identify the company's Web site.

Because millions of companies are now online with more to come, the likelihood of consumer confusion of a trademark with another company's domain name will surely be a necessary concern of every online corporation. An e-business's *brand-name equity* is intellectual property, and it is considered one of the valuable elements of its goodwill that should be guarded and legally protected. This chapter examines the laws that provide legal recourse to a company whose distinctive trademark and/or trade name has been infringed in cyberspace.

►http://

- See the entire Uniform Dispute Resolution Policy at **http://www.icann.org/udrp/udrp.htm**

TRADEMARK INFRINGEMENT AND DILUTION

Businesses spend a lot of money protecting their names and building goodwill. They are therefore protective of their trademarks. But trademarks can be devalued without being duplicated or stolen. Trademark infringement and trademark dilution can do great harm to a company. As the commercial world enters e-business, companies should be aware that the online environment makes them even more exposed to trademark infringement and dilution.

Trademark Infringement

A **trademark infringement** occurs when a party uses a trademark that causes a "likelihood of confusion" (see Figure 3.4) between goods or the relationship between the parties that make the goods. It generally takes place between competing companies and causes an immediate likelihood of confusion with the consumers. For example, if

FIGURE 3.4   **Ten Factors Used to Determine a Likelihood of Confusion:**
Interpace Corp. v. Lapp, Inc., **721 F.2d 460 (3d Cir. 1983)**

Lapp Factors

1. Strength of the mark: Generic marks are not given protection.
2. Kind of mark: Descriptive marks are given less protection.
3. Similarity of the goods: Goods should be related.
4. Channel of trade: Concurrent markets in cyberspace may be evidence of a likelihood of confusion.
5. Consumer sophistication: Internet consumers are more sophisticated than offline users and should be able to distinguish competitors.
6. Wrongful intent: Not necessary to prove confusion, but if found it is strong evidence of confusion.
7. Actual confusion: Would a reasonable prudent consumer be confused?
8. Zone of natural expansion: Plaintiff must provide proof of expanding in the marketplace of the defendant.
9. Length of time the defendant used the mark: The longer it was used without actual confusion the weaker the plaintiff's case.
10. Same sales efforts: The extent to which the parties have the same sales efforts is evidence of confusion.

Dunkin' Donuts were to use Starbucks's registered trademark and also use its own trademark, Dunkin' Donuts, it would give the confusing impression that Dunkin' Donuts has an affiliation with Starbucks. Starbucks would be entitled to sue Dunkin' Donuts for trademark infringement.

In the following case, *Checkpoint Systems, Inc. v. Check Point Software Technologies, Inc.*, the court considered the factors used in determining a likelihood of confusion of a similar trademark.

Checkpoint Systems, Inc. v. Check Point Software Technologies, Inc.
269 F.3d 270 (3rd Cir. 2001)

Facts

Checkpoint Systems, Inc. has been manufacturing and distributing commercial electronic security control systems since 1967. Its devices are designed to track the physical location of goods and are sold to retailers to prevent merchandise theft. It is one of the two dominant manufacturers in the retail security products market. Since 1967, Checkpoint Systems has used the "CHECKPOINT" mark, which is registered with the USPTO.

Defendant Check Point Software Technologies, Inc. writes computer programs that protect and manage access to information. Check Point Software's principal product is "firewall" technology.

At the time Check Point Software was founded in Israel in 1993, its founders were unaware of Checkpoint Systems. They adopted the "Check Point" mark because they believed their computer firewall technology, which limited access to data, resembled military checkpoints that prevent access to restricted areas.

In early 1996, Checkpoint Systems attempted to register the Internet domain name *http://www.checkpoint.com*, but discovered it was registered by Check Point Software. After its request to discontinue use was rebuffed, Checkpoint Systems filed suit alleging trademark infringement and unfair competition under the Lanham Act. In a nonjury trial, the District Court held Check Point Software neither violated the Lanham Act nor infringed Checkpoint Systems's trademark. In this appeal, Checkpoint Systems contends the District Court improperly evaluated the Lapp factors in its likelihood of confusion analysis.

Judicial Opinion *(Judge Scirica)*

To prove likelihood of confusion, plaintiffs must show that "consumers viewing the mark would probably assume the product or service it represents is associated with the source of a different product or service identified by a similar goods. [W]e set forth the relevant standards on likelihood of confusion in noncompeting goods cases, commonly known as the *Lapp* factors:

1. [The] degree of similarity between the owner's mark and the alleged infringing mark;
2. the strength of the owner's mark;
3. the price of the goods and other factors indicative of the care and attention expected of consumers when making a purchase;
4. the length of time the defendant has used the mark without evidence of actual confusion;
5. the intent of the defendant in adopting the mark;
6. the evidence of actual confusion;
7. whether the goods, though not competing, are marketed through the same channels of trade and advertised through the same media;
8. the extent to which the targets of the parties' sales efforts are the same;
9. the relationship of the goods in the minds of consumers because of the similarity of functions; and
10. other facts suggesting that the consuming public might expect the prior owner to manufacture a product in the defendant's market or that he is likely to expand into that market.

None of these factors is determinative in the likelihood of confusion analysis and each factor must be weighed and balanced one against the other. Not all factors must be given equal weight. The weight given to each factor in the overall picture, as well as the weighing for plaintiff or defendant, must be done on an individual fact-specific basis. The Lapp test is a qualitative inquiry. Not all factors will be relevant in all cases; further, the different factors may properly be accorded different weights depending on the particular factual setting.

Similarity of Marks

Although the degree of similarity between the owner's mark and the alleged infringing mark is but one factor in the multi-factor confusion analysis, we have recognized that when products directly compete, mark similarity "may be the most important of the ten factors in Lapp."

Strength of Mark

The strength of a mark is determined by (1) the distinctiveness or conceptual strength of the mark and (2) its commercial strength or marketplace recognition.

The District Court was correct in stating, "Checkpoint [Systems] has used its name and mark in connection with its electronic article surveillance products for more than thirty years continuously, extensively, and in a substantially exclusive manner, and that long use renders the mark strong within the physical surveillance field."

Factors Indicative of the Care and Sophistication of Purchasers

When consumers exercise heightened care in evaluating the relevant products before making purchasing decisions, courts have found there is not a strong likelihood of confusion. Where the relevant products are expensive, or the buyer class consists of sophisticated or professional purchasers, courts have generally not found Lanham Act violations. Both plaintiff's products and defendant's products are expensive. The purchasers of these respective products are, for the most part, highly sophisticated, and the sale process is lengthy. . . . Plaintiff's and defendant's products are not impulse purchases, but rather are subject to long sales efforts and careful customer decision making.

The District Court properly evaluated the care exercised by consumers of these products in making purchasing decisions. The evidence supports the finding that the purchase of both parties' products involve a significant investment and even smaller commercial consumers exercise a heightened degree of care in evaluating the products and making purchasing decisions. We see no clear error.

The Evidence of Actual Confusion

Courts have recognized that evidence of intentional, willful and admitted adoption of a mark closely similar to the existing marks weighs strongly in favor of finding the likelihood of confusion. Here, the District Court found, "there is no evidence or even inference that defendant chose its name with plaintiff's name or products in mind." We agree.

Relationship of Goods in the Minds of Consumers Because of the Similarity of Product Functions

The District Court did not clearly err. The "relatedness" analysis is intensely factual. Goods may fall under the same general product category but operate in distinct niches.

When two products are part of distinct sectors of a broad product category, they can be sufficiently unrelated that consumers are not likely to assume the products originate from the same mark.

The Extent to Which the Parties' Goods Are Marketed Through the Same Channels of Trade

As the District Court found, "There is no evidence that plaintiff 's products and defendant's products were offered at the same time in any magazine, trade show, or distribution network. . . . That there is no overlap in the places these parties market their products tends to diminish the chance that someone who is a specialist in network security will even come across an advertisement for plaintiff, and vice versa." We see no clear error.

The Extent to Which Targets of the Parties' Sales Efforts Are the Same

We have recognized that when parties target their sales efforts to the same consumers, there is a stronger likelihood of confusion. This analysis too is intensely factual.

The District Court found the parties market their products to different users. Checkpoint Systems markets its products to physical security consumers. Check Point Software markets its products to MIS professionals. Even though many companies often purchase both types of products, most rely on information specialists to make purchasing decisions about network security systems, especially since Check Point Software's firewall systems must be installed as part of the overall architecture of a business's total computer system. But information specialists are not essential to make purchasing decisions about physical article security systems.

Evidence of Converging Markets

We have held that evidence that the markets in which the parties sell their goods are converging is "pivotal in non-competing products."

Additionally, there is little evidence that either party currently operates in both the physical security and network security markets. We see no clear error.

We also hold the District Court properly evaluated the evidence of initial interest confusion and did not clearly err in finding this evidence did not weigh heavily in favor of finding likely confusion. For the foregoing reasons, we will affirm the judgment of the District Court.

Case Questions

1. Why did the court find there was no likelihood of confusion between the two similar trademarks?
2. Did the court find that one of the ten factors in Lapp was more important than the others? Is so, explain why.
3. Is it ethical to use a similar trademark that may not legally infringe but may cause some consumer confusion?

Trademark Dilution

The **Federal Trademark Dilution Act of 1996** (15 U.S.C. Sec. 1125) amended the Lanham Act to protect companies against dilution of *famous and distinctive marks* in the United States. The Federal Trademark Dilution Act defines a dilution as "the lessening of the capacity of a famous mark to identify and distinguish goods or services, regardless of the presence or absence of (1) competition between the owner of the famous mark and other parties, or (2) the likelihood of confusion or mistake or to deceive" (see Figure 3.5).

It is important to note that a trademark dilution creates a new federal statutory remedy and differs from a trademark infringement. A **trademark dilution** occurs when a trademark is used by another company in such a manner as to cause its identity to diminish over a period of time. It need not cause immediate confusion in the mind of the consumer. Dilution can take place without consumer confusion regarding the identity of the goods, even when the mark is used on unrelated noncompeting goods or services. Although trademark dilution is actionable under about half of the states' statutory laws, it was not actionable under the Lanham Act prior to the 1996 amendment. You can expect trademark dilution to be used extensively in domain name disputes by *famous trademark* owners against any party using a registered domain name that will lessen the value of their mark.

http://

- For a discussion of the Federal Trademark Dilution Act, see **http://www.bitlaw.com/trademark/dilution.html**

A trademark dilution will allow a registered trademark owner of a famous mark to bring a claim against the registered owner of a similar or identical domain name used for commercial purposes. When a domain name in some fashion causes a dilution of a "famous" registered trademark, there could be a violation of the act.

In a dilution case, there is no requirement that consumers be "likely confused" about an association between the unauthorized using company and the trademark owner, or that the user be a competitor. The defendant may be an unrelated business

FIGURE 3.5   The Plaintiff's Burden of Proof and Defenses in a Trademark Dilution Case

Plaintiff

1. Must prove it owns the trademark (e.g., registered in the USPTO).
2. The mark is *distinctive and famous.*
3. The defendant's use is *causing* dilution.

Defendant's Defenses

1. Ownership of a registered trademark.
2. *Fair use* of the mark in promoting its goods or identifying competing goods.
3. Noncommercial use of the mark.
4. Any form of news reporting or commentary.

using a famous trademark online. The trademark owner who has the "famous mark" may bring a claim against the unrelated business causing dilution of the distinctive quality of the mark.

"Famous" Trademarks. In order to be eligible to sue under the Federal Trademark Dilution Act the plaintiff company must first prove its trademark is a **famous trademark**.

When a court must determine whether a mark is distinctive and famous, it applies guidelines to the facts of the trademarks use. (See Figure 3.6 for guidelines to determine when a mark is famous.) The burden of proving the mark is famous is often accomplished in court by an expert witness testifying about surveys made in response to questions based on the guidelines in Figure 3.6. For instance, the trademark *Oracle,* although relatively new, may qualify as a "famous" trade name because it is readily recognized in the computer world. Note that the best method in qualifying a trademark as famous should be to register it in the Principal Register at the USPTO and then to engage in an extensive advertising campaign.

In *Washington Speakers Bureau, Inc. v. Leading Authorities, Inc., 33* F. Supp. 2d 488 (E.D. Va., 1999), the court held that the defendant's use of the domain name "washingtonspeakers.com" infringed on the plaintiff's name, Washington Speakers Bureau, and caused a likelihood that consumers would be confused by the defendant's use of a "colorable imitation" of the plaintiff's trademark in its domain name. The services the parties offered the public were virtually identical, and the court found the defendant adopted the domain name in bad faith to attract the plaintiff's business. However, the court also found no trademark dilution because the plaintiff's trademark was not famous. Note that a trademark dilution claim cannot be brought unless the plaintiff can prove the trademark is famous within the guidelines already stated.

The following case illustrated the reasons why it refused to apply the Federal Trademark Dilution Act to the facts of the case. Note the extensive revenues spent on advertising alone where not sufficient to make the name "famous."

A.B.C. Carpet Co., Inc., et al. v. Naeini
Case No. 00-CV-4882 (FB), 2002 U.S. Dist. Lexis 1129 (E.D. N.Y., January 22, 2002).

Facts

Plaintiffs have used the marks "ABC" and "ABC Carpet" in connection with their operation of retail stores offering carpets, rugs, and other merchandise since 1961. Plaintiffs have used the mark "ABC Carpet and Home" since 1992, and they federally registered the marks "ABC" and "ABC Carpet and Home" in 1998 in the USPTO.

Defendant Mehdi Naeini has operated a business under the name American Basic Craft Carpet and Home Restoration since 1980. This business offers carpets and carpet cleaning services to the public.

In 1998, Naeini registered the domain name "ABCcarpetandhome.net" for use in connection with this business. At the time he registered this domain name, he was aware of plaintiffs' prior use of the marks in question.

Plaintiffs commenced this suit, charging that defendant's conduct infringed plaintiffs' trademarks in violations of the Lanham Act and diluted their marks in violation of the Federal Trademark Dilution Act. Plaintiffs also claimed that defendant had registered the domain name at issue in bad faith in violation of the Anticybersquatting Consumer Protection Act ("ACPA").

Judicial Opinion *(District Judge Block)*

The Court denied plaintiffs' motion for summary judgment, holding that issues of fact precluded it from resolving the parties' disputes at this time. To prevail on a trademark infringement claim, a plaintiff must show that its mark is protectable, and that defendant's use of this mark is likely to cause consumer confusion. In analyzing whether use of a mark will cause such confusion, courts in the Second Circuit examine the following eight factors:

1. the strength of plaintiff's marks;
2. the similarity of the parties' marks;
3. the proximity of the parties' products or services in the marketplace;
4. the likelihood that the plaintiff will bridge the gap between the products or services;
5. actual confusion;
6. the defendant's intent in adopting the mark;
7. the quality of the defendant's product; and
8. the sophistication of the relevant consumer group.

The court found that each of the first four factors enumerated above favored the plaintiffs. Thus, the court found that the plaintiffs ABC's mark was arbitrary, and hence strong, that defendant had used a mark identical to plaintiffs', and that plaintiffs and defendant were competitors offering carpet-related sales and services. Nonetheless, the court denied plaintiffs' motion, finding that issues of fact precluded it from determining whether defendant had acted in good faith when selecting the domain name at issue. At this stage in the proceedings, the court was unwilling to find that defendant had acted in bad faith, given his claim that he had adopted the domain name at issue, "abccarpetandhome.net", as an abbreviation of the name under which he had been doing business since 1980 "American Basic Craft Carpet and Home Restoration." For similar reasons, the court denied plaintiffs' motion for summary judgment on its ACPA claim. To establish an ACPA claim, the plaintiff must establish that defendant acted in bad faith, a finding the court was not prepared to make at this stage of the proceedings.

Lastly, the court denied plaintiffs summary judgment on their Federal Trademark Dilution Claim. To establish such a claim, the trademark holder must establish that its mark is famous, a burden the court held that plaintiffs failed to meet on the evidence before it. Said the court:

> The Second Circuit has held that under the FTDA marks qualify as "famous"
> only if they carry "a substantial degree of fame," approaching the level of fame

enjoyed by "household" names such as Dupont, Buick, or Kodak. Here the Court concludes that ABC's submissions fail to establish that there is no material fact as to whether its marks are "famous" under the FTDA. ABC has not established the type of national, "household" name recognition required by the FTDA, and its sales and advertising expenditures are lower than those of other companies whose marks were found insufficiently famous.

Importantly, the court reached this conclusion despite the plaintiffs' claims that they had spent $15 million advertising their marks between 1993 and 1998, during which period they sold over $550 million dollars worth of goods and services.

Case Questions

1. Explain why the court was unwilling to find the defendant acted in "bad faith."
2. Explain why the trademark ABC is an arbitrary mark and therefore inherently distinctive.
3. Was it ethical for the court to base its finding of a famous mark on competing companies' sales and advertising?

Dilution by Tarnishment. **Dilution by tarnishment** occurs when the plaintiff's mark has been associated by the defendant's conduct with unwholesome, unsavory, or shoddy quality products or when consumers are likely to associate the lack of prestige or quality of the product with the plaintiff's unrelated goods. A 1996 case, *Hasbro, Inc. v. The Internet Entertainment Group*, pitted the maker of a child's game against a pornographer. The famous family board game Candyland was being used as a domain name by a pornographic Web site. The plaintiff sued for trademark infringement, trademark dilution, and unfair competition of its federally registered trademark "Candyland" for use with its board game, alleging the toy maker's wholesome image was being tarnished by the adult-oriented site.

FIGURE 3.6   Guidelines to Determine If a Trademark Is Famous

- The degree of inherent or acquired distinctiveness of the mark.
- The duration and extent of use of the mark in connection with the goods or services with which the mark is used.
- The duration and extent of advertising and publicity of the mark.
- The geographical extent of the trading area in which the mark is used.
- The channels of trade for the goods or services with which the mark is used.
- The degree of recognition of the mark in the trade.
- The nature and extent of use of the same or similar marks by third parties.
- Whether the mark was registered on the Principal Register.

The court enjoined the defendant from using the domain name. It stated that the defendant's use of the pornographic Web site was a trademark dilution by tarnishment and would degrade the quality of the Candyland mark.

In *Toys "R" Us v. Akkaoui*, the court held that the defendant's use of the mark in association with sexual products was inconsistent with the image that Toys "R" Us had acquired in the commercial market. The Court found that the Toys "R" Us family of marks were famous and distinctive before defendants began identifying themselves as Adults "R" Us. "Plaintiffs have used the . . . trademark[s] continuously. Because of the plaintiffs' promotional activity and because of the inherent peculiarity, the "R Us" family of marks have acquired a strong degree of distinctiveness. Toys "R" Us and Kids "R" Us thus qualify as famous, distinctive marks eligible for protection from dilution."

In *Toys "R" Us., et al. v. Richard Feinburg, et al.*, the Court held defendant's use of the domain name "gunsareus.com" for an e-business selling firearms neither infringed or diluted the famous plaintiff's Toys "R" Us trademark and trade name. Note that there were two claims in this case: one for trademark infringement and the other for trademark dilution. The Court found that consumers were not likely to be confused by defendant's use of the domain name "gunsareus" with the "R" Us company. The defendant sold firearms out of a small retail store, and on their Web site defendant's domain name would neither blur nor tarnish plaintiff's name because consumers could not relate the defendant's business to the plaintiff's.

This was a weak argument with respect to the trademark dilution. The "R" Us family sells children's toys, and any parent that sees the "gunsareus.com" Web site could easily believe there is an affiliation with the plaintiff. Remember that the likelihood to deceive or confuse the consumer is not necessary in a trademark dilution case. Further, there is no way of knowing the size of the retail gun store by viewing a Web site. This case was later overruled on appeal.

Dilution by Blurring. **Dilution by blurring** occurs over an extended period of time when a famous trademark's value will be diminished by its use on dissimilar products. For example, if an online clothing company were allowed to use "www.fidelity.com" as its domain name, blurring would eventually dilute this world-famous trademark. Although the consuming public can distinguish mutual funds from a noncompeting clothing e-business, over a period of time the Fidelity trademark would be diminished.

TRADEMARKS IN CYBERSPACE: CYBERPIRACY AND INTERNET TECHNOLOGY

Anticybersquatting Consumer Protection Act (ACPA)

Domain names have become valuable commodities, so *cyberpirates* have registered domain names with Network Solutions, Inc. or other domain name registrars that are famous trademarks. The cyberpirates then attempt to sell the registered domain name to the trademark owner for a large amount of money. Keep in mind that the first person to register a dot.com domain name secures all rights to use the name as a URL.

The 1999 U.S. **Anticybersquatting Consumer Protection Act** made several changes to the Lanham Act (federal trademark law) to protect trademark owners from online cyberpiracy. The ACPA states in part that "A person shall be liable in a civil action by the owner of a mark, including a personal name which is protected as a mark . . . if that person has a bad faith intent to profit from the mark." The act does not define *bad faith,* although it does define nonexclusive factors as guidelines in determining bad faith (see Figure 3.7).

The act also makes it illegal to register the domain name of a living person without the person's consent with the specific intent to profit by selling the name for financial gain. Under the act, a plaintiff may elect *statutory damages* in lieu of *actual damages* (loss of profits) in the amount of at least $1,000 but not more than $100,000 per domain name, as the court considers just (see Figure 3.8). It may also order the transformation of the domain name to the owner of the trademark, as well as reasonable attorney fees. The intent of the law is to make cybersquatters accountable to the holders of famous trademarks who have spent years and large amounts of money in advertising the federally registered trademark. In the following case, the plaintiff, E and J Gallo, sued Spider Webs Ltd. under the ACPA based on a "bad faith" domain name registration of a similar name.

E & J Gallo Winery v. Spider Webs Ltd.
129 F. Supp.2d 1033 (S.D. Tex. 2001),
aff'd 286 F.3d 270 (5th Cir. 2002)

Facts

Ernest & Julio Gallo Winery ("Gallo") registered the trademark "Ernest & Julio Gallo" on October 20, 1964 with the United States Patent and Trademark Office, as Registration Number 778,837. Gallo has registered a number of other trademarks, as well as Internet domain names, but had not registered the domain name at issue here. Gallo has sold more than four billion bottles of wine and has spent more than $500 million promoting its brands.

The individual defendants, brothers Steve and Pierce Thumann, and their father, Fred Thumann, trustee, run a family-owned prehanging millwork business named Doortown, Inc. In June 1999, they created Spider Webs Ltd. as a limited partnership. According to Steve Thumann, Spider Webs's business plan is to develop Internet address names. It has registered more than two thousand Internet domain names through Network Solutions, Inc., one of the companies responsible for the registration of Internet domain names. Approximately three hundred of these domain names contained names that could be associated with existing businesses, including "ernestandjuliogallo.com," "firestonetires.com," "bridgestonetires.com," "bluecross-blueshield.com," "oreocookies. com," "avoncosmetics.com," and others. As the trial court found, because Internet domain names cannot contain ampersands or spaces, and because all Internet domain names must end in a top-level domain such as ".com," ".org," ".net," etc., "ernestandjuliogallo.com" is effectively the same thing as "Ernest & Julio Gallo."

Spider Webs sells some of the names it has registered on its Web site on the Internet auction site eBay (and apparently has refused to accept any bids of less than $10,000), although it has not yet offered "ernestandjuliogallo.com" for sale. Steve Thumann admitted in his deposition that "ernestandjuliogallo.com" is valuable because of the goodwill that Gallo had developed in its name. However, Spider Webs did not initiate any contact with Gallo, nor did it attempt to sell the domain name to Gallo.

Approximately six months after Gallo brought this lawsuit, Spider Webs published a Web site at "ernestandjuliogallo.com" that discussed the lawsuit, the risks associated with alcohol use, and alleged misrepresentations by corporations. It contained a picture of the upper half of a wine bottle with the words "Whiney Winery" ("the Whiney Winery website"). Spider Webs Ltd. registered the Internet domain name "ernestandjuliogallo.com" (the "domain name"). Gallo sent Spider Webs a letter requesting that they release or transfer the domain name to Gallo, but Spider Webs refused to do so. Gallo sued Spider Webs under the Anti-Cybersquatting Consumer Protection Act ("ACPA"), and under federal and Texas anti-dilution, trademark infringement, and unfair competition laws. After this litigation began, Spider Webs hosted a Web site at the domain name that was critical of this litigation, of alcohol, and of corporate America. The parties consented to proceed before a magistrate judge, who granted summary judgment to Gallo on the ACPA and Texas Anti-Dilution Statute ("ADS") claims, issued an injunction under the ADS, ordered the transfer of the domain name to Gallo under the ACPA, and awarded statutory damages to Gallo under the ACPA. Spider Webs appeals. We AFFIRM.

Judicial Opinion (Judge Jolly)

We turn now to consider the bad-faith factors as they apply to this case. Spider Webs has no intellectual property rights or trademark in the name"ernestandjuliogallo," aside from its registered domain name. The domain name does not contain the name of Spider Webs or any of the other defendants. Spider Webs had no "prior use" (or any current use) of the domain name in connection with the bona fide offering of goods or services. Under the fourth factor, Spider Webs's use is commercial, and there is no indication that it is a fair use. Steve Thumann admitted that the domain name was valuable and that they hoped Gallo would contact them so that they could "assist" Gallo in some way. Further, at least two other courts have found that when a defendant registers a domain name that is identical to someone else's trademarked name and thereby impacts the trademark owner's business by preventing internet users from reaching the trademark owner's own web site, this is impacts the trademark owner's business and is a use "'in connection' with goods and services."

Additionally, there is uncontradicted evidence that Spider Webs was engaged in commerce in the selling of domain names and that they hoped to sell this domain name some day. Although Spider Webs did not offer "ernestandjuliogallo.com" for sale, it has offered for sale other domain names that it has registered. Steve Thumann stated that Spider Webs intended to wait until the ACPA is declared unconstitutional before selling the domain name here.E. &. J. Gallo. Spider Webs admitted that Gallo had a valuable trademark, and that when they registered the domain name they hoped Gallo would contact them so they could "assist" Gallo. Indeed, the Ninth Circuit had found that one can be in the "business" of "register[ing] trademarks as domain names and then sell[ing] them to the rightful trademark owners. The ACPA was passed to address situations just like this one: "For example, many cybersquatters are now careful to no longer offer the domain name for sale in any manner that could implicate liability under existing trademark dilution law. And, in cases of warehousing and trafficking in domain names, courts have sometimes declined to provide assistance to trademark holders, leaving them without adequate and effective judicial remedies."

Additionally, there is no evidence that Spider Webs actually used the domain name until after the lawsuit began. Under the bad faith factor, the fact that Spider Webs hosted a website using Gallo's trademarked name, at which it disparaged the instant litigation and alcohol, is evidence of intent to harm Gallo's goodwill and to tarnish its mark Although Spider Webs has not offered this domain name for sale, it has registered other domain names that are identical or similar to the names of well-known businesses and products, has offered other domain names for sale, and has refused to accept less than $10,000 per name. These factors all favor a finding of bad faith.

Considering the statutory factors and all the circumstances of this case, the trial court's conclusion that Spider Webs acted with a bad faith intent to profit and its grant of summary judgment to Gallo on this issue were appropriate.

Case Questions

1. Is it a violation of the ACPA to sell a domain name on eBay.com?
2. Is it a violation of the ACPA to warehouse a famous domain name? Is that evidence of "bad faith"?
3. Was the defendant, Spider Webs Ltd., acting ethically in this case?

Internet Technology and Trademark Infringement

Internet technology, the code used in software, provides three areas of concern with respect to trademark infringement and dilution. They include *deeplinking, metatags,* and *framing.* (See Chapter 1 for a technical explanation of these terms.) Surfers seeking information about a product or service without having the correct URL often use a search engine that generates a list of sites based on a key term provided by the user. The following explains various ways that a Web designer may violate a trademark right by using Internet technology.

Deep Linking. The very culture of the World Wide Web involves a process known as **hyperlinking** that allows a user to conveniently move from one site to another by a predetermined highlighted area on a Web page. A hyperlink is created by the Web designer inserting a URL (universal resource locator) into HTML (hypertext

FIGURE 3.7   **Bad Faith Guidelines Under the ACPA**

Any of the following may constitute bad faith by the domain-name holder:

- The trademark rights of the owner of the federally registered trademark will be diminished.
- The domain-name owners intend to cause consumers to divert the goodwill represented by the trademark, either for profit or to tarnish or disparage the trademark, by creating a likelihood of confusion in the minds of the consumers.
- The domain-name owners offer to sell the name to the trademark owner or a third party for financial gain.
- The holder of the domain-name applied for it by providing false information.
- The holder applied for multiple domain-names registration that were known to be identical or confusingly similar to others.

markup language) code that, upon a left click of the mouse, allows the user to access the new linked site automatically. The home page of this new Web site is called a *surface link*. Because a surface link is merely an address of a site and does not involve a copying, there is generally no copyright violation and may usually be provided without the owner's consent. (See Chapter 4, "Copyrights.") A **deeplink** goes beyond the home page to other pages within the Web site. In most cases only the home page will show a banner advertisement and the Web site owners' trademark. Because a home page often displays "banner ads" that pay the Web site owner a fee based on the number of "hits," a deeplink can result in an enormous amount of lost income. This is especially true for a noncommercial site that often depends on "banner ads" as its sole source of revenue. Deeplinking that bypasses the home page may give the end user the false impression that the product or service described or shown belongs to the wrong company.

FIGURE 3.8   **Remedies of a Trademark Owner Against a Cyberpirate**

Sue for *actual damage* (i.e., loss of profits to the company) and reasonable attorney fees plus cancellation of the domain name.

or

Sue for *statutory damages*—minimum of $1,000 up to $100,000 per domain name and reasonable attorney fees and cancellation of the domain name.

or

Transfer the domain name to the plaintiff trademark owner.

Metatags. A **metatag** is an invisible code imbedded in the hypertext markup language (HTML) used to create Web sites. Its primary use is to assist a search engine to index and summarize sites. For example, a person looking for a bookstore would type in "amazon" and find its URL. When a user seeks information on a search engine about a company (e.g., Amazon.com), a competing company (e.g., Barnes & Noble) with an invisible metatag on its Web site could lead the user to believe there is an affiliation with that company. An unethical Web site owner can easily use a competitor's trade name with a similar product or service by placing the competitor's name on its metatags. This could constitute a trademark infringement, trademark dilution, or unfair competition.

An e-business can determine if a corporation is using its trademark as a metatag by entering its trademark as a search term on a search engine, such as www.yahoo.com. It could then note the Web site listed as a "hit" on which the trademark does not visibly appear. If it views the HTML version of those pages on a Netscape Navigator by right-clicking the mouse on View and then the Document Source, it will illustrate the key terms included in the metatag. The infringing company can be using a registered trademark that has nothing to do with the company and simply attempts to lure users to its site. This is often referred to as *invisible trademark infringement.*

In a 1999 decision, *Brookfield Communications, Inc. v. West Coast Entertainment Corporation,* the court described a metatag trademark infringement this way:

> Using another's trademark in one's metatags is much like posting a sign with another's trademark in front on one's store.

> Suppose West Coast's competitor (let's call it "Blockbuster") puts up a billboard on a highway reading—"West Coast Video: 2 miles ahead at Exit 7"—where West Coast is really located at Exit 8 but Blockbuster is located at Exit 7. Customers looking for West Coast's store will pull off at Exit 7 and drive around looking for it. Unable to locate West Coast, but seeing the Blockbuster store right by the highway entrance, they may simply rent there. Even consumers who prefer West Coast may find it not worth the trouble to continue searching for West Coast since there is a Blockbuster right there. Customers are not confused in the narrow sense: they are fully aware that they are purchasing from Blockbuster and they have no reason to believe that Blockbuster is related to, or in any way sponsored by, West Coast. Nevertheless, the fact that there is only initial consumer confusion does not alter the fact that Blockbuster would be misappropriating West Coast's acquired goodwill.

One can question the ethics of an e-business using metatags to entice consumers to a Web site and thereby steal its hard-earned goodwill.

In the following case, the court held a former Playboy Playmate of the Year, who used metatags in her Web site that identified herself in that fashion, was fair use of the metatag PLAYBOY and PLAYMATE.

Playboy Enterprises Inc. v. Welles
162 F.3d 1169 (9th Cir. 2002)

Facts

Playboy Enterprise Inc. (PEI) owns federally registered trademarks for the terms *Playboy, Playmate, Playmate of the Month,* and *Playmate of the Year.* Defendant Terri Welles is a self-employed model and spokesperson who began her modeling career with *Playboy* magazine in 1980. In May 1980, Welles appeared on the cover of *Playboy* magazine and was subsequently featured as the Playmate of the Month in the December 1980 issue. Defendant claims that she has always referred to herself since 1980 as a Playmate or Playmate of the Year with the knowledge of PEI.

Defendant uses the terms *Playboy* and *Playmate* along with other terms within the keywords section of the meta tags, which constitutes the internal index of the Web site used by some search engines. PEI appeals the district court's grant of summary judgment.

Judicial Opinion *(Judge Nelson)*

Defendant, Ms. Welles, has used the terms Playboy and Playmate as meta tags for her site so that those using search engines on the Web can find her website if they were looking for a Playboy Playmate. The problem in this case is that the trademarks that defendant uses, and the manner in which she uses them, describe her and identify her. This raises a question of whether there is a "fair use" of these marks pursuant to 15 U.S.C. §§ 1115(b)(4) and 1125(c)(4). See New Kids, 971 F.2d at 306 (noting that the "fair use" defense arises when the trademark also describes a person, a place or an attribute of a product). Terri Welles was and is the "Playmate of the Year for 1981." Plaintiff has conceded this fact and has not submitted any evidence for the Court to conclude that PEI may prevent defendant from using that term to identify herself and her award; as noted above, PEI conceded that there are no contractual agreements between it and defendant which restrict her use of any of the marks. Thus, defendant has raised a "fair use" defense which must be overcome by the plaintiff before a potential infringement under Section 43(a) of the Lanham Act or trademark dilution under Section 43(c) of the Lanham Act may be found.

With respect to the meta tags, the court finds there to be no trademark infringement where defendant has used plaintiffs trademarks in good faith to index the content of her website. The meta tags are not visible to the websurfer although some search engines rely on these tags to help websurfers find certain websites. Much like the subject index of a card catalog, the meta tags give the websurfer using a search engine a clearer indication of the content of a website. Other factors weigh in defendant's favor. Though she is using the trademarks, she has done nothing else to make her use identical to the Playboy trademark. There is no bunny logo, the font for the terms is different, and there is no other indication that PEI is sponsoring the website. Plaintiff has presented no empirical evidence to show that there is actual confusion among consumers. Though not necessary, the lack of any such demonstration weighs in defendant's favor. Finally, it appears that defendant has used the trademarks in good faith. She has removed some of the references per PEI's request, has not used the bunny logo, and has added a disclaimer to the vast majority of her free web pages. See *Consumers Union of U.S. v. General Signal Corp.,* 724 F.2d 1044, 1053 (2d Cir. 1983).

Conclusion

In *Prestonettes v. Coty,* 264 U.S. 359, 368 (1924), Justice Holmes explained the purpose of trademark protection and noted that "[w]hen the mark is used in a way that does not deceive the public, we see no such sanctity in the word as to prevent its being used to tell the truth. It is not taboo." In this case, Ms. Welles has used PEI's trademarks to identify herself truthfully as the Playmate of the Year 1981. Such use is not "taboo" under the law. Based on the foregoing analysis, the court finds that plaintiff has failed to demonstrate that a preliminary injunction is warranted since there is not a strong likelihood of success on the merits. Consequently, the Court cannot find that the balance of harm tips strongly enough in plaintiff's favor to overcome the lack of meritoriousness the court has found. See *Stokely-Van Camp Inc. v. Coca-Cola Co.,* 2 U.S.P.Q. 2d 1225, 1227 (N.D. Ill. 1987). In addition, it is unclear that irreparable harm would ensue from the continued operation of Ms. Welles' website since plaintiff has not demonstrated that there is a likelihood of confusion. We affirm the district court's grant of summary judgment.

We affirm the district court's grant of summary judgment.

Case Questions

1. Why did the court allow Welles to use the term *Playboy* in her metatags?
2. Was there any actual confusion among consumers based on her use of the metatags?
3. Was she acting ethically in using the metatags?

Framing. **Framing** is an Internet technology that allows a Web site user to view content from another Web site while still viewing the home page of the original site. If the framing site's domain name remains displayed at the top of the Web page, this could lead to consumer to believe there is an affiliation with the framed Web site.

INTERNATIONAL REGULATION AND ENFORCEMENT OF TRADEMARK LAW

Trademark law is primarily a creature of national law. However, international law sets down guidelines of uniform definition and protection, and establishes ways to make it easier for owners to acquire rights in different countries. The following discussion provides examples of leading international trademark laws and problems.

Key International Trademark Treaties

The Agreement on Trade-Related Aspects of Intellectual Property Rights (TRIPS).[1]
TRIPS is one of the World Trade Organization's (WTO) multilateral agreements. Like the other WTO multilateral agreements, the WTO member countries are automatically members of the TRIPS Agreement. TRIPS establishes a comprehensive set of rights and obligations governing international trade in intellectual property. To accomplish this, the agreement establishes a common minimum of protection for intellectual property rights within the territories of all WTO member countries.

The TRIPS Agreement has a number of important points. First, WTO members countries are required to observe the substantive provisions of the following multilateral intellectual property agreements: the **International Convention for the Protection of Industrial Property (Paris Convention)**, the Berne Convention for the Protection of Literary and Artistic Works (Berne Convention), the International Convention for the Protection of Performers, Producers of Phonograms, and Broadcasting Organizations (Rome Convention), and the Treaty on Intellectual Property in Respect of Integrated Circuits (IPIC Treaty). TRIPS supplements these multilateral intellectual property agreements. For example, the agreements sets the minimum term of copyrights at 50 years, patents at 20 years, and trademarks at 7 years.

Second, TRIPS establishes criteria for the effective enforcement of intellectual property rights. WTO member countries are bound by the WTO's Dispute Resolution Understanding agreement. This understanding establishes a mechanism for settling intellectual property disputes between WTO member countries.

Third, the agreements extends the basic international trade principles established in the General Agreement on Tariffs and Trade to the field of international intellectual property rights. TRIPS requires nations to follow various international principles. The "national treatment principle" requires each member country to extend to nationals of other members treatment "no less favorable" than that which it gives its own nationals regarding intellectual property rights. The "transparency principle" requires member countries to publish and to notify the WTO's TRIPS Council of all relevant laws, regulations, and practices, and to promptly respond to other member countries' requests for information about its intellectual property rules. The "most-favored-nation treatment principle" requires a member country to grant to the nationals of all other member countries the most favorable treatment that it grants to the nationals of any one of them.

Finally, there is a transition period for less developed member countries to bring their intellectual property rules into compliance with TRIPS. Developing members and those transitioning to a market economy had to be in full compliance by January 1, 2000. The least developed member states have until January 1, 2006 to reach TRIPS standards.

---

[1]The text of the TRIPS Agreement is posted at *http://www.wto.org/english/tratop_e/trips_e/trips_e.htm*

The International Convention for the Protection of Industrial Property (Paris Convention).[2] The Paris Convention establishes a "union" of countries responsible for protecting industrial property rights. Industrial property rights include patent, trademarks, and industrial designs. Member countries are required to comply with three "principles:" (1) "National treatment" (which is the same principle set out in the TRIPS Agreement); (2) "Right of priority," which provides that an applicant for protection in one country has up to twelve months to file an application in other countries, and that those other countries must then treat the application as if it were filed on the same day as the original application; and (3) "Common rules" establish basic minimum criteria and procedures for granting industrial property rights.

Trademark Law Treaty.[3] The **Trademark Law Treaty** seeks to achieve uniformity in various trademark procedures. The treaty was signed at the Diplomatic Conference in Geneva on October 27, 1994, by thirty-five countries, including the United States, Russia, China, the United Kingdom, Australia, and Japan (with limited reservations). The key features of the treaty seek to harmonize the following rules: (1) the initial and renewal terms of registering trademarks is ten years; (2) service marks now have equal protection as trademarks under the Paris Convention; and (3) various procedures related to renewal applications, powers of attorney, authentication, and others have been streamlined.

Madrid Protocol.[4] The **Madrid Protocol** establishes a single international trademark application and registration system that provide trademark protection in a number of countries. Managed by the WIPO, international registration has the same effect as if registration was made in each of the signatory countries. If a particular national office does not refuse protection, the trademark has the same protection in that country as any other. The Madrid system significantly simplifies trademark management. Companies may record subsequent changes (i.e., change of ownership, change of address of the holder, even renewal of registration) with a single procedural step. A number of countries have signed the Madrid Protocol, such as China, France, Poland, Russia, Spain, the United Kingdom, and Switzerland. After some initial reluctance related to EU voting rights, the U.S. approval of the protocol is now winding its way through Congress and the Executive Branch. Most commentators conclude that U.S. ratification of the protocol is imminent.

International Trademark Disputes of Internet Domain Names

As described in Chapter 1, an Internet domain name is a naming system that attaches an Internet World Wide Web address to a unique Internet protocol number. Disputes as to who owns a domain name (the owner of the real-world trademark or the owner of the domain name online) have raged both within the United States and throughout

[2]The Paris Convention text is posted at *http://www.wipo.org/treaties/ip/paris/index.html*
[3]The Trademark Law Treaty is posted at *http://www.wipo.org/treaties/ip/tlt/*
[4]The Madrid Protocol is posted at *http://www.wipo.int/madrid/en/legal_texts/index.html*

the world. Unfortunately, no single overarching rule exists regarding the trademark status. Court rulings seem highly fact dependent and have not developed an international consensus. International arrangements have started to develop, but they do not have complete international acceptance. Next are examples of national and international initiatives related to defining ownership of a domain name trademark.

United Kingdom. UK courts have ruled against cybersquatters, concluding that various defendants have "passed off" the trademark holder's well-known marks by cybersquatting on domain names. In addition, a UK court found that it had jurisdiction over a German Web site because the UK plaintiff alleged harm and damages resulting within the UK. The UK plaintiff cited section 2 of the Brussels convention, which permits lawsuits to be heard where the unlawful event occurred.

France. French courts, relying on the Brussels convention, have not hesitated to assert jurisdiction over Web sites that are broadcasted into their jurisdiction. For example, a French software company demanded an injunction from Brokat, a German company located in Stuttgart, from using the term *payline*. The French company had trademarked the term *payline*. The French court found jurisdiction and issued the injunction against Brokat. The French court justified the decision by stating that the German Web site was broadcast into French territory and therefore France was the locale for its trademark infringement. The court barred Brokat from using the trademark payline anywhere in France, including online. Foreign companies seeking to protect their domain name trademark in France should both file with the national trademark office and register their company domain names with the French top-level domain ".fr".

Asia. Disputes over domain names appear far less common in Asia. This may be because most Asian countries have very few Internet users as compared to Europe and the United States. When these disputes do occur, they usually center on an international firm attempting to protect its trademarked domain name from local infringement. For example, in India, Yahoo! sued to stop an Indian company from acquiring and using the domain name Yahooindia.com without a license. Yahooindia raised a number of common defenses, such as placing disclaimers placed on its Web site disassociating itself with Yahoo!, citing the sophistication of Internet users, claiming its registration of the domain name is a complete defense, and asserting that because India did not have legislation protecting service marks it could not be restrained. The Indian court rejected Yahooindia's arguments, reasoning that a disclaimer does not reduce confusion, and stating that trademark law applies with equal force online as well as in the physical world. Other Asian countries have also witnessed trademark domain name disputes. In China, Yahoo! prevailed in securing the domain name yahoo.com.cn from various cybersquatters. In New Zealand, quokka.com, which had a license to use the America's Cup Trademark, filed a complaint against two New Zealanders who registered an Internet address using the trademark. Lawsuits were filed in both New Zealand and the United States. Hours before a U.S. federal judge was to rule in the case, the parties settled, and the two New Zealanders agreed to transfer the domain names.

The Problem of Enforcement. Even if a company with a valid trademark discovers a potentially infringing cybersquatter, enforcing that trademark on an international scale may pose significant difficulties. First, a popular trademark is subject to dilution online because of the plethora of available domain names with deceptively similar marks. For example, the Web site att.com has attracted such deceptive imitators as attt.com, at-t.com, attcellular.com, attweb.com, attonline.com, attnetwork.net, and others. Second, even if a cybersquatter is found, effective judicial service on the squatter may be difficult, as addresses given are often fictitious. Third, if a deceptive domain name holder is found and served with a cease and desist notice, the holder could transfer the domain name to a third party. Finally, the holder's name may remain listed for a time with Network Solutions, Inc. (NSI), the entity responsible for many domain name allocations, even if it does not pay registration fees or loses a lawsuit. The best strategy for protection domain name trademarks may be a good offensive stance. Purchase a domain name and its related terms as quickly as possible before a cybersquatter grabs it.

Dispute Resolution. The WIPO has established a **Uniform Dispute Resolution Policy (UDRP)** that aids in resolving domain main disputes between trademark holders and domain name owners. The UDRP holds that if a domain name registrant refuses in bad faith to transfer the domain name over to a valid trademark holder of the name, the trademark holder may obtain cancellation of the domain through the UDRP. A UDRP complainant must show three things in order to retrieve the domain from the respondent:

- the respondent's domain name is identical or confusingly similar to the trademark,
- the respondent has no rights in the domain name, and
- the respondent has registered the domain name and possesses it in bad faith.

Unlike traditional trademark infringement, where subjective intent is relevant, under the UDRP showing the respondent's bad faith is mandatory. Bad faith includes, for example, purchasing the domain name with the intent to resell it at a higher price, prevent the trademark owner from obtaining the name, disrupt a competitor's business, or attract the trademark holder's potential customers for commercial gain.

"Metatagging" and Misuse of Another's Trademark

Metatags are words in a Web page that a search engine uses to categorize that Web page according to topic or interest. These tags are similar to "subject words" found in a library catalog. These words are usually hidden from the user and are only available in the source code of the document.

Through the use of metatags, a Web site can repeatedly use another company's trademark in its metatags in order to attract attention to its Web site. For example, a creative vegetarian group may fill its metatags with the word *McDonald's*, in order to greet any user using a search engine to find information about the restaurant with its own propaganda. Such misuse of metatags has attracted the attention of the trademark holder, who often demands an injunction against the use of metatags. For example, in *Playboy Enterprises v. Calvin Designer Label*, Playboy demanded an injunction against Calvin, claiming that Calvin used the trademarks Playboy and Playmate as metatags on its Web site. The federal court granted the injunction, ruling that use of Playboy's metatags violated that company's trademark rights.

Although no litigated cases have appeared, this metatagging problem can certainly be reproduced on an international scale. A UK company, for example, could place within its Web site trademarked metatags of a U.S. firm. Such disputes might generally follow the same path as established by international courts in normal domain cases. The real-world owner of the trademark would probably prevail in such a dispute against the metatagging company. One commentator offers three suggestions regarding the control of metatag misuse.[5]

- the prohibition of the use of spamdexing, when there is no relation of the metatag to the content of the Web site;
- the approval of the use of metatags in an effort to raise awareness of a competing product, to promote comparative advertising, to increase competition, and to lower costs to consumers; and
- the organization of a system to monitor use and to penalize violators.

Summary

Yahoo!, AOL, and Amazon.com are household words that did not exist a short time ago. They are now famous trademarks that have acquired a special meaning on the Internet. A successful e-business must establish a dominance on the Web by brand-name recognition. This business strategy requires a great deal of money and a legal strategy to protect the domain name, company name, its logo, and advertising slogans from being infringed and/or diluted by others.

Our legal system provides for federal registration of trademarks granting the owner federal statutory rights against infringers and dilutors. These rights extend to certain technological devises such as the wrongful use of metatags, deeplinking, and framing. A sound legal strategy of federal registration in the USPTO must protect the trade name, domain name, its logo, and advertising slogans as valuable intellectual property of the e-business.

In addition, managers must consider the international protection of their trademarks. A number of key treaties regulate international registration and enforcement of trademarks. The trend in international law seems to favor the trademark holder over the cybersquatter in domain-name disputes, but uncertainties still remain. Trademark infringement by misuse of "metatags" may also be an issue, and managers should take steps to prevent this infringement on both a national and international scale.

---

[5]Joseph T. Kucala Jr. "Putting the Meat Back in Meta-Tags." *Journal of Law, Technology & Policy* (2001): 129.

Key Terms

trademark, *48*
Lanham Act, *48*
U.S. Patent & Trademark Office (USPTO), *49*
domain name, *49*
service mark, *50*
trade dress, *50*
inherently distinctive, *52*
secondary meaning, *52*
Supplemental Register, *52*
Principal Register, *52*
Network Solutions, Inc. (NSI), *52*

Internet Corporation for Assigned Names and Numbers (ICANN), *52*
trademark infringement, *58*
Federal Trademark Dilution Act of 1996, *63*
trademark dilution, *63*
famous trademark, *64*
dilution by tarnishment, *66*
dilution by blurring, *67*
Anticybersquatting Consumer Protection Act, *68*
hyperlinking, *70*
deeplink, *71*

metatag, *72*
framing, *74*
Agreement on Trade-Related Aspects of Intellectual Property Rights (TRIPS), *75*
International Convention for the Protection of Industrial Property (Paris Convention), *75*
Trademark Law Treaty, *76*
Madrid Protocol, *76*
Uniform Dispute Resolution Policy (UDRP), *78*

Manager's Checklist

√ Register a company's domain name with the U.S. Patent & Trademark Office. If possible, it should be the same as its trade name.

√ Be aware of what constitutes a "famous" trademark and consider doing whatever is possible to acquire that status. Remember that a claim against an online noncompetitor for trademark dilution requires that the plaintiff's trademark be "famous."

√ Constantly review, with your lawyer, the duration of the trademark and any renewal that may be necessary.

√ Register with an accredited registrar of Internet Corporation for Assigned Names and Numbers as many derivative domain names relative to your product and/or services as possible to prevent others from doing so. Consider federal registration of these derivative domain names with the PTO.

√ Be aware that the online use of a "famous" trademark by your company or another noncompeting company may constitute "blurring" or "tarnishment" under the Federal Dilution Trademark Act.

√ Display the circled ® on your Web page wherever the registered trademark appears. For a service mark, use the sm initials. Although not required by law, this provides actual notice of federal registration.

√ Be aware that federal registration of a trademark does not grant international protection. This is a very real problem because an online company using its trademark has a global presence and may have to register the mark in every country in which it is doing business. This can be a very costly process.

√ Be sure your Web designer avoids deeplinking and framing and does not use another company's trade name in its metatags.

√ Be aware of any changes to international law related to trademarks. Also be aware of the procedures under the Madrid Protocol for international trademark registration.

√ Although ownership of domain names seems to favor the trademark holder internationally, the best practice is to obtain the trademarked domain name as early as possible and avoid an international conflict.

√ Ethical Considerations

Is there an ethical justification for surface linking to another company's Web site without the site owner's permission? Assume your Web site was linked to a pornographic Web site. Would that change your answer?

Case Problems

1. Plaintiff, AOL, uses the phrase "You Have Mail" to notify its subscribers of their receipt of e-mail. AOL has a pending application for the trademark "You Have Mail." Defendant, AT&T, operates a competing service offering a feature that it describes as "You Have Mail," which notifies subscribers of notification of their receipt of e-mail. AOL contends that AT&T's use of the phrase "You Have Mail" infringed and diluted its trademark and brought suit under the Lanham Act. AT&T counterclaimed alleging AOL's trademark "You Have Mail" is a generic mark and not entitled to trademark protection. Decide. [*America Online Inc., v. AT&T Corp.*, 243 F.3d 812 (4th Cir. 2001)]

2. Defendant used the phrase "Barbie's Playhouse" on its Web site in a font and colors virtually identical to those used by plaintiff to market its products. It used plaintiff's federally registered trademark "Barbie" to advertise the sale of adult entertainment services. Plaintiff sued defendant under the Federal Trademark Dilution Act. Decide. Explain the elements of the federal statute and why they do or do not apply in this case. [*Mattel, Inc. v. JCom, Inc. and Brand McBride*, 97 Civ. 7191 (SS) (S.D. N.Y. 1998)]

3. Plaintiff, Kraft Foods Holdings, Inc. ("Kraft"), is the manufacturer and distributor of Velveeta brand cheese products. Kraft has owned the Velveeta trademark since 1923. Defendant, Stuart Helm nicknamed "King Velveeda" in 1985, has operated a Web site since 1990 at *http://www.cheesegraphics.com* that contains photographs, drawings and other material of an adult nature and provides non-cheese merchandise or services for sale to the public. One of the items Helm designed and sells on this site is a comic book called *VelVeeda*. Helm's Web site and its use of the name brought on a lawsuit from Kraft claiming Helm is tarnishing the Velveeta trademark, in violation of the "Lanham Act" and the "Illinois Anti-Dilution Act." Decide and state your reasons why Kraft should be granted a preliminary injunction. [*Kraft Foods*

Holdings, Inc. v. Stuart Helm a/k/a "King VelVeeda," 205 F. Supp. 2d 942 (2002)]

4. Avery Dennison Corp. is an office supply company with the federally registered trademark *Avery.* Sumpton and Poplawski registered the domain name avery.com with Network Solutions, Inc. Avery claims they registered the name to extort payment for the sale of the domain name. Advise Avery of its rights using the analytical framework for trademark infringement cases. [*Avery Dennison Corp. v. Sumpton and Poplawski,* 999 F. Supp. 1337 (C.D. Cal. 1998)]

5. Prince Sports Group, Inc., a U.S. manufacturer of sports equipment, sought to stop a UK defendant, Prince plc, an information technology company, from using the domain *name prince.com.* Both parties had valid trademarks supporting use of the name. Prince plc held valid common law rights in the UK to use the prince mark; the U.S. firm completed valid trademark registrations of the word *prince* in both the United Kingdom and the United States. Who owns the domain name prince.com? [*Prince plc v. Prince Sports Group, Inc., Chancery Division* (July 30, 1997)]

Additional Readings

- Beatty, Sally Goll. "Alta Vista Alters Its Vision of the Market." *Wall Street Journal* (December 18, 1996), p. B9.

- Halpern, Marcelo, and Mehrotra, Ajay K. "From International Treaties to Internet Norms: The Evolution of International Trademark Disputes in the Internet Age." *University of Pennsylvania Journal of International Economic Law* 21 (2000): 523.

- Lessig, Lawrence. *Code and Other Laws of Cyberspace,* Chapter 10, "Intellectual Property." New York: Basic Books, 1999.

- Quick, Rebecca. "Can't Get There from Here May Be Web's New Motto." *Wall Street Journal* (July 2, 1997), p. B6.

COPYRIGHTS

Napster harms the market in "at least" two ways: it reduces audio CD sales among college students and it raises barriers to plaintiffs' entry into the market for the digital downloading of music.

—*Judge Beezer in* **A & M Records, Inc., et al. v. Napster,**
114 F. Supp. 2d 896 at 913 (9th Cir. 2001)

LEARNING OBJECTIVES

After you have read this chapter you should be able to:

1. Explain what subject matter may be copyrighted on an e-business Web site.
2. Explain and discuss the exclusive statutory rights granted to the online owner of a federally registered copyright.
3. Explain the statutory limitations on the exclusive statutory rights of an online copyright owner.
4. Understand the elements that make up the defense of "fair use" in the online context.
5. Explain the duration of copyright protection.
6. Explain and understand the difference between direct, contributory, and vicarious infringement.
7. Explain copyright liability to online service providers.
8. Understand the significance of the Digital Millennium Copyright Act.
9. Explain the legal remedies for a copyright infringement.
10. Understand the various international copyright treaties.
11. Explain the factors involved in determining when an international copyright can be enforced in a U.S. court.

http://

- Additional material on copyright law may be found at the Bentley College Cyberlaw Center Web site (**http://ecampus.bentley.edu/ dept/cyberlaw**) under Intellectual Property—Copyright Laws.

INTRODUCTION

Napster, discussed later in this chapter, would be a thriving business today were it not for copyright law. This chapter will help you understand the copyright issues relevant to an e-business and assist you in reviewing e-commerce from a copyright law perspective.

An e-business has two major concerns regarding copyright law: first, to protect its Web site from potential infringers who may copy parts or all of their content without permission, and second, to be sure its Web pages are not infringing on another owner's copyrighted material. Furthermore, your Web site may link to another site that displays copyrighted material without the owner's consent. Could your e-business be sued under a theory of copyright infringement? Is there a legal strategy to be utilized that may limit this potential liability exposure? This chapter discusses these and other issues relevant to copyright protection and liability.

Digital content, transmitted over the Internet, creates unique copyright issues. Web page words, videos, music, Terms of Use and privacy policies, providing they are "original works," may be the appropriate subject matter of copyright protection and federal registration in the U.S. Copyright Office. Copyright law does not protect ideas, systems, or business methods. For example, copyright law does not protect your ideas and graphs expressed in an original business plan, but the original written and graphic description is protected. In addition to copyright law, you should exercise your *trade secret* rights in your business plan (discussed in Chapter 5).

►http://

- Visit the U.S. Copyright Office at
  http://lcweb.loc.gov/copyright

Federal copyright law provides the owner of an original work of authorship with exclusive statutory rights, discussed in this chapter. Because Web site design and development are costly ventures, legally protecting them with copyright ownership incurs a special significance on the Internet. Furthermore, the improper use of e-mail may implicate copyright liability. For example, an e-mail user may send, without the owner's permission, an attached copy of a copyrighted document that is reproduced in perfect form to a vast global audience. This inappropriate use of electronic communication poses special and unique problems for copyright protection on the Internet.

As previously stated in Chapter 3, "Trademarks," copyright law has historically been a form of intellectual property along with trademarks, patents, and trade secrets. Trademarks, not copyrights, legally protect business names, advertising slogans, and short phrases used to distinguish goods and/or services sold in interstate commerce. Patents, not copyrights, may protect business methods, discussed in Chapter 5, "Business Methods Patents and Trade Secrets." Copyright legally protects a vast array of "original works of authorship fixed in a tangible medium of expression" including

- computer software and architecture (code)
- movies and other audiovisual works, including those on a Web site
- musical compositions, including the lyrics of the song
- novels, including e-books
- poetry
- literary works, including Web site content
- dramatic works
- sound recordings, including Web site audio transmissions
- pantomimes and choreographic works

- sculptural works
- architectural works

The origin of U.S. copyright law is found in the first English copyright act, the 1710 Statute of Anne. Although the common law provides the author of "original and creative works" with copyright protection as soon as it is "fixed in a tangible form," filing the work for registration in the U.S. Copyright Office is a prerequisite for initiating a legal claim for copyright infringement in the federal court system [*M.C.B. Homes, Inc. v. Ameron Homes Inc.*, 903 F.2d 1486, 1488 (11th Cir. 1990)].

Copyright law is federal law found in the Copyright Act [17 U.S.C. 101-1205] that protects the authors from copyright infringement for "original works of authorship fixed in a tangible medium of expression" [17 U.S.C. Sec. 40l (d)]. Because the original content on Web pages qualifies for federal registration of the site in the U.S. Copyright Office, one of the first orders of business of an e-business should be to file for federal copyright registration of its Web pages.

Providing the entire content of the Web pages are "original works of authorship," the online venture satisfies the statutory requirement that it be "fixed in a tangible medium of expression." Web site developers must be especially aware of copyright issues that may have legal consequences at a later time when a great deal of effort and cost have been expended to create or update an e-company's Web site.

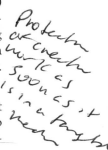

- Visit the federal Copyright Office Web site to see detailed information on copyright law: **http://lcweb.loc.gov/copyright**

Because designing, producing, and maintaining a sophisticated Web site is very expensive, protecting content ownership is extremely important. Electronic commerce will continue to be highly competitive. As Web sites become more and more interactive with consumers, their creation, design, and maintenance place enormous demands on innovative marketing techniques that should be legally protected.

Framers of the U.S. Constitution knew the value of protecting exclusive rights in the owner of creative works. The authority of Congress to enact copyright laws is found in Article I, Section 8, clause 8: The Constitution grants power in Congress *"to promote the progress of science and useful arts, by securing for limited times to authors and inventors the exclusive right to their respective writings and discoveries."* This exclusive property interest gives the copyright owner of a Web site a monopoly in the work. However, the free flow of information that is the very culture and value of the World Wide Web may conflict with this copyright interest. The First Amendment's history of freedom of speech encourages the currency of ideas and their expression, no matter how controversial. Creative information and, indeed, commerce itself, depends on the development of commercial expression. Balancing these competing interests is the purpose of the U.S. Copyright Act and the federal courts.

Keep in mind that never before has it been so easy to violate a copyright owner's exclusive right to copy the material. Common copyright violations are employees

accepted

forwarding or attaching copyrighted e-mail without the consent of the author. Both methods may violate the owner's exclusive statutory right to copy the document.

The uploading of information and making multiple copies of online material could also be a copyright violation, as well as the downloading of MP3 files (*http://www.mp3.com*). Companies and individuals that are not aware of these copyright infringements may find themselves liable under legal theories discussed later.

Copyright law is a strict liability statute. This means it is possible to be liable as an unintentional infringer, and hence the importance of an e-business working closely with its lawyers cannot be overestimated. This chapter reviews the copyright laws of e-commerce and acquaints you with some of the copyright problems relative to the online environment. Suggestions are made throughout the chapter as to how an e-business manager can legally protect copyright ownership and limit a company's copyright liability (see Figure 4.1).

COPYRIGHT ACT OF 1976

changes for the better

In order to implement the congressional authority as stated in the U.S. Constitution of granting exclusive rights to copyright owners, Congress adopted in 1790 the first U.S. copyright law. The statute has gone through numerous amendments, resulting in a comprehensive revision in 1909. As our mass media evolved from radio to movies to VCRs, to audio and videotapes, Congress again saw fit to amend the Copyright Act in 1976. The act took effect on January 1, 1978.

The federal courts' function is to interpret the Copyright Act within the context of our current environment of information technology. As stated by the U.S. Supreme Court, "From the beginning, the law of copyrights has developed in response to significant changes in technology" [*Sony Corp. v. Universal Studios, Inc.*, 464 U.S. 417 (1984)]. The role of the court, however, remains constant. It must maintain the del-

---

FIGURE 4.1   E-Business Copyright Objective and Legal Strategy

---

E-business objective: Protect the Web pages of the company's Web site from being copied by other companies and protect the company from any copyright infringement suits.

Legal strategy:

- Register the copyright of the Web pages.
- Include appropriate disclaimers in the Terms of Use for copyright infringement by linked companies.
- Monitor bulletin boards and chat rooms for known copyright infringements by third parties.

---

icate balance between the exclusive rights of copyright owners and the public's right to have access to information (discussed later under the "fair use" doctrine).

Subject Matter of Copyrights

Copyright ownership can be registered for (1) literary works, (2) musical works, (3) dramatic works, (4) pantomimes/choreographic works, (5) pictorial, graphic, and sculptural works, (6) motion pictures and audiovisual works, (7) sound recordings, and (8) architectural works.

In order for this material to be registered in the Copyright Office as a copyright, it must be *"an original work of authorship* fixed in any tangible medium of expression from which they can be perceived, reproduced, or otherwise communicated either directly or with the aid of a machine or devise" [17 U.S.C. Sec.102 (a)]. This requirement may fit the application of the material found on Web pages, allowing them to be federally registered with the U.S. Copyright Office (see Figure 4.2).

The nature of its originality requires the work be a creative document not copied from another source. It must be the independent work of the author. Under the Copyright Act, a **fixed creative work** is fixed "when its embodiment in a copy or phonorecord . . . is sufficiently permanent or stable to permit it to be perceived, reproduced, or otherwise communicated for a period of more than transitory duration" (17 U.S.C. Sec. 101). Fixed creative works must be fixed in a tangible medium of expression in order to be copyrighted. Web pages fit this statutory requirement and may be federally registered. The Copyright Act clearly states that an original work of authorship does not extend to any idea, procedure, process, system, method of operation, concept, principle, or discovery, unless fixed in a tangible form [17 U.S.C. Sec. 102(b)]. Copyright law protects the expression of an idea and not the idea itself.

Although you cannot copyright a creative and original idea, once the idea is expressed in a fixed, tangible form, it may acquire copyright protection. For example, the contents on a Web page were once original and creative ideas, but when coded and fixed in floppy disks, compact disks, or other digital storage devices, printed copies of this material may be sent with the application to the Copyright Office for federal copyright registration. Notice that a system or method of operation is not a subject matter for a copyright. However, an appropriate "business method" may be patentable. (See Chapter 5, "Business Methods Patents and Trade Secrets.")

FIGURE 4.2   Criteria for Copyright Protection of a Web Page

√ *Originality*—The Web site may not copy a similar site and should strive for a unique presentation (e.g., *http://www.consumerreview.com*).

√ *Creativity*—The Web site need not be novel, as in a patent requirement, but should be an independent creation (e.g., *http://www.landsend.com*).

√ *Fixed form*—The application of the content to the Web site is sufficient to create a fixed form for copyright protection purposes.

Original and creative digital works fixed in a tangible medium of expression will receive exclusive statutory rights under copyright law. This is the basis for Web site federal registration in the U.S. Copyright Office.

Requirements for Registration in the Copyright Office

Registration of a copyright in the Copyright Office requires a completed registration form and a submission of the original work. The Copyright Office will then issue to the owner a certificate of registration. In a copyright infringement case, the plaintiff will submit this certificate to prove copyright registration and ownership. The certificate of registration constitutes prima facie evidence of the validity of the copyright and allows the owner to sue an infringer in the federal court and pursue statutory remedies. So the importance of federal registration of the e-business Web site cannot be overestimated. It provides the e-business with a property interest in the Web site that is legally protected.

Duration of Copyright

In October 1998, Congress enacted the **Sonny Bono Copyright Term Extension Act (CTEA)**. It extends the term of most copyrights by twenty years. These changes harmonize U.S. law with European copyright laws.

Thus copyrights for works created prior to January 1, 1978, generally endure for a term of 28 years with the option to renew for a further term of 67 years. Prior to the CTEA, the renewal term was for 47 years [17 U.S.C. sec. 304].

Copyrights for works created on or after January 1, 1978, generally endure for a term consisting of the life of the author plus an additional 70 years after the author's death. Prior to the CTEA the term after death was for 50 years [17 U.S.C. sec. 302].

CONSTITUTIONAL CHALLENGE TO THE SONNY BONO COPYRIGHT TERM EXTENSION ACT

The U.S. Supreme Court heard the case of *Eldred v. Ashcroft*, on the issue of whether or not the constitutional limits of congressional power to extend the term of copyright for twenty years has been exceeded as provided in the Copyright Clause that states, "Congress has the authority to issue copyrights "for limited times" in order to "promote the progress of science and useful arts." The plaintiffs argued that copyright protection is a legal monopoly giving exclusive rights to the copyright owner, with some limitations for fair use, during the copyright duration. The traditional basis for that entitlement was to give the authors an incentive to write and publish material and at the same time to promote the progress of the arts. Petitioners argued that at some point this copyright protection should end and the copyrighted material should fall into the realm of public domain. They further argued to assure a vast public domain of free works is available for the common good, the retroactive extension for twenty years granted in the Sonny Bono Copyright Term Extension Act of 1998 was an abuse of congressional authority. As you read the case, note how the U.S. Supreme

Court responded to the objection that the copyright extension has an adverse effect on the public domain's reception of expired copyrighted works and the right of Congress to grant a monopoly to copyright owners is subject to the limited time provision of the U.S. Constitution.

Eldred v. Ashcroft
123 S. Ct. 769

Facts

This case concerns the authority the Constitution assigns to Congress to prescribe the duration of Copyrights. The Copyright and Patent Clause of the Constitution, Art. I, Sec. 8, cl. 8, provides as to copyrights: "Congress shall have Power . . . [t]o promote the Progress of Science . . . by securing [to Authors] for limited Times . . . the exclusive Right to their . . . Writings." In 1998, in the measure here under inspection, Congress enlarged the duration of copyrights by twenty years [Copyright Term Extension Act (CTEA), Pub. L. 105-298, Sec. 102(b) and (d), 112 Stat. 2827-2828 (amending 17 U.S.C. Sections 302, 304)]. As in the case of prior extensions, principally in 1831, 1909, and 1976, Congress provided for application of the enlarged terms to existing and future copyrights alike.

Petitioners are individuals and businesses whose products or services build on copyrighted works that have gone into the public domain. They seek a determination that the CTEA fails constitutional review under both the Copyright Clause's "limited times" prescription and the First Amendment's free speech guarantee.

In accord with the District Court and the Court of Appeals, we reject petitioners' challenges to the CTEA. In that 1998 legislation, as in all previous copyright term extensions, Congress placed existing and future copyrights in parity. In prescribing that alignment, we hold, Congress acted within its authority and did not transgress constitutional limitations.

Petitioners' suit challenges the CTEA's constitutionality under both the Copyright Clause and the First Amendment.

We granted certiorari to address two questions: whether the CTEA's extension of existing copyrights exceeds Congress' power under the Copyright Clause; and whether the CTEA's extension of existing and future copyrights violates the First Amendment. We now answer those two questions in the negative and affirm.

Judicial Opinion *(Justice Ginsburg)*

We address first the determination of the courts below that Congress has authority under the Copyright Clause to extend the terms of existing copyrights. Text, history, and precedent, we conclude, confirm that the Copyright Clause empowers Congress to prescribe "limited Times" for copyright protection and to secure the same level and duration of protection for all copyright holders, present and future.

To comprehend the scope of Congress' power under the Copyright Clause, "a page of history is worth a volume of logic." *New York Trust Co. v. Eisner,* 256 U.S. 345, 349

(1921) (Holmes, J.). History reveals an unbroken congressional practice of granting to authors of works with existing copyrights the benefit of term extensions so that all under copyright protection will be governed evenhandedly under the same regime.

Congress' consistent historical practice of applying newly enacted copyright terms to future and existing copyrights reflects a judgment stated concisely by Representative Huntington at the time of the 1831 Act; "[J]ustice, policy and equity alike forb[id]" that an "author who had sold his [work] a week ago, be placed in a worse situation than the author who should sell his work the day after the passing of [the] act." 7 Cong. Deb. 424 (1831). The CTEA follows this historical practice by keeping the duration provisions of the 1976 Act largely in place and simply adding 20 years to each of them. Guided by text, history, and precedent, we cannot agree with petitioners' submission that extending the duration of existing copyrights is categorically beyond Congress' authority under the Copyright Clause.

Satisfied that the CTEA complies with the "limited Times" prescription, we turn now to whether it is a rational exercise of the legislative authority conferred by the Copyright Clause. On that point, we defer substantially to Congress. *Sony*, 464 U.S., at 429 stated ("[I]t is Congress that has been assigned the task of defining the scope of the limited monopoly that should be granted to authors . . . in order to give the public appropriate access to their work product.")

The CTEA reflects judgments of a kind Congress typically makes, judgments we cannot dismiss as outside the Legislature's domain.

The CTEA may also provide greater incentive for American and other authors to create and disseminate their work in the United States. "[M]atching th[e] level of [copyright] protection in the United States [to that] in the EU can ensure stronger protection for U.S. works abroad and avoid competitive disadvantages vis-à-vis foreign rightholders."

In addition to international concerns, Congress passed the CTEA in light of demographic, economic, and technological changes.

In sum, we find that the CTEA is a rational enactment; we are not at liberty to second-guess congressional determinations and policy judgments of this order, however debatable or arguably unwise they may be. Accordingly, we cannot conclude that the CTEA—which continues the unbroken congressional practice of treating future and existing copyrights in parity for term extension purposes—is an impermissible exercise of Congress' power under the Copyright Clause.

Petitioners separately argue that the CTEA is a content-neutral regulation of speech that fails heightened judicial review under the First Amendment. We reject petitioners' plea for imposition of uncommonly strict scrutiny on a copyright scheme that incorporates its own speech-protective purposes and safeguards. The Copyright Clause and First Amendment were adopted close in time. This proximity indicates that, in the Framers' view, copyright's limited monopolies are compatible with free speech principles. Indeed, Copyright's purpose is to *promote* the creation and publication of free expression. "[T]he Framers intended copyright itself to be the engine of free expression. By establishing a marketable right to the use of one's expression, copyright supplies the economic incentive to create and disseminate ideas." As we read the Framers' instruction, the Copyright Clause empowers Congress to determine the intellectual property regimes that, overall, in that body's judgment will serve the ends of the Clause. The wisdom of Congress' action, however, is not within our province to second guess. Satisfied that the legislation before us remains inside the domain the Constitution assigns to the First Branch, we affirm the judgment of the Court of Appeals.

Case Questions

1. What were the petitioners' grounds for this appeal?
2. What is the relationship of this case to the copyright law of the European Union?
3. Why did the court hold that the extended copyright duration for an additional twenty years did not violate the First Amendment's free speech guarantee?

EXCLUSIVE STATUTORY RIGHTS OF A COPYRIGHT OWNER

E-business owners of a federally registered copyright work have the following **exclusive statutory rights** that collectively define the scope of the copyright:

- To reproduce the copyrighted work
- To sell, rent, lease, or otherwise distribute copies of the copyright work to the public
- To prepare derivative works based on the copyright work
- To perform and display publicly the copyright work

Right to Reproduce the Work

Copyright infringement in the online environment often involves a violation of the reproduction right that occurs by transferring data from one computer to another. An early 1984 case, *Apple Computer v. Formula International*, 594 F. Supp. 617, held that copies stored in random access memory (RAM) were temporary, and running a computer program from RAM does not create an infringed copy.

However, in a 1993 case, *MAI Systems Corp. v. Peak Computer, Inc.* 1991 F.2d 511 (9th Cir. 1993), software was downloaded into RAM when the defendant turned the computer on in the course of performing maintenance. In doing so, the defendant was able to view the software program to assist him in diagnosing the problem. The court found that the copy created in RAM was sufficiently permanent and "fixed" to satisfy the Copyright Act and cause an infringement of the software. This case should alert the e-business manager that an unauthorized downloading of software onto RAM and using it for personal gain constitute both a "copying" and infringement.

Other instances of an unauthorized reproduction and copyright infringement are "scanning" a copyrighted printed document into a digital file and uploading and/or downloading a digital copyrighted file to a bulletin board system.

Right of Distribution: Selling, Renting, or Leasing Copies

Because a copyright is the exclusive property of the owner, the right to exercise property interests, such as selling, renting, or leasing the copyright, is protected by the court. A person who does not own the copyright and makes it available on a bulletin board service can be liable for copyright infringement.

In *Playboy Enter. Inc., v. Frena,* 839 F. Supp. 1552 (M.D. Fla. 1993), the court held that when unauthorized photographs of Playboy Enterprises were downloaded to a bulletin board system by the defendant's subscribers, the plaintiff's exclusive right of distribution was infringed by customers of the defendant. Notice how a bulletin board operator, as the defendant in this case, has an obligation to monitor its system to ensure that copyrighted documents are not being displayed and "downloaded" by its customers.

The same rationale regarding the copyright owner's exclusive right of distribution applies to e-mail *attached* or *forwarded* without the permission of the copyright owner. This has become common company practice, and managers should be aware of the potential employer's copyright infringement liability.

In a 1997 case, *Marobie-Fl. Inc. v. National Ass'n of Fire Equip. Distribs.,* 983 F. Supp. 1167 (N.D. Ill.), unauthorized copies of the plaintiff's electronic clip art files were placed on the defendant's Web page. The court held that this constituted an infringing distribution because the files were available for downloading by Internet users. Because this has become a common practice, Web designers as well as managers should be careful in obtaining permission from the owner of clip art if they want to use it on their Web sites.

Linking to a Web Site. Linking to a *surface page* (i.e., a home page that often displays the Web site's trademark, copyright, and "banner ads") by listing its URL (universal resource locator) is similar to giving directions to the listed site and is not a "copying" within the Copyright Act. Hence a surface link to a home page does not generally require permission. This position is based on the theory that going online creates an implied license for anyone with a computer to view the Web site.

However, the terms of use published in many sites restrict the user to making only one copy for personal use of any information displayed. This interactive feature of the WWW to hyperlink defines its very culture, distinguishing it from any other communications medium. E-business Web sites often link to other sites that provide the user with merchandise, helpful information, or resources related to the product and/or service being offered. It would be a prudent business practice to obtain permission to link. Entering into a Web-linking agreement with the linked site will avoid any misunderstanding regarding a copyright infringement.

Creators of a Web site who wanted assurance it was not linked to a pornographic or shabby site could place a prohibition in its Terms of Use similar to, "Do not link to this site without our express consent." This could negate any implied license to link by merely going online.

➤ http://

- For an example of linking to multiple sites, see **http://www.mapquest.com**

Databases. Databases may be subject to copyright registration if the author is creative in selecting and arranging the data and does not merely display the data as facts. In a copyright infringement suit before the U.S. Supreme Court, defendant was the publisher of a telephone directory that reproduced over one thousand of the plaintiff's telephone numbers without its consent. The court found for the defendant and held that the plaintiff's mere arrangement of facts lacked originality because "there is nothing remotely creative about arranging names alphabetically. . . ." [*Feist Publications, Inc. v. Rural Telephone Services Inc.,* 499 U.S. 340 (1991)]. Note that the court denied copyright protection on the basis that the mere alphabetical listing of names and telephone numbers lacked originality.

A federal court in deciding an online case involving the "Red Book" that listed the retail value of used automobiles held the book would be granted copyright protection. The listings in the defendant's "Red Book" were found to be original because the compilation included the selection of optional features in a unique fashion, made an adjustment for mileage in 5,000-mile increments, and used the concept of an "average" vehicle as the subject of evaluation [*CCC Information Services, Inc., v. McAllen Hunter Market Reports, Inc.,* 44 F.3d. 61 2nd Cir. 1994)].

This case is especially important in the online environment because information acquired from consumers is often compiled in a database, and in some instances it is sold to other merchants. (See Chapter 9, "Privacy.") To acquire copyright protection for the consumer database, it must be an original coordination and arrangement of the data. You could accomplish this by dividing the information into regional areas based on customer preference, and so on. Managers should be careful of being in compliance with the privacy policy posted on the company's Web site that makes representations to the users how the information will be used.

http://

- See **http://www.ebay.com** for a "privacy policy" statement on a Web page.

Right to Prepare Derivative Works

Web designers often examine various Web sites and select their most attractive features. The designers must be careful not to infringe on the copyright of another site by preparing a derivative work based on the original presentation.

The Copyright Act defines **derivative work** as "a work based upon one or more preexisting works, such as a translation, musical arrangement, dramatization, fictionalization, motion picture version, sound recording, art reproduction, abridgment, condensation, or any other form in which a work may be recast, transformed or adopted" (17 U.S.C. sec. 101). A derivative work includes "a work consisting of editorial revisions, annotations, elaborations, or other modifications, which, as a whole, represent an original work of authorship. . . (17 U.S.C. sec. 101).

A federal court held that a "Game Genie" device that altered features in Nintendo's videogame cartridges did not create a derivative work. The "Game Genie" enhanced the audiovisual displays without incorporating the underlying work in any permanent form [*Lewis Galoob Toys, Inc. v. Nintendo, Inc.,* 964 F.2d. 965 (9th Cir. 1962)].

To avoid a possible copyright infringement suit based on it being a derivative work, the Web site should not be an adaptation of another site. Managers should consider an indemnity contract with the Web site designer that will repay them for any loss sustained from this potential liability.

Right to Perform and Display Publicly a Copyright Work

The Copyright Act defines as **public performance** the performance that occurs at a place open to the public. It also includes a semipublic place or any place where a substantial number of persons outside of a normal circle of a family and its social acquaintances are gathered (17 U.S.C. Sec. 101).

In *Columbia Pictures, Ind. v. Aveco, Inc.*, 800 F.2d 59 (3rd. Cir. 1986), the defendant improperly authorized public performances by renting videotapes and allowed customers to see the tapes in viewing rooms. The court held that this constituted "a place open to the public" within the meaning of Sec. 101, on the theory that the rooms were open for "any member of the public to avail themselves of this service." Business managers who display Web material on a computer monitor in employee training programs, without the consent of the owner, may be opening this to the public. Within the statutory definition of a *public place,* you should obtain permission from the owner before doing so. Courts have held that making available videotape over the Internet without authorization and posting unauthorized copies of electronic clip art on Web pages could violate the copyright owner's exclusive statutory right of public display [*Michaels v. Internet Entert. Group, Inc.*, 5 F. Supp. 2d 823 (C.D. Cal. 1998)].

THEORIES OF LIABILITY FOR COPYRIGHT INFRINGEMENT

There are three theories of copyright infringement liability: direct, contributory, and vicarious.

Direct Infringement

The direct infringer is the direct actor who, with or without a specific intent to infringe, is the primary party that violates one of the copyright owner's exclusive statutory rights. This is the person or company that actually carries out the **direct infringement**. The Copyright Act is a strict liability statute, meaning that knowledge or intent of infringement need not be proved by the plaintiff.

Bulletin board operators may be liable for the unauthorized distribution and display of images uploaded to and downloaded from their systems. A Florida court held that it was irrelevant the bulletin board system operator did not make the copies itself and thus found it liable for direct infringement [*Playboy Enters., Inc. v. Frena*, 839 F. Supp. 1552 (M.D. Fla. 1993)].

A California court took a more realistic position and held there was no direct infringement of the statutory exclusive rights under the Copyright Act when the infringement was initiated by a third party. In now-famous legal language, the court stated, "although copyright is a strict liability statute, there should still be some element of *volition or causation* which is lacking where a defendant's system is merely used to create a copy by a third party." The court reasoned that it would be inappropriate to apply direct infringement liability to a party such as an Internet service provider that acts like a conduit of information [*Religious Tech. Ctr. v. Netcom On-Line Communications Services, Inc.*, 907 F. Supp. 1361 (N.D. Cal. 1995), discussed in full later in this chapter].

Contributory Infringement

Contributory infringement is the tort (civil wrong not based on contract) of contributing to the direct infringement of another. Although not mentioned in the Copyright Act, the legal theory developed by court decisions supporting contributory infringement liability is based on the fact that a person with knowledge or reason to know of the infringing activity causes or materially contributes to the conduct of the direct infringer. For there to be a contributory infringement claim *there must first be a direct infringement* by another person.

In *Sega Enterprises Ltd. v. Maphia*, the court *did not find direct copyright infringement* by the operator of an electronic bulletin board service but, nevertheless, found him liable for contributory infringement. The users of the bulletin board service were the direct infringers. The *Sega Enterprises Ltd. v. Maphia* case is one of the leading cases on contributory infringement. If a person has knowledge that a user is copying a document or could monitor such activity and carelessly avoided doing so, there is contributory copyright infringement. E-business managers must be aware of direct infringing taking place by their subordinates. For example, a company could be liable for contributory infringement if a manager knows an employee is consistently using e-mail to forward or attach copyrighted material to others and allows this to continue.

Vicarious Infringement

Vicarious infringement occurs when a company receives direct financial benefit from the infringement by another party and had the right and ability to supervise the infringement activity. Courts have held that vicarious liability requires neither knowledge nor participation in the direct infringement.

In the following case the court dismissed a claim of vicarious liability against an Internet service provider because the plaintiff could not prove any evidence of direct financial benefit received by the provider from posting the infringed material.

Religious Technology Center v. Netcom On-Line Communication Services, Inc.
907 F. Supp. 1361 (N.D. Cal. 1995)

Facts

Plaintiffs Religious Technology Center (RTC) and Bridge Publications, Inc. (BPI) hold copyrights in the unpublished and published works of L. Ron Hubbard, the late founder of the Church of Scientology. Defendant Dennis Ehrlich is a former minister of Scientology turned vocal critic of the church, whose pulpit is now the Usenet newsgroup alt.religion scientology (a.r.s.), an online forum for discussion and criticism of Scientology. Ehrlich posted portions of these copyrighted works on a.r.s. Ehrlich gained his access to the Internet through defendant Thomas Klemesrud's computer bulletin board service (BBS). Klemesrud is the operator of the BBS, which is run out of his home and has approximately 500 paying users. Klemesrud's BBS is not directly linked to the Internet, but gains its connection through the facilities of defendant Netcom On-Line Communications.

After failing to convince Ehrlich to stop his postings, plaintiffs contacted defendants Klemesrud and Netcom. Plaintiffs demanded to defendants that Ehrlich be kept off their systems. Klemesrud responded by asking plaintiffs to prove they owned the copyrights to these posted works. Netcom responded that it would be impossible to prescreen Ehrlich's postings, and that to kick Ehrlich off the Internet meant kicking off the hundreds of users of Klemesrud's BBS.

Plaintiffs filed suit against Ehrlich, Klemesrud, and Netcom. Issues of Ehrlich's liability were addressed in a previous court order. That order concluded in part that a preliminary injunction against Ehrlich was warranted. This case continues as to defendants Klemesrud and Netcom. They are named as defendants in this action for copyright infringement. Netcom made a motion for summary judgment. Klemesrud made a motion for judgment on the pleadings and alternatively filed a motion for summary judgment.

Judicial Opinion *(District Judge Whyte)*

This case concerns an issue of first impression regarding intellectual property rights in cyberspace.

Cyberspace is a popular term for the world of electronic communications over computer networks. Specifically this order addresses whether the operator of a computer bulletin board service, and the Internet access provider that allows the BBS to reach the Internet, should be liable for copyright infringement committed by a [third party] subscriber of the BBS.

I. Netcom's Motion for Summary Judgment of Noninfringement

Because the court is looking beyond the pleadings in examining this motion, it will be treated as a motion for summary judgment rather than a motion to dismiss. Summary judgment is proper when 'the pleadings, depositions . . . show that there is no genuine issue as to any material fact and that the moving party is entitled to judgment as a matter of law.' The court, however, must draw all justifiable inferences in favor of the nonmoving parties, including questions of credibility and of the weight to be accorded particular evidence.

To establish a claim of copyright infringement, a plaintiff must demonstrate (1) ownership of a valid copyright and (2) 'copyrighting' of protectable expression by the defendant. Infringement consists of the unauthorized exercise of one of the exclusive rights of the copyright holder. These rights include the right to reproduce, the copyrighted work, the right to prepare derivative works, the right to distribute copies to the public, and the right to publicly display the work. Plaintiffs argue that, although Netcom was not itself the source of any of the infringing materials on its system, it nonetheless should be liable for infringement, either directly, contributorily, or vicariously. Netcom disputes these theories of infringement and further argues that it is entitled to its own fair use defense.

The court will address the relevant facts to determine whether a theory of direct infringement can be supported based on Netcom's alleged reproduction of plaintiffs' works. The parties do not dispute the basic processes that occur when Ehrlich posts his allegedly infringing messages to a.r.s. Once on Netcom's computers, [these] messages are available to Netcom's customers and Usenet neighbors, who may then download the messages to their own computers. Unlike some other large online service providers, such as CompuServe, America Online, and Prodigy, Netcom does not create or control the content of the information. It also does not monitor messages as they are posted. Netcom admits that, although not currently configured to do this, it may be possible to reprogram its system to screen postings. Netcom, however, took no action after it was told by plaintiffs [about] Ehrlich . . . instead claiming that it could not shut out Ehrlich without shutting out all the users of Klemesrud's BBS.

In the present case, there is no question . . . that 'copies' were created, as Ehrlich's act of sending a message to a.r.s. caused reproductions of portions of plaintiffs' works. Even though the messages remained on their systems for at most eleven days, they were sufficiently 'fixed' to constitute . . . copies under the Copyright Act. Netcom argues that Ehrlich, and not Netcom, is directly liable for the copying. The court believes that Netcom's act of designing or implementing that [system which] creates temporary copies of all data sent through it is not unlike that of the owner of a copying machine who lets the public make copies with it. [The court thus declines to find] direct infringement. The court does not find workable a theory of infringement that would hold the entire Internet liable for activities that cannot reasonably be deterred.

[The court finds,] [h]owever, the evidence reveals a question of fact as to whether Netcom knew or should have known that Ehrlich had infringed plaintiffs' copyrights following receipt of plaintiffs' letter. Thus, it is fair, assuming Netcom is able to take simple measures to prevent further damage to plaintiffs' copyrighted works, to hold Netcom liable for contributory infringement.

Assuming plaintiffs can prove a violation . . . , there is no infringement if the defendant's use is fair. Congress has set out four nonexclusive factors to be considered in determining the availability of the fair use defense:

1. the purpose and character of the use;
2. the nature of the copyrighted work;
3. the amount . . . used in relation to the whole;
4. the effect of the use upon the . . . value of the copyrighted work.

In balancing the various factors, the court finds . . . Netcom has not justified its copying plaintiffs' works to the extent necessary to establish entitlement to summary judgment.

[As to Klemesrud,] [t]he allegations [of direct infringement] fail for the same reason. Klemesrud's *computer,* not Klemesrud himself, created additional copies. [As for contributory infringement,] [f]or the reasons discusses in connection with Netcom's motion, the court finds plaintiffs' pleadings sufficient to raise an issue of contributory infringement. The court denies Netcom's motion for summary judgment and Klemesrud's motion for judgment on the pleadings.

Case Questions

1. When did the court say summary judgment is appropriate?
2. What is necessary to establish a claim of copyright infringement?
3. Was it ethical for the court to provide a different standard of liability for Netcom than for other online service providers such as CompuServe, American Online, and Prodigy?

LIMITATIONS ON COPYRIGHT OWNERS' EXCLUSIVE RIGHTS

Limitations on copyright owners' exclusive rights include fair use, the first sale doctrine, public domain use, and other statutory exemptions on copyright owners' exclusive rights.

Fair Use Doctrine

The **fair use doctrine** is a statutory limitation on the exclusive rights of a copyright owner. Think of fair use as the first cousin to free speech. It is a policy position taken by Congress that the public interest is best served by placing statutory limitations on the copyright owner's monopoly to its original work. Certain fair uses of a copyright are authorized by law and do not require the consent of the copyright owner. They may even be used over the owner's objection and are a defense to a copyright infringement lawsuit. For example, limited copyrighted material may be used as handout material in a college classroom over the objection of the copyright owner.

Congress has set out in the Copyright Act (U.S.C. 17, Sec. 107) the following four nonexclusive factors to be considered in determining whether the defense of fair use is appropriate.

1. *The purpose and character of the use, including whether its use is of a commercial or educational nature:* The first test is to determine if the purpose of the use was *commercial* or *nonprofit educational*. In *Sony Corp. v. Universal City Studios, Inc.,* 464 U.S. 417 (1984), the U.S. Supreme Court stated that commercial use of copyright material raises a presumption of unfair use that must be rebutted by the defendant.

Although nonprofit educational institutions that distribute copyright material are inclined to have the benefit of fair use, they must be aware of its limitations. Courts have found copyright infringement for teachers distributing substantial photocopies of portions of books in class and the classroom unauthorized use of videotaped material [*Marcus v. Rowley,* 695 F.2d 1171 (9th Cir. 1983), and *Encyclopedia Britannica Ed. Corp. v. Crooks,* 558 F. Supp. 11247 (W.D. N.Y. 1983)].

2. *The nature of the copyright material:* Courts will examine the nature of the work to determine if it is merely informational or factual. Newsworthy events and mere information are generally subject to fair use.

3. *The amount and substantiality of the copyright material in relation to the copyright work as a whole:* This criterion is quantifiable and relates to the number of pages used. Distribution of a page or two may be appropriate, but a small critical portion may implicate infringement liability. [*Harper & Row Publishers, Inc. v. Nation Enter.,* 471 (U.S. 539 1985)]. This limitation may be of special importance if a user in a nonprofit institution should download an entire program.

4. *The impact of the use on the potential market value of the copyright material:* The courts will be unwilling to find fair use if the plaintiff can prove that due to the defendant's copying, the value of the copyright material will diminish. This economic loss can occur either currently or potentially. Even with the first three criteria satisfied, there will not be fair use if the potential market of the copyright material is lost [*American Geophysical Union v. Texaco, Inc.* 37 F.3d 881 2nd Cir. (1994)].

The U.S. Supreme Court has stated, "Fair use, when properly applied, is limited to copying by others which does not materially impair the marketability of the work copied" [*Harper & Row Publishers, Inc., v. Nation Enter.,* 471 U.S. 539 (1985)].

First Sale Doctrine

The **first sale doctrine** (Sec. 109(a) of the Copyright Act) limits the copyright owner's exclusive right to distribute publicly a copy of the work when the copyright material was lawfully acquired by another. Under the Copyright Act, "the owner of a . . . copy . . . is entitled, without the authority of the copyright owner, to sell . . . that copy." (17 U.S.C., Sec. 19). You could and probably will sell this textbook, and can do so without violating its copyright. However, the sale, rental, or lease of a licensed computer program without permission of the copyright owner may constitute an infringement.

Consider the case of a textbook purchase in electronic form, transferred and delivered to a student through the Internet. If the student resold the textbook electronically, it would involve the infringing acts of reproduction and public display of the textbook that are not permitted under the first sale doctrine. The first student who owned the book also retained a copy, so the first sale doctrine does not permit the distribution and reproduction of a copy through the Internet.

Public Domain

Materials in public domain are not subject to the exclusive statutory rights of the copyright owner. Public domain falls into two categories: (1) all works of the U.S. government (e.g., the Congressional Record and court decisions), and (2) works whose copyright term has expired (refer back to the explanation of the duration of a copyright).

Other Statutory Exemptions on Copyright Owners' Exclusive Rights

The owner of a copy of a computer program may make a copy as an essential step in using the program in a computer and may make limited copies of that program unless prohibited by the terms of the license (Copyright Act, Sec. 117). See Figure 4.3 for burden of proof in a copyright infringement suit.

FIGURE 4.3   **Burden of Proof in a Copyright Infringement Case**

COPYRIGHT INFRINGEMENT LAWSUIT

PLAINTIFF	v.	DEFENDANT

PLAINTIFF

A. Owner of the registered copyright
B. Violation of an exclusive statutory
   right under copyright law
C. Theory of liability
   (1) direct infringement
   (2) contributory infringement
   (3) vicarious infringement

v.

DEFENDANT

doctrine of fair use applies
or
public domain

Since 1989, under the Berne Convention Implementation Act, there is no longer a requirement that the copyright owner display use of the copyright material by the symbol ©. Although it is now optional, copyright owners should use the circled © with online activities. This will assist the owner in proving that the defendant had knowledge the content was copyrighted.

REMEDIES FOR COPYRIGHT INFRINGEMENT

A plaintiff in a copyright infringement lawsuit has a number of remedies available against the defendant.

1. *Monetary damages.* The plaintiff may sue for actual damages and for the return of any profits made by the defendant by its use of the copyright material.

2. *Statutory damages.* If the copyright has been registered in the Copyright Office prior to the commission of the infringement, the plaintiff is entitled to statutory damages in lieu of actual damages. **Statutory damages** under the Copyright Act are set at $500 to $20,000 per work infringed. *Willful* infringement may result in damages up to $100,000 per work infringed. *Innocent* infringement may be reduced to a minimum of $200 per infringed work. Under the Intellectual Property and Communication Omnibus Reform Act 1999, S. 1948, statutory damages will be increased to $750 to $30,000 per work infringed and willful infringement has been raised to $150,000.

3. *Attorney's fees.* A successful plaintiff in a copyright infringement case may recover reasonable attorney's fees from the defendant.

4. *Preliminary Injunction (PI) or a Temporary Restraining Orders (TRO).* A plaintiff in a copyright infringement case may ask the court for a PI or a TRO in the event there would be irreparable harm in allowing the infringement to continue pending the upcoming trial. This is important because of the long wait before a trial in the federal courts is available.

In 1997, Congress passed the **No Electronic Theft Act**. The statute establishes criminal copyright liability, even without economic gain to the user, when the copyrighted material consisted of one or more works with a total retail value of more than $2,500. The act was based on a 1994 case involving a Massachusetts Institute of Technology undergraduate student who was acquitted of criminal charges after he offered copyrighted software for free on his electronic bulletin board. This is one of many statutes that could make *hacking* a crime even without economic gain.

The Digital Millennium Copyright Act (DMCA)

On October 28, 1998, Title 17 of the Copyright Act was amended by the **Digital Millennium Copyright Act (DMCA)**. Its general purpose is to protect copyright owners from the circumvention of technologies used by them to manage the control and use of the digital content of their copywritten works. The broader purpose of the DMCA is to have the copyright act comply with the World Intellectual Property Organization (WIPO) copyright treaty adopted by many countries.

Anti-Circumvention of "Digital Locks"

Digitized material appearing as content on a Web site allows a user to make perfect multiple copies at practically no expense. For example, digitized music, movies, video games, and e-books, unless technologically protected, can be reproduced and sent to countless others in violation of the copyright owner's exclusive statutory rights. Copyright owners may prevent massive reproductions of their protected works by utilizing software products that provide *technological locks* and controls. The DMCA prohibits a user from decrypting digital locks by circumvention access commonly referred to as the *anti-circumvention provision* [17 U.S.C., sec. 1201 (a)(l)(A)].

Copyright and Management Systems

The DMCA prohibits the circumvention of a "digital lock" on a digitized product such as a DVD, e-book, or video game. The statute makes it illegal to "descramble a scrambled work, to decrypt an encrypted work, or otherwise avoid, bypass, remove, deactivate, or impair a technological protection measure" [17 U.S.C. sec. 1201 (a)(2000)]. Companies adopt management systems that utilize "digital locks" on their copyrighted works, thereby denying access to the digitized product. It is now a violation of the DMCA to circumvent this *access control*, including the free distribution of software that might provide such anti-circumvention, or linking to a site with information on anti-circumvention software.

The DMCA provides copyright owners with the right to use circumvention technology that gives them the ability to manage the use of their copyrighted works with respect to how many copies, if any, can be made of the work, how long the copyrighted digitized work will last, or any other control they may wish to place on the reproduction of the original copyrighted work. As software engineers continue to discover ways of controlling digitized products, there is a growing controversy regarding the balance in the copyright act between the rights of the copyright owner and the "fair use" of others.

Trafficking in Circumvention Tools

The DMCA defines the distribution of circumvention tools as "the manufacture, import, offer to the public, to provide or otherwise 'traffic' circumvention tools." This trafficking provision was addressed in a DVD encryption case entitled *Universal v. Corley,* 273 F.3d 429 (2nd Cir. 2001).

In that case, digitized movies have been encoded on digital video discs (DVD) as a *copyright management tool* to protect the mass distribution of Universal's digitized products. The defendant, Corley, used a computer program called DeCSS to decrypt the DVD content. The court granted an injunction of the online posting and distribution of DeCSS that was an *anti-circumvention software product* used to decrypt the DVD movie. One of the troubling questions raised by the case is whether or not merely providing a link to a Web site that contains the anti-circumvention software qualifies as trafficking in an anti-circumvention tool.

SAFE HARBOR FOR ONLINE SERVICE PROVIDERS UNDER THE DMCA

In 1998, Congress codified the online copyright Infringement Liability Limitation Act as Section 512 of the Digital Millennium Copyright Act. The purpose behind the safe harbor is to provide to those entities that qualify as *network systems providers* federal immunization from claims brought against them by copyright owners based on a theory of secondary liability.

Online Service Providers (OSPs)

Search engines, Internet service providers, hosting services, and Web sites with multiple links to third parties provide network access to subscribers and customers who may post materials that infringe on copyrights. In that capacity the customers are *direct infringers,* violating the copyright owner's exclusive statutory rights to reproduce the work. The direct infringer is held *primarily liable* for the infringement.

Secondary Liability. However, copyright law also allows claims against secondary infringers under the tort theories of *contributory infringement* and *vicarious infringement.* For example, suppose your Web site provides multiple links to other sites that post infringed material as "direct infringers." Does that linking create potential contributory infringement liability? A contributory infringer is a person or entity that has knowledge of the direct infringement and provides a facility for that infringing process. A vicarious infringer need not have *knowledge of the direct infringement* but incurs a *financial benefit* as a result of the direct infringement. Both contributory infringement and vicarious infringement are referred to as *secondary liability* and represent potential claims by a copyright owner.

Exemption from Secondary Liability. These theories of secondary copyright infringement become a significant copyright claim in view of the function of online service providers. So long as the online service providers are in compliance with the DMCA by using *proper notification of its policy* regarding alleged copyright infringement and establishing a company agent to be notified in the event of such infringement, they are exempt from secondary liability. This does not mean that entities such as search engines, Internet service providers, hosting services, and Web sites with multiple links can be casual about this exemption. Strict compliance with the DMCA, section 512, is an important function of copyright management by such entities. If the entity qualifies for the DMCA safe harbor exemption, only the direct infringers will be held liable for copyright damages.

Online Service Provider. Section 512 (k)(1)(A-B) defines an online service provider as "an entity offering transmission, routing, or providing connections for digital online communications, between or among points specified by a user, or material of the user's choosing, without modification to the content of the material has sent or received" or "a provider of online services or network access, or the operator of facilities there."

This vast definition provides a broad umbrella for various entities to function as online service providers. As sophisticated e-commerce Web sites become more and more interactive, the use of search engines, bulletin board systems, chat rooms, instant messaging, and Web sites with multiple links to other Web sites may qualify as online service providers under this broad definition.

An e-business with multiple links to other sites should review with its legal counsel the "safe harbor" provisions of the DMCA to assure compliance in the event of a claim by a copyright owner based on a theory of secondary copyright liability.

SECTION 512 OF THE DIGITAL MILLENNIUM COPYRIGHT ACT (DMCA) AND THE NAPSTER CASE

The Digital Millennium Copyright Act was discussed in the Napster case [*A&M Records, Inc., et al. v. Napster, Inc.*, 239 F.3d 1004 (9th Cir. 2001)] as a defense argued by Napster. The facts of the case are summarized as follows:

> Napster makes music available for free on its web site using MusicShare software. A user downloads this software, then seeks to access the Napster system. Once on the system it reads a list of MP3 files the user has elected to make available to other users and sends that list to Napster's servers.

> If the user wants to locate a particular MP3 file, the user enters the name of the song or band on the search page in the MusicShare program on his/her computer. This software then searches the current directory on Napster's servers, and generates a list of files responsive to the request. To download one of these files, the user selects that file from the list. The Napster server then communicates this request to the computer on which the file is stored, which request is read by the MusicShare software found on that computer.

Napster moved for partial summary judgment, claiming that DMCA section 512(a) [17 U.S.C. 512(a)] limited the relief that could be awarded against it. Section 512(a) exempts qualifying service providers from monetary liability for direct, vicarious and contributory infringement, and limits the injunctive relief that may be issued by the court.

The court found section 512(a) limits a service provider's liability for copyright infringement by reason of the service provider's "transmitting, routing or providing connections for material through a system or network controlled or operated by or for the service provider." The court held that Napster's role in the transmission of MP3 files by and among the various users of its system was not entitled to protection under Section 512(a) because such transmission does not occur through Napster's system. Rather, all files transfer directly from the computer of one Napster user through the Internet to the computer of the requesting user. Similarly, any role that Napster plays in providing a connection between these two computers does not occur through its system. Said the court:

> Although the Napster server conveys address information to establish a connection between the requesting and host users, the connection itself occurs through the Internet. The legislative history of section 512 demonstrates that Congress intended the 512(a) safe harbor to apply only to activities "in which a service provider plays the role of a 'conduit' for the communications of others." . . . Napster enables or facilitates the initiation of connections, but these connections do not pass through the system within the meaning of subsection 512(a).

To be entitled to such protection, a service provider must meet the requirements of section 512(i) of the DMCA, which, among other things, obligates the service provider to "adopt and reasonably implement and inform subscribers and account holders of the service provider's system or network of a policy that provides for the termination in appropriate circumstances of subscribers and account holders of the service provider's system or network who are repeat infringers." The court held that issues of fact existed as to whether Napster had appropriately adopted and informed its users of such an effective policy which precluded at this time any relief to Napster under the DMCA.

INTERNATIONAL REGULATION AND ENFORCEMENT OF COPYRIGHT LAW

A basic international purpose of copyright law is to encourage creativity by recognizing a property right in the artist's creation. The creator of the work should have the power to regulate dissemination of the creation as well as profit from it. Like trademark law, copyright law is generally regulated on a nation-by-nation basis. The following section discusses key issues related to international copyright law and cyberspace.

Key International Copyright Initiatives

The Agreement on Trade-Related Aspects of Intellectual Property Rights (TRIPS).[1] **TRIPS** is one of the World Trade Organization's (WTO) multilateral agreements. Like the other WTO multilateral agreements, the WTO member countries are automatically members of the TRIPS Agreement. TRIPS establishes a comprehensive set of rights and obligations governing international trade in intellectual property. To

---

[1]The text of the TRIPS Agreement is posted at *http://www.wto.org/english/tratop_e/trips_e/trips_e.htm*

accomplish this, the agreement establishes a common minimum of protection for intellectual property rights within the territories of all WTO member countries. The TRIPS Agreement and its relevance to intellectual property law are discussed in more detail in Chapter 3, "Trademarks."

The Berne Convention for the Protection of Literary and Artistic Works (Berne Convention). [2] The **Berne Convention** creates a union of countries responsible for protecting literary and artistic rights (that is, copyrights). Four principles define the members' obligations: (1) "National treatment"; (2) "Nonconditional protection" means that no formalities (such as the use of the copyright symbol ©) may be required to protect artistic property; (3) "Protection independent of the country of origin" means that artistic property that is protected in one member country is protected in all; (4) "Common rules" (as with the Paris Convention) establish basic minimum criteria and procedures for granting literary artistic rights.

A great many of the cyberlaw cases heard by courts around the world involved claims of copyright infringement in violation of the national laws that implement the Berne Convention. Examples include the case of *Wang Meng v. Century Internet Communications Technology Co.*, in which a court in Beijing, China, held that the defendant had violated the copyrights of several authors by posting their works on a Web site without their permission, and the case of *Int'l Federation of the Phonographic Industry v. Olsson*, in which a Swedish court held that a teenager had not infringed any copyrights by posting links to copyright recordings on his Web site. [3]

European Union Copyright Directive (EUCD). The **European Union Copyright Directive (EUCD)** was formally adopted by the European Parliament on February 14, 2001. The EUCD provides harmonization of copyright protection for rightholders. The EUCD establishes a universal definition of non-commercial private copying. Also, the EUCD authorizes the imposition of penalties against any person who attempts to circumvent security measures from digital files. Article 6 outlaws devices or products "designed to circumvent technological measures" that thwart piracy. The EUCD permits limited replication of copyrighted material for "transient and incidental" reproductions that are an essential part of computer transmission, such as the distribution of files on computer networks. EU members had until summer 2002 to comply with the directive.

WIPO Copyright Treaty (WCT). [4] The **WIPO Copyright Treaty (WCT)** was adopted in Geneva on December 20, 1996. The WCT builds on the foundation of the Berne Convention, and explicitly states that it does not "derogate from existing obligations" of that convention. The WCT gives copyright holders the power to authorize publication of their works in both wire and wireless modes, in a manner established by the copyright holder. The determination of when infringement occurs is left to the individual member state's national law. However, Article 12 states that signatories must

---

[2] The text of the Berne Convention is posted at *http://www.wipo.int/clea/docs/en/wo/wo001en.htm*
[3] Summaries of these cases are posted at *http://www.perkinscoie.com/casedigest/default.cfm*
[4] The WIPO Copyright Treaty is posted at *http://www.wipo.int/treaties/ip/wct/index.html*

provide legal remedies to copyright holders whose works have been illegally copied through the circumvention of antipiracy technologies. Injunctions and other speedy legal tools must be available to enforce the copyright. Although the WCT requires that signatories develop enforcement measures, the WCT does not have a specific enforcement provision similar to TRIPS.

WIPO Performances and Phonograms Treaty.[5]   Adopted in Geneva on December 20, 1996, the **WIPO Performances and Phonograms Treaty** expands on the protection for sound recordings established in prior agreements. Articles 6 through 10 of the treaty give performers the right to control public distribution, manipulation, and rental rights of their works. A record company would have to obtain permission from the performer before distributing the performer's work under this treaty. Enforcement of these rights is controlled by the legislation of the nation where the performer claims protection.

Extraterritorial Enforcement of Domestic Copyrights

Another option for U.S. online firms is to enforce infringement of copyrights abroad through the extraterritorial application of U.S. copyright law. Although U.S. courts rarely allow such application, it may be permitted under certain limited circumstances.

The U.S. Judicial Reluctance Toward Extraterritorial Enforcement.   A general presumption exists in American law that, unless Congress intends otherwise, legislation passed is only meant to apply within the territorial boundaries of the United States. This is based on the principle that a nation cannot extend its reach beyond its own boundaries. Also, Congress is reluctant to infringe on international law when it enacts domestic legislation. This reluctance becomes particularly important in a cyberspace forum, where online artists are increasingly vulnerable to copying and infringement by anyone around the world with access to the Internet.

The same presumption exists in copyright law. For example, the court in *Subafilms, Ltd v. MGM-Pathe Communications* (1994),[6] considered whether a domestic authorizer of foreign infringement could be held liable for copyright infringement under U.S. law. In 1967, Subafilms and its partner Hearst Corporation entered into agreements with the United Artists, now owned by the defendant, to license and distribute the film *Yellow Submarine*. When the defendant authorized international video-cassette distribution of the famous Beatles film, Subafilms and Hearst objected and filed a lawsuit alleging U.S. copyright infringement. The court concluded that the plaintiffs could not sue for U.S. copyright infringement because U.S. copyright law did not extend to conduct engaged in wholly beyond U.S. borders.

Exceptions to the Presumption Against Extraterritorial Enforcement of U.S. Copyright Law.   Although courts generally refuse to enforce U.S. law for infringements abroad, courts occasionally allow it. For example, in *Steele v. Bulova Watch Co.* (1952),[7] an

---

[5]The text of the WIPO Performances and Phonograms Treaty is posted at *http://www.wipo.int/treaties/ip/wppt/index.html*
[6]24 F.3d 1088 (9th Cir.) (en banc), cert. denied, 513 U.S. 1001 (1994).

American citizen named Steele moved his watch manufacturing business to Mexico and registered the mark "Bulova" there. He then assembled watches in Mexico with U.S. parts, stamped the Bulova name on them, and sold them in Mexico. The watches found their way across the border, and the Bulova Watch Company received complaints from jewelers who were being asked to repair the Mexican watches. Even though the infringement occurred in Mexico, the court allowed U.S. law to apply against Steele. The court relied on the facts that Steele purchased parts from the United States, Steele's watches found their way into the United States, and Steele's watches adversely impacted the reputation of the Bulova Watch Company. Although this case addressed trademark infringement, its ruling applies with equal relevance to copyrights.

Future courts expanded on the *Steele* decision and developed a multifactored test to determine whether extraterritorial application is appropriate. In *Vanity Fair Mills, Inc. v. T. Eaton Co.* (1956),[8] the Second Circuit court identified the following three factors for determining whether the Lanham Act applies to foreign conduct. First, does the defendant's conduct have a substantial effect on U.S. commerce? Second, is the defendant a U.S. citizen? Third, would extraterritorial application conflict with any trademark rights established under foreign law. These factors have been developed and reshaped by courts over time,[9] but these fundamental elements still apply. If these factors are more or less present, the court will likely permit extraterritorial application of U.S. trademark law.

Summary

An e-business's Web site is a composition of content that is unique and constantly being revised. It represents a large capital investment and must be legally protected from those that would copy and use it without the owner's consent and payment of royalties. Our legal system provides a process for federal copyright registration of the Web pages that grants the owner exclusive statutory rights. These rights are limited by the fair use doctrine, which has guidelines that must be complied with for the doctrine to be upheld in court.

Because most e-business Web sites have a bulletin board or chat room to interact with the customer, it is important to monitor the material posted to ensure there is no known copyright violation. The e-business could be held liable as a contributory infringer if it knew of the copyright material posted by the customer and actively allowed it to remain online.

---

[7]344 U.S. 280 (1952).

[8]234 F.2d 633 (2d Cir.), cert. denied, 352 U.S. 871 (1956).

[9]Federal courts outside the Second Circuit have developed their own variants of the *Vanity Fair Mills* test. For example, the Fifth Circuit requires some effect on U.S. commerce for extraterritorial application to apply. See *American Rice Growers*, 701 F.2d 408 (5th Cir. 1983). The Ninth Circuit has established a more complex multitiered test. See *Star-Kist Foods, Inc. v. P.J. Rhodes & Co.*, 769 F.2d 1393 (9th Cir. 1975). Nevertheless, the fundamental principles established in *Vanity Fair Mills* almost fifty years ago remain.

An e-business must have its lawyers review and register with the Copyright Office its Web pages. In addition, e-commerce firms must register and protect their copyrights from infringement internationally. Although worldwide enforcement of copyright infringement may have to occur in the nation where the infringement occurred, exceptions do exist that allow a U.S. company to stop infringement of copyright law in other countries in a U.S. court.

Key Terms

fixed creative work, *87*
Sonny Bono Copyright
 Term Extension Act
 (CTEA), *88*
exclusive statutory rights,
 91
derivative work, *93*
public performance, *94*
direct infringement, *94*
contributory infringement, *95*

vicarious infringement, *95*
fair use doctrine, *98*
first sale doctrine, *99*
statutory damages, *100*
No Electronic Theft Act,
 101
Digital Millennium Copy-
 right Act (DMCA), *101*
The Agreement on Trade-
 Related Aspects of Intel-

lectual Property Rights
 (TRIPS), *104*
Berne Convention, *105*
European Union Copyright
 Directive (EUCD), *105*
WIPO Copyright Treaty
 (WCT), *105*
WIPO Performances and
 Phonograms Treaty, *106*

Manager's Checklist

√ Employee training programs that use videotapes and display Web sites on a computer monitor may be violating the copyright owner's exclusive right to display the work publicly. Managers should obtain the authorization of the copyright owner.

√ When linking to a Web site, consider entering a "Web-linking agreement" with the linked site owner to avoid any possible violation of a Term of Use that may prohibit this practice.

√ Web designers and their clients should be careful not to violate the copyright owner's exclusive right to prepare a derivative work.

√ Databases should be arranged in an original and creative manner in order to qualify for copyright registration.

√ Managers should be aware of the theories of contributory and vicarious liability.

√ Managers should obtain an indemnification contract from the Web site designer in the event of a copyright infringement suit against the company.

√ Managers must be prepared to follow the various international copyright laws. This includes mounting a defense of one's copyright in a non-U.S. judicial forum.

√ Managers must anticipate in their contracts with others that international copyright issues may arise. The contract should resolve clearly who holds these copyrights and under what circumstances.

√ **Ethical Considerations**

Is it ethical for copyright law to hold a person liable as a direct infringer if she had access to the original copyrighted material and her work was substantially similar? With easy access to the WWW, almost everybody has the original copyright material available. Does that necessarily mean a similar work was copied?

Case Problems

1. Plaintiff Robert Hendrickson, the copyright owner of the documentary "Manson" (dba Tobann International Pictures), filed suit against eBay, an online service provider that "enables trade on a local, national and international basis" for copyright infringement, alleging, among other things, that eBay is liable for the sale of unauthorized copies of the film "Manson" by users on eBay's Web site. Defendant eBay filed for summary judgment. Decide if "DMCA" offers protection to eBay? What role does the Safe Harbor under Section 512 (c) play here? [*Robert Hendrickson, Plaintiff, v. EBay Inc.*, 165 F. Supp. 2d 1082 (2001)]

2. Plaintiff Leslie Kelly, a professional photographer who has copyrighted many of his images of the American West, licenses those images to other Web sites. Defendant is Arriba Soft Corp., an Internet search engine that displays its results in the form of small pictures. Arriba copied 35 of Kelly's images to its database without Kelly's permission and used them on its Web site so users could click on those small picture "thumbnails" to view a large version of the picture. When Kelly discovered this, he brought suit against the defendant for copyright infringement. What critical factors are analyzed in determining whether the use of a particular case is a fair use? Decide if Arriba Soft Corp.'s use of the pictures is a fair use. [*Leslie A. Kelly v. Arriba Soft Corporation*, 280 F.3d 934 (2002)]

3. Plaintiff Mist-On Systems, Inc. brought a lawsuit against defendants Gilley's European Tan Spa and Dan Gilley for copyright infringement, claiming the defendant's Web site FAQ mirrors Mist-On Systems' FAQ page, resulting in irreparable damage and sustained lost profits, thus seeking monetary relief and a permanent injunction. "To succeed on its copyright infringement claim, plaintiff must show (1) ownership of a valid copyright and (2) copying of constituent elements of the work that are original." "Unauthorized copying can be established when the plaintiff can show both that 'the defendant has access to the copyrighted work' and 'the accused work is substantially similar to the copyrighted work'." Decide what test should be used for "substantial similarity." In order for the court to award attorney fees, what should be done? [*Mist-On Systems, Inc. v. Gilley's European Tan Spa, et al.*, U.S. Dist., W.D. Wis. (2002)]

4. Plaintiff Harlan Ellison, author of many works of science fiction, is the owner of the copyrights of those works. Defendant Stephen Robertson scanned, uploaded, and copied Ellison's fictional works without Ellison's permission onto his USENET Internet server. USENET is a newsgroup network that shares a variety of topics over its network, including the Internet; AOL became a peer since 1994. By its agreement, one peer's servers automatically transmit and receive newsgroup messages from another peer's server. This data is automatically transmitted to and received by AOL's USENET servers accessible by its users when they reach the particular system through AOL's newsgroup service. By its retention policy for USENET messages, AOL kept the data on the company servers for fourteen days. On April 24, 2000, plaintiff filed suit against AOL and other defendant, alleging copyright infringement and contributory infringement. AOL motioned for summary judgment. Discuss the safe harbor provisions of section 512(a) of the Digital Millennium Copyright Act. Decide. [*Harlan Ellison v. Stephen Robertson, an individual;* America Online, Inc., et al., 189 F. Supp. 2d 1051 (2002)]

Additional Readings

- Blanke, Jordan M. "Vincent van Gogh, 'Sweat of the Brow,' and Database Protection." *American Business Law Journal* 39:4 (Summer 2002): 645–682.

- Burgunder Lee B. "Reflections on Napster: The Ninth Circuit Takes a Walk on the Wild Side." *American Business Law Journal* 39:4 (Summer 2002): 683–707.

- Lessig, Lawrence. *Code and Other Laws of Cyberspace*, Chapter 10, "Intellectual Property." New York: Basic Books, 1999.

- O'Sullivan, Michael J. "International Copyright: Protection for Copyright Holders in the Internet Age." *New York International Law Review* 1 (2000): 13.

- Rivette, Kevin, and David Kline. "Surviving the Internet Patent Wars." *The Industry Standard* (December 13–20, 1999): 180–182.

- "Web Posting of Book Portions Can Be Contributory Copyright Infringement." *E-Commerce Law Weekly* 1:9 (1999): 216.

BUSINESS METHODS PATENTS AND TRADE SECRETS

Patents such as yours are the first step in vitiating the Web, in raising the barriers to entry not just for your competitors, but for the technological innovators who might otherwise come up with great new ideas that you could put to use in your own business.

—Letter from Tim O'Reilly, technical publisher to Jeff Bezos, CEO, Amazon.com, January 2000 (see http://www.oreilly.com/ask_tim/ amazon_patent.html).

LEARNING OBJECTIVES

After you have red this chapter, you should be able to:

1. Understand the sources of patent law.
2. Summarize the policy reasons for the laws, regulations, and practices.
3. Explain the criteria for granting a patent.
4. Understand the strategies involved in writing patent claims.
5. Understand patent infringement litigation.
6. Understand the sources of trade secret law.
7. Summarize the reasons for these laws and why a business might choose to protect assets through a trade secret strategy rather than through the patent process.
8. Describe the process of protecting assets as trade secrets.
9. Understand how trade secrets are misappropriated.
10. Understand trade secret litigation.
11. Understand international issues related to business methods patents.
12. Understand the challenges of protecting trade secrets on a global scale.

http://

- Additional material on patents and trade secrets may be found at the Bentley College CyberLaw Center Web site (**http://ecampus.bentley. edu/dept/cyberlaw**) under Intellectual Property—Patent Laws and Trade Secret Laws.

INTRODUCTION

The *patent* system of protection for inventions is recognized in the U.S. Constitution. As with copyrights, the power to grant patent protection resides with Congress. It represents an effort "to promote the progress of science and useful arts, by securing for limited times in authors and inventors the exclusive right to their respective writings and discoveries."

The patent system was designed to act as an important incentive for inventors. It was also construed as an important engine for the development and growth of new technologies, and thus a direct link to the improvement of the domestic economy. These considerations have not changed over the last two centuries, yet what has changed is the content and character of the inventions and creations. Now, instead of patenting improvements to the making of pot ash and pearl ash (essential ingredients for making soap, glass, dyeing fabrics, baking, saltpeter and gunpowder, and other such tangible products—see U.S. Patent Number 1), we see patents for business processes and software programs, such as one-click ordering systems (Amazon), micro-payment methods (PayPal), and online auction software (eBay). Although there are various classes of patents (including utility, design and plant patents), we focus on business methods patents only (a subclass of utility patents), because of their high relevance to e-commerce. We examine what business methods are patentable and how patent infringement claims are litigated.

Trade secrets, another method of protecting digital intellectual property assets, are perhaps the least understood and the most used. Essentially, a trade secret strategy requires the establishment and maintenance of the secret, a continuous managerial effort. The trade secret need not be novel, obvious, or useful, and the secret carries on indefinitely, potentially beyond the limited term of patent protection. Thus the protections of trade secrets can be broader and longer than patents, yet are perhaps more susceptible to theft and misappropriation. We look at how trade secrets are developed and managed. Finally we examine how claims are litigated.

BUSINESS METHODS PATENTS

Legal Framework of Patents

By way of background, it is helpful to describe what a patent is, and is not, before we discuss its relevance to e-commerce and cyberspace law. A **patent** is the grant of a property right to inventors by the U.S. Patent and Trademark Office (USPTO) for an invention, for a term of twenty years from the date on which the application was filed. It is, in essence, a government-sponsored monopoly to recognize and reward inventors by granting inventors exclusive control of the patent subject matter. The grant of a patent gives inventors the right to *exclude others* from making, using, offering for sale, or selling the invention. It is not the right to make, use, offer for sale, or sell the invention—although these possibilities of commercialization are available to patent holders. The legal environment of patent laws consists of the interplay of the Constitution, congressional enactments, agency interpretation of those laws, and judicial review of those laws as applied to commercial transactions.

U.S. Constitution. Article 1, Section 8, of the U.S. Constitution is the source of patent regulation. It states, "Congress shall have power . . . to promote the progress of science and useful arts, by securing for limited times to authors and inventors the exclusive right to their respective writings and discoveries."

The regulation of patents is a constitutional grant of power to Congress to create a federal law of patents. Congress has the exclusive power to make all laws relating to patent review and administration, including the length of term for the protection of patented inventions. This power preempts state legislation and regulation. The patent system is meant to create economic incentive for entrepreneurship and inventiveness. The primary goal of patent laws is to create an incentive to innovate through the conferral of a monopoly. This secures the invention for the benefit of the public and advances the useful arts and sciences. Secondarily, patent laws are designed to be a barrier to theft. Thus the term becomes sort of an economic balancing act: the term *granted* is meant to motivate and repay inventors and act as a complete, but temporary barrier to entry. The original length of patent protection granted was set at four years. The first patent examiner, Thomas Jefferson, was conflicted over the patent system. Although his goal was to promote inventions, he was dismayed by the system's collateral effect of promoting protection. This debate continues today.

- To read more about this early Patent Office history, see **http://etext.lib.virginia.edu/journals/ EH/EH40/walter40.html** and **http://earlyamerica.com/review/ winter2000/jefferson.html**
- To read Article 1, see **http://www.law.cornell.edu/ constitution/constitution.articlei. html#section8**

Congressional Powers. Under this constitutional grant of power, Congress possesses the power to regulate patents. Pursuant to this, it has enacted patent laws, beginning in 1790, and most notably, it enacted the modern law through the Patent Act of 1952. (Congress later incorporated other statutes into this act, including the American Inventors Protection Act and Patent Cooperation Treaty.) Congress has delegated oversight power to the **U.S. Patent & Trademark Office (USPTO)**.

Patent Act The **Patent Act** is the main patent statute, providing among other things, that "whoever invents or discovers any new and useful process, machine, manufacture, or composition of matter, or any new and useful improvement thereof, may obtain a patent therefore, subject to the condition and requirements of" this statute. (These requirements are discussed in detail later.) In essence, the Patent Act makes a bargain with inventors: in exchange for complete information on the invention, it grants a monopoly. Thus all secrets in the process are turned over for public review and scrutiny—and are helpful to competitors. (This is in contrast with a strategy of protecting information under the trade secret laws, wherein nothing is publicly revealed.)

Also, as with copyright protection, the term of protection has increased over the years. Congress extended the original four-year term length to fourteen years; and again extended it to its current term of twenty years (for utility and plant patents only; design patents have a term of fourteen years). The length of the term is (or if not, it should be) calculated to maximize these values, but also, not so overly long as to be oppressive, thus thwarting the very innovation it was intended to promote. Critics assert that the present overly long patent protection is oppressive and counter to the Framers' intent. This debate has a parallel in copyright law, with respect to the recently decided *Eldred v. Ashcroft* case challenging the Copyright Term Extension Act. (See Chapter 4, "Copyrights," for an explanation of the *Eldred* case.)

http://

- To read the Patent Act, see **http://www4.law.cornell.edu/ uscode/35/**

American Inventors Protection Act of 1999 The **American Inventors Protection Act** is a series of amendments to the Patent Act that are intended to strengthen an inventor's rights in relation to other later inventors and patent promotion companies. It also strengthens third parties' right to examine and comment on patent applications. The act guarantees a minimum term length of protection, sets application fees, creates study commissions, and so forth.

Agency Enforcement of Patent Laws

USPTO. The USPTO administers the patent laws, examines new applications, grants patents, publishes issued patents, publishes applications for patents, records assignments of patents, and maintains a database in order to search patents. The USPTO site offers a range of services and invaluable information on the patent process.

Courts. Courts are the final authority on patent matters. A special judicial framework has been created in order to construe patent laws uniformly and resolve patent disputes. A separate circuit court, the Court of Appeals for the Federal Circuit, hears all patent appeals. Any appeals from this circuit are heard by the Supreme Court. Patent suits usually involve a range of issues; many include challenges to inventorship, validity, misuse, and infringement.

►http://

- To read more about the American Inventors Protection Act, see **http://www.uspto.gov/web/offices/dcom/olia/aipa/index.htm**
- To see the site and search for filed applications or existing patents, visit **http://www.uspto.gov**
- For completing and submitting a patent application, see **http://www.uspto.gov/web/patents/howtopat.htm**
- The Federal Circuit's site is at **http://www.fedcir.gov/**

PATENT LAW AS IT RELATES TO BUSINESS PRACTICES

Patentable Subject Matter

The Patent Act specifies what may be patented. The three main requirements are set forth here. Historically, patent subject matter pertained to physical inventions. The patent subject matter of today is much more abstract. In an information economy, where assets are in digital format, inventors are understandably interested in protecting their investment in creating those assets, and later, ensuring a return on them. Examples of such inventions include innovations from R&D labs in software development, computer science, robotics, artificial intelligence, biotechnology, life science, and genetics. The exploitation of these assets and commercialization of such inventions depends in large part on the patent system where patent owners may develop the process into commercial products or services, and even transfer or license the process to others.

What is deserving of a patent: the requirements:

An invention or discovery (such as of a machine, article, process, or composition) that is:

- Novel;

- Useful; and

- Nonobvious

As simple as this definition seems, these issues continue to be litigated.

An Invention or Discovery. An invention or discovery is patentable if it produces a "useful, concrete and tangible result" [*State Street Bank & Trust Co. v. Signature Financial Group, Inc.*, 149 F.3d 1368 (1998)]. This is construed to "include anything under the sun that is made by man" [*Diamond v. Chakrabarty*, 447 U.S. 303, 309 (1980)]. Inventions and discoveries may be related, to both natural and human-made creations.

Inventions that are *not* patentable are "laws of nature, natural phenomena, and abstract ideas" [*Diamond v. Diehr*, 450 U.S. 175, 185 (1981)]. These include the following:

- purely mental processes/abstract ideas,
- naturally occurring phenomena, and
- scientific laws.

Exceptions to this rule of no patentability are when these things produce a *useful* result. For example, an *application* of abstract ideas (not just pure math) is patentable subject matter. See *In re Alappat*, 33 F.3d 1526 (Fed. Cir. 1994) (*en banc*). So, whereas the sun itself is *not* patent subject matter, a *use* of the sun, such as the design and manufacture of photovoltaic cells that transform sunlight into energy, may be patent subject matter. (Finally, patents are not allowed for inventions useful solely for nuclear and atomic weapons.)

Novel. The invention must not have been invented, patented, or published before. This requires that this particular invention was never patented before the inventor invented it; never before described in a publication; and never before in public use or for public sale more than one year preceding the date on which an application for a patent was filed.

http://

- For further understanding of this concept, see
  http://www.uspto.gov/web/offices/ pac/doc/general/novelty.htm

When there is this **prior art**, the invention is not patentable. Currently, there is a trend by those critical of the patenting process to "defensively publish" a description of the invention on the Web *before* it is patented by the inventor. This creates prior art and thereby deprives inventors of the opportunity to patent the invention. Prior art may be found in the USPTO site, trade publications, books, journals, and conference proceedings. Novelty is a fiercely contested issue in business methods patent litigation.

Useful. This requires that somehow the invention operates/does/performs/accomplishes something useful. It has to have a practical benefit, in fact anything whatsoever. (This is not construed to mean the invention must have a commercial/marketable application.)

http://

- For further reading on the usefulness requirement, see http://www.uspto.gov/web/offices/pac/doc/general/what.htm

The limits of "useful arts" is not known at this time. The USPTO has deemed the following two examples useful—and thus patentable subject matter.

1. U.S. Patent 5,443,036: Method of exercising a cat

Abstract

A method for inducing cats to exercise consists of directing a beam of invisible light produced by a hand-held laser apparatus onto the floor or wall or other opaque surface in the vicinity of the cat, then moving the laser so as to cause the bright pattern of light to move in an irregular way fascinating to cats, and to any other animal with a chase instinct.

2. U.S. Patent 5,993,336: Method of executing a tennis stroke

Abstract

A method of executing a tennis stroke includes covering a knee of a tennis player with a knee pad during tennis play. The covered knee of the player is placed on a tennis court surface with the knee pad positioned between the knee and the surface. The tennis racket is swung toward a tennis ball so as to hit the tennis ball with the racket either while the covered knee is on the tennis court surface, or just prior to the knee contacting the tennis court surface.

There are many such inventions as these that have been awarded patents, too.

Nonobvious. This is the inventive step that takes the patent subject matter out of the realm of the obvious and easily anticipated. This requires that the invention must not be obvious/anticipated to a person having ordinary skill in the particular field of invention. An invention is not patentable if the differences between the invention and the prior art are such that the invention would have been obvious. For example, a civil engineering innovation in bridge building is not patentable if it is mere substitution of one material for another or just changes in dimensions. It has to amount to an "inventive step," an innovation that is *not* obvious to the average civil engineer.

http://

- Some helpful sites in this initial search are as follows:
  Patent site: http://www.uspto.gov
  Nonpatent reviewers:
  http://bustpatents.com
  Reward for prior art/anticipation:
  http://www.infotoday.com/searcher/default.shtml
- In addition, refer to the Electronic Official Gazette at http://uspto.gov/web/patents/patog/

This issue of nonobviousness is also hotly contested with regard to business methods patents, where critics note that many of these Internet applications (of such commonplace events as shopping and browsing) could have been easily anticipated and were an obvious next step given the direction of e-commerce, rather than an inventive step.

To assure that an invention is patentable, therefore, it is extremely important to make a detailed, thorough research effort, utilizing patent as well as nonpatent literature (such as trade magazines and sites), in order to determine whether this subject matter is new, useful, and nonobvious.

In a recent case, Trilogy Software sued CarsDirect over U.S. Patent No. 5,825,651 covering a system for choosing options when buying a car online. This would seem to cover the mere automation of the car salesperson's job. In another recent case, Sight-Sound sued NsK over U.S. Patent No. 5,191,573 covering online sales of music. This would seem to be an easily anticipated new application of the present way of conducting music sales.

Types of Patents

There are three classes of patents: *utility patents* (new and useful process, machine, article of manufacture, compositions of matter, or improvements thereof—this class includes business methods patents); *design patents* (new, original, and ornamental design for articles of manufacture); and *plant patents* (inventions or discoveries relating to reproducing any distinct and new variety of plants). Because business methods patents are the only ones directly related to the focus of this text, the Internet and e-commerce, we limit our discussion to this one subclass of patents.

What Claims Are Covered

The value of a patent depends on many factors, including how inventive it is. But more particularly, the writing of the claims is of critical importance. In patent applications, inventors describe exactly what the patent, if issued, would cover in detail. The Patent Act requires inventions to describe their work in "full, clear, concise, and exact terms" [35 U.S.C. section 112]. A patent agent or attorney states in the application the broadest possible statement of the invention first—that will cover the most claims. Then the parties progress through a restatement of the claims in an effort to narrow, or reduce, the number of claims the patent holder will ultimately control. To the extent the Patent Office allows more claims, the patent is broader. In fact, the reach of the patent may extend beyond even those claims granted, by virtue of the judicially created doctrine of equivalents—that excludes inventions that are a copy, or "equivalent" to the patented ones.

First to Invent versus First to File a Patent

This issue arises when two inventors file a patent on the same invention at the same time. Under the first-to-invent system, the one who invented the process earliest wins. Under a first-to-file system, the one who files earliest wins.

The U.S. Patent Office, since its inception over two centuries ago, worked on a first-to-invent system. Under this system, inventors need only keep records of their inventions as they make progress. Inventors have time to make refinements, get feedback, and generally mature the invention. All of this is done before filing for patents. This system, by its nature, favors inventors, inventiveness, and innovation.

Under a first-to-file system, there is an incentive to rush and file the application. First-to-file rules discourage feedback and discourse among inventors and instead create an atmosphere of secrecy lest another inventor wins in the race to file. This system favors large organizational entities with a corps of support staff. This system though, is simpler and greatly reduces interferences, a process that is declared when there is a dispute over who is the first to invent the process. The European Community and other states follow the first-to-file system, and so it is likely the United States will adopt this system in order to harmonize American intellectual property laws with those of Europe.

THE PATENTABILITY OF SOFTWARE AND BUSINESS METHODS PATENTS

Software Patents

In 1981, the Supreme Court first recognized the patentability of software in the *Diamond v. Diehr* case. In this suit the Court was asked to consider whether a process for curing synthetic rubber employing a mathematical formula and a programmed digital computer is patentable subject matter under the Patent Act. (Previously this process was done by employees regularly checking the temperature of the rubber. The company came up with an algorithm that would more precisely do the same job.) In this case, the patent examiner rejected the application because it involved an algorithm, which was historically not patentable subject matter. In a 5–4 decision, the Court rejected this approach, instead deciding it was patentable subject matter. It reasoned that the process created a new useful and nonobvious result. (The Court cautioned, however, that the algorithm, *by itself*, was a nonpatentable abstract idea and not inherently useful.) The Court reaffirmed that patent law is not confined to new machines or compositions of matter, but extends to any novel, nonobvious, and useful art, process, or manufacture—even software.

Recall in Chapter 4 that we discussed the copyright protection available for software. There is an overlap between patent and copyright law as they relate to software development. Software programs consist of both language and function. To the extent the software expresses ideas (through source code), it may be copyright protected. To the extent it produces a new, useful, and nonobvious result (through object code), it is patentable subject matter. (For a case applying these concepts, see the *Universal Studios, Inc. v. Corley* case in Chapter 11. That case involves a decryption program that circumvents the code written into DVDs.)

Software patents are reaching into areas that are almost incomprehensible today—with the realities of animal cloning firmly established and the possibility of human cloning on the horizon. By patenting DNA code of living organisms and living animals with engineered genetic codes, the range of patentable subject matter is perhaps exceeding the public good. *Diamond v. Diehr* paved the way for consideration of another expansion of the range of patentable subject matter—business methods patents.

Justice Stevens's dissent in *Diamond v. Diehr* is important and relevant to our discussion today over what a business methods patent is and whether it is statutory subject matter. He makes several points. Most notably, he found that the process was merely a high-tech rendition of what the company had already been doing—that is, curing rubber. So, in effect, the transference of the job from a manual system to an automated one was neither new nor nonobvious. No inventive concept was disclosed/introduced beyond the algorithm; the process was the same, and this one minor change was easily anticipated. He considered this not to be patentable subject matter, therefore. Second, he questioned the merits of the majority's decision because no rules have been established for the patentability of program-related inventions. If there are no standards, how can the law develop in any rational way?

Business Methods Patents

With the patentability of software established and widespread recognition of the utility of computer programs to accomplish a variety of tasks, it became a matter of time before the question arose over the patentability of business methods. As Justice Stevens pointed out, there are no firm rules for these patents, and to exacerbate the situation, there is no precise definition. **Business methods patents** are considered to include any process involving data processing, calculations, conversions, and so on, used for business operations and management.

The USPTO groups them with the class of patents known as utility patents that protect inventions and formulae, and defines them as follows:

Class 705

DATA PROCESSING: FINANCIAL, BUSINESS PRACTICE, MANAGEMENT, OR COST/PRICE DETERMINATION

Class Definition:

This is the generic class for apparatus and corresponding methods for performing data processing operations, in which there is a significant change in the data or for performing calculation operations wherein the apparatus or method is uniquely designed for or utilized in the practice, administration, or management of an enterprise, or in the processing of financial data. This class also provides for apparatus and corresponding methods for performing data processing or calculating operations in which a charge for goods or services is determined.

The leading case establishing that business methods are patentable subject matter is *State Street Bank & Trust*. Again, courts had to consider the breadth of the Patent Act and whether it encompassed a conceptual process: a business method that made use of algorithms to transform data. The result of this case is to abolish a hundred years of law holding that business methods patents were not patentable subject matter. This case greatly expands the universe of subject-matter patentability. This case will always be a benchmark and reference point (and poster case) for the controversial issues surrounding business methods patents.

http://

- To read the entire definition, see **http://www.uspto.gov/web/offices/ac/ido/oeip/taf/def/705.htm**
- To read insightful commentary, visit **http://www.bustpatents.com**
  http://www.patnewsinc.com/
  http://www.cptech.org/ip/business/
  http://www.oreillynet.com/policy

State Street Bank & Trust Co. v. Signature Financial Group, Inc.
149 F.3d 1368 (Fed. Cir. 1998), cert. denied, 525 U.S. 1093 (1999)

Facts

Signature is the assignee of U.S. Patent No. 5,193,056 (the '056 patent), which is entitled "Data Processing System for Hub and Spoke Financial Services Configuration." The '056 patent issued to Signature in 1993 named R. Todd Boes as the inventor. It is generally directed to a data processing system for implementing an investment structure developed for use in Signature's business as an administrator and accounting agent for mutual funds. The system facilitates a structure whereby mutual funds (the Spokes) pool their assets in an investment portfolio (the Hub) organized as a partnership. It determines the percentage share that each Spoke maintains in the Hub, as well as daily changes in net asset value. Additionally it tracks all relevant data for tax purposes. This investment configuration provides the administrator of a mutual fund with the advantageous combination of economies of scale in administering investment coupled with the tax advantages of a partnership.

Speed and accuracy in calculation are essential for this system because shares in the investments are sold to the public and quoted daily. A computer is a virtual necessity to perform these complex tasks. Thus the claims encompass a *machine* (definitely patentable subject matter) as it relates to a *business method* (heretofore questionable whether it is patentable subject matter).

State Street and Signature are both in the business of acting as custodians and accounting agents for multitiered partnership fund financial services. State Street negotiated with Signature for a license to use the '056 patented data processing system. When negotiations broke down, State Street brought a declaratory judgment action asserting invalidity, unenforceability, and noninfringement. The federal district court held for State Street, and Signature appealed.

Judicial Opinion *(Judge Rich)*

The substantive issue on hand, whether the '056 patent is invalid for failure to claim statutory subject matter under section 101, is a matter of both claim construction and statutory construction. Claim 1, properly construed, claims a machine, namely, a data processing system . . . which machine is made up of . . . specific structures disclosed in the written description and corresponding to the means-plus-function elements.

This does not end our analysis, however, because the [trial] court concluded that the claimed subject matter fell into one of two judicially-created exceptions to statutory subject matter. The first exception [is] the 'mathematical algorithm' exception and the second exception [is] the 'business method' exception. Section 101 reads:

> Whoever invents or discovers any new and useful process, machine, manufacture,
> or composition of matter, or any new and useful improvement thereof, may

obtain a patent therefore, provided it meets the other requirements for patentability set for in Title 35.

[Section 101 specifies that statutory subject matter must also satisfy the other 'condition and requirements' of Title 35, including novelty, nonobviousness, and adequacy of disclosure and notice.]

The plain and unambiguous meaning of section 101 is that any invention falling within one of the four stated categories of statutory subject matter may be patented. The use of the expansive term 'any' in section 101 shows Congress's intent not to place any restrictions on the subject matter for which a patent may be obtained beyond those specifically recited in section 101. Indeed, the Supreme Court has acknowledged that Congress intended section 101 to extend to 'anything under the sun that is made by man.'

The "Mathematical Algorithm" Exception

The Supreme Court has identified three categories of subject matter that are unpatentable, namely 'laws of nature, natural phenomena, and abstract ideas.' Of particular relevance to this case, the Court has held that mathematical algorithms are not patentable subject matter to the extent that they are merely abstract ideas. To be patentable an algorithm must be applied in a 'useful' way. [For example] in *Alappat*, we held that data transformed by a machine through a series of calculations to produce a smooth waveform display on a monitor, constituted a practical application of an abstract idea.

Today, we hold that the transformation of data, representing discrete dollar amounts, by a machine through a series of mathematical calculations into a final share price, constitutes a practical application of a mathematical algorithm, because it produces a 'useful, concrete and tangible result'—a final share price—[and thus it is] statutory subject matter.

The question of whether a claim encompasses statutory subject matter should not focus on which of the four categories of subject matter a claim is directed to—process, machine, manufacture, or composition of matter—but rather on the essential characteristics of the subject matter, in particular, its practical utility.

The "Business Method" Exception

As an alternative ground for invalidating the '056 patent under section 101, the [trial] court relied on the judicially-created, so-called 'business method' *exception* to statutory subject matter. We take this opportunity to lay this ill-conceived exception to rest. [A business method] is as patentable as anything else, and is not in fact, any *exception* to patent law at all. Business methods are always patentable subject matter, provided they meet the other requirements of the statute. Claim 1 is therefore statutory subject matter—a business method that is patentable. Whether the claims are directed to subject matter within section 101 should not turn on whether the claimed subject matter does 'business' instead of something else.

REVERSED.

Case Questions

1. Why were algorithms historically not patentable?

2. What are Signature's business options following this opinion?

3. What are State Street's business options following this opinion?

The *State Street Bank & Trust* case therefore recognized the validity of both software patents and business methods patents, and it paved the way for Internet-related patents, including software for databases, shopping rewards, ordering systems, reverse auctions, incentive programs, and so forth.

Immediately following the *State Street Bank & Trust* case, the Federal Circuit decided *AT&T Corp. v. Excel Communications, Inc.*, 172 F.3d 1352, *cert. denied*, 528 U.S. 946 (1999). This case involved a "Call Message Recording for Telephone Systems." The court once again examined the scope of the Patent Act and found the claimed subject matter—here, a mathematical algorithm that transformed data—and held it was patentable subject matter.

The result of these two cases has been an explosion in the number of these conceptual patents on business practices, and questions are being raised about the quality of these patents that the USPTO is granting. Moreover, this decision prompted a change of tactics by Internet businesses, the majority of which heretofore protected business methods with a trade secret strategy. Patenting business methods became a viable and appealing alternative to trade secrets, because patent protections carry on even when trade secret protection is lost because of such events as reverse engineering or public disclosure of the secrets.

What May Be Done with the Patent

Patent Commercialization and Knowledge Transfer Strategies. A patent does not in and of itself represent any return on investment. That is up to the patent owner to make business decisions on how best to exploit the value of the claims covered by the patent. The mere fact of ownership of a patent creates two values. One is the financial/monetary/market value in the patent property itself. The other related value is the monopoly effect. The value of owning a certain property, the first of its kind, is in knowing you may exclude all others. It is a land grab of sorts, albeit temporary. This creates huge barriers to entry, where patent owners have an enormous competitive advantage. How a patent is utilized is a pure business decision, whether and how to create value with the patent. Other strategies for patent use include technology transfers, assignments, and licensing. These create revenue for the inventors with somewhat less risk.

Note too, how patents relate to business valuation. It is quite a challenge to value intangible assets such as these, as they are susceptible to rapid and dramatic changes, and they have a limited lifetime of up to only twenty years. In the 1950s, for example, tangible assets represented 78 percent of the assets of U.S. nonfinancial corporations. In 2002, the proportion is 53 percent. This has contributed to market volatility and has created a great deal of market uncertainty as to how much assets are worth [Greg Ip, "The Rise and Fall of Intangible Assets Leads to Shorter Company Life Spans," *Wall Street Journal* (April 4, 2002), p. 1].

Shop Rights and Ownership of Patents. Inventorship and ownership of patents are separate statuses. For the most part, patents are owned by the inventors, but these rights may be assigned, licensed, or transferred. Complex issues arise when inventorship is unclear or the duties to assign are not clear. The patent application must be filed in the name of the inventor. Whether inventors are obligated to assign their patents to employers, unless there is a contractual agreement to do so, can become a major issue.

The shop rights issue arises when an invention is invented by an employee who is under no duty to assign patent ownership but developed the invention using employer resources. Employers enjoy a shop right in the patent, entitling them to a royalty-free nonexclusive license to the patent.

Other issues arise, such as in cases where coinventors are working together, but located in different places and working on different aspects of the same process. The best method of avoiding all of these possibilities is for businesses to include within their employment agreements policies outlining resource allocation, development and ownership of inventions, creations, and trade secrets.

The following case is a challenge to inventorship, involving one of the best known business methods patents, and the case shows how even seemingly simple questions become muddled in the Patent Office.

Marketel International, Inc. v. Priceline.com
138 F. Supp. 2d 1210 (N.D. Cal. 2001)

Facts

Plaintiff claims that its employees, Perell, Martinez Hughes-Hartogs and Weiss (the *alleged* inventors), were the *actual* inventors of the business method and apparatus claimed in U.S. Patent No. 5,794,207 (the '207 patent) that was registered by Priceline. Plaintiff asserts that the alleged inventors explained the substance of their inventions to agents of defendants in confidential documents and conversations—before defendants sought and received a patent on the disputed invention. Plaintiff seeks relief in the form of an order correcting inventorship in the '207 patent so plaintiff's employees are added to the certificate naming inventorship, as the only inventors.

Defendant motioned for summary judgment arguing that (1) plaintiff's asserted conception of the subject matter is not corroborated; and (2) plaintiff's asserted communication of the invention to defendants is not corroborated.

U.S. Patent No. 5,794,207:

'Method and apparatus for a cryptographically assisted commercial network system designed to facilitate buyer-driven conditional purchase offers'

The Abstract of the Invention:

The present invention is a method and apparatus for effectuating bilateral buyer-driven commerce. The present invention allows prospective buyers of goods and services to communicate a binding purchase offer globally to potential sellers, for sellers conveniently to search for relevant buyer purchase offers, and for sellers potentially to bind a buyer to a contract based on the buyer's purchase offer. In a preferred embodiment, the apparatus of the present invention includes a controller which receives binding purchase offers from prospective buyers. The controller makes purchase offers available globally to potential sellers. Potential sellers then have the option to accept a purchase offer and thus bind the corresponding buyer to a contract. The method and apparatus of the present invention have applications on the Internet as well as conventional communications systems such as voice telephony.

The Listed Inventors are: Walker; Jay S. (Ridgefield, CT); Schneier; Bruce (Oak Park, IL); Jorasch; James A. (Stamford, CT)

The Patent was assigned to: Walker Asset Management Limited Partnership (Stamford, CT)

35 U.S.C. section 256 authorizes federal courts and the PTO to resolve inventorship contests. Inventors may be added, and there may be a complete substitution of one inventor for another. The person name in an issued patent is presumed to be the true inventor. This presumption is a powerful one, and the burden of showing misjoinder or nonjoinder of inventors is a heavy one, and must be proved by *clear and convincing evidence.*

Judicial Opinion *(Judge Legge)*

It is axiomatic that 'conception is the touchstone of inventorship.' Conception is the formation in the mind of the inventor, of a definite and permanent idea of the complete and operative invention, as it is hereafter to be applied in practice. Thus, facts relevant to inventorship are those showing the conception of the invention, for others may provide services in perfecting the invention conceived by another without becoming an 'inventor' by operation of law. To establish priority of invention, a party must show: (1) possession of every feature recited in the disputed claim; and (2) every limitation of the claim was known to the inventor at the time of alleged invention. To establish that the named inventor derived the invention from another, a party must show: (1) prior conception of the claimed subject matter, and (2) communication of the conception to the named inventor. The determination of whether there was a prior conception is a question of law.

An inventor's testimony . . . cannot, standing alone, rise to the level of clear and convincing proof. An alleged inventor *must* supply independent evidence to corroborate the essential aspects of his testimony. [Here] Plaintiff asserts that the alleged inventors explained the substance of their inventions to agents of Defendant in confidential documents and conversations before Defendants sought and received a patent on the disputed invention. Plaintiff argues that 'numerous Marketel documents corroborate Marketel witnesses' account of the process by which Marketel invented and developed the trade secrets misappropriated by Defendants. But instead of presenting this evidence and relating it to the elements of the cause of action, Plaintiff merely states that such evidence has been 'described in great detail.'

Plaintiff's showing is insufficient. When the moving party (Defendant—for summary judgment) points to an absence of proof and the nonmoving party will bear the burden of proof . . . the nonmoving party must . . . 'designate specific facts showing that there is a genuine issue for trial.' Plaintiff has designated no specific facts. Even if the court were to agree [with Plaintiff] that there is a 'remarkable correlation' between Defendants' patent claims and Plaintiff's alleged trade secrets, this does not address (1) which of the particular claims . . . were conceived by the alleged inventors; (2) the timing of the alleged inventors' purported conception; (3) communication of the alleged inventors' supposed inventions to Defendants'; or (4) the individual contributions, and therefore the basis for the claims to inventorship. General reference to . . . declarations of [parties do not] carry the day. The court is not obliged to sort through all of Ps declarations to locate evidence on its behalf. Given that the record on these summary judgment motions measures at least six feet in height, the concerns addressed . . . are very real here.

[Finally finding some documentation, the court then decides] the declaration of Martinez and Perell, CEO and CFO of Marketel respectively, begin to flesh out the history of Marketel and its innovative business method plans from its inception. At first blush, this appears to be the type of evidence required. On closer inspection, however, this is only the undeveloped germ of an inventorship correction claim [as the documents relate mainly to private placement documents and short, and long-term plans]. Without more, this does not establish the existence or communication of a 'definite and permanent idea of the complete and operative invention' needed to support prior conception. The testimony from two of the alleged inventors is insufficient to raise a triable issue, and there is insufficient corroborative evidence to substantiate their claims.

The court GRANTS summary judgment in favor of Defendants, for inventorship correction.

IT IS SO ORDERED.

Case Questions

1. Do plaintiffs have any other possible cause of action after this case?
2. What is the significance to Priceline of actually owning, rather than licensing, this patent?
3. Say plaintiffs invent some refinements to the '207 patent. Should they seek a patent on these?

ENFORCING PATENT RIGHTS: PLAINTIFF'S CASE

Businesses need to keep abreast of their products and services in the marketplace, and there is even more incentive to do so where the assets have the additional protections of a patent. To enforce rights of control that a patent affords, there are two theories of patent infringement that plaintiffs may allege.

http://

- To read the statutory section, see http://www4.law.cornell.edu/uscode/35/271.html
- A good patent infringement resource site can be found at http://www.lawnotes.com/patent/lawsuit.html

Literal Infringement

Under the Patent Act, **infringement** is defined as one who makes, offers, uses, offers to sell, or sells any patented invention, or actively induces infringement on any of the claims covered by the patent. Patent litigation is a civil matter. Importantly for plaintiffs, there is a presumption that a patent is valid. The statute allows for equitable relief, as well as damages for any infringement. Damage claims may include lost profits on lost sales, price deterioration, lost royalties, and lost licensing opportunities.

The following decision is perhaps the most notorious of the business methods patent cases. Although litigation carried on even after this decision, the parties settled the matter in 2002. This case remains important reading regarding issues of literal patent infringement and validity, how the patent process works, and the necessity of checking on the existence of prior art.

Amazon.com, Inc. v. Barnesandnoble.com, Inc.
239 F.3d 1343 (Fed. Cir. 2001)

Facts

This case involves U.S. Patent No. 5,960,411 (the '411 patent) which issued on September 28, 1999, and is assigned to Amazon. On October 21, 1999, Amazon brought suit against barnesandnoble.com (B&N) alleging infringement of the patent and is seeking a preliminary injunction.

Amazon's Patent: 'A method and system for placing an order to purchase an item via the Internet.'

Patent Abstract:

The order is placed by a purchaser at a client system and received by a server system. The server system receives purchaser information including identification of the purchaser, payment information, and shipment information from the client system. The server system then assigns a client identifier to the client system and associates the assigned client identifier with the received purchaser information.

The server system sends to the client system the assigned client identifier and an HTML document identifying the item and including an order button. The client system receives and stores the assigned client identifier and receives and displays the HTML document. In response to the selection of the order button, the client system sends to the server system a request to purchase the identified item. The server system receives the request and combines the purchaser information associated with the client identifier of the client system to generate an order to purchase the item in accordance with the billing and shipment information whereby the purchaser effects the ordering of the product by selection of the order button.

Inventors: Hartman; Peri (Seattle, WA); Bezos; Jeffrey P. (Seattle, WA); Kaphan; Shel (Seattle, WA); Spiegel; Joel (Seattle, WA)

Assignee: Amazon.com, Inc. (Seattle, WA) Appl. No.: 928951

Amazon developed the patent to cope with what it considered to be frustrations presented by what is known as the 'shopping cart model' purchase system for e-commerce transactions. That model required a number of steps to perform several actions before achieving the goal of a placed order. The '411 patent sought to reduce the number of actions required from a consumer to effect a placed order; such that only a single action needs to take place after the products are chosen. The '411 patent has 26 claims, 4 of which are independent; some are for method, others are for apparatus. B&N developed a standard shopping cart system, and another system, called the Express Lane, which it consistently advertised as a 1-click ordering system. [Incidentally, B&N trademarked the name 'Express Lane'.] B&N began using the Express Lane system in May 1998.

The trial court granted Amazon's request for a preliminary injunction enjoining B&N from using any feature of the '411 patent, finding it likely that there was infringement. [They reached this decision in spite of some evidence of prior art.] B&N's appeal attacks the trial court's decision on two grounds: that either its method does not infringe the 'single action' limitation—or that the 'single action' feature of the patent is invalid.

Judicial Opinion *(Judge Clevenger)*

Both infringement and validity are at issue in this appeal. It is well settled that an *infringement analysis* involves two steps: the claim scope is first determined, and then the properly construed claim is compared with the accused device to determine whether all of the claim limitations are present either literally or by a substantial equivalent. [T]he first step of an *invalidity analysis* based on anticipation and/or obviousness is view of prior art references is no different from that of an infringement analysis. A claim must be construed before determining its validity just as it is first construed before deciding infringement. Only when a claim is properly understood can a determination be made whether the claim 'reads on' an accused device or method (patent infringement), or whether the prior art anticipates and/or renders obvious the claimed invention (patent invalidity).

Patent Infringement: [The court extensively analyzed the 1-click process, including the prosecution history of the '411 patent, written description and file history. It concluded that] when the correct meaning of the single action limitation is read on the accused B&N system, it becomes apparent that the limitations of claim 1 are met by the accused [B&N]

system [and thus it is infringing]. After a full review of the record before us, we conclude that under a proper claim interpretation, Amazon has made the showing that it is likely to succeed at trial on its infringement case. Given that . . . Amazon has demonstrated likely literal infringement . . . we need not consider infringement under the doctrine of equivalents. The question remaining, however, is whether the [trial] court correctly determined that B&N failed to mount a substantial challenge to the validity of the claims in the '411 patent.

Patent Invalidity: [I]n an invalidity analysis, the district court must assess the meaning of the prior art references. [The district court found likely infringement by BN, and so it did not focus its analysis on the validity issue.] In this case, we find that the district court committed clear error by misreading the factual content of the prior art references cited by B&N. [E]ach of the [4] asserted references [by B&N] clearly teach key limitations of the claims of the patent in suit. One of the references . . . the 'CompuServe Trend System,' . . . appears to have used 'single action ordering technology.' [Also] B&Ns expert, Dr. Lockwood testified that he developed an on-line ordering system called 'Web Basket,' an embodiment of a 'shopping cart ordering component,' [because of its] 'cookie specifications.' [Also] an excerpt from a book . . . [explains how to] modify shopping cart ordering software to skip unnecessary steps. [Finally] a web page describing the 'Oliver's Market' ordering system [features this line]: 'A single click on its picture is all it takes to order an item.'

Conclusion

While it appears . . . that Amazon has carried its burden with respect to demonstrating the likelihood of success on infringement, it is also true that B&N has raised substantial questions as to validity of the '411 patent. For that reason, we must conclude that the necessary prerequisites for entry of a preliminary injunction are presently lacking. We therefore vacate the preliminary injunction.

Case Questions

1. What observations do you have about Amazon's strategy of what is, in essence, a preemptive strike in court to establish its patent rights?
2. What business decisions should Amazon make immediately following this decision?
3. How may B&N modify its online order system following this decision?

Amazon and B&N eventually settled out of court. The terms of the parties' settlement are confidential, with Amazon reportedly pleased to put this matter behind it, and Jeff Bezos reportedly suggesting a shorter term for BMPs, rather than the standard twenty years for other classes of patents [Nick Wingfield, "Amazon, Barnes & Noble.com Settle Long-Lasting Technology Patent Suit," *Wall Street Journal* (March 6, 2002), p. 1].

The Doctrine of Equivalents

This second theory of patent infringement was judicially created by the Supreme Court 150 years ago, in *Winans v. Denmead*, 15 How. 330, 347 (1854). The **doctrine of**

equivalents is a rule that competitors cannot simply make insignificant changes to a patented object to avoid infringement claims. This rule takes the incentive away from reverse engineering and making minor changes so as to avoid literal infringement charges. It further extends the reach of patent claims to prevent "copycats" from reaping benefits from the patented inventions of others. This policy grants patent holders a right to control inventions *beyond* even those claims covered in the patent. Thus doctrine of equivalents permits a finding of patent infringement, even when the claims are not literally infringed.

The Supreme Court decided a challenge to the doctrine of equivalents in the case *Festo Corp. v. Shoketsu Kinzoku Kogyo Kabushiki Co., Ltd*, 122 S. Ct. 1831, 2002 U.S. LEXIS 3818 (May 28, 2002). The Supreme Court unanimously upheld this doctrine and ruled that it is up to the patent holder to prove the doctrine of equivalents applies against copycats. This decision affirms the worth of existing patents in that it encourages competitors to invest in their own innovative products, rather than attempt to copy existing products.

Defendant's Case

Filing a patent infringement case, even with the presumption in plaintiff's favor, does not mean automatic liability for defendants. There are a number of theories under which defendants may escape liability. Defendants may be able to challenge the patent itself, with proof that it is invalid, that the listed inventors are not the real inventors, and so forth. These defenses are as follows.

Noninfringement

Defendants must prove their process is not the same, in every way, as plaintiff's process—that it is qualitatively different from plaintiffs' and not a copycat. In one case, *ACTV, Inc. v. Walt Disney Co.*, 2002 U.S. Dist. LEXIS 9267 (May 24, 2002), a federal court considered a noninfringement defense that defendant raised. Plaintiffs patented a system for synchronizing Internet programming drawn from sites throughout the Web—with video and television programming. Defendants' system offers subscribers the ability to synchronize certain Disney television programs with certain Disney Web sites. The court agreed with Disney and found noninfringement because the accused device (Disney's) did not meet every limitation of plaintiff's patent, either literally or by equivalents.

Invalidity

Defendants must prove that one of the conditions for patentability was not met by the plaintiffs in the first place. For example, the USPTO should never have issued a patent to plaintiff, because plaintiff's process was not new, or useful, or nonobvious. This could be due to the existence of prior art (defendants publicly used that process for one year prior), or that plaintiff's process was easily anticipated, or that it did not produce a useful result. There is a strong presumption of patent validity—as to each claim. This means defendant's burden of establishing invalidity is very difficult to

http://

- To read the text of patent defenses, see **http://www4.law.cornell.edu/ uscode/35/282.html**

prove because invalidity must be shown by "clear and convincing evidence." Patent invalidity is the main assertion behind Justice Stevens's dissent and the rationale of those who object to the concept of business methods patents.

The Federal Circuit recently heard a public use case. In *Netscape Communications Corp. v. Microsoft Corp.*, 2002 U.S. App. LEXIS 13840 (Fed. Cir. July 9, 2002), the court reviewed patents that allow computer users to access and search a database residing on a remote computer. The developer gave demonstrations to others of prototypes of his invention at his laboratory. The court considered whether this was a public use that would negate anyone else's patent for this process. The court noted that inventors may test their inventions in public without it being a public use, and it would look to see whether any confidentiality provisions were made and how ready the process was for patenting.

Remedies

http://

- For the remedies provided for in the Patent Act, see **http://www4. law.cornell.edu/uscode/35/plIIch29. html**
- For some interesting invention stories, visit **http://www.uh.edu/ engines/keywords.htm**

Patent infringement law is civil and there are no criminal provisions, as there are for the other three types of intellectual property. Plaintiffs are limited to the remedies described here. The statute of limitations for filing a patent infringement suit is six years.

1. *Equitable remedies* This is the most important of the remedies. Courts have the power to assign patents, rewrite inventorship, and prevent violations of any rights secured by the patent
2. *Damages* Successful plaintiffs are entitled to at least the amount of what a reasonable royalty would have been, plus interest and costs, and any lost profits, if they can be proven. Court may increase by three times this amount for cases of willful infringement.
3. *Attorney's fees* Successful plaintiffs are entitled, in exceptional cases, to reasonable attorney fees.

THE FUTURE OF BUSINESS METHODS PATENTS: THE PROBLEMS/VULNERABILITIES IN THE PRESENT SYSTEM

Prior Art

The collection of prior art for tangible assets is a great deal easier than collecting the same for intangible assets such as software. Moreover, whereas prior art has been collected for all classes of patents since the issuance of Patent No. 1, no prior art was collected on software or business methods prior to the *State Street Bank & Trust* decision. There has been no discussion of retroactively collecting and cataloging prior art for business method patents either, and that begs the question of how good these patents are. You need only refer back to the *Amazon* case to know the answer.

Additionally, although Rule 56 of the Patent Code requires patent applicants to supply all relevant prior art that is "known" to them, it does not require applicants to *search actively* for prior art that could invalidate their own applications. This has a sort of ostrich effect.

Valuation Issues

This question relates to how much business methods patents are worth. Intangible assets are by definition harder to value than tangible assets. This rush to patent every conceivable process is driven in part by business efforts to create value/shareholder wealth. Potential and actual investors rely on this information, yet how valuable are these intellectual property assets? And how accurate are the accountants' estimates? It is a guess at this time. Accounting standards are not yet fully developed in this respect, leading to uncertainty and volatility in those companies that have a relatively large intellectual property portfolio. A second and related question is whether patents create value. This is unclear. There is a perception that the costs of business methods patent protection exceed the benefits. For example, in efforts to create open code projects, developers stall when there is a question whether some business may have a patent that may involve the technology—this is the hold-up phenomenon where business methods patents impinge business development. A secondary effect is that the patents act as a concentrator of economic power, excessively enriching those who were first to file at the Patent Office.

Lock-Up on Information

The Internet was designed as an open platform: it is the ultimate open and free communication system. It was built without patents, but patents are being grafted onto the very structure of the Internet (i.e., ordering systems, ad displays, transfer protocols, etc.). When we patent such processes, we are taking away parts of the open and free structure, replacing it with gateways, tollbooths, and worse: we are stifling the very openness that is the Internet's hallmark.

It is an open question, too, whether these patents on business methods actually "promote the useful arts and sciences," as the patent system is meant to do. Business methods patents are monopolies on information goods. These are inherently different from tangible goods (for which the patent system is better equipped). Information goods are nonrival goods, meaning there is no rival, no real, perfect substitute for them. This begs the question of why a patent is needed for a good that has no true rival. We are thereby locking up information and not necessarily promoting the useful arts and sciences.

In one lawsuit, for example, British Telecom filed an infringement suit against Prodigy seeking royalty payments for its 1989 U.S. Patent No. 4,873,662 covering hyperlink technology. Do we owe British Telecom a royalty every time we click on a link?

http://

- The American Intellectual Property Law Association has recommended that the USPTO step up its efforts to collect prior art. See **http://www.aipla.org** and go to Michael K. Kirk's statements at the Oversight Hearing on Business Methods Patents, April 4, 2001.

http://

- For a helpful general patents site, visit **http://www.genuineideas.com**
- For a compelling critique of the patent system as it exists today, visit **http://lpf.ai.mit.edu/Patents/patents.html**

The Patent Office

The PTO is paid by the number of patents it issues. Clearly an alternative fee structure needs to be established. There needs to be other incentives for the USPTO to generate quality work. This is under study, per the American Inventors Protection Act. They are now encouraging consistency, focus on finding the invention and searching strategies, and developing a mandatory search scope. Examiner training in substantive patent areas, such as advanced networking, financial transactions, smart cards, accounting, and insurance will add a second-level review before allowance of patent.

INTERNATIONAL RECOGNITION AND ENFORCEMENT OF BUSINESS METHODS PATENTS

Patent Cooperation Treaty

International protection for patents is essential in a global information economy. Recognizing the need to harmonize laws, as well as centralize the administration of patents, the **World Intellectual Property Organization (WIPO)** plays a central role in these efforts. Before this centralization, it was necessary for patent holders to prosecute and register their patents in *every* country they wished to conduct business in and comply with as many laws and regulations.

The **Patent Cooperation Treaty (PCT)** simplifies and reduces the costs of obtaining international patent protection and facilitates public access to a wealth of technical information relating to inventions. By filing one international patent application under the PCT, inventors can simultaneously gain protection in over a hundred nations. (See the WIPO site mentioned earlier.) Inventors would first file their patent application with the PTO and also file an international application with the PTO, which acts as a receiving office for WIPO. Unfortunately, Europe's interpretation of the PCT has been less than friendly to business methods patents. In February 2002, the European Patent Office (EPO), an organization formed to establish a uniform patent system in Europe, announced it will not function as a searching authority under the PCT for business methods patents filed by U.S. nationals. Although business methods patents are now recognized in the United States their status globally is far from clear. A number of nations and international organizations are struggling with the issue of whether to recognize business methods patents. Surprisingly, very few other nations have followed the U.S. lead in fully recognizing business methods patents.

European Union (EU)

The **European Union (EU)**, through the European Patent Office (EPO), complies with the European Patent Convention. There appears to be only a limited amount of oppor-

http://

- To review the Patent Cooperation Treaty, visit **http://www.wipo.org/pct/en/**

tunities to secure business process patents in Europe. The
EU treats business methods in two classes—those that contain technical features and those that do not. Business
methods that possess both technical and nontechnical components may be patentable if the technical feature provides
a sufficient patentable contribution. Therefore, U.S. patent
filers of business processes must ensure that any European
application contains a sufficient technical contribution.

- For further examination of the
  European Patent Convention, see
  **http://www.european-patent-
  office.org**

   In 2000, the EU Directorate General for the Internal Market published a paper on
the patentability of computer-implemented inventions. It represents an attempt to
reconcile the exclusion of the patentability of computer programs with the reality of
thousands of patented technical inventions found in computer programs. They concluded that a computer-implemented invention which merely automates a known
process does not involve an inventive step.

World Intellectual Property Organization (WIPO)

WIPO is an international organization dedicating to the promotion of human creativity and the protection of intellectual property. In WIPO's "Primer on Electronic
Commerce and Intellectual Property Issues," WIPO recognizes that patents have
been increasingly granted in the United States for financial services, Internet advertising, and e-commerce billing methods. However, WIPO recognizes that commentators have criticized e-commerce business methods patents because they do not
reflect new ways of doing business and the only aspect different from traditional business methods is that they occur in cyberspace.

Japan

In November 2000, the Japanese Patent Office (JPO) published a draft document
titled, "Policies Concerning 'Business Methods Patents.'" The policy was motivated in
part by advancements of Internet-related technology and provides that "as personal
computers and the Internet become popular, 'business method-related inventions' utilizing known computers and communication technology come to attract attention from
service industries, financial or advertising etc., which have
not formerly been interested in the Patent System." Japanese
patent law recognizes patents only for inventions that have
industrial applicability and exploit the laws of nature.

http://

- For further examination of
  Japanese patent laws, see
  http://www.jpo.go.jp

   In January 2001, the JPO published final guidelines that
focus on the patentability of software-related inventions.
The JPO currently requires that inventions have a "statu-
tory invention" and an "inventive step." The statutory invention prong requires "a
creation of technical ideas using the law of nature." The inventive step requires in
essence that the patent not be obvious to someone versed in the field. These steps
allow for the filing and approval of business methods patents, but are limited to
software-related applications. Because many Internet-related business methods

patents involve software, the patentability of such methods in Japan may soon equal the breadth under U.S. law.

Extraterritorial Enforcement of Business Methods Patents

The differing view of the validity of business methods patents worldwide presents significant obstacles for U.S. businesses. Applicants for business methods patents must consider both the current and future trends in international patent law when deciding on a strategy to pursue. Limited opportunities exist to protect American holders of business methods patents outside the United States.

The most obvious choice for enforcing business methods patents is to bring suit in the United States against the infringing party. Section 402(1)(c) of the Restatement of Foreign Relations provides that a country has "jurisdiction to prescribe law with respect to . . . conduct outside its territory that has or has intended to have a *substantial effect* within its territory." However, U.S. courts would apply the law only if that foreign state's law recognizes the patentability of business methods.

Another provision, section 271(g) of the Patent Act of 1994, allows businesses to block the importation of infringing products into the United States. The patent holder must show a connection between the alleged infringement and the imported product. If the product is a direct result of a violation of the patent, the patentee may block the importation of that product. However, to invoke this law, it must be shown the patent was an essential part of the development or manufacturing process. In most situations, infringers can escape persecution because *alternative* methods of production exist.

TRADE SECRETS: AN ALTERNATIVE STRATEGY TO PATENTING

Legal Framework of Trade Secrets

A **trade secret** is secret information owned or developed by a business that gives it a competitive advantage. The laws relating to trade secrets were developed by judges at common law, in order to provide a remedy for businesses that suffer economic damages related to the improper disclosure or theft of proprietary secrets to competitors. These laws were originally based on theories related to breach of fiduciary duty or breach of contract. A series of statutes have been enacted, and so there are a variety of state and federal remedies to pursue for such injuries.

Trade secret protection is an alternative to patent protection, and it may accomplish the same goals, and more. Trade secret protection is not secured with the grant of a government-sponsored monopoly, as is the case with copyrights and patents. Rather, trade secret protection is developed with no government intervention at all (this is similar to trademarks where rights arise from use rather than registration). Trade secret protection is accomplished through proprietary efforts by the business to develop and then continually maintain the secret. The scope of subject matter that may be treated as a trade secret differs as well. Trade secret protection covers potentially anything of economic value to a business, and so coverage is greater than say, for example, patents, where the subject matter must be novel, useful, and nonobvious.

For example, although customer lists or invoices do not qualify as patentable subject matter, they clearly have economic value and may be protected as trade secrets. The Patent Office demands that all relevant information for patents be publicly disclosed, but a trade secret is just that—secret and potentially never available to the public. Finally, whereas patents have a limited lifetime, trade secrets have a potentially unlimited lifetime, protected as long as the company engages in continuous efforts at confidentiality.

Trade Secret Laws. Trade secret laws are enforced by a patchwork of federal and state laws. First, there is the **Economic Espionage Act**. Subtle differences exist in the laws, but trade secret laws have three elements in common. A trade secret (1) is known only to the business; (2) it affords the business a competitive advantage over others in its industry; and (3) is kept secret continuously by means of reasonable steps. Owners of trade secrets can enforce rights against those who disclose, misappropriate, or steal the secrets, but most significantly, they cannot enforce rights against those who independently develop or reverse-engineer the secrets.

Economic Espionage Act (EEA) This is the federal act addressing trade secrets. More about this statute appears in Chapter 12. According to the EEA,

> 'Trade Secret' means all forms and types of financial, business, scientific, technical . . . information, whether tangible or intangible . . . if:
>
> (A) the owner thereof has taken reasonable measures to keep such information secret; and
>
> (B) the information derives the independent economic value . . . from not being generally known . . . and not being readily ascertainable through proper means by, the public. . . .

http://

- To read the Economic Espionage Act, see **http://www4.law.cornell. edu/uscode/18/pIch90.html**
- To read the Uniform Trade Secrets Act, adopted by a number of states, see **http://nsi.org/Library/ Espionage/usta.htm**

Uniform Trade Secrets Act (UTSA) The language of the **Uniform Trade Secrets Act** is virtually identical to the Economic Espionage Act in its definition of a trade secret). This model law has been adopted by approximately forty-one states.

State Laws Because the Uniform Act has not been adopted by every state, it is important to consult the law of the forum state. (This inevitably leads to forum shopping.) We cite the California trade secret law here because California is frequently a forum for litigation in this area, and in fact it is handling the DVD Copyright Control Association case.

California Civil Code section 3426, Uniform Trade Secrets Act (in part) states,

> 'Trade Secret' means information, including a formula, pattern, compilation, program, device, method, technique, or process, that:
>
> (1) Derives independent economic value, actual or potential, from not being generally known to the public or to other persons who can obtain economic value from its disclosure or use; and

- To read the entire California statute, see **http://www.calbar.org/ ipsection/tradesecret/**

(2) Is the subject of efforts that are reasonable under the circumstances to maintain its secrecy.

Trade Secret Law as It Relates to Business Practices

Trade Secret Subject Matter. A trade secret may encompass more and different types of information than would be patentable and may include general information, procedures, billing, account information, lists/compilations, formulae, patterns, program devices, methods, techniques, processes, strategies, marketing plans, and pricing information.

Some example of trade secrets are Colonel Sanders's secret recipe, McDonald's special sauce, Smith's Black Cough Drops, Kodak, and the Coca-Cola formula. (The Listerine formula was initially protected by a trade secret until its formula was published in a journal.)

Maintaining Trade Secrets. The most difficult part of controlling trade secrets is maintaining it as a secret. The standard for information to be considered a trade secret is that it must be the subject of continuous efforts that are reasonable under the circumstances to maintain its secrecy. Businesses must formulate a strategy that controls all points where trade secrets might be leaked: the network, employees, or others who have a working relationship with the business.

Employee Duties Employees have a fiduciary duty to their employers not to disclose company secrets.

As more trade secrets are in digital format, they are ever easier to steal, misappropriate, or publish on the Internet. It is a critical management task to control employee access, knowledge, and use of trade secrets.

Trade Secret Agreements Strategies to protect trade secrets, therefore, take on a heightened importance. To accomplish this goal, businesses often require employees and others with insider knowledge (such as vendors, suppliers, partners, and clients) to sign nondisclosure agreements, noncompetition agreements, and/or nonsolicitation agreements.

Nondisclosure agreements prohibit parties from disclosing confidential information. Defining what is, and is not, confidential information is crucial. Such agreements should also cover acceptable (and unacceptable) uses of the information, as well as the duration of the agreement. These agreements are appropriate for employees, officers, directors, vendors, suppliers, partners, clients, and even bankers, lawyers, and accountants who are privy to quite a bit of insider information.

Noncompetition agreements prohibit parties from competing with the business for a period of time and within a certain geographic area. These agreements are appropriate for employees and officers of the business. Noncompetition agreements are generally enforceable if they protect a legitimate business interest and are reasonable in scope, duration, and geographic limitation. Significantly, California does not recognize noncompetition agreements. In one recent case, eBay (based in California) and Amazon (based in Washington) were in litigation over an executive who left Amazon to go to eBay, and one of the most contested points was where the suit should be heard—because the location is dispositive in many of these cases.)

Finally, businesses use **nonsolicitation agreements** that prohibit parties from attempting to lure away employees who may have knowledge or access to trade secrets. These agreements are appropriate for the business's partners. Note how these agreements, which are used for important and legitimate reasons, negatively impact job mobility and opportunities for employees.

Maintaining Physical and Network Security Where it is possible to have trade secrets in digital format, it becomes an easy endeavor to steal them and then post them on the Internet, so they lose their status as a trade secret—and never get caught because the perpetrators did this anonymously. Controlling access to the secrets, and locking them up, for example in an encrypted file, is an almost necessary strategy in establishing that the trade secrets were the subject of continuous reasonable efforts to maintain their secrecy. The actual securing of trade secrets is an issue that deserves more attention from businesses. (Refer also to Chapter 11 on this issue.)

How Trade Secrets Rights Are Lost. Trade secrets can be lost in a number of ways: when the secret is reverse-engineered, independently developed, or published, or when the business fails to continuously maintain secrecy. Note how with respect to these occurrences that although the trade secret protection is lost, had these secrets been patented, the patent protection would have continued, in spite of these negative events.

Trade Secret Litigation: Plaintiff's Case

Plaintiffs must prove the elements of the statutes they are filing suit under. For example, they must show the existence and ownership of a trade secret that derives independent value from not being generally known and they have continuously maintained. They will need to prove that defendants had access to the trade secrets; that they had notice the information was protected as a trade secret (this could be accomplished by use of the agreements mentioned); and that defendants used the trade secrets. Then plaintiffs allege any of the following causes of action. (Note that in many of the corporate defamation/cybersmear lawsuits that the posters are, in most instances, publishing trade secrets. (Refer to Chapter 11, "Defamation.")

Misappropriation. It is illegal to misappropriate or use improper means to acquire a trade secret. A claim is made when the following exists:

- Ownership of a trade secret; and
- Theft, bribery, misrepresentation, breach, or inducement of a breach of a duty to maintain secrecy or espionage through electronic or other means; or
- **Misappropriation** (the acquisition of a trade secret by one who knows or has reason to know the trade secret was acquired by improper means or wrongful disclosure of a trade secret to another without consent).

Breach of Contract. Breach of contract claims usually are due to a breach of the employment agreement, specifically the noncompetition, nondisclosure, or nonsolicitation clauses. These agreements generally create a legal duty not to disclose the trade secrets without permission.

Inevitable Disclosure. The claim of **inevitable disclosure** is used when the former employee had access to inside information and trade secrets, thereby possessing extensive and intimate knowledge about company operations and strategy. The business may sue to prevent the former employee from going to work for a competitor under the inevitable disclosure doctrine, which holds that the employee would inevitably disclose the trade secrets of his or her former employer and so may not be trusted to protect the former employer's trade secrets. This theory effectively presumes that employees are going to do something wrong; the theory works best when the former and new business share or potentially share many of the same customers and markets. For a case on this doctrine, see *PepsiCo, Inc. v. Redmond*, 54 F.3d 1262 (7th Cir. 1995) (the former Pepsi employee was not allowed to assume his duties with Quaker, where he was to oversee the Gatorade and Snapple brands).

Trade Secret Litigation Continued: Defendant's Case

To be successful, defendants have to disprove any of plaintiff's proofs. For example, defendants would have to show the information was not a protected trade secret (due to disclosure, inadequate protections, etc.) or that defendants did not have access to the trade secret, or notice it was a trade secret, or did not use the trade secret.

Public Disclosure/Publication of the Trade Secret. A trade secret cannot be a secret if the contents of it have been disclosed. So defendants would have to prove a publication of the secret, which is relatively easy to do. In terra firma, public disclosure occurs when the trade secret is published in print form or becomes well known throughout that industry. In cyberspace, however, public disclosure is a matter of a few clicks; it occurs when the trade secret is published anywhere on the Internet. In fact, there are instances of anonymous publishers (usually disgruntled present or former employees) of trade secrets on the Internet. The trade secret loses its status as a trade secret, and the posters of the trade secret are in a sense judgment proof because they cannot be found.

Consider this important and recent disclosure case:

DVD Copy Control Association v. Bunner
93 Cal. App. 4th 648, 2001 Cal. App. LEXIS 1179
(November 1, 2001)

This decision was withdrawn, however, because the California Supreme Court granted a petition for review: 41 P.3d 2, 2002 Cal. LEXIS 614 (February 20, 2002). This case is still pending.

Facts

The DVD Copy Control Control Association (the Association) is an industry-sponsored not-for-profit group responsible for licensing the Digital Versatile Disk (DVD) industry's Content Scrambling System, known as CSS. CSS is an encryption system and designed so DVDs may be played only on CSS-equipped players or drives. (It also—to some extent—prevents unauthorized use.) The typical licensees are manufacturers of stand-alone DVD players and DVD drives installed in computers that run Windows operating systems. No DVD players or drives were licensed for computers running alternative operating systems such as Linux. In October 1999, a fifteen-year-old Norwegian boy, Jon Johansen, reverse-engineered the CSS, thereby making it possible to play an encrypted DVD on a non-CSS-equipped DVD player or drive. He named this program DeCSS. The first posting of DeCSS appeared in October 1999, and soon thereafter it appeared on a number of sites worldwide. Andrew Bunner republished the DeCSS program. (Other individuals posted only links to the DeCSS program, without actually republishing the DeCSS.) The Association filed suit in late December 1999 against more than fifty Web site operators who allegedly posted information about DeCSS on their sites.

The Association initiated an action under the UTSA, charging that the master codes in the CSS and, consequently, the DeCSS are protected trade secrets. The Association is suing Bunner and others in order to suppress their dissemination of DeCSS over the Internet. The Association alleges that it protected this proprietary information by (1) limiting its disclosure to those who had signed licensing agreements, and (2) prohibiting disclosure to all others. The license agreement states that the CSS is a confidential trade secret. It is unclear in the pleadings whether the Association's licensing agreements, or other user agreements (click-wrap, browse-wrap, etc.) contained any clause prohibiting the act of reverse-engineering CSS. DVD CCA requested equitable relief in the form of a temporary restraining order and a preliminary injunction. The state trial court agreed with the Association and ordered Bunner and others to refrain from republishing DeCSS. The state appeals court reversed this order for a preliminary injunction, concluding it amounted to an impermissable prior restraint on speech in violation of Bunner's First Amendment rights.

What are the issues on appeal and how should they be resolved?

The Association's Arguments

- It has a trade secret (valuable information and reasonable efforts to keep it a secret.
- Bunner's actions violated the UTSA because DeCSS discloses the trade secret master keys; the master key was obtained by improper means; and Bunner had reason to know this.
- DeCSS was substantially derived from proprietary information property or trade secrets of the CSS.
- The applicable law is California law, not the law of Norway, and the Association need only show that improper means were used to gain the information.
- The Association concedes that computer code is speech, but argues it is entitled to relief because it would suffer severe and irreparable harm.
- The Association suggests it has a License Agreement that restricts reverse engineering (but it is unclear whether their licensing agreements are explicit on this point).

Bunner's Arguments

- Posting of DeCSS, or any code, for that matter is an expressive right protected by the First Amendment, and the government may not burden that right—unless it has a compelling reason to do so, and the means chosen are narrowly tailored to achieve that end.
- There is no evidence that he knew, or should have known, that DeCSS was created by improper use of any proprietary information. He was merely a republisher.
- He was never an employee of the Association and so never breached any agreement about nondisclosure.
- In Norway, for example, reverse engineering of software is permitted for the purpose of achieving interoperability, despite any agreement to the contrary.
- Publication of programs such as DeCSS, decrypting supposedly secure encryption (in this case by a fifteen-year-old) actually serves a very beneficial public interest—by notifying the makers and the public of security flaws in software.
- He saw DeCSS on the slashdot.org site, and merely republished it so other programmers could modify and improve DeCSS—in the way that open-source programmers collaborate to improve programs. He alleges he had no reason to believe it was improperly reverse engineered or misappropriated.
- Finally, he asserted that the repeated postings of this alleged trade secret caused it to become public knowledge anyway, and so the code lost its status as a trade secret.

http://

- To follow developments in this case, see http://www.eff.org/IP/Video/DVDCCA_case/ and http://eon.law.harvard.edu/openlaw/DVD/

As improbable as it seems, the Association revealed—in an open court session—the trade secrets it said Bunner improperly released. Realizing its blunder, the Association then requested the court to seal the documents, and the judge obliged.

An important observation in this case that deserves discussion: note how the trial court's decision impacts Bunner's rights of speech. This speech issue is more fully developed in Chapter 10, "Obscenity," and Chapter 13, "Internet and Computer Crime."

In a recent case, Ingenix filed suit against a former employee. It asked the court for an injunction to prevent the former employee from using or disclosing any of Ingenix's business, customer, pricing and marketing information, and from soliciting business from any of Ingenix's clients. The court granted the plaintiff's request where it found that the information was maintained as a series of trade secrets; that the former employee had access to it and notice of its trade secret status, and that it would be used. The former employee's e-mails proved this, and so did audit logs of his computer use [*Ingenix, Inc. v. Lagalante*, 2002 U.S. Dist. LEXIS 5795 (E.D. La. March 28, 2002)].

Reverse Engineering. **Reverse engineering** is a defense to trade secret misappropriation claims. Although under patent law, it is unlawful infringement to reverse-engineer an invention, it is not illegal under trade secret law. But most digital products or services contain agreements, such as click-wraps and browse-wraps that prohibit reverse engineering. So, even though plaintiffs could not bring a trade secret misappropriation claim, they may still have available a breach of contract claim for the act of reverse engineering.

Independent Derivation. The **independent derivation** defense arises when the same secret was developed independently by another. Courts must undertake an extremely detailed fact-specific investigation, including dates of development, the state of this knowledge in the industry, and so forth.

Remedies. If plaintiffs prove their case, there are a number of applicable remedies:

1. *Injunction* By virtue of a court order, plaintiffs may be able to regain control of the trade secret or stop use of the trade secret.
2. *Damages* Compensatory damages are available. In exceptional cases, punitive damages (up to twice the compensatory damages) as well as attorney fees are available.
3. *Imprisonment* Criminal penalties are invoked for cases of trade secret theft. (Refer to Chapter 12.)

International Recognition and Enforcement of Trade Secret Laws

Global Recognition of Trade Secret Laws. Unlike business methods patents, trade secrets have received significant international recognition and protection for some time. For example, the **Paris Convention** prohibits unfair trade practices among its members. The Paris Convention states that unfair trade practices include "[a]ny act of competition which is in conflict with the fair customs of industry and trade." Although examples provided by the Paris Convention do not explicitly include trade secrets, trade secret infringement could likely be interpreted as a form of "unfair competition" under its provisions.

Trade-Related Aspects of Intellectual Property Rights (TRIPS). TRIPS is a widely recognized international agreement that reaffirms earlier intellectual property treaties such as the Paris Convention and requires signatories to afford equal intellectual property treatment to nationals of signatory nations. TRIPS also requires nations to develop laws to protect intellectual property, establish dispute settlement procedures, and enforce these intellectual property rights.

The most relevant TRIPS provision to trade secret protection is Article 39(2), which states,

> Natural and legal persons shall have the possibility of preventing information lawfully within their control from being disclosed to, acquired by, or used by others without their consent in a manner contrary to honest commercial practices so long as such information:
>
> (a) is secret in the sense that it is not, as a body or in the precise configuration and assembly of its components, generally known among or readily accessible to

persons within the circles that normally deal with the kind of information in question;

(b) has commercial value because it is secret; and

(c) has been subject to reasonable steps under the circumstances, by the person lawfully in control of the information, to keep it secret.

Although this section does not use the phrase "trade secret," it clearly contemplates protection for undisclosed commercial information. Article 39(2) requires that the information must be secret and not generally known among individuals knowledgeable in the field. Also, the information must have some commercial value in the marketplace. Finally, the owners of the information must have taken some steps to keep the information from public disclosure.

The phrase "manner contrary to honest commercial practices" arguably encompasses a broad range of improper disclosures such as breach of confidence by a confidant and the acquisition of the information by third parties who knew or should have known the practice in question was a trade secret. Thus the violation of trade secrets under TRIPS may include unlawful disclosers as well as third-party acquirers of secret information.

North American Free Trade Agreement (NAFTA). NAFTA, an agreement that regulates trade between the United States, Canada, and Mexico, contains a section that establishes uniform minimum trade secret standards. Article 1711(1) states,

Each Party shall provide the legal means for any person to prevent trade secrets from being disclosed to, acquired by, or used by others without the consent of the person lawfully in control of the information in a manner contrary to honest commercial practices, in so far as:

http://

- To examine the NAFTA treaty further, see **http://www.nafta-sec-alena.org**

(a) the information is secret in the sense that it is not, as a body or in the precise configuration and assembly of its components, generally known among or readily accessible to persons that normally deal with the kind of information in question;

(b) the information has actual or potential commercial value because it is secret; and

(c) the person lawfully in control of the information has taken reasonable steps under the circumstances to keep it secret.

NAFTA protection practically mirrors the protection provided by TRIPS. However, some differences do exist. For example, NAFTA more broadly defines sufficient value as having "actual or *potential* commercial value." TRIPS does not make this distinction. In addition, Article 1711(3) and (4) prohibits NAFTA members from placing any limits on the duration of trade secret protection. TRIPS does not similarly discuss duration of trade secrets.

Global Enforcement of Trade Secret Laws. A company trying to protect its trade secrets may be required to bring the violator to court. The company has two choices: sue the discloser in the United States, or in the foreign country where the violations occurred.

Enforcing Trade Secret Protection in an International or Foreign Forum Traditionally, legal actions for trade secret violations in another country would have to be pursued in that country. This leaves U.S. companies at the mercy of different, and potentially lax, trade secret protections in that nation.

TRIPS attempts to solve this problem. TRIPS requires members to establish national enforcement systems that resolve intellectual property violations. Article 63 requires that any law, regulation, administrative ruling, or court decision related to TRIPS must be available for public examination. A TRIPS council exists to monitor compliance with this and other provisions. The enforcement provisions of TRIPS (Articles 41–47) require members to establish evidence production requirements and permit remedies such as injunctions and compensatory damages. Any TRIPS member should have viable enforcement and judicial mechanisms in place for extraterritorial protection of trade secrets. If the company holds a valid judgment in the United States, that judgment is recognized in other member countries as binding.

Enforcing Foreign Trade Secret Judgments in the United States A trade secret judgment in a foreign country may influence the decision of a U.S. court. Although case law is unsettled on this point, some legal principles seem clear. A majority of states have enacted the **Uniform Foreign Money-Judgments Recognition Act**, providing that foreign judgments are generally recognizable, with exceptions, including for fraud, repugnance to public policy, or conflict with another judgment.

Summary

Business methods patents and trade secrets protection represent additional important and useful methods for managing intellectual property assets. Patenting business methods is a key strategy in the new economy, both as a way to control product and service development upstream and to license or assign rights downstream. It remains to be seen whether business methods patents can withstand the present criticism and scrutiny of their worth and economic value. Protecting assets by way of trade secrets offers greater flexibility and a potentially unlimited life span, but at the cost of making a diligent, concerted, and continuous effort to protect those secrets. Both of these methods offer legal protections, and they should be considered as complementary for businesses making decisions on intellectual property asset protection and control. Business methods patents and trade secrets must also be protected on a global level. Although most patents are recognized internationally, business methods patents receive limited or no protection in many nations. Similarly, trade secrets may not be recognized in countries without developed trade secret laws.

Key Terms

patent, *112*
U.S. Patent & Trademark Office (USPTO), *113*
Patent Act, *113*
American Inventors Protection Act, *114*
prior art, *115*
business methods patents, *119*
infringement, *126*
doctrine of equivalents, *128*
World Intellectual Property Organization (WIPO), *132*
Patent Cooperation Treaty (PCT), *132*

European Union (EU), *132*
trade secret, *134*
Economic Espionage Act, *135*
Uniform Trade Secrets Act, *135*
nondisclosure agreements, *136*
noncompetition agreements, *136*
nonsolicitation agreements, *137*
misappropriation, *137*
inevitable disclosure, *138*

reverse engineering, *140*
independent derivation, *141*
Paris Convention, *141*
Trade-Related Aspects of Intellectual Property Rights (TRIPS), *141*
North American Free Trade Agreement (NAFTA), *142*
Uniform Foreign Money-Judgments Recognition Act, *143*

Manager's Checklist

√ Patent law is a specialized area, and any discussion of patent strategies and procedures should take place with legal counsel.

√ Software has expressive as well as functional components and may be proper subject matter for copyright and/or patent protection.

√ Patents have many uses, and a comprehensive strategy should be considered to maximize these assets.

√ In deciding whether to protect information as a patent or a trade secret, consider the many features of each method, and, again, consult legal counsel.

√ With regard to the risks associated with trade secrets, the major security vulnerability is with those most closely associated with the company: employees, consultants, vendors, suppliers, clients, and consultants. Manage the risk accordingly.

√ Consider agreements with each of these groups so as to control information, use, and disclosure.

√ Be aware that business methods patent protection varies widely among countries. For example, they are least protected in Europe, somewhat protected in Japan, and fully recognized in the United States.

√ Investigate carefully any foreign company you share trade secret information with. A specific contract should be drafted to regulate control of any trade secrets disclosed.

√ Structure your business relationship so there is motivation to preserve your company's trade secrets. If it is profitable for the foreign company to keep the secret confidential, then it will be more likely that it remains so.

√ **Ethical Considerations**

- Companies should make clear policies for ownership of patentable subject matter that employees invent on company time.

- Companies should consider defensive strategies to competitors' patent applications.

- When an inventor offers a company the opportunity to purchase and develop patentable subject matter or a trade secret at the company, the company must consider its obligations to the inventor and how to properly recognize the inventor.

- Companies should consider the use of restrictive agreements, such as non-compete or disclosure clauses, but also be aware of the impact on employees' job mobility.

Case Problems

1. Telular filed a patent infringement suit against Vox2. For pretrial discovery, Telular wants its expert to have access to Vox2 documents. Vox2 objects because these documents are trade secrets. What is the result? [*Telular Corp. v. Vox2, Inc.*, 2001 U.S. Dist. LEXIS 7472 (June 4, 2001)]

2. Mr. Antonious is the owner of U.S. Patent No. 5,482,279 ("the 279 patent"), which is directed to an improved perimeter weighting structure for metal golf club heads. Spalding sells the Intimidator golf club line. The Intimidator line includes drivers and fairway woods that use what Spalding refers to as "titanium insert technology." Antonious saw several Spalding Intimidator metal wood-type golf clubs in retail stores. He purchased one of the Intimidator drivers and cut open the club head. After inspecting the interior of the club head, Antonious concluded that Spalding's club infringed his 279 patent. What are Antonious's legal options? [*Antonious v. Spaulding and Evenflo Co.*, 275 F.3d 1066 (Fed.Cir. 2002)]

3. Multi-Tech filed a lawsuit in February 2000 alleging patent infringement by Dialpad. Multi-Tech contends that even after it filed suit, Dialpad continued its infringing activities. Now the deadline for amending the pleadings has passed, yet Multi-Tech seeks to amend its complaint, in order to add a claim of willful infringement (thus entitling Multi-Tech to seek punitive damages). How should the court handle this request? [*Multi-Tech Systems, Inc. v. Dialpad.com, Inc.*, 2001 U.S. Dist. LEXIS 23575 (D. Minn. August 28, 2001)]

4. Plaintiffs read a case study in business school about X-IT. The study contained a lot of detailed information about the company including its customers. X-IT

manufactures and sells mesh rope-style emergency escape ladders, both in stores and through its Web site. After school, plaintiffs bought X-IT and subsequently entered into discussions with Kidde Portable Equipment about a potential deal with X-IT; pursuant to this the parties signed a confidentiality agreement about the negotiations. X-IT's customer account lists (which included Home Depot) were shown to Kidde during these negotiations. X-IT alleges that a Kidde representative told Home Depot that X-IT was in negotiations to be sold to Kidde. X-IT lost business because of this. X-IT alleges that the list was a trade secret and was misappropriated. What is the result? [*X-IT Products, LLC v. Walter Kidde Portable Equipment, Inc.*, 155 F. Supp.2d 577 (E.D. Va. 2001)] (This is a helpful case detailing a start-up business.)

5. Pepsi-Cola Bottling seeks an order compelling Kansas Vending to produce all records, invoices, purchase orders, and so on, from any transactions with Sam's Club or any other wholesale merchandiser, for any of Pepsi's products. Kansas Vending objected to the subpoena order, on the grounds that these documents are trade secrets. What is the result? [*Pepsi-Cola Bottling Co. v. PEPSICO, Inc.*, 2001 U.S. Dist. LEXIS 20153 (D. Kan. November 28, 2001)]

6. The Church of Scientology sued a former member for copyright infringement and trade secret misappropriation for allegedly copying a few church documents and posting them on the Internet. These documents were publicly available due to an earlier court action. What is the copyright result? What is the trade secret result? [*Religious Technology Center v. F.A.C.T.Net, Inc.*, 901 F. Supp. 1519 (D. Col. 1995)]

7. A medical foundation used IDX's medical billing software. IDX's competitor is Epic. Two Epic employees left and went to work directly for the medical foundation, and soon thereafter, the foundation switched its software supplier—to Epic. IDX alleges that these two employees used their new positions to transfer valuable information to Epic, about how IDX software works, and so on, thus enabling Epic to enhance its own software package. IDX filed suit alleging the two employees misappropriated IDX's trade secrets. What is the result? *IDX Systems Corp. v. Epic Systems Corp.*, 285 F.3d 581 (7th Cir. 2002)]

8. Ford Motor Company filed suit requesting an order barring the operator of a Web site, Robert Lane, who was *not* a company employee, from posting confidential company documents containing information about its future plans and product plans. Ford alleges that posting these documents disclosed its trade secrets. What is the result? [*Ford Motor Co. v. Lane*, 67 F. Supp. 2d 745 (E.D. Mich. 1998)]

9. E. Circuit Sales hired Randall and he signed an employment agreement that contained both nondisclosure (of trade secrets or confidential information) and noncompetition clauses. N.E. later filed suit against Randall in an effort to

enforce the employment agreement, after he resigned to go work for a direct competitor of N.E. Circuit Sales. What is the result? [*New England Circuit Sales, Inc. v. Randall*, 1996 U.S. Dist. 9748 (D. Mass. 1996)]

10. Pfizer, a U.S. company, sued a Chinese company that manufactures a flavor enhancer in violation of Pfizer's patent. This first Chinese company does not import the product into the United States. Rather, it sells the enhancer to a second Chinese company—that in turn sells it to a U.S. importer, F&S Alloys and Minerals. Is the first Chinese company liable for patent infringement? What about F&S? [*Pfizer, Inc. v. Aceto Corp.*, 853 F. Supp. 104 (S.D. N.Y. 1994)]

11. Pilkington Bros., a British company, licensed its "float glass" technology to a U.S. company. When the British company became concerned the U.S. company would sell and thereby expose its technology, it filed an action before an arbitration panel in England. The British panel issued an interim injunctive order in favor of Pilkington. Pilkington then sought to enforce the British order in the United States. Should the U.S. court recognize this interim British order? [*Pilkington Bros. P.L.C. v. AFG Industries, Inc.*, 581 F. Supp. 1039 (D. Del. 1984)]

Additional Readings

- Bouchoux, Deborah E. "Protecting Your Company's Intellectual Property: A Practical Guide to Trademarks, Copyrights, Patents and Trade Secrets." (2001).

- Gleick, James. "Patently Absurd." *New York Times Magazine* (March 12, 2000); republished at *http://www.around.com/patent.html*.

- Lessig, Lawrence. "The Future of Ideas." (2001).

- Myers, Timothy F. "Foreign Infringement of Business Method Patents." *Willamette Journal of International Law and Dispute Resolution* 7 (2000): 101.

Part 3

Business and Financial Issues in Cyberspace

ONLINE CONTRACTING

6

E-commerce has grown geometrically, and is rapidly establishing itself as a major economic force. It provides an important outlet of advertising and sales for a wide variety of businesses, from multinational corporations to fledgling entrepreneurs operating in basements and garages.

—Clapper v. Freeman Marine Equipment, Inc.,
2000 WL 33418414, LC No. 97-737513-CK (Mich. App. 2000)

The overriding purpose of any commercial code is to facilitate commerce by reducing uncertainty and increasing confidence in commercial transactions. We believe that [the Uniform Computer Information Transactions Act] fails in this purpose. Its rules deviate substantially from long-established norms of consumer expectations. We are concerned that these deviations will invite overreaching that will ultimately interfere with the full realization of the potential of e-commerce in our states.

—The Attorneys General of Connecticut, Idaho, Indiana,
Iowa, Kansas, Maryland, Nevada, New Mexico, North Dakota,
Oklahoma, Pennsylvania, Vermont, and Washington and the
Administrator of the Georgia Fair Business Practices Act

http://◄

- Additional material on online contracting may be found at the Bentley College CyberLaw Center Web site (**http://ecampus.bentley. edu/dept/cyberlaw**) under Business and Financial Issues—Contracting.

LEARNING OBJECTIVES

After you have read this chapter you should be able to:

1. Understand the fundamental terms and models of electronic commerce.
2. Describe the basic laws governing the formation of contracts.
3. Identify requirements establishing the validity of electronic signatures.
4. Comprehend key legal issues in drafting software licensing agreements.
5. Explain the legality and function of shrink-wrap agreements.
6. Summarize important legal issues in prevailing uniform electronic commerce laws.
7. Understand how insurance laws and agreements affect online business risks.
8. Identify key international laws relating to electronic commerce.

INTRODUCTION

A *contract* is an agreement to exchange property or services that is legally enforceable in a court of law. For business, the value of a contract cannot be overestimated. Contracts make business transactions predictable. Without contracts, businesses could not dependably buy, sell, lease, or license their goods and services. Contracts allow the parties to establish precisely what they intend before the agreement is executed.

One of the most rapidly growing forums for forming agreements is online. Online contracting is also known as electronic commerce, or **e-commerce**, is a general term that encompasses any commercial transaction involving the exchange of goods, services, or information over the Internet.

Why Is Online Contracting Law Important?

No doubt some have asked this question: Why is e-commerce law different than any traditional contract law? You may contend that online contracts are really no different than traditional contracts and need not be discussed separately with regard to the Internet. Some may see e-commerce law as a mere fad that will pass into obscurity as the Internet matures as a commercial mechanism.

However, online contracting is substantially different and requires separate study for a number of reasons. First, companies transacting in e-commerce have developed novel contractual arrangements to take advantage of the Internet as a new method of doing business. These arrangements found on online auction sites and in business-to-business (B2B) marketplaces may have only a distant similarity to real-world exchanges. These new approaches require a fresh look at potential legal issues that may arise.

Second, online contracting is changing at a very rapid pace. E-commerce arrangements are shifting quickly to take advantage of new technological innovations. Meanwhile, changes in traditional contract law occur at an almost glacial pace. Online contracting law takes into account the ever-shifting patterns of information technology and their effects on online agreements.

Third, e-commerce is evolving an increasingly international focus. A product or service can be advertised and sold through the Internet to almost anywhere in the world. At no time in history have so many companies had access to so many consumers across the globe. As these transactions cross national boundaries, border-related legal issues will inevitably arise between parties. Jurisdictional questions, tax issues, import/export disputes, and many other international issues will all become critical matters in the e-commerce legal environment.

History and Development of Online Contracting

E-commerce is not the first and only forum for online contracting. Online contracts date back to the 1970s when banks used electronic funds transfers (EFT) through secure private networks. In the 1980s, electronic transactions occurred through electronic data interchange, which required a dedicated data link between a customer and supplier to communicate purchasing and other needs. Business documents were also sent between companies in a computerized form. Such exchanges were put in place to save time, reduce paper, and improve automation of transactional processes. Electronic contracts constituted a minuscule percentage of all commercial agreements.

Even as late as 1995, it was nearly impossible to anticipate how profoundly advances in information technology would change the contractual landscape in which business would be conducted. That was the first year of significant recorded Internet commerce, with generated sales totaling just over $435 million. By 2000, released estimates of e-commerce sales by retail establishments alone totaled $25.8 billion. More recent data reveals that sales continue to rise (see Figure 6.1). The U.S. Department of Commerce reported that e-commerce transactions increased 19.3 percent from the first quarter of 2001 to the first quarter of 2002. Projections for B2B e-commerce in 2003 and beyond range from $1.2 to $10 trillion in total sales.

Even with such dramatic growth, online transactions represent a very small part of all commerce, just 1 to 2 percent of all sales. Traditional "real-world" contracting still dominates the marketplace, but e-commerce represents a rapidly growing practice.

http://

- For the latest reports on the increasing amount of electronic commerce in the U.S. economy, visit **http://www.census.gov** and click on "E-stats."

Terms of E-Commerce

A number of acronyms represent the different kinds of e-commerce prevalent on the Internet today. The most familiar kind of e-commerce involves retail sales from a business to a consumer. This is generally referred to as business-to-consumer or *B2C, e-commerce*. One of the most common examples of B2C is Amazon.com. Amazon.com, which specializes in filling orders for books, movies, electronics, music,

FIGURE 6.1   **Estimated Quarterly U.S. Retail E-Commerce Sales (in billions of dollars) 4th Quarter 1999–3rd Quarter 2002**

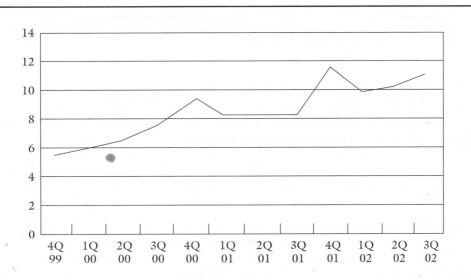

and many other products. Consumers may even create a wish list that Amazon.com will try to fulfill if an unavailable product becomes available again. Other B2C Web sites (and there are many) include landsend.com, sears.com, and a multitude of others.

E-commerce transactions may occur between two businesses. These agreements are called *B2B e-commerce* and can take a variety of forms. One common example is called a *vertical portal model*, which offers a collection of information, services, and goods to a particular industry. Such a portal provides matchmaking and other services to bring businesses together. For example, coalcamp.com is a B2B vertical portal that provides a marketplace exchange of goods and supplies for various segments of heavy industry. Another kind of B2B is a "supply chain" model. For example, a single Web site can find parts, identify suppliers, and order parts for a business. Partminer.com is an example of such a site.

A subset of business-to-business transactions, called *B2B2C*, involves Internet-enabling and streamlining an entire business value chain, from its initial supplier to the finished product that is delivered to a consumer. An example of this would be General Motors allowing consumers to purchase a vehicle online. GM procurement systems would find the lowest price parts through online vendors and route them to the nearest manufacturing plant. Shipping systems would find the most competitively priced trucking company to deliver the vehicle to a nearby dealer for sale. Such a system would be fully Internet enabled throughout the entire value chain.

E-Commerce Business Models

Numerous e-commerce models exist on the Internet within the general categories of B2B, B2B2C, and B2C. These models originate from two sources. First, many models are replicated from traditional business contracting methods. Second, some models are genuinely unique to e-commerce and the Internet.

A number of traditional commerce models are alive and well on the Internet. The *mail-order model*, typified by Amazon.com, allows a Web site to sell physical goods in response to orders from its customers online. Such operations have strong real-world foundations and in fact may be considered traditional retail shops using an Internet venue. This model is the most common among e-commerce transactions. Other models, though less common, also thrive on the Internet. A *subscription-based model* provides access to digital products, such as music, for a specified period of time. The *direct marketing model* involves sending unsolicited commercial e-mail called *spam* to a mass market in hopes the recipients will respond and purchase the advertised product. Spam is almost universally abhorred by users and has a response rate as low as .0025 percent from consumers. The *real estate model* rents or sells Web space or domain names. The *free trial model* allows free use of software for a limited time, after which a fee must be paid to use the software permanently.

E-commerce models developed predominantly online involve the *information barter model*, which allows consumers and businesses to exchange goods and services. The *digital delivery model* provides digital products ordered online, as compared with Web sites that deliver a physical good through the Internet. Finally, the *access-*

provision model sells access to the Internet in exchange for a fee. Such a service is usually provided by established Internet service providers (ISPs) like Earthlink and AOL.

Benefits to Consumers

E-commerce benefits consumers as well as businesses. The most significant beneficial impact is that consumers can monitor the price and availability of goods and services. Consumers can compare goods far more quickly than would be possible with store-to-store comparisons. Also, buyers can access detailed product, warranty, repair, and pricing information before deciding to complete a final sale. Many consumers now have an "online store" of their own, auctioning collectibles and other goods. E-commerce represents an increasingly important form of trade that will fundamentally improve available opportunities for both businesses and consumers alike.

FUNDAMENTAL PRINCIPLES OF CONTRACT LAW

Although e-commerce law is a separate and important legal topic, any understanding of the legal aspects of online contracting must be based on some knowledge of traditional contract law. This section introduces you to contracts and describes the basic requirements for forming a legally binding agreement.

Simply stated, contract law is a matter of both common law (judge made) and statutory law. The common law contract rules are summarized in the **Restatement Second of the Law of Contract**. This is an unofficial but highly respected synopsis of the rules set out in U.S. court cases.

Statutory contract law—the contract law enacted by the U.S. Congress and state legislatures and federal and state administrative agencies—is remarkably similar throughout the United States. In part, this is due to the efforts of the National Conference of Commissioners on Uniform State Laws (NCCUSL), which has drafted model uniform state codes. Although the drafts must be adopted by state legislatures before they come into force in a state, nearly all states have done so. The NCCUSL draft law for commercial transactions is the **Uniform Commercial Code (UCC)**, which has been adopted by all fifty states (although Louisiana has adopted only part of it), as well as the District of Columbia. Article 2 of the UCC sets out the rules governing the sale of goods and Article 2A the rules governing the leasing of goods.

THE REQUIREMENTS OF A CONTRACT

In order for persons to enter into a valid and enforceable contract, several **requirements of a contract** must be met:

1. **Mutual Assent.** The parties to a contract must manifest by words or conduct their intent to enter into a contract. This is usually done by one of them making an offer and the other accepting it.
2. **Consideration.** Each party to the contract must exchange something of value.

3. **Capacity.** The parties must have the legal ability to enter into a contract. Persons judicially declared incompetent lack contractual capacity. Others, including minors and intoxicated persons, have limited contractual capacity.
4. **Legality.** The object of a contract cannot be criminal, tortious, or otherwise against public policy.
5. **Form.** A few contracts must be in a particular form. That is, they must be in writing and signed.

In the following sections, each of these elements is discussed in more detail.

Mutual Assent

Section 3 of the Restatement Second of the Law of Contracts defines the making of an agreement that constitutes a contract as "the manifestation of a mutual assent on the part of two or more persons." In other words, the parties to a contract must give some outward indication of their intention to be bound. Ordinarily, the parties show their mutual assent through an offer and an acceptance. One party proposes (offers) by words or conduct and the other agrees (accepts) by words or conduct. A contract expressed in words (whether oral or written) is an *express contract*. A contract formed by conduct is known as an *implied contract*. In determining whether or not both parties have actually agreed to the contract, the law applies an *objective standard*. That is, it looks to see if the intent of each of the parties can be ascertained from that party's words or actions. The law is not concerned with subjective intent (i.e., with what a party may have thought at the time of expressing an intent).

Offer. An offer does not have to be in a particular form. However, it must (1) manifest an intent to enter into a contract, (2) be communicated (by the person making the offer—the *offeror*—to another—the *offeree*), and (3) be definite and certain.

- *Intent.* An offer must convey the offeror's intent to enter into a contract. A proposal that is made in jest ("Ha, ha. You bet, I'll give you $10,000 for your old 486 computer!") is not an offer. Similarly, a preliminary inquiry ("How much is that laptop?") is not an offer.

  An advertisement on an Internet Web page does not constitute an offer. If it did, the merchant might not be able to deliver the promised property or services if too many people were to accept. Recognizing this, the law treats advertisements, newsletters, quotation sheets, merchandise displays, and the like, as informational notices rather than offers.

  A company that runs an auction, like eBay, is likewise not making an offer to sell goods, software, or other property that it lists for sale. It is, rather, soliciting offers. The persons placing bids are offering to buy the listed items. Only when the auction company declares the auction is closed and a bid has been accepted is there a binding contract.

  If an auction is advertised or announced as being *without reserve*, the auction company may not withdraw an item put up for sale unless no bid is received within a reasonable time. If there is no advertisement or announcement of this sort, then the auction is *with reserve* and the auction company may withdraw the items put up for sale at any time, even after several bids have been made.

- *Communication.* An offeror must intend to communicate an offer to an offeree and must actually do so. In other words, the offer is ineffective unless the offeror means to communicate it to a particular offeree. For example, Ann may send an e-mail to Bob offering to sell him her laser printer for $200. She likes Bob and wants to give him a special price. Bob doesn't need the printer, but he knows that Charlie does, so he forwards Ann's e-mail to Charlie. Charlie's acceptance of Ann's offer would not be effective, because Ann made the offer to Bob, not Charlie.

  Additionally, the offeror must actually deliver the offer to the offeree. For instance, assume that Dale sends an e-mail message offering to sell his cell phone to Elvira. Because of a server error, the message never gets to Elvira. If Elvira were to call Dale on the phone and tell him she wants to buy Dale's cell phone, she would not be accepting the e-mail offer, because it never got to her. Instead, she would be making her own offer to Dale, and the terms of that offer would govern their contractual relationship, not the terms in Dale's e-mail message.

- *Definiteness.* The terms of an offer must be reasonably certain and complete. This is so a court will be able to enforce the resulting contract if asked to do so.

  If too many terms are missing, a court may hold that the parties did not intend to form a contract. Because contracts take many forms, it is not possible to list the essential terms necessary to form a contract. However, for most contracts, the material terms would include the subject matter, quantity, quality, price, payment terms, and duration.

Acceptance. An acceptance is a positive and unequivocal expression of an offeree's intent to enter into a contract on the terms set out in the offer. Only when an offer is accepted does a contract come into existence. An offeree usually is under no legal obligation to reply to an offer. The offeree's silence or inaction, therefore, will not constitute an acceptance. However, silence or inaction can constitute acceptance if the parties agree in advance that it will, or if custom, usage, or a prior course similarly so provide. For example, when a person becomes a member of a mail-order book club, the person agrees that failure to return a notification card rejecting offered goods will constitute acceptance of the club's offer to sell the member the goods.

Time When Acceptance Is Effective. Unlike an offer (as well as a revocation, counteroffer, and rejection), an acceptance is ordinarily not effective when it is received. Rather, it has effect *from the moment of its dispatch by the offeree.* This is so unless at least one of the following conditions apply:

1. The offer specifically provides otherwise.
2. The offeree uses an unauthorized method of acceptance (such as mailing a response by ordinary mail when the offer requires that the response be by e-mail).
3. The acceptance is sent after the offeree sends a rejection (in which case, the communication that gets to the offeror first will be the one that is effective).

Acceptance with Modifications. It is not uncommon for an offeree to want to change or add terms to an offer. Under the common law, the *mirror image rule* applies: an acceptance must exactly mirror the offer. Any change or addition will constitute a rejection of the offer and the making of a counteroffer. The UCC relaxes the mirror image rule under certain circumstances, allowing contracts between merchants to be formed if no different material terms exist between the offer and the acceptance.

Consideration

In order for a contract to be enforceable, it must be supported by consideration. *Consideration* is something of value that is given (or given up) in exchange for getting something back. If a contract is bilateral, the promises exchanged by each party are the consideration. If a contract is unilateral, the consideration of one party is its promise; the performance of an act is the consideration of the other party. Any agreement must be supported by consideration to be a valid contract. Otherwise, the promise is a mere gift and usually cannot be enforced in court.

Exceptions to the Requirement of Consideration. There are a few exceptions to the requirement that a contractual promise be supported by consideration. For example, a modification of a sale of goods contract does not need consideration to be binding. In addition, if a merchant promises to keep open an offer to buy or sell goods for a period of time, that promise is enforceable even if it is not supported by consideration. Finally, the doctrine of *promissory estoppel* states that a person who reasonably relies on the promise of another, and suffers injury as a result, may force the promisor to keep his or her promise, even if it is unsupported by consideration. For example, suppose an Internet service provider tells a client it is welcome to set up a Web site for free on the ISP's Web server. Because of this, the client spends several thousand dollars to have a Web site designed. The ISP cannot later change its mind and refuse to let the client put the Web site on its server.

Capacity

Persons who enter into contracts must understand they are doing so. Someone who does not understand the consequences of what he or she is promising to do lacks contractual capacity. Ordinarily, the law assumes that everyone has the capacity to contract. There are three main exceptions to this rule. Minors, intoxicated persons, and the mentally incompetent are often held to lack contractual capacity.

In most states, a minor is anyone under the age of eighteen. Minors are allowed to avoid contracts they have entered into, unless the contract is one for basic goods or services called *necessaries*. On the Internet, many online sites rely on circumstantial criteria for determining if a customer is an adult. Commonly, they require a customer to provide an employment address, a credit card number, and a statement that the client is an adult. A person who is so intoxicated that he or she is unaware they are entering into a contract is not bound by the promise. Similarly, persons declared incompetent in a court proceeding lack the capacity to contract, and any contract they enter into is said to be void. Persons not yet declared incompetent, but who are unable to appreciate the effect of their contractual promises, have the right to disaffirm such a promise.

Legality

Contracts must be legal to be enforceable. If they require a party to commit an illegal act, they are said to violate public policy. That is, they violate accepted standards of behavior and they are *void*. When a contract is void, courts generally take no action, leaving the parties in the situation they have put themselves.

The following are examples of illegal contracts that the courts regard as void:

- Contracts to commit a crime or tort
- Gambling contracts (unless authorized by law)
- Exculpatory contracts (contracts that attempt to limit the liability of a person who sells goods or services to the public)
- Contracts meant to restrain or restrict trade

Unconscionable Contracts. In an **unconscionable contract**, one party uses its significantly superior bargaining power to take advantage of the other party in an agreement. Courts refused to enforce unconscionable contracts because the agreements are considered fundamentally unfair. Two factors usually exist when a contract is considered unconscionable. First, oppression, whereby the entity with the superior bargaining power exerts its leverage to force an unfair contract on the weaker entity. Second, surprise, whereby one party does not fully understand the implications of the contract or does not have the opportunity of understanding the implications of the contract before signing. Under these conditions, the agreement is considered to shock the conscience of the court, which would refuse to enforce all or part of the agreement's terms.

Contracts to Restrain Trade. Of these illegal contracts, those involving a restraint of trade are the most likely to affect online contracting. Section 1 of the Sherman Antitrust Act, the principal federal law dealing with the regulation of competition, prohibits contracts, combinations, and conspiracies in restraint of trade or commerce. The most common contract in restraint of trade is *price fixing*: an agreement among competitors to set the same price for their products. Because an agreement to set prices in advance rather than letting the forces of the marketplace determine the price is anticompetitive, injurious to consumers, and a restraint of trade, it violates the Sherman Antitrust Act and is illegal. Other arrangements that amount to restraints of trade are *noncompetition agreements*—agreements not to sell competing products or services; *tying agreements*—agreements to purchase one product or service as a condition or prerequisite to purchasing a second product; and *grant back agreements*—agreements requiring one party to turn over to a second party any improvements the first party makes to a technology licensed to it by the second party.

Form

Most contracts do not have to be any particular form. As a general rule, they may be written, oral, or even unstated, and still be enforceable. Certain contracts, however, must be in writing. These are contracts described in a law known as the *Statute of Frauds*. Originally adopted by the English Parliament in the seventeenth century, all of the U.S. states now have their own statutes of frauds. For example, these statutes require that the following contracts be in writing:

- Contracts involving the sale of an interest in land
- Contracts that cannot be performed within one year
- Collateral contracts to pay the debt of another person

The Uniform Commercial Code, which has its own Statute of Frauds provisions (UCC §§ 2-201 and 2A-201), requires that these additional contracts be in writing:

- Contracts for the sale of goods for $500 or more
- Contracts for the lease of goods for $1,000 or more

Complying with the Statute of Frauds. The writing requirement of the statutes of fraud does not require that a writing be in any particular form, that it describe the entire agreement, or that it even prove the contract is binding. All that is required is that a writing or memorandum prove a contract was made. It must do the following: (1) Specify the parties to the contract, (2) Specify with reasonable certainty the subject matter and the essential terms of that part of the contract not yet performed, and (3) Be signed by the party against whom the contract is to be enforced. Compliance with the Statute of Frauds online is discussed later in the chapter.

- *The Signature.* The *signature* required on a writing or memorandum may be a person's name, initials, or any other symbol, as long as the party intends for it to authenticate the writing. Although the legality of signatures in traditional contracts is well settled, special requirements for online agreements exist. The electronic signature acts that have now been adopted in most states establish procedures for making valid electronic signatures or establish criteria for determining if a signature is valid.

Exceptions to the Statute of Frauds' Writing Requirement

There are several exceptions to the Statute of Frauds' requirement that some contracts have to be in writing. The *doctrine of part performance* applies to contracts for the sale of an interest in land. This says that when a purchaser of land makes value improvements to it, or when the purchaser takes possession of the land after having paid part of the purchase price, a writing is not needed to make the contract enforceable.

There are several exceptions to UCC Statute of Frauds rules that sales of goods for more than $500 and leases of goods for more than $1,000 have to be in writing. UCC §§ 2-201 and § 2A-201 state that a writing is not required for the following:

- Contracts for goods specially manufactured for the buyer on which the seller has begun performance
- Contracts for which payment has been made and accepted or for which the goods have been received and accepted
- Contracts in which the party being sued admits in a court or in the pleadings that the contract was made

In addition, for sales of goods (but not for leases of goods), a writing is not required for contracts between merchants, if the merchant being sued received a written notice from the other merchant confirming the existence of the contract and if the merchant being sued did not object to the confirmation within ten days of its receipt.

The Parol Evidence Rule. The *parol evidence rule* applies to contracts that are in writing, whether or not they are required to be so by the Statute of Frauds. This rule states that the parties to a complete and final written contract cannot introduce evidence in court to change the meaning of the terms of the contract. See UCC § 2-202 and § 2A-201.

The parol evidence rule only excludes evidence of oral or other agreements made at the time of, or prior to, the making of the written contract. It does not exclude evidence of a modification made after the written contract was agreed to, or which is introduced to explain (but not change the meaning of) a contractual term.

For example, suppose Imogene, a seller, told Jake, a buyer, that the computer system he wanted to buy included a 16-gigabit hard drive and a DVD drive. Later, when Jake signed the contract to buy the system, the written contract said there would be a hard drive, but it did not specify the size. Also, instead of a DVD drive, it said a CD-ROM drive would be provided. Jake may testify in court to explain the hard drive was meant to be a 16-gigabit drive, because his testimony would help the court understand the meaning of the term *hard drive*. However, he may not testify that the CD-ROM drive was supposed to be a DVD drive, because this would change the meaning of that term.

WARRANTIES, DISCLAIMERS, AND TERMS OF USE

Almost every Web site selling a good or service contains specific contractual language that governs any transactions involving that Web site. This language, usually called the *Terms of Use*, can establish payment methods, list Web site rules, define external linking and attribution permissions, and articulate statements of privacy. However, one of the most common purposes of the Terms of Use Web page is to affirm or disclaim warranties of a product or service sold from that site.

A **warranty** is an assurance in a contract that a product will satisfy certain standards. Three types of warranties exist. First, an *express warranty* (UCC § 2-313) is an explicit statement of fact made by the seller about the quality or other characteristic of the product. For example, the statement that "the computer's hard drive will contain 80 gigabytes of storage capacity" is an express warranty of the hard drive's performance. Second, an *implied warranty*, which is not explicitly stated, may arise as a result of the conduct of the parties. Most products contain an *implied warranty of merchantability* (UCC § 2-314), which guarantees that goods are reasonably fit for their ordinary purpose. Some products have an *implied warranty for fitness of a particular purpose* (UCC § 2-315). Such a warranty states that the goods are fit for a particular activity if the buyer is relying on the seller's skill and expertise in selecting goods for the buyer.

Dell Computer Corporation is a popular seller of personal computers to individuals and businesses. Here is an excerpt of Dell's Terms of Use that establishes some of its limited warranties:

90-Day Limited Warranty (United States Only)

Dell Computer Corporation ("Dell") manufactures its hardware products from parts and components that are new or equivalent to new in accordance with industry-standard practices. Dell warrants that the hardware products it manufactures will be free from defects in materials and workmanship. The limited warranty term is 90-days beginning on the date of invoice, as further described in the following text.

Damage due to shipping the products to you is covered under this limited warranty. Otherwise, this limited warranty does not cover damage due to external causes, including accident, abuse, misuse, problems with electrical power, servicing not authorized by Dell, usage not in accordance with product instructions, failure to perform required preventive maintenance, and problems caused by use of parts and components not supplied by Dell.

This limited warranty does not cover any items that are in one or more of the following categories: software; external devices (except as specifically noted); accessories or parts added to a Dell system after the system is shipped from Dell; accessories or parts added to a Dell system through Dell's system integration department; accessories or parts that are not installed in the Dell factory . . . all other monitors, keyboards, and mice (including those sold through the DellWare program) are not covered.

During the ninety-day period beginning on the invoice date, Dell will repair or replace products covered under this limited warranty that are returned to Dell's facility. To request limited warranty service, you must contact Dell's Customer Technical Support within the limited warranty period. Refer to the chapter titled "Getting Help" or "Contacting Dell" in your documentation to find the appropriate telephone number for obtaining customer assistance. . . . Dell will ship the repaired or replacement products to you freight prepaid if you use an address in the continental United States, where applicable. Shipments to other locations will be made freight collect.

Dell also presents a disclaimer of certain warranties. A *disclaimer* (UCC § 2-316) is a statement that a particular warranty does not apply to the agreement. Dell's agreement also limits available remedies to its customers if a dispute were to arise involving Dell. A seller is allowed to disclaim most available warranties in its contract. Also, businesses like Dell also include a limitation of available remedies (UCC § 2-719). A limitation of remedy clause states that if Dell does breach a warranty, the consumer may recover only a limited amount of damages. The following language highlights Dell's warranty disclaimers and remedy limitations:

> ALL EXPRESS AND IMPLIED WARRANTIES FOR THE PRODUCT, INCLUDING BUT NOT LIMITED TO ANY IMPLIED WARRANTIES OF AND CONDITIONS OF MERCHANTABILITY AND FITNESS FOR A PARTICULAR PURPOSE, ARE LIMITED IN DURATION TO THE LIMITED WARRANTY PERIOD SET FORTH ABOVE AND NO WARRANTIES, WHETHER EXPRESS OR IMPLIED, WILL APPLY AFTER SUCH PERIOD. SOME STATES (OR JURISDICTIONS) DO NOT ALLOW LIMITATIONS ON HOW LONG AN IMPLIED WARRANTY LASTS, SO THE ABOVE LIMITATION MAY NOT APPLY TO YOU.

> DELL DOES NOT ACCEPT LIABILITY BEYOND THE REMEDIES SET FORTH IN THIS LIMITED WARRANTY STATEMENT OR LIABILITY FOR INCIDENTAL OR CONSEQUENTIAL DAMAGES, INCLUDING WITHOUT LIMITATION ANY LIABILITY FOR PRODUCTS NOT BEING AVAILABLE FOR USE OR FOR LOST DATA OR SOFTWARE. SOME STATES (OR JURISDICTIONS) DO NOT ALLOW THE EXCLUSION OR LIMITATION OF INCIDENTAL OR CONSEQUENTIAL DAMAGES, SO THE ABOVE EXCLUSION OR LIMITATION MAY NOT APPLY TO YOU.

This language is quite common in computer-related contracts and generally serves to protect the business from claims of extraordinary losses or from arguments that other warranties exist that are not stated in the agreement. Notice that the language is in all capital letters. This represents Dell's efforts to make its disclaimers and liability limitations prominent to the consumer. Placing the language in all capital letters helps deter the argument that the consumer missed this language because it was hidden in the fine print.

http://

- For a further examination of Dell's terms and conditions, visit **http://www.dell.com** and click on "Terms and Conditions of Sale."

Other Terms of Use: PayPal, Inc.'s User Agreement

PayPal is an online payment service that allows a business or private individual to send and receive payments via the Internet. A PayPal account holder sends money by informing PayPal of the intended recipient's e-mail address and the amount to be sent by designating a credit card, bank account, or PayPal account as a funding source. PayPal accesses the funds and makes them available to the intended recipient. PayPal generates its revenues through transaction fees and the interest it derives from holding funds until they are sent.

The prospective customer assents to the agreement by clicking a box at the bottom of an application page that reads, "[you] have read and agree to the User Agreement and [PayPal's] privacy policy." A link to the text of the user agreement is located at the bottom of the application. The link to user agreement need not be opened for the application to be processed. If the prospective customer does click on the user agreement link, he is presented with a lengthy document consisting of twenty-five printed pages and eleven sections. Each section contains a number of subparagraphs that establish the parties' duties and obligations. The following paragraphs show some of the highlights of that agreement. The PayPal user agreement begins with the following statement:

> This User Agreement ("Agreement or "User Agreement") is a contract between you and PayPal, Inc. and applies to your user of the PayPal payment services and any related products and services (collectively the "Service"). This Agreement affects your rights and you should read it carefully. We encourage you to print the Agreement or copy it to your computer's hard drive for your reference.

> [Y]ou agree to the terms and conditions of this Agreement, the PayPal Privacy Policy, and any documents incorporated by reference. You further agree that this User Agreement forms a legally binding contract between you and PayPal, and that this Agreement constitutes "a writing signed by You" under any applicable law or regulation.

Many user agreements contain an arbitration clause requiring any disputes to be settled through binding arbitration instead of through traditional litigation. Section II(19) of the PayPal user agreement contains the following arbitration clause:

> **Arbitration.** Any controversy or claim arising out of or relating to this Agreement or the provision of Services shall be settled by binding arbitration in accordance with the commercial arbitration rules of the American Arbitration Association. Any such controversy or claim shall be arbitrated on an individual basis, and shall not be consolidated in any arbitration with any claim or controversy of any other party. The arbitration shall be conducted in Santa Clara County, California, and judgment on the arbitration award may be entered in any court having jurisdiction thereof. Either you or PayPal may seek any interim or preliminary relief from a court of competent jurisdiction in Santa Clara County, California necessary to protect the rights or property of you or PayPal, Inc. (or its agents, suppliers, and subcontractors) pending the completion of arbitration.

Online user agreements often grant the drafter significant discretion regarding the management and termination of its customer's accounts. The following terms of use are found in section V(3) of PayPal's user agreement:

> PayPal, at its sole discretion, reserves the right to close an account at any time for any reason, including but not limited to a violation of this Agreement, upon notice to the User and payment to the User of any unrestricted funds held in custody. PayPal, at its sole discretion, also reserves the right to periodically retrieve and review a business and/or consumer credit report for any account, and reserves the right to close an account based on information obtained during this credit review process.

> PayPal, at its sole discretion, also reserves the right to restrict withdrawals from an account for any one of the events listed below. If the dispute covers only a

specific transaction, we will only restrict funds related to that particular transaction. If your account is restricted, you will be notified by e-mail and requested to provide information relevant to your account. PayPal will investigate the matter promptly. If the investigation is in your favor, we will unrestrict your account. If the investigation is not in your favor, PayPal may return funds to the sender and unrestrict the remainder of your account, continue the restriction for up to 180 days as to funds necessary to protect PayPal against the risk of reversals, or may close your account by giving you notice and mailing a check for any funds in your account (minus funds that are in dispute) to the address that you have provided. If you are later determined to be entitled to the funds in dispute, PayPal will make an additional payment of those funds to you. Any of the following events may lead to a restriction of your account . . . [omitting list of nineteen provisions that include "Receipt of potentially fraudulent funds," "Refusal to cooperate in an investigation," "Opening multiple Personal accounts," and "Logging in from a country not included on PayPal's permitted countries list."] . . . PayPal will use reasonable efforts to investigate accounts that are subject to a restriction and to reach a final decision promptly.

This Agreement is subject to change by PayPal without prior notice (unless prior notice is required by law), by posting of the revised Agreement on the PayPal Web site. Descriptions of material amendments to this Agreement will be posted in advance on the PayPal Web site in the "Policy Updates" section that is displayed to you when you log in to your account. You can also set your Preferences to receive e-mail notification of all policy updates. You may review the current Agreement prior to initiating a transaction at any time at our User Agreement page.

Take a close look at the terms and conditions just stated. Do these terms favor PayPal or the customer? Do any of the terms seem particularly unfair or harsh? What portions of the user agreement appear to give PayPal an almost unrestricted right to amend, freeze, or terminate its customers' accounts? Does the arbitration clause appear fair to consumers? Does PayPal give itself the right to change any portion of the agreement, at any time, for any reason without prior notice to the customer?

By now it may become clear that online user agreements such as PayPal's generally contain terms that protect the company at the expense of the customer. Perhaps we may conclude that these terms are so unfair as to be unenforceable. At least two customers and one noncustomer of PayPal believed so, and the terms are the basis of a lawsuit described in the next section.

Disputing the Terms of Use: *Comb v. PayPal*

In *Comb v. PayPal, Inc.*, 218 F. Supp. 2d 1165 (N.D. Cal. 2002), two subscribers and one nonsubscriber to PayPal's electronic disbursement service sued PayPal, alleging that PayPal improperly held or removed funds from their bank accounts, triggering various penalty fees by the plaintiffs' banks and other damages. PayPal required that the plaintiffs submit their claims to arbitration pursuant to a clause in the user agreement that required all claims to be submitted to binding arbitration in California.

The plaintiffs argued that the arbitration clause and other terms of the user agreement were so unfair as to be unconscionable. Thus PayPal could not enforce these terms against them. The court found that the agreement, and in particular the arbitration clause, was unconscionable. The contract was a "contract of adhesion" that relegated the subscribing party to the contract with only the opportunity to "take it or leave it," without the possibility of negotiation. This left PayPal's unsophisticated customers unduly vulnerable to the terms of the user agreement. The court also reasoned that the user agreement was unconscionable because PayPal held unrestricted power to resolve disputes, close accounts, and procure ownership of any funds held in its possession.

The arbitration clause prohibited any consolidation of consumer claims. The court found this unconscionable because in practice most claims would involve consumers seeking a small amount of money and the costs of recovering those funds would be so high it would create the "potential for millions of customers to be overcharged small amounts without an effective method of redress." Finally, PayPal's insistence that all consumer disputes (most are under $100) be resolved in "PayPal's backyard" of Santa Clara County, California, "serves to shield PayPal from liability instead of providing a neutral forum in which to arbitrate disputes." The court concluded that such one-sidedness, without the presence of meaningful alternatives, constituted an unconscionable contract that could not be enforced against the consumer.

The *Comb* decision informs us that courts will not blindly accept all user agreements proffered by the purveyor of computer-related services. The user agreement in *Comb* contained so many unfair terms that the court found the agreement unenforceable against the consumer. Although the decision represents a major victory for end users, the *Comb* decision is only binding on a small part of California. It remains to be seen whether the *Comb* decision takes hold as the jurisprudential law of the land.

THE DEVELOPING UNIFORM E-COMMERCE LAW: UCITA AND UETA

The **Uniform Computer Information Transactions Act (UCITA)** is a set of commercial rules designed to regulate transactions of computer information and licensing of software. UCITA laws are not themselves binding. Rather, they must be enacted in a state before they are enforceable in that state. UCITA is one of the most significant developments in online contracting because it attempts to provide a uniform system for most computer transactions in all fifty states. As a result, UCITA has become very controversial, with a number of groups advocating is passage or rejection.

►http://

• For a copy of the act and interesting commentary supporting it, see **http://www.ucitaonline.com**

History and Development

As the volume of software sales grew dramatically in the early 1990s, it became obvious that the Uniform Commercial Code would not be applicable to most software transactions. Article 2 of the UCC regulates the sale of tangible goods, and software is considered electronic information that constitutes intangible property. In addition, the purchase of software does not usually grant the owner full rights in the application. Rather, most software sales are completed as a software license, which also falls outside the Article 2 sales of goods. As a result, a new regulatory framework needed to be put in place.

UCITA is a draft of legislation created by the National Conference of Commissioners on Uniform State Laws (NCCUSL) and the American Law Institute (ALI).[1] The first efforts at development focused on modifying Article 2 of the UCC to include the licensing of goods. Many were reluctant to tamper with well-settled Article 2 provisions. As a result, drafters proposed that a separate UCC Article 2B be developed to address the commercial practice of electronic transactions. However, despite many years of negotiation, ALI and NCCUSL could not reach an agreement on the final form of Article 2B. ALI had "significant reservations about both some of its key substantive provisions and its overall clarity and coherence." The ALI, which supported incorporation of all other articles of the UCC, rejected Article 2B.

After ALI declined to support implementation of Article 2B, the NCCUSL went forward on its own and established the provisions under an independent act, naming it UCITA. The NCCUSL proceeded to recommend adoption of UCITA by the states. So far, only two states have followed. In Maryland, UCITA was signed by the governor on April 25, 2000, and became effective on October 1, 2000. In Virginia, UCITA was signed by the governor on March 14, 2000, and became effective on July 1, 2001. Bills have been introduced in a number of other states.

UCITA: A Controversial Measure

Why is UCITA so controversial? A host of consumer groups and other organizations such as the Motion Picture Industry of America, the Recording Industry of America, and the Newspaper Association of America oppose UCITA for a number of reasons. Some claim UCITA is poorly drafted and unnecessarily complex. There is also a widespread belief that UCITA favors the software industry by allowing software companies to restrict legal action to venues favorable to them. Finally, some claim that UCITA permits software companies to block consumers from having presale access to software terms and conditions, thus requiring consumers to agree to all terms before using the product.

http://

- See **http://www.ali.org** and **http://www.nccusl.org**
- For more criticisms of UCITA, see **http://www.ucitaonline.com**

Supporters of UCITA contend it is the most effective response to the information revolution and fairly considers the rights of consumers. Supporters note that UCITA allows parties to opt out of its provisions. In addition, software developers note that limitations of liability and warranty inherent in UCITA are essential for the industry. Finally, some claim that UCITA actually improves, rather than degrades, consumer

---

[1]The American Law Institute was founded in 1923 by a distinguished group of lawyers, judges, and law teachers with the goal of preparing "an orderly restatement of the general common law of the United States, including in that term not only the law developed solely by judicial decision, but also the law that has grown from the application by the courts of statutes that were generally enacted and were in force for many years." Wolkin, "Restatements of the Law: Origin, Preparation, Availability," 21 Ohio B.A. Rept. 663 (1940).

rights. Supporters note that UCITA retains existing consumer protection laws, adopts UCC consumer protection laws in Article 2, and only gives small additional protections to the software industry.

UCITA: Key Provisions

Scope and Coverage of the Act. The UCITA applies to "computer information transactions," which section 102(11) of the act defines as an agreement to "create, modify, transfer, or license computer information or informational rights in computer information." Computer information transactions include, among other things, contracts to develop a program, databases accessed online, e-books, and the license or purchase of software. However, embedded programs, such as when a program is inseparably embedded to a traditional good, are not covered under UCITA. Examples of embedded programs are found in stereos, television sets, and medical equipment. The UCITA specifically excludes a number of transactions. UCITA does not apply to agreements involving the following:

1. Financial services transactions;
2. Cable, satellite, or other broadcast media;
3. Movies, sound recordings, or musical works;
4. Compulsory licenses;
5. Employment, except if the individual is an independent contractor providing computer information; or
6. Subject matter within the scope of Articles 3 through 8 of the Uniform Commercial Code.

Formation of a UCITA Contract. Many contract formation issues follow real-world guidelines. However, the UCITA adds some interesting changes to contract formation requirements. For example, Section 2-208 of the UCC allows for silence to serve as acceptance only where a single contract involves "repeated occasions for performance."

UCITA § 112(f) expands on this, allowing the parties in one transaction to agree that acceptance by inaction will apply to any "future transactions between the parties." The state attorneys general who object to UCITA cite this provision as one that invites abuse. If the UCITA comes into force, consumers and other purchasers will have to read carefully the fine print of every software license they are offered before they agree to be bound by its terms. If they do not, they may be agreeing to accept the offeror's future software products unless they respond negatively to them.

The UCITA also discusses writing requirements. Section 201 of UCITA requires a writing for contracts for the licensing of informational rights for more than $5,000 and contracts for the licensing of informational services that cannot be performed in less than one year. In an online forum, a writing or memorandum may be any permanent record showing that the parties entered into a contract. Most states have adopted electronic signature acts that define writings so they include information stored in an electronic medium retrievable in a perceivable form. Similarly, UCITA Section 106 provides that an electronic record is to be regarded as a writing and Section 107 states that "[a] record . . . may not be denied legal effect or enforceability solely because it is in electronic form."

Exceptions to the writing requirement do exist in UCITA, and they are analogous to those in the UCC. For example, UCITA Section 201 says that a writing is not required for the following:

- Contracts for which payment has been made and accepted or for which the information has been received and accepted
- Contracts in which the party being sued admits in a court or in the pleadings that the contract was made
- Contracts between merchants, if the merchant being sued received a written notice from the other merchant confirming the existence of the contract and if the merchant being sued did not object to the confirmation within ten days of its receipt

Warranties. As noted earlier, a warranty is an assurance in a contract that a product will satisfy certain standards. When the UCITA applies, several new obligations are placed on the contracting parties. For example, Section 401 states it is the licensor's obligation to see that no third-party claim of infringement of an intellectual property right or of misappropriation affects the delivered information. Delivery of the product must be free of any such claims. Section 403 creates an implied warranty of merchantability of computer programs. Like the UCC, it requires the software to be "fit for the ordinary purpose" for which programs of its type are used. Section 404 creates an implied warranty of information. This implied warranty affirms that no inaccuracies in the informational content exist as a result of the merchant's failure to use reasonable care.

Section 405 implies a warranty with respect to information provided for a particular purpose. A "particular purpose" differs from the ordinary purpose for which the information is used in that it envisions a specific use by the licensee peculiar to the nature of its business. In comparison, the ordinary purposes for which the computer information is used are contemplated under the concept of merchantability. Section 405 obligates any integration of system components to be fit for the purpose for which it is being implemented and function together as a system. Section 409 extends warranty protection to all individual consumers in the family or household if the individual's use should have been expected by the licensor. Section 803 states that consequential damages for personal injury cannot be disclaimed for a computer program contained in consumer goods.

These warranties are not irrefutable and the seller may disclaim them. Section 403 permits disclaimers of certain implied warranties if the seller uses the words *merchantability* or *quality* (or similar words) and sets apart the disclaimer in a clear conspicuous manner such as all capital letters. Disclaimers of other warranties require similar specific and conspicuous language.

Authentication and Attribution of the Agreement. Section 107 of UCITA clearly accepts electronic signatures, otherwise known as authentications, stating, "A record or authentication may not be denied legal effect or enforceability solely because it is in electronic form." UCITA equates electronic authentications with traditional hand signatures for contracts within its scope. If a party uses an electronic agent for signature, that party is bound by the operations of the electronic agent, even if no individual was aware of or reviewed the agent's operations. For example, if Bob agrees to buy a thousand computers from Sue, Bob cannot deny the contract's existence merely because the signature for the contract was transmitted electronically.

UCITA also provides a mechanism for attribution. Section 102(5) describes an attribution procedure as simply a means to verify an electronic authentication is that of a particular person or to detect changes or errors in information. An attribution procedure may be any security device that is commercially reasonable under the circumstances. In other words, UCITA does not favor one signature encryption technology over another. The party relying on the attribution has the burden of establishing its validity.

Mass-Market Licensing. Section 102(45) defines a mass-market license as a consumer contract or a transaction with an end-user licensee who acquired the license in a retail transaction. This definition encompasses most ordinary consumer purchases of software. For example, a shrink-wrap license (see later) purchased at a computer store contains a mass-market license. These licenses are automatically enforceable as long as the terms are made readily available and the licensee is given an opportunity to review them. If the licensee does not agree to the license, he or she may return the software. Mass-market licenses may be presented after initial general agreement from the licensee. This means the licensor does not have to reveal the license terms until *after* the licensee has purchased the software product.

Electronic Self-Help and Remedies. The licensor may exercise "self-help" if the licensee breaches the license agreement. Such self-help can include cancellation, repossession, and prevention of continued use of the software. For example, if Mega-Soft, Inc., discovers copies of its software are used illegally online, the company can disable the pirated software and prevent its further use. The licensor may enforce his or her license rights through both nonelectronic and electronic means. Self-help is not unlimited, however. For example, Section 816(b) states that electronic self-help is not permitted in mass-market transactions. Also, self-help is only available to the licensor if the parties explicitly agreed to it beforehand. Like most contracts, the aggrieved party under UCITA may cancel the contract, seek liquidated damages that have been preestablished in the agreement, and receive compensatory damages for injuries incurred. However, an aggrieved party may not recover consequential damages in most situations.

The UETA

The **Uniform Electronic Transactions Act (UETA)** is another uniform law relevant to online contracting. Less controversial than UCITA, the UETA does not create substantive rules for electronic contracts. Rather, the UETA supports the validity of electronic contracts as a viable medium for agreement. The UETA is similar to the

UCITA in many ways. Both proposals affirm the equivalency of computer records to traditional writings. Both proposals also approve of e-signatures, e-agents, and electronic attribution. The two are not identical, however. For example, the UETA addresses all commercial transactions, not just computer information like the UCITA. In addition, the UETA only applies to parties that agree to use e-commerce. The UCITA applies to any contract within its scope, regardless of the nature of the format. At least twenty-eight states have adopted UETA (compared to only two that have adopted UCITA) as binding law.

ELECTRONIC SIGNATURES

Many contracts require a signature to make a transaction enforceable. A significant issue arising in electronic commerce is the viability of electronic signatures in electronic contracts. According to Section 2(8) of the UETA, an electronic signature is an electronic sound, symbol, or process attached to or logically associated with an electronic acquisition or contract record and executed or adopted by a person with the intent to sign the record. Section 2(13) of the UETA defines a record as "information that is inscribed on a tangible medium or that is stored in an electronic or other medium and is retrievable in perceivable form."

Digital signatures are typically generated through a public key or an asymmetric cryptosystem. An asymmetric cryptosystem is based on the use of two software keys— a public key and a private key. A user makes his or her public key available to individuals who may need to decode their transmission. The user transmits information with his or her private key, and the public key is able to recognize when a document has the proper private key from the user. The two keys are related, but the mathematical algorithms that connect them are so complex, they are almost impossible to untangle.

Other signature technology captures a sender's handwritten signature and attaches that signature in an encrypted format to all transmitted documents. The signature is captured through a stylus pad or other device. The format is known as *signature dynamics*. Under this capturing system, third-party verification through a public key is not necessary. Although signature dynamics signatures are easier to comprehend by the average user, they do not provide the level of security inherent in public key systems, which are immediately verifiable with a third-party issued certificate.

http://

- For a closer look at California's electronic signature law, see **http://www.ss.ca.gov/digsig/code165.htm**

Many states already have electronic signature laws in place. For example, the Washington State *Electronic Authentication Act* establishes a procedure for creating valid digital signatures through the licensing of certifying authorities. By comparison, California has enacted rules for identifying electronic signatures [California Code § 16.5(a) (2002)]. This provides that an electronic signature is valid under these conditions:

1. It is unique to the person using it.
2. It is capable of verification.

3. It is under the sole control of the person using it.

4. It is linked to the data in such a manner that if the data is changed the signature is invalidated.

5. It conforms to regulations adopted by the appropriate state agency.

In line with the California rules, the UCITA would provide for the authentication of an electronic record both by human action and by means of an electronic agent (i.e., by a program that can independently initiate an action or respond to an electronic message or request without review or action by an individual). UCITA § 107(d) states,

> A person that uses its own electronic agent for authentication, performance, or agreement, including manifestation of assent, is bound by the operations of the electronic agent, even if no individual was aware of or reviewed the agent's operations or the results of the operations.

Current Electronic Signature Legislation: E-Sign

On June 30, 2000, President Clinton signed the Electronic Signatures in Global and National Commerce Act. The act, widely known as **E-sign**, gives electronic signatures and contracts the same validity as traditional handwritten and copy signatures. The law eliminates uncertainty in electronic commerce by improving the ease in which a valid online contract may be formed and enforced.

Although E-sign affirms the validity of electronic signatures and forms, it does not affect any substantive rights that may arise out of the agreement. For example, E-sign does not change any common law or statutory rules regarding formation of contracts, breach, and damages. All E-sign does is establish the validity of electronic records as bases for binding agreements.

The new E-sign law helps provide uniformity in electronic contracting nationwide by overriding state laws that are inconsistent with E-sign. At least eighteen states have adopted some form for federal signature laws. However, these state laws are not uniform. For example, California law differs from many electronic signature laws in that it does not recognize certain documents with e-signatures. Further, E-sign preempts any state law that is not technology neutral. For example, in 1995, Utah passed one of the first electronic signature laws that specifically addressed, and impliedly endorsed, public key implementation of signatures. Congress through E-sign preempted laws like Utah's to the extent that they give greater status to the use of a specific technology.

Although E-sign provides broad coverage, it does contain several exceptions. E-sign does not apply to wills, testamentary trusts, or family law records. E-sign also does not apply to cancellation of utility services, repossession and foreclosure, cancellation of health or life insurance benefits, and hazardous product recalls. E-sign also does not apply to any contracts formed under the Uniform Commercial Code, except those formed under Articles 2 and 2A, which relate to the sales of goods, personal property, and leases.

E-sign also requires special procedures for consumer transactions. Section 106 of the act defines consumers as "an individual who obtains, through a transaction, products or services which are used primarily for personal, family, or household purposes." If a state or federal law requires consumer notices, Section 101 of E-sign requires certain procedures to be used if notices are sent electronically. The consumer must affirmatively consent to receiving communications electronically and must be provided with a "clear and conspicuous statement" that consent is optional and may be withdrawn at any time. The consumer must also demonstrate access to the electronic information, and the business must inform the consumer how to obtain a hard copy of any electronic records at issue.

The Relationship between E-Sign and the UETA. E-sign was enacted with consideration of states' adoption of UETA. If a state adopts the official version of the UETA, that adoption will override E-sign, even though the UETA varies from E-sign in several respects. In general, the UETA is more comprehensive than E-sign. Section 9 of UETA states that an electronic signature must be "attributable to a person" by examining the circumstances surrounding that signature. E-sign does not address attribution issues. The UETA also allows the parties to vary the signature creation and attribution formats by an agreement between the parties. E-sign is for the most part silent on this issue. Under the UETA and most electronic signature laws, evidence of an electronic record or signature may not be excluded merely because that record or signature is in electronic form. Thus a state may enact the UETA and receive its additional protections without running the risk of being preempted by E-sign.

SOFTWARE LICENSING

One of the most prominent industries tied to electronic commerce is the U.S. software industry. Although software sales can be lucrative, the industry is facing an increasingly competitive environment. Users demand ever-increasing complexity, flexibility, and utility in their software products. Substantial price cuts and lower margins pervade the industry. Thus more software must be distributed on a high-volume, mass-market basis in order to be profitable. At the same time, the breath of software applications is as broad as the imagination. Far beyond traditional applications such as word processors and spreadsheets, software components are critical parts of numerous industries and businesses. These rapidly changing business conditions compel the need for a contracting mechanism that can meet the flexible demands of software developers who want to sell the right to use software, but not the right to own the program. That solution lies in the widely used practice of *software licensing*.

Software licensing, at least at its core, is no more complicated than this. When the owner of software decides to transfer to another person the use and enjoyment of his creation, while still retaining the ownership of his creation, that owner provides the user with a license to use that software. With proprietary software, the software code is copyrighted and then distributed under a *license agreement* that gives its users special rights. These licenses usually restrict users to installation of only one copy of their software. As a general rule, only those that have purchased the software may use it under the license. Licensing agreements help the owners preserve their market share, provide a higher return on their investment, and safeguard their intellectual property rights.

Key Terms/Components of a Software Licensing Agreement

Key provisions must be considered whenever drafting or signing a license agreement. These issues should be a part of any software licensing agreement.

Define the Scope of the Agreement. Granting a license assumes, of course, that the licensor holds all applicable rights in the software. The agreement should clearly establish the proprietary rights of the license holder, whether in the United States or worldwide. The scope of the license should address the physical territory in which the licensee may use the software. Such a scope may limit use to a particular geographical region or a particular purpose. For example, the agreement may limit use only to "personal use within the United States." This gives the licensor the right to assert claims against the licensee for exceeding the bounds of the scope of the license.

The scope of the agreement can be very broad (e.g., "to use, distribute copies, prepare derivate works, and display the software publicly") or can be contoured to a specific, limited purpose (e.g., "to execute a single copy of the software on a single computer for the sole purpose of entering data of the licensee"). The license should specifically list certain prohibited actions that would violate the license agreement (e.g., "the licensee may not directly or indirectly copy, publish, or print all or any part of the software"). The license should note that a breach of the license agreement could constitute a basis for a breach of contract claim and a claim for infringement of intellectual property rights.

Any grant of a software license should specify whether the licensee would receive access to the software's source code. If yes, then the license should also state whether or not the licensee may modify or correct that code. Some license agreements allow for a kind of "source code escrow," whereby the licensee obtains access to the source code if the licensor becomes unable to perform corrections or maintenance for the licensee.

Another important part of the scope of a license agreement is the term of the license. A software license may be for a fixed term or a perpetual term. The agreement may be subject to the licensor's ability to revoke or terminate the license at any time. The license should state whether or not the licensee has the power to grant a sublicense to third parties. In essence, a sublicense would grant the third party a subset of the powers given to the original licensee. For example, a software resale or distribution agreement may involve a reseller who can grant sublicenses to end users.

The license should also specify whether or not the licensee may transfer the license to third parties. Unlike a sublicense, such a transfer would be a complete shift of rights from the original licensee to a new licensee. The license may be transferable, but with an exception that it may not be transferred to competitors of the licensor.

The licensee may even wish to be given an exclusive license to the software. Such a license would prohibit the licensor from providing a similar license to another licensees in that software. A licensee may wish such a license because it plans to grant sublicenses to clients and does not want competition from other sources. A geographically selective license may provide the licensee some benefit while allowing the licensor to sell the software elsewhere.

Finally, the license agreement should state that the only licenses granted are those expressly stated in the written agreement. No additional licenses should exist that are being granted by implication or otherwise.

Provide Delivery and Acceptance Provisions. If relevant, the parties should agree on a specific manner of delivery. For example, the licensor may have a password-protected Web site and facilitate the delivery of the software by downloading from the Web site. Software may also be delivered by CD-ROM.

The software license agreement should also specify when the licensee has accepted the conditions of the license. Acceptance of license terms may occur by signing a written contract. Alternatively, acceptance may occur through a special shrink-wrap agreement. A *shrink-wrap agreement*, discussed later in this chapter, informs the licensee before installation to review the agreement and affirmatively assent to the terms by mouse clicks or other affirmative act. The license may grant the licensee a fixed period to review the software for any defects or nonconformance. If nonconformities are found, the license may require the licensee to accept or reject the software or it may require the licensor to cure the defects in the software.

If the license states that source code will be placed in escrow, the agreement should state the manner and deliver of the source code and the particular location of the stored code. Further, the license should also affirm that any updates or patches should be escrowed in the future.

Establish Warranties. Like any commercial contract, a software license should pay particular attention to the presence or absence of any express warranties made by the licensor to the licensee. The warranty may state that the software will perform according to its specifications as described in the documentation (e.g., "Licensor represents and warrants to Licensee that the Software, when properly installed by Licensee and used with the Designated Equipment, will perform substantially as described in University's then current Documentation for such Software for a period of sixty (60) days from the date of shipment."). This is probably one of the most important warranties, as the licensee is no doubt interested in the software reliably performing its described functions without fail. If the software is experimental or new, the warranty may be qualified so it does not require perfect performance (e.g., "perform substantially in all material respects").

Another related warranty establishes that the software is free from defects in its materials and workmanship. This would be most relevant with software delivered by a physical media such as a CD-ROM or diskette. This term would be less relevant if the software were being delivered through the Internet.

The licensor should also warranty that use of the software or its documentation does not infringe on the intellectual property of another. This term affirms that the licensor actually possesses the proper intellectual property rights to grant the license.

If this poses a problem for the licensor, this term may be qualified (e.g., "to the knowledge of the licensor, this software does not infringe . . ."). However, an unqualified statement affirming intellectual property rights will be key for any licensee who wants unfettered use of the software or who wishes to sell sublicenses. Although this may not initially seem a problem for most licensors, the licensor may not be able to determine whether a patent has been filed that the software infringes. Many companies use "submarine patents," which are patents filed but not issued and not made public until a number of infringers emerge. Then, the patent holder suddenly appears and attempts to halt their activities. A licensor cannot know if such patents exist, and thus cannot always affirm with certainty that their software does not infringe on established intellectual property rights.

The licensor should warranty against any defects arising from using the software on or after a particular date (e.g. "the Software will function without error or interruption related to date data, specifically including errors or interruptions from functions which may involve date data from more than one century."). This protects against any future date-related computer glitches that may unexpectedly arise.

The agreement should warranty against the presence of any disabling or malicious code that would destroy or debilitate data entered by the licensee. For example, some software providers place code in the software that prevents unauthorized use of the software. This may give the licensor significant leverage over the licensee's uses that the licensee may not wish the licensor to have. The agreement should also specify that the software is free of viruses.

Provide Limitations of Liability. Virtually all software license agreements contain licensor limitations of liability. Most agreements disclaim liability for consequential, indirect, special, incidental, and punitive damages. Liability may also be limited to a refund of the cost of the software or a specific dollar amount. Agreements may also contain an indemnification provision, requiring the licensee to indemnify the licensor against any claim while using the software outside the scope of the license.

CLICK-WRAP, SHRINK-WRAP, AND BROWSE-WRAP AGREEMENTS

The mass production and sale of software has created the problem of requiring the user to agree to the terms of the software license without a face-to-face meeting between the developer and the user. This problem has been largely solved by the implementation of a **shrink-wrap agreement**, stated inside the box in which the software is packaged. Software is commonly packaged in a container or wrapper that advises the purchaser that the use of the software is subject to the terms of the agreement. The agreement, either presented as a physical shrink wrap or later during installation of the software, states that if the purchaser does not want to enter into the contract, he or she must return the product for a refund, and failure to return it may constitute assent to the license terms.

Much litigation has ensued over the enforceability of shrink-wrap licenses and related agreements. One possible reason is that most users simply do not read them. One study found that 90 percent of the respondents indicated they never read the entire user click-wrap agreement. Also, 55 percent of respondents did not believe they entered into a legally binding contract when they clicked on the "I agree" button. Must buyers of shrink-wrap software obey the terms of shrink-wrap licenses? Does a shrink-wrap or related agreement bind the user to its terms even if the user has never seen them? The following case examines these and other interesting questions.

ProCD, Inc. v. Zeidenberg
86 F.3d 1447 (7th Cir. 1996)

Facts

ProCD, the plaintiff, has compiled information from more than three thousand telephone directories into a computer database [called SelectPhone]. . . . The "shrink-wrap license" gets its name from the fact that retail software packages are covered in plastic or cellophane "shrink-wrap," and some vendors, though not ProCD, have written licenses that become effective as soon as the customer tears the wrapping from the package. Vendors prefer "end-user license," but we use the more common term. . . .

Every box containing its consumer product declares that the software comes with restrictions stated in an enclosed license. This license, which is encoded on the CD-ROM disks as well as printed in the manual, and which appears on a user's screen every time the software runs, limits use of the application program and listings to noncommercial purposes.

Matthew Zeidenberg bought a consumer package of SelectPhone in 1994 from a retail outlet in Madison, Wisconsin, but decided to ignore the license. He formed Silken Mountain Web Services, Inc., to resell the information in the SelectPhone database. The corporation makes the database available on the Internet to anyone willing to pay its price—which, needless to say, is less than ProCD charges its commercial customers. Zeidenberg has purchased two additional SelectPhone packages, each with an updated version of the database, and made the latest information available over the World Wide Web, for a price, through his corporation. ProCD filed this suit seeking an injunction against further dissemination that exceeds the rights specified in the licenses.

Judicial Opinion *(Judge Easterbrook)*

Must buyers of computer software obey the terms of shrinkwrap licenses? The district court held not, for two reasons: first, they are not contracts because the licenses are inside the box rather than printed on the outside; second, federal law forbids enforcement even if the licenses are contracts . . . and we disagree with the district judge's conclusion on each. Shrinkwrap licenses are enforceable unless their terms are objectionable on grounds applicable to contracts in general (for example, if they violate a rule of positive law, or if they are unconscionable).

Transactions in which the exchange of money precedes the communication of detailed terms are common. . . . Someone who wants to buy a radio set visits a store, pays, and walks out with a box. Inside the box is a leaflet containing some terms, the most important of which usually is the warranty, read for the first time in the comfort of home. By Zeidenberg's lights, the warranty in the box is irrelevant; every consumer gets the standard warranty implied by the UCC in the event the contract is silent; yet so far as we are aware no state disregards warranties furnished with consumer products. Drugs come with a list of ingredients on the outside and an elaborate package insert on the inside. The package insert describes drug interactions, contraindications, and other vital information—but, if Zeidenberg is right, the purchaser need not read the package insert, because it is not part of the contract.

Next consider the software industry itself. Only a minority of sales take place over the counter, where there are boxes to peruse. A customer may place an order by phone in response to a line item in a catalog or a review in a magazine. Much software is ordered over the Internet by purchasers who have never seen a box. Increasingly software arrives by wire. There is no box; there is only a stream of electrons, a collection of information that includes data, an application program, instructions, many limitations ("MegaPixel 3.14159 cannot be used with BytePusher 2.718"), and the terms of sale. The user purchases a serial number, which activates the software's features. On Zeidenberg's arguments, these unboxed sales are unfettered by terms—so the seller has made a broad warranty and must pay consequential damages for any shortfalls in performance, two "promises" that if taken seriously would drive prices through the ceiling or return transactions to the horse-and-buggy age. . . .

Zeidenberg has not located any Wisconsin case—for that matter, any case in any state—holding that under the UCC the ordinary terms found in shrinkwrap licenses require any special prominence, or otherwise are to be undercut rather than enforced. In the end, the terms of the license are conceptually identical to the contents of the package. Just as no court would dream of saying that SelectPhone must contain 3,100 phone books rather than 3,000, or must have data no more than 30 days old, or must sell for $100 rather than $150—although any of these changes would be welcomed by the customer, if all other things were held constant—so, we believe, Wisconsin would not let the buyer pick and choose among terms. Terms of use are no less a part of "the product" than are the size of the database and the speed with which the software compiles listings. Competition among vendors, not judicial revision of a package's contents, is how consumers are protected in a market economy. ProCD has rivals, which may elect to compete by offering superior software, monthly updates, improved terms of use, lower price, or a better compromise among these elements. As we stressed above, adjusting terms in buyers' favor might help Matthew Zeidenberg today (he already has the software) but would lead to a response, such as a higher price, that might make consumers as a whole worse off.

THE JUDGMENT IS REVERSED AND REMANDED.

Case Questions

1. Should a buyer be forced to abide by an agreement he or she has not read? Why or why not?
2. According to Judge Easterbrook, when is a shrink-wrap contract formed?
3. What if ProCD placed outrageous terms in the shrink-wrap agreement? Would the terms still be enforceable?

Decisions subsequent to *ProCD* have followed its logic when viewing the validity of similar terms and conditions. For example, in *Brower v. Gateway 2000, Inc.,* 676 N.Y. S.2d 569 (N.Y. App. Div. 1998), Tony Brower sued Gateway alleging that Gateway broke its promise of twenty-four-hour free technical assistance because it was nearly impossible to contact technical support as Gateway promised. Gateway sought to dismiss the lawsuit and to settle the dispute through arbitration as required by the "Standard Terms and Conditions Agreement," which Brower accepted when he purchased his Gateway computer.

Brower claimed that prohibitive filing fees, travel costs, and legal expenses arising from the arbitration clause made the clause unconscionable and established an improper contract of adhesion. Citing the *ProCD* case, the court rejected Brower's arguments, stating that no "take it or leave it proposition" existed because Brower had thirty days to return the merchandise if not satisfied with the agreement. The court also noted that payment preceding the revelation of full contract terms is particularly common in a number of industries. The consumer's failure to read or understand the contract does not invalidate the contract's terms. The court rejected most of Brower's claims and sent the case back to the lower court for further proceedings.

Although *ProCD* has been widely accepted as a leading case on shrink-wraps and computer merchandise agreements, not all software-related agreements are equally valid. The next case highlights the enforceable limits of shrink-wrap-type agreements in software.

[handwritten margin note: contract of adhesion]

Specht v. Netscape Communications Corp.
150 F. Supp. 2d 585 (S.D. N.Y. 2001)

Facts

Defendant Netscape, a provider of computer software programs that enable and facilitate the use of the Internet, offers its "SmartDownload" software free of charge on its Web site to all those who visit the site and indicate, by clicking their mouse in a designated box, that they wish to obtain it. SmartDownload is a program that makes it easier for its users to download files from the Internet without losing their interim progress when they pause to engage in some other task, or if their Internet connection is severed. . . .

Visitors wishing to obtain SmartDownload from Netscape's Web site arrive at a page pertaining to the download of the software. On this page, there appears a tinted box, or button, labeled "Download." By clicking on the box, a visitor initiates the download. The sole reference on this page to the License Agreement appears in text that is visible only if a visitor scrolls down through the page to the next screen. If a visitor does so, he or she sees the following invitation to review the License Agreement: "Please review and agree to the terms of the *Netscape SmartDownload software license agreement* before downloading and using the software." Visitors are not required affirmatively to indicate their assent to the License Agreement, or even to view the license agreement, before proceeding with a download of the software. . . .

Judicial Opinion *(Judge Hellerstein)*

Plaintiffs allege that usage of the software transmits to Defendants private information about the user's file transfer activity on the Internet, thereby effecting an electronic surveillance of the user's activity in violation of two federal statutes. . . . Defendants move to compel arbitration and stay the proceedings, arguing that the disputes reflected in the Complaint, like all others relating to use of the software, are subject to a binding arbitration clause in the End User License Agreement ("License Agreement"), the contract allegedly made by the offeror of the software and the party effecting the download. Thus, I am asked to decide if an offer of a license agreement, made independently of freely offered software and not expressly accepted by a user of that software, nevertheless binds the user to an arbitration clause contained in the license.

Unless the Plaintiffs agreed to the License Agreement, they cannot be bound by the arbitration clause contained therein. My inquiry, therefore, focuses on whether the Plaintiffs, through their acts or failures to act, manifested their assent to the terms of the License Agreement proposed by Defendant Netscape. More specifically, I must consider whether the web site gave Plaintiffs sufficient notice of the existence and terms of the License Agreement, and whether the act of downloading the software sufficiently manifested Plaintiffs' assent to be bound by the License Agreement.

In order for a contract to become binding, both parties must assent to be bound. . . .

[This principle enjoys] continuing vitality in the realm of software licensing. The sale of software, in stores, by mail, and over the Internet, has resulted in several specialized forms of license agreements. For example, software commonly is packaged in a container or wrapper that advises the purchaser that the use of the software is subject to the terms of a license agreement contained inside the package. The license agreement generally explains that, if the purchaser does not wish to enter into a contract, he or she must return the product for a refund, and that failure to return it within a certain period will constitute assent to the license terms. These so-called "shrink-wrap licenses" have been the subject of considerable litigation. [The court then summarized the *ProCD* case and its conclusions.]

For most of the products it makes available over the Internet (but not SmartDownload), Netscape uses another common type of software license, one usually identified as "click-wrap" licensing. A click-wrap license presents the user with a message on his or her computer screen, requiring that the user manifest his or her assent to the terms of the license agreement by clicking on an icon. The product cannot be obtained or used unless and until the icon is clicked. For example, when a user attempts to obtain Netscape's Communicator or Navigator, a web page appears containing the full text of the Communicator/ Navigator license agreement. Plainly visible on the screen is the query, "Do you accept all the terms of the preceding license agreement? If so, click on the Yes button. If you select No, Setup will close." Below this text are three button or icons: one labeled "Back" and used to return to an earlier step of the download preparation; one labeled "No," which if clicked, terminates the download; and one labeled "Yes," which if clicked, allows the download to proceed. Unless the user clicks "Yes," indicating his or her assent to the license agreement, the user cannot obtain the software. The few courts that have had occasion to consider click-wrap contracts have held them to be valid and enforceable. . . .

The SmartDownload License Agreement in the case before me differs fundamentally from both click-wrap and shrink-wrap licensing. . . . Click-wrap license agreements and the shrink-wrap agreements . . . require users to perform an affirmative action unambiguously expressing assent *before* they may use the software, that affirmative action is equivalent to an express declaration stating, "I assent to the terms and conditions of the license agreement" or something similar. For example, Netscape's Navigator will not function without a prior clicking of a box constituting assent. Netscape's SmartDownload, in contrast, allows a user to download and use the software without taking any action that plainly manifests assent to the terms of the associated license or indicates an understanding that a contract is being formed. . . .

Netscape argues that the mere act of downloading indicates assent. However, downloading is hardly an unambiguous indication of assent. The primary purpose of downloading is to obtain a product, not to assent to an agreement. In contrast, clicking on an icon stating "I assent" has no meaning or purpose other than to indicate such assent. Netscape's failure to require users of SmartDownload to indicate assent to its license as a precondition to downloading and using its software is fatal to its argument that a contract has been formed.

Furthermore, unlike the user of Netscape Navigator or other click-wrap or shrink-wrap licensees, the individual obtaining SmartDownload is not made aware that he is entering into a contract. SmartDownload is available from Netscape's web site free of charge. Before downloading the software, the user need not view any license agreement terms or even any reference to a license agreement, and need not do anything to manifest assent to such a license agreement other than actually taking possession of the product. From the user's vantage point, SmartDownload could be analogized to a free neighborhood newspaper, readily obtained from a sidewalk box or supermarket counter without any exchange with a seller or vender. It is there for the taking.

The only hint that a contract is being formed is one small box of text referring to the license agreement, text that appears below the screen used for downloading and that a user need not even see before obtaining the product: "Please review and agree to the terms of the *Netscape SmartDownload software license agreement* before downloading and using the software."

Couched in the mild request, "Please review," this language reads as a mere invitation, not as a condition. The language does not indicate that a user *must* agree to the license terms before downloading and using the software. While clearer language appears in the License Agreement itself, the language of the invitation does not require the reading of those terms or provide adequate notice either that a contract is being created or that the terms of the License Agreement will bind the user.

The case law on software licensing has not eroded the importance of assent in contract formation. Mutual assent is the bedrock of any agreement to which the law will give force. Defendants' position, if accepted, would so expand the definition of assent as to render it meaningless. Because the user Plaintiffs did not assent to the license agreement, they are not subject to the arbitration clause contained therein and cannot be compelled to arbitrate their claims against the Defendants.

For the reasons stated, I deny Defendants' motion to compel arbitration.

SO ORDERED.

Case Questions

1. What is the difference between a click-wrap license, a shrink-wrap license, and the license in *Specht*?
2. Why is the license not enforceable? What makes it different than the agreement in *ProCD*?
3. What should Netscape have done to make SmartDownload's agreement enforceable in court?

E-COMMERCE AND INSURANCE: INSURING ONLINE CONTRACTING RISK

No matter how careful we try to be, we are always subject to risk—accidents, injuries, fire, flood, vandalism, and other catastrophes. With thousands of traditional businesses selling their goods and services online, and a host of e-entrepreneurs starting new businesses every day, inevitably companies large and small will suffer from damage, accidents, or other mishap. No doubt, with business comes risk, and with risk comes insurance. Most traditional companies have a standard commercial general liability policy that protects the company against liabilities imposed on the insured from claims that the insured's conduct somehow caused injury to the person or property of another.

Most insurance is based on basic principles. An insurance contract is called a *policy*. An individual or business that obtains protection of an insurance policy, often called the *insured*, pays a premium to the insurance company in exchange for the insurance coverage. One of the most common kinds of policies purchased by businesses is a commercial liability insurance policy. Broadly defined, a **liability insurance policy** is an insurance policy purchased to provide insurance protection against liability to third persons for covered losses. It is one of the oldest forms of insurance in the United States.

In the electronic commerce context, companies confront claims or lawsuits by customers or others who complain that the insured's software or other electronic product caused them to incur "property damage." For example, an insured software manufacturer may sell a defective program to a retail store. The software malfunctions, causing the store to close temporarily and lose revenue. The store sues the software manufacturer, which then demands a defense and payment by its insurance company. The critical issue in the case would be whether the injured party suffered the type of harm for which such insurance is written. The standard commercial general liability policy contains a specific definition of the term *property damage*, usually defined as "physical injury to tangible property, including all resulting loss of use of that property or loss of use of tangible property that is not physically injured."

The question of whether traditional insurance policies cover electronic commercial mishaps is far from settled. The following two cases represent opposing views on the issue.

State Auto Property & Casualty Insurance Company v. Midwest Computers & More
147 F. Supp. 2d 1113 (W.D. Okla. 2001)

Facts

Defendant's business is computer sales, repair, and service. Plaintiff is an insurer who issued a business owners' liability policy to defendant. The policy provides coverage for "property damage" to "tangible property." The pertinent definition in the policy states,

> "Property damage" means:
>
> a. Physical injury to tangible property, including all resulting loss of use of that property . . . ; or b. Loss of use of tangible property that is not physically injured. . . . In 1999, William C. Spray and Patricia Spray d/b/a Spray Appraisals purchased a computer from defendant and hired defendant to perform certain computer services. The Sprays filed suit against defendant in June 2000 alleging that negligent performance of service work on the computer system had caused [loss of] . . . extensive amounts of appraisal data and other business information which was stored on their computer system. Defendant has made a claim against the policy for coverage to defend the Sprays's lawsuit and to indemnify defendant for any damages that it becomes liable to pay as a result of the lawsuit.

By this action, plaintiff seeks a declaratory judgment that its policy does not cover the Sprays's alleged loss and thus that it has no duty to indemnify or defend its insured with respect to the lawsuit. Defendant has countersued for breach of the insurance contract. By the present motions, both parties seek summary adjudication of their coverage dispute. They agree on the relevant facts and a legal issue to be decided: "Is the [Sprays's] computer data, allegedly destroyed by the acts of the Defendant, 'tangible' property within the meaning of the Defendant's insurance policy?"

Judicial Opinion (Judge Alley)

According to Oklahoma law, an insurance policy is a contract. If the terms are unambiguous, clear, and consistent, they are to be accepted in their ordinary sense and enforced to carry out the expressed intentions of the parties. Here, the parties ask the Court to decide the meaning of a single term, "tangible property;" no ambiguity in the policy is alleged or presented. Were the Court to decide this question, it would conclude that computer data is intangible, not tangible, personal property. "Terms of an insurance policy must be considered not in a technical but in a popular sense, and must be construed according to their plain, ordinary, and accepted sense in the common speech of men, unless it affirmatively appears from the policy that a different meaning was intended" [*Webb v. Allstate Life Ins. Co.*, 536 F.2d 336, 339 (10th Cir. 1976)]. Ordinary meanings of "tangible," according to a commonly used English dictionary, include "capable of being perceived esp. by the sense of touch: palpable [;] . . . capable of being precisely identified or realized by the mind [;] . . . capable of being appraised at an actual or approximate value (assets)" [*Webster's Ninth New Collegiate Dictionary*, p. 1205 (1985)].

None of these definitions fits data stored on a computer disk or tape. Although the medium that holds the information can be perceived, identified, or valued, the information itself cannot be. Alone, computer data cannot be touched, held, or sensed by the human mind; it has no physical substance. It is not tangible property.

Therefore, under the undisputed facts and record presented, plaintiff's insurance policy does not cover defendant's claim concerning the loss of computer use and computer data alleged in the Sprays' lawsuit. Plaintiff is entitled to judgment as a matter of law on the coverage issue and on defendant's counterclaim for breach of contract.

Plaintiff's Motion for Summary Judgment is GRANTED; Defendant's Motion for Summary Judgment is DENIED. Judgment will be entered accordingly.

Case Questions

1. What is the difference between "physical injury to tangible property" and "loss of use"? Which clause in the policy would more likely be helpful to a software company?
2. What could the insured have done to prevent the result in this case?

As a general rule, liability policies require injury or loss of use to *tangible property*, generally defined as property that has physical form and substance. It is property that may be seen, weighed, measured, felt, touched, or is in any manner perceptible to the senses. Insurance companies have increasingly argued that data, information stored on computer drives and other electronically captured material, does not constitute tangible property under liability insurance policies. Where a computer glitch causes actual physical injury to goods, there would appear to be injury to tangible property. However, where the error results simply in loss of data, causing business interruption, loss of goodwill, or remediation costs to restore the data, nothing tangible is damaged, and the claim is more likely a traditional breach of contract or warranty action between the customer and the supplier of the computer or software.

The next case also addresses insurance coverage, but takes a more expansive view of the term *physical damage*. As you read, consider which case, *Ingram Micro* or *Midwest Computers,* makes more sense in a twenty-first century economy.

American Guarantee & Liability Insurance Company v. Ingram Micro, Inc.
2000 WL 726789, No. 99-185 TUC ACM (D. Ariz. April 18, 2000)

Facts

Ingram is a wholesale distributor of microcomputer products. The company uses a worldwide computer network (the Impulse System) to track its customers, products, and daily transactions. . . . All of Ingram's orders are processed through Impulse, and Ingram's entire business operation depends on the proper functioning of Impulse.

In October 1998, Ingram procured an insurance policy from American which insured Ingram's "[r]eal, and personal property, business income and operations in the world wherever situated except for U.S. Embargo Countries." The policy insured against "All Risks of direct physical loss or damage from any cause, howsoever or wheresoever occurring, including general average, salvage charges or other charges, expenses and freight." Ingram's computers, including Impulse, are insured under the policy.

At approximately 8 A.M. on the morning of December 22, 1998, the Data Center experienced a power outage that was apparently caused by a ground fault in the fire alarm panel. Although electrical power service to the building itself was not disrupted, all of the electronic equipment at the Data Center, including the computers and telephones, stopped working. . . .

Connections between Tucson and six Impulse locations in the United States and Europe were interrupted and Ingram could not conduct business. After working for hours to determine the source of the problem, Ingram employees finally brought the network back up to operation by means of bypassing a malfunctioning matrix switch. Impulse was restored to full operation by 4 P.M., approximately eight hours after the shutdown.

In the days following the power outage, Ingram employees determined that when the power outage occurred, all of the programming information disappeared from the random access memory. The custom configurations that existed prior to the outage were different than the default settings after the outage. So when power was restored to the matrix switch, the custom configurations remained lost. The matrix switch had to be reprogrammed with the necessary custom configurations before communications with the six Impulse locations could be restored.

[As a result of the power outage, Ingram filed a claim under its policy to American. American denied the claim. American then filed a complaint for declaratory relief against Ingram. Ingram responded by filing a breach of contract claim against American. Each side filed a motion for summary judgment, both attempting to dismiss the opposing party's action before trial.]

Judicial Opinion (*Judge Marques*)

American and its expert witnesses admit that Ingram's mainframe computers and the matrix switch did not function as before the power outage and that certain data entry and reconfiguration processes were necessary to make Impulse operate as it had before the power outage. American argues, however, that the computer system and the matrix switch were not "physically damaged" because their capability to perform their intended functions remained intact. The power outage did not adversely affect the equipment's inherent ability to accept and process data and configuration settings when they were subsequently reentered into the computer system.

Ingram argues that the fact that the mainframe computers and the matrix switch retained the ability to accept the restored information and eventually operate as before does not mean that they did not undergo "physical damage." Ingram offers a broader definition of this term and contends that "physical damage" includes loss of use and functionality.

At a time when computer technology dominates our professional as well as personal lives, the Court must side with Ingram's broader definition of "physical damage." The Court finds that "physical damage" is not restricted to the physical destruction or harm of computer circuitry but includes loss of access, loss of use, and loss of functionality. . . .

Lawmakers around the country have determined that when a computer's data is unavailable, there is damage; when a computer's services are interrupted, there is damage; and when a computer's software or network is altered, there is damage. Restricting the Policy's language to that proposed by American would be archaic. . . .

In this case, Ingram *does* allege property damage—that as a result of the power outage, Ingram's computer system and worldwide computer network physically lost the programming information and custom configurations necessary for them to function. Ingram's mainframes were "physically damaged" for one and one half hours. It wasn't until Ingram employees manually reloaded the lost programming information that the mainframes were "repaired." Impulse was "physically damaged" for eight hours. Ingram employees "repaired" Impulse by physically bypassing a malfunctioning matrix switch. Until this restorative work was conducted, Ingram's mainframes and Impulse were inoperable. . . .

Accordingly,

IT IS ORDERED THAT INGRAM'S MOTION FOR PARTIAL SUMMARY JUDGMENT IS GRANTED.

IT IS FURTHER ORDERED THAT AMERICAN'S CROSS-MOTION FOR SUMMARY JUDGMENT REQUESTING DECLARATION OF "NO COVERAGE" IS DENIED.

Case Questions

1. How does the court interpret the term *physical damage*?
2. What does the court mean when it says, "restricting the policy's language to that proposed by American would be archaic"?
3. What do you think would happen to the cost of insurance premiums if this case became the law? How could this decision ultimately affect the price of goods for online consumers?

As the decisions here reveal, the viability of traditional commercial general liability policies for electronic commerce is far from certain. What should electronic commerce business do in order to ensure protection? The obvious answer is to obtain insurance that specifically encompasses coverage for online-related damage.

For example, a business may insure for damages caused by computer viruses. Viruses cost business over $1.6 trillion a year and about 40,000 human years of productivity worldwide. Companies may also wish to insure against online fraud and theft. Also, business interruption insurance may also be necessary for online companies that depend on a constant stream of Internet access to survive. Internet insurance policies are increasingly customized by policyholders and insurance companies to face the diverse needs of online business. Business owners need to determine for themselves what kinds of electronic commerce risks they may be exposed to and what kind of damage could result from those risks.

INTERNATIONAL ASPECTS OF ELECTRONIC CONTRACTING

As electronic commerce transforms into a truly global phenomenon, the need for international regulation of the area has developed along with it. A number of international regulatory frameworks exist that attempt to govern the global cyber-marketplace. Although none of these frameworks are binding everywhere, each provides guidance on a number of issues regarding electronic commerce.

UN Convention on Contracts for the International Sale of Goods

The **UN Convention on Contracts for the International Sale of Goods (UNCISG)** represents the fundamental international framework addressing international goods commerce. Widely accepted among nations, the U.S. Senate ratified the UNCISG and it became U.S. law on January 1, 1988. Thus, if a U.S. buyer contracts for goods with a seller that has also ratified the convention, UNCISG will govern the contract. Unless the parties opt out of UNCISG, it applies automatically.

Much of the UNCISG is similar to the Uniform Commercial Code. However, some key differences do exist. For example, under the UCC a contract for goods over $500 must be in writing to be enforceable. The UNCISG has no such writing requirement. The UCC states that an offer is irrevocable only if it is in writing and for a fixed period. The UNCISG permits some offers to be irrevocable even if not in writing. When an acceptance of a contract between merchants contains new minor terms, the UCC generally allows the contract to form. The UNCISG, however, requires that the acceptance be a "mirror image" of the offer and replicate the offer in all respects. Otherwise, the UNCISG considers the nonmatching acceptance a rejection of the offer. Nevertheless, the UNCISG represents the predominant framework regulating goods contracts internationally.

Solution for Internation commerce by UN

UNCITRAL Model Law on E-Commerce

The **United Nations Commission on International Trade Law (UNCITRAL)** model law on electronic commerce is the international standard for developing a coherent global regulatory system. In 1996, the UN General Assembly recommended that the model law be adopted by all members. This document represented the culmination of a decade of international cooperation.

The model law focuses on general rather than specific prescriptions. The model law does not describe in detail how to create legally binding electronic documents. Also, the law does not require the use of a particular technology in order to meet any requirements. Electronic documents are legally effective if they satisfy the functional equivalence of paper documents. Regarding signatures, Article 7 of the model law requires not only that a method be used that both identifies the originator and confirms the originator's approval, but also be "as reliable as was appropriate" for its intended purpose. Article 10 recognizes that information initially set out on paper may be transferred to an electronic medium and still satisfy record requirements for an original. Similarly, messages are also given equal respect to admissibility and evidentiary weight in legal proceedings. Finally, Article 14 discusses determining receipt of a message, focusing on whether or not a data message was received and not on whether it has been read, as the critical factor for acknowledgment.

The model law has three general limitations. First, the model law does not establish specific provisions relating to consumers, perhaps because of the difficulty of defining a consumer in a global context. Second, the model law limits itself to commercial activities only, although governments are also looking to the model law for the delivery of services and programs. Third, the model law does not contain significant enforcement and liability provisions.

EU Directive Concerning E-Commerce

European Union (EU) representatives have been gradually developing a legal framework regulating electronic commerce through a number of initiatives over the past ten years. The EU does not yet have a unifying framework like UCITA but is developing electronic commerce initiatives in a number of areas. For example, in 1998, EU representatives proposed harmonizing legislation in the following four areas: commercial communications, online formation of contracts, liability of intermediaries, and enforcement issues. In addition, the EU has produced a selling directive that places limitations on online contracts to consumers in the fifteen member states. Other work by the EU has focused on database protection, protection of personal data, electronic signatures, and contract negotiations.

↘http://

- For more information on EU directives addressing electronic commerce, see **http://www.europa.eu.int**

Summary

A contract is a legally enforceable promise. The parties must manifest by words or conduct their *mutual assent* to a contract. Usually this is done when one of them makes an offer and the other accepts it. Additionally, the contract must involve an exchange of *consideration;* the parties must have the legal *capacity* to contract; and the contract itself must be *legal.* Also, some contracts must be in *writing*; in the United States, the most common contracts that must be in writing are those involving a sale of goods for more than $500.

The making of contracts electronically has presented the law with the challenge of applying traditional legal concepts to new circumstances. Contracts made electronically present the parties with the unique problem of complying with writing and signature requirements. Electronic signature acts are meant to solve this problem, but they have not been adopted in all states. Software licensing represents a major forum of electronic commerce with a number of pitfalls for both the licensor and the licensee. In addition, click-wrap contracts made by large software vendors are increasingly under scrutiny by courts.

The UCITA and the UETA have made efforts to develop a uniform law, but with varying degrees of success. The UCITA has proven to be very controversial, and consumer groups oppose it because it would preempt existing state consumer protection laws. Manufacturers and retailers support it because it simplifies and validates contracts made electronically.

Problem solution

Even if various acts exist to govern electronic commerce, companies will inevitably expose themselves to business risk. Traditional insurance is not sufficient to protect against liability. Insurance directly addressing electronic commerce is necessary to protect the interests of a modern firm. Finally, a developing international law exists to add stability and uniformity to international transactions. Virtually all electronic commerce contains a global component, and any manager that ignores international law issues in e-commerce does so at his or her peril.

Key Terms

e-commerce, *152*
Restatement Second
   of the Law of
   Contract, *155*
Uniform Commercial
   Code (UCC), *155*
requirements of a
   contract, *155*
unconscionable contract, *159*
warranty, *161*

Uniform Computer Infor-
   mation Transactions Act
   (UCITA), *166*
Uniform Electronic Trans-
   actions Act (UETA), *170*
E-sign, *172*
shrink-wrap agreement,
   176
liability insurance
   policy, *182*

UN Convention on Con-
   tracts for the International
   Sale of Goods (UNCISG),
   187
United Nations Commission
   on International Trade
   Law (UNCITRAL),
   187

Manager's Checklist

√ The UCITA is the predominant uniform code regulating electronic commerce in the United States. However, only two states have adopted it, and its provisions remain highly controversial.

√ Software licenses much be specifically tailored to meet the needs of both the license and the licensee.

√ Be aware that some courts as well as the UCITA regard shrink-wrap and click-wrap licenses as valid.

√ Be aware that the law is unsettled as to whether a minor who misrepresents his or her age will be able to avoid a contract entered into online.

√ Most (but not all) states have adopted electronic signature acts that give legal effect to electronic records and signatures.

√ Online firms should minimize their risk of doing business by purchasing insurance that specifically addresses electronic commerce issues.

√ Although U.S. law requires that contracts for the sale of goods for more than $500 must be in writing, this is not required for most international sales or for sales between merchants in other countries.

√ Ethical Considerations

Consider whether or not a binding arbitration clause buried within a lengthy user agreement violates a business's ethical responsibility to avoid unfair surprises for the consumer.

Consider whether or not it is unethical for a company to establish contract terms that may be accessed only after the product is purchased by the consumer.

Case Problems

1. The Wisconsin Pharmacy Examining Board censured the Walgreen Company for accepting and filling drug prescriptions by e-mail because Wisconsin state law requires prescriptions to bear a signature. Walgreen appealed, contending that filling prescriptions by e-mail was similar to filling prescriptions over the telephone, and that state law does not require a pharmacy to receive a signed prescription in such a case. What is the result? [*Walgreen Co. v. Wisconsin Pharmacy Examining Board*, 577 N.W. 2d 387, 1998 WL 65551 (Wis. Ct. App. 1998)]

2. Prospective subscribers to the Microsoft Network are prompted by Microsoft software to view multiple screens of information, including a membership agreement containing a forum selection clause. The forum selection clause requires that any claims against Microsoft must be litigated only in the state of Washington. Prospective subscribers must assent to the clause by clicking on an "I agree" button to receive the subscription. Steve Caspi, a subscriber, sued Microsoft in New Jersey, claiming that Microsoft improperly rolled over his membership into a more expensive category without notice. Microsoft sought to dismiss the action, citing the presence of the forum selection clause. What is the result? [*Caspi v. Microsoft Network, LLC*, 732 A. 2d 528 (N.J. App. Div. 1999)]

3. Microsoft entered into a software licensing arrangement with Sun Microsystems that entitled Microsoft to include Sun's Java software code in Microsoft's Internet Explorer 4 Web browser and to include a statement on the browser's packaging that it is Java compliant. Microsoft used the code but made changes

to it so it would not work with other browsers, contrary to the agreement made with Java. Sun sued for contract infringement and for an injunction forbidding Microsoft from releasing the browser with the noncompliant code and the "Java compliant" statement. Should Sun's request be granted? [*Sun Microsystems Inc. v. Microsoft Corp.* 21 F. Supp. 2d 1109 (N.D. Cal. 1998)]

4. Seagate Technology manufactured disk drive storage devices for personal computers and small business machines. Amstrad, a United Kingdom corporation, purchased Seagate disk drives for its personal computers and sold personal computers in which the Seagate drives were incorporated. Amstrad sued Seagate, alleging the drives were defective. Seagate demanded insurance coverage and defense protection from its carrier, St. Paul Fire & Marine Insurance Company. Seagate had purchased insurance from St. Paul covering "bodily injury and property damage liability," which insured against loss due to physical damage and loss of use of "tangible property." Does the sale of defective hard drives constitute loss of "tangible property" under the insurance policy? [*Seagate Technology, Inc. v. St. Paul Fire and Marine Insurance Co.,* 11 F. Supp. 2d 1150 (N.D. Ca. 1998)]

5. The M. A. Mortenson Co. licensed software from Timberline Software Corp. that was to be used by contractors for preparing construction bids. The license contained the following disclaimer:

> LIMITATION OF REMEDIES AND LIABILITY. NEITHER TIMBERLINE NOR ANYONE ELSE WHO HAS BEEN INVOLVED IN THE CREATION, PRODUCTION, OR DELIVERY OF THE PROGRAMS OR USER MANUALS SHALL BE LIABLE TO YOU FOR ANY DAMAGES OF ANY TYPE, INCLUDING BUT NOT LIMITED TO, ANY LOST PROFITS, LOST SAVINGS, LOSS OF ANTICIPATED BENEFITS, OR OTHER INCIDENTAL, OR CONSEQUENTIAL DAMAGES ARISING OUT OF THE USE OR INABILITY TO USE SUCH PROGRAMS, WHETHER ARISING OUT OF CONTRACT, NEGLIGENCE, STRICT TORT, OR UNDER ANY WARRANTY, OR OTHERWISE, EVEN IF TIMBERLINE HAS BEEN ADVISED OF THE POSSIBILITY OF SUCH DAMAGES OR FOR ANY OTHER CLAIM BY ANY OTHER PARTY. TIMBERLINE'S LIABILITY FOR DAMAGES IN NO EVENT SHALL EXCEED THE LICENSE FEE PAID FOR THE RIGHT TO USE THE PROGRAMS.

Mortenson installed and used the software to prepare a bid. It encountered an error while doing so, but it nevertheless submitted the bid generated by the program. After submitting the bid, Mortenson discovered the bid was $2 million less than it should have been. Mortenson subsequently sued Timberline for breach of contract for failing to deliver operable software. Timberline argued that its disclaimer excused it from liability. Is Timberline liable? [*M. A. Mortenson Co. v. Timberline Software Corp.,* 998 P. 2d 305 (Wash. 2000)]

Additional Readings

- Brinson, J. Dianne, and Radcliffe, Mark F. *Internet Law and Business Handbook*. Port Huron, MI: Lasera Press, 2000.

- Kennedy, Dennis M. "Key Legal Issues in E-Commerce: The Law Comes to a New Frontier," *Thomas M. Cooley Law Review* 18 (2001): 17.

- Maggs, Gregory E. "Regulating Electronic Commerce." *American Journal of International Law* 50 (2002): 665.

- Rustad, Michael L., and Daftary, Cyrus. *E-Business Legal Handbook*. New York: Aspen Law and Business, 2002.

SALES TAX IN E-COMMERCE

The growing inability of states to collect sales and use tax from remote sales impacts the future of states' primary consumption tax. The general sales and use tax provides about one-third of state revenue—over $150 billion in 1998—with most of the funds dedicated to finance K–12 education. For six states, sales tax revenue accounts for over 50 percent of all state revenue. According to the Center for Business Research at the University of Tennessee, by 2003 states will lose $11 billion in sales tax revenue due to the emergence and growth of electronic commerce.

—**Testimony of Senator Steven Rauschenberger, Illinois State Senate, Co-Chair, National Conference of State Legislatures Task Force on State and Local Taxation of Telecommunications & Electronic Commerce before the Finance Committee, U.S. Senate, October 26, 2000**

LEARNING OBJECTIVES

After you have read this chapter you should be able to:

1. Explain the requirements for a state to obtain tax jurisdiction over an out-of-state e-business.
2. Understand a *tax nexus*.
3. Explain the U.S. Constitution's limitations on tax jurisdiction.
4. Understand and explain a sales tax and how it is used in e-commerce transactions.
5. Understand and explain a use tax and how it may be used in e-commerce.
6. Understand state statutory exemptions on sales taxes.
7. Explain the Internet Tax Freedom Act of 1998.
8. Explain the role of the Advisory Commission on Electronic Commerce under the Internet Tax Freedom Act of 1998.
9. Explain the significance of the *Quill Corp v. North Dakota* case to the taxation of e-commerce transactions.
10. Understand international initiatives coordinating global Internet taxation.
11. Define and explore the meaning of "permanent establishment."
12. Discuss the impact of the EU value-added tax on Internet sales.

- Additional material on taxation may be found at the Bentley College CyberLaw Center Web site (**http://ecampus.bentley.edu/dept/cyberlaw**) under Business and Financial Issues—Taxation.

INTRODUCTION

Senator Steven Rauschenberger's statement, quoted at the beginning of this chapter, is a clear indication of the enormous revenues lost by a state's inability to require online companies to collect and remit sales taxes from its customers simply because they have no physical presence in the state. In June 2000, the U.S. General Accounting Office published a study of estimated sales tax losses from remote out-of-state sellers in a report entitled *Sales Taxes: Electronic Commerce Growth Presents Challenges; Revenue Losses Are Unknown*. It estimated national sales tax losses from remote sales to be as high as $20 billion in the year 2003.

http://

- The General Accounting Office report, *Sales Taxes: Electronic Commerce Growth Presents Challenges; Revenue Losses Are Unknown*, is found at **http://www.gao.gov/new.items/g600165.pdf**

This chapter discusses the latest developments on reforming the state sales tax system in an attempt to collect sales tax from e-commerce ventures with no physical presence in a state. Online services and products are generally sold from remote locations to consumers in a manner similar to a mail-order catalog purchase. The out-of-state e-business must have a **nexus**, or physical connection, with the taxing state where the customer is located, before it is obligated to collect and remit to the state the sales tax. E-tailers that have this physical connection (nexus) with the state are collectors of tax revenue from consumers.

For example, if you purchase a book at a Barnes & Noble brick-and-mortar bookstore in a state with a sales tax, you pay the tax at the point of sale. If you buy the same book online from Amazon.com in a state with no retail store or warehouse, you do not pay the sales tax.

Should an e-business without a retail store, doing business in a state with a sales tax, be exempt from collecting the tax from the online shopper and paying the state the sales tax? Should e-commerce retail transactions in the same state be treated any differently from Main Street brick-and-mortar shops, simply because the e-business has no physical store in that state? Companies have often moved to a state or country because of its favorable tax treatment. This has always been a costly step involving an assessment of the foreign country's political stability, its labor market, infrastructure, and other considerations. A pure e-business can easily move from one state to another with no sales tax to avoid tax liability.

An e-business should always explore the tax consequences of the state where it will do business and consider selecting a desirable tax site. For example, an online consumer in Maryland purchases a computer from a New Hampshire e-business that is shipped from a New Hampshire warehouse. Because New Hampshire has no sales tax, the Web merchant, with no physical presence in Maryland, has no obligation to collect a sales tax from the online consumer. If the same consumer purchased the computer in a retail store in Maryland, the local merchant would have to collect sales tax. This chapter focuses on the e-commerce sales transactions with special emphasis on sales and use taxes. It also discusses how the U.S. Constitution's due process and commerce clauses place limitations on the state's authority to tax an e-business.

Taxation in Cyberspace

Taxation in cyberspace assumes various forms. The states may impose a sales tax or a use tax on a resident consumer and, provided it has sufficient nexus (i.e., a connection with the out-of-state e-business), compel the seller to collect the sales tax and remit it to the state. Both the sales and use tax are based on a flat rate, usually between 3 percent and 8 percent of the gross receipts of the sale. What would the Internet economy's tax base represent within this context?

Sales tax is paid by the consumer at the point of purchase on tangible personal property and collected by the seller/vendor. It is charged on the gross amount of the sale or leased transaction and collected where the sales tax originated.

Most states rely on sales tax for much of their revenue. The Advisory Commission on Intergovernmental Relations reports that about 7,500 state and local jurisdictions impose sales and use taxes.

Currently only five states do not charge a sales tax: Alaska, Delaware, Montana, New Hampshire, and Oregon. Forty-five states do have a sales tax, and eleven applied it to Internet sales transactions prior to October 1, 1998. **Use tax** is imposed on the consumer for tangible goods purchased out of state for use within the taxing state. For example, if a resident of Massachusetts buys a computer in New Hampshire where there is no sales tax and intends to use the computer in Massachusetts, the purchaser should pay a use tax to the state of Massachusetts.

Usually because this tax is self-assessed, it is generally *not* paid (see Figure 7.1). The emerging and sustained conflict on Internet taxation revolves around the state's ability and willingness to tax sales transactions in e-commerce and the obstacle to e-commerce growth resulting from this taxation. In addition to the fifty states, various local counties would like to impose a sales tax on e-commerce transactions.

As we already mentioned, this amounts to more than 7,500 tax jurisdictions. Imagine the confusion caused by the various tax rules and regulations imposed on an e-business with the obligation of charging and collecting a sales tax on its transactions. Violation of these tax statutes imposes a sales tax liability on the Web merchant and, if intentional, could result in criminal prosecution. Is this an unreasonable burden to impose on an out-of-state e-business that has no brick-and-mortar store in the state and does not use the tax-supported infrastructure that offline stores rely on? Certain sales transactions are generally exempt by state statue from sales and use tax. They commonly include food, clothing, and nontangible transactions such as services. Because these exemptions differ from state to state, it is important to review the state tax statute.

State Tax Jurisdiction Under the U.S. Constitution

Before a state may tax a sales transaction, it must have tax jurisdiction over the out-of-state merchant. Tax jurisdiction requires a company to have a physical presence in the state, referred to as a *substantial nexus*. The physical presence requirement usually takes the form of a retail store, warehouse, employees, or sales representatives doing business in the taxing state. The taxing state must prove this nexus before an out-of-state

FIGURE 7.1   Use Tax Form

FORM ST-11
(Rev. 4/96)

Massachusetts Department of Revenue
Individual Use Tax Return

Name

Social Security number

Address   State   Zip

Return is due with payment on or before April 15 for purchases made in the prior calendar year. Make check payable to the Commonwealth of Massachusetts. Mail to: **Massachusetts Department of Revenue, PO Box 7009, Boston, MA 02204.**

I declare under the penalties of perjury that this return has been examined by me and to the best of my knowledge and belief is a true, correct and complete return.

Signature

1. Year purchases made **1**

2. Total purchases from line 9 on reverse **2**

3. Use tax (5% of line 2) **3**

4. Total credit for sales/use tax paid to other states or jurisdictions. From line 10 on reverse **4**

5. Balance. *Subtract line 4 from line 3.* Not less than "0" **5**

6. Penalty **6**

7. Interest **7**

8. Total amount due **8**

Date

Date of purchase	Name of seller, city and state	Quantity and description of property purchased	A. Sales price	B. Sales/use tax paid to other jurisdictions *or* 5% of sales price — *whichever is less*

9. Total purchases. Add all of the purchase prices listed in column A. Enter the result here and in line 2 on the front. ▶ | $

10. Total sales/use tax paid to other states or jurisdictions. Add all of the amounts listed in column B. Enter the result here and in line 4 on the front. ▶ | $

Attach an additional statement if more space is necessary

9M 3/98 CRP0198

company is required to collect the tax from the buyer and remit it to the state. This tax jurisdiction requirement has for years, prior to electronic commerce, given mail-order companies an advantage over local retail stores.

Mail-Order Transactions

Mail-order companies include catalog sales, direct marketing, and cable television shopping. Because they have no physical presence in an out-of-state sale, they generally do not have to collect and remit the sales tax. Mail-order forms usually list the states where consumers must pay a sales tax and request them to submit it with the purchase order (see Figure 7.2).

FIGURE 7.2 Order Form

Sur La Table

CATALOG DIVISION
1765 6TH AVENUE SOUTH
SEATTLE, WASHINGTON
98134-1608

ORDER TOLL FREE
800 243-0852
24 HOURS A DAY

ORDERED BY:
Name and address should be that of person placing order. Please make corrections as necessary.

SHIP TO:
☐ Same ☐ Different ☐ See gift forms below

Name
C/o
Address
City, State, Zip
E-mail Address
▶ Day Phone ( )

Please fill in order form completely, including item numbers.

LINE	QTY	ITEM #	DESCRIPTION	✓GIFT WRAP	UNIT PRICE	TOTAL
1						
2						
3						
4						
5						
6						
GIFT #1	Name		Gift Message			
	Address					
	City State Zip		Recipient's Phone ( )			
7						
8						
GIFT #2	Name		Gift Message			
	Address					
	City State Zip		Recipient's Phone ( )			
9						
10						

PAYMENT METHOD:
☐ Check or Money Order ☐ VISA ☐ MasterCard
☐ American Express ☐ Novus

Expiration Date ________ Signature ________

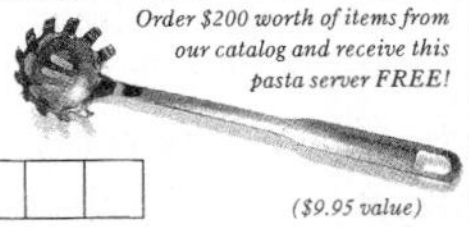

Order $200 worth of items from our catalog and receive this pasta server FREE!

($9.95 value)

Merchandise Total	
Add $5 for each Gift Wrap	
Subtotal	
Add Delivery Charges per Address (*see ordering information*)	
Additional Shipping Charges (*AK, HI, 2nd day and overnight delivery*)	
State Sales Tax*	
GRAND TOTAL	

ORDER TOLL FREE 800 243-0852 • FAX 206 682-1026 • www.surlatable.com

Local Main Street retail stores find this unjust and discriminatory because they have to charge and collect the sales tax, whereas an out-of-state mail-order house or e-business with no physical presence in the state is exempt. A Web out-of-state merchant doing e-business in a foreign state where it has no physical presence is treated for sales tax purposes like a mail-order business. It must charge and collect sales if its home state has a sales tax, but there is no obligation to do so if it has no physical presence there.

In the following leading tax case, *National Bellas Hess, Inc. v. Dept. of Rev. of the State of Ill.,* 386 U.S. 753, 1967, a Missouri mail-order house had no property, office, outlets, or any sales representatives in Illinois. The court ruled that the imposition by the state of Illinois that the Missouri mail-order house collect a sales tax on the sale of its products to Illinois residents violated the due process clause and the **commerce clause** of the U.S. Constitution (see Figure 7.3).

FIGURE 7.3   Commerce Clause Test for Tax Purposes

- E-business needs a substantial nexus with the taxing state
- The tax must be fairly apportioned
- Tax cannot discriminate
- Tax must be fairly related to the services provided by the state

National Bellas Hess, Inc. v. Dept. of Rev. of the State of Illinois
386 U.S. 753 (1967)

Facts

National Bellas Hess is a mail-order house with a principal place of business in North City, Missouri. It is licensed to do business in only that state and in Delaware, where it is incorporated.

Although the company has neither outlets nor sales representatives in Illinois, the Department of Revenue obtained a judgment from the Illinois Supreme Court that National is required to collect and pay to the state a use tax. Because National's constitutional objections to the imposition of this liability present a substantial federal question, we noted probable jurisdiction of its appeal. National does not maintain in Illinois any office, distribution house, sales house, warehouse, or any other place of business; it does not have in Illinois any agent, salesman, canvasser, solicitor, or other type of representative to sell or take orders, to deliver merchandise, to accept payments, or to service merchandise it sells. It does not own any tangible property, real or personal, in Illinois, it has no telephone listing in Illinois, and it has not advertised its merchandise for sale in newspapers, on billboards, or by radio or television in Illinois. All of the contacts that National does have with the state are via the U.S. mail or common carrier. Twice a year catalogs are mailed to the company's active or recent customers throughout the nation, including Illinois. This mailing is supplemented by advertising flyers, which are occasionally mailed to past and potential customers. Orders for merchandise are mailed by the customers to National and are accepted at its Missouri plant. The ordered goods are then sent to the customers either by mail or by common carrier.

This manner of doing business is sufficient under the Illinois statute to classify National as a "retailer maintaining a place of business in this State," because that term includes any retailer "engaging in soliciting orders within this State from users by means of catalogues or other advertising, whether such orders are received or accepted within or with this State" [Ill. Rev. Stat. C. 120, 439.2 (1965)].

Bellas Hess must also "keep records, receipts, invoices and other pertinent books, documents, memoranda and papers as the State shall require, in such form as the State shall require, and must submit to such investigations, hearings, and examinations as are needed by the State to administer and enforce the use tax law." Failure to keep such records or to give required receipts is punishable by a find of up to $5,000 and imprisonment of up to six months. Finally, to allow service of process on an out-of-state company like National, the statute designates the Illinois secretary of state as National's appointed agent, and jurisdiction in tax collection suits attaches when process is served on him and the company is notified by registered mail.

Judicial Opinion *(Justice Stewart)*

National argues that the liabilities which Illinois has thus imposed violate the Due Process Clause of the Fourteenth Amendment and create an unconstitutional burden upon interstate commerce. These two claims are closely related. For the test of whether a particular state exaction is such as to invade the exclusive authority of Congress to regulate trade between the States, and the test for a State's compliance with the requirements of due process in this are similar. As to the former, the Court has held that "State taxation falling on interstate commerce . . . can only be justified as designed to make such commerce bear a fair share of the cost of the local government whose protection it enjoys." And in determining whether a state tax falls within the confines of the Due Process Clause, the Court has said that the "simple but controlling question is whether the state has given anything for which it can ask return." The same principles have been held applicable in determining the power of a State to impose the burdens of collecting use taxes upon interstate sales.

Here, too, the Constitution requires "some definite link, some minimum connection, between a state and the person, property or transaction it seeks to tax." In applying these principles the Court has upheld the power of a State to impose liability upon an out-of-state seller to collect a local use tax in a variety of circumstances. Where the sales were arranged by local agents in the taxing state, we have upheld such power. We have reached the same result where the mail-order seller maintained local retail stores. In those situations the out-of-state seller was plainly accorded the protection and services of the taxing State.

But the Court has never held that a State may impose the duty of use tax collection and payment upon a seller whose only connection with customers in the State is by common carrier or the United States mail.

In order to uphold the power of Illinois to impose use tax burdens on National in this case, we would have to repudiate totally the sharp distinction which these and other decisions have drawn between mail-order sellers with retail outlets, solicitors, or property within a State, and those who do no more than communicate with customers in the State by mail or common carrier as part of a general interstate business. But this basic distinction, which until now has been generally recognized by the state taxing authorities, is a valid one, and we decline to obliterate it. And if the power of Illinois to impose use tax burdens upon National were upheld, the impediments upon the free conduct of its interstate business would be neither imaginary nor remote. For if Illinois can impose such burdens, so can every other State, and so, indeed, can every municipality, every school district, and every other political subdivision throughout the National with power to impose sales and use taxes. The many variations in rates of tax, in allowable exemptions, and in administrative and record-keeping requirements could entangle National's interstate business in a virtual welter of complicated obligations to local jurisdictions with no legitimate claim to impose "a fair share of the cost of the local government."

The very purpose of the Commerce Clause was to ensure a national economy free from such unjustifiable local entanglements. Under the Constitution, this is a domain where Congress alone has the power of regulation and control.

The judgment is reversed.

Reversed *(Judge Fortas, dissenting)*

There should be no doubt that this large-scale, systematic, continuous solicitation and exploitation of the Illinois consumer market is a sufficient "nexus" to require Bellas Hess to collect from Illinois customers and to remit the use tax, especially when coupled with the use of the credit resources of residents of Illinois, dependent as that mechanism is upon the State's banking and credit institutions. Bellas Hess is not simply using the facilities of interstate commerce to serve customers in Illinois. It is regularly and continuously engaged in "exploitation of the consumer market" of Illinois by soliciting residents of Illinois who live and work there and have homes and banking connections there, and who, absent the solicitation of Bellas Hess, might buy locally and pay the sales tax to support their State. Bellas Hess could not carry on its business in Illinois, and particularly its substantial credit business, without utilizing Illinois banking and credit facilities. Since the case was tried on affidavits, we are not informed as to the details of the company's credit operations in Illinois. We do not know whether it utilizes credit information or collection agencies or similar institutions. The company states that it has "brought no suits in the State of Illinois." Accepting this as true, it would nevertheless be unreasonable to assume that the company does not either sell or assign its accounts or otherwise take measures to collect its delinquent accounts, or that collection does not include local activities by the company or its assignees or representatives.

Bellas Hess enjoys the benefits of, and profits from the facilities nurtured by, the State of Illinois as fully as if it were a retail store or maintained salesmen therein. Indeed, if it did either, the benefit that it received from the State of Illinois would be no more than it now has—the ability to make sales of its merchandise, to utilize credit facilities, and to realize a profit; and, at the same time, it would be required to pay additional taxes. Under the present arrangement, it conducts its substantial regular, and systematic business in Illinois and the State demands only that it collect from its customers—users—and remit to the State the tax which is merely equal to the sales tax which resident merchants must collect and remit. To excuse Bellas Hess from this obligation is to burden and penalize retailers located in Illinois who must collect the sales tax from their customers.

Case Questions

1. What are the circumstances, mentioned in the court's decision, when a state may impose liability on an out-of-state seller to collect a local use tax?
2. What were the arguments presented by the dissenting opinion for Bellas Hess to collect and remit the use tax?
3. Who would have the best ethical arguments for use tax collection, the majority or dissenting opinion? Explain.

The following leading U.S. Supreme Court case, *Quill v. North Dakota,* 504 U.S. 298 (1992), held that the interstate commerce clause of the U.S. Constitution requires an out-of-state merchant to have a physical presence before it can be obligated to collect its taxes. Notice how the Supreme Court refused to overrule the 1967 *National Bellas Hess* case. Be aware as you read this case how the Court distinguished between the commerce clause that provides a different nexus requirement from the due process clause.

Quill Corp. v. North Dakota
504 U.S. 298 (1992)

Facts

Quill is a Delaware corporation with offices and warehouses in Illinois, California, and Georgia. None of its employees work or reside in North Dakota, and its ownership of tangible property in that State is either insignificant or nonexistent. Quill sells office equipment and supplies; it solicits business through catalogs and flyers, advertisements in national periodicals, and telephone calls. Its annual national sales exceed $200 million, of which almost $1 million are made to about three thousand customers in North Dakota. It is the sixth-largest vendor of office supplies in the state. It delivers all of its merchandise to its North Dakota customers by mail or common carrier from out-of-state locations.

As a corollary to its sales tax, North Dakota imposes a use tax on property purchased for storage, use, or consumption within the state. North Dakota requires every "retailer maintaining a place of business in" the state to collect the tax from the consumer and remit to the state. In 1987, North Dakota amended the statutory definition of the term *retailer* to include "every person who engages in regular or systematic solicitation of a consumer market in the state." State regulations, in turn, define "regular or systematic solicitation" to mean three or more advertisements within a twelve-month period. Thus, since 1987, mail-order companies that engage in such solicitation have been subject to the tax even if they maintain no property or personnel in North Dakota.

Quill has taken the position that North Dakota does not have the power to compel it to collect a use tax from its North Dakota customers. Consequently, the state, through it tax commissioner, filed this action to require Quill to pay taxes (as well as interest and penalties) on all such sales made after July 1, l987. The trial court ruled in Quill's favor, finding the case indistinguishable from *Bellas Hess;* specifically, it found that because the state had not shown that it had spent tax revenues for the benefit of the mail-order business, there was no "nexus to allow the state to define retailer in the manner it chose." The North Dakota Supreme Court reversed, concluding that "wholesale changes" in both the economy and the law made it inappropriate to follow *Bellas Hess* today. The principal economic change noted by the court was the remarkable growth of the mail-order business "from a relatively inconsequential market niche" in 1967 to a "goliath" with annual sales that reached "the staggering figure of $183.3 billion in 1989."

Moreover, the court observed, advances in computer technology greatly eased the burden of compliance with a "welter of complicated obligations" imposed by state and local taxing authorities.

Judicial Opinion *(Justice Stevens)*

As in a number of other cases involving the application of state taxing statutes to out-of-state sellers, our holding in *Bellas Hess* relied on both the Due Process Clause and the Commerce Clause. Although the "two claims are closely related," the clauses pose distinct limits on the taxing powers of the States. Accordingly, while a State may, consistent with the Due Process Clause, have the authority to tax a particular taxpayer, imposition of the tax may nonetheless violate the Commerce Clause.

The two constitutional requirements differ fundamentally, in several ways. The Due Process Clause and the Commerce Clause reflect different constitutional concerns. Moreover, while Congress has plenary power to regulate commerce among the States and thus may authorize state actions that burden interstate commerce, it does not similarly have the power to authorize violations of the Due Process Clause.

Thus, although we have not always been precise in distinguishing between the two, the Due Process Clause and the Commerce Clause are analytically distinct.

In "modern commercial life" it matters little that solicitation is accomplished by a deluge of catalogs rather than a phalanx of drummers: the requirements of due process are met irrespective of a corporation's lack of physical presence in the taxing State. Thus, to the extent that our decisions have indicated that the Due Process Clause requires physical presence in a State for the imposition of duty to collect a use tax, we overrule those holdings as superseded by developments in the law of due process.

In this case, there is no question that Quill has purposefully directed its activities at North Dakota residents, that the magnitude of those contacts are more than sufficient for due process purposes, and that the use tax is related to the benefits Quill receives from access to the State. We therefore agree with the North Dakota Supreme Court's conclusion that the Due Process Clause does not bar enforcement of that State's use tax against Quill.

The State contends that the nexus requirements imposed by the Due Process and Commerce Clauses are equivalent, and that if a mail-order house that lacks a physical presence in the taxing State nonetheless satisfied the due process "minimum contacts" test, then that corporation also meets the Commerce Clause "substantial nexus" test. We disagree. Despite the similarity in phrasing, the nexus requirements of the Due Process and Commerce Clauses are not identical. The two standards are animated by different constitutional concerns and policies.

Due process centrally concerns the fundamental fairness of governmental activity. Thus, at the most general level, the due process nexus analysis requires that we ask whether an individual's connections with a State are substantial enough to legitimate the State's exercise of power over him. We have, therefore, often identified "notice" or "fair warning" as the analytic touchstone of due process nexus analysis. In contrast, the Commerce Clause, and its nexus requirement, are informed not so much by concerns about fairness for the individual defendant as by structural concerns about the effects of state regulation on the national economy. Under the Articles of Confederation, State taxes and duties hindered and suppressed interstate commerce; the Framers intended the Commerce Clause as a cure for these structural ills. It is in this light that we have interpreted the negative implication of the Commerce Clause. Accordingly, we have ruled that the Clause prohibits discrimination against interstate commerce.

Undue burdens on interstate commerce may be avoided not only by a case by case evaluation of the actual burdens imposed by particular regulations or taxes, but also, in some situations, by the demarcation of a discrete realm of commercial activity that is free from interstate taxation.

Bellas Hess followed the latter approach and created a safe harbor for vendors "whose only connection with customers in the [taxing] State is by common carrier or the United States mail." Under *Bellas Hess*, such vendors are free from state imposed duties to collect sales and use taxes.

A bright line rule in the area of sales and use taxes also encourages settled expectations and, in doing so, fosters investment by businesses and individuals. Indeed, it is not unlikely that the mail-order industry's dramatic growth over the last quarter century is due in part to the bright line exemption from state taxation created in *Bellas Hess*.

In sum, although in our cases subsequent to *Bellas Hess* and concerning other types of taxes we have not adopted a similar bright line, physical presence requirement, our reasoning in those cases does not compel that we now reject the rule that *Bellas Hess* established in the area of sales and use taxes. To the contrary, the continuing value of a bright line rule in this area and the doctrine and principles of *stare decisis* indicate that the *Bellas Hess* rule remains good law. For these reasons, we disagree with the North Dakota Supreme Court's conclusion that the time has come to renounce the bright line test of *Bellas Hess*.

This aspect of our decision is made easier by the fact that the underlying issue is not only one that Congress may be better qualified to resolve, but also one that Congress has the ultimate power to resolve. No matter how we evaluate the burdens that use taxes impose on interstate commerce, Congress remains free to disagree with our conclusions. Indeed in recent years Congress has considered legislation that would "overrule" the *Bellas Hess* rule. Its decision not to take action in this direction may, of course, have been dictated by respect for our holding in *Bellas Hess* that the Due Process Clause prohibits States from imposing such taxes, but today we have put that problem to rest. Accordingly, Congress is now free to decide whether, when, and to what extent the States may burden interstate mail order concerns with a duty to collect use taxes.

Indeed, even if we were convinced that *Bellas Hess* was inconsistent with our Commerce Clause jurisprudence, "this very fact [might] give us pause and counsel withholding our hand, at least for now. Congress has the power to protect interstate commerce from intolerable or even undesirable burdens." In this situation, it may be that "the better part of both wisdom and valor is to respect the judgment of the other branches of the Government." The judgment of the Supreme Court of North Dakota is reversed and the case is remanded for further proceedings not inconsistent with this opinion.

IT IS SO ORDERED.

Case Questions

1. Explain why the Court distinguishes the due process clause from the commerce clause for tax purposes.

2. Why did the Court state that "[T]he underlying issue is not only one that Congress may be better qualified to resolve, but also one that Congress has the ultimate power to resolve"?

3. Is it ethical for a mail-order company doing substantial business in a state not to pay state sales tax simply because it has no "physical presence" in that state?

Although the *Quill* decision explicitly allows Congress to enact legislation for the states to impose sales and use taxes on products sold by an out-of-state merchant, it has to date failed to do so. In view of the enormous loss of state revenue, you can expect state representatives to continue their request to tax remote sales for mail-order and e-commerce transactions.

Physical Presence Nexus Test for E-Commerce

An out-of-state Web merchant may have a physical presence for tax jurisdiction purposes without having a retail store in the taxing state. In order to avoid being subject to collecting and paying a sales tax to the taxing state, an online company should be aware of other reasons for establishing a tax nexus with the e-business that are the foundation of the **physical presence test**:

1. Renting an office or a warehouse in the taxing state

2. Holding trade shows where employees or agents take orders from customers in the taxing state

3. Using a Web merchant's server

4. Working with a server in the taxing state

5. Maintaining inventory in a taxing state

6. Licensing software to licensees in a taxing state

7. Hiring agents in the taxing state

8. Maintaining a business relationship with a brick-and-mortar affiliated company in the taxing state

9. Falling under the market maintenance theory

Next we examine each reason in detail.

Renting an Office or Warehouse. An e-business that leases office or warehouse space is considered to have a "nexus" for tax purposes even if the office or warehouse is not used to generate sales. Because most e-commerce retailing requires the inventory to be stocked in a warehouse and often shipped by UPS or FedEx to the remote customer, this is an important consideration. An e-business should consider leasing an office or warehouse in one of the five states that does not impose a sales tax.

Holding Trade Shows. Suppose your e-business sells software and you send a few employees to an e-commerce trade show to display and sell your products. If the state where the trade show is located has a sales tax, the sales transactions of your employees or agents at the trade show could result in a nexus for state tax jurisdiction. Tax nexus depends on how long the employees attended the trade show and how much revenue was generated. Managers should consult with their tax advisers to determine the tax effect of trade show attendance. Even though your company has no physical presence at the trade show in a taxing state, having agents who are sales representatives, employees, or independent contractors working on sales on behalf of your company may constitute a tax **nexus by attribution** and a resulting obligation to collect the sales tax.

Using a Web Merchant's Server. One of the perplexing questions regarding state taxation of e-commerce is whether having a server in a state constitutes a physical and a substantial tax nexus. It may be possible for a Web merchant who owns, leases, or rents a server in a state with a sales or use tax to have a tax nexus in that state. If your server is in a jurisdiction where you fill orders, you may be subject to sales tax liability in that state.

Maintaining Inventory in a Taxing State. An e-business that maintains a warehouse for inventory purposes can result in a tax nexus for those states imposing a sales or use tax. Warehoused property that is sold may result in a sales tax imposed by the state where the warehouse is located when the buyer is a resident of that state. For example, assume a book is purchased by an Arizona resident from Amazon.com located in the state of Oregon. If its *warehouse* were in Arizona, Amazon would have to collect the sales tax and remit it to the state of Arizona.

The sale of digital software products over the Internet creates special sales tax problems because software is not tangible personal property, and it can be sold and delivered electronically. An online buyer of software generally pays with a credit card number that does not identify the address of the buyer. Because the sale is made by allowing the buyer to download the software, there is no physical delivery of a tangible product, and the e-business vendor may not know where the sale was made. This prevents the e-business from complying with a sales tax in the state of purchase. Software stacked in a warehouse in a state with a sales tax may subject the vendor to collecting the sales tax. At issue is whether the software is tangible personal property. Nineteen states impose sales tax on the sale of intangible goods sold over the Internet. A company selling software online should try to avoid having a Web-based business in those states taxing the online sale of software.

Licensing Software to Licensees in a Taxing State. Suppose a Web company develops software and licenses it in a state with a sales tax. Depending on the number of licensees in the taxing state, the licensor may have a tax nexus and be required to collect the sales tax. Failure to do so will result in a penalty tax on the licensor.

Hiring Agents in the Taxing State. A Web merchant's agent (independent contractor or sales representatives) in the foreign state may create nexus for sales and use tax purposes. It is not necessary that the vendor's agents be its employees in order to create a tax nexus in the foreign state. In the following U.S. Supreme Court case, the court ruled that independent agents soliciting sales in Florida for an out-of-state retailer created a tax nexus in Florida. Notice how the Court found a connection between the state and the out-of-state merchant based on sales solicitations by independent sales agents of Scripto, Inc.

A Pure E-Business Maintaining a Business Relationship with a Brick-and-Mortar Affiliated Company. Barnes & Noble.com is an independent company from Barnes & Noble, Inc., its brick-and-mortar affiliate. The latter has several stores in California and distributed to its customers $5 Barnes & Noble.com coupons in promotional shopping bags with B&N on one side and "bn.com" on the other. The California Board of Equalization ruled in The Petition for Redetermination of Barnes & Noble.com, No. 89872 (September 12, 2002) that Barnes & Noble.com, through its relationship with B&N, Inc., had a sufficient physical presence within California to obligate it to collect sales tax from its California customers. Not all states would follow this California decision. In *Bloomingdale's v. Dept. of Revenue*, 527 Pa. 347, cert. denied, 504 U.S. 955 (1992), the acceptance of returns by a brick-and-mortar company affiliate was not a physical nexus for sales tax purposes when there were independent reasons for accepting the returns that were an insignificant quantity.

Falling Under the Market Maintenance Theory. Tax nexus between an out-of-state vendor and the taxing state may be based on the **market maintenance theory**, when the vendor's state activities are significantly associated with the taxpayer's ability to establish and maintain a market in the state for its sales. In *Tyler Pipe Industries, Inc. v. Dept. of Revenue*, 483 U.S. 232 (1987), the court ruled that through sales contacts, the representatives maintained and improve the name recognition, market share, goodwill, and individual customer relations of the company and, therefore, subjects the company to the state's tax nexus.

Notice how in each of the nine tests of establishing a tax nexus for sales tax purposes, an e-business must be aware of subtle business associations that are very difficult to determine. The business must work closely with its tax adviser as it pursues expanding markets.

Internet Tax Freedom Act of 1998

In an effort to prevent the states from enacting new tax legislation that would tax Internet transactions, in October 1998 Congress passed the **Internet Tax Freedom Act (ITFA)** as part of H.R. 4328, the supplemental omnibus appropriations bill, preventing federal, state, and local governments from enacting new Internet taxes for a period of three years, that was in effect until 2001. Critics contended the moratorium discriminated against traditional retail stores that subsidized the out-of-state Internet retailer.

The 19-member **Advisory Commission on Electronic Commerce**, created by the ITFA, heard testimony from various interest groups and made recommendations to

Congress that the moratorium be extended until November 2003. The ITFA required a membership on the Advisory Commission consisting of 3 representatives from the federal government (comprised of the secretary of commerce, the secretary of the treasury, and the U.S. trade representative), 8 representatives from the state and local governments, and 8 representatives from the electronic commerce industry, telecommunications carriers, local retail business, and consumer groups. The contentious discussions by the Advisory Commission, consisting of 19 members, is evidenced by the simple majority of only 10 members that voted for the no new taxes extension. Congress has voted to extend the act to November 2003.

Sales Tax and the Dormant Commerce Clause

The Commerce Clause of the U.S. Constitution, in Article 1, Section 8, Clause 3, provides that, "The Congress shall have power. . . . to regulate commerce . . . among the several states." The dormant aspect of this clause (the commerce clause) is a judge-made doctrine first articulated by Chief Justice Marshall in *Wilson v. Black-bird Creek Marsh Co.*, 27 U.S. 245 (1949), when he described a "power to regulate commerce in its dormant state." The theory behind the dormant commerce clause is that even when Congress does not regulate interstate commerce, the power given to Congress is dormant, and the states may not regulate interstate commerce.

If Congress should not extend the ITFA in November 2003, would a state law that imposes a sales tax collection burden on an out-of-state Internet sales transaction violate the dormant commerce clause doctrine? In *New Energy Co., of Ind. v. Limbach*, 486 U.S. 269, 273-74 (1988), the Supreme Court ruled the dormant commerce clause "prohibits economic protectionism—that is, regulatory measures designed to benefit in-state economic interests by burdening out-of-state competitors." One could argue a sales tax collection burden on an out-of-state e-tailer would violate this holding.

In *Santa Fe Natural Tobacco, Inc. v. Spitzer* (S.D. N.Y. 2000), the court ruled a New York statute that prohibited out-of-state retailers from selling cigarettes in New York through the Internet discriminated against interstate commerce in favor of local retailers was per se invalid. The court stated that although the New York statute was enacted "for the purpose of protecting in-state retailers from competition from out-of-state direct sellers . . . such protection, while welcomed by in-state retailers, is impermissible under the commerce clause." We can surely expect to see further litigation on Internet sales as the states attempt to impose a sales tax collection burden on out-of-state e-tailers who argue that doing so interferes with free trade in interstate commerce.

A NEW SALES TAX SYSTEM: THE STREAMLINE SALES TAX PROJECT (SSTP)

As previously discussed, our present sales tax system requires a retail company with a tax nexus in the state or county to collect and remit the appropriate tax collected from

►http://

- See the Streamline Sales Tax Project Web site at **http://www.streamlinedsalestax.org/index.html**

the buyer. An e-business doing business in all states has a potential sales tax obligation in over 7,500 taxing jurisdictions, each with its own definition of what is taxable, the rate to be charged, the tax form to be used, when the tax is due, and where to register. No wonder the online companies are opposed to any new sales taxes.

An initiative by state and local governments, with input from the private sector, called the *Streamlined Sales Tax Project* (STSP), has an objective to simplify and modernize sales and use tax collection and administration for remote online and offline sales transactions. This SSTP represents a national momentum to upgrade the sales tax system to a level consistent with e-commerce in the twenty-first century. The SSTP objective is to unify definitions for key terms in the tax base, including sales tax exemptions, and the use of technology to reduce the burden on the merchant to collect and remit the sales tax to the state.

The SSTP is comprised of two phases. The first phase, the Uniform Sale and Use Tax Administration Act (USUTA), has proposed model state legislation with uniform definitions of sales tax provisions such as sales price, purchase price, retail stores, delivery charges, clothing, and food. This enabling legislation authorizes the adopting states to enter into the second phase, entitled the *Streamlined Sales and Use Tax Agreement* (STUTA).

http://www.streamlinedsalestax.org/index.html

Alabama	Arkansas	District of Columbia	Florida	Illinois	Indiana	Iowa	Kansas	Kentucky	Louisiana	Maine	Maryland	Michigan
Minnesota	Mississippi	Missouri	Nebraska	New Jersey	Nevada	North Carolina	North Dakota	Ohio	Oklahoma	Pennsylvania
Rhode Island	South Carolina	South Dakota	Tennessee	Texas	Utah	Vermont	Washington	West Virginia	Wisconsin	Wyoming

Streamlined Sales Tax Project
promoting a streamlined sales tax system for the 21st century

- SSTP Home
- About the Project
- Meetings & Materials
- Press Releases
- Issue Papers
- Library
- St. Legislative Status
- 2002-03 Timeline
- Collection Cost Study
- Resolutions

Sites You May Wish To Visit
Federation of Tax Administrators

Latest News and Developments

1/06/03 – Updated Executive Summary – December 2002

12/05/02 – New Advisory Group
In an effort to make sure we all get off to a good start drafting our legislation and educating our legislators, we have created a committee to act as a resource to you as you draft legislation, rules, regulations and policies implementing the SST Agreement. Our hope is that this group is large enough to make sure someone has an answer to any question that gets asked, but if it isn't we will draw in the topic experts as needed. The questions you ask will be the start of the interpretation of the agreement. We will sort and publish all questions and answers. To help ensure quality control and consistency, please send your questions to everyone on the attached list. Thank you for your continued support of this project.
Scott Peterson

11/12/02 – Final SSTIS Agreement

PROJECT MISSION
The Streamlined Sales Tax Project will develop measures to design, test and implement a sales and use tax system that radically simplifies sales and use taxes.

STEERING COMMITTEE
Co-Chairs
Diane Hardt (WI)
Scott Peterson (SD)

Members
Carol Fischer (MO)
Harold Fox (NJ)
R. Bruce Johnson (UT)
Eleanor Kim (TX)
Tom Kimmett (PA)
Charlotte Quarles (KY)
Marshall Stranburg (FL)

Twenty-nine states have currently adopted both phases of the SSTP. There are currently thirty-eight states actively engaged in the SSTP. Enabling legislation or executive orders by the governors has authorized thirty-two of these states as voting participants. The remaining six states are nonvoting participants and are awaiting authorization by the legislature or governor to become voting members of the SSTP.

The SSTP attempts to unify the 7,500 sales tax jurisdictions in the United States that impose different definitions of personal tangible property and tax exemptions, along with different tax rates. Because most e-businesses without a physical presence in the taxing state are not required to collect and remit sales taxes, state governors can see a substantial loss in sales tax revenues. The traditional Main Street retailer sees a discrimination based on the pure online retailer that is not required to collect a sales tax.

Sales Tax Simplification Under the SSTP

The SSTP has stated a plan for sales tax simplification consisting of the following aspects:

Uniform Definitions. State legislators will continue to have the authority to determine what personal property will be subject to a state sales tax and what property will be exempt. However, there will be a common definition for key terms found in the tax base.

Simplified Sales Tax Exemption Administration. The current practice of the merchant/seller acting in "good faith" and being responsible for identifying and verifying a buyer's sales tax exemption status will be replaced by the buyer being liable for an incorrect claimed exemption. Buyers will be required to display identifying information and reasons for claiming the sales tax exemption at the point of purchase. The merchant/vendor would then be legally protected if the buyer was not in compliance.

Simplified Sales Tax Rates. The current practice of states and local tax authorities changing the sales tax rate will be changed to require the state to give adequate notice of any change in the tax rate. The individual states would be responsible for the administration of all local taxes and would distribute the revenues to the local governments. Both state and local governments would be required to use a common tax base. Because thousands of local governments levy a sales tax, this would relieve the remote merchant's burden in tracking sales tax rate changes.

Simplified Sales Tax Returns. A merchant must not only collect and remit the sales tax but is also required to file state sales tax returns. Because currently all states and some local governments have different sales tax returns, this provision would allow one uniform sales tax return and relieve the merchant of the costly administrative burden of multiple filings.

Standardized Tax Remittance Schedule. A timely sales tax remittance is difficult for the merchant/vendor operating in multiple states because the states and local governments have different due dates for remitting the tax revenue collected from the consumers. The SSTP would require a standard schedule of sales tax remittance among the taxing authorities.

Standardized Audit Procedures. The SSTP provides for a Streamlined Sales Tax Pilot project that provides for advanced technology models to simplify and reduce the cost of collecting the sales tax and, if adopted by a merchant, would assure the merchant is not subject to a sales tax audit or will have a limited audit, depending on the selected technology used. The Streamlined Sales Tax Pilot grants the state the authority to "certify" the technology used by the merchant to collect the sales tax and remit it to the state. A merchant using state-certified technology to collect and remit the sales tax that fails to function properly would be granted a "safe harbor" from a sales tax assessment resulting from a sales tax audit.

State Payment for the Sales Tax System. In order to reduce the cost of implementing the advanced technology of the sales tax collecting system, the states will pay for part of the system by allowing the merchant to keep a portion of the sales tax collected. Although about half of the states currently allow the merchant to keep a portion of the sales tax collected on its behalf, the SSTP would require all participating states to keep a portion of the collected sales tax.

Streamlined Sales Tax Pilot: Technology Models. The Streamlined Sales Tax Pilot would allow the merchant/vendor to utilize one of three technological models. All of the models must be certified first by the taxing state before being used by the merchant.

- *Model I. Certified Service Provider.* Under this technological program, the software performs all of the merchant/vendor's tax obligations imposed by the taxing state. The program collects the tax from the consumer at the point of purchase, computes the correct sales tax assessed by the state, remits the sales tax collected to the state within a timely fashion, and prepares and files the sales tax return on behalf of the merchant. This model is especially appropriate because it relieves the merchant from the entire tax burden with the exception of oversight and internal auditing to assure tax compliance.
- *Model II. Certified Automated System.* This technological model is a software program that performs only the sales tax calculation function and requires the merchant to collect and remit the sales tax to the state and file the sales tax return. It may be of value to a small e-business that wants control over the relatively few sales tax transactions in cross-border states.
- *Model III. Internal System Certified by the State.* A substantial national business that can afford a self-developed sales tax software system may do so, but the system must be certified by each state where it transacts business. Any software model selected by an e-business must be approved by each state where the

merchant/vendor is doing business. The SSTP will continue to review technological models based on pilot testing.

Streamline Sales Tax Pilot: Sales Tax Compliance by an Outside Certified Service Provider (CSP)

The Streamlined Sales Tax Pilot is part of Phase II of the Streamline Sales Tax Project found in the Streamlined Sales and Use Tax Agreement. A function of the pilot project, that began on October 1, 2000, is to continue testing available sales tax software technology that helps outside vendors calculate, collect, remit, and file sales tax returns on behalf of the merchant/vendor.

Internet Tax Moratorium and Equity Act (S. 512)

In the 107th Congress, the Internet Tax Moratorium and Equity Act (ITMEA) was introduced on March 9, 2001, by its sponsor, Senator Byron Dorgan (D-N.D.), and referred to the Senate Commerce Committee. The bill states that Congress may facilitate equal taxation regarding a traditional retail establishment with mail order, telephone, or the Internet, consistent with the U.S. Supreme Court's decision in *Quill Corp. v. North Dakota*. Of great significance are the similar provisions of the ITMEA found in the Streamlined Sales Tax Project. It provides for the development of a streamlined sales and use tax system by Congress, the states and localities that address the issues of the SSTP such as a centralized, one-stop, multiregistration system for sellers, uniform definitions for goods or services that may be included in the tax base, uniform procedures for the treatment of purchases exempt from sales and use taxes, a uniform procedure for the certification of software that sellers rely on to determine sales and use tax rates, a uniform format for tax returns and remittances forms, and uniform audit procedures. The net effect of the ITMEA would be to allow a taxing state that has adopted the compact consistent with the act's guidelines to require the remote "pure-play" e-business retailer to collect and remit the sales tax in the same manner as the Main Street retailer.

INTERNATIONAL INTERNET TAXATION

Companies have made tremendous investments developing electronic commerce operations that further global sales of their goods and services. Billions of dollars are already exchanged over the Internet, and that amount is guaranteed to grow. A necessary companion to any volume of transactions is the question of when and how those transactions should be taxed. The sheer volume of electronic commerce has provoked an unprecedented debate among nations and international organizations regarding the proper status of international Internet taxation.

Organization of Economic Cooperation and Development Initiatives

The *Organization of Economic Cooperation and Development (OECD)* is an international body dedicated to addressing the economic, social, and governance challenges of its thirty member countries. Members include most European countries, Japan, Korea, and the United States. The OECD has been examining international taxation issues for some time and has presented a number of initiatives aiming at developing an overarching framework addressing international Internet taxation.

http://

- Documents relating to the OECD can be found at **http://www.oecd.org**

Committee on Fiscal Affairs Report, 1998. In October 1998, the OECD Committee on Fiscal Affairs presented a report at the OECD conference titled *A Borderless World, Realising the Potential of Electronic Commerce* in Ottawa, Canada. This report outlined a number of general principles for developing a system of fair and efficient taxation of electronic commerce. These principles have focused on a number of areas.

- *Neutrality.* The OECD concluded that taxation should be neutral and equitable among the various forms of electronic commerce. Online firms should be motivated to make decisions based on business considerations, not tax matters. Similar taxpayers executing similar transactions should be susceptible to comparable taxation costs.
- *Efficiency.* Tax administrators should minimize the cost of Internet taxation for themselves and e-commerce taxpayers as much as possible. Lowering costs can be achieved through a number of technological developments and streamlined procedures.
- *Effectiveness and Fairness.* Taxation should impose the appropriate tax at the appropriate time. Measures must be implemented to minimize tax avoidance.
- *Flexibility.* E-commerce taxation systems must be flexible and dynamic to ensure they keep up with both technological and commercial developments.
- *Certainty and Simplicity.* Taxpayers should be able to anticipate with certainty when taxes are due and how much tax is owed. Tax rules should be clear and easy to understand.

The Permanent Establishment Problem. Defining where profits of a multinational online company should be taxed is controversial. Two principles of taxation are most common. The *source-based taxation principle* states that income derived from a source in a particular country will be taxed by that country as income. Although seemingly simple, source-based taxation presents a number of problems. For example, the taxing government may experience difficulty in enforcing its source-based taxes. Given the borderless nature of the Internet and the speed of its transactions, nations will not easily be able to find and impose tax on businesses around the globe with no connection to the source-based tax country other than the Internet sale. In contrast, the *residence-based taxation principle* states that the residence of the company earning income determines where that company is taxed. In the United States, for example, U.S. residents pay income taxes on their income from whatever source derived, including income generated overseas.

OECD Guidelines on Defining Permanent Establishment. In addition to the question of which taxation principle applies, nations must define what constitutes a "permanent establishment." Article 5 of the OECD Model Convention defines a permanent establishment as a "place of management, a branch, a factory, a workshop, and mine . . . or any other place of extraction of nature resources." A permanent establishment does not include the use of facilities for the sole purpose of storing, displaying, or delivering goods. It also does not include a fixed place of business that carries on activities that are merely "preparatory or auxiliary" in nature.

On December 22, 2000, the OECD Committee on Fiscal Affairs published a report applying the "permanent establishment" definition to electronic commerce transactions. The committee reached a number of conclusions. For example,

- A Web site cannot, without more, constitute a permanent establishment.
- If an Internet service provider (ISP) hosts the Web site of another enterprise on its own servers, the location of the hosting servers will not be a permanent establishment for the Internet company.
- ISPs do not constitute an agent of the enterprises to which the Web sites belong and thus do not establish a permanent establishment for the hosting Web site. They do not have the authority to conduct contracts on the company's behalf.
- A distinction exists between software/data and server equipment for establishing permanent establishment. A Web site, which is a combination of software and data, is not tangible property and therefore does not have a location that can constitute a place of business. The server where the Web site exists, however, is tangible property and under certain circumstances can constitute a permanent establishment.
- Computer equipment at a location may only constitute a permanent establishment if it is fixed. A server will have to be located in a certain place for a "sufficient" period of time in to become fixed.
- The presence of human intervention is not necessary to establish a permanent establishment in a particular place.

National Initiatives Defining Permanent Establishment

Individual national programs are also underway to form underlying principles of international Internet taxation. The following countries exemplify national efforts around the globe.

Germany. The German Federal Ministry of Finance followed OECD reports and concluded that a server used for electronic commerce, without more, does not automati-

http://

- The text of the December 22, 2000, OECD report is available at **http://www.oecd.org/pdf/ M000015000/M00015535.pdf**
- To view the text of the press release and other information related to the UK's views on taxation of e-commerce, see **http://www.inlandrevenue.gov.uk/ e-commerce/ecom15.htm** (and links there).

cally create a permanent establishment. However, German courts have not yet resolved this issue. On September 6, 2001, a lower German court considered whether tax authorities could attribute income to a company with a computer server located in Switzerland. The server was connected with Germany by a dedicated line and operated without on-site human assistance. Information was fed through the server and distributed to Swiss television sets for a fee. The court concluded that this arrangement constituted a permanent establishment and was taxable by German authorities. The case is currently on appeal.

India. In September 2001, the Indian government officials published a report recommending that India banish the concept of permanent establishment altogether. The "High-Powered Committee on Electronic Commerce and Taxation" stated source state taxation, combined with a physical presence requirement, is not reasonable in the era of electronic commerce. India is a net importer of goods. Thus India would lose significant taxation opportunities from companies selling to India from Web sites that have no presence there. Following this principle, India would likely conclude that any e-commerce activity within its borders constitutes taxable income, regardless of physical presence. The Indian government is still debating the position. A moratorium is in place preventing additional duties on electronic commerce until 2004.

United Kingdom. The UK has generally followed the OECD's establishment of the permanent establishment concept. The Inland Revenue Department (the UK version of the IRS) defines it as a "fixed place of business through which the business of an enterprise is wholly or partly carried on." On April 11, 2000, the Inland Revenue Department issued its first press release on the subject, stating, "In the UK, we take the view that a web site of itself is not a permanent establishment. And we take the view that a server is insufficient of itself to constitute a permanent establishment of a business that is conducting e-commerce through a Web site on the server. We take that view regardless of whether the server is owned, rented or otherwise at the disposal of the business." This policy is similar to OECD guidelines.

European Union Value-Added Tax on Internet Sales

On May 7, 2002, the European Union approved rules requiring non-EU vendors to collect and remit a value-added tax (VAT) when selling electronic goods such as music and software in EU member states. The EU intends to help Europe's Internet-based business compete against their American counterparts, who obtain no taxes from online consumers. The new rules require U.S. businesses to levy the tax against European consumers, thus raising their prices and removing the tax-free advantage U.S. businesses would have in selling to European consumers. Rules require non-EU vendors to register in one EU country. When the European consumer pays the VAT, the VAT is then reallocated to the customer's country of residence. The tax would be enforced beginning July 1, 2003, and applies only to retail sales. This places U.S. businesses in the challenging position of determining the consumer's nation of origin, levying the appropriate VAT, and then remitting it to the EU. The EU is also considering a similar requirement on shipped goods, such as books, for the future.

Summary

An out-of-state e-business with a tax nexus in the state must be aware of any local sales tax that obligates it to collect a sales tax from the buyer and remit it to the state. Failure to do so could result in the state collecting the taxes due from the e-business, plus imposing a penalty tax for late payment. If it has reason to believe the tax evasion was intentional, there could be criminal prosecution.

This is a daunting task for the e-business tax adviser because each state, and some local communities, have their own version of the amount to be taxed and what items may be exempt. It is no wonder that Congress in 1998 passed the Internet Tax Freedom Act that created a three-year moratorium on any new Internet taxes. Proponents for keeping the Internet tax free argue that imposing taxes on the Internet will impede our electronic-driven economy. The opposition, consisting of some state governors and brick-and-mortar businesses, complain of tax discrimination with a tax-free Internet advantage to the online merchant. The e-businesses argue that they do not use the infrastructure the state tax base supports, and for the states to require them to charge and collect a sales tax on their behalf is unfair.

We can only be assured that the report and legislative suggestions to Congress, rendered by the Advisory Commission on Electronic Commerce, will continue to be vigorously debated.

Questions of Internet taxation are also being debated globally. The OECD leads the way in developing fair and uniform taxation principles. Countries will continue to wrestle with the "permanent establishment" question as it relates to the virtually intangible forum of cyberspace. The challenge of international Internet taxation will continue to grow as an increasing number of people from around the world complete transactions in cyberspace.

Key Terms

nexus, *194*
sales tax, *195*
use tax, *195*
commerce clause, *197*

physical presence test, *204*
nexus by attribution, *205*
market maintenance
   theory, *206*

Internet Tax Freedom
   Act (ITFA), *206*
Advisory Commission on
   Electronic Commerce, *206*

Manager's Checklist

√ An e-business should determine in which states it has nexus for sales and use tax purposes. Managers should work with their tax advisers to discover what products and services are taxable and at what rate.

√ A Web company should determine if the products or services it sells are taxable in the nexus state. For instance, downloaded software is subject to sales and use tax in Alabama, Illinois, Louisiana, Nebraska, New York, North Dakota, Texas, Washington, and Wisconsin.

√ Be aware that the tax law in this area is subject to change and managers should work closely with their tax advisers.

√ Remember that noncompliance with tax law can incur substantial penalties to the e-business, and an intentional violation may be criminal. A Web company that does not collect the sales tax from the buyer at the time of the sale will forever lose that opportunity.

√ A Web merchant who owns, leases, or rents a server in a state with a sale and/or use tax may be subject to a tax nexus in that state.

√ Attendance at e-commerce trade shows by a Web company's employees or sales representatives may establish a tax nexus in that state.

√ Be aware of international taxation requirements wherever an online company plans to do business.

√ Note that the definition of "permanent establishment" for taxation purposes varies widely from country to country. Political and economic issues may cause that term to be changed over time.

√ Be aware that the EU value-added tax may represent a significant financial and reporting burden for U.S. companies transacting with EU customers. The 2002 rules may even create a competitive disadvantage for U.S. companies, not just level the playing field.

√ Ethical Considerations

Consider the ethics of a pure online business without any physical presence in a state that generates substantial revenues from consumers in that state and has no legal obligation to collect sales tax. Is this in any manner fair to the local retail store that has the legal burden of collecting sales tax for the same product sold offline?

Case Problems

1. Taxpayer X markets and sells physical and digital gift certificates, gift cards, and other related products over the Internet. The core of Taxpayer X's business involves the sale of Merchant Certificates, which Taxpayer purchases from participating merchants at a discount and keeps in its inventory until a customer orders from Taxpayer X's Web site. Then the Merchant Certificate, attractively packaged, is shipped by Taxpayer X via a third-party courier service to a recipient, who is usually a person other than the customer. Taxpayer X has a record of the credit card information and address for a physical certificate purchaser and e-mail address, street address, and credit card information, and the e-mail address of the recipient for a digital certificate purchaser. Is the sale at issue a tangible personal property sale? If not, how do you characterize the receipts from the sale? [STATE-CASE-TAX-CT, NY-TAXRPTR, ¶404-186, New York

Commissioner of Taxation and Finance, TSB-A-02(3)C, Deloitte & Touche (Advisory Opinion) (2002)]

2. Petitioner Borders.com, an out-of-state corporation, sells books, videos, music, and gift items via the Internet. The goods sold to California purchasers are delivered by common carrier from outside California. Borders, Inc. ("Borders") that sells similar goods in brick-and-mortar stores throughout California is a separate and distinct legal entity from Borders.com. California customers could return items purchased at borders.com to Borders Books and Music store, get cash refunds, or exchange items from Borders. Borders provides return services to petitioner's competitors, too. Does borders.com have substantial sales and use tax nexus with the state of California? [STATE-CASE-TAX-CT, CA-TAXRPTR, ¶403-191, In the Matter of the Petition for Redetermination Under the Sales and Use Tax Law of: Borders Online, Inc. (2001)]

3. Petitioner Pegasus Internet, Inc. provides Web site design and development services to customers both within and outside New York State. The finished Web sites are placed on a hosted server to deliver services. "On occasion, Petitioner will send its customer a copy of the Web site on a compact disk." Petitioner also purchases prewritten software for use in its Web site development services. Some are customized software designed and developed to Petitioner's specifications. Discuss taxability of those transactions in e-commerce. Are charges for Web site design and development services subject to New York State sales tax? [STATE-CASE-TAX-CT, NY-TAXRPTR, ¶404-234, New York Commissioner of Taxation and Finance, TSB-A-02(13)S, Pegasus Internet, Inc. (Advisory Opinion) (2002)]

4. Petitioner Journey Education Marketing, Inc., currently registered as a vendor with the state of New York, is in the business of reselling educational software products. Headquartered in Carrollton, Texas, Petitioner used to have a Texas sales representative travel to New York State to meet customers and attend trade shows, but not to accept sales orders. Petitioner stopped this physical presence in New York since December 31, 1999, and has focused its marketing channels in mail-order catalogs and through its Internet Web site. With an expected annual sale of less than $750,000, Petitioner would like to formally withdraw its sales tax registration in New York because "it no longer has a physical presence in the state, and no longer has employees or independent representatives soliciting sales in the state." Did Petitioner's nexus with New York State end when it discontinued the practice stated above? [STATE-CASE-TAX-CT, NY-TAXRPTR, ¶404-240, New York Commissioner of Taxation and Finance, TSB-A-02(19)S, Journey Education Marketing, Inc. (Advisory Opinion) (2002)]

5. Petitioner, a financial consulting firm, provides online interactive educational services to financial professionals. Its principal services, for which Petitioner charges an annual fee, are risk management analysis and forecasting services in market risk assessment and credit risk assessment. A client usually has a specific portfolio whose risk characteristics need analysis. Petitioner also provides its clients, free of charge, with publications that keep them up to date with developments in the field. Those publications are open to the public upon request. Decide if the education services are subject to sales and compensating use tax, if the market risk management analysis and forecasting services are subject to sales and use tax, and if the credit risk management analysis and forecasting services are subject to sales and use tax. [STATE-CASE-TAX-CT, NY-TAXRPTR, ¶403-575, The RiskMetrics Group LLC (Advisory Opinion) (2000)]

6. A Dutch corporation supplied oil and oil-related products through a fully automated, remote-controlled underground pipeline in Germany. The Dutch company had no employees in Germany and used independent contracts to perform all maintenance work. Does the Dutch oil pipeline constitute a "permanent establishment" in Germany for taxation purposes? How is this dispute over oil pipelines relevant for understanding international cyber-taxation?

Additional Readings

- Eisenstein, M. I. "The Constitutional Limits on Sales Taxation of Cyberspace." *State Tax News* (February 24, 1997).

- Frieden, Karl, and Porter, Michael. "The Taxation of Cyberspace: State Tax Issues Related to the Internet and Electronic Commerce." 1996 *State Tax Notes* 1363, 1367 (1996).

- Grierson, R. Scott. "State Taxation of the Information Superhighway: A Proposal for Taxation of Information Services." *Loyola of Los Angeles Entertainment Law Journal* 16 (1995): 200.

- Kaywood, Jr., Sam K. "International Tax Aspects of Internet & E-Commerce." *Practicing Law Institute/Tax* 715 (2002): 534.

ONLINE SECURITIES OFFERINGS AND TRANSACTIONS

Recent advances in information technology—particularly the Internet— are revolutionizing commerce. The securities industry, most significantly on-line brokerage, is at the forefront of this revolution.

—*On-Line Brokerage: Keeping Apace of Cyberspace, Executive Summary (2001) (http://www.sec.gov/news/studies/cyberspace.htm)*

LEARNING OBJECTIVES

After you have read this chapter, you should be able to:

1. Understand there are a variety of ways to finance businesses.
2. Understand what an investment is.
3. Know how the Internet has changed methods of raising capital.
4. Determine whether an offering is for a security or not.
5. Explain the regulatory role of the Securities and Exchange Commission.
6. Understand the purpose of the Securities Act of 1933, the Securities Exchange Act of 1934, and the Investment Company Act of 1940.
7. Explain where the vulnerabilities are in online trading systems.
8. Understand the importance of quality information/ data and fair trading systems.
9. Understand the principles underlying international cooperation in securities law enforcement.
10. Determine whether an online securities offer constitutes an "offshore offering" under Regulation S.

http://

- Additional material on securities offerings and transactions may be found at the Bentley College CyberLaw Center Web site (**http:// ecampus.bentley.edu/dept/cyberlaw**) under Business and Financial Issues—Online Securities.

INTRODUCTION

Consider how start-ups, or even existing businesses, secure funding for any number of reasons, including operations, expansion, improvements, equipment, research and development, sales and marketing, new product development, and so forth. One method of raising capital is to issue securities to investors in return for their cash investment into the business. Such transactions were formerly the exclusive domain of investment bankers. And subsequent transactions in these securities, such as buying and selling stock, were the exclusive domain of stockbrokers. Securities offerings as well as trading are among the myriad of commercial applications to migrate to the Internet. This has improved access to capital markets, especially for small businesses, and has resulted in major changes to the securities industry.

The first part of this chapter focuses on defining a security and raising capital through offering securities online. The second part focuses on Internet transactions following the initial offering—the trading of securities online. Particular attention is paid to the legal and regulatory framework as it continually adapts to the phenomenon of online offerings and transactions. The final part focuses on international aspects of securities offerings and transactions. We address the regulatory framework as well as the management of **offshore offerings**.

RAISING CAPITAL: ONLINE SECURITIES OFFERINGS

One of the most attractive alternatives for businesses to secure capital is to issue equity securities to investors. Although there are a number of other methods to finance businesses, such as through loans or issuing bonds, these create an immediate financial burden for the business. For example, the business must first qualify for a loan. The evaluation and underwriting process is rigorous because lenders are increasingly interested in financing only later-stage companies with established earnings, rather than start-ups with speculative earnings potential. If a loan even materializes, the interest/repayment rate may be substantially above the prime lending rate, and thus prohibitively expensive. This type of financing represents another expense on profit and loss statements, as well as a liability on balance sheets. Bonds have the same effect, although repayment may be delayed for some years. Such investment monies are loans to the business and must be paid back. Another avenue to raise capital is for companies to take in angel or venture capital investors, but management often loses control and/or ownership of the company to these investors.

This is perhaps why offering securities as a form of ownership in the business, in exchange for investors' cash, is a particularly attractive way for businesses to secure financing. Businesses are able to raise capital, yet they have no definite repayment obligation. Access to capital increases (although ownership in the company becomes diluted). However, control is not correspondingly diluted. Investors generally do not participate in internal operations and strategies. Controlling shareholders create a market for their shares in the company. Liquidity is thereby improved dramatically because now there will be a market for the shares. Also, the image of the company may improve along with becoming more widely known. Finally, companies may be able to attract and retain key personnel, because now stock options and bonuses can be tied to company stock and share price performance. Such offerings may be issued repeatedly over the life of the company: at the start, for early-stage financing; during operations for expansion financing; and finally, before the initial public offering (IPO) or merger/acquisition, exit financing. And from the investors' standpoint, they have ownership in a potentially profitable enterprise with two ways of increasing their wealth: through dividend payments and through an appreciation in the price of their shares. The first issue to be considered, then, is what defines securities.

What Is a Security?

Because there are many varied investment schemes, the first question is whether the interest being sold is actually a security interest, also known as an *equity*. If it is, the protection of the federal and state securities laws may be invoked for the benefit and protection of investors, against the fraudulent practices of those who solicit investors under the guise of offering a legitimate investment. If the interest is *not* a security interest, the securities laws are inapplicable, and the only recourse for defrauded investors is claims based on tort or criminal law statutes under theories of negligence, theft, or racketeering, for example.

The **Securities Act of 1933** defines a **security** in broad and general terms that include a variety of instruments. Section 3(a)(10) provides:

> The term 'security' means any note, stock, treasury stock, bond, debenture, certificate of interest or participation in any profit-sharing agreement . . . or pre-organization certificate or subscription, transferable share, investment contract . . . certificate of deposit . . . any put, call, straddle, option . . . or in general, any instrument commonly known as a security.

The **Securities and Exchange Commission (SEC)**, as administrator of the securities laws, and the courts have indicated they do not intend to be bound by legal formalisms and what a transaction is called. The leading case construing the definition of a security interest is *Securities and Exchange Commission v. W. J. Howey Co.*, 328 U.S. 293 (1946). The Court was asked to decide whether the sale of an interest in a citrus grove was a security, and thus subject to the securities laws. The Court created a "risk capital" analysis and concluded an interest in the grove was a security because the transaction evidenced (1) an investment, (2) in a common enterprise, (3) with a reasonable expectation of profits, and (4) to be derived from the efforts of others. Although the *Howey* transaction—manifested by shares in an enterprise—is the quintessential security, notes may, or may not be, securities.

The Supreme Court decided this question in *Reves v. Ernst & Young*, 494 U.S. 56 (1990). The Court considered whether uncollateralized and uninsured promissory notes payable on demand that paid a variable rate of interest were securities. The Court declined to follow the *Howey* test, and instead it adopted a "family resemblance" test for deciding whether notes are securities. The Court began with the presumption that they are securities, rebuttable by a showing that the notes more closely resemble the family of instruments that are *not* securities. The Court assessed (1) the motivations of the buyer and seller; (2) the plan of distribution of the notes; (3) the reasonable expectations of the buyer; and (4) whether there were other laws regulating the transaction, rendering application of the securities laws unnecessary.

The Securities Act's definition of security may seem to address every possible investment that could be found to be a security, but this threshold question of what is a security, such that the securities laws may be invoked, continues to evolve. In fact, the SEC as recently as June 2002 added futures contracts to its definition of a security [SEC Release Nos. 33-8091; 34-45769]. The following case highlights this issue of what is a security from the perspective of an Internet scheme involving "virtual shares" in "virtual companies."

Securities and Exchange Commission v. SG Ltd.
265 F.3d 42 (1st Cir. 2001)

Facts

SG operated the StockGeneration Web site, offering visitors an opportunity to purchase shares in eleven different "virtual companies" listed on the site's "virtual stock exchange." SG arbitrarily set the purchase and sale prices of each of the imaginary companies in biweekly rounds and guaranteed that investors could buy or sell any quantity of shares at posted prices. SG placed no upper limit on the amount of funds that investors could spend on the virtual offerings.

On the site, SG advised potential purchasers to pay "particular attention" to shares in the "privileged" company. It boasted the investing in those shares was a "game without any risk." To this end, the site represented that the privileged company's shares would unfailingly appreciate, boldly proclaiming the share price is supported by the owners of SG, and this is why its value constantly rises; on average at a rate of 10 percent monthly (which is approximately 215 percent annually). Although SG conceded that a decline in the share price was theoretically possible, it represented that the privileged company shares were supported by several distinct revenue streams: from new participants, share sales commissions, the bid-ask spread on transactions, and so forth. SG posted lists of "big winners," featuring testimonials from supposedly satisfied participants.

At least eight hundred U.S. residents, paying real cash, purchased virtual shares in the virtual companies listed on the defendants' virtual stock exchange. SG deposited these millions of dollars into Latvian and Estonian banks. In late 1999, participants began to experience difficulties redeeming their virtual shares. SG then unilaterally suspended all redemption requests. It the executed a reverse stock split, which caused the share price of privileged company to plummet to 1/10,000 of its previous value. Meanwhile, SG continued soliciting new participants on its site.

The district court granted SG's motion to dismiss the complaint for failure to state a claim, on the ground that the virtual shares were a clearly marked and defined game lacking a business context, and thus was not a transaction in securities. The Securities and Exchange Commission appealed this decision.

Judicial Opinion *(Judge Selya)*

SG asseverate[s] that the virtual shares were part of a fantasy investment game created for the personal entertainment of Internet users, and therefore, that those shares do not implicate the federal securities laws. The Securities and Exchange Commission . . . counters that substance ought to prevail over form, and that merely labeling a website as a game should not negate the applicability of the securities laws. The appeal turn[s] on whether the SEC alleged facts which, if proven, would bring this case within the jurisdictional ambit of the federal securities laws. Consequently, we focus on the type of security that the SEC alleges is apposite here: investment contracts.

The applicable regulatory regime rests on two complementary pillars: the Securities Act of 1933 . . . and the Securities Exchange Act of 1934. These statutes employ nearly identical definitions of the term 'security.' Included in this array [of what is a security] is the elusive, essentially protean, concept of an investment contract. Judicial efforts to delineate what is—and what is not—an investment contract are grounded in the seminal case of *SEC v. W. J. Howey* Co. The Supreme Court has long espoused a broad construction of what constitutes an investment contract, aspiring 'to afford the investing public a full measure of protection.'

What remains is to analyze whether purchases of the privileged company's shares constitute investment contracts. **Investment of Money.** The determining factor is whether an investor chose to give up a specific consideration in return for a . . . financial interest with the characteristics of a security. SG represent[ed] that participants could firmly expect a 10% profit monthly on purchases of the privileged company's shares. We conclude that the SECs complaint sufficiently alleges the existence of this factor. **Common Enterprise.** [C]ommonality requires more than pooling (of investors' funds) alone; it also requires that investors share in the profits and risks of the enterprise. [T]he arrangement . . . fairly can be characterized as either a Ponzi or pyramid scheme (as evidence of pooling), and that it provides the requisite profit-and-risk sharing to support a finding of . . . commonality. **Expectation of profits solely from the efforts of others.** The Supreme Court has recognized an expectation of profits in two situations, namely, (1) capital appreciation from the original investment, and (2) participation in earnings resulting from the use of investors' funds. These situations are to be contrasted with transactions in which an individual purchases a commodity for personal use or consumption. The SEC posits that SG's guarantees created a reasonable expectancy of profit from investments in the privileged company, whereas SG maintains that participants paid money not to make money, but, rather, to acquire an entertainment commodity for personal consumption. In our view, [SGs] profit-related guarantees constitute a not-very-subtle form of economic inducement. SG has a plausible argument . . . that no participant in his or her right mind should have expected guaranteed profits from purchases of privileged company shares. [But nevertheless] SG enjoyed direct operational control over all aspects of the virtual stock exchange.

[W]e hold that the SEC has alleged a set of facts which, if proved, satisfy the three-part *Howey* test and support its assertion that the opportunity to invest in the shares of the privileged company . . . constituted an invitation to enter into an investment contract within the jurisdictional reach of the federal securities laws.

REVERSED AND REMANDED.

Case Questions

1. Why was SG so eager to prove the transaction was merely part of a game, rather than an offering of securities?
2. What is the practical effect of the court's decision?
3. Based on this decision, what recommendations do you have for site operators who wish to offer virtual stock market games?

The Securities Laws: Governing the Issuance, Administration, and Transactions in Securities

One of the major purposes of the federal securities laws is to require companies making a public offering of securities to disclose material business and financial information in order that investors may make informed investment decisions.

—Securities and Exchange Commission

Once it is determined that the offering is in fact for a security instrument, a number of securities laws become applicable to every aspect of transactions in that security. The Supreme Court supports an expansive interpretation of what amounts to fraud in connection with the purchase and sale of securities, and it reiterated this support in *Securities and Exchange Commission v. Zandford*, 2002 U.S. LEXIS 4023 (June 3, 2002). Most important are the Securities Act, Securities and Exchange Act, and the Investment Company Act, followed by a series of additional laws targeting specific parties or practices (see Table 8.1.)

➤http://

- To access the full text of the Securities Act of 1933, see **http://www4.law.cornell.edu/uscode/15/**, and click on Chapter 2A.
- For a listing of initial public offerings (IPOs) for the last three years, see **http://online.wsj.com/documents/ipopipe.htm**

Securities Act of 1933, 15 U.S.C. Sections 77a–77aa. Congress enacted this statute primarily to ensure full disclosure of all material facts about the offering in *advance* of the purchase of the securities. Congress mandates a range of registration, delivery, and filing requirements for companies raising capital through the public offer and sale of securities. The requirements are, for the most part, applicable to offerings in excess of $10 million. Other offerings (which is usually the case for Internet start-ups), such as those offered under Regulation A (Reg A), Regulation D (Reg D), or Private Placement Offerings, are exempt from many of the registration requirements (discussed later in the chapter). Information that must appear in the offering circular, known as the **Prospectus**, include:

- Offering summary
- Description and number of shares offered
- Underwriting—discounts, commissions, plan for distribution of the shares
- Use of proceeds
- Dilution, if any, of outstanding shares
- Dividend policy
- Risk factors, financial data, competitors, dependence on key personnel, lack of operating history, adverse economic conditions in that industry
- Other matters, such as property, plant and equipment, legal proceedings, management information, and large contracts
- Financial statements

The following case details an offering that was never registered with the SEC—for essentially nonexistent securities. The SEC brought charges under the Securities Act of 1933 for violations of its registration provisions.

FIGURE 8.1   **Additional Investment Acts**

Act	Code	Purpose
Investment Advisers Act of 1940	15 U.S.C. § § 80b-1 - 80b-20 (1999) 17 C.F.R. Parts 275, 279 (1999)	This act regulates investment advisers and seeks to check the power of advisers over company directors.
Private Securities Litigation Reform Act of 1995	15 U.S.C. § § 77k, 77l, 77z-1, 77z-2, 78j-1, 78t, 78u, 78u-4, 78u-5 (1999)	This act imposes certain limitations on private lawsuits imposing stricter pleading standards for class actions and limitations on discovery.
Public Utility Holding Company Act of 1935	15 U.S.C. § § 79 - 79z-6 (1999) 17 C.F.R. Part 250 (1999)	This act attempts to protect consumer interests and correct abuses in the holding company device, especially in the gas and utility industries.
Securities Investor Protection Act of 1970	15 U.S.C. § § 78 aaa - 77lll (1999) 17 C.F.R. § 200.30-3- .30-18 (1999)	This act attempts to stop the failure or instability of a significant number of brokerage firms; to restore investor confidence in capital markets; upgrade financial responsibility of registered representatives; and establish a fund for claims against firms.
National Securities Markets Improvement Act of 1996	15 U.S.C § 77r (1999)	Codifies rules giving SEC power in exempting SEC transactions from duplicative regulation.
Securities Litigation Uniform Standards Act of 1997	H.R. 1689, 105th Cong. (1997); S. 1260, 105th (1997)	Legislation proposing preemption of certain state securities fraud litigation and vesting exclusive jurisdiction of litigation over nationally traded securities in federal courts.
Trust Indenture Act of 1939	15 U.S.C. § § § 77aaa- 77bbbb (1999) 17 C.F.R. Part 260 (1999)	This act attempts to eliminate fraudulent practices and improve disclosure of indenture provisions to include such features as financial condition and relationship with underwriters.

Securities and Exchange Commission v. Abacus International Holdings Corp.
2001 U.S. Dist. LEXIS 12635 (N.D. Cal. Aug. 16, 2001)

Facts

The SEC filed its complaints against Abacus and its sole owner and employee, Agustin, on May 11, 1999, alleging that Agustin, acting by and through Abacus and its Web site, had since July 1998 fraudulently offered and sold nonexistent securities. The SEC alleged his acts violated the securities registration antifraud provisions of the Securities Act of 1933 and the antifraud broker-dealer registration provisions of the Securities Exchange Act of 1934. The complaint alleges that Agustin promised extravagant, risk-free investments with guaranteed returns of 80 percent per month and higher. At least one investor was induced to invest approximately $170,000 in Abacus's securities, $60,000 of which Agustin allegedly misappropriated for personal use.

The SEC also claimed that Agustin used materials and statements from other Web sites to deceitfully describe Abacus as an international company with access to a wide variety of investment opportunities, when, in fact, it was nothing more than a Web site that Agustin operated out of his home. Agustin, through the Abacus Web site, allegedly made numerous material misrepresentations and omissions regarding the investments. Most importantly, the investments that Abacus offered did not exist, and the statements about them were purely fraudulent.

The SEC served the complaint on Abacus and Agustin personally. After no response from the defendants, the SEC filed a Motion for Judgment by Default and also sought to permanently enjoin defendants from future violations of the Securities Act and the Securities Exchange Act. The SEC also sought civil remedies, including a repayment of the $170,000 plus prejudgment interest.

Judicial Opinion (Judge Henderson)

The Court may consider [when] determining whether to award a default judgment . . . the merits of plaintiff's claims. Th[is] . . . require[s] that plaintiff's allegation 'state a claim on which (plaintiff) may recover.'

Section 5 c of the Securities Act provides that 'it shall be unlawful for any person, directly or indirectly, to make use of any means or instruments of transportation or communication in interstate commerce or of the mails to offer to sell or offer to buy through the use or medium of any prospectus or otherwise any security, unless a registration statement has been filed as to such security. The SEC has plead a prima facie case of a section violation. It contends (1) that the non-existent financial instruments and investments that Abacus offered are securities, [and] (2) that since Agustin, through Abacus, offered and sold securities to the public through the Internet, interstate commerce, he was subject to the requirements of section 5, and (3) that Agustin is liable under section 5 because he sold securities to the public for his own financial gain without registering with the SEC.

Section 17(a) of the Securities Act . . . prohibit[s] acts, transactions, and practices or courses of businesses that operate with fraud or deceit, including misrepresentations and omissions of a material fact, in connection with the offer, purchase or sale of securities. The SEC has alleged all the prima facie elements for a violation of these provisions. It claims (1) that Agustin . . . made numerous material misrepresentations and omissions regarding the investments offered; (2) that these representations were fraudulent on their face, and (3) that it is clear that Agustin and Abacus acted with the requisite degree of scienter [knowledge].

A district court has the discretion to fashion whatever equitable relief it deems necessary to deprive defendants of their wrongful gains.

A. Injunctive Relief. The SEC asks this Court to permanently enjoin Agustin from future violations of the securities laws. [Courts] grant permanent injunction[s] against future violations if the defendant's past conduct indicates . . . that there is a reasonable likelihood of further violations in the future. In this case the complaint details multiple violations which resulted from a premeditated scheme, carried out over a period of time, to misappropriate client funds. In these circumstances, the Court finds that injunctive relief is appropriate.

B. Disgorgement and Prejudgment Interest. To prevent unjust enrichment and to deter others from violating the securities laws, courts have broad equity powers to order defendants to disgorge illicit gains and impose prejudgment interest on those gains. The amount of disgorgement should be measured by the defendant's unjust enrichment or personal benefit, not by the damages inflicted upon purchasers and sellers of the relevant securities. The Court finds that disgorgement is appropriate, since Agustin has been unjustly enriched in the amount of $170,000.

C. Civil Penalties. [P]enalties are available when the securities law violation 'involved fraud, deceit, manipulation. . . . The law provides that [3rd tier civil penalties are] not to exceed the greater of $110,000 for a natural person, or the 'gross amount of pecuniary gain' to the defendant as a result of the violation. [Agustin's] fraudulent conduct and reckless disregard of regulatory requirements warrants the imposition of civil penalties.

CONCLUSION

Accordingly, and given all of the above, the SECs Motion for Judgment by Default is GRANTED.

IT IS SO ORDERED.

http://

- For the complete text of the Securities Exchange Act of 1934, see **http://www4.law.cornell.edu/uscode/15/**, and click on Chapter 2B.

Case Questions

1. Do you think Abacus could have effected this fraud without the aid of the Internet?
2. What is the most effective strategy for the SEC to use to find such fraudulent schemes on the Internet?
3. Do you think the penalties are serious enough to provide a deterrent to future conduct? Do you think this case should have been prosecuted as a crime?

Securities Exchange Act of 1934, 15 U.S.C. Sections 78a–78mm. The **Securities Exchange Act of 1934** was enacted primarily to govern the administration and filing of periodic reports, *after* the initial purchase of securities, to ensure accurate information on a continual basis. Under this law, the SEC mandates accounting and record-keeping procedures for domestic large capitalization companies. Information that must be reported includes:

- Operations
- Financial condition
- Management
- Financial statements
- Elections
- Mergers, acquisitions, tender offers
- Beneficial ownership of shares and share transactions by insiders
- Compliance with the Foreign Corrupt Practices Act rules, outlawing bribes

The following case outlines the standards that plaintiffs (at least in the Fifth Circuit) must meet in order to prove successfully that defendants are liable for securities fraud under the Securities Exchange Act. Note, too, how important accurate financial statements are in company valuations.

Haack v. Max Internet Communications, Inc.
2002 U.S. Dist. LEXIS 5652 (N.D. Tex. April 3, 2002)

Facts

Max Internet manufactures and markets Max i.c. Live, a personal computer Internet media processor card (the live card). The live card was designed to enhance a computer's video and audio functions by delivering the power to conduct true-motion, synchronized video and audio communications, as well as video and audio streaming and browsing over a broadband Internet connection. Max reported its first quarter fiscal 2000 results (F00) on November 12, 1999. According to the complaint, Max represented to the investing community that it successfully launched the live card and that the product was "positioned to become the industry's standard for video processing over the Internet." It further represented that improving sales of the live card would result in strong earnings per share growth for the company. It further reported that a financial analyst initiated coverage of the Max stock and issued a "buy" recommendation. Because of these events, Haack asserts that Max artificially inflated by 600 percent the forecast for the growth of its stock.

Shortly thereafter, on May 12, 2000, Max restated its earnings for the first half of F00. It disclosed that the majority of sales during F00 were from Brazil and were booked in reliance upon documentation—documentation that was later found to be falsified. As a result, Max restated its earnings, resulting in a loss of 46 cents per share based on 16,248,188 weighted average shares outstanding.

Because of this disclosure, Haack claims that Max's stock price plummeted 69 percent from $28 per share on February 9, 2000, to a low of $4 3/16 per share on May 12, 2000. Haack contends that Max's statement during the period "were false and misleading when issued because Max's financial results were presented in violation of Generally Accepted Accounting Principles." In particular, Haack maintains that Max falsified its financial earnings by recognizing revenue that never occurred. Instead, Max recorded nonexistent sales to a Brazilian subsidiary and then shipped live cards to wholesalers, wherein payment was contingent on resale. Haack further contends the live cards did not work on many of the major operating system platforms.

Haack filed suit in August 2000 against Max and its officers and directors, alleging that they committed securities fraud in violation of section 10(b) and Rule 10b-5 of the Securities Exchange Act of 1934. Haack further asserted claims against the individual defendants for intentional and negligent breach of fiduciary duties. The defendants filed motions to dismiss the complaints for failure to state claims. Max claims the company's alleged misstatements are not actionable as a matter of law (essentially that they are mistakes; there was no knowledge of the problems and thus do not amount to fraud). Subsequently, the trial judge held a status conference and thereafter ordered the parties to mediation. That process failed to resolve the dispute.

Judicial Opinion *(Judge Fish)*

Before the court are the motions of the defendants . . . to dismiss the case.

A. Legal Standard

To establish a violation of section 10(b) of the Exchange Act and Rule 10b-5, the plaintiffs must allege, in connection with the purchase or the sale of securities, a misstatement or an omission of material fact made with scienter [knowledge] on which the plaintiff relied, that proximately caused [the plaintiff's] injury. [Moreover] a plaintiff's claims for a violation of section 10(b) . . . must satisfy the strict pleading requirements for fraud.

Standard for Dismissal [The Federal Rules] authorize dismissal of a complaint for 'failure to state a claim upon which relief can be granted.' [This is] granted only if it appears beyond doubt that the plaintiff could prove no set of facts in support of his claims that would entitle him to relief. In the securities context . . . dismissals are difficult to obtain because the cause of action deals primarily with fact-specific inquiries.

B. Grounds for Dismissal

[The court examines each of the following elements to determine whether the plaintiff's claims can survive the defendants' motions to dismiss: Materiality; Scienter; Reliance . . .]

1. *Materiality.* To satisfy the first element of a Rule 10b-5 claim, a plaintiff must allege facts showing that the defendant made an untrue statement of material fact, or failed to state a material fact necessary to make the statements that were made, not misleading. A statement or omission is only material if a reasonable investor would consider it important in determining whether to buy or sell stock. While some courts have held that statements classified as 'corporate optimism' are not actionable . . .

because they amount to puffing . . . the court finds, after a careful review of the complaint, that Haack's fraud claims satisfy the materiality element of a Rule 10b-5 claim. First, the complaint sets forth a series of detailed allegations. Further, Haack's complaint makes specific allegations about Max's financial affairs and internal operations.

2. *Scienter.* A plaintiff may meet his scienter pleading obligation based on conscious behavior, severe recklessness, or motive and opportunity. The defendants argue that the complaint fails, because Haack has not pled a viable motive for fraud, conscious misbehavior, or severe recklessness. After a careful review . . . the court finds that Haack has sufficiently pleaded fraudulent intent. Haack's complaint alleges a viable theory of severe recklessness . . . [defined as] those highly unreasonable omissions or misrepresentations that involve not merely simple or even inexcusable negligence, but an extreme departure from the standards of ordinary care, and that present a danger of misleading buyers or sellers which is either known to the defendant or is so obvious that the defendant must have been aware of it. [T]he complaint supports the strong inference that the defendants acted with fraudulent intent.

3. *Reliance.* Haack may assert reliance based on the fraud-on-the-market theory in connection with his cause of action under Rule 10b-5. [This] theory allows a plaintiff to satisfy the reliance element of securities fraud without proving direct reliance on false representations. [It] is based on the hypothesis that, in an open and developed securities market, the price of a company's stock is determined by the available material information regarding the company . . . misleading statements will therefore defraud purchases of stock even if they do not directly rely on the misstatements. [This] presumption [of reliance] may be rebutted by showing that the stock price was not affected by the misrepresentation or that purchasers or sellers did not trade in reliance on the integrity of the market price. [The element of reliance is satisfied.]

►http://

- For the full text of the Investment Companies and Advisers Act, see **http://www4.law.cornell.edu/uscode/ 15/**, and click on Chapter 2D.

CONCLUSION

Accordingly, the motions to dismiss by Max . . . and the individual defendants are DENIED.

SO ORDERED.

Case Questions

1. Do you think the fraud-on-the-market theory should be applicable to these serious federal charges, even though the theory is merely a presumption and not direct proof?
2. How could the system of reporting earnings be improved to avoid or minimize the market pressures?
3. What responsibility should the accounting industry share for misstatements of earnings?

Investment Company Act, 15 U.S.C. Sections 80a-1–80a-64. The **Investment Company Act** was primarily enacted to regulate the companies, such as mutual fund companies, that invest, reinvest, and trade in securities, and whose own securities are publicly offered. The law attempts to minimize the conflicts of interest that frequently arise in these enterprises. Information that must be reported includes:

- Financial condition
- Investment objectives
- Investment policies
- Company structure and operations

Exemptions from These Laws: Small Business/Small Offering Exemption from Registration and Reporting Requirements

If a business qualifies as a "small business issuer," a simplified registration statement may be used. This includes businesses with less than $25 million in yearly revenues, with outstanding stock worth not more than $25 million. The exemptions most commonly used by small and start-up businesses are described next.

Intrastate Offering Exemption, 15 U.S.C. Section 3(a)(11). This exemption, although difficult to qualify for, has application to purely local operations. To qualify, the company must

- Be incorporated in the state where the offering is conducted;
- Carry out a significant amount of business in that state; and
- Make offers and sales to only that state's residents.

These following exemptions, known as Reg A and Reg D, are commonly called **Private Placement Offerings (PPOs)**, in large part because the offerings are not available to every investor and the subsequent resale of the shares is restricted.

Reg A, 15 U.S.C. Section 3(b). The exemption from registration requirements, called the **Reg A Exemption**, is available to businesses for public offerings up to $5 million. The offering process is streamlined and simplified. Most importantly, Reg A offerings allow companies to test the waters—to first determine whether there is even sufficient investor interest in the offering before the company produces all of the offering materials. Basically, companies are soliciting for interest, not capital. Some states do not allow testing the waters, however. (This is another recurring issue in our federalist government, whereby there are layers of law, federal and state, that must be reconciled.) Other important features of Reg A offerings are as follows:

- Available to all investors, accredited and non-accredited;
- Not subject to any minimum share price requirement;
- Nonaudited financial statements may be used; and
- Not subject to resale restrictions.

Reg D, 17 C.F.R. Section 230.501–508. The **Reg D Exemption** establishes three separate exemptions from registration requirements: Rule 504, Rule 505, and Rule 506. The differences among them primarily relate to the size of the offering. For example, Rule 504 applies to offerings up to $1 million; Rule 505 to offerings up to $5 million, and Rule 506 to offerings in excess of $5 million.

Rule 504
- No limitation on solicitation or advertising to the public;
- Offering is available to all investors;
- No limitation on the number of investors;
- No specific disclosure requirements;
- Shares are subject to resale restrictions; and
- No requirement that financial statements be audited.

Rule 505
- Solicitation or advertising prohibited;
- Offering is available to an unlimited number of accredited investors, plus thirty-five other investors. (Accredited investors are defined as officers or directors of the offering company, other businesses, employee benefit plans, high net worth individuals, large trusts or charitable organizations.);
- Shares are subject to resale restrictions; and
- Financial statements must be audited.

Rule 506
- Solicitation or advertising prohibited;
- Offering is available to an unlimited number of accredited investors, plus up to thirty-five other investors, who must be "sophisticated." (*Sophisticated investors* are defined as having sufficient knowledge and experience in financial and business matters so they are capable of evaluating merits and risks of a prospective investment.);
- Shares are subject to resale restrictions; and
- Financial statements must be audited.

The Process of Conducting a Securities Offering

The first part of the process is known as the **prefiling period**, in which no statements regarding sale of the securities may be made. After this is known as the **waiting period**, between the **registration and effective period**, in which only oral statements may be made about the securities. It is during this time that companies typically undertake an advertising campaign to publicize the offering in what is known as a **road show**. It is critical that any information be verified. Should investors rely on any misstatements of material facts, civil or criminal liability may be imposed. The offering is valued and shares are priced during this time. The securities are sold in what is known

http://
- A complete list of the laws, rules, and forms required for any of these offerings may be found on the SEC's Web site, at **http://www.sec.gov**

as the *offering*. This could be an **initial public offering (IPO)**—the very first time that shares in a company are offered to the public for sale—or it could be a follow-on or secondary offering. A number of shares in offerings are allocated to large institutional investors, such as mutual or pension funds; a portion of shares is allocated to smaller, retail investors. Finally, there is the **post-effective period** when securities are already being traded. For a look at current offerings, otherwise known as what is in the pipeline, refer to any major financial newspaper on Mondays, and check out the offerings for the week ahead. (For example, *http://www.nytimes.com/business*, and click on Markets, or *http://www.wsj.com*, and click on Markets.)

Historically, investment bankers have underwritten/sponsored all securities offerings. They promise to use their best efforts to market and sell the shares, and in return, they receive commissions, fees, and shares. Traditional offerings are usually for those businesses with seasoned management who have engaged established attorneys, accountants, and underwriters. The underwriters offer expertise in industry segments and are (hopefully) capable of making judgments on the ability of the offering company to grow and attract investors. Underwriters aggressively sell the offerings, and they offer support after the offering in an attempt to minimize price volatility; they act as a certification of market fitness that the fundamentals of the offering company are sound.

There is an inherent bias in this formula, though, in favor of offerings by established, name-brand large-capitalization (large-cap) companies that offer recognizable products, wide distributions systems, and, most importantly, earnings. This traditional public offering system does not work well, though, for promising early-stage micro-cap companies with products in the pipeline, localized distributions systems, and no history of earnings—or as is oftentimes the case, a five-year history of losses. The Internet creates the possibility of bypassing the traditional public offering system and instead selling shares directly to the public.

Internet Public Offerings/Direct Public Offerings. The phenomenon of these offerings is related to the relaxation of the legal and regulatory requirements for offerings over the past twenty years, and to the Internet, which has made information and transactions online possible. Companies now have viable offering alternatives under the Reg A and Reg D programs, whereas before, it was cost prohibitive for small early-stage companies to conduct offerings. Combined with the Internet, where online offerings may now be made direct from companies to investors, Internet offerings represent a low-cost, and potentially lucrative, alternative to raising capital for small businesses. Most importantly, the Internet helps bridge the phenomenon known as the *capital gap*, representing the difference between that amount of capital companies need for their operations and that amount of capital investors have available to invest in companies. The Internet aggregates information in ways previously not known.

The Internet also closes the capital gap between *Fortune* 500 large-cap companies and small-cap and micro-cap companies. These small companies, by virtue of the Internet, are able to participate in offerings. The Internet has made three important changes to corporate finance: it levels the field to the extent that small companies may vie for funds; improves the efficiency of the capital markets; and bridges the information gap between companies, analysts and favored clients, and individual investors.

It is evident, though, that in these start-ups, investors are usually taking on a higher level of risk and volatility combined with a lower level of liquidity—but possibly reaping outsize returns on their investment. Although traditional investment bankers may decline to underwrite many of these start-up/early-stage offerings, an industry has developed for marketing these offerings online. Internet offerings, however, are mostly characterized as a passive effort, because the offering company is usually waiting for a hit on its offering site. In fact, most of the investors in Internet offerings are similar to those in **direct public offerings (DPOs)**, and are from what is known as *affinity groups,* such as the company's suppliers, customers, officers, directors, employees, and friends. Also, there may not be a ready market for these shares once investors wish to sell theirs. On balance, although the cost savings is considerable for Internet offerings, the long-term success and liquidity of such offerings is more precarious and uncertain.

The Requirements for Online Delivery of Offering Materials, Including Prospectuses and Sales Literature. Formerly, underwriters/sponsors of the offerings apportioned shares to selected brokers. From there, brokers would sell these securities to their clients. Brokers also knew clients' income, asset allocation, risk tolerance, and other pertinent data. Brokers would first send out a prospectus to their clients detailing the investments, and then they would discuss this investing option first before making any purchases on their behalf. The Internet has had a tremendous impact on this system. The advent of electronic delivery of offering materials means the possibility of nameless, faceless, essentially anonymous transactions, and to the extent that investors are not screened properly by online brokerages, a new level of risk is added to the process of investing.

In 1995, the SEC endorsed the use of the Internet for delivery of offering materials and other transactions, in Release 33-7233:

> Given the numerous benefits of electronic media, the Commission encourages
> further technological research, development, and application . . . the use of electronic media should be at least an equal alternative to the use of paper-based
> media. Accordingly, issuer or third party information that can be delivered in
> paper . . . may be delivered in electronic format.

In 2000, the SEC updated this information in Release Nos. 33-7856, 34-42728, IC-24426, specifically addressing three areas of concern: e-delivery of documents; issuer's liability for Web site content; and conduct of issuers and market intermediaries.

The first offering conducted over the Internet took place in 1996. Spring Street Brewing Company posted a Reg A IPO prospectus on its Web site and raised $1.6 million. No commissions were paid to underwriters, exchanges, or brokers. Thirty-five hundred investors paid $1.85 per share for stock that had no market yet. (Spring Street is not listed on any exchange at this point, and there is no longer any Web site for this company.)

To address the risks inherent in Internet offerings, the SEC developed guidelines for acceptable practices. Next, we mention this in the context of five areas of heightened concern for Internet offerings.

1. *Delivery of Offering Materials.* These are the guidelines to ensure successful delivery of any offering materials:
   - Notice: timely and adequate notice that offering information is available;
   - Access: to a medium of delivery. The offering information may be delivered in the form of paper, e-mail, disk, CD-ROM, audio, or video, and the format may not be so burdensome that recipients cannot effectively access the information; and
   - Evidence of Delivery: The SEC requires reasonable assurance of delivery—such as by e-mail confirmation, return receipt, and so forth.

2. *Private Placement Offerings (PPOs).* This issue relates to offerings that are subject to bans on solicitation. PPOs, by their nature, are private, and so to offer them on the Internet, which is wide open, is problematic. The SEC has indicated it would approve of password-protected sites accessible only to those investors who otherwise meet the statutory requirements. This brings up an interesting question of identification and authentication of investors. How may Internet investment sites attempting to raise capital under PPOs verify the information that investors provide them with? The anonymity of the Internet creates these additional risks.

3. *Road Shows.* Before the Internet, company management conducted live presentations to a restricted audience of high net worth or institutional investors in an attempt to generate interest in the offering during the waiting period. With the advent of Web-casting technology, anyone with an Internet connection may view a Web-cast road show. Like PPOs, these are for a restricted audience, and so controlling access to the road show is problematic. The SEC takes the position that Internet road shows are permissible, if the issuer:

   - Denies access to its Web site to all except those the seller has confirmed its reasonable belief regarding their qualifying status;
   - Assigns confidential passwords to each buyer unique to a specific road show;
   - Receives confirmation from each seller about the qualified status of each buyer; and
   - Has no actual knowledge or reason to believe the buyer is not qualified.

4. *Dissemination of Information.* There are two major issues relating to releasing information. The first relates to *who* is disclosing financial information. The Internet is an open forum, capable of reaching millions of users simultaneously at almost no cost and targeting them by interest, or income, and so forth. Chat rooms, bulletin boards, and other sites—financial and gossip—are devoted to individual stocks and offerings. The quality of the information

disseminated on these sites is often questionable, yet they enjoy a devoted following. As an example of a bulletin board site, go to *http://finance.yahoo.com*, enter the symbol for a stock, and click on messages. Some information may be true, but because there is no editorial control over these postings, much information is not verified, and some of it may even violate the securities laws, as well as other laws, such as laws prohibiting defamation. (For further discussion, refer to Chapter 11, "Defamation.")

The second issue related to the dissemination of information concerns *what* is being disclosed to whom. Concerned with the selective disclosure of material information by issuers to favored clients, analysts, or institutions about important information such as advance warning on earnings results, the SEC enacted Reg FD (Fair Disclosure). (Previously, issuers released advance information given to insiders and favored clients ahead of releasing it to the general public.) The SEC likened this practice to "tipping," and it enacted this rule that is *designed to promote the full and fair disclosure of material information by issuers*, so all investors are privy to the same information. And so although the *quantity* of information available has grown exponentially due to the Internet, issuers, analysts, and others in the financial industry complain that the *quality* of the information has gone down because Reg FD has a chilling effect on communications between issuers and analysts, for example. Companies must now develop a formal policy for disclosure of material information. Because this regulation is so new, there is no litigation on it yet. Considering the controversy surrounding this regulation, too, it is likely the SEC will reconsider this rule.

5. *Allocation of Shares.* This is the final topic of discussion relating to Internet offerings before we discuss Internet transactions. Issuers and underwriters enjoy the perquisite of allocating shares in IPOs. This was an especially attractive feature for companies during the IPO boom of the late 1990s. However, it is apparent that companies and underwriters abuse the allocation of shares. In one recent instance, Credit Suisse First Boston (CSFB) settled charges with the SEC after CSFB offered clients IPO share in exchange for kickbacks from clients, and clients promised to buy more shares. The aftermarket order for additional shares at higher prices is a practice known as *laddering*. This clearly represents a manipulation of stock prices in violation of the securities laws. Charges stemming from share allocation schemes have been filed against a number of other underwriters, too, including Goldman Sachs, J.P. Morgan Chase, and Lehman Brothers. In 2001, charges of illegal share allocations accounted for the majority of securities fraud claims against companies and their underwriters.

http://

- To read the complete final rule, see http://www.sec.gov/rules/final/33-7881.htm
- To read more on this issue, the settlement order may be found at http://www.sec.gov/litigation/complaints/judglr17327.htm

The following case relates to the republication of false company financial information, a case that shows both how easy it is to manipulate information, and how there are repercussions to disseminating unverified information. Although this information relates to transaction in shares, rather than an initial offering of shares, this case has application to both scenarios.

Hart v. Internet Wire, Inc. & Bloomberg L.P.
163 F. Supp. 2d 316, and 145 F. Supp. 2d 360 (S.D. N.Y. 2001)

Facts

On August 25, 2000, defendants were the unwitting victims of a criminal hoax, created by Mark Simeon Jakob, to manipulate the stock of Emulex Corporation. Jakob sold shares of Emulex stock short on August 24, 2000, and incurred a paper loss in excess of $97,000. Because of this, he faced a margin call from his stockbroker. So Jakob decided to try to manipulate the price of Emulex stock and cause it to fall and have the effect of lessening the amount he owed his broker. Jakob, a previous employee of Internet Wire, used his knowledge about the news business in his scheme. Jakob sent an e-mail to Internet Wire from a Yahoo! account he opened that evening. The e-mail contained a fake press release and was delivered to Internet Wire under the false name of "Ross Porter" of the fictitious public relations firm of "Porter and Smith" on the account of porterandsmith@ yahoo.com. Jakob's e-mail instructed Internet Wire to issue a press release that was attached to the e-mail, and it stated that "this release is extremely important and I would like it to go out . . . at 9:30 A.M. EST . . . tomorrow morning, Friday, August 25th."

Internet Wire distributed this release to the major news services, including Bloomberg, which were all duped into publishing and distributing it. These news services had no role in the authorship or content of the release. The release announced that Emulex said that the company's president and chief executive officer had resigned, that the SEC was conducting a formal investigation of accounting irregularities at the company, and that the company would revise its fourth quarter results to reflect losses rather than profits. The release was entirely false.

At 9:30 A.M. EST on August 25, 2000, Emulex stock opened at $110.6875 per share. Thereafter the stock began a precipitous decline, and it crashed to a price of below $44 per share by 10:28 A.M. At this point, NASDAQ issued a halt to all trading in Emulex stock. Emulex learned of the news release and branded it a hoax, and several news organizations published the repudiation immediately. Trading began again, and at the end of the day, Emulex shares closed at $105 per share.

Plaintiffs are a group of individuals who sold common stock or call options in Emulex, or purchased put option in Emulex on August 25, 2000, after the opening of the market until trading was halted. Because they are individuals, rather than the government, attempting to enforce the securities laws, they must bring their suit under the Private Securities Litigation Reform Act (PSLRA). The PSLRA makes it compulsory to assert detailed factual pleadings of the essential grounds for a federal securities fraud suit.

Internet Wire is a private business that distributes corporate news, including press releases. Bloomberg is a worldwide publisher of financial, legal, and business news to financial professionals via a network of desktop computer terminals. It regularly retransmits to the general public press releases prepared by professional agencies, such as Internet Wire.

Judicial Opinion *(Judge Pollack)*

The PSLRA sought to curb abusive class action stock market litigation and the filing of cases largely to obtain hoped-for discovery of a legal basis for speculative claims, and to head off unwarranted settlements. [Plaintiffs still have to allege as a basis for their claim under the 1934 Act, fraudulent intent. Therefore] no private cause of action for damages will lie under 10(b) and Rule 10b-5 in the absence of any allegation of 'scienter'—intent to deceive, manipulate, or defraud.

Because Plaintiffs' complaint fails to plead recklessness inferring fraud and fraudulent intent they have failed to allege scienter and [the] suit should not have been brought. The [Plaintiffs'] Amended Complaint seeks to bolster this inadequate charge of federal securities fraud on the notion that red flags in the content and submission of the Fake Press Release, when disregarded by Defendants, rose to a sufficient case of fraudulent intent to participate in a hoax. However, as each flag cited is examined separately and in unison, they fall short of spelling a sufficient claim of federal securities fraud. [T]he content of the release gave no meaningful hint of the falsity thereof. None of the red flags suffice to show a plausible motive or intent to defraud investors. [Case law indicates] that allegations as to what defendant 'should have turned up' constituted 'negligence at best,' and are insufficient . . . to plead securities fraud.

While Section 10(b) is aptly described as a catchall provision . . . what it catches must be fraud. A 10b-5 case requires intentional misconduct and this is not a 10b-5 case. The Plaintiffs' suggestion that defendants should have detected signs of Mark Jakob's fraud, without more, is palpably insufficient to . . . establish . . . liability as long as defendants did not deliberately shut their eyes to the facts.

The Second Amended Class Action Complaint is dismissed.

SO ORDERED.

Case Questions

1. Identify two ways in which the Internet made it easier for Jakob to advance his scheme.
2. What recommendations do you have for Internet Wire, bloomberg.com, and other publishers of the hoax? What are the financial and time costs of your recommendations?
3. Because this conduct falls outside of the federal securities laws, how would you amend the current laws to address this type of scheme?

ONLINE TRANSACTIONS IN SECURITIES

The first part of this chapter outlined Internet issues related to *offerings* of securities. Now we detail Internet issues related to *transactions* in securities that have already been sold. This section outlines the issues that will be presented for legal resolution in future lawsuits as the e-trading industry matures and as the markets fluctuate. The Internet presents new complications because there were a great many filters in place acting as quality checks/certifications of fitness of particular investments, for individual clients. For example, pre-Internet, information was generated by the financial industry as reported by the major financial newspapers. Information complied with SEC rules, newspaper stories were checked by editors before going to press, and so forth. Post-Internet, information comes from a variety of sources and, except for company publications, there are no editorial checks on any of this information. Another example: pre-Internet, shares of stock could be bought only through registered and licensed broker-dealers. They are under a series of legal obligations to buy only those investments for individuals that are appropriate and suitable. Post-Internet, individuals are making their own representations about what their net worth and liquidity and financial needs are, largely unverified by e-brokerages, and these individuals are engaging in their own trading, without the advice or direction of broker-dealers. Clearly problems existed in the securities industry before the Internet, but the Internet has greatly added to the regulatory challenges of protecting investors.

The migration of securities transactions to the Internet represents a tremendous opportunity to capitalize on savings through less expensive investment information, transaction fees; and greater market-making opportunities when selling, yet it has quickly become apparent that a number of risks are involved due to the many vulnerabilities in online trading systems. We present the major issues as they are developing, grouped them into two categories.

Security Vulnerabilities

Privacy. Through data mining and other data extraction techniques that observe client behavior and transaction history, e-brokerages are developing investor profiles. This customer-relationship-management (CRM) software that aggregates all of this data creates a real privacy concern for clients, and it makes the e-brokerage sites and their servers potential targets for privacy invasions and other criminal acts. How seriously are e-brokerages taking this important issue of privacy? Privacy breaches through hacking and identity theft are leading causes of crime. Another related issue is whether the companies may sell/share data with business partners, subsidiaries, other companies, or even the government. (For further discussion of this particular issue, refer to the Gramm-Leach-Bliley Act.) Acceptable data collection, protection, and sales practices must be formulated and standardized throughout the industry.

Identification and Authentication (I&A) of Clients. How can e-brokerages effectively accomplish I&A of its clients? This security issue (generally addressed in Chapter 12,

"Internet and Information Security") is of paramount importance, because relationships are not face to face for the most part anymore. E-brokerages need to ensure the veracity of their data and systems and develop appropriate software to accomplish this goal. The SEC is charged with maintaining the integrity of the markets, and it is incumbent on the commission to mandate e-brokerage security. What are the best ways to accomplish this? What will e-brokerages' liability be for cases when they execute transactions for individuals who break through I&A systems and trade in someone else's name?

Quality Vulnerabilities

Investor Suitability. Brokers are obliged to recommend only those investments that are suitable for customers. Defining what a recommendation is in the online environment is difficult. Further, online firms now use data-mining technology to develop client profiles and customize information, and they base their trading recommendations on this computer-generated profile. Investor suitability claims will inevitably arise.

Best Execution. Brokers are required to seek the most advantageous terms reasonably available for client transactions. This duty of best execution for trades evolves with technology and the way in which different markets are developing. How can the best execution be evaluated when there are so many different portals (refer to page 241 for more information on portals), e-brokerages, and so forth, available? And because portals are not registered with the SEC, this duty potentially does not exist for them.

Market Data. The law requires the SEC to ensure that market participants and the public can obtain market information in terms that are fair and reasonable. Now there is delayed, as well as real-time, data. Real-time data is now accessible to anyone on the Internet; previously, individual investors were able just to receive delayed data. What should the access charges be for real-time data—and will this discriminate between certain groups of investors and between those who are connected and those who are not?

System Capacity/Access Problems Due to Volume, Lack of Adequate Trading Infrastructure. As e-transactions in securities continue to grow at a phenomenal pace, it is important to consider system infrastructure and capacity. Highly publicized outages and delays are reported with regularity, and these clearly negatively impact the SEC's duty to maintain fair and orderly markets, as well as brokers' duty of best execution. System capacity becomes a pressing issue due to the Internet: it is now much more difficult to determine where exactly the system has failed. Execution errors and failures are a serious concern. Moreover, the Internet is a decentralized structure, where subgroups of a group of data are broken into packets and sent; each packet travels through different connection points before it is reassembled at the destination point. Communications failures can occur at any point along these pathways. This impact is greater on those e-brokerages with a geographically dispersed client base. How should brokerages respond? How should they reimburse clients for failures? How can e-brokerages mitigate client losses? How can we ensure that each e-brokerage system hosts a minimally functional network that includes a backup data system, a backup power source, and a method to speedily identify and remediate the failure points?

Investor Education. All investing information formerly filtered down to investors through registered representatives. Now investors have access to a myriad of information sources, some helpful and some not. This vast data stream combined with the option of directly ordering stocks is a powerful incentive for investors to bypass the middle person—leading (as the Internet has in so many other industries) toward disintermediation. Investors save on fees, yet do they lose in other ways? Are they investing in qualitatively better ways? Is the investor experience better than before the Internet? Investor complaints have skyrocketed, mainly attributed to investors who are not experienced in the investment field. How should the SEC and the **Federal Trade Commission (FTC)** educate the public so that they are knowledgeable, competent investors? (Recently, the SEC posted six fake investment Web sites in order to show investors how easy it is to get scammed. The sites received hundreds of thousands of hits from interested investors. One of them, for example, is *http://www.mcwhortle.com*.)

Online Discussion Forums. Before the Internet, there were limited sources of financial information, and it was always clear who said what. The Internet has made possible online discussion forums where there are seemingly endless sources of financial information, and it is oftentimes unclear who said what (refer back to the *Hart* case). Many times postings are akin to useless chatter and gossip and relatively harmless. But postings are potentially more lethal, to the extent they are written by present or former disgruntled employees. The issue of postings is further exacerbated when they are anonymous or pseudonymous. Postings are responsible, to a degree, for market volatility, and they impact the functioning of the markets in other ways. How should companies respond to postings, especially when they purport to speak about information that would, if true, be considered "material"? How closely should companies monitor online discussion forums?

Portals. These gateways to the Internet include such sites as AOL's Personal Finance, Yahoo! Finance, and so forth. Portals are not registered with the SEC, yet they directly compete with e-brokerages, and they charge brokers a fee to link from their sites. These fees are usually based on performance factors, such as transactions completed. Yet the SEC prohibits the receipt of transaction-based compensation by non-broker dealers. What is the best way, then, for e-brokerages to compensate these sites that are not registered with the SEC?

Enforcement Issues

Enforcement of the securities laws is a multitiered effort representing the combined resources of the SEC, the FTC, as well as state and federal consumer protection agencies and prosecutors. The SEC is charged with maintaining market integrity and investor protection. Yet, as a civil agency, it has no authority to pursue criminal charges against perpetrators. Its power is limited to issuing **No-Action Letters** (indicating that it will not take any action at this time, and so the transaction does not violate any laws as interpreted by the SEC); ordering repayment of losses; the payment of fines; and barring wrongdoers from participating in the capital markets in the future. Resolution of SEC actions often takes up to three years (although the threat of an SEC investigation or the publicity of a heavy fine is a deterrent effect as well.) FTC authority overlaps with the SEC because it is charged with preventing fraudulent, deceptive, and unfair business practices against consumers. Again, its enforcement actions are civil in nature.

State and federal prosecutors are perhaps the biggest threat to those who violate the securities laws. They have the power to pursue criminal charges, prison sentencing, as well as monetary penalties. Moreover, prosecutions and sentencing happen quickly as compared to SEC actions. Although this would seem to undermine SEC authority, the agency actually welcomes and consults in prosecutions because these actions are an important deterrent to securities crimes. In one recent case involving allegedly fraudulent transactions in the stock of ImClone, the SEC began an investigation simultaneously with federal prosecutors. Federal prosecutors have an array of laws on which to charge defendants, including theft, fraud, and racketeering—commonly known as mail or wire fraud. A leading case on the applicability of the mail and wire fraud statutes to securities transactions is *Carpenter v. United States*, 484 U.S. 19 (1987). Further enforcement changes recently began, as a direct result of the 9/11 terrorist action. The USA Patriot Act requires mutual funds and other financial services companies, effective July 2002, to file **Suspicious Activity Reports (SARs)** with the Treasury Department whenever the conduct of clients or even potential clients indicates possible money laundering activities. Previously banks were only required to report cash deposits in excess of $10,000. All other transactions escaped reporting requirements, even those in smaller denominations that when added up exceeded $10,000. Suspicious activity is loosely defined, and we are sure to see litigation on this issue. This reporting requirement adds another layer of regulation and impacts the entire financial services industry to the extent they accept third-party checks, international wire transfers, and even cashier's checks.

INTERNATIONAL ASPECTS OF ONLINE SECURITIES OFFERINGS

One of the unique characteristics of the Internet is its users' capacity to send securities-related information across national boundaries. This has made international enforcement of securities laws critical. Regulators are focusing on a variety of securities law topics and their application in a global format. Regulators have to balance the need to prevent securities fraud with the ability to use the Internet efficiently. The SEC and other organizations around the world are now making significant efforts to regulate the flow of capital in cyberspace and enforce securities laws online.

Regulation of the International Movement of Capital

The intergovernmental organization (IGO) that has taken the leading role in regulating the international movement of capital is the **Organization for Economic Cooperation and Development (OECD)**. Its **Code of Liberalization of Capital Movements**, first adopted in 1961 and last amended in 1989, requires the OECD member countries to progressively abolish their restrictions on the movement of capital. That is, it encourages member countries to let foreigners invest locally and to allow residents to invest abroad. The code applies to all kinds of investments, including investments in equity and debt securities, such as stocks, bonds, money market transactions, and even swaps, options, and other derivative instruments. Although the OECD Code allows member states to retain controls that existed when the code was first adopted, by the early 1990s, OECD member countries had abolished all significant restrictions on the international movement of capital.

The other IGO that has taken an interest in capital movements is the Council of Europe. Its 1989 **Convention on Insider Trading** establishes a cooperative mechanism for supervising securities markets. In particular, "because of the internationalization of markets and the ease of present-day communications," the Convention focuses on uncovering insider trading activities "on the market of a state by persons not resident in that state or acting through persons not resident there." *Insider trading* is the use of nonpublic information by a company insider (such as a corporate officer or director) about a company or the securities market to buy or sell securities for personal gain. The Convention, in essence, allows the regulatory agencies in one country to request the assistance of those in another country to uncover conduct by an individual or individuals that constitutes insider trading in the requesting country.

Aside from the Council of Europe's multilateral Convention on Insider Trading, the other international efforts to stop insider trading are found in bilateral "Memoranda of Understanding" (MOUs) between the U.S. Securities and Exchange Commission and its counterpart in seventeen other, mostly European, countries.[1] The MOUs provide a mechanism for exchanging information and for mutual cooperation in the investigation of securities violations.

International Cooperation and Securities Law Enforcement

International Organization of Securities Commissions and the SEC. The **International Organization of Securities Commissions (IOSCO)** is a multinational body of governmental and nongovernmental organizations concerned with the regulation of securities fraud on a global scale. IOSCO's members include organizations from at least a hundred countries, including the U.S. SEC. IOSCO seeks to promote high standards of international regulation, exchange information between members, unify international legal and surveillance standards, and provide mutual assistance in order to promote integrity in the markets. Its members have also articulated five principles regarding international securities regulation of the Internet:

http://

- For a more in-depth look at IOSCO, visit **http://www.iosco.org**

---

[1]The countries are Argentina, Australia, Brazil, Chile, Costa Rica, France, Hungary, Italy, Japan, Luxembourg, Mexico, the Netherlands, Norway, Spain, Sweden, Switzerland, and the United Kingdom. In addition, the U.S. Securities and Exchange Commission has agreements with the Canadian provinces of British Columbia, Ontario, and Quebec.

1. Regulators should not inhibit legitimate securities-related uses of the Internet.
2. Regulators should strive for transparency and consistency in the application of international securities laws.
3. Regulators of different jurisdictions should cooperate with one another.
4. Regulators should maintain a flexible approach to applying securities laws that accounts for continuous development of technology.
5. Regulators should ensure that fundamental policies underlying securities regulation—protection of investors, efficiency and transparency of markets, and the reduction of systemic risk—should also govern Internet-based actions.

IOSCO also believes that, although the existing securities law framework can be applied to Internet activities, regulators should examine current laws for the presence of gaps and inconsistencies when being applied to an online forum.

International Internet Surf Days. Members of IOSCO periodically cooperate with one another and perform coordinated securities enforcement sweeps of the Internet. For example, the SEC and other IOSCO members participated in "International Internet Surf Days," in March 2000 and April 2001. Regulators search the Internet for fraudulent solicitation of investors, stock manipulation, false or misleading information, or other illicit activity. In the March 2000 sweep, for example, 300 individuals from 41 countries examined more than 27,000 Web sites. More than 2,400 Web sites examined were tagged for follow-up attention. IOSCO has commented that in light of the increasingly international nature of securities Internet fraud, such surf days will inevitably continue.

International Securities Fraud

Even with the most thorough of enforcement from the SEC and international organizations, new Web sites continuously appear offering securities with the lure of incredible short-term returns. The following case as an excellent example of current issues in international Internet securities enforcement.

Securities and Exchange Commission v. Gold-Ventures Club (d/b/a www.gold-ventures.net)
Case No. 1:02-CV-1434 (CAP) (N.D. Ga., filed May 28, 2002)

COMPLAINT FOR INJUNCTIVE AND OTHER RELIEF

Facts

Plaintiff Securities and Exchange Commission ("Commission") alleges that:

Defendants

Gold-Ventures Club is an entity that operates an Internet investment website (the "Website"). The Website provides an e-mail address to contact Gold-Ventures, but no address or telephone number. The Commission has been unable to locate an address for Gold-Ventures. EarthLink and its server, which host Gold-Ventures' Website, are located in Atlanta, Georgia. Alexander Khamidouline is at least one of the people responsible for the investment program offered by Gold-Ventures and operating the Gold-Ventures Website. The Commission believes Khamidouline resides in Irkutsk, Russia.

Jurisdiction and Venue

This Court has subject matter jurisdiction. This Court has personal jurisdiction over the Defendants by virtue of the Defendants' activities directed at the United States and the Northern District of Georgia. The Defendants contracted with an Atlanta-based server to host their Website, consented to personal jurisdiction in Georgia in that contract, sent e-mails to United States residents advertising the fraudulent securities, accepted money from United States residents to invest in the fraudulent investment program, contracted with a domain name registrar in the United States to register the name of the Website, and impersonated a Commission attorney located in the United States.

The Fraudulent Scheme

Since at least March 2002, the Defendants have offered an investment program through the Gold-Ventures Website (www.gold-ventures.net). The Defendants' short-term investment program promises an exorbitant 200% return on principal investments of $250.00 to $5000.00 in only 14 days. The Defendants claim to remit a 200% return on the principal invested in a single payment at the end of each 14-day investment term.

The Defendants represent on the Gold-Ventures Website that the investments in, and returns from, the investment program are guaranteed, risk-free, and require no investor participation. For example, the "About" section of the Website states that "our group gives guarantees that in 14 days we will DOUBLE every amount you deposit (From 250 to 5000 $USD) with no risk for you! We do it when you sleep, walk, go to work or make shopping. We need no effort on your part to work with your investments and pay you high returns."

On the Website, the Defendants further represent that Gold-Ventures' organizers can generate 200% profits for investors every 14 days due to their knowledge of, and "by working with[,] the real world financial markets." The Website also maintains that Gold-Ventures is "based on a real business model," maintains "a large fund of reserve capital" in the event of any "unforeseen situation[s]," and makes "payouts" to investors through a "pool" of funds. . . . Gold-Ventures and Khamidouline raised money from at least four investors, two of whom are in the United States.

The representations described . . . were materially false and misleading as the investment in, and return on investments from, the Gold-Ventures Club investment program are not and cannot be risk-free or guaranteed. Among other things, investing in global financial markets by its nature involves undertaking risk. Thus, Gold-Ventures could not guarantee exorbitant risk-free returns on investments made during all 14-day business cycles throughout the year. . . . The investment terms the Defendants offer—short-term, fixed financial returns that are both exorbitant and risk-free—are patently fraudulent . . . . Therefore, the Defendants knew or were reckless in not knowing that [their] representations . . . were false.

On May 2, 2002, a Commission attorney sent by e-mail a letter addressed to Khamidouline, informing him that the Commission was conducting an informal inquiry into Gold-Ventures' operations. The letter requested numerous documents of Gold-Ventures to aid in the inquiry. Not only did Gold-Ventures and Khamidouline ignore the request, but they apparently used the letter in an attempt to blackmail a former investor into giving them more money. On May 6, 2002, just four days after the Commission sent its letter, the former investor received an e-mail purportedly from a Commission attorney with an almost identical name to the attorney who sent the letter to the Defendants. The fake letter stated that the Commission was investigating the investor, but would end its investigation if the investor sent money to Gold-Ventures' EvoCash account. The e-mail contains the Commission's actual file number of the Gold-Ventures investigation.

Relief Requested

WHEREFORE, the Commission respectfully requests that the Court:

1. Declare, determine and find that Defendants Gold-Ventures and Khamidouline committed the violations of the federal securities laws alleged in this Complaint.
2. Issue a Temporary Restraining Order, a Preliminary Injunction and a Permanent Injunction, restraining and enjoining Defendants Gold-Ventures and Khamidouline, and their officers, agents, servants, employees, attorneys, and all persons in active concert or participation with them, and each of them, from violating [various securities laws].
3. Issue an Order temporarily freezing the assets of Defendants Gold-Ventures and Khamidouline until further Order of the Court, and requiring accountings by Gold-Ventures and Khamidouline.
4. Issue an Order requiring Defendants Gold-Ventures and Khamidouline to disgorge all ill-gotten profits or proceeds that they have received as a result of the acts and conduct complained of, with prejudgment interest.
5. Issue an Order requiring Defendants Gold-Ventures and Khamidouline to take necessary steps to repatriate to the territory of the United States all funds and assets of investors described in the Commission's Complaint in this action.

Case Questions

1. How can the SEC legally file this action in the United States when the fraudulent activity occurred in Russia?
2. How did the defendants perpetrate their alleged fraud on unwary investors? What should have investors looked for that would make them suspicious?
3. How can the SEC prevent such fraudulent activities from happening when the basis of operations is in another country?

Although final resolution of the case is still pending (see SEC Litigation Release No. 17537, May 28, 2002), the SEC won a significant victory because the government won a temporary restraining order, an asset freeze, and other relief from the court ordering the defendants to stop violating U.S. securities laws.

Investments in Offshore Securities and the Internet: Regulation S

History and Development. During the 1970s and 1980s, global capital markets experienced significant growth. European offerings of common and preferred stock increased from $200 million in 1983 to $20 billion in 1987. By 1987, U.S. investors' purchases of non-U.S. stocks climbed to a record $187 billion, and foreign purchasers of U.S. stocks topped $481 billion. The SEC realized the number of international securities transactions would continue to grow. As uncertainty arose regarding the specific extent of the SEC's regulatory powers, the SEC established set boundaries for regulation. These boundaries were ultimately developed into Regulation S (Reg S).

Understanding Regulation S. Section 5 of the Securities and Exchange Act of 1933 bars any person in interstate commerce from selling a security unless a registration statement is in effect regarding that security. The **Reg S Exemption** states that securities offers and sales that occur *outside* the United States do not fall within Section 5 of the act. In other words, foreign offers of securities outside the United States do not have to comply with U.S. registration requirements. Reg S supports the SEC's theory that U.S. securities laws exist to protect U.S. capital markets and investors who purchase securities in these domestic markets. This protection extends to foreign nationals as well.

Meeting the Basic Requirements of Reg S Offshore Offerings. An issuing company must satisfy two fundamental requirements in order to qualify for the safe harbor of Reg S and thus escape U.S. registration requirements. First, no directed selling efforts must be made into the United States. For example, directed selling efforts include marketing campaigns or seminars in the United States designed to induce the purchase of securities supposedly being distributed abroad.

Second, the offer or sale of the security must be for an "offshore transaction." An offer or sale is for an offshore transaction when the offer is not made to a person in the United States and, when the buy order is originated, the buyer is outside the United States—or the seller reasonably believes the buyer is outside the United States. Alternatively, Reg S offers two "safe harbors" that constitute a transaction outside the United States. An offer to a person not in the United States is an offshore transaction when it occurs through a physical trading floor of an established foreign securities exchange. In the case of resales of securities, the seller may complete the transaction through a "designated offshore securities market." Reg S further classifies securities into three categories, and each category has specific further requirements for securities offerings and resales.

http://

- To review Regulation S in its entirety, see **http://www.sec.gov/divisions/corpfin/forms/regs.htm**

Internet Offerings and Reg S. The SEC developed guidelines for solicitations published over the Internet. The SEC has noted that Internet publication of an offer or sale of securities may remove the issuer from the exemption of Reg S. In other words, placing an offer or sale of securities on the Internet may require the issue to file registration requirements with the SEC. The SEC reasons that anyone who has access to the Internet can obtain access to a Web site unless the Web site sponsor adopts special procedures to restrict access.

Fortunately for issuers, the SEC suggests steps that issuers can take that will limit SEC scrutiny. For example, foreign issuers should place a prominent disclaimer on their Web site clearly stating the offer is directed only to countries other than the United States. The site could also state that the securities or services are not being offered in the United States or to U.S. persons, or it could specify those jurisdictions (other than the United States) in which the offer is being made. The statements should be located on the same screen as the offering material or on a screen that must be viewed before reaching the offering materials.

The securities offeror also may use certain preventative measures to ensure that any purchaser is not in the United States. This could include ascertaining the prospective purchaser's residence before the sale and declining to send information to certain geolocations. Issuers may also wish to implement password-type protection in order to limit access.

Conversely, the SEC may also construe certain statements on a Web site as enticements to U.S. investors. For example, if a securities offeror emphasizes that the offer allows the investor to reduce or avoid payment of U.S. income taxes, the SEC would regard such a site as *not* an "offshore offering." Sham offshore offerings that exist offshore in name only will also not be considered to fall under Reg S. Accidental sales to U.S. persons do not automatically result in disqualification from Reg S status, but the SEC recommends that if the issuer discovers it is unwittingly selling to U.S. persons, it take immediate steps to assure against future accidental sales.

http://

- For a review of an SEC regulation addressing Internet publication of securities offers and solicitations, see **http://www.sec.gov/rules/ interp/33-7516.htm#body17**

International Internet Securities Offerings and "Blue Sky" Laws

International securities offerings in cyberspace also present the difficult question of whether cyber-offerings on a Web site may be regulated by the *state* securities laws (also known as **Blue Sky laws**) where the Web site may be viewed. If each state could regulate every securities offering that was viewable by a Web site in that state, then potentially each state could impose its own restrictions on any securities offering. As a general rule, mere passive presence of a Web site in a state does not sufficiently develop the basis for jurisdiction of that state's laws over the Web site.

If passive presence is not sufficient, then how "active" must a securities offeror be in order to trigger state blue sky laws? In response to this question, the **North American Securities Administrators Association (NASAA)** developed a model rule that establishes that states will not attempt to establish jurisdiction over a Web offering if that offering has specific disclaimers stating that no offers or sales are being made to the resident of that particular state. The disclaimer may be presented in the home page. Also, the Web site may wish to request the Web site visitor's address or zip code before the visitor can access offering materials. At least thirty-nine states have adopted a version of the NASAA model rule.

Summary

There is a close interplay between issuing companies and regulators. Companies are in effect making the rules of the game by creating new offering and trading systems and then requesting No-Action Letters from the SEC. Gradually, a body of law is developing from the SECs No-Action Letters, Litigation Releases, Settlements, and Enforcement Proceedings. The Internet has effectively created a new, less expensive, better targeted method to raise capital, boding especially well for small, start-up, and low capitalization companies. Investors, too, benefit from online offerings, trading, and information previously available only to large institutional investors and other favored clients. Many of the DPOs, however, carry a higher investment risk and lower liquidity than traditional offerings and share transactions. Risks also extend to purchases of international securities in cyberspace. Various international organizations, as well as the SEC, are establishing procedures to combat cross-border securities cyberfraud. The SEC is also establishing its own boundaries by defining when Internet offerings of securities constitute an offshore transaction not covered by SEC rules and regulations.

Key Terms

offshore offering, *220*
Securities Act of 1933, *221*
security, *221*
Securities and Exchange Commission (SEC), *221*
Prospectus, *224*
Securities and Exchange Act of 1934, *228*
Investment Company Act, *231*
Private Placement Offering (PPO), *231*
Reg A Exemption, *231*
Reg D Exemption, *232*
prefiling period, *232*

waiting period, *232*
registration and effective period, *232*
road show, *232*
initial public offering (IPO), *233*
post-effective period, *233*
direct public offering (DPO), *234*
Federal Trade Commission (FTC), *241*
No-Action Letter, *241*
Suspicious Activity Reports (SARs), *242*
Organization for Economic

Cooperation and Development (OECD), *242*
Code of Liberalization of Capital Movements, *242*
Convention on Insider Trading, *243*
International Organization of Securities Commissions (IOSCO), *243*
Reg S Exemption, *247*
Blue Sky laws, *248*
North American Securities Administrators Association (NASAA), *248*

Manager's Checklist

√ Issuers must work closely with accountants, auditors, and attorneys who have experience in the type of offering that is under consideration to ensure full compliance with the federal securities laws.

√ Issuers must take steps to ensure that their offerings are targeted to only qualifying investors as defined by the laws, a particularly challenging task because of the open architecture of the Internet.

√ Issuers should be aware there is a dual layer of securities regulations, and they must comply with federal as well as any relevant state laws in which their securities are sold.

√ Publishers, republishers, as well as bulletin board sponsors of company financial data, may incur liability for publication of false financial data.

√ Investors must be aware of the significant potential for international cyberfraud that exists with offshore investments, especially from Web sites that seem to promise fantastic returns in a short time.

√ Issuers must take steps to ensure that their Web site explicitly excludes U.S. investors in order to qualify for the Reg S offshore exemption.

√ Ethical Considerations

Companies must continually evaluate the legality and ethics of new practices in cases where government oversight does not yet exist.

Compliance with securities regulations must be considered and integral component to the capital-raising process, rather than a marginal and costly expense item to the process.

Companies should evaluate the merits of conducting domestic offerings versus offshore offerings.

Companies should make every effort to manage their publicity and reputation during the capital-raising process.

Case Problems

1. Critical Path, Inc., a leader in electronic messaging systems for companies, went public in 1997. In 2000, its revenues were below analysts' estimates for the third and fourth quarters. In an effort to maintain its share price, Critical Path's president booked nonexistent revenue on its income statements. (He did this through a software swap with one company and by securing an extension on re-payments to another company.) The company thereafter announced that it achieved its earnings estimates. Is this conduct within the reach of the federal securities laws? [*SEC v. Thatcher, http://www.sec.gov/litigation/admin/ 34-45393.htm*]

2. Razorfish is an Internet consulting company that went public in 1999. It acquired another Internet consulting company, i-Cube. Shortly thereafter, the company made statements regarding the results of the acquisition or related matters. By way of example, here are two of the twelve allegedly fraudulent statements: (a) "Our strong sequential, quarter-over-quarter growth of 22% has Razorfish hitting on all cylinders now that we have successfully integrated our acquisitions and built global, scaleable capabilities. . . . ," and (b) "[Statement by defendant Michael Pehl] I could not be more pleased with our accomplishments to date, in particular the successful integration of i-Cube into Razorfish. . . ." In the wake of the NASDAQ correction in 2000, Razorfish's

share price dropped dramatically. Plaintiffs, unhappy shareholders, contend that these and the other statements were false because the integration was neither successful nor complete, and Razorfish's statements amount to securities fraud. What was the result? [*In re Razorfish, Inc.*, 2001 U.S. Dist. LEXIS 14756 (S.D. N.Y., Sept. 21, 2001)]

3. Homestore.com, an online provider of home and real estate–related information, issued a release of positive second quarter results, causing its stock price to rise 25 percent the next trading day. Later, the company released positive third quarter results; immediately thereafter, Homestore slashed its revenue projections for the future, citing a decline in its business. Shares fell by more than 50 percent on the next trading day. Shareholders filed suit, alleging that Homestore overstated revenue and assets during these quarters in violation of SEC rules. What is the best strategy for preventing accounting fraud allegations in the first instance? (This is an extremely common claim—and echoes the claims involved in the Enron/Arthur Anderson case.) ["Homestore.com Faces Shareholder Lawsuit over Executives' Actions Since Mid-July," December 27, 2001, *http://www.wsj.com*, and click on Tech Center]

4. New World Web Vision.com, Inc. made numerous claims that it was preparing to conduct an IPO. It offered and sold "pre-IPO shares" at $.60 per share and told investors their shares would be worth $6 to $16 per share when the company went public. The company accomplished this by using two Web sites and sending thousands of unsolicited e-mail messages. Are these pre-IPO shares considered securities, and thus under the jurisdiction of the securities laws? [*Securities and Exchange Commission v. New World Web Vision.com*, Inc., Litigation Release No. 17442, March 27, 2002, *http://www.sec.gov*]

5. PacketSwitch.com raised more than $3.7 million as a start-up technology company. It mainly generated funds from affinity groups. The company represented that it had new proprietary technology for wireless broadcasting as well as established revenue sources. After the company experienced financial hardship, investors filed suit, alleging the statements were material, false, and fraudulent; the company asserted they were not, and instead amounted to optimistic puffery. Evidence showed there was some business being conducted, that it was a start-up, but the technology a commercial off-the-shelf product that had no capability to broadcast wirelessly. What was the result? [*Securities and Exchange Commission v. Packetswitch.com*, Litigation Release No. 17268, December 12, 2001, *http://www.sec.gov*]

6. Emsanet Internet Services, Inc., an ISP start-up company, planned to raise further funds by selling stock to investors through a PPO. In the offering materials, they stated that Emsanet officers had substantial industry experience. They predicted that by the end of 2001, its ISP service would have 1.7 million

subscribers and the company would generate $254,800,000 in revenues. One underwriter posted messages on various Internet bulletin boards, stating that Emsanet planned to conduct an IPO at $20 per share and any investors who purchased shares in the PPO at $3.50 per share would be able to sell those shares. Evidence showed that the officers did not have substantial industry experience; at this stage it lacked any operational infrastructure, and so the financial projections were speculative; and it had not undertaken steps to conduct an IPO. Are these three statements materially misleading, amounting to securities fraud? What was the result? [*Securities and Exchange Commission v. Emsanet Internet Services, Inc.*, Litigation Release No. 17336, January 24, 2002, *http://www.sec.gov*]

7. International Alliance Trading, Inc. and Sun Pacific Capital Group, Inc. published reviews of securities offerings on their Web site, Investors Edge. The reviews touted the merits of the issuers and published favorable and purportedly independent reviews. The reviewers did not disclose that they received options to buy shares in the offering in exchange for promoting the offering. Was any securities law violated? [*Securities and Exchange Commission v. Volmer*, Litigation Release No. 15952, October 27, 1998, *http://www.sec.gov*]

8. Knight Trading Group, the largest dealer for NASDAQ stocks, found that its stock price declined more than 50 percent in trading before the market opened. NASDAQ halted trading in the stock. Traders attributed the drop to a rumored federal inspection of Knight's books. An investigation revealed that a software problem caused a succession of automatic sell orders. Knight corrected the software glitch. What should NASDAQ do about the trades that occurred during this period of time? What should NASDAQ do about the rumors of pending federal investigations? ["Software Problem Hurts Knight Trading's Shares," June 4, 2002, *http://www.nytimes.com*, and click on Technology]

9. Alan Carr, owner of Europe and Overseas Commodity Traders, was solicited via phone and fax while in Florida by a foreign company to purchase shares in a bond futures fund. Carr placed some buy orders from his Florida residence. The foreign company hid various characteristics of the fund from Carr, and Carr sustained substantial losses. Carr is a Canadian citizen, Carr's company is Panamanian, and the defendant companies are all non-U.S. Can the defendants claim coverage under Regulation S? [*Europe and Overseas Commodity Traders v. Banque Paribas London*, 147 F.3d 118 (2nd Cir. 1998)]

Additional Readings

- Hatlestad, Luc. "Diary of an Internet IPO." *Red Herring* (July 1999) (*http://www.redherring.com/mag/issue68/inv-critical.html*).

- SEC. "Internet Fraud: How to Avoid Internet Investment Scams." (*http://www.sec.gov/investor/pubs/cyberfraud.htm*).

- SEC. "On-Line Brokerage: Keeping Apace of Cyberspace." The Executive Summary is found at *http://www.sec.gov/news/studies/cyberspace.htm*. The Full Report is found at *http://www.sec.gov/pdf/cybrtrnd.pdf*.

- Silber, Jordan. "Online Securities Trading: Triggering the Cycle of Technological Innovation and Congressional Response." *Yale Symposium on Law & Technology* 5 (2001): 4 (*http://lawtech.law.yale.edu/symposium/s01/note_silber.htm*).

- Wang, S. Eric. "Investing Abroad: Regulation S and U.S. Retail Investment in Foreign Securities." *University of Miami Business Law Review* 10 (2002): 329.

Part 4

Special Issues in Cyberspace

PRIVACY

Recent Inventions and business methods call attention to the next step which must be taken for the protection of the person, and for securing to the individual what Judge Cooley calls (Cooley on Torts, 2nd edition) the right "to be let alone."

—**Samuel D. Warren and Louis D. Brandeis,**
"The Right to Privacy," **Harvard Law Review 193 (1890): 4.**

LEARNING OBJECTIVES

After you have read this chapter you should be able to:

1. Understand federal and state constitutional sources of the right to privacy.
2. Discuss the four common law torts for invasion of the right to privacy.
3. Discuss the privacy issues and laws related to the collection and disclosure of financial- and health-related personal information.
4. Discuss selected federal laws that regulate privacy in cyberspace with major emphasis on the Electronic Communication's Privacy Act of 1986.
5. Explore the privacy issues surrounding spamming and online profiling with emphasis on the Federal Trade Commission's efforts to enforce its regulations in this area.
6. Explore workplace privacy issues, in particular, the monitoring of employee computer use and electronic mail (e-mail).
7. Discuss the impact of the European Union (EU) Directive on privacy in cyberspace.
8. Understand the U.S./EU safe harbor rules and how U.S. firms may satisfy them.
9. Comprehend other international initiatives to regulate online privacy.

http://

- Additional material on privacy may be found at the Bentley College CyberLaw Center Web site (**http://ecampus.bentley.edu/dept/cyberlaw**) under Social Issues—Privacy.

INTRODUCTION

At the time Warren and Brandeis talked about the concept of a "right to privacy," none had been recognized constitutionally or otherwise. They fervently believed in and advocated that right, and they were also prophetic. When they referred to "recent inventions and business methods," one wonders if they could have foreseen the time when that right to be let alone would be increasingly threatened by global positioning systems that allow auto rental agencies to track the speed and direction of its customers, the FBI's use of advanced technology such as thermal global imaging to penetrate the walls of a house to determine if marijuana was growing inside (see *Kyllo v. U.S.*, 121 S. Ct. 2038, 2001 presented in Chapter 12), surveillance cameras in public places to monitor our activities, employers monitoring employees' computer usage in the workplace, parents not being able to adequately prevent online Web sites from collecting personal information about their children without permission or notice, or a federal law passed as a result of the most tragic and fearsome foreign threat to the security of our homeland in our history that provides new search and seizure powers to the government in order to assist its efforts to combat and protect us against acts of terrorism. All these no doubt would have made Brandeis and Warren's "top ten" list of major threats to our privacy.

In this chapter we discuss the evolution of the right to privacy and its application to cyberspace. We also explore important cyberspace privacy considerations precipitated by the privacy laws related to the use of the Internet with major emphasis on the workplace.

The enormous growth of the Internet, not only as a means by which we communicate electronically with one another via e-mail but also a marketing tool for e-businesses, continues to present major privacy issues and concerns. For example, every time we visit a Web site, we leave a kind of footprint containing personal demographic information. To gather this information, businesses use computer files called *cookies* capable of tracking our visits to sites and depositing facts about us on our hard drives. What is bothersome, and has the potential for legal and ethical problems, is the use of this private information for commercial purposes without our permission.

Later in this chapter, we discuss some of the uses of this information including spamming (the bulk e-mailing of unsolicited advertisements) and online profiling of personal information (information about users accessed and gathered by Internet advertisers and others). Also later in this chapter, to illustrate the privacy issues raised by these practices, we study one of the most important cases: *In Re DoubleClick Inc., Privacy Litigation.*

You should first be aware that if you searched the Bill of Rights and all twenty-seven amendments to the U.S. Constitution, you would not find an expressed or enumerated right to privacy. Rather, the right to privacy is a penumbral, or implied right, under the U.S. Constitution. The sources of this right require us to consider the Fourth, Fifth, and Ninth Amendments to the U.S. Constitution as applied to the states by the Fourteenth Amendment. Keep in mind, these amendments protect us from unwarranted government intrusions.

SOURCES OF THE RIGHT TO PRIVACY

U.S. Constitution

The **Ninth Amendment** provides:

> The enumeration in the constitution of certain rights shall not be construed to
> deny or disparage others retained by the people.

This amendment was probably the genesis used by the courts and legal scholars including Warren and Brandeis to create a kind of right to privacy. In addition, the Fourth and Fifth Amendments are also sources of the "right to privacy." The **Fourth Amendment** provides:

> The right of the people to be secure in their persons, houses, papers, and effects, against unreasonable searches and seizures, shall not be violated; and no Warrants shall issue, but upon probable cause, supported by oath or affirmation, and particularly describing the place to be searched, and the persons or things to be seized.

In *Griswold v. Connecticut* (1965), the U.S. Supreme Court declared unconstitutional a state law prohibiting the use of birth control devices and the giving of advice concerning their use. The Court also recognized that the Bill of Rights provided us with what it deemed to be "zones of privacy," or areas or locations where privacy is expected.

Later cases held that an important element of this right was to establish the existence of a "reasonable expectation of privacy" (discussed later in more detail) in the particular zone of privacy. The following are minimum requirements for establishing a "reasonable expectation of privacy":

1. A person exhibits an actual expectation of privacy. Consider what you expect when entering an area or location, such as your bedroom, which you desire to be "off limits" to others. Or consider what level of privacy an employee should anticipate with regard to his or her office, desk, file cabinet, or floppy disk.
2. Society recognizes the expectation as reasonable. In addition to your privacy expectation, what do others believe to be your expectation of privacy when you close the door to your bedroom or your office, enter a public phone booth, send an e-mail, or surf a Web site?

For purposes of our discussion of establishing privacy rights associated with cyberspace, these requirements, at a minimum, will have to be satisfied concerning the mass of information, some of a personal nature, being disseminated and accumulated over the Internet.

We next focus on the provision of the **Fifth Amendment** that protects us from government actions that could result in self-incrimination. That provision reads in part:

> No person . . . shall be compelled, in any criminal case, to be a witness against himself.

This does not apply when a person voluntarily turns over documents, records, files, and papers to a law enforcement agency or official. Similarly, the public records of a corporation are not subject to this provision, even if they contain incriminating evidence.

An interesting cyberlaw application of the Fifth Amendment involves the act of encrypting a file that contains possible incriminating information. Encryption involves using encoding methods (using key codes and secured passwords) to block access to certain documents. In *Doe v. United States*, 487 U.S. 201 (1988), the Supreme Court held that an individual could "be forced to surrender a key to a strongbox containing incriminating documents, but not to reveal the combination to his wall safe . . . by word or deed." This case seems to imply that a law enforcement agency, pursuant to a valid search warrant, could obtain an encrypted file. However, the decision in *Doe* would likely prevent the agency from forcing a defendant to supply the private key, password, or code that could enable decryption or decoding, thereby allowing access. *Doe* raises issues regarding employees who store potentially criminal information on their employer's computers. If the information belongs to the employer and not the employee, it is possible a court would allow the employer to access it and use it not only to fire the employee but also to provide it to law enforcement officials. Of course, this presupposes that if the employee has encrypted the material sought, the company has the ability either through stated company policy or the law to require the employee to allow access.

State Constitutions

In addition to the U.S. Constitution, state constitutions are a source of privacy rights. In general, these rights mirror the amendments mentioned earlier in content and, similarly, apply only to public employees. However, some states afford greater protection to government violations of privacy. States have afforded privacy protection to electronic eavesdropping (wiretapping), medical, insurance, school records, credit and banking information, and so on. You should also recognize that the states, under the common law, grant privacy protection to what are called certain "privileged" communications. For example, with very limited exceptions, what a client tells an attorney or what a patient tells a physician is private and not available to anyone, including government officials, unless voluntarily disclosed by the client or patient.

Attorney-Client Privilege and the Use of E-Mail

A growing privacy concern involves the extensive use of e-mail, via computers and Palm Pilots, by attorneys (in 2000, the American Bar Association estimated 94 percent use it) to communicate with their clients and the possibility of unauthorized access of this information by others, thereby jeopardizing the confidentiality of the communications. Thus far, the issue of e-mail and the attorney-client privilege has yet to be decided by the courts. Attorneys and others (doctors, psychiatrists, etc.) who electronically communicate confidential information to their clients or patients should, at the very least, seek the most effective methods such as encryption to protect them.

http://

- Check your state's government to see what privacy rights are provided under state law from links at **http://www.law.cornell.edu/states/listing.html**

COMMON LAW TORTS FOR INVASION OF PRIVACY

Our focus next shifts to the four types of torts recognized at common law and by the Restatement (Second) of Torts. These provide monetary and injunctive relief for an unreasonable or unwarranted invasion of the right to privacy. Conceivably, they could also provide remedies for a cause of action in cases involving privacy rights in cyberspace. These torts are **Intrusion upon Seclusion; Public Disclosure of Private Facts**

Causing Injury to Reputation; Publicly Placing Another in a False Light; and **Misappropriation of a Person's Name or Likeness Causing Injury to Reputation.**

Intrusion upon Seclusion

On occasion, most of us have wished to enjoy what Judge Cooley recognized as a basic "right to be let alone," to go to a place of seclusion. Of course, like most of our legal rights, this right is not absolute. However, when another individual, without permission or legal justification, violates that place of seclusion, this tort could provide a remedy. The Restatement (Second) of Torts defines Intrusion upon Seclusion as:

> Intentionally intruding, physically or otherwise, upon the solitude or seclusion of another or his private affairs or concerns.

In order to succeed, a plaintiff would have to prove the following elements:

- There was intent to intrude or knowledge that the intrusion would be wrong.
- There was a reasonable expectation of privacy.
- Intrusion was substantial and highly offensive to a reasonable person.

Intent or Knowledge. The tort of intrusion to seclusion, similar to the other three that follow, requires that the defendant acted with intent to intrude or violate the plaintiff's privacy or with knowledge that actions would result in a privacy intrusion.

Reasonable Expectation of Privacy. Expanding on our earlier discussion, the level or amount of privacy we should expect depends on whether we are in what is usually considered to be a public or private place. What is done in the privacy of one's home should be entitled to more privacy than what one does in a public park or airport. However, laws may prohibit certain acts even if they occur in the privacy of one's home (see the discussion of the possession of child pornography in Chapter 10). Also, be aware that state laws can prohibit what consenting adults do in the privacy of their home. These laws usually refer to sexual activity deemed by the state to constitute "acts against nature." Similarly, the fact that an individual is in a "public" place does not deprive the person of all rights to privacy. In fact, in right to privacy cases, courts have focused on protecting the person rather than the place. In the following landmark case, the U.S. Supreme Court had to decide the privacy that an individual should expect when making a phone call in a public phone booth, even where the call involved criminal activity.

Katz v. United States
389 U.S. 347 (1967)

Facts

The petitioner, Katz, was convicted of transmitting wagering information from Los Angeles to Miami to Boston in violation of a federal statute. At trial, over the petitioner's objection, the government was permitted to introduce evidence of the phone calls obtained by FBI agents who had attached an electronic listening and recording device to the outside of a public phone booth from which the calls had been placed. The Court of Appeals affirmed the conviction, finding there was no Fourth Amendment violation because there was no "physical entrance into the area occupied by the petitioner." The Supreme Court granted certiorari in order to determine if the government's eavesdropping activities violated the petitioner's rights under Fourth Amendment "search and seizure" provisions.

Judicial Opinion *(Justice Stewart)*

Because of the misleading way the issues have been formulated, the parties have attached great significance to the telephone booth from which the petitioner placed his calls. The petitioner has strenuously argued that the booth was a "constitutionally protected area." The Government has maintained with equal vigor that it was not. But this effort to decide whether or not a given "area," viewed in the abstract, is "constitutionally protected" deflects attention from the problem presented by this case. For the Fourth Amendment protects people, not places. What a person knowingly exposes to the public, even in his own home or office, is not a subject of Fourth Amendment protection. . . . But what he seeks to preserve as private, even in an area accessible to the public, may be constitutionally protected. . . .

The Government stresses the fact that the telephone booth from which the petitioner made his calls was constructed partly of glass, so that he was as visible after he entered it as he would have been had he remained outside. But what he sought to exclude when he entered the booth was not the intruding eye—it was the uninvited ear. He did not shed his right to do so simply because he made his calls from a place where he might be seen. No less than an individual in a business office, in a friend's apartment, or in a taxicab, a person in a telephone booth may rely upon the protection of the Fourth Amendment. One who occupies it, shuts the door behind him, and pays the toll that permits him to place a call, is surely entitled to assume that the words he utters into the mouthpiece will not be broadcast to the world. To read the Constitution more narrowly is to ignore the vital role that the public telephone has come to play in private communication.

The Government contends, however, that the activities of its agents in this case should not be tested by Fourth Amendment requirements, for the surveillance technique they employed involved no physical penetration of the telephone booth from which the petitioner placed his calls. It is true that the absence of such penetration was at one time thought to foreclose further Fourth Amendment inquiry, *Olmstead v. United States.* . . . For that Amendment was thought to limit only searches and seizures of tangible property. But "[t]he premise that property interests control the right of the Government to search and seize has been discredited." *Warden v. Hayden,* 387 U. S. 294, 304, . . . Thus, although a closely divided Court supposed in *Olmstead* that surveillance without any trespass and without the seizure of any material object fell outside the ambit of the Constitution, we have since departed from the narrow view on which that decision rested. Indeed, we have expressly held that the Fourth Amendment governs not only the seizure of tangible items, but extends as well to the recording of oral statements, overheard without any "technical trespass under . . . local property law." *Silverman v. United States,* 365 U. S. 505, 511. Once this much is acknowledged, and once it is recognized that the Fourth Amendment protects people—and not simply "areas"—against unreasonable searches and seizures, it becomes clear that the reach of that Amendment cannot turn upon the presence or absence of a physical intrusion into any given enclosure.

The Government's activities in electronically listening to and recording the petitioner's words violated the privacy upon which he justifiably relied while using the telephone booth and thus constituted a "search and seizure" within the meaning of the Fourth Amendment. The fact that the electronic device employed to achieve that end did not penetrate the wall of the booth can have no constitutional significance.

The question remaining for decision, then, is whether the search and seizure conducted in this case complied with constitutional standards? In that regard, the Government's position is that its agents acted in an entirely defensible manner: They did not begin their electronic surveillance until investigation of the petitioner's activities had established a strong probability that he was using the telephone in question to transmit gambling information to persons in other States, in violation of federal law. Moreover, the surveillance was limited, both in scope and in duration, to the specific purpose of establishing the contents of the petitioner's unlawful telephonic communications. The agents confined their surveillance to the brief periods during which he used the telephone booth, and they took great care to overhear only conversations of the petitioner himself. Accepting this account of the Government's actions as accurate, it is clear that this surveillance was so narrowly circumscribed that a duly authorized magistrate, properly notified of the need for such investigation, specifically informed of the basis on which it was to proceed, and clearly apprised of the precise intrusion it would entail, could constitutionally have authorized, with appropriate safeguards, the very limited search and seizure that the Government asserts in fact took place . . .

The Government urges that, because its agents relied upon the decisions in *Olmstead and Goldman,* and because they did no more here than they might properly have done with prior judicial sanction, we should retroactively validate their conduct. That we cannot do. It is apparent that the agents in this case acted with restraint. Yet the inescapable fact is that this restraint was imposed by the agents themselves, not by a judicial officer. They were not required, before commencing the search, to present their estimate of probable cause for detached scrutiny by a neutral magistrate. They were not compelled, during the conduct of the search itself, to observe precise limits established in advance by a specific court order. Nor were they directed, after the search had been completed to notify the authorizing magistrate in detail of all that had been seized. In the absence of such safeguards, this Court has never sustained a search upon the sole ground that officers reasonably expected to find evidence of a particular crime and voluntarily confined their activities to the least intrusive means consistent with that end. Searches conducted without warrants have been held unlawful "notwithstanding facts unquestionably showing probable cause," . . . for the Constitution requires "that the deliberate, impartial judgment of a judicial officer . . . be interposed between the citizen and the police . . ." . . . "Over and again this Court has emphasized that the mandate of the [Fourth] Amendment requires adherence to judicial processes," and that searches conducted outside the judicial process, without prior approval by judge or magistrate, are per se unreasonable under the Fourth Amendment—subject only to a few specifically established and well-delineated exceptions.

It is difficult to imagine how any of those exceptions could ever apply to the sort of search and seizure involved in this case. Even electronic surveillance substantially contemporaneous with an individual's arrest could hardly be deemed an "incident" of that arrest. Nor could the use of electronic surveillance without prior authorization be justified on grounds of "hot pursuit." And, of course, the very nature of electronic surveillance precludes its use pursuant to the suspect's consent.

The Government does not question these basic principles. Rather, it urges the creation of a new exception to cover this case. It argues that surveillance of a telephone booth should be exempted from the usual requirement of advance authorization by a magistrate upon a showing of probable cause. We cannot agree. Omission of such authorization "bypasses the safeguards provided by an objective determination of probable cause and substitutes instead the far less reliable procedure of an after-the-event justification for the . . . search, too likely to be subtly influenced by the familiar shortcomings of hindsight judgment." *Beck v. Ohio,* 379 U.S. 89, . . .

And bypassing a neutral predetermination of the scope of a search leaves individuals secure from Fourth Amendment violations "only in the discretion of the police." Id., at 97. . . .

These considerations do not vanish when the search in question is transferred from the setting of a home, an office, a hotel room to that of a telephone booth. Wherever a man may be, he is entitled to know that he will remain free from unreasonable searches and seizures.

The Government agents here ignored "the procedure of antecedent justification . . . that is central to the Fourth Amendment," a procedure that we hold to be a constitutional precondition of the kind of electronic surveillance involved in this case. Because the surveillance here failed to meet that condition, and because it led to the petitioner's conviction, the judgment must be reversed.

IT IS SO ORDERED.

Case Questions

1. What if the government suspected illegal bets were being placed by e-mail nationwide and the FBI, without warrants, accessed and traced the e-mails resulting in criminal charges against the alleged perpetrators?
2. Would Katz's privacy have been violated if instead of a bet he were planning a robbery?
3. Can the legal wiretapping of a "private place" ever be ethically justified?

Based on the holding in Katz, what level of privacy can we reasonably expect regarding our e-mail, use of cellular phones, and other online communications including those in chat rooms? Currently, there are no strict prohibitions imposed for collecting and using the personal information we voluntarily disclose in e-mail and other communications (later in this chapter, we discuss the laws governing unauthorized use of this information). Internet service providers (ISPs) and others utilize channels of communication easily accessible by others. Therefore, unless security measures are employed by the user to prevent access and ensure privacy, or a law recognizes a right to privacy exists, we should not expect any degree of privacy in the online information we volunteer or allow to be accessed. (*Note:* Again, the best method for insuring security is encryption.) This is similar to the easy access to cellular phone conversations.

Privacy in the Use of Cellular Phones

When using a cell phone, certainly we should expect less in the way of privacy than was afforded Katz in the phone booth, especially because scanners and other technology can be used to randomly access and intercept cell phone calls. The public or openness methods generally used to make cell calls lead to the same conclusion.

What about the courts? Some guidance regarding cell phone privacy was provided by the U.S. Supreme Court in *Bartnicki v. Vopper*, 121 S. Ct 1753 (2001) where one of the plaintiffs, the chief negotiator for a teacher's union, made a cell phone call to another plaintiff, the union president, in which they discussed ongoing contentious union negotiations that had also been widely reported in the media. An unknown person illegally intercepted the call and mailed a tape of it to one of the defendants. He in turn sent it to the other defendant, a talk show host who played it on his radio program. The plaintiffs sued claiming their privacy rights had been violated under state and federal wiretap laws (Electronic Communications Privacy Act, discussed later). The defendants argued that because the conversation contained information of importance to the public, they were entitled to First Amendment protection. The Court agreed with the defendants and decided, at least based on the facts of this case, that the privacy concerns of the plaintiffs were outweighed by the freedom of speech and press rights of the defendants to communicate or publish information, even though wrongfully intercepted, that was truthful and of significant interest to the public.

As far as the privacy rights of employees are concerned, we will discover that there is virtually little or no reasonable expectation of privacy in the workplace, *and* if an employee were to be successful in proving an invasion of a right to workplace privacy, probably Intrusion upon Seclusion provides the best (remedy) theory for recovery.

Substantial and Highly Offensive to a Reasonable Person. Most of the case law and the Restatement (Second) of Torts concerning this tort require that the defendant's conduct and resultant intrusion shock or outrage the conscience of a reasonable person. The actions of the FBI in the Katz case would satisfy this element. Similarly, as we see later with workplace privacy, monitoring telephone or e-mail messages without justification or consent would probably also constitute an intrusion sufficient for this element.

Public Disclosure of Private Facts Causing Injury to Reputation

This tort allows recovery when highly personal facts or information about another are publicly disclosed or transmitted whereby injury to reputation results. In some instances, this tort is associated with the tort of defamation, and both may be used as separate causes of action arising out of the same case.

In addition to the elements of "intent or knowledge" and "highly offensive to a reasonable person" previously discussed, the public disclosure of private facts causing injury to reputation requires the following:

- The facts must be private.
- Communication or publicity must be disclosed to a significant segment of the community.

Facts Must Be Private. If the information disclosed were obtained with consent, voluntarily, or was already in the public domain, this tort likely will not be successful. This can result when we sign a consent form authorizing the release of personal information about us related to medical or insurance reports. It could also be true regarding highly personal information we volunteer to ISPs or companies operating online. This information ends up stored in their vast databases, available for any number of purposes, including the sale to others.

If the information is not obtained as described and subsequently is disclosed, the issue again focuses on establishing that the plaintiff had a reasonable expectation the facts disclosed would be kept private.

Communication or Publicity to a Significant Segment of the Community. Recovery here is based on disclosure to a large enough group of people so the information about the plaintiff becomes common knowledge. Therefore, it would be insufficient "to communicate a fact concerning the plaintiff's private life to a single person or even a small group of persons" [Restatement (Second) of Torts].

Publicity Placing Another in a False Light

This tort also is associated with the tort of defamation and involves falsely connecting a person to an immoral, illegal, or embarrassing situation resulting in injury to one's reputation. In general, the elements of this tort mirror those already discussed. To date, it has not been the subject of much, if any, litigation involving the invasion of privacy in cyberspace.

Misappropriation of a Person's Name or Likeness Causing Injury to Reputation

This tort usually applies in cases where the name or picture of a living person is used for commercial (non-newsworthy) purposes without the person's permission or consent. In some states, such as New York, it can result in both criminal and civil liability. Consider *Stern v. Delphi Services Corporation*, 626 N.Y.S. 2d 694 (N.Y. Sup. Ct. 1995), where, as a publicity stunt, Howard Stern, the plaintiff and controversial radio "shock jock" and self-proclaimed "king of all media," facetiously ran for governor of New York. The defendant operated an online news service and to promote its products, he took out a full-page ad in two New York publications in which a photo of Stern in leather pants with his buttocks exposed ran without his permission. Stern alleged that the picture violated a New York statute prohibiting commercial use of an individual's name or picture without permission. The statute provided for an "incidental use exception" that allowed news providers to publicize newsworthy communications. Such was the case here. Stern's candidacy was newsworthy because of his celebrity and candidacy. Therefore, his right to privacy was not violated. The court stated that to restrict the defendant from informing the public of the nature and subject of its service would constitute an impermissible restriction of its First Amendment rights. Cases like *Stern* demonstrate the difficulty and exceptions courts can recognize when dealing with the privacy rights of celebrities.

Another interesting case involving this tort and the duty of a pharmacy to maintain the confidentiality of information concerning its customers is *Weld v. CVS Pharmacy, Inc., et al.*, 1999 WL 494114 (Mass. Sup. Ct. June 29, 1999), where CVS, without the knowledge or consent of its customers, released their names, addresses, phone numbers, and other personal information, including the nature of their illnesses and diseases, to drug manufacturers, who then sent to them information specific to their ailment. The court allowed the case to proceed to trial to determine if the tort of misappropriation of private information and an invasion of privacy occurred given the fact that a pharmacy owes a duty of confidentiality to its customers.

A similar case at the federal level, *In the Matter of Eli Lilly*, Docket No. 0123214, January 18, 2002, involved a complaint brought by the FTC against Eli Lilly, Inc., a huge drug company that manufactures drugs including the antidepressant Prozac. Lilly maintained and offered several Web sites, including *http://www.prozac.com*, which provided information about the drug Prozac and also offered an e-mail prescription refill reminder service called Medi-messenger. Some 669 Prozac users opted for the service and automatically received personal e-mail reminders to take their medication or to refill their prescriptions. However, in June 2001, a decision was made to terminate the program, and one of Lilly's employees created a program to e-mail each customer of the site's termination. Instead, the employee accidentally sent the e-mail to all 669 members simultaneously, rather than individually, thereby disclosing their identities to one other. Despite Lilly's claims that they had implemented adequate customer privacy and confidentiality policies, the FTC disagreed, deciding Lilly's actions were deceptive because it failed to maintain or implement adequate internal procedures including proper employee training to protect and ensure the privacy and confidentiality of the personal information. Lilly admitted they were negligent and agreed to create and implement a new information security program.

http://

- For more about the Lilly case, visit **http://www.ftc.gov/opa/2002/01/elilily.htm**

This case is significant because it represents a shift by the FTC in its efforts to protect consumer privacy. It appears that liability for privacy violations of the type involved in *CVS* and *Lilly* will arise even where the defendant's actions, although unintentional, demonstrated a lack of reasonable care and resulted in actionable negligence and potential liability. Recall that all four common law torts for invasion of privacy require the element of intent.

FEDERAL PRIVACY LAWS

Congress began passing laws designed to protect privacy in the 1970s (see Figure 9.1). These laws deal primarily with the requirements for keeping and using personal data about individuals by the government. In this part of the chapter we focus on the most significant of those acts as well as those that affect nongovernment or private

FIGURE 9.1   Federal Privacy Laws

- Privacy Protection Act, 1980 (PPA)
- Privacy Act, 1994
- Cable Communications Protection Act, 1984 (CCPA)
- Video Privacy Protection Act, 1988 (VPPA)
- Telephone Consumer Protection Act, 1991 (TCPA)
- Fair Credit Reporting Act, 1970 (FCRA)
- Computer Fraud and Abuse Act, 1986 (CFAA)
- Electronic Communications Privacy Act, 1986 (ECPA)
- Gramm-Leach-Bliley Act, 1999 (GLB)
- Bank Secrecy Act, 1970
- Right to Financial Privacy Act, 1978
- Health Insurance Portability and Accountability Act, 1996 (HIPAA)
- Children's Online Privacy Protection Act, 1998 (COPPA)

entities. Keep in mind that the Uniting and Strengthening America by Providing Appropriate Tools Required to Intercept and Obstruct Terrorism Act (**USA Patriot Act**) of 2001 has amended many of these.

Privacy Protection Act (PPA) (1980), 42 U.S.C. § 2000

The **Privacy Protection Act (PPA)** applies to law enforcement agencies and allows Fourth Amendment protection against the unreasonable searches and seizures of:

> Work product materials possessed by a person reasonably believed to have a purpose to disseminate to the public, a newspaper, book, broadcast, or other similar form of public communication, in or affecting interstate commerce.

The PPA could apply to those qualifying as electronic publishers who use the Internet for the interstate transmission of their messages. If there were probable cause to believe the materials sought from these publishers were being used for a criminal purpose, a court would likely uphold a search of them as long as Fourth Amendment requirements were met. The same would be true if the search was necessary to prevent a person's injury or death. (See the *Scarfo* case in Chapter 12, "Internet and Information Security.")

Privacy Act of 1974, 5 U.S.C. § 552a Amended

The **Privacy Act** was passed because Congress was concerned with curbing the surveillance and investigation of individuals by federal agencies precipitated by the Watergate break-in scandal during the Nixon administration, and also with the potential negative impact on privacy rights that could arise from the government's increased use of computers to access, collect, and store personal data and its ability to retrieve it by simply using an individual's Social Security number.

Nearly thirty years later, the USA Patriot Act has diminished those concerns wherever outweighed by interests of national security. The Privacy Act has been described as a kind of "omnibus" code of fair information practices (discussed later) designed to regulate the collection, maintenance, use, and disclosure of personal information by federal agencies by establishing requirements that must be satisfied before government agencies or departments can disclose records and documents in their possession that contain personal information about individuals. The act only applies to records and documents that identify an individual by name, Social Security number, or other means of personal identification such as a photograph, fingerprint, or voiceprint. Thus, in order for the act to apply to the Internet, personal information about a person would have to be stored in a file containing one of these identifying features. The individual's name alone would be insufficient for the act to apply.

In addition, the act requires the agency or department to do the following:

1. Obtain the written consent of the individual unless the purpose of the disclosure is consistent with that for which the records are being retained.
2. Furnish copies of the records to the individual upon request.
3. Allow the individual to correct any misinformation contained in the records.
4. Make a reasonable effort to inform the individual that his or her records have been disclosed.

In general, the exceptions to these requirements apply to certain government law enforcement activities, situations that concern the health or safety of an individual, and court-ordered disclosures. Violations of the act can result in lawsuits by the injured party against the agency for money damages, remedies at equity such as an injunction, or both.

Cable Communications Protection Act (CCPA) (1984), 47 U.S.C. § 551

The **Cable Communications Protection Act (CCPA)** applies to cable television operators and is concerned with the privacy rights a subscriber should expect regarding personal data or information about them that a cable television operator gathers. In general, the operator is required to do the following:

1. Obtain the permission of its subscribers before collecting personal data about them.
2. Notify subscribers annually regarding the extent to which personal information about them is used or disclosed, and the purposes for which it is gathered.
3. Allow the subscriber to examine the data and make corrections of any errors or mistakes.
4. Not disclose the data except as may be required by law or court order.

(*Note:* This requirement also applies to government requests for personal information about cable subscribers.)

Failure to follow these requirements can result in lawsuits by affected subscribers. Seemingly, the CCPA could apply to the operator of a Web site that offers cablelike entertainment (adult or otherwise) or goods and services, and where its visitors wish to remain anonymous.

Video Privacy Protection Act (VPPA) (1988), 18 U.S.C. § 2710

The **Video Privacy Protection Act (VPPA)** expands the Cable Communications Protection Act. Specifically, it prohibits the use and disclosure of personal information about the videocassettes and related products an individual rents or purchases unless their written permission is obtained. This act could be applied to rentals and purchases of videos and related products via the Internet.

Telephone Consumer Protection Act (TCPA) (1991), 47 U.S.C. § 227

The **Telephone Consumer Protection Act (TCPA)** was passed as a direct result of the telemarketing activities arising from the transmission of telephone solicitations originating from automatic dialers. The TCPA directs the Federal Communications Commission (FCC) to promulgate and implement rules and regulations directed at these solicitations. Basically, the TCPA provides the following:

1. It is illegal to make a phone call by means of an automatic dialing system or prerecorded (or artificial) voice that results in the party called being charged for the call. (This also applies to calls made to a cellular phone number.)
2. It prohibits the use of any device to send an unsolicited advertisement to a telephone facsimile machine.
3. Companies engaging in telephone telemarketing are required to set up "do not call" lists for consumers who do not wish to receive these types of calls.

Consumers also have the right to have their names removed or excluded from existing lists. These "do not call" lists generally allow a telemarketer one call before civil liability arises. In general, industry efforts have been virtually ineffective, which has resulted in more than half of the states establishing their own "do not call lists." In December 2002, the FTC amended the Telemarketing Sales Rule to require and establish a national "do not call" registry effective July 2003. Many would like a similar "do not spam" rule to apply to spamming (the mass or bulk mailing of unsolicited e-mails containing advertisements for goods or services). Spamming is discussed in greater detail later in this chapter.

➤http://

- See New York's "Do Not Call" Telemarketing Registry at **http://www.consumer.state.ny.us/**

It should be noted that a federal district court has given exclusive jurisdiction to the states in suits brought under the TCPA. [*Erienet, Inc., et al. v. Velocity Net, Inc., et al.,* 1998 U.S. App. Lexis 23931 (3rd Cir., September 25, 1998)].

FEDERAL LEGISLATION: CREDIT AND FINANCIAL RECORDS

The Fair Credit Reporting Act (FCRA) of 1970, 15 U.S.C. § 1681

The purpose of the **Fair Credit Reporting Act (FCRA)** is to ensure that the credit reports furnished by consumer credit reporting agencies, including requests sent online, are accurate, impartial, and respect privacy. Also, in general, before an agency can release or use credit information about an individual, his or her permission must be obtained. An example would be when a credit card, insurance company, or financial institution uses credit information to profile or "prescreen" consumers for unsolicited e-mail (spam) marketing offers.

The FCRA also gives consumers the right to obtain information about their credit status from credit bureaus and check or correct any errors that exist. Another provision requires credit-reporting agencies to maintain a toll-free phone number so representatives are available to consumers seeking to discuss their credit reports. The Federal Trade Commission (FTC) has jurisdiction over the FCRA, usually basing its complaints under Section 5 of its regulations that prohibit unfair or deceptive business practices that affect business.

Failure to comply with the FCRA requirements can result in civil and criminal liability. In 2000, three major credit-reporting agencies, Equifax, Trans Union, and Experian, entered into a consent decree with the Federal Trade Commission whereby they agreed to pay $2.5 million to settle claims that they violated the FCRA for not maintaining a consumer toll-free phone number allegedly by blocking millions of consumer calls from reaching the number and by keeping others on hold for extraordinarily long periods of time.

The Computer Fraud and Abuse Act (CFFA) of 1986 (Amended 1994), 18 U.S.C. § 1030

The primary purpose of the **Computer Fraud and Abuse Act** (also discussed in Chapter 13, "Internet and Computer Crime") is to protect national security by prohibiting the intentional access of data stored in computers belonging to or benefiting the U.S. government. The CFFA makes it a felony for an individual to obtain this data without authority. Of significance to our discussion of privacy is another provision of the act that makes it a felony to intentionally access personal identifiable information about a consumer contained in the financial records of a financial institution or in a file of a consumer reporting agency.

FEDERAL LEGISLATION: PRIVACY IN PERSONAL FINANCIAL INFORMATION

Congress has passed other federal laws intended to protect privacy rights in personal identifiable information (PII) contained in our financial records and data. These include the **Bank Secrecy Act** of 1970 that essentially makes it illegal to launder money and use secret foreign bank accounts for illegal purposes. It also requires that financial institutions (banks, credit unions, etc.) and nonfinancial institutions (casinos, brokerages, etc.) report to the U.S. Treasury Department any cash transaction over $10,000. The Treasury Department can share this information with other law enforcement agencies.

It should be obvious that this act would be extremely beneficial in helping law enforcement and other agencies (charged with protecting homeland security) in their efforts to follow any trail of money destined for enemies of the United States or monies illegally obtained through fraudulent schemes (insider trading, tax fraud, etc.). The act also authorizes the Treasury Department to require financial institutions to keep records of their customers' personal financial transactions, including those conducted online that have "a high degree of usefulness in criminal, tax and regulatory investigations and proceedings."

Additionally, the Treasury is authorized to require that a financial institution report to the Treasury any "suspicious transaction" carried out by a customer that could result in or be relevant to possible violations of laws or regulations. The privacy concern here is that this is done without the knowledge or permission of the customer and the law enforcement agency does not have to be suspicious of an actual crime before it accesses a report and no court order, search warrant, subpoena, or written request is needed.

http://

- For more about the Bank Secrecy Act, visit **http://www.occ.treas.gov/handbook/bsa.pdf**
- For more about the Right to Financial Privacy Act, visit **http://www.4.law.cornell.edu/uscode/12/ch35.html**

Brief mention should also be made here of the **Right to Financial Privacy Act** of 1978, 29 U.S.C. § 3401, passed by Congress to provide some semblance of privacy protection to customers of banks and other financial institutions by requiring the government, subject to exceptions under the Patriot Act, to obtain a search warrant before being allowed to access financial records and information.

The most significant federal law passed by Congress pertaining to privacy protection for the disclosure and use of PII collected and contained in financial records is the **Gramm-Leach-Bliley Act (GLB)** of 1999, also known as the Financial Services Modernization Act of 1999.

Gramm-Leach-Bliley Act of 1999, 15 U.S.C. § 6801 *et seq.*

As you study the GLB Act, keep in mind that the Computer Fraud and Abuse Act makes it a felony to intentionally access, *without authorization,* personal identifiable information about a consumer contained in the financial records of a financial institution or credit bureau. Also, be aware that the major federal administrative agencies that have regulatory and enforcement powers regarding the GLB include the Securities and Exchange Commission, the Federal Reserve Board, and the Federal Trade Commission.

The GLB Act applies to all financial institutions that offer financial goods and services including but not limited to banks, credit unions, mortgage companies, insurance companies, and brokerages. Specifically, Title V of the GLB Act provides privacy protection for personal identifiable information (PII) collected by financial institutions. The GLB Act effectively repealed the sixty-six-year-old Glass-Steagall Act that prohibited financial institutions from affiliating or combining with one another and disclosing and sharing PII about their customers. The GLB Act now allows both affiliations and the sharing of information. Examples of acceptable affiliations include Charles Schwab and the U.S. Trust Company, Citizens Bank and Travelers Insurance, and Solomon-Barney and Citicorp.

Title V of the GLB Act provides notice and consent requirements that financial institutions must satisfy before they can disclose or share personal identifiable financial information about their customers with *nonaffiliated* businesses. If the GLB Act notice and consent requirements are met (discussed later), these institutions may share personal financial information about their customers with each other. Such information would include the name of the customer along with his or her account balance. The same is true for ISPs and nonaffiliated companies with whom the financial institution has an agreement, the terms of which allow these companies to market their goods and services to customers of the financial institution.

Notice and Consent Requirements: Nonaffiliates

At the beginning (and annually thereafter) of the business relationship between the customer and its bank or other financial institution, the GLB Act requires the bank to provide the customer with a privacy notice that indicates how it collects, discloses, and uses their "nonpublic" or personal identifiable (financial) information (PII). The institution must also provide the customer with the opportunity and methods to be used in order to "opt-out" or deny permission to the bank to share PII with nonaffiliates. Typically these methods include:

- Letter or form provided by the institution
- Toll-free phone number to be called
- Online, if this is the usual method for doing business with the institution.

Note that if a specific method for opting out is prescribed and not followed by the customer, the institution may or may not accept it.

In any event, the procedure clearly puts the burden on the customer to take appropriate action, and recent estimates indicate that only about 5 percent have met that burden and have actually opted out. Some of the reasons privacy advocates have advanced for this low rate include consumer indifference, lack of knowledge of the privacy issues surrounding their financial information, and the inconvenience an opt-out policy presents. As a result, these advocates have criticized the GLB Act as being ineffective in protecting privacy rights and, along with members of Congress, have sought, albeit unsuccessfully, new federal legislation that would require financial institutions to implement an "opt-in" policy. This would require a financial institution to obtain permission from the customer *before* being allowed to collect and use the information, effectively shifting the burden.

Some states such as Vermont and New Mexico have adopted "opt-in" policies. It is important to note, if state law provides greater privacy protection for consumers, the GLB Act provides that such laws preempt its application. You should be aware that the GLB Act also contains requirements that attempt to prevent the crimes of identity theft and "pretexting," both of which severely threaten and invade our privacy.

Identity Theft

A major threat to privacy is identity theft as it relates to personal financial information. Prohibited under Title V of the GLB, **identity theft** occurs when personal identifiable information (PII) such as an account number or Social Security number is stolen and used to obtain financial services. Examples include obtaining a loan, credit card, or

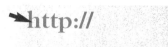

bank account in the name of the person whose identity was stolen. The Identity Theft and Assumption Deterrence Act of 1999,18 U.S.C. § 1028, gives the FTC jurisdiction to process identity theft complaints and to assist victims and direct them to the proper law enforcement agency.

- For the FTC's identity theft complaint form, see **http://www. consumer.gov/idtheft**

In 2001, the FTC reported it had received complaints from over 86,000 victims of identity theft. In Chapter 13, "Internet and Computer Crime," you will learn more about this crime.

Pretexting

Pretexting is also prohibited under Title V of the GLB Act and results when personal financial information such as a bank account number is fraudulently or falsely obtained by contacting the victim's bank or financial institution under the pretext of being or impersonating the actual customer.

FEDERAL LEGISLATION: PRIVACY IN HEALTH AND MEDICAL RECORDS

Personal identifiable information (PII) contained in our health and medical records has also become a major focus of privacy concerns. In response, Congress passed the very complicated **Health Insurance Portability and Accountability Act (HIPAA)** of 1996, P.L. 104-191.

Health Insurance Portability and Accountability Act (HIPAA) of 1996, P.L. 104-191

HIPAA applies to what it classifies as "covered entities" including health care providers, health care clearinghouses, and health plans, including those offered by employers to their employees, as well as to others providing services to them who transmit health information electronically. Essentially, HIPAA covers the receipt, transmittal, and disclosure of personal health information and data related to health plans, health care clearinghouses, and health care providers (hospitals, physicians, insurance companies, employers, etc.) that use electronic communications for processing and disclosing personal health information (PHI) surrounding health claims, payments, and other related services. HIPAA attempts to protect the confidentiality of our health records without creating obstacles for quality health care. Its provisions were so extensive and difficult, extra time was needed for implementation and compliance. HIPAA did not become fully effective until April 14, 2003. HIPAA will be implemented by the U.S. Department of Health and Human Services (HHS).

In general, HIPAA requires a covered entity to give written notice to a patient at the time of their treatment as to how their personal health information (PHI) will be used and disclosed. It also gives a patient the right to receive a copy of their medical records and inspect and correct PHI if they so choose. Further, HIPAA requires that covered entities give patients an opportunity to opt in (not opt out as allowed under

GLB) by giving their *written* authorization or permission before releasing patient related PHI. Originally, HIPAA distinguished between routine matters related to treatment, payment, and health care operations for which patient consent was to be required. However, in August 2002, HHS promulgated an amendment eliminating the strict requirement that a health care provider obtain a patient's written consent for information related to routine matters regarding treatment, payment, and health care operations. Now, a health care provider need only make a "good faith" effort to obtain consent before disclosing or using this information. Legal challenges to this amendment are likely because it appears to diminish Congress' intent in passing HIPAA to protect patient privacy. A final point to remember is that state laws that provide greater protection than HIPAA and GLB preempt and prevail over them.

PRIVACY PROTECTION FOR CHILDREN FROM THE COLLECTION OF ONLINE PERSONAL INFORMATION

The Children's Online Privacy Protection Act of 1998 (COPPA), 15 U.S.C. § 6501 *et seq.*

The **Children's Online Privacy Protection Act (COPPA)** protects children under age thirteen and applies to commercial operators that collect or store data containing personal identifiable information (PII) concerning children who visit or use their Web sites. The FTC is charged with implementing COPPA and has established requirements that these operators must satisfy before they collect PII from children under age thirteen. Essentially, they must:

- Provide a clear and conspicuous link, on their home page and/or wherever such information is collected, to a description of their information collection practices.
- Indicate what types of information is collected and how it is to be used.
- Indicate if it will be disclosed to third parties along with a description of the nature of the third party's business.

COPPA's most important privacy protection provision requires that operators obtain verifiable parental consent before collecting, disclosing, or using PII obtained from children. Although COPPA allows a parent to indicate consent via an e-mail, the operator must confirm the consent by phone, letter, or e-mail sent to the parent.

Since its passage, the FTC has successfully brought several complaints under COPPA. The first, and one of the most publicized, was *FTC v. Toysmart.com, LLC*, District of Massachusetts, Civil Action No. 00-11341-RGS, 2000. Toysmart.com was a company that sold educational toys online. Its privacy statement contained a promise that it would *never* disclose or sell PII it collected from its customers, some of whom were children under age thirteen. Toysmart.com filed for bankruptcy and, pending that proceeding, wanted to sell its customer databases containing the customer PII. The FTC claimed this was a misrepresentation and sought to prevent the sale, seeking an injunction alleging unfair and deceptive business practices under Section 5 of the FTC Act and a failure to obtain verifiable parental consent as required by COPPA. The FTC succeeded in enjoining the sale except to a "qualified buyer" who would have to agree to abide by the promise contained in the privacy statement. Subsequently, the

http://

- For other FTC actions under COPPA, see http://www.girlslife.com, http://www.bigmailbox.com, http://www.insidetheweb.com. Also http://www.ftc.gov/os/2001/04/index. htm and jollytime.com at http://www. ftc.gov/os/2002/02/index.htm

settlement was challenged by thirty-nine state attorneys general who alleged that *any* sale even to a qualified buyer would violate COPPA as well as Toysmart's policy and promise. The U.S. Bankruptcy Court agreed and, in August 2000, overturned the settlement requiring Toysmart to obtain court approval before selling its databases.

COPPA: Safe Harbor

COPPA provides a safe harbor for those operators who engage in some form of self-regulation program such as those offered by so-called seal organizations sanctioned by the FTC program. Examples include the Children's Advertising Review Unit of the Council of Better Business Bureaus, TRUSTe, and the Entertainment Software Rating Board that establish policies and rules for meeting the privacy provisions of statutes like COPPA. The FTC has also set up an informational link on its home page for children, parents, operators, and service providers called *Kidz Privacy.*

The Electronic Communications Privacy Act (ECPA) of 1986, 18 U.S.C § 2510

One of the most important federal statutes regarding privacy in cyberspace is the **Electronic Communications Privacy Act (ECPA)** of 1986. In 1968, no doubt influenced by cases including *Katz v. United States* (discussed earlier in this chapter) that demonstrated the ability of the government to monitor and record telephone conversations, Congress passed Title III of the Omnibus Crime Control and Safe Streets Act (18 U.S.C. § 2510), the so-called wiretap statute. This statute established Fourth Amendment requirements that government agencies would have to satisfy in order to carry out legal wiretaps. These included obtaining a valid search warrant

http://www.ftc.gov/bcp/conline/edcams/kidzprivacy/

based on a showing of probable cause that the phone call to be intercepted was related to a criminal activity.

By the 1980s, advancements in technology and the creation of new and more sophisticated modes of wire and electronic communications, including e-mail, caused concerns that existing wiretap laws were inadequate to protect the rights of individuals. Congress responded by passing the ECPA, which amended the Omnibus Crime Control and Safe Streets Act. The ECPA applies to ISPs and other commercial online service providers engaged in the transmission, interception, and storage of electronic communications, including e-mail "to the public" that affects interstate or foreign commerce.

The meaning of "to the public" under the ECPA was a major issue before the court in *Andersen Consulting LLP v. UOP*, 991 Fed. Supp.1041 (N.D. Ill. 1998). In *Andersen*, the defendant maintained an internal e-mail system and allowed the plaintiff, *UOP*, to use it. The defendant disclosed some of the plaintiff's e-mail messages to a newspaper that published them and the plaintiff sued under the ECPA. The court dismissed the suit, interpreting the phrase "to the public" as meaning the "community at large." Here, the defendant intended its e-mail system to be for internal communication purposes and not for transmission to the public or community at large. The defendant certainly had not intended to affect interstate commerce. Therefore, the disclosure did not violate the ECPA.

Essentially, the ECPA contains three major provisions, Title I (also known as the Wiretap Act) applies to the interception and disclosure of wire, oral, and electronic communications. Title II (also known the Stored Communications Act) applies to stored wire, transactional, and electronic communications. Title III (also referred to as the Pen Register Act) applies to wiretaps via telephone pen registers and trap and trace devices. Violations of the ECPA can result in criminal and civil liability. Note that the ECPA does not, in the absence of an agreement to the contrary, prohibit disclosure of the contents of an e-mail message by the intended recipient to another person.

Title I (§§ 2510–2522)—Interception and Disclosure of Wire, Oral, and Electronic Communications.
Title I prohibits the unauthorized interception and disclosure of wire, oral, and electronic communications. The ECPA defines an electronic communication as:

> Any transfer of signs, signals, writing, images, sounds, data, or intelligence of any nature transmitted in whole or in part by a wire, radio, electromagnetic, photo-electronic or photooptical system that affects interstate or foreign commerce.

Examples include transmissions by radio paging devices (excluding "tone-only" devices), cellular phones, computer-generated transmissions, and e-mail. The ECPA covers all communication carriers or persons who provide or operate facilities for communications that affect interstate or foreign commerce.

Specifically, Title I prohibits, with exceptions:

1. Any person from intentionally intercepting any wire, oral, or electronic communication;

2. Any person from intentionally using or disclosing the contents of any wire, oral, or electronic communication to another person;

3. An Internet service provider (ISP) from intentionally disclosing the contents of a communication to any person or entity other than the addressee or intended recipient.

In *McVeigh v. Cohen et al.*, 983 F. Supp. 215 (D.D.C., 1998), the plaintiff, Timothy McVeigh, was discharged from the U.S. Navy because he was gay, a fact disclosed to the navy by America Online (AOL), an ISP. AOL had discovered McVeigh's sexual orientation after identifying him as the sender of an anonymous e-mail and as an individual described in its membership directory as gay. In issuing a preliminary injunction preventing the navy from discharging McVeigh, the Court of Appeals ruled the navy was in violation of its "Don't ask, don't tell" policy. The Court was also aided in its decision by the actions of AOL in intentionally disclosing information about McVeigh and his e-mail, resulting in a direct violation of the ECPA.

Note: The ECPA does not prohibit access or disclosure of electronic communications placed on a site intended to be readily accessible by the public.

There are four *major* exceptions to Title I:

1 Internet service providers (ISPs)
2. **Business Extension Rule**, or "Ordinary Course of Business"
3. Prior consent to interception of electronic communications
4. Government and law enforcement agencies—interception and disclosure of electronic communications. (These exceptions also apply to Title II and III.)

1. *Internet Service Providers (ISPs).* An online operator, officer, employee, or agent of a provider of wire or electronic communication service may, in the normal course of employment, intercept, disclose, or use an electronic communication "which is a necessary incident to the rendition of" their service or to the "protection of the rights or property of the provider of that service." (*Note:* Random observing or monitoring of a communication are not allowed under this exception except for mechanical or quality control purposes.) This exception would apply to outside e-mail service providers such as Prodigy, CompuServe, and America Online, as well as to an internal e-mail system operated by the employer. In *United States v. Mullins*, 992 F. 2d 1472 (9th Cir. 1992), an employee and agent of American Airlines was investigating discrepancies in reservations being made by a travel agent on an online travel reservations system maintained by American. The employee intercepted some of these reservations and the travel agent sued, arguing the employee's actions violated Title I of the ECPA. The court disagreed, deciding that American Airlines was a service provider acting to protect its rights and property interests. Therefore, the interception of the communication was allowable under the exception just described and did not violate the ECPA.

2. *Business Extension Rule or Ordinary Course of Business.* The business extension rule focuses on the ECPA section that requires a plaintiff to prove the defendant used an "electronic, mechanical, or other device," capable of intercepting an electronic communication. Specifically, it exempts from liability under the ECPA any device furnished to the subscriber or user by a provider of wire or electronic communication service in the ordinary course of business and being used by the subscriber or user in the ordinary course of its business.

This exception would allow the interception of e-mail and other communications by an employer, provided certain qualifications are met. More follows in the discussion of workplace privacy later in this chapter. For now, suffice it to say that the employer would have to prove it had established a monitoring policy and certain employees knew about it in advance of the interception, and that the interception was business related. Therefore, it appears an employer could monitor an employee's phone calls or e-mail messages in order to make sure they were business related and not purely "personal" in nature.

3. *Prior Consent.* The interception of an electronic communication is permitted when one of the parties to the communication, either the sender or the recipient, has given prior consent to the interception unless the communication is intercepted for purposes of committing a crime or tort.

4. *Government and Law Enforcement Agencies—Interception and Disclosure of Electronic Communications.* Here the ECPA distinguishes between an electronic communication accidentally intercepted by a service provider and those sought from an ISP or other provider by a government or law enforcement agency official.

A service provider who accidentally intercepts a communication containing evidence of an illegal act may, without liability under the ECPA, disclose the communication to the proper authorities. However, law enforcement officials must follow the provisions of the ECPA. Essentially, they require the official to apply to a judge for a court order, search warrant, or, in the case of private documents, a subpoena. In the application, the official will have to establish there is sufficient probable cause to believe the person named in the application is, has, or is about to commit a crime. The official will also have to describe in particular detail the place and items to be searched.

If the communication sought is associated with an emergency situation that poses an *immediate* threat of death or serious injury to a person, a threat to national security, or involves criminal activity associated with organized crime, the interception may occur without the application and court order, warrant, or subpoena. However, within forty-eight hours after the interception, the agent must then comply with the above application procedure. If the application is not approved and a court order, warrant, or subpoena is not issued, the interception will be declared to have been obtained in violation of the ECPA and would be, most likely, inadmissible in a criminal prosecution brought against the person who was the subject of the application.

In most cases where the government has requested access to a subscriber's e-mail messages or other stored data, the ECPA requires the service provider to notify the subscriber of the request. The subscriber then has fourteen days from the date of the notice to challenge the request in a court proceeding. An interesting question is posed by an electronic communication containing a message that is encrypted. Obviously, a service provider could not accidentally intercept this type of message.

What about a law enforcement agency seeking to intercept a message it believes contains evidence of a criminal activity? Currently, there is no law that expressly gives law enforcement officials the right to access encrypted messages even with a court order. The FBI and other law enforcement agencies have asked for laws requiring that encryption software be sold with key features (a kind of "back door") that would allow a message to be decrypted and accessible by law enforcement agencies. In *U.S. v. Scarfo,* presented in Chapter 12, "Internet and Information Security," you will discover that the court exercised its interpretive muscle to fashion a unique application of a federal statute, the Classified Information Procedures Act, in order to strike a balance between individual privacy rights and the need for law enforcement agencies to employ new technology to investigate and prosecute criminal activity, especially post 9/11. The decision in *Scarfo* appears to have provided at least a partial answer to the FBI's request. In Chapter 12, you will also learn about Carnivore (also known by its less ominous name, DCS 1000) and other surveillance key logger tools the FBI and law enforcement agencies use to help fight terrorism and other crimes. Here, we briefly mention the privacy concerns raised by Carnivore.

Carnivore

Carnivore is a device the FBI likens to a pen register (a device that records phone numbers dialed from another phone) that allows the FBI pursuant to a court order to search ("sniff") and sift through the e-mail and other Internet traffic passing through a suspect's ISP and intercept what it believes indicates evidence of criminal activities. One of the major privacy concerns raised is that *all* traffic is searched, even that of individuals not named in the original court order. The FBI is able to obtain sender and recipient's addresses as well as the subject matter contained in their e-mail.

This being the case, privacy advocates and critics of Carnivore are concerned that the volume and extent of the data gathered pose privacy threats to innocent citizens and liken Carnivore to a wiretap for which stricter Fourth Amendment scrutiny would be required. The FBI claims that its use of electronic surveillance has led to over 25,000 criminal convictions in the past thirteen years and is therefore vital to its crime fighting efforts.

Of course, remember in the interest of national security the USA Patriot Act has increased the authority and ability of the federal government to monitor and access electronic communications and Internet activities. Some have observed this to result in a diminution of Fourth Amendment and privacy rights and protections.

Title II (§ 2701)—Unlawful Access to Stored Communications. The purpose of Title II is to protect data stored in transit and at the point of destination from being accessed and disclosed. This usually involves data stored in RAM (random access memory) or on computer discs and other similar devices.

Subject to exceptions similar to those under Title I, § 2701 basically does the following:

1. It prohibits any person from intentionally accessing without authorization a facility through which an electronic communication service is provided or

intentionally exceeding authorization to access that facility and thereby obtaining, altering, or preventing authorized access to a wire or electronic communication while it is in electronic storage in such a system.

Although similar to those provided under Title I, one additional exception should be mentioned: § 2701 (c) (2) exempts from liability conduct authorized *by a user of a wire or electronic communication service with respect to a communication of or intended for that user.* The application of this exception and the ECPA are discussed later in this chapter in the *DoubleClick* case and in the *Konop* case dealing with workplace privacy.

It was also an issue in *Sega Enterprises v. MAPHIA,* 948 F. Supp. 923 (N.D. Ca. 1996). In deciding the copyright infringement issue before it, the court had to look at whether Sega's employee's actions in using a pseudonym to access data stored on MAPHIA's bulletin board system (BBS) violated this section of the ECPA. The BBS was readily accessible to the public at large by use of pseudonyms and Sega had collected the information by having one of its employees gain access to the BBS under a pseudonym using information supplied by an authorized user who was an informant. Because the data were available on a public BBS, the court decided Sega's actions did not violate this section of the ECPA.

2. It prohibits a person or entity providing an electronic communication service to the public from knowingly divulging to any person or entity the contents of any communication while in electronic storage by that service.

3. A person or entity providing remote computing service to the public is prohibited from knowingly divulging to any person or entity the contents of any communication that is carried or maintained on that service. In the following class action case, the court had to decide if a company's use and placement of cookies on the plaintiff's computer hard drives in order to collect nonpersonal identifiable information violated Title II of the ECPA or met one of its exceptions.

In Re DoubleClick Inc., Privacy Litigation
154 F. Supp. 2d 497 (S.D. N.Y., 2001)

Facts

DoubleClick is the largest provider of Internet advertising products and services in the world, specializing in collecting, compiling, and analyzing nonpersonal identifiable information about Internet users and using it to target online advertising. It promises its clients to place ads in front of viewers who match their clients' demographic target and has placed billions of ads online. Its services reach a majority of the Internet users in the United States.

By placing cookies on the hard drives of its users' computers, DoubleClick is able to collect the information when the user accesses a DoubleClick affiliate. A user may take simple steps to prevent DoubleClick's use of cookies by "opting out" (denying permission to place them on the hard drive) or by reconfiguring the browsers on their computers in order to block any cookies from being deposited.

The plaintiffs brought this action on behalf of themselves and all others who, since January 1, 1996, have had information collected about them by Doubleclick as a result of viewing products or services on the Internet or who have had cookies placed on their computer hard drives by DoubleClick. The plaintiffs allege that these actions constituted an invasion of their privacy and violated Title II of the ECPA, § 2701 that prohibits unauthorized access of stored communications. They also alleged violations of other federal and state laws. DoubleClick argued that because its clients consented to the gathering of the information, it met the requirements of the prior consent exception. In seeking a motion to dismiss, . . .

Judicial Opinion *(District Judge Naomi Reice Buchwald)*

Assuming the communications are considered to be in "electronic storage," it appears that DoubleClick's conduct constitutes an offense under the Electronic Communications Privacy Act of 1986 (ECPA), 18 U.S.C. § 2701(a), absent an exception.

§ 2701 (a) provides:

> Whoever intentionally accesses without authorization a facility through which an electronic information service is provided and thereby obtains access to a wire or electronic communication while it is in electronic storage in such system, shall be punished.

> Subsection (a) shall not apply with respect to conduct authorized by a user of that [wire or electronic communication] service with respect to a communication of or intended for that user.

Therefore, the issue is whether DoubleClick's conduct falls within the exception. The issue has three parts: (1) what is the relevant electronic communication service? (2) were DoubleClick-affiliated websites "users" of this service? (3) did the DoubleClick-affiliated websites give DoubleClick sufficient authorization to access plaintiffs' stored electronic communications "intended" for those websites? Obviously, in the broad sense, the "Internet" is the relevant communications service. However, it is important that we define Internet service. Plaintiff argues that the electronic communication service is "Internet access" and the " ISP" (Internet Service Provider). The difference is important. An ISP is an entity that provides access to the Internet (America Online, etc.). Access to the Internet is the service an ISP provides. Therefore, the "service that provides to users thereof the ability to send or receive wire or electronic communications" is "Internet Access."

The ECPA defines a "user" as "any person who uses an electronic communication service; and is duly authorized by the provider of such service to engage in such use." DoubleClick-affiliated websites appear to be users. They are "entities" that use Internet access and are authorized to use Internet access by ISPs to which they subscribe. One could imagine a facially sensible argument that websites are not "users" of Internet access because they are passive storage receptacles for information; the human is the "user" and the website is what is used. However, the Internet's engineering belies this description. Indeed, no direct connection ever exists between the human user and the website. Rather, the human sends a request to which the website must actively respond. Indeed, websites are among the most active "users" of Internet access—their existence and utility depend on it. Therefore, we find as a matter of law that the DoubleClick affiliated websites are "users" of Internet access under the ECPA.

Plaintiffs have proffered no proofs to support their bare assertion that DoubleClick's access was unauthorized. Every fact they do allege supports the inference that the DoubleClick-affiliated Web sites did authorize DoubleClick's access.

The very reason clients hire DoubleClick is to target advertisements based on users' demographic profiles. Title II in no way outlaws collecting personally identifiable information or placing cookies. Therefore, we find that the DoubleClick-affiliated Web sites consented to Doubleclick's access of plaintiffs' communications to them. DoubleClick did not need anyone's authorization to access them. Their long-term residence on plaintiffs' hard drives places them outside of § 2510's definition of "electronic storage" and Title II's protection. Even if they were in "electronic storage," DoubleClick is authorized to access its own communications.

Plaintiffs have offered no explanation as to how the Doubleclick-affiliated Web sites could have played such a central role in the information collected and not have authorized DoubleClick's access.

Therefore, we find that DoubleClick-affiliated Web sites consented to Doubleclick's access of plaintiffs' communications to them. DoubleClick's practices and consumers privacy concerns with them are unknown to Congress. Indeed, Congress is currently considering legislation that specifically recognizes the online harvesting of user information.

For the foregoing reasons, DoubleClick's motion to dismiss is granted.

IT IS SO ORDERED.

Case Questions

1. How did the court determine that the Web sites authorized DoubleClick to access plaintiffs' electronic communications?
2. Why did the court decide the cookies placed on users' hard drives were not in temporary "electronic storage"?
3. How can DoubleClick's practice in placing the cookies be justified ethically?

(*Postscript:* After this decision, the plaintiffs filed appeals in the federal Court of Appeals and the California Superior Court. In March 2002, pending the outcome of these appeals, a settlement was reached whereby DoubleClick agreed to pay $1.8 million in damages to the plaintiffs. In August 2002, in order to end an investigation spearheaded by New York's attorney general Eliot Spitzer and ten other states to determine if DoubleClick created consumer profiles unlawfully, DoubleClick agreed to pay $450,000 in damages, to better disclose how it tracks consumers online, to allow consumers to access the profiles created about them, and to allow for an independent audit of its privacy policies for several years.)

http://

- For more discussion of the changes to the ECPA the Patriot Act provides, visit The American Library Association site at **http://www.ala.org/washoff/patriot.html** and link to Matrix of the USA Patriot Act Provisions.

Title III (U.S.C. §§ 3121-3127): The Pen Register Act

Title III applies to wiretaps, pen registers, and trap and trace devices. Recall that a pen register records phone numbers dialed from another phone. A trap and trace device records the phone numbers where incoming calls originated. Before a government agency can use either, Title III requires that it obtain a court order which will only be granted if the information sought is relevant to an ongoing criminal investigation. Also, note that if the facts indicate the monitoring was excessive, a court could rule it was more like a wiretap than a pen register for which a search warrant rather than a court order would be required. The result could render any evidence obtained to be in violation of the Fourth Amendment and therefore inadmissible.

Keep in mind that the USA Patriot Act amended Title III of the ECPA (and at least fifteen other federal statutes) by broadening the surveillance powers of the federal government to combat threats of terrorism, some argue at the expense of the rights to privacy of innocent individuals or individuals suspected of nonterrorist crimes for which they are entitled to more Fourth Amendment protection. These powers extend to monitoring e-mail and computer usage. You will study the effect of the USA Patriot Act in more detail in Chapters 12 and 13.

PRIVACY AND SPAM ("UNSOLICITED COMMERCIAL E-MAIL")

No doubt you have been online when an unsolicited and perhaps unwanted (spam) ad appears on your screen. Estimates are that each of us will receive a **spam** over two thousand times this year and by 2006, over four thousand times. As you already learned, the Telephone Consumer Protection Act, state laws, and the FTC proposed initiative give us the right not to be called by a telemarketing company. To date, no such right applies to spam and, for those who have not given permission to receive these ads, they have become just as much an annoyance as those unwanted telemarketing calls.

Efforts by members of Congress to pass federal antispam laws have not been successful. The position of the FTC has consistently been that self-regulation (more discussion later) rather than federal legislation is the most effective way to control spam. More than half the states disagree with the FTC and have adopted antispam laws or have imposed strict requirements and controls for its use. It should also be mentioned that international laws on spam differ from country to country. Austria, Denmark, and Italy require consumers to opt in; England, Canada, and France require them to opt out before receiving spams.

http://

- For examples of state anti-spam laws, see **http://www.spamlaws.com/state/**

A state case involving spam is *State of Washington v. Heckel*, 24 P. 3d 404 [(Supreme Court of Washington, 2001, certiorari denied, 122 S. Ct. 467 (2001)], where a state act prohibited sending spam that "misrepresents or disguises the message's point of origin or transmission path or uses a misleading subject line." It also prohibited a spammer from failing to provide an e-mail address to which the recipient of the spam could respond. The act was challenged on the basis that it was discriminatory against out-of-state businesses and therefore imposed a burden on interstate commerce in violation of the dormant Commerce Clause of the U.S. Constitution. The dormant clause that applies to a state law where there is no applicable federal law limits and, in some cases, prohibits the power states have to pass laws to regulate *interstate* commerce.

The court in *Heckel* held that the state antispam law was not discriminatory on its face because it applied equally to intrastate as well as interstate businesses. The court also held that the benefits of the act outweighed any burdens imposed. It would reduce the Internet traffic jam caused by mass spam, protect the owners of domain names, and help reduce the Internet access costs for unwanted e-mail paid for by its recipients be they businesses or individuals. In essence, the court said the "only burden the Act places on spammers is the requirement of truthfulness, a requirement that does not burden commerce at all but actually facilitates it by eliminating fraud and deception."

Thus we can see that unless there is a state antispam law or you have taken steps to prevent spam by opting out (consumers have complained that clicking "Remove me" or similar buttons has been ineffective) or installing blocking software, there is very little you can do regarding spam. Note, in the past five years, the FTC reports having received over 250,000 spam complaints resulting in over thirty enforcement actions. Why has spam become so prevalent a marketing and advertising tool? E-businesses maintain that spam is a relatively inexpensive method to reach huge numbers of prospective customers and is very profitable (2002 retail sales online were estimated to be over $72 billion, a 41 percent increase over 2001). Amazon estimated its sales for 2002 to be $850 million. It would be difficult to determine the effect of spam on those figures. Again, for many, the spam serves only to annoy, invade privacy, and create a kind of online "traffic jam."

> **http://**
> - For the FTC's suggestions for reducing spam, see **http://www. ftc.gov/bcp/online/features/spam.htm**
> - For more information, visit the FTC site at **http://www.ftc.gov**

You are probably aware where these e-commerce companies get our names and other personal information about us for spamming and other purposes. As we indicated in the introduction to this chapter, and as we discovered in the *DoubleClick* case, every time we visit a Web site we leave a "fingerprint" of information about ourselves in the form of a cookie. Not only is personal information about us stored on the cookie, but also other information such as our buying habits and preferences. E-commerce businesses are willing to pay for this valuable information. Thus the gathering of such data has evolved into big business for many companies specializing in the sale of it in the form of lists. This has led to what is called *online profiling*. Privacy concerns arise because these lists and profiles are sold without our consent or knowledge and are often the catalyst for spam. E-businesses argue that these profiles are useful in targeting interested consumers for receiving customized information about their products or services, special events, and other matters of interest. It should be obvious that as long as the profiling process and the resultant solicitations meet the requirements of the law, they will likely be protected as exercises of free speech or enterprise.

One of the most significant industry self-regulation initiatives recommended by the FTC for Web sites that collect personal identifiable information (PII) is that their online privacy policies be drafted in accordance with the **fair information practices** (see Figure 9.2) (first suggested in 1973 by the Department of Health Education and Welfare's Advisory Committee on Automated Data Systems and advocated by the FTC in its Reports to Congress). Keep in mind, there are a number of concerned consumer watchdog groups such as the Electronic Privacy Information Center (EPIC), Center for Democracy and Technology, the Electronic Frontier Foundation, and the Privacy Rights Clearinghouse, whose agendas focus on monitoring and safeguarding personal privacy online and who also recommend policies based on the practices (see Figure 9.3).

Is Self-Regulation Working?

The FTC conducted a survey in 2000 consisting of a sample random group of 335 Web sites ("Random Sample") and 100 of the busiest sites. The results indicated that nearly 100 percent of the sites collected some type of PII and posted a privacy policy, but only 50 percent met the basic *Notice* and *Choice* requirements of the FIP.

http://

- For particulars about the FTC 2000 Privacy Survey, see the 2000 FTC Report to Congress at **http://www.ftc.gov/reports/ privacy2000/privacy2000.pdf**

The FTC is not completely convinced that self-regulation is the answer to controlling spam but will allow it to continue focusing its efforts on continuing to apply and enforce its regulations against deceptive and fraudulent spams and inadequate privacy policies. It did so in the following case involving spam. In *FTC v. GM Funding, Inc., Global Mortgage Inc., et al.*, SACV 02-1026 DOC—U.S. District Court, CA (2002), the FTC charged the defendant with "**spoofing**," which was described as disguising an e-mail to make it appear it was mailed from an address different from the one from which it was actually mailed without the permission of the user of the actual "spoofed" address. In this case, spams were sent in the name of and along with the trademarks of well-known financial institutions that offered, among other services, mortgages and other financial services. Those "spoofed" included Prudential, Radian Corporation, and the Fannie Mae Corporation.

The spams requested personal financial information from consumers including income and credit ratings under the pretense it would be used to help the consumers obtain mortgages. Attempts by the consumers to stop the spam failed. In fact, the information was sent to an IP address registered to the defendant, who transferred it to another defendant who could then solicit the consumers about obtaining mortgages.

The FTC charged the defendants with unfair and deceptive practices under Section 5 of the FTC Act and with violating Section 521 of the GLB Act, 15 U.S.C. § 6821, which prohibited obtaining customer personal financial information of a financial institution by false, fictitious, or fraudulent statements. The court agreed and issued an injunction preventing these practices in the future. (*Note:* The defendants did not admit guilt but opted to avoid a trial by agreeing to the injunction.)

FIGURE 9.2   FTC's Fair Information Practices

Web sites that collect personal identifying information (PII) about or from consumers should comply with the following:

- **Notice:** Indicate information collection practices before collection.
- **Choice:** Inform how information is to be used along with opportunities to deny or grant permission for collection of PII.
- **Access:** Allow access to information already collected to determine and correct, if necessary, inaccurate or incomplete information.
- **Security:** Make sure information is protected from unauthorized use, access, or disclosure.
- **Enforcement:** Implement procedures to subject themselves to outside monitoring to ensure compliance with appropriate sanctions and remedies for violations.

FIGURE 9.3   Industry Attempts to Address Spam and Related Privacy Issues

- **World Wide Web Consortium (W3C), Platform for Privacy Preferences (P3P):** A leader in developing technical specifications for the Web's infrastructure in order to further and enhance its growth and operation. Over 450 member Web sites post their privacy policies automatically, making them viewable by visitors who may then choose what information they will or will not allow to be collected. (See *http://www.w3.org.*)
- **TRUSTe:** An independent, nonprofit Internet privacy organization sponsored by AOL, Microsoft, and others, comprised of more than six hundred member companies. Its major function is to monitor the sites of its members making sure their information practices are fair and sensitive to privacy rights. Members are also required to inform users about how personal information about them is used and to establish oversight and consumer complaint procedures. Those in compliance receive a trustmark (a type of online "seal of approval"). (See *http://www.etrust.org.*)
- **Network Advertising Initiative:** Its members include DoubleClick, Avenue A, and other online providers of advertising services and products, all of whom are committed to providing the privacy protections associated with the fair information practices (FIP). (See *http://www.networkadvertising.org.*)
- **Direct Marketing Association (DMA):** Provides information and guidance to its members. In 2002, approved and *mandated* a set of online information guidelines for its members who operated Web sites and engaged in bulk e-mail solicitations. (See *http://www.the-dma.org/library/guidelines/onlineguidelines. shtml.*)
- **Netiquette** is an unofficial attempt at self-regulation by businesses engaged in cyberspace. It proscribes a kind of ethical code of etiquette to be followed when dealing with customers or users online. Generally, it seeks to require courtesy and respect online. It also seeks to ensure that bandwidths are not clogged.

For insight as to how federal courts have treated other cases involving spam, consider the following two cases. In the first case, *Cyber Promotions v. America Online, Inc.*, the court had to balance First Amendment guarantees of freedom of speech associated with commercial speech, against the rights of the individual to be free from what they perceive to be an annoying interference with privacy rights.

In the second case, *CompuServe, Inc., v. Cyber Promotions,* the court was asked to apply the common law theory of trespass to the sending and receiving of electronic signals. The judges in both cases categorized the issues presented for decision as "novel."

Cyber Promotions, Inc., v. America Online, Inc.
948 F. Supp. 436 (E.D. Pa. 1996)

Facts

The plaintiff, Cyber Promotions, is a private company incorporated in Pennsylvania. It provides advertising services for companies and individuals. One of its business activities is sending unsolicited e-mail advertisements through the Internet to America Online (AOL) subscribers.

AOL is a private company offering computer online services. Its members pay prescribed fees for use of AOL resources, access to AOL, and access and use of AOL's e-mail system and connection to the Internet.

AOL's computer servers have a finite, though expandable, capacity to handle e-mail. It allows its subscribers to send and receive e-mail to and from AOL, as well as non-AOL, members. Under either scenario, these services require the use of AOL's computer hardware and software. AOL subscribers pay a monthly service fee, and AOL is responsible for processing all of this information, including the e-mail.

In a letter dated January 26, 1996, AOL advised Cyber that it was upset with Cyber's dissemination of unsolicited e-mail to AOL subscribers. Apparently these advertisements continued despite the letter. AOL subsequently sent a number of "bombs" to Cyber's Internet service providers (ISPs). Cyber has stated that the "bombs" occurred when AOL gathered all unsolicited e-mail sent by Cyber to undeliverable AOL addresses, altered their return, and then sent the altered e-mail in a bulk transmission to Cyber's ISPs in order to disable the ISPs. Cyber filed suit first, alleging that as a result of the bombing, two of its ISPs terminated their relationship with Cyber, and a third ISP has refused to enter into a contract with Cyber. The complaint asserts claims under the Computer and Fraud Abuse Act, and state law claims such as intentional interference with contractual relations.

Two weeks later, AOL filed a complaint against Cyber for, *inter alia,* service and trade name infringement and violations of the Virginia Consumer Protection Act and the Electronic Communications Privacy Act. One month later, Cyber added a declaratory judgment claim seeking a "declaration that [it] has the right to send to AOL members, via the Internet, unsolicited e-mail advertisements." AOL has vehemently argued throughout the brief history of these suits that Cyber has no right to send literally millions of e-mail messages each day to AOL's Internet servers, free of charge, resulting in the overload of the e-mail servers. Cyber argues, however, that by providing these services, AOL has opened up this domain for public use, and as such performs a public function open to the public.

The trial judge consolidated the two cases because they arise from the same nucleus of operative facts. AOL motioned for partial summary judgment on Cyber's First Amendment claim.

Judicial Opinion (Memorandum Opinion and Order, District Judge Weiner)

These cases present the novel issue of whether, under the First Amendment to the United States Constitution, one private company has the unfettered right to send unsolicited e-mail advertisements to subscribers of another private online company over the Internet and whether the private online company has the right to block the e-mail advertisements from reaching its members. The question is important because while the Internet provides the opportunity to disseminate vast amounts of information, the Internet does not, at least at the present time, have any means to police the dissemination of that information.

Under Federal Rule of Civil Procedure 56(c), summary judgment may be granted when, 'after considering the record of evidence in the light most favorable to the non-moving party, no genuine issue of material fact exists and the moving party is entitled to judgment as a matter of law.' In its motion . . . AOL contends that Cyber has no First Amendment right to send unsolicited e-mail . . . because AOL is not a state actor.

The First Amendment to the United States Constitution states that 'Congress shall make no law . . . abridging the freedom of speech, or of the press.' Only recently the Supreme Court has stated that 'the guarantees of free speech . . . guard only against the encroachment by the government and erect no shield against merely private conduct.' In the case *sub judice*, the parties have stipulated that AOL is a private online company that is not owned in whole or in part by the government. They have also stipulated that there has been no government involvement in AOL's business decision to institute . . . a block directed to Internet e-mail sent by Cyber to AOL members or subscribers.

Despite these stipulations, Cyber argues that AOL's conduct has the character of state action. As a general matter, private action can only be considered state action when 'there is a sufficiently close nexus between the State and the challenged action [of the private entity] so that the action of the latter may be fairly treated as that of the state itself.'

Pursuant to the Court's directive, the parties have stipulated to the following facts: 'No single entity—academic, corporate, governmental, or non-profit—administers the Internet. Although the Internet is accessible to all persons, . . . the constituent parts . . . are owned and managed by private entities.'

In sum, we find that since AOL is not a state actor and there has been no state action by AOL's activities under any of the . . . tests for state action enunciated by our Court, Cyber has no right under the First Amendment to send unsolicited e-mail to AOL's members. The motion of America Online, Inc., for partial summary judgment on First Amendment issues is GRANTED.

IT IS SO ORDERED.

Case Questions

1. How did Cyber's spamming activities interfere with AOL's contractual relations?
2. What provisions of the ECPA do you believe were violated by Cyber?
3. Is it ethical to allow an ISP to block all spam messages, especially in cases where a subscriber does not object to receiving them?

CompuServe, Inc., v. Cyber Promotions
962 F. Supp. 1015 (S.D. Ohio 1997)

Facts

CompuServe is one of the major national commercial online computer services. In addition to its other services, CompuServe also provides its subscribers with a link to the much larger resources of the Internet. This allows its subscribers to send and receive electronic messages, known as "e-mail," by the Internet. CompuServe subscribers use CompuServe's domain name together with their own unique alphanumeric identifier to form a distinctive e-mailing address. E-mail sent to CompuServe subscribers is processed and stored on CompuServe's proprietary computer equipment and subscribers electronically retrieve those messages.

Defendants, Cyber Promotions, Inc., and its president Sanford Wallace, are in the business of sending unsolicited e-mail advertisements on behalf of themselves and their clients to hundreds of thousands of Internet users, many of whom are CompuServe subscribers threatening to discontinue service unless CompuServe prohibits mass mailers from using its equipment. CompuServe receives no payment from the mass mailers and asserts that the volume of e-mail messages generated places a significant burden on its equipment, which has finite processing and storage capacity. Subscribers pay for their access to CompuServe's services in increments of time, and thus the processing of unsolicited e-mail costs them money.

CompuServe notified defendants that they are prohibited from using its computer equipment to process and store the unsolicited e-mail. In an effort to shield its equipment from defendants' bulk e-mail, CompuServe has implemented software programs designed to screen out messages and block their receipt. Allegedly, defendants have been able to continue sending messages to CompuServe's equipment in spite of CompuServe's protests and protective efforts.

CompuServe brought suit, alleging the defendants have trespassed on their personal property. CompuServe motioned this court for a preliminary injunction to prevent defendants from sending them unsolicited advertisements. Defendants assert that they possess the right to continue to send these communications under the First Amendment constitutional guarantee of free speech.

Judicial Opinion *(District Judge Graham)*

This case presents novel issues regarding the commercial use of the Internet. [The court first addressed CompuServe's request for a Temporary Restraining Order in which it enjoined defendants] from performing any of the acts . . . described during the pendency of this litigation.

CompuServe predicates . . . its motion for a preliminary injunction on the common law theory of trespass to personal property or to chattels, asserting that defendants' continued transmission of electronic messages to its computer equipment constitutes an actionable tort.

Trespass to chattels has evolved from its original common law application, concerning primarily the asportation of another's tangible property, to include the unauthorized use of personal property:

Its chief importance now is that there may be recovery . . . for interferences with the possession of chattels which are not sufficiently important to be classed as conversion, and so to compel the defendant to pay the full value of the thing with which he has interfered. Trespass to chattels survives today, in other words, largely as a little brother of conversion.

While authority under Ohio law respecting an action for trespass to chattels is extremely meager, it appears to be an actionable tort. Both plaintiff and defendant cite the Restatement (Second) of Torts to support their respective positions. In determining a question unanswered by state law, it is appropriate for this Court to consider such sources as the Restatement of the law and decisions of other jurisdictions.

The Restatement § 217 (b) states that a trespass to chattels may be committed by intentionally using or intermeddling with the chattel in possession of another. Electronic signals generated and sent by computer have been held to be sufficiently physically tangible to support a trespass cause of action in California. [The] Indiana Supreme Court recogniz[ed] in dicta that a hacker's unauthorized access to a computer was more in the nature of trespass than criminal conversion. [A Washington state court held] computer hacking as the criminal offense of 'computer trespass' under Washington law. It is undisputed that plaintiff has a possessory interest in its computer systems. Further, defendants' contact with plaintiff's computers is clearly intentional.

Under Restatement § 252, the owner of personal property can create a privilege in the would-be trespasser by granting consent to use the property. Defendants argue [just this]. Their argument is analogous to the argument that because an establishment invites the public to enter its property for business purposes, it cannot later restrict . . . access . . . , a proposition which is erroneous under Ohio law.

In response to the trespass claim, defendants [also] argue that they have the right to continue to send unsolicited . . . under the First Amendment. The United States Supreme Court has recognized that "the constitutional guarantee of free speech is a guarantee only against abridgement by the government." In the present action, CompuServe is a private company. Defendants' . . . use is an actionable trespass to plaintiff's chattel. The First Amendment to the United States Constitution provides no defense for such conduct.

Plaintiff has demonstrated a likelihood of success on the merits . . . [and] has shown that it will suffer irreparable harm without the grant of a preliminary injunction. Based on the foregoing, plaintiff's motion for a preliminary injunction is GRANTED. The temporary restraining order . . . is hereby extended in duration until final judgment is entered in this case.

IT IS SO ORDERED.

Case Questions

1. What "irreparable harm" will the plaintiff suffer without the injunction?
2. Do you agree that electronic signals should be classified as physically tangible personal property?
3. How can a company ethically justify engaging in a business that appears to create an annoyance and invasion of privacy?

The day after the AOL decision, Sanford Wallace, the so-called spam king, entered into a settlement agreement with AOL. The agreement provided that AOL be allowed to install what it calls "PreferredMail." This allowed AOL subscribers the option to receive or block unsolicited e-mail advertisements such as those offered by companies like Cyber Promotions. Both sides considered this settlement a victory. However, you should recognize that this settlement applied only to Cyber Promotions and AOL.

WORKPLACE PRIVACY

Employees' inappropriate e-mail and usage of computers owned and maintained by employers continue to provide a fertile environment for privacy issues and litigation. From the employer's perspective, employee workplace privacy rights, whether they exist under the Fourth Amendment search and seizure provisions, other statutes, or common law torts, are overcome by the employer's vested economic interest in ensuring employee productivity and protection of the employer from potential liability for harassment, discrimination, obscenity, and defamation as well as protection of trademark, trade secret, and other proprietary interest violations that could result from inappropriate and unsupervised employee computer usage.

This right to search an employee's office, desk, and files was recognized in *O'Connor v. Ortega*, 480 U.S. 709 (1987), where the U.S. Supreme Court held that a *public* or *government* employer could do so provided the search was "reasonable under all circumstances." The Court stated that the employee's legitimate expectation of privacy had to be "balanced against the government's need for supervision, control and the efficient operation of the workplace." As we will discover, the rationale used for the decision in *Ortega* is the similar to that used by other courts in workplace privacy cases involving employees in the private sector.

How Common Is the Problem of Employee Inappropriate Computer Use?

In 1999, a study conducted by the Elron Software Corporation determined that over 85 percent of the employees responding indicated they used employer e-mail systems for personal use, and over 60 percent indicated they visited adult Web sites with more than 50 percent receiving inappropriate e-mails. Although the law has yet to be settled in this area and there are virtually no U.S. Supreme Court cases in this area, there are some trends or precedents that provide possible guidance and predictability concerning employer liability.

Employer liability appears to be greatly diminished, *but not eliminated,* where the employer has developed a clear and written computer-monitoring and usage policy communicated on a regular basis to all employees. Obtaining employee consent to the monitoring is also a mitigating factor for liability (also under the ECPA's exceptions). Keep in mind that the employer's rights are not limitless even with a valid policy and with employee consent to monitoring. For example, an employer would have difficulty justifying around the clock ("24/7") monitoring in the absence of a business-related reason (*Sanders v. Bosch*, 38 F. 3d 736 [1994]). The same could be true where the employer's monitoring policy *only* applied to business messages and personal messages were intercepted and accessed (*Watkins v. L.M. Berry & Co.,* 704 F.2d 577 [11th Cir. 1983]).

How prevalent are such policies? A workplace privacy survey in 2000 conducted by the Society for Human Resource Management and West Group indicated that 70 percent of the 722 human resource managers reported having computer and e-mail monitoring policies and 94 percent reported the policies were communicated to their employees. In companies that have policies, employees experience difficulty in proving that they enjoyed a reasonable expectation of privacy in their computer use and especially their e-mail. Recall our earlier discussion in the *Katz* case and of the tort of intrusion upon seclusion where the element of a reasonable expectation of privacy was critical to proving an invasion of privacy rights. This element continues to be one of the most critical discussion points in many of the cases decided in this area. Without such a policy, the employer can be exposed to liability.

In *Nardinelli et al., v. Chevron*, N0.945302, Superior Court, CA (1995), Chevron had an anti-harassment policy but none for computer usage or monitoring. Nardinelli and other employees sued Chevron, claiming they were sexually harassed by e-mails sent to them by other employees that offered *25 reasons why beer was better than women*. Chevron settled out of court with the employees for $2.2 million.

In a more recent case, an employer had no monitoring policy regarding its online bulletin board outside the workplace on which employees could post messages. Defendant's employees posted harassing comments on the bulletin board about the plaintiff. Although the employer was informed about them, it did nothing, believing the bulletin was not outside the workplace. The court took a different view, ruling that even though the bulletin board did not have a physical presence in the workplace, it was close enough so harassment posted on it would be considered to have occurred in the workplace. Further, the court made a point of the fact that once the employer knew of the comments, it had a legal duty to stop them. The plaintiffs in that case were awarded $1.7 million in damages (see *Blakey v. Continental Airlines*, 751 A. 2d 538 (N.J. 2000).

In the following case, an employer promised it would neither read employee e-mail nor terminate or reprimand an employee based on the content of the e-mail. The employer did intercept the employee's e-mail, found it unprofessional and inappropriate, and fired him.

Michael A. Smyth v. Pillsbury Company
914 F. Supp. 97 (E.D. Pa., 1996)

Facts

Plaintiff, an at-will employee, received certain e-mail communications from his supervisor over defendant's e-mail system on his computer at home. At some later date, contrary to the assurances of confidentiality made by defendant, defendant intercepted plaintiff's e-mail messages. The messages concerned statements about the sales management and contained threats to "kill the backstabbing bastards." They also referred to the planned holiday party as the "Jim Jones Koolaid affair."

As a result, plaintiff is terminated for transmitting what the defendant deemed to be inappropriate and unprofessional comments over defendant's e-mail system.

Judicial Opinion *(Judge Weiner)*

As a general rule, Pennsylvania law does not provide a common law cause of action for the wrongful discharge of an at-will employee such as the plaintiff. An employer "may discharge an employee at-will with or without cause, at pleasure, unless restrained by some contract."

Henry v. Pittsburgh & Lake Erie Railroad Co., 139 Pa. 289, 21 A. 157 (1891). However, in the most limited circumstances, exceptions have been recognized where discharge of an at-will employee threatens or violates a clear mandate of public policy. This public policy exception is an especially narrow one. To date, the Pennsylvania Superior Court has only recognized three such exceptions. First, an employee may not be fired for serving on jury duty.

Second, an employer may not deny employment to a person with a prior conviction.

And finally, an employee may not be fired for reporting violations of federal regulations to the Nuclear Regulatory Commission.

As evidenced above, a public policy exception must be clearly defined. Plaintiff claims that his termination was a violation of public policy, which precludes an employer from terminating an employee in violation of the employee's right to privacy as embodied in Pennsylvania common law. In support for this proposition, plaintiff directs our attention to a decision by our Court of Appeals in *Borse v. Piece Goods Shop, Inc.*, 963 F. 2d 611 (3rd Cir. 1992). In *Borse,* the plaintiff sued her employer alleging wrongful discharge as a result of her refusal to submit to urinalysis screening and personal property searches at her workplace pursuant to employer's drug and alcohol policy. After rejecting plaintiff's argument that the employer's drug and alcohol program violated public policy embodied in the United States and Pennsylvania Constitutions, our Court of Appeals stated "our review of Pennsylvania law reveals other evidence of public policy that may, under certain circumstances, give rise to a wrongful discharge action related to urinalysis or to personal property searches. Specifically, we refer to Pennsylvania common law regarding invasion of privacy." One of the torts Pennsylvania recognizes as encompassing an action for invasion of privacy is the tort of "intrusion upon seclusion." The Restatement (Second) of Torts defines the tort as follows:

> One who intentionally intrudes, physically or otherwise, upon the solitude or seclusion of another or his private affairs or concerns, is subject to liability to the other for invasion of his privacy, if the intrusion would be highly offensive to a reasonable person.

Liability only attaches when the intrusion is "substantial and would be highly offensive to the 'ordinary reasonable person.'" *Borse,* 963 F. 2d at 621. Although the Court of Appeals in *Borse* observed that "the Pennsylvania courts have not had occasion to consider whether a discharge related to an employer's tortious invasion of an employee's privacy violates public policy," the Court of Appeals predicted that in any claim where the employees claimed that his discharge related to an invasion of his privacy, "the Pennsylvania Supreme Court would examine the facts and circumstances surrounding the alleged invasion of privacy. If the court determined that the discharge was related to a substantial and highly offensive invasion of the employee's privacy, we believe that it would conclude that the discharge violated public policy." In determining whether an alleged invasion of privacy is substantial and highly offensive to a reasonable person, Pennsylvania would adopt a balancing test which balances the employee's privacy interest against the employer's interest in maintaining a drug-free workplace. Because the Court of Appeals in *Borse* could envision at least two ways in which an employer's drug and alcohol program might violate the public policy protecting individuals from tortious invasion of privacy, the Court vacated the district court's order dismissing the plaintiff's complaint and remanded the case to the district court with directions to grant Borse leave to amend the complaint to allege how the defendant's drug and alcohol program violates her right to privacy.

Applying the Restatement definition of the tort of intrusion upon seclusion to the facts and circumstances of the case *sub judice,* we find that plaintiff has failed to state a claim upon which relief can be granted. In the first instance, unlike urinalysis and personal property searches, we do not find a reasonable expectation of privacy in e-mail communications voluntarily made by an employee to his supervisor over the company e-mail system, notwithstanding any assurances that management would not intercept such communications. Once plaintiff communicated the alleged unprofessional comments to a second person (his supervisor) over an e-mail system, which was apparently utilized by the entire company, any reasonable expectation of privacy was lost. Significantly, the defendant did not require plaintiff, as in the case of a urinalysis or personal property search, to disclose any personal information about him. Rather, plaintiff voluntarily communicated the alleged unprofessional comments over the company e-mail system. We find no privacy interests in such communications.

In the second instance, even if we found that an employee had a reasonable expectation of privacy in the contents of his e-mail communications over the company e-mail system, we do not find that a reasonable person would consider the defendant's interception of these communications to be a substantial and highly offensive invasion of privacy. Again, we note that by intercepting such communications, the company is not requiring the employee to disclose any personal information about him or invading the employee's person or personal effects. Moreover, the company's interest in preventing inappropriate and unprofessional comments or even illegal activity over its e-mail system outweighs any privacy interest the employee may have in those comments.

In sum, we find that the defendant's actions did not tortiously invade the plaintiff's privacy and, therefore, did not violate public policy. As a result, the motion to dismiss is granted.

IT IS SO ORDERED.

Case Questions

1. Do you think Smyth should have been given a warning he would be terminated the next time he made these kinds of comments? Were they that serious?
2. How can a court justify the "chilling effect" employer interception of employee e-mail appears to have on an employee's freedom of speech?
3. Was it ethical for the employer to break the promise not to read employee e-mail or terminate or reprimand an employee based on the content of the e-mail?

In a more recent case, *McLaren v. Microsoft*, Case No. 05-97-00824, 1999 Tex. App. LEXIS 4103 (Tex. Ct. of App.1999), McLaren was fired after his employer, Microsoft, broke into and accessed his personal folders that were protected by a password known only to McLaren and discovered files that contained evidence of sexual harassment. McLaren argued that because Microsoft allowed him to have a password for his personal folders, a reasonable expectation of privacy was created and Microsoft's actions resulted in violations of the Fourth Amendment, the tort of intrusion upon seclusion, and an invasion of privacy. However, the court decided for Microsoft, reasoning that because the e-mails had to first travel through various points in Microsoft's e-mail system before reaching McLaren's folder, Microsoft could have accessed them before they reached his folder, thereby eliminating any reasonable expectation of privacy. The court offered reasoning similar to that in *Smyth*, providing the following guidelines for similar future cases:

- Microsoft's actions would not be considered highly offensive to a reasonable person.
- The folders were business related and not personal.
- The e-mails belonged to Microsoft and the employees.
- Microsoft had a right to prevent inappropriate and unprofessional comments or potential illegal activities such as sexual harassment and this right outweighed any privacy rights enjoyed by McLaren.

Smyth and *McLaren* serve notice to employees that they should expect little or no privacy in the workplace. Particular attention should be paid to the similar reasoning employed by both courts. It provides some guidelines and predictability for cases of these types. However, remember that the law is still unsettled in this area so other courts could decide differently in cases involving similar facts. A Massachusetts trial court appears to have done exactly that in *Restuccia v. Burk Technology*, 5 Mass. L. Rptr, No. 31, 712 (Middlesex Superior Court, 1996), where the employer suspected the employee of sending inappropriate personal e-mails through the employer's e-mail system. The employer allowed the employees to have personal passwords, send personal e-mails, and never told them their e-mails could be accessed. In effect there was no monitoring policy. Without offering reasoning, the court believed there existed a question of fact to be decided by a jury as to whether the employees enjoyed a reasonable expectation of privacy that was violated by the employer's intrusion (upon seclusion) resulting in an invasion of privacy.

Impact of the ECPA on Workplace Privacy

Recall that Title I of the ECPA prohibits the unauthorized interception of an electronic communication including e-mail in transmission and Title II prohibits accessing and disclosing such communications if they are in storage. As mentioned earlier, both titles provide for exceptions.

In the following case, the plaintiff brought claims alleging violations of the ECPA and the Railway Labor Act for wrongful interference with union organizing activities. The case was originally tried in federal district court and was appealed to the federal court of appeals twice. The second appeal is presented here.

Robert Konop v. Hawaiian Airlines
302 F.3d 868 (9th Cir. 2002)

Facts

Konop was a pilot for Hawaiian Airlines (HA) and operated a secure Web site accessible only by a password he would assign to users. He also created a list of "users." During union negotiations, he posted messages critical of his employer, its officers, and the union to which he belonged. He also urged employees to seek alternative union representation. Davis, HA's vice president, believed Konop was posting false allegations on his Web site and enlisted the aid of Wong, another pilot who had a password but had never logged on to the Web site. Davis used Wong's name and password to access the Web site and discovered the comments. He disclosed them to other officers of the company and to the union. Konop files suit in federal district court claiming these actions violated his privacy under Title I of the ECPA (referred to in the case as the Wiretap Act) and Title II of the ECPA (referred to in the case as the Stored Communications Act) prohibitions against interception of electronic communications, alleging that HA viewed his secured Web site and disclosed the contents of the messages he had posted. Further, he alleged the actions resulted in unauthorized surveillance of union activities prohibited by the Railway Labor Act (RLA). The district court ruled against Konop as to his claims under Title I, holding there was no "interception" of the message by Davis because it occurred when the message was "in storage" and not when it was "in transmission" as required by Title I.

The district court also ruled against Konop in his Title II claim holding that the actions were covered by an exception to Title II that allows access "without authority" where the "conduct is authorized by a user of that service with respect to a communication of or intended for that user." The exception required that a "user" actually *use* or access the Web site, not merely possess a password to do so. Wong had never accessed the Web site and without evidence of that fact, the court ruled both Wong and Davis were users and therefore there was no Title II violation. The court did find a violation of the RLA had occurred. In the first appeal to this court in January 2001, the court reversed the decision of the district court as to the ECPA claims, ruling there were violations of both Title I and II. It affirmed the decision regarding the RLA (236 F.3d 1035 (9th Cir. 2001). HA filed a petition for a rehearing that became moot when the court withdrew its January 2001 opinion leading to this appeal.

Judicial Opinion *(Circuit Judge Boochever)*

For a website such as Konop's to be "intercepted in violation of the Wiretap Act (Title I of the ECPA), it must be acquired during transmission not while it is in storage. This conclusion is consistent with the ordinary meaning of "intercept" which is to "stop, seize, or intercept in progress of course before arrival." (Webster's Dictionary) More importantly, it is consistent with the structure of the ECPA, which created the Stored Communications Act (SCA) for the express purpose of addressing "access to stored . . . electronic communications and transactional records." The level of protection provided stored communications under the SCA is considerably less than that provided under the Wiretap Act. The SCA details the procedures law enforcement must follow to access contents of stored communications and these are less burdensome than those required to obtain a wiretap order under the Wiretap Act. Thus, if Konop's position were correct and acquisition of a stored electronic communication were an interception under the Wiretap Act, the government would have to comply with the more burdensome and restrictive procedures under the Wiretap Act to do exactly what Congress intended it to do under the less burdensome procedures of the SCA. Congress could not have intended that result. We conclude that for a website such as Konop's to be "intercepted" in violation of the Wiretap Act, the electronic communication must be acquired during transmission and not while it is in storage.

Davis' conduct did not constitute an "interception of an electronic communication" in violation of the Wiretap Act. We affirm the district court's grant of a summary judgment against Konop on his wiretap claim.

Konop also argues that by viewing his secure website, Davis accessed a stored electronic communication without authorization in violation of the SCA (Title II of the ECPA). The parties agree that the relevant "electronic communication service" is Konop's website, and that the website was in electronic storage. Davis' conduct constituted "access without authorization" to "a facility through which an electronic communication is provided."

We address only the narrow question of whether the district court properly found Hawaiian Airlines exempt from liability under § 2701 (c) (2) which allows a person to authorize a third party's access to an electronic communication if the person is (1) a "user" of the "service" and (2) the communication is "of or intended for that user." The district court concluded that Wong had the authority under § 2701 to consent to Davis' use of the website because Konop put them on the list of eligible users. As intended recipients of wire and electronic communications, they were allowed to authorize third parties to access those e-mail communications. The district court did not make any finding on whether Wong actually used Konop's website. We cannot find any evidence that Wong ever used Konop's website and we must assume that he was not a "user" under § 2701 (c) (2) at the time he authorized Davis to view it. We therefore reverse the district court's summary judgment to Hawaiian on Konop's CA claim.

For the foregoing reasons, we affirm the district court's judgment with respect to Konops' Wiretap Act claims (and those under the RLA) and reverse the district court's judgment on Konop's claims under the SCA.

AFFIRMED IN PART, REVERSED IN PART, AND REMANDED.

Case Questions

1. Would the decision in this case have been different if Konop's Web site was accessible by a nonprotected password?
2. What facts were critical to the court of appeals' determination that Davis had violated the Stored Communications Act (Title II of the ECPA)?
3. How do the facts in this case differ from those in *Smyth*?

Conclusion

From our discussion, it should be obvious that employee privacy rights in the workplace are virtually nonexistent. However, in order to balance the interests of the employer with those of the employee, and create a workplace environment characterized by productivity, high morale, and mutual respect, *all* employers would be well advised to develop and implement a written computer usage policy, including a right to monitor, applicable to company-owned computers and electronic communications whether used on the business premises or at another location. From a legal stand-point, the policy should stress that employees have no reasonable expectation of privacy in company-owned property. The policy should be developed in consultation with the company attorney and other relevant individuals and departments including the employees or their representatives. Proper consideration should be given to the company culture. Figure 9.3 *suggests* the elements of a computer usage policy that a court could look to in employee privacy cases. Also, keep in mind that proper implementation of the policy is important. Courts will look to see if:

- Appropriate training programs regarding company requirements for computer usage are provided.
- The policy is in writing and conspicuously displayed in company employee literature (manuals, etc.).
- Every employee executes a written acknowledgment that they have received.
- Employees are reminded of the policy yearly.

Keep in mind that the policies listed in Figure 9.4 are not yet mandatory either under federal or state law. There is no guarantee that even with a policy the employer will be

FIGURE 9.4   Suggested Elements of an Employee Workplace Computer Use Policy

- Indicate the reasons for the policy.
- Indicate that employees should expect no privacy in company-owned property. Apply the policy to all employees including the CEO.
- Inform employees that computers issued to them are to be used for business purposes only (delineate any allowable personal uses).
- Indicate the nature and extent of computer monitoring, that it can be done at any time without notice, and describe the use of any related software or other methods for that purpose. Indicate the nature and extent of the impact imposed on the company by the USA Patriot Act.
- Inform employees that all communications, data, and documents stored in computers are confidential unless made public by the company. If relevant, inform employees on the methods to be used in handling such information.
- Zero tolerance will apply to offensive, harassing, or discriminating communications or e-mails and visits to inappropriate Web sites.
- Prohibit employee encryption of e-mail without company permission.
- Establish requirements for employee personal Web sites (indicate that the company name should not be posted on the site).
- Indicate the penalties for violations of the policy.
- Indicate that password protection does not guarantee freedom from employer access.

totally immune from liability for employee privacy claims. However, from the cases we have seen and others that have been decided, courts look favorably on employers who adopt an effective and well-implemented computer usage policy.

GLOBAL ISSUES OF PRIVACY IN CYBERSPACE

As an ever-increasing number of people access the Internet from all over the world, the question of what privacy should exist in cyberspace becomes all the more important. As national and international initiatives develop around the globe, significantly different perceptions of privacy begin to emerge, some in conflict with U.S. policy. The following section presents key initiatives around the world related to the issue of privacy in cyberspace.

European Union Directive on Privacy Protection

One of the most significant efforts protecting data privacy is the *European Union's (EU) Directive on Privacy Protection*, which became effective on October 25, 1998.[1] The directive 95/46/EC of the European Parliament and the Council of October 24,1995, requires EU member states to adopt legislation that protects the "fundamental rights and freedoms" of an individual, particularly the right to privacy as it relates to the processing and collection of personal data. Under the directive, "personal data" is defined as "information that relates to an identified or identifiable natural person." Corporations are not included under this definition. The definition of "processing" personal data is "any operation or set of operations performed upon personal data" and includes its collection, storage, disclosure, and destruction.

http://

- Read the text of the directive at **http://www.cdt.org/privacy/ eudirective/EU_Directive_.html**

The provisions of the legislation also apply to nonmember states doing business with member states. Specifically, Article 6 of the directive requires member states involved in the collection and possession of personal data to ensure that the data are:

- Processed fairly and accurately.
- Collected for specified and legitimate purposes and not further processed in a way incompatible with those purposes.
- Adequate, relevant, and not excessive for the purposes for which they are collected and/or further processed.
- Accurate and, where necessary, updated.
- Kept in a form that permits identification of data subjects for no longer than is necessary.

---

[1]The official name of the directive is the *Directive 95/46/EC of the European Parliament and of the Council of 24 October 1995 on the protection of individuals with regard to the processing of personal data and on the free movement of such data.*

Additionally, Article 7 of the directive states that personal data may only be processed if the person or corporation in control of the data can prove at least one of the following:

- The consent of the data subject has been given unambiguously.
- The processing of the data is necessary for the performance or preparation of a contract to which the data subject is a party.
- The processing of the data is necessary in order to protect the vital interests of the data subject.
- The processing of the data is in the public interest or in the exercise of official authority of the controller of the data or a third party.
- The processing is necessary for the legitimate interests of the controller or a third party except where the data subject's privacy rights are greater.

One of the most important directives is Article 25. This article prohibits the export of personal data to nonmembers countries that do not have laws that "adequately" protect personal data. "Adequate" does not have a specific term, but is rather defined on a case-by-case basis "in light of all circumstances surrounding a data transfer operation or set of data transfer operations."

Article 25 has significant implications for U.S. businesses and other EU non-members. This article requires EU members to follow vague minimum standards regarding the protection of personal data. For nations like the United States where its laws do not conform to the strictures of the directive, U.S. companies may be denied access to the EU marketplace. If U.S. companies "misuse" EU privacy information, they may be subjected to monetary penalties. Industries that heavily rely on personal data, such as services, travel, and health care companies, are most drastically affected.

Early implementation of the privacy directive has been quite stringent against EU nonmembers. For example, a Swedish privacy watchdog group demanded that American Airlines delete all health and medical information about Swedish passengers after each flight unless the passenger gave express consent otherwise. This would require American Airlines to delete details about allergies, asthma, and dietary needs, which are routinely collected in the United States, and not transmit that data to its SABRE reservation system in the United States. The Swedish court agreed with the privacy group, and transmission of this information was suspended.

This example also shows how easily anyone can take action against an infringing non-EU company. The directive permits any of the over 350 million EU citizens to file an action against a company claiming abuse of personal data that can be pursued to the highest echelons of the EU court system. At any time during this process, courts can mandate injunctions, suspend data flow, and halt business operations of an infringing firm. This first directive reveals how far apart the EU and other countries (especially the United States) are in their views of international data privacy.

The United States/European Union Safe Harbor Agreement

In response to the EU directive, the United States released draft "safe harbor" principles that purported to protect the privacy of data through a mix of government regulation, registration, and industry self-policing. After significant negotiations, the EU and the United States reached an agreement on March 14, 2000, that established safe harbor privacy principles accessible to both parties. This agreement, known as **The US–EU Safe Harbor Agreement**, establishes fixed requirements that U.S. companies must satisfy in order to meet the EU's minimum standards of privacy protection. Meeting this standard would allow U.S. companies to avoid experiencing interruptions in their business dealings with the EU or avoid prosecution by European authorities under European privacy laws. Certifying to the safe harbor assures the EU that U.S. companies provides "adequate" privacy protection, as defined by the EU Directive. At least 130 companies have joined the list, with more additions on the horizon.

> http://◄
>
> • For a checklist of how to satisfy the safe harbor rules, see **http://www.export.gov/safeharbor/checklist.htm**

The safe harbor standard is focused on seven basic principles. The **Seven Principles of the Safe Harbor Agreement**, as stated by the U.S. Department of Commerce, are as follows:

1. **Notice:** Organizations must notify individuals about the purposes for which they collect and use information about them. They must provide information about how individuals can contact the organization with any inquiries or complaints, the types of third parties to which it discloses the information, and the choices and means the organization offers for limiting its use and disclosure.

2. **Choice:** Organizations must give individuals the opportunity to choose (opt out) whether their personal information will be disclosed to a third party or used for a purpose incompatible with the purpose for which it was originally collected or subsequently authorized by the individual. For sensitive information, an affirmative or explicit (opt in) choice must be given if the information is to be disclosed to a third party or used for a purpose other than its original purpose or the purpose authorized subsequently by the individual.

3. **Onward Transfer** (Transfers to Third Parties): To disclose information to a third party, organizations must apply the notice and choice principles. Where an organization wishes to transfer information to a third party that is acting as an agent (1), it may do so if it makes sure the third party subscribes to the safe harbor principles or is subject to the Directive or another adequacy finding. As an alternative, the organization can enter into a written agreement with such a third party requiring that the third party provide at least the same level of privacy protection as is required by the relevant principles.

4. **Access:** Individuals must have access to personal information about them that an organization holds and be able to correct, amend, or delete that information where it is inaccurate, except where the burden or expense of providing access would be disproportionate to the risks to the individual's privacy in the case in question or where the rights of persons other than the individual would be violated.

5. **Security:** Organizations must take reasonable precautions to protect personal information from loss, misuse, and unauthorized access, disclosure, alteration, and destruction.

6. **Data integrity:** Personal information must be relevant for the purposes for which it is to be used. An organization should take reasonable steps to ensure that data is reliable for its intended use, accurate, complete, and current.

7. **Enforcement:** In order to ensure compliance with the safe harbor principles, there must be (a) readily available and affordable independent recourse mechanisms so each individual's complaints and disputes can be investigated and resolved and damages awarded where the applicable law or private sector initiatives so provide; (b) procedures for verifying that the commitments companies make to adhere to the safe harbor principles have been implemented; and (c) obligations to remedy problems arising out of a failure to comply with the principles. Sanctions must be sufficiently rigorous to ensure compliance by the organization. Organizations that fail to provide annual self-certification letters will no longer appear in the list of participants and safe harbor benefits will no longer be assured.

If an organization fails to comply with the safe harbor after certifying it has done so, it will be actionable under federal and state law provisions prohibiting unfair or deceptive acts. If the failure to comply continues, the company will no longer be entitled to benefit from the safe harbor coverage, and the company must notify the U.S. Department of Commerce.

Other National Efforts at Regulating Internet Data Privacy

Nations outside the U.S. and EU spheres have also developed data privacy initiatives. The following efforts are examples of attempts to regulate data privacy around the globe.

http://

- For more detailed information on the act, see **http://www.law.gov.au/privacy/royalinfo.html**

Australia. Australia has recently enacted the **Privacy Amendment (Private Sector) Act 2000,** which establishes a national program for managing personal information by private firms. The act also allows industries in place of the legislative framework to develop privacy codes of their own that are tailored to their own industry needs. The legislation has been in force since December 21, 2001, although small businesses have an additional year to comply.

This legislation establishes ten *National Privacy Principles (NPP)* that are the minimum standards for the privacy sector.[2] They regulate the collection, use and disclosure, and overseas transfer of personal data. The NPPs require that personal information is accurate, up to date, and secure. NPPs require that companies must disclose how they manage personal information, provide access and correction rights, and must allow individuals to deal with them anonymously if possible.

---

[2]The ten principles are collection, use and disclosure, data quality, data security, openness, access and correction, identifiers, anonymity, transborder data flows, and sensitive information.

The act limits transmittal of information across borders. An organization can transfer personal information to someone in a foreign country only if the foreign individual is subject to a law or scheme that upholds principles of fair data handling that are substantially similar to Australia's NPPs. Alternatively, the data may also be transferred if the individual who the information describes consents or it is necessary to perform or complete a contract. An individual who suffers harm from a violation of the act may collect damages from the controller or collector of the data.

Canada. Canada's most recent endeavor in the privacy arena is the enactment of the **Personal Information Protection and Electronic Documents Act**, which became effective January 1, 2001. The act establishes basic ground rules regarding how private sector companies may collect, use, or disclosure personal information collected by them in the course of their commercial activities.

With certain exceptions, the act requires a company to obtain an individual's consent when it collects, uses, or discloses personal information. The act also requires companies to supply a consumer with a product or a service even if the consumer refuses to consent to the collection, use, or disclosure of personal information, unless the information is essential to the transaction. Companies must provide personal information policies that are clear, understandable, and readily available. Any information held by a company that remains after a transaction is completed with a consumer should be destroyed, erased, or made anonymous when that data is no longer necessary. The act does not apply to information held by individuals for personal use (e.g., a personal greeting card list), provincial or territorial governments, an employee's basic personal information, and the collection of information solely for journalistic, artistic, or literary purposes.

If a complaint is filed, the privacy commissioner will investigate the complaint and attempt to resolve the dispute through mediation. That failing, the individual can ask for a hearing in the federal court. That court may award damages when appropriate. The court may also impose a fine as high as $62,790 ($100,000 Canadian) against any entity who inhibits a commissioner's investigation.

Since passage of the act in 2000, Canada and the European Union have been working toward an agreement confirming an equivalent level of privacy protection in both jurisdictions. Part of the process examined whether the legislation was "adequate" under the EU Directive on Data Protection. In January 2001, the Article 29 Working Party (Data Protection), composed of privacy commissioners from all EU member states, considered the Canadian legislation and issued a favorable opinion on the level of privacy protection in Canada.

Russia. The Russian Federation has taken a diametrically opposed view to data privacy. In short, the Russian government has given itself the power to spy on its citizens when they use the Internet. Further, Russia can punish Internet service providers (ISPs) that will not help. In 1999, Russia's Federal Security Bureau (FSB), formerly known as the KGB, introduced an addendum to a regulation called **System for Operational-Investigative Activities (SORM)**. The addendum requires an Internet service provider to install government-supplied "black boxes" that monitor electronic communications. ISPs are required to pay for the new technology. ISPs that refuse may be shut down. Security agencies may be tempted to bypass the legal requirement for a warrant before monitoring private correspondence. In early 2000, that power was expanded beyond the FSB to seven other federal security agencies, including the tax and interior ministry police.

Summary

This chapter discussed the common law and constitutional sources of the right to privacy, applying them to cyberspace. It also discussed the many federal statutes that have been passed to protect this right, including those related to personal identifiable information contained in financial and health care related records and data. Major emphasis was placed on the Electronic Communications Privacy Act. Employer-employee workplace privacy issues and policies were also explored. Spamming and its conflicts with First Amendment rights were also highlighted.

Finally, in the international arena the EU data privacy directive has set the standard for global data management. U.S. companies may now satisfy the directive requirements by applying under the US–EU Safe Harbor Agreement reached in 2000.

Key Terms

Fourth, Fifth, and Ninth Amendments to the U.S. Constitution, *258–259*

Intrusion upon Seclusion, *260*

Public Disclosure of Private Facts Causing Injury to Reputation, *260*

Publicly Placing Another in a False Light, *261*

Misappropriation of a Person's Name or Likeness Causing Injury to Reputation, *261*

USA Patriot Act, *268*

Privacy Protection Act (PPA), *268*

Privacy Act, *268*

Cable Communications Protection Act (CCPA), *269*

Video Privacy Protection Act (VPPA), *270*

Telephone Consumer Protection Act (TCPA), *270*

Fair Credit Reporting Act (FCRA), *270*

Computer Fraud and Abuse Act, *271*

Bank Secrecy Act, *271*

Right to Financial Privacy Act, *272*

Gramm-Leach-Bliley Act (GLB), *272*

identity theft, *273*

pretexting, *274*

Health Insurance Portability and Accountability Act (HIPAA), *274*

Children's Online Privacy Protection Act (COPPA), *275*

Electronic Communications Privacy Act (ECPA), *276*

Business Extension Rule, *278*

Carnivore, *280*

spam, *284*

fair information practices, *286*

"spoofing," *286*

netiquette, *287*

The US–EU Safe Harbor Agreement, *303*

Seven Principles of the Safe Harbor Agreement, *303*

Privacy Amendment (Private Sector) Act 2000, *304*

Personal Information Protection and Electronic Documents Act, *305*

System for Operational-Investigative Activities (SORM), *305*

Manager's Checklist

√ Make sure company use of the Internet and Web are mindful of rights to privacy.

√ Establish and implement effective company privacy policies regarding e-mail and computer usage. Make sure you establish a level of privacy employees should "reasonably expect."

√ Take steps to protect privacy and confidentiality of company-related proprietary interests and data, especially related to personnel.

√ Make sure you and your employees are aware there is very little privacy protection afforded to online communications.

√ If your company collects and stores information about its customers, make sure you provide them with an easy-to-read privacy policy (follow the fair information practices) with an opt-in rather than opt-out provision.

√ Be familiar with all applicable privacy laws and regulations, especially the fair information practices recommended by the FTC. Consider adopting the TRUSTe or other seal of approval for your Web site.

√ Implement a policy of self-regulation regarding privacy rights, including the kind of netiquette that others have established.

√ Ensure that any international data gathering effort complies with the EU directive on privacy. Satisfying the safe harbor provisions should be considered a perquisite for doing online business in Europe.

√ Be aware that national approaches to data privacy vary widely. Russia, for instance, has little if any privacy protections for consumers and businesses.

√ **Ethical Considerations**

Be truthful and forthright with employees regarding monitoring and computer usage policies and expectations. You and other company executives must adhere to them as well.

If your company collects and uses personal identifiable information about its customers and expresses a concern for their privacy, ensure that concern is reflected in actions and not merely words.

Support industry initiatives such as P3P, TRUSTe, and Netiquette.

Case Problems

1. Curtis and other plaintiffs, former at-will employees of Citibank, brought this action for sexual harassment under Title VII of the Civil Rights Act of 1965

against DiMaio and other defendants alleging the defendants created a hostile work environment when they used Citibank's e-mail system to send them e-mails that contained *two* racially and ethnically jokes offensive to African Americans. The defendants admitted the jokes were insensitive but that sending only two jokes was not severe or pervasive enough to have created a hostile workplace and satisfy the requirements of Title VII. How should the court decide? Give reasons for your answer. [*Curtis v. DiMaio*, 46 F. Supp. 2d 206 (E.D. N.Y. 1999), affirmed, 205 F.3d 1322 (2d Cir. 2000)].

2. Plaintiff, Steve Jackson Games (SJG), publishes books, magazines, role-playing games, and related products. In the mid-1980s, it began operating a BBS that offered its customers services by which could be sent and received. Private e-mail could be stored on the hard drive of its BBS until retrieved by the addressee. An investigator for the Bell Company discovered SJG was distributing a computerized text file containing information about Bell's emergency 911 call system. The Secret Service was notified and obtained a warrant and seized SJG's computer that operated the BBS, thereby closing it down. No 911 document belonging to Bell was found. When it was returned sometime later, SJG discovered 162 e-mail messages had been read and deleted. SJG sued the Secret Service, claiming violations of the Privacy Protection Act and Title I and II of the ECPA. The lower court found a violation of Title II because the Secret Service unlawfully seized stored electronic documents. However, because the Secret Service did not "intercept" the e-mail wrongfully (it had not acquired its contents contemporaneously with its transmission), it held there was no violation of Title II. Do you agree with the court's findings? [*Steve Jackson Games v. U.S. Secret Service*, 816 F. Supp. 432 (W.D. Tex. 1993), aff'd 36 E. 3d 457 (5th cir. 1994)]

3. The plaintiff, a senior executive-level employee, is allowed to use the defendant's company-owned computer for work at home. He agreed to and acknowledged the defendant's computer usage and monitoring policy. The defendant monitors and inspects the computer, discovering the plaintiff had been accessing pornographic Web sites. The plaintiff claims the Web sites had simply "popped up" on his computer screen. He is fired and sues for wrongful termination alleging that because the computer was provided as a perk for senior executives so they could work at home, he enjoyed a reasonable expectation of privacy. The defendant disagreed, claiming his actions were legal. What result? [*Zieminski v. TBG Insurance Services, Inc.*, No. B153400 (Cal. Super. Ct., 2002)]

4. GeoCities operates a very popular Web site with more than 2 million members (200,000 are between the ages of 3 and 15), which it refers to as "Homesteaders." Geo provides numerous services to its members, including free and fee-based home pages and free e-mail service. To join, individuals must com-

plete a new member application form in which mandatory personal information is required. The application also requests other "optional" information about level of education, income, marital status, and occupation. In the form, members were told their information would only be used to "provide members the specific advertising offers and products and services they requested and that the 'optional' information would not be released to anyone without the member's permission." The Federal Trade Commission (FTC) issues a complaint against Geo, alleging it engaged in deceptive practices by selling or disclosing personal information about its members, including children, to third parties other than those agreed to. These third parties would then be able to send unsolicited advertisements to these members. Geo denies the allegations.

What should GeoCities do in order to avoid claims that its actions are violating the privacy rights of its members including those between the ages of 3 and 13?

5. Plaintiffs are consumers who visit the Web sites of the defendants who are drug companies. These companies hired co-defendant, Pharmatrak, a provider of Internet traffic tracking services, to place cookies on plaintiffs' hard drives in order to secretly intercept and access the plaintiffs' electronic communications and visits to the defendant's Web sites. This was done without plaintiffs' knowledge, authorization, or consent. Personal information was collected about the plaintiffs related to their browsing habits and health. Pharmatrak provided monthly traffic reports to the drug companies. There was no evidence the information collected was being used unlawfully. The plaintiffs claim the actions of the defendants violated their privacy rights under Title I and II of the ECPA. The defendants claim they qualify for the "consent" exception provided under § 2511 (2)(d) of the ECPA. Are they correct? Do the plaintiffs have any privacy rights under HIPAA? [*In Re Pharmatrak Privacy Litigation*, 2002 WL 1880387 (D. Mass)]

6. In May 1999, officials from the Spanish Data Protection Authority carried out an inspection of Microsoft's subsidiary in Spain. The authority found that Microsoft possessed a database filled with the personal information of their Spanish consumers. It was later determined that Microsoft was transferring Spanish employee information from Spain to a Web server in the United States. Under current international law, what was the result?

Additional Readings

- Crutchfield, George, Lynch, Patricia, and Marsnik, Susan J. "U.S. Multinational Employers: Navigating Through the 'Safe Harbor' Principles to Comply with the EU Data Privacy Directive." *American Business Law Journal* 38 (2001): 735.

- Davis, Carrie. "Kiss Your Privacy Goodbye: Online Anonymity Post-9/11." *The Internet Law Journal* (January 21, 2002).

- Hatlestad, Luc. "Online Privacy Matters." *Red Herring* (January 16, 2001) (*http://redherring.com/industries/2001/*).

- Verton, Dan. "Government Data Mining Raises Privacy Concerns." *Computerworld* (January 17, 2003) (*http://www.computerworld.com*).

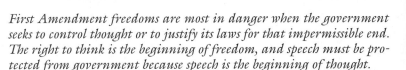

OBSCENITY

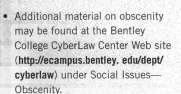

10

First Amendment freedoms are most in danger when the government seeks to control thought or to justify its laws for that impermissible end. The right to think is the beginning of freedom, and speech must be protected from government because speech is the beginning of thought.

—*U.S. Supreme Court Justice Anthony M. Kennedy writing for the majority in* **Ashcroft v. Free Speech Coalition,** *122 S. Ct. 1389, 2002 U.S. LEXIS 2789 (2002)*

LEARNING OBJECTIVES

After you have read this chapter, you should be able to:

1. Understand the *Miller* three-prong test used for determining obscenity and its application to material disseminated via the Internet.
2. Discuss the elements in proving or establishing liability for transmitting obscene material.
3. Explain how federal, state, and local laws attempt to regulate and affect the transmission, sale, and possession of obscene material, including child pornography.
4. Discuss the elusive nature of obscenity as a global concept.
5. Understand the existing treaties regulating obscenity.
6. Explore national efforts to regulate obscenity around the globe.

http://

- Additional material on obscenity may be found at the Bentley College CyberLaw Center Web site (**http://ecampus.bentley. edu/dept/ cyberlaw**) under Social Issues— Obscenity.

INTRODUCTION

With the continuing growth of literally thousands of adult-oriented sexually explicit Web sites, concern and controversy have arisen regarding censorship and the legal issues surrounding it. Some of the facts and statistics demonstrate just how enormous this market has become:

- The number-one search word or term used on search engines is the word "sex." (Alexa Research)
- In 1998, $970 million was spent on visits to adult Web sites, an amount that could rise to $3 billion by 2003. (*U.S. News & World Report,* March 27, 2000).
- In January 2002, 27.5 million Internet surfers visited porn sites of which 72 percent were men and 28 percent women. (Nielsen Net/Ratings)
- Seventy percent of all Web porn traffic occurs between 9 A.M. and 5 P.M. (Industry Standard)

- There are currently over 100,000 sexually explicit Web sites. (Log-On Data Corporation)
- In 1998, 25 percent of U.S. teenagers visited Web sites containing nudity (PC Meter, Inc.), and in 2000, 65 percent, 21 percent of whom were under fourteen, spent more time on porno sites than on those providing games. (NetValue Report on Minors Online, December 2000)
- The FBI has documented over four thousand cases of online child pornography.

http://

- To learn more about the FBI's Operation Candyman and its efforts to combat online child pornography, visit **http://www.fbi.gov**
- For views on censorship and obscenity, visit **http://www.aclu.org**, **http://www.eff.org**, **http://www.cdt.org**, and **http://www.cc.org**

Traditionally, governments and courts have found it difficult to define or distinguish prohibited obscene or indecent materials from those entitled to protection under First Amendment guarantees of freedom of expression. Courts have always taken a dim view regarding the dissemination of material considered to be harmful to children. A somewhat more fettered approach has been taken when dealing with the regulation of obscene material possessed by an adult for use in the privacy of one's home. As you read this chapter, keep in mind that much of the difficulty concerning the transmission of **cyberporn** results from a lack of consensus on how it should be defined. Public interest groups such as the American Civil Liberties Union (ACLU), the Free Speech Coalition, the Electronic Frontier Foundation (EFF), and the Center for Democracy and Technology oppose Internet censorship and legislation. Other groups such as the Christian Coalition are the driving forces behind legislation directed at prohibiting obscenity and indecency on the Internet.

FIRST AMENDMENT PROTECTION: FREEDOM OF EXPRESSION

Before we discuss the test currently employed for determining whether questionable materials transmitted or displayed via the Internet are to be protected or prohibited, we should look at the First Amendment's provision regarding freedom of expression. It basically puts limitations on the government's ability to regulate our rights to freedom of speech and expression. However, as you have probably observed in other contexts, our rights under the Constitution or, for that matter those provided by other federal and state laws, are not absolute (as we see in Chapter 11, "Defamation," speech that is defamatory is not protected).

In the landmark case *Roth v. United States,* 354 U.S. 476 (1957), Roth, the defendant, operated a business involving the sale of books, photographs, and magazines, some of which were obscene. He was convicted under a federal obscenity statute for mailing obscene materials. In upholding Roth's conviction, the Supreme Court held that obscenity was not within the area of constitutionally protected speech or press. Specifically, the Court declared:

> The protection given speech and press was fashioned to assure unfettered interchange of ideas for the bringing about of political and social changes desired by

the people. [All] ideas having even the slightest redeeming social importance—unorthodox ideas, controversial ideas, even ideas hateful to the prevailing climate of opinion—have the full protection of the guaranties, unless excludable because they encroach upon the limited area of more important interests. But implicit in history of the First Amendment is the rejection of obscenity as utterly without redeeming social importance.

The Test for Obscenity

Whether questionable materials transmitted via the Internet will be prohibited or protected may be determined by applying the three-prong test for obscenity announced in the following landmark U.S. Supreme Court case and highlighted in Figure 10.1.

Miller v. California
413 U.S. 15 (1973)

Facts

This case involves the application of California's state criminal obscenity statute to a situation in which sexually explicit materials have been thrust by aggressive salespeople on unwilling recipients who had in no way indicated a desire to receive such materials. It was proven at the criminal trial that Marvin Miller distributed obscene material when he caused to be mailed unsolicited brochures advertising various illustrated books and a movie, all euphemistically called "adult material." The charges arise specifically to an incident in which Miller mailed an envelope of this material to a California restaurant. The manager of the restaurant opened the envelope with his mother. They had not requested the brochure and later complained to the police.

At the time of the commission of the alleged offense, the California Penal Code read in part: [§ 311.2] "(a) Every person who knowingly sends or causes to be sent, or brings or causes to be brought, into this state for sale or distribution, or into this state prepares, publishes, prints, exhibits, distributes, or offers to distribute, or has in his possession with intent to distribute or exhibit, any obscene matter is guilty of a misdemeanor." As used in this chapter, (a) Obscene means that to the average person, applying contemporary standards, the predominant appeal of the matter, taken as a whole, is to prurient interest, that is, a shameful or morbid interest in nudity, sex, excretion, which goes beyond customary limits of candor in description or representation of such matters and is matter which is utterly without redeeming social importance.

After a jury trial, Miller was convicted under this law of a misdemeanor charge of knowingly distributing obscene material. The state appellate court affirmed the judgment without opinion. The U.S. Supreme Court granted certiorari to consider the application of the First Amendment's protections for expression to a state criminal obscenity statute. The Chief Justice wrote the Supreme Court's opinion, and it enunciated a three-part test still in use today. The Court was sharply divided, 5–4, with this opinion garnering a slim majority.

Judicial Opinion *(Chief Justice Burger)*

This is one of a group of "obscenity-pornography" cases being reviewed by the Court in a reexamination of standards enunciated in earlier cases involving what Mr. Justice Harlan called "the intractable obscenity problem." This case involves the application of a State's criminal obscenity statute to the First Amendment. This Court has recognized that the States have a legitimate interest in prohibiting dissemination or exhibition of obscene material when the mode of dissemination carries with it a significant danger of offending the sensibilities of unwilling recipients or the exposure to juveniles.

It is in this context that we are called upon to define the standards which must be used to identify obscene material that a State may regulate without infringing on the First Amendment as applicable to the States through the Fourteenth Amendment. [T]he Court now undertakes to formulate standards more concrete than those of the past, [and] it is useful for us to focus on two of the landmark cases in the somewhat tortured history of the Court's obscenity decisions. In *Roth v. United States,* [f]ive Justices joined in the opinion stating: "All ideas having even the slightest redeeming social importance—controversial ideas, even ideas hateful to the prevailing climate of opinion—have the full protection of the [First Amendment]." But implicit in the history of the First Amendment is the rejection of obscenity, as utterly without social importance.

Nine years later in *Memoirs v. Massachusetts,* the Court . . . articulated a new test for obscenity. The plurality held . . . three elements must "coalesce: it must be established that, [inter alia] the material is utterly without redeeming social value." While Roth presumed "obscenity" to be "utterly without redeeming social value," Memoirs required that to prove obscenity it must be affirmatively established that the material is "*utterly* without redeeming social value." Thus, even as the repeated words of *Roth,* the *Memoirs* plurality produced a drastically altered result that called upon the prosecution to prove a negative, i.e., that the material was "*utterly* without redeeming social value"—a burden virtually impossible to discharge under our criminal standards of proof.

The basic guidelines for the trier of fact must be:

1. whether "the average person, applying contemporary *community standards*" would find the work, taken as a whole, appeals to the prurient interest,
2. whether the work depicts or describes, in a *patently offensive* way, sexual conduct specifically defined by state law,
3. whether the work, taken as a whole, *lacks serious literary, artistic, political, or scientific value.*

We do not adopt as a constitutional standard the . . . test of *Memoirs*. The Judgment of the . . . Superior Court . . . is vacated and remanded to that court for further proceedings not inconsistent with the First Amendment standards established by this opinion.

VACATED AND REMANDED.

Mr. Justice Douglas, Dissenting

The idea that the First Amendment permits government to ban publications that are "offensive" to some people puts an ominous gloss on freedom of press. I do not think we, the judges, were ever given the constitutional power to make definitions of obscenity. If it is to be defined, let the people debate and decide by a constitutional amendment what they want to ban as obscene.

Case Questions

1. Would the Court have decided differently if the restaurant owner had ordered the materials?
2. Does the decision propose actual obscenity regulations or merely guidelines for the states to follow?
3. What ethical dilemmas are posed by the three-prong test?

Applying the Three-Prong *Miller* Test to Material Transmitted Online (Cyberporn)

The three-prong *Miller* test resulting from the *Miller v. California* case defines obscene material as having the following attributes:

1. It arouses "Prurient interest" that does not conform to "contemporary community standards."
2. It is "patently offensive."
3. It "lacks serious literary, artistic, political or scientific value."

"Prurient" Interest and "Contemporary Community Standards." What did the Court mean by **prurient interest** and **contemporary community standards**? The courts have been inconsistent in providing predictable answers to this question, making it difficult, if not impossible, for transmitters of online materials to predict protection or prohibition of its materials. In *Roth,* mentioned earlier, the U.S. Supreme Court may have provided the *Miller* Court with some guidance in defining the terms. In arriving at its decision to affirm Roth's conviction, the Court found that the materials dealt with sex in a manner appealing to "prurient interest" in that they had a "tendency to excite lustful thoughts." The Court also applied to the facts the definition of *prurient* found in Webster's *New International Dictionary* (Unabridged, 2nd ed. 1949),

---

FIGURE 10.1   *Miller* Test

1. "Prurient interest and contemporary community standards"
2. "Patently offensive"
3. "Lacks serious literary, artistic, political, or scientific value"

---

deciding that the materials in question demonstrated an "Itching; longing; uneasy with desire or longing; of persons, having itching, morbid, or lascivious longings; of desire, curiosity, or propensity, lewd." The Court further expanded the above by applying to it the definition of obscene as contained in the Model Penal Code Section 207.10(2) (Tent. Draft No. 6, 1957):

> A thing is obscene if, considered as a whole, its predominant appeal is to prurient interest, i.e., a shameful or morbid interest in nudity, sex, or excretion, and if it goes substantially beyond customary limits of candor in description or representation of such matters.

Miller also requires that the material be viewed in the context of the relevant local "contemporary community standards." A question that arises concerns which community's standards are to be used. With online transmissions, a court could either use the community standards where the transmission originated or where it was downloaded. The standards for each might be different, depending on the demographics or culture of the relevant community. Thus material deemed obscene in one community might escape such a designation in another. Determining which community's standards are to be used is critical in establishing protection or prohibition for the material under scrutiny. Therefore, it is likely that operators of chat rooms, bulletin board services, and other Internet users will have difficulty in determining, with any predictability, whether a transmission would be deemed obscene or protected free speech or expression. The following case illustrates this difficulty.

United States v. Thomas
74 F.3d 701 (6th Cir.), cert. denied 117 S. Ct. 74 (1996)

Facts

Defendants, Robert Thomas and his wife Carleen, operated the Amateur Action Computer Bulletin Board System (AACBBS) from their home in California. The AACBBS was a computer bulletin board system that operated by using telephones, modems, and personal computers. Its features included e-mail, chat lines, public messages, and files that members could access, transfer, and download to their own computers and printers. By means of a scanner, Thomas converted sexually explicit magazine pictures into computer files called *graphic interchange format files,* or GIF files. Thomas also sold adult videotapes to members, shipping them by United Parcel Service.

In July 1993, a U.S. postal Inspector, Agent David Dirmeyer, received a complaint regarding the AACBBS from a Tennessee resident. Subsequently, Dirmeyer used an assumed name and sent in the $55 to join AACBBS. Thomas called Dirmeyer at his undercover telephone number in Memphis, Tennessee, acknowledging receipt of his application and authorizing him to log on with his personal password. Dirmeyer downloaded obscene materials and ordered adult videotapes, which Thomas sent to him. The Thomases were indicted by a federal grand jury in Tennessee. They were tried and convicted in a Tennessee federal district court for violating obscenity laws under Title 18 of the U.S. Code. They appealed their convictions to the U.S. Circuit of Appeals.

Judicial Opinion *(Judge Nancy G. Edmunds)*

Defendants challenge venue in the Western District of Tennessee. They argue that since it was Dirmeyer, who, without their knowledge, accessed and downloaded the GIF files and caused them to enter Tennessee, the case should have been heard in California. We disagree. The Government must prove that a defendant knowingly used a facility or means of interstate commerce for the purpose of distributing obscene materials. The Government is not required to prove that defendants had specific knowledge of the destination of each transmittal at the time it occurred. "Venue lies in any district in which the offense is committed," and the Government is required to establish venue by a preponderance of the evidence.

Substantial evidence introduced at trial demonstrated that the AACBBS was set up so members located in other jurisdictions could access and order GIF files which would then be instantaneously transmitted in interstate commerce. Moreover, AACBBS materials were distributed to an approved AACBBS member known to reside in Tennessee. Some of these GIF files were clearly marked "Distribute Freely." In light of the above, the effects of the defendant's criminal conduct reached Tennessee and that district was suitable for accurate factfinding.

Accordingly, we conclude venue was proper in that judicial district.

In *Miller v. California*, 413 U.S. 15 (1973) the Supreme Court set out a three-prong test for obscenity. It inquired whether (1) "the average person applying 'contemporary community standards' would find that the work, taken as a whole appeals to the prurient interest"; (2) it "depicts or describes, in a patently offensive way, sexual conduct specifically defined by applicable state law"; and (3) "the work, taken as a whole, lacks serious literary, artistic, political, or scientific value."

Under the first prong of the *Miller* test, the jury is to apply "contemporary standards." Defendants acknowledge the general principle that, in cases involving interstate transmission of obscene material, juries are properly instructed to apply the community standards of the geographic area where the materials are sent. Nonetheless, defendants assert that this principle does not apply here for the same reasons they claim venue was improper. This argument cannot withstand scrutiny. The computer-generated images were electronically transferred from defendants' home in California to Tennessee. Accordingly, the community standards of that judicial district were properly applied in this case.

Issues regarding which community's standards are to be applied are tied to those involving venue. It is well established that: venue for federal obscenity prosecution lies "in any district from, through, or into which" the allegedly obscene material moves. This may result in prosecutions of persons in a community to which they have sent materials which are obscene under that community's standards though the community from which it is sent would tolerate the same material.

Defendants argue that the computer technology used here requires a new definition of community, i.e., one that is based on the broad-ranging connections among people in cyberspace rather than the geographic locale of the federal district court of the criminal trial. Without a more flexible definition, there will be an impermissible chill on protected speech because BBS operators cannot select who gets the material they make available on their bulletin boards. Therefore, they contend, BBS operators like the defendants will be forced to censor their materials so as not to run afoul of the standards of the community with the most restrictive standards. If defendants did not wish to subject themselves to liability in jurisdictions with less tolerant standards for determining obscenity, they could have refused to give passwords to members in those districts, thus precluding the risk of liability.

Thus, under the facts of this case, there is no need for this court to adopt a new definition of "community" for use in obscenity prosecutions involving electronic bulletin boards.

For the foregoing reasons, this court AFFIRMS Robert and Carleen Thomas's convictions and sentences.

Case Questions

1. Would the decision be different if the defendants had only operated a dial-a-porn (telephone) service?
2. How did the Court determine the defendants knew where the materials were being received?
3. Analyze ethically the actions of the government in using Agent Dirmeyer to apprehend the Thomases.

"Patently Offensive." The second prong of the test is concerned with whether the material/transmission depicts or displays, "in a **patently offensive** way, sexual conduct specifically defined by the applicable state law." *Miller* would require the transmissions exhibit hard-core "ultimate sexual acts, normal or perverted, actual or simulated" that include "masturbation, excretory functions, and lewd exhibition of the genitals." As with prurient interest, whether an online transmission would be prohibited or protected would have to be viewed in the context of local community standards, which would raise the same issue of predictability.

"Lacks Serious Literary, Artistic, Political, or Scientific Value." Unlike the first two prongs of the test that view the material in the context of relevant local community standards, leaving it to a jury to decide, the third prong—**literary, artistic, political**, and **socially redeemable value**—would require a more objective determination based on a "reasonable person" test.

For example, in *Pope v. Illinois,* 481 U.S. 497 (1987), the Supreme Court ruled that the proper inquiry was not whether an ordinary member of any given community would find serious value in the allegedly obscene material but whether a reasonable person would find such value in it, taken as a whole. Thus we should reiterate that the factors and standards for obscenity vary greatly, depending on the culture of the state, city or town, or, for that matter, foreign country. This makes it virtually impossible for a provider and others to determine, with any degree of predictability, whether the material they distribute, transmit, post, and so on, would be deemed obscene.

Proving the Case

In earlier cases, if the material failed to satisfy the three-prong test and was deemed obscene, in order to establish liability the government had to prove the defendant had actual knowledge that the contents of the transmission were obscene and that the defendant was an adult who consented to view the material.

The Knowledge Requirement (Scienter). Given the huge number of files and documents owned by a provider, establishing the knowledge requirement could be difficult and could provide a valid defense to prosecution. Thus the later cases seem to reflect a less stringent burden of proof, requiring the interstate transmission of the material together with proof the provider had knowledge of the character and nature of the material rather than knowledge that it was obscene.

The "Consenting Adults" Defense. In *Paris Adult Theatre I v. Slaton* (413 U.S 49, 1973), the owners of two Atlanta theaters were charged under a Georgia statute that prohibited the showing of hard-core pornographic films. They raised the **consenting adults defense** that because their customers consented to viewing the films, they should be entitled to the same First Amendment and privacy protection they would enjoy as if they were at home. The Supreme Court did not agree with the analogy and reaffirmed its holding in *Roth*. Essentially, the Court upheld the right of a state to regulate, if it so chose, specifically defined sexual conduct between consenting adults as long as the regulation was within limits designed to prevent infringement of First Amendment rights.

If consenting adults viewed the pornographic films described in Slaton at home, would they be afforded First Amendment and privacy protection? The Supreme Court answered that question in *Stanley v. Georgia* (394 U.S. 557, 1969), where it created a zone of privacy in one's home. In that case, the defendant, Stanley, was suspected of bookmaking activities. With a warrant to search his home for evidence, the law enforcement authorities discovered pornographic films stored in his bedroom. In reversing the conviction for possession of obscene material and remanding the case, the Court extended freedom of speech, press, and privacy protection to the right to receive information and ideas in one's home regardless of their social worth. In writing for the Court, Justice Thurgood Marshall stated, "If the First Amendment means anything, it means that a state has no business telling a man, sitting alone in his home, what book he may read or what films he may watch."

GOVERNMENT REGULATION OF CYBERPORN

Once material has been declared obscene, our focus shifts to a review of some of the important laws that attempt to regulate it. These laws, both state and federal, have been challenged constitutionally, sometimes successfully, and in other instances, they have been the subject of controversy and criticism because of their impact on our personal freedoms.

The **Communications Decency Act (CDA)** of 1996 (Title V of the Telecommunications Act of 1996; 47 U.S.C. § 223) represents the first attempt by Congress, albeit, as we shall discover, unsuccessful, to protect minors from pornography. The CDA makes it a crime for anyone to knowingly transport obscene material for sale or distribution either in foreign or interstate commerce or through the use of an interactive computer service. The CDA has been the subject of criticism as being overburdensome and overbroad in its attempt at regulation. As we shall see, parts of it have been declared unconstitutional while others have passed constitutional scrutiny.

The CDA provides for fines of up to $100,000 and imprisonment of up to five years for a first offense and up to ten years for each subsequent offense. The CDA specifically applies to what it terms *matter*—in particular, books, magazines, pictures, paper, film, videotape, and audio recordings.

Another provision of the CDA prohibits and makes it a crime for anyone to knowingly transmit obscene online communications that involve "comments, requests, suggestions, proposals, images, or other communication which is obscene, lewd, lascivious, filthy or indecent made with the intent to annoy, abuse, threaten, or harass another person." A separate part of this provision makes it a crime to knowingly transmit the described material to a person under the age of eighteen, irrespective of whether the maker placed the call or initiated the communication.

Allowable Defenses

The CDA allows certain defenses to liability. One defense is based on the distinction between an *access service provider* and a *content provider*. Specifically, criminal liability is imposed on the content provider who transmits obscene materials to a minor, rather than on the Internet service provider who provides access or connection to a network and has nothing to do with content.

A second defense applies to a person who has made a good faith effort or attempt to restrict or prevent access by minors to the types of communications prohibited under the CDA. To raise this defense successfully, a defendant has to prove it made use of available technology to block the transmission. Examples include the use of a "v" chip, verifiable credit card to gain access, a debit account, an adult access code, or adult personal identification number.

Similarly, it could be possible for a content provider to avoid liability by raising this defense. The content provider would have to prove that it took all available steps (e.g., warning labels, sign-on requirements, etc.) to restrict access to its site by minors.

Keep in mind that many argue that the responsibility for monitoring or preventing a minor's access to obscene Web sites is best placed on the minor's parent or guardian and not technology.

A third defense is the **Good Samaritan defense** for blocking and screening offensive material. It protects an online provider or user of an interactive computer service from civil liability as a publisher or speaker of any information provided by another content provider.

You should be aware that certain expressions involving ideas and information about sexuality, reproduction, and the human body could be afforded protection under the

CDA, even if received by a minor. A court could deem these to have social value, thereby eliminating liability for their transmission. Figure 10.2 summarizes the defenses to liability under the CDA.

The CDA Under Constitutional Attack

Congress can regulate speech or expression that is harmful to minors. This may not include "indecent" speech or expression. The problem with Sections 223 (a) and (d) of the CDA is that they do not clearly define what is considered to be "indecent" speech or expression, nor do they sufficiently distinguish "indecent" from "obscene." The U.S. Supreme Court and the Federal Communications Commission (FCC) provide some assistance. The Supreme Court has defined *indecent* as referring to *"nonconformance with accepted standards of morality"* [See *FCC v. Pacifica Foundation*, 438 U.S. 726 (1978)]. The FCC, using the second prong of the *Miller* test only, defines *indecent* as *"language or material that depicts or describes, in terms patently offensive as measured by contemporary standards in the broadcast medium, sexual or excretory activities or organs."*

In *Reno v. American Civil Liberties Union (Reno I)*, 521 U.S. 844 (1997), the U.S. Supreme Court declared §§ 223 (a) and (d) as applied to indecent material to be unconstitutional under the freedom of speech and expression protections of the First Amendment, deciding these sections were too broad and restrictive in their application to content-based speech "effectively suppressing a large amount of speech that adults have a constitutional right to receive." For our discussion, this would include information on the Internet that a parent deemed appropriate for their children to receive who were less than eighteen years of age. For example, if these sections were enforceable, a parent could be subject to a fine and/or imprisonment for e-mailing birth control information to a seventeen-year-old college freshman son or daughter. The court left alone the provisions regarding "obscene" materials as far as minors were concerned.

In the following case, an adult-oriented cable television operator challenged the "scrambling" (filtering) provision and requirement of the CDA.

FIGURE 10.2   Defenses to Liability Under the Communications Decency Act

---

- Access service provider v. content

  Criminal liability is imposed on content provider, rather than the ISP

- Efforts to block access to the site

  Defendant must prove it used technology to block transmission of cyberporn

- Good Samaritan defense

  Online provider or user is protected from publishing information provided by another content provider

- Social value

  Material with social value is protected against criminal liability

---

U.S. v. Playboy Entertainment Group, Inc.
529 U.S. 803 (2000)

Facts

Section 505 of the Telecommunications Act of 1996 (Communications Decency Act) requires cable television operators providing channels "primarily dedicated to sexually-oriented programming" either to "fully scramble or otherwise fully block" those channels or to limit their transmission to hours when children are unlikely to be viewing, between 10 P.M. and 6 A.M. Even before § 505's enactment, cable operators used signal scrambling to limit access to certain programs to paying customers. Scrambling could be imprecise, and either or both audio and visual portions of the scrambled programs might be heard or seen, a phenomenon known as "signal bleed." The purpose of § 505 is to shield children from hearing or seeing images resulting from signal bleed.

Not all scrambling technology is perfect. And cable television analog systems may not prevent signal bleed, so discernible pictures may appear from time to time on the scrambled screen. Digital technology may one day provide another solution, as it presents no bleed problem at all. However, because most cable operators had an analog system, in order to comply with § 505, the majority of the operators adopted a "time channeling" approach, so that, for two-thirds of the day, no viewers, including adults, in their service areas could receive the programming in question. Playboy Entertainment Group, Inc., filed this suit challenging § 505's constitutionality on First Amendment grounds. A three-judge District Court concluded that § 505's content-based restriction on speech violates the First Amendment because the government might further its interests in protecting children by less restrictive ways. One plausible, less restrictive alternative could be found in § 504 of the act, which requires a cable operator, "[u]pon request by a cable service subscriber . . . without charge, [to] fully scramble or otherwise fully block" any channel the subscriber does not wish to receive. As long as subscribers knew about this opportunity, the court reasoned, § 504 would provide as much protection against unwanted programming as would § 505 and consequently declared § 505 unconstitutional. The court also required Playboy to insert notice provisions in its contracts with cable operators who in turn would then inform their subscribers that certain channels broadcast sexually oriented programs, that signal bleed may appear which could be viewed by children without parental consent or permission, and that blocking devices were available free of charge and only a phone call away. The United States directly appealed to this court.

Judicial Opinion *(Justice Kennedy)*

Two essential points should be understood concerning the speech at issue here. First, we shall assume that many adults themselves would find the material highly offensive; and when we consider the further circumstance that the material comes unwanted into homes where children might see or hear it against parental wishes or consent, there are legitimate reasons for regulating it. Second, all parties bring the case to us on the premise that Playboy's programming has First Amendment protection. As this case has been litigated, it is not alleged to be obscene; adults have a constitutional right to view it; the Government disclaims any interest in preventing children from seeing or hearing it with the consent of their parents; and Playboy has concomitant rights under the First Amendment to transmit it. These points are undisputed.

The speech in question is defined by its content; and the statute which seeks to restrict it is content based. Section 505 applies only to channels primarily dedicated to "sexually explicit adult programming or other programming that is indecent." The overriding justification for the regulation is concern for the effect of the subject matter on young viewers. Section 505 is not justified without reference to the content of the regulated speech. This is the essence of content-based regulation. Since § 505 is content-based, it can stand only if it satisfies strict scrutiny. It must be narrowly tailored to promote a compelling Government interest, and if a less restrictive alternative would serve the Government's purpose, the legislature must use that alternative. Cable systems have the capacity to block unwanted channels on a household-by-household basis. No one disputes that § 504 is narrowly tailored to the Government's goal of supporting parents who want sexually explicit channels blocked. The question here is whether § 504 can be effective. Despite empirical evidence that § 504 generated few requests for household-by-household blocking during a period when it was the sole federal blocking statute in effect, the District Court correctly concluded that § 504, if publicized in an adequate manner, could serve as an effective, less restrictive means of reaching the Government's goals. When the Government restricts speech, the Government bears the burden of proving the constitutionality of its actions.

The First Amendment requires a more careful assessment and characterization of an evil in order to justify a regulation as sweeping as this. The Government has failed to establish a pervasive, nationwide problem justifying its nationwide daytime speech ban. The Government also failed to prove § 504, with adequate notice, would be ineffective. There is no evidence that a well-promoted voluntary blocking provision would not be capable at least of informing parents about signal bleed (if they are not yet aware of it) and about their rights to have the bleed blocked (if they consider it a problem and have not yet controlled it themselves).

Basic speech principles are at stake in this case. When the purpose and design of a statute is to regulate speech by reason of its content, special consideration or latitude is not accorded to the Government merely because the law can somehow be described as a burden rather than outright suppression. The history of the law of free expression is one of vindication in cases involving speech that many citizens may find shabby, offensive, or even ugly. It follows that all content-based restrictions on speech must give us more than a moment's pause. If television broadcasts can expose children to the real risk of harmful exposure to indecent materials, even in their own home and without parental consent, there is a problem the Government can address. It must do so, however, in a way consistent with First Amendment principles. Here the Government has not met the burden the First Amendment imposes.

The Government has failed to show that § 505 is the least restrictive means for addressing a real problem; and the District Court did not err in holding the statute violative of the First Amendment. The judgment of the District Court is affirmed.

IT IS SO ORDERED.

Case Questions

1. Are there more effective methods for blocking sexually oriented programs other than requiring the subscriber to notify their cable operator to do so? If so, what are they?
2. How important to the Court's decision was the fact that the government failed to establish that "signal bleed" was a pervasive, nationwide problem?
3. Time channeling restricts programming prior to 10 P.M. If 30 to 50 percent of all adult viewing occurs prior to 10 P.M., should the Court take into account the negative effect this would have on cable-generated revenue?

CHILD PORNOGRAPHY

Federal and state laws regulating child pornography are very strict and generally make it a crime to create, distribute, sell, or possess child pornography. Similar to the CDA, these laws have been successfully attacked on constitutional grounds, and have been, in general, ineffective in combating access to child pornography in cyberspace. What follows is a discussion of additional attempts by Congress at passing federal legislation that seeks to eliminate child pornography and to protect minors from sexual exploitation either as participants in the production of child pornography or from being harmed by exposure to it online.

Federal Regulation of Child Pornography

Child Pornography Prevention Act of 1996 (CPPA), 18 U.S.C. § 2256. For our purposes, § 2256 is the most significant section of the **Child Pornography Protection Act**. It prohibits and criminalizes the use of computer technology to knowingly produce child pornography that contains both depictions of real children as well as "virtual" or fictitious children. Section 2256 defines child pornography as

"any depiction, including any photograph, film, video, picture, or computer or computer-generated image or picture, whether made or produced by electronic, mechanical, or other means, of sexually explicit conduct, where—

(A) the production of such visual depiction involves the use of a minor engaging in sexually explicit conduct;

(B) such visual depiction is, or appears to be, of a minor engaging in sexually explicit conduct;

(C) such visual depiction has been created, adapted, or modified to appear that an identifiable minor is engaging in sexually explicit conduct; or

(D) such visual depiction is advertised, promoted, presented, described, or distributed in such a manner that conveys the impression that the material is or contains a visual depiction of a minor engaging in sexually explicit conduct."

This language, particularly the phrases "appears to be" and "conveys the impression," has created some problems of interpretation, resulting in a split in case decisions at the Federal Circuit Court of Appeals level. At issue is whether these terms are so vague and overbroad that a person of ordinary intelligence would find it difficult to determine the age of those depicted and to understand exactly what the CPPA prohibits, thereby rendering it unconstitutional. Some courts have ruled the language to be specific enough to fulfill the purposes of Congress to protect children from the evils of pornography. These courts have decided that the content of the language was sufficiently narrow to satisfy Congress's intention to eliminate child pornography by singling out and banning a particular category of expression, child pornography, based on its content. See *U.S. v. Hilton*, 167 F.3d 61 (1st Cir. 1999), where the court upheld the defendant's conviction for possession of child pornography, deciding that "child pornography was an unprotected category of expression identified by its content" and, therefore, was allowed to be "freely regulated." The decision did not distinguish between images of real children and those that were fictitious or imaginary.

A later Florida case, *U.S. v. Acheson*, No. 98-3559 (11th Cir. Nov. 12, 1999), reached a similar conclusion. However, in a California case, *Free Speech Coalition v. Reno*, 198 F.3d 1083 (9th Cir. 1999), the court reached an opposite conclusion. It viewed the definition of *child pornography* under the CPPA as vague and too broad because it applied to both real and fictitious depictions of children. Therefore, it held that the First Amendment prohibited Congress from enacting a statute that makes it a crime to create images of fictitious children engaged in imaginary but explicit sexual conduct. It would be virtually impossible for a person looking at the images to determine if the depiction was a minor or an adult with a youthful appearance. Furthermore, the court said that the CPPA represented a change in the original intent of Congress in enacting child pornography statutes. Originally, these statutes were aimed only at real children. The CPPA shifted from "defining child pornography in terms of the harm inflicted upon real children to a determination that child pornography was evil in and of itself, whether it involved real children or not." This, the court concluded, violated the First Amendment. In *Ashcroft v. Free Speech Coalition* (discussed in detail in Chapter 13, "Internet and Computer Crime"), 122 S. Ct. 1389, U.S. LEXIS 2789 (April 16, 2002), the U.S. Supreme Court revisited *Free Speech Coalition v. Reno*, again having to decide the issue of whether depicting images of virtual children in sexually explicit acts violated § 2256 of the CPPA or qualified as protected speech under the First Amendment. The Court held that the images were protected speech because no real children were harmed and the coverage of § 2256 was overly broad. The decision rendered the CPPA ineffective pending future consideration by the courts, leaving this area of the law unsettled.

Yet another attempt by Congress to regulate child pornography in cyberspace is the Child Online Protection Act of 1998 (COPA), which Congress intended as a substitute to the parts of the CDA that were declared unconstitutional.

Child Online Protection Act of 1998 (COPA), 47 U.S.C. § 231. In passing the **Child Online Protection Act of 1998 (COPA)**, Congress narrowed the provisions of the CPPA to include online transmissions by service providers and e-commerce site providers. It expressed the following rationale for this new legislation:

1. The Internet presents opportunities for minors to access materials through the Web in a manner that could frustrate parental control or supervision.
2. The protection of the physical and psychological well-being of minors by shielding them from materials that are harmful to them presents a compelling governmental interest.
3. Industry attempts to provide ways to help parents and others restrict a minor's access to harmful materials have not been totally successful.
4. Prohibiting the distribution of material harmful to minors, combined with legitimate defenses, is currently the most effective and least restrictive means to protect minors.
5. Parents, educators, and industry must continue efforts to find ways to protect children from being exposed to harmful materials found on the Internet, notwithstanding protections that already limit the distribution over the Web of material that is harmful to minors.

http://

- For examples of other blocking or filtering, parental control software, visit **http://www.cyberpatrol.com** and **http://www.netnanny.com**

COPA requires commercial site operators who offer material deemed to be "harmful" to minors to use bona fide methods to establish the identification of visitors seeking to access their site. Failure to do so can result in criminal liability with fines of up to $50,000 and six months in jail for each offense. Specifically, COPA states:

"Whoever, in interstate or foreign commerce, by means of the World Wide Web, knowingly makes any communication for commercial purposes that includes any material that is harmful to minors without restricting access to such material by minors pursuant to subsection (c) shall be fined not more $50,000, imprisoned not more than 6 months, or both.

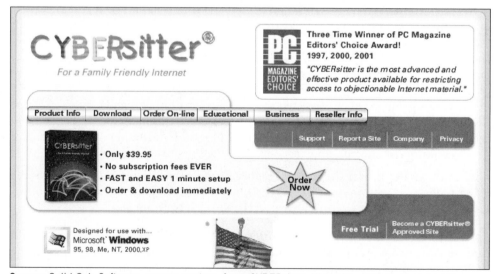

Source: Solid Oak Software, screen capture from CYBERsitter Web site, *http://www.cybersitter.com.* Reprinted with the permission of Solid Oak Software, Inc.

Under COPA, Congress defined harmful material as:

"any communication, picture, image, graphic image file, article, recording, writing, or other matter of any kind that is obscene or that—

(A) the average person, applying contemporary community standards, would find, taking the material as a whole and with respect to minors, is designed to appeal to, or is designed to pander to, the prurient interest;

(B) depicts, describes, or represents, in a manner patently offensive with respect to minors, an actual or simulated sexual act or sexual contact, an actual or simulated normal or perverted sexual act, or a lewd exhibition of the genitals or post-pubescent female breasts; and

(C) taken as a whole, lacks serious literary, artistic, political, or scientific value for minors."

The constitutionality of COPA was challenged almost immediately after its enactment. In *ACLU et al. v. Reno* (referred to as *Reno II*), 31 F. Supp. 2d 473 (E.D. Pa. 1999), the plaintiffs sought a temporary restraining order to enjoin implementation of the statute. The federal district court granted the injunction agreeing with the plaintiffs that COPA violated the First and Fifth Amendments, that the affirmative defenses provided by COPA were technologically and economically unavailable to many of the plaintiffs, and that it overly burdened speech protected as to adults. Additionally, the plaintiffs successfully argued that the impact of COPA could result in denying adults and older minors access to protected educational materials that could contain information about art, science, medicine, or sex.

The court was also concerned that commercial and noncommercial service providers and operators would be fearful of prosecution under COPA. This would result in self-censorship of their online materials. This would have a chilling effect on speech and would cause irreparable harm to the plaintiffs both constitutionally and economically.

Further, the court expressed concern that, although the public has an interest in protecting minors, that interest would not be served by enforcing an unconstitutional law that would likely fail to survive strict scrutiny analysis. Instead, the court indicated that the public interest would be best served by maintaining the status quo until some time in the future when a more thorough examination of the constitutionality of COPA could be explored. That examination occurred when the district court's temporary restraining order was appealed to the U.S. Court of Appeals, 217 F.3d 162 (3rd Cir. 2000), which, interestingly, opted not to focus on the findings of the district court, per se, as already discussed, but rather on COPA's requirement that "contemporary community standards" (a part of the *Miller* test) be used to identify material harmful to minors.

The court decided that this use was overbroad because Web site operators would find it impossible to limit access to their sites based on the geographic location of particular Internet users. To protect itself from liability under COPA, the Web site publisher would have to place material deemed harmful by the most conservative community behind an age or credit card verification system, thereby placing an unconstitutionally overburdensome requirement on the publisher. The following case is an appeal of this 2000 decision brought by U.S. attorney general John Ashcroft (Janet Reno's successor) in an attempt to preserve at least a modicum of regulation and protection for minors from pornography provided by COPA.

Ashcroft v. American Civil Liberties Union
523 U.S. 1037 (2001)

Facts

In *Reno v. ACLU*, 521 U.S. 844 (1997), this Court found the Communications Decency Act (CDA) violated the First Amendment and was therefore unconstitutional because it was overly broad in its scope. Thereafter, in 1998, Congress again attempted to regulate child pornography by passing the Children's Online Protection Act (COPA). Unlike the CDA, which applied to the entire Internet, COPA applied to the World Wide Web, the publishing medium for the Internet (the global network). Also, COPA covered only commercial communications and only "material harmful to children." In deciding whether or not material is harmful to children, COPA uses the three-part obscenity test announced in *Miller*" thereby requiring a judge or jury to use "contemporary community standards" in their decision. Respondents who post or have members that post adult-oriented material on the Web challenged the constitutionality of COPA on its face before it took effect. The federal district court issued a preliminary restraining order on constitutional grounds without considering the issue of community standards. The U.S. Court of Appeals (3rd Circuit), rather than addressing the grounds used by the district court, nevertheless affirmed its decision declaring the *community standards* requirement under COPA to be unconstitutional.

Judicial Opinion *(Justice Thomas)*

This case presents the narrow question whether the Child Online Protection Act's (COPA or Act) use of "community standards" to identify "material that is harmful to minors" violates the First Amendment. We hold that this aspect of COPA does not render the statute facially unconstitutional.

In their complaint, respondents alleged that, although they believed that the material on their Web sites was valuable for adults, they feared that they would be prosecuted under COPA because some of that material "could be construed as 'harmful to minors' in some communities." Respondents' facial challenge claimed that COPA violated adults' rights under the First and Fifth Amendments because it (1) "create[d] an effective ban on constitutionally protected speech by and to adults"; (2) "[was] not the least restrictive means of accomplishing any compelling governmental purpose"; and (3) "[was] substantially overbroad."

The Court of Appeals, however, concluded that this Court's prior community standards jurisprudence "has no applicability to the Internet and the Web" because "Web publishers are currently without the ability to control the geographic scope of the recipients of their communications." We therefore must decide whether this technological limitation renders COPA's reliance on community standards constitutionally infirm.

The tremendous breadth of the CDA magnified the impact caused by differences in community standards across the country, restricting Web publishers from openly displaying a significant amount of material that would have constituted protected speech in some communities across the country but run afoul of community standards in others.

COPA, by contrast, does not appear to suffer from the same flaw because it applies to significantly less material than did the CDA and defines the harmful-to-minors material restricted by the statute in a manner parallel to the *Miller* definition of obscenity. To fall within the scope of COPA, works must not only "depic[t], describ[e], or represen[t], in a manner patently offensive with respect to minors," particular sexual acts or parts of the anatomy, they must also be designed to appeal to the prurient interest of minors and "taken as a whole, lac[k] serious literary, artistic, political, or scientific value for minors."

When the scope of an obscenity statute's coverage is sufficiently narrowed by a "serious value" prong and a "prurient interest" prong, we have held that requiring a speaker disseminating material to a national audience to observe varying community standards does not violate the First Amendment.

If a publisher chooses to send its material into a particular community, this Court's jurisprudence teaches that it is the publisher's responsibility to abide by that community's standards. The publisher's burden does not change simply because it decides to distribute its material to every community in the Nation. Nor does it change because the publisher may wish to speak only to those in a "community where avant-garde culture is the norm," but nonetheless utilizes a medium that transmits its speech from coast to coast. If a publisher wishes for its material to be judged only by the standards of particular communities, then it need only take the simple step of utilizing a medium that enables it to target the release of its material into those communities.

We have no reason to believe that the practical effect of varying community standards under COPA, given the statute's definition of "material that is harmful to minors," is significantly greater than the practical effect of varying community standards under federal obscenity statutes. It is noteworthy, for example, that respondents fail to point out even a single exhibit in the record as to which coverage under COPA would depend upon which community in the country evaluated the material. As a result, if we were to hold COPA unconstitutional because of its use of community standards, federal obscenity statutes would likely also be unconstitutional as applied to the Web, a result in substantial tension with our prior suggestion that the application of the CDA to obscene speech was constitutional.

Respondents argue that COPA is "unconstitutionally overbroad" because it will require Web publishers to shield some material behind age verification screens that could be displayed openly in many communities across the Nation if Web speakers were able to limit access to their sites on a geographic basis. "[T]o prevail in a facial challenge," however, "it is not enough for a plaintiff to show 'some' overbreadth. Rather, "the overbreadth of a statute must not only be real, but substantial as well."

At this stage of the litigation, respondents have failed to satisfy this burden, at least solely as a result of COPA's reliance on community standards. Because Congress has narrowed the range of content restricted by COPA in a manner analogous to Miller's definition of obscenity, we conclude, that any variance caused by the statute's reliance on community standards is not substantial enough to violate the First Amendment.

The scope of our decision today is quite limited. We hold only that COPA's reliance on community standards to identify "material that is harmful to minors" does not by itself render the statute substantially overbroad for purposes of the First Amendment. We do not express any view as to whether COPA suffers from substantial overbreadth for other reasons, whether the statute is unconstitutionally vague, or whether the District Court correctly concluded that the statute likely will not survive strict scrutiny analysis once adjudication of the case is completed below. While respondents urge us to resolve these questions at this time, prudence dictates allowing the Court of Appeals to first examine these difficult issues.

Petitioner does not ask us to vacate the preliminary injunction entered by the District Court, and in any event, we could not do so without addressing matters yet to be considered by the Court of Appeals. As a result, the Government remains enjoined from enforcing COPA absent further action by the Court of Appeals or the District Court. For the foregoing reasons, we vacate the judgment of the Court of Appeals and remand the case for further proceedings.

IT IS SO ORDERED.

Case Questions

1. If the Court had decided COPA was constitutional in all aspects, do you believe it would be effective in aiding the government's intent in passing it to regulate child pornography?
2. What effect does this decision have on the government's ability to prosecute violations under COPA?
3. Would it be more beneficial to determine whether material is harmful or not to minors by a national rather than a community standard? What obstacles could such a standard meet?

Keep in mind, that although eight of the nine justices in *Ashcroft* ruled that using community standards to judge obscene material did not render COPA unconstitutional on its face, six of the nine had significant constitutional reservations about applying them to electronic communications online. This division of opinion, and the fact that the decision as a whole is convoluted, leaves the law still unsettled and the attempt by Congress to regulate child pornography unfulfilled.

Another, albeit controversial, attempt by Congress to regulate child pornography is the **Children's Internet Protection Act (CIPA)** of 2000. This act is a congressional attempt to regulate computer access to adult-oriented Web sites in public schools and libraries.

Children's Internet Protection Act (CIPA) of 2000, 47 U.S.C. § 254

The CIPA provides that, for public schools and libraries to receive federal funds and grants, they must certify they have installed filtering technology that prevents adults from accessing obscene or pornographic depictions and minors from accessing material deemed harmful. Similar to COPA, almost immediately objections were raised by free speech advocates including the ACLU and the American Library Association. They maintain that CIPA places unconstitutional restraints on speech and privacy because the technology employed could block nonpornographic or otherwise protected speech. These objections resulted in a case challenging the constitutionality of CIPA. In *American Library Association* (ALA) *v. United States*, 201 F. Supp. 2d 401 (May 31, 2002), a federal district court decided the blocking provisions under CIPA were overbroad in their effect on both the libraries and their patrons. Consequently, CIPA was declared unconstitutional and invalid under the First Amendment. The court based its decision on the fact that CIPA required libraries to block patrons from accessing substantial amounts of protected speech as a precondition to receiving federal funds. (*Note*: The United States appealed this decision directly to the U.S. Supreme Court, *U.S. v. American Library Association*, No. 02-361 (2003). The decision is pending.)

One piece of federal legislation that so far as survived attacks on its constitutionality is the **Protection of Children from Sexual Predators Act of 1998**, Title 18 U.S.C., whose focus is aimed at the producers of child pornography.

Protection of Children from Sexual Predators Act of 1998, Title 18 U.S.C. § 302. The **Protection of Children from Sexual Predators Act of 1998** expands the liability we discussed earlier to those who attempt to use the Internet for purposes of child pornography. This statute specifically targets commercial pornographers and makes it a crime to knowingly make a communication for commercial purposes harmful to minors (sixteen years old and younger) or to use the Internet for purposes of engaging in sexual activities with minors.

http://

- For more information about this act, visit **http://www.ussc.gov/sexpred/predlegh.pdf**

State Regulation

In addition to federal regulations, bulletin board system (BBS) operators, online service providers, and Web site operators may be subject to state statutes prohibiting the possession, distribution, and sale of child pornography. State laws usually mirror the federal standards with some modifications, particularly regarding the *Miller* test. In *New York v. Ferber*, 458 U.S. 747 (1982), the U.S. Supreme Court upheld New York's strict standards concerning child pornography. In that case, the defendant owned a bookstore and was convicted of selling material depicting children less than sixteen years of age in certain prohibited sexual activities. The United States upheld the constitutionality of the statute, stating, "the prevention of sexual exploitation of children constitutes a government objective of surpassing importance." The Court also modified the *Miller* test, holding that:

1. The material need not appeal to the prurient interest of the average person.
2. The sexual activity need not be done in a patently offensive manner.
3. The material need not be considered as a whole.

Remember that the prosecution must still prove the defendant had knowledge (*scienter*) of the "character and content" of the material. Additionally, many states including New York allow a defendant to avoid liability if they can prove they had a good faith and reasonable belief the actors in the materials were of legal age. Also note that a city or town that has adopted conservative "community standards" under *Miller*, particularly as they relate to minors, could apply its obscenity laws to sexually explicit music CDs, music videos, books, and other forms of expression available online. The same could result for those whose content advocates violence.

The Consenting Adults Defense in Child Pornography

In the case of child pornography, the consenting adults defense is not applicable. In the following case, although the U.S. Supreme Court reversed and remanded the decision on procedural grounds, it upheld a state statute that was designed to protect minors from pornography.

As far as cyberspace is concerned, it should be obvious that individuals who possess, sell, and distribute child pornography in e-commerce will be held criminally liable, irrespective of where or in what context the pornographic material is disseminated and accessed.

Osborne v. Ohio
495 U.S. 103 (1990)

Facts

Defendant Osborne was arrested after police, pursuant to a valid search warrant, searched his home and found four photographs of a nude male adolescent (minor) posed in sexually explicit positions. Osborne was convicted under a Ohio statute that prohibited any person from possessing or viewing any material or performance showing a minor who is not his child or ward in a state of nudity involving a lewd exhibition. Osborne argued that his privacy and First Amendment rights were violated and the statute was unconstitutionally overbroad. The state intermediate appellate court and State Supreme Court rejected these arguments and upheld his conviction.

Judicial Opinion *(Justice White)*

The threshold question in this case is whether Ohio may constitutionally proscribe the possession and viewing of child pornography or whether, as Osborne argues, our decision in *Stanley v. Georgia,* 394 U.S. 557 (1969), compels the contrary result. In Stanley, we struck down a Georgia law outlawing the private possession of obscene material. Georgia primarily sought to proscribe the private possession of obscenity because it was concerned that obscenity would poison the minds of its viewers. We recognized that the statute impinged upon Stanley's right to receive information in the privacy of his home. *Stanley* should not be read too broadly. Assuming, for the sake of argument, that Osborne has

First Amendment interests in viewing and possessing child pornography, we nonetheless find this case distinct from *Stanley* because the interests underlying child pornography prohibitions far exceed the interests justifying the Georgia law at issue in *Stanley*. The State does not rely on a paternalistic interest in regulating Osborne's mind. Rather, Ohio has enacted its law on the basis of its compelling interests in protecting the physical and psychological well-being of minors and in destroying the market for the exploitative use of children by penalizing those who possess and view the offending materials. Moreover, Ohio's ban encourages possessors to destroy such materials, which permanently record the victim's abuse and thus may haunt him for years to come, and which, available evidence suggests, may be used by pedophiles to seduce other children.

To conclude, although we find Osborne's First Amendment arguments unpersuasive, we reverse his conviction and remand for a new trial in order to ensure that Osborne's conviction stemmed from a finding that the State had proved each of the elements of the statute.

SO ORDERED.

Case Questions

1. What if the parents or guardian have consented to the taking and displaying of the photographs of the minor?
2. What methods could be employed by states to destroy the market for child pornography other than penalizing the possession of child pornography?
3. Is it ethical for the operator of a BBS or Web site to transmit child pornography, even if it is intended for use at home?

EMPLOYEES' ACCESS TO ADULT-ORIENTED WEB SITES

In our discussion of privacy and employer monitoring, the emphasis was placed on the employer's right to monitor e-mail and computer usage from a privacy perspective. We also learned that this right extended to the problem of improper surfing and visits to adult-oriented Web sites. In 1999, a study was conducted by Elron Software, Inc., whereby they were hired to install monitoring software on computers used by employees working for some 110 corporations, educational institutions, and government agencies with employees numbering from 50 to 15,0000. The study lasted for three days and determined that 62 percent of the monitored employees accessed adult-oriented, sexually explicit Web sites. Employers must be particularly wary of the possibility that such usage can sometimes result in cases of sexual harassment as prohibited under provisions of Title VII of the Civil Rights Act of 1965, as amended.

http://➤

- For more information about Elron Software and Internet monitoring, see **http://www.elronsoftware.com**

One of the ways this could result is from the sending of unwelcome sexually charged messages or jokes to other employees, thereby creating a hostile work environment. Of course, using a computer to request sexual favors as a condition of employment, promotion, pay raise, and so on, could also be considered a form of sexual harassment. As discussed in Chapter 9, "Privacy," for ethical and economic reasons, it is incumbent on employers to develop and implement policies that limit or deny employees the right to access adult-oriented Web sites. However, in exercising their rights under such policies, *remember* an employer must also be aware of the requirements for a valid search and seizure of an employee's computer under the Fourth Amendment [*U.S. v. Slanina,* 283 F.3d 670 (5th Cir. 2002)]. The following obscenity case involves the First Amendment and the attempt by the state of Virginia to restrict access to certain Web sites for "educational purposes" by a group of college professors employed at its public colleges and universities.

Urosky et al. v. Gilmore
167 F.3d 191 (4th Cir., Feb. 10, 1999)

Facts

A Virginia act (statute) restricted access to sexually explicit material by state employees unless written approval for access was obtained from the appropriate agency head. Approval would only be granted if the materials sought were to be used for a "bona fide" research project or for a similar use. Urosky and other professors at Virginia state colleges wanted to access sexually explicit sites for a variety of educational purposes. These included student online research assignments involving "indecent" speech, professors' online research involving gay and lesbian studies, the human sexual experience, and sexually explicit poetry. Urosky and other professors filed suit in a U.S. District Court, arguing the statute violated First Amendment rights to free speech. Virginia argued that state employee computer use was not protected speech because the employees were acting as government employees and not as public citizens. It also contended the statute was passed in order to help maintain an efficient workplace and to prevent the creation of a sexually hostile work environment that could lead to sexual harassment and other workplace claims.

The court decided that the statute violated the First Amendment and also did not satisfy its intended purposes. It stated that the statute was both underinclusive and overinclusive: *underinclusive* because it did not address other types of online distractions such as video games, news services, and chat rooms that could negatively impact the workplace, nor did it address racially, ethnically or religiously offensive material; *overinclusive* because the statute restricted access to sexually explicit Web sites to be used for academic, artistic, literary, historical, or philosophical purposes.

Virginia appealed the decision to the Circuit Court of Appeals.

Judicial Opinion *(Circuit Judge Wilkins)*

As its language makes plain, the Act prohibits state employees from accessing sexually explicit material on computers owned or leased by the Commonwealth. But the Act does not prohibit all access by state employees to such materials, for a state agency head may give permission for a state employee to access such information if the head deems such access to be required in connection with a bona fide research project or other undertaking. Plaintiffs maintain that this restriction—the denial of access to sexually explicit material when permission has not been given—is violative of their First Amendment right to freedom of expression and hinders their ability to perform their employment duties, *e.g.,* teaching and researching.

It is well settled that citizens do not relinquish all of their First Amendment rights by virtue of accepting public employment. Nevertheless, the state, as an employer, undoubtedly possesses greater authority to restrict the speech of its employees than it has—as sovereign to restrict the speech of the citizenry as a whole . . .

First Amendment requires "a balance between the interests of the [employee], as a citizen, in commenting upon matters of public concern and the interest of the State, as an employer, in promoting the efficiency of the public services it performs through its employees." This balancing involves an inquiry first into whether the speech at issue touches upon a matter of public concern, and, if so, whether the employee's interest in First Amendment expression outweighs the public employer's interest in what the employer has determined to be the appropriate operation of the workplace. Thus, our threshold inquiry is whether the Act regulates speech by employees of the Commonwealth as citizens upon matters of public concern.

Speech involves a matter of public concern when it affects a social, political, or other interest of a community. When a public employee's speech does not touch upon a matter of public concern, that speech is not "totally beyond the protection of the First Amendment." The challenged aspect of the Act does not regulate the speech of the citizenry in general, but rather the speech of state employees in their capacity as employees. It cannot be doubted that in order to pursue its legitimate goals effectively, the Commonwealth must retain the ability to control the manner in which its employees discharge their duties and to direct its employees to undertake the responsibilities of their positions in a specified way. Because Plaintiffs assert only an infringement on the manner in which they perform their work as state employees, they cannot demonstrate that the speech to which they claim entitlement would be made in their capacity as citizens speaking on matters of public concern. The Act regulates the speech of individuals speaking in their capacity as Commonwealth employees, not as citizens, and thus the Act does not touch upon a matter of public concern. Consequently, the speech may be restricted consistent with the First Amendment.

REVERSED.

(*Note:* The Virginia House of Delegates amended the act in *Urofsky* requiring the Virginia Department of Personnel and Training to adopt and implement an acceptable computer use policy. In addition, the act now applies to material that is lascivious. An appeal of the decision was denied by to the U.S. Supreme Court [2001 U.S. LEXIS 134, 2001)].

Case Questions

1. Would the Virginia act apply to employees allowed to take home their computer?
2. What would constitute a "bona fide" agency-approved research project that might involve accessing sexually explicit materials?
3. Would it be ethical for a professor to assign a research project that would require students to access adult-oriented Web sites?

INTERNATIONAL REGULATION OF OBSCENITY

The nations of the world have each formulated laws governing forms of speech usually reflective of what they deem to be in the best interest of its culture and society. As is the case in the United States, in foreign countries the standards for obscenity vary, making it virtually impossible to establish predictability as to whether online material will be allowed or prohibited. Such issues surround the importation and exportation of pornography and attempts to regulate it. As you read this section, keep in mind the following factors that affect and determine the ability or inability to achieve a worldwide agreement on prohibiting obscene materials:

1. There is only a minimal body of international law governing the transmission or receipt of obscene material and no universal definition or set of standards regarding it.
2. Cultural, moral, and legal characteristics usually form the basis of a country's views on obscene and other forms of speech.
3. It is difficult for one country to impose or enforce its laws on another country.
4. A provider in a country with strict obscenity standards may transmit materials to a country with more liberal standards, and from there it is accessible worldwide by a simple click.

In addition, a number of UN organizations have explicitly affirmed a nation's right to uphold its own public morals. Indeed, most governments have placed at least some restrictions on domestic obscenity. The following material discusses the various international approaches relevant to regulating and limiting obscenity online.

The Act of State Doctrine and the Regulation of Obscene Transmissions

The **Act of State Doctrine** creates a judicial exception to the rule that U.S. courts have the power to adjudicate all claims over which they hold jurisdiction. This doctrine prevents courts from adjudicating claims against foreign countries when those claims address conduct within that foreign country's territory. Therefore, a U.S. court would lack jurisdiction and be powerless to rule on what occurs within the borders of a foreign country, even if it violates U.S. laws. For example, both the United States and Germany have laws protecting free speech. However, German law criminalizes speech that denies the existence of the Holocaust or that fosters Nazism, so-called *hate speech*.

U.S. law would likely afford such speech First Amendment protection. Therefore, if these types of hate speech were received by a user in the United States, and challenges to their legality under U.S. law were raised, the Act of State Doctrine would prevent a U.S. court from prohibiting their dissemination, notwithstanding German law.

A question arises as to whether a foreign court would have the power to regulate transmissions by a U.S. service provider that were prohibited under the laws of a foreign country. This was the issue in a 1995 case brought in a German court against CompuServe Germany, a wholly owned subsidiary of CompuServe USA. CompuServe Germany provided local dial-up access for German subscribers to CompuServe USA's facilities. As a result of an investigation, the German police found a list of almost three hundred Internet newsgroups stored on CompuServe USA's servers containing alleged images of pornographic materials illegal under German law. Some of these sites did not contain prohibited materials.

Nevertheless, faced with prosecution, CompuServe USA blocked access to these sites by its over 4 million U.S. and worldwide subscribers. Subsequently, CompuServe made parental control software available to its subscribers and proceeded to unblock the sites. Later, the German police discovered the newsgroups still contained illegal materials. Felix Somm, the general manager of CompuServe Germany, was then indicted, tried, convicted, and sentenced to two years in jail for failing to block access to the sites. The court declared CompuServe USA an accomplice with Somm for its failure to block access and the financial benefits realized therefrom.

Obscenity as a Global Concept

Admittedly, obscenity is hard to define. One Supreme Court justice famously commented when asked to define obscenity, "I know it when I see it." Accordingly, not all countries agree on the same definition of obscenity. For example, in the UK, obscenity encompasses sexually explicit material, extreme violence, and advocacy of drug use. The United States, in contrast, limits its definition of obscenity to sexually explicit material. However, three basic concepts seem to underlie most national definitions of obscenity.

First, obscenity is determined by whether or not it is *immoral*. Immoral obscene acts directly contravene moral norms and arguably weaken the prevailing moral fabric. The second notion of obscenity views it as *counter-majoritarian*. This view determines obscenity by whether or not the majority of the society finds the material is offensive and believes it should be regulated. Third, obscenity may be determined by whether or not it *promotes harmful behaviors*. Under this concept, obscenity is classified by its ability to promote destructive acts that should thus be criminalized. Under any definition, the significant presence of obscenity online is forcing nations around the globe to rethink their views of obscenity within an increasingly multinational online world.

Multilateral Treaties Regulating Obscenity

Two multilateral agreements, albeit old, regulate obscenity. First, the *Arrangement Between the United States and Other Powers Relative to the Repression of the Circula-*

tion of Obscene Publications, enacted in 1910 and ratified in the United States in 1911, invites cooperation among signatories to control dissemination of obscene materials and to share information regarding regulations and sentencing. The treaty points to national law as a solution, stating that obscene materials will be confiscated "within the scope of municipal legislation." The second agreement, the *International Convention for the Suppression of the Circulation of and Traffic in Obscene Publications*, enacted in 1923, regulates the information change provisions of the prior treaty and grants jurisdiction to countries where offenders commit any element of the crime. Also, nations where the offenders are nationals also have jurisdiction. The United States is not a party to this treaty.

U.S. Views on the Importation and Exportation of Cyberporn

Importation. Title 19 of the U.S. Code bans the importation of:

> Any obscene book, pamphlet, paper, writing, advertisement, circular, print, picture, drawing, or other representation, figure, or image on or of paper or other material, or . . . article which is obscene or immoral.

Liability under Title 19 could be imposed on a service provider who had knowledge of the contents of prohibited material originating in a foreign country yet who allowed it to be downloaded. The same liability may be imposed on a user who searches and downloads prohibited material from a foreign source.

Exportation. Service providers are subject to the obscenity laws of those countries in which they solicit or obtain customers. As we have seen, these laws may be strict or liberal, except in the case of child pornography, where the laws are generally extremely strict. We have already seen the restrictions Germany places on speech dealing with the Holocaust and Nazism. This same speech (hate speech) would be protected under the laws of some other countries. China and Singapore are even more restrictive than Germany.

Other National Efforts to Regulate Internet Obscenity

China. China's laws on obscenity prohibit access to Web sites including *Playboy*, *Penthouse*, and so on. These sites are not considered obscene and, in general, are protected by the laws of the United States, the United Kingdom, Canada, and so on. China also restricts access to Web sites it believes contain materials that are politically incorrect. These include the *New York Times*, the *Wall Street Journal*, Cable News Network (CNN), Amnesty International, and the Taiwan Government Information Office. You should also be aware that before any ISP is allowed to transmit in China, approval must be obtained from the Chinese Ministry of Posts and Telecommunications.

Singapore. In Singapore, any Web site containing pornographic material is banned, along with those containing issues related to political criticisms, religions, and race. Scrutiny is particularly strict regarding political parties whose Web sites must be approved by the agencies of the Singapore government. Also note that unlike the United States, libraries and schools are held to higher standards of supervision regarding access to the Internet.

United Kingdom. The UK defines obscenity by the type of person who obtains the material. The *UK Obscene Publications Act of 1959* states that if a viewer is likely to be corrupted and or depraved by material, that material is considered obscene. Access to paper-printed material is tightly controlled, whereas Internet access is available to everyone. If the likely pool of viewers changes, nonobscene print material may turn into obscene material when placed online. The *Public Order Act of 1994* extended the 1959 act to cover obscene material viewed through the transmission of electronically stored data. This act also makes Internet service providers (ISPs) liable for content even in some circumstances where they did not consent to the publication of the material.

Summary

This chapter discussed obscenity and the attempts at regulating its transmission via the Internet, particularly regarding child pornography. It should be obvious that no matter how vigilant those in society are regarding censorship of what they believe to be questionable materials, there exist no foolproof methods for preventing or blocking their online transmissions.

From a legal liability perspective, the best way to avoid prosecution under state, federal, and international law is to take whatever steps are necessary to comply with all relevant laws. Parents or guardians are probably the first and best defense for protecting children from obscenity and other harmful material. Similarly, employers have a legal and ethical obligation to prevent employees from visiting adult-oriented Web sites in the interest of ensuring a productive workplace that is free from hostilities.

Key Terms

cyberporn, *312*
prurient interest, *315*
contemporary community standards, *315*
patently offensive, *318*
literary, artistic, political, or socially redeemable value, *318*

consenting adults defense, *319*
Communications Decency Act (CDA), *319*
Good Samaritan defense, *320*
Child Pornography Protection Act, *324*

Child Online Protection Act of 1998 (COPA), *325*
Children's Internet Protection Act (CIPA), *330*
Protection of Children from Sexual Predators Act of 1998, *331*
Act of State Doctrine, *336*

Manager's Checklist

√ Make sure your company's written computer usage and monitoring policy specifically addresses improper access to pornographic Web sites.

√ Penalties and procedures for violations of the policy should be established and publicized.

√ If an employee is suspected of computer misuse, make sure you verify the identity of the employee before taking any action.

√ Determine whether installing appropriate filtering software or other means could protect company computers from being downloaded with undesirable materials especially by employees who are minors.

√ From time to time, employer/employee open discussions may be helpful in establishing an acceptable, or at least comfortable, business environment regarding computer use.

√ Obscenity is not limited to sexual interests. Online firms selling or posting extremely violent material or advocating drug use may be in violation of obscenity laws.

√ Be aware that global views of obscenity are difficult to harmonize. Each nation has its own defined obscenity laws that vary widely.

√ Ethical Considerations

Consider joining industry and other efforts to help combat child pornography.

Online service providers have an ethical if not legal obligation to take a more proactive role in restricting access to sexually explicit Web sites by minors.

Case Problems

1. Defendant took sexually explicit pictures of his thirteen-year-old niece in New Hampshire. According to testimony, he intended to develop the pictures in Massachusetts and put them on the Internet on a computer in Massachusetts. He was convicted under a federal child pornography law that required the defendant "knew or had reason to know" that the pictures would be transported in interstate commerce. On appeal, the defendant argued he was not engaged in interstate commerce. The government argues his intent was sufficient to support a conviction under the law and that transmitting the pictures via the Internet constitutes interstate commerce. How should the court decide? [*United States v. Carroll,* 105 F.3d 740 (1st Cir. 1997)]

2. The parents of children who use the town's public library are aware that some of the children have been visiting adult-oriented Web sites. Concerned that some of these sites may contain obscene material including child pornography, a group of the parents complain to the trustees of the library. As a result, the library purchases and installs software on all library computers blocking access to these sites. Another group of citizens file a lawsuit, claiming the actions of the library restrict their rights to access these sites. How should the court decide? Suggest other methods the library could use to prevent the children from accessing these sites. [*Mainstream Loudoun v. Board of Trustees of the Loudoun County Library,* 24 F. Supp. 2d 552 (E.D. Va. 1998)]

3. John is allowed to take his company computer home on weekends to do work. One weekend he downloads pornographic pictures and sends them to a co-worker,

Bob, instructing him not to open them at work. While in his office cubicle, Bob proceeds to view them. Linda, their supervisor, comes into Bob's cubicle to ask him a question and sees the materials. Subsequently, both John and Bob are fired. John argues that because the downloading occurred at home, his rights to privacy and free speech have been violated. Bob argues that because he did not intend for Linda to see the material and he was in a cubicle away from other employees, his same rights were violated. Do you agree with their arguments? Does it matter whether the company had a policy on appropriate computer use?

4. Angevine was a professor of architecture at Oklahoma State University (OSU). OSU's computer usage policy allowed it to view, at any time without any notice, files or e-mails stored on its computers. Angevine downloaded three thousand pornographic images of young boys on his OSU computer. Under the policy, OSU searched Angevine's computer and discovered the images. In his trial for possession of child pornography in a federal district court, he brought a motion to exclude or suppress the evidence of the pornographic images on the grounds that he had a reasonable expectation of privacy in the use of his computer and therefore a warrant was required for the search under the Fourth Amendment. The court denied his motion and Angevine conditionally pled guilty to the charges but reserved the right to appeal the denial of his motion. He now seeks to appeal his conviction on Fourth Amendment grounds. What result? [*U.S. v. Angevine.* No. 01-6097 (10th Cir. Feb. 22, 2002)]

5. Defendant used America Online to transmit child pornography in violation of federal law. In addition to large fines and imprisonment, the law had a forfeiture provision that allowed the government to seize the pornographic materials and other assets belonging to the defendant. In this case, the government ordered the defendant to forfeit his home. The defendant argued this was an "excessive fine," unconstitutional under the Eighth Amendment. Do you agree? How can you justify the forfeiture? [*United States v. Ownby,* 926 F. Supp. 558 (W.D. Va. 1996)]

6. Japan's law regulating obscene material is one of the most relaxed in the industrialized world. Japan has a statute prohibiting "forced indecency," but it protects only Japanese children under age thirteen, and then only from child prostitution and pornography. Further, the law may only be enforced if the child or a representative raises a claim within six months of the incident. Japan's only protection for children over thirteen is its general criminal code regulating pornography, which classifies it through the display of sexual organs. What effects, if any, does Japan's leniency in this area have on global online obscenity regulation?

Additional Readings

- "Pornography on the Internet—The Red-Light District of Cyberspace." CWA Library, May 1999 (*http://www.cwfa.org/library.asp?category=pornography*).

• Sayle, Amber Jene, Note and Comment. "Net Nation and the Digital Revolution: Regulation of Offensive Material for a New Community." *Wisconsin International Law Journal* 18 (2000): 257.

• Wilks, Fred L. "The Community Standards Conundrum in a Borderless World: Making Sense of Obscenity Laws in Cyberspace." UCLA Online Institute for Cyberspace Law and Policy (1998) (*http://www.gseis.ucla.edu/clp/flwilks.htm*).

DEFAMATION

Reputation is an idle and most false imposition; oft got without merit, and lost without deserving.

—*William Shakespeare,* **Othello,** *Act II, Scene 3*

LEARNING OBJECTIVES

After you have read this chapter, you should be able to:

1. Understand the common law tort of defamation and its two forms, slander and libel.
2. Discuss the elements of proof required and the defenses available in a cause of action for defamation.
3. Discuss the liability for defamation of online and Internet service providers and others operating in cyberspace.
4. Understand the application of the Communications Decency Act of 1996 to online service providers.
5. Understand some of the jurisdictional and conflict of laws questions related to defamation.
6. Discuss the legal issues related to discovering the identity of users who post defamatory messages anonymously on the Internet (so-called John Doe cases).
7. Learn about SLAPP suits used by government officials and entities and corporations to stifle online public criticism about them.
8. Comprehend the varying international efforts at regulating cyber-defamation.
9. Explore the issues related to the liability of Internet service providers for defamatory statements posted by their subscribers.
10. Be familiar with the choice of law issue and how it relates to online defamation claims.

> **http://**
>
> - Additional material on defamation may be found at the Bentley College CyberLaw Center Web site (**http://www.ecampus.bentley.edu/ dept/cyberlaw**) under Social Issues—Defamation.

INTRODUCTION

As we have seen, the First Amendment of the U.S. Constitution provides us with the rights of free speech and expression, and, as with other rights, these are not entitled to absolute protection. They can be limited if, in practice, they infringe or violate the rights of others. This chapter focuses on one such limitation, the common law tort of defamation as it relates to the reputations of individuals and e-businesses communicating in cyberspace. As you proceed through this chapter, remember that not only do the laws we discuss pertain to the reputation of an individual, but also to that of a business or its product or service. Also keep in mind that many of the cases brought for defamation can also include claims for invasion of privacy and intentional infliction of emotional distress.

The laws regarding defamation differ from state to state and country to country. This fact poses some interesting questions of jurisdiction, conflict of laws, and choice of laws. In general, courts consider the impact and injurious effect of the statements on the plaintiff's reputation in the community where the plaintiff resides. Most likely, the damage to reputation would be greatest where others know the plaintiff. Therefore, a court could apply the law of that place. This may yield a just result for non-public figures. However, a different situation is presented if the plaintiff is a public figure whose fame extends domestically and internationally.

Whose laws would be used? Where should the suit be brought? What if the laws of one state or country conflict with those of another? For some insight into these issues and what factors courts could use in online defamation cases, recall the discussion of jurisdiction in Chapter 2, especially involving long-arm statutes and *minimum contacts*. A brief mention is made here of three important factors courts will consider in determining a court's authority to exercise person jurisdiction over an out-of-state resident who posts defamatory information online:

- Whether there was a direct electronic activity into the state
- An intent to conduct business or other interactions in the state
- The activity must create in a person within the state a cause of action recognizable by the courts of that state.

The court applied these factors to *Stanley Young v. The New Haven Advocate*, et al., No. 01-2340 (4th Cir. 2002) and held the plaintiff, a Connecticut newspaper with no subscribers in Virginia, that "merely posted" an allegedly defamatory article on a Virginia Web site about the defendant, a Virginia resident, did not satisfy any of the factors and the Virginia federal courts lacked personal jurisdiction over the plaintiff. The court found that the plaintiff's articles and Web sites were aimed at Connecticut residents and not those of Virginia. Therefore, it engaged in no direct electronic activity in Virginia over which the Virginia courts would have jurisdiction. Further, because the plaintiff had no subscribers in Virginia, the plaintiff had not manifested intent to conduct business there (no "minimum contacts" and the long-arm statute was inapplicable to the facts), nor did the activity it conducted create a cause of action recognized by the Virginia federal courts. (See also *ALS Scan, Inc., v. Digital Services Consultants, Inc.*, 293 F.3d 707, 2002, for a similar decision.)

The likelihood in the future of more defamation litigation, including those similar to the issues presented in *Stanley*, is inevitable, given the personal nature of electronic communications, publications, e-mail messages, and so on, and the relative ease by which it is possible to virtually *instantaneously* publish and transmit to millions of other online users worldwide. The potential for harm to one's reputation can be significant if these messages contain defamatory material. Also, keep in mind our previous discussions of employer policies regarding employee computer usage and monitoring. Here a court could hold the employer liable, along with the employee, for online defamatory statements, especially those directed at competition, posted by an employee under the common law theories of vicarious liability and *respondeat superior*. These theories hold an employer or principal liable for the torts of an employee or agent as long as the tort was committed within the "scope" of the terms of the employment. Once again, employers would be well advised to address defamation in the policies they establish and disseminate.

Complicating these issues is the fact that online users can communicate anonymously whether in chat rooms or in newsgroups. In addition, those communicating online sometimes engage in what has become known as **flaming** (i.e., a kind of cyberspace online word battle where individuals engage in heated discussions directed at each other, sometimes rising to the level of defamatory language). These communications are not private, may be accessible by others, and may lead to potential liability for the flamers.

In order for us to understand the nature of defamation and its significance to cyberspace, we must first explore some background regarding the common law tort of defamation.

THE TORT OF DEFAMATION

Defamation may be defined as oral or written false statements that wrongfully harm a person's reputation. The oral form is called **slander**, and the written or published form is **libel**. (*Note:* If the defamatory remarks are directed against the goods or services of one's business, the tort is called *business* or *product disparagement*. See *Cubby, Inc. v. CompuServe Inc.,* discussed later in this chapter.) In all cases, the harm to reputation must be severe enough so as to lower the esteem of the plaintiff in the community by subjecting the individual to ridicule, contempt, or even hatred.

DEFAMATION IN CYBERSPACE: SLANDER OR LIBEL?

Because most material communicated on the Internet can be classified as published (bulletin boards, e-mail, chat rooms, etc.) and has a degree of permanence, if it satisfies the elements of proof needed for defamation, it will likely be classified as libel and not slander.

Elements of Proof Required for Defamation

In suits for the tort of defamation, the Restatement (Second) of Torts requires proof of certain elements (see Figure 11.1). We consider their applicability to libel in cyberspace.

First, a false and defamatory statement, usually of fact and not opinion, must be made about another's reputation or business. Direct evidence, innuendo, insinuation, or reference may establish this. What is necessary to establish is that the statement made is understood by others to be "of or concerning" the plaintiff. Note that this tort, like some others, is considered personal. Therefore, if the individual who is the subject of the defamation is deceased at the time it is published, no cause of action for defamation exists.

FIGURE 11.1   Elements of Proof Required in a Suit for Defamation

- A false statement of fact, not opinion, about the plaintiff
- Publication of the statement without a privilege to do so
- Fault or negligence
- Damages—actual or presumed

Second, an unprivileged publication is made or communicated to a third party. Generally, there is no liability if the defendant did not intend the publication to be viewed by anyone other than the plaintiff. However, it is common knowledge that very few online communications, especially those concerning e-mail, are considered private. They are accessible and capable of interception by literally millions of others worldwide. Therefore, it is unlikely that a defendant would be able to argue he or she did not intend others to view defamatory statements published online.

Third, depending on state law or whether the plaintiff is considered a public official or figure, the plaintiff may have to establish some degree of fault or negligence on the part of the defendant. As discussed later in more detail, a plaintiff who is a public official or figure will have to prove the defamatory remarks were made with *actual malice* (with knowledge the remarks were false or with reckless disregard as to whether they were false or not). If the plaintiff is a private individual, one not famous in the community, then the burden of proof is less demanding, depending on the state's requirement for "fault" regarding this element. Typically, those states with such a requirement require a plaintiff to prove the defendant failed to exercise reasonable care in determining the truth or falsity of the statements published.

Fourth, the defamatory statements must result in actual or presumed damages. If the words qualify as libel, damages are presumed to exist. The permanent nature of a libelous statement, the ability, especially via the Internet, to distribute it widely, store it indefinitely, and the fact that, in general, written words require more premeditation than those spoken, have led courts to allow recovery for libel without proof of actual or special damages.

However, if the words qualify as slander, a plaintiff will have to establish actual or special damages unless the false accusations fall into one of the following categories known as **slander per se** where damages are presumed to exist:

1. Accusing another of committing a serious crime
2. Accusing another of having a loathsome or communicable disease
3. Injuring another in their business or profession
4. In some states, accusing a woman of being unchaste

Defenses to Defamation

There are defenses to defamation suits available to a defendant. *Truth* is an absolute or complete defense to defamation. If what is stated about the plaintiff is true, there is no basis for recovering damages, even where the defendant is motivated by malice (ill will, spite, or revenge) (see Figure 11.2).

In certain situations, the law allows an individual an **absolute privilege** to speak freely about another without regard to liability for defamation. This defense usually extends to statements associated with the effective furtherance of the operations of government. Thus members of the judicial, legislative, and executive branches of government are protected from liability for publishing false statements as long as they relate to their particular function. The law recognizes that these individuals must be free to express their opinions freely without fear of a lawsuit.

A **qualified privilege** attaches to other situations. Such is the case where an individual who is defamed by another publishes a reasonable rebuttal to the statements made about them. This defense is also recognized where the publisher and the third party have a common and legitimate interest in the plaintiff, as where a prospective employer seeks a reference from a prior employer of a prospective employee. The statements contained in the reference must relate to the employee's job performance.

Note that in some states, the privilege is lost if the former employer knows the information furnished is false or the employer is motivated by malice toward the employee. When dealing with public officials or figures, the law imposes a stricter burden of proof than that required of private figures. Here, the law attempts to strike a balance between the right of individuals to protect their reputation and the right of the public to know about the newsworthy activities of public figures and officials.

Before discussing the burden of proof, we must define what the law recognizes as public officials and figures. In *Rosenblatt v. Baer*, 383 U.S. 75 (1966), the Supreme Court defined public officials as "those among the hierarchy of government employees who have or appear to have substantial responsibility over the conduct of governmental affairs." Individuals elected to office and others such as police and fire chiefs qualify under this definition.

The courts have found it more difficult to define who is a public figure. *Gertz v. Robert Welch, Inc.*, 418 U.S. 323 (1974) held that in order to qualify as a public figure, plaintiffs would be required to show "clear evidence" they have established fame or notoriety in the community. World-famous celebrities like Jennifer Lopez or Mohammed Ali would meet this test and, if defamed online or elsewhere, would be classified as *public figures*.

FIGURE 11.2   Defenses to Defamation

- Truth
- Absolute privilege
- Qualified privilege

Turning our attention to liability and privilege, the press and other media have a *qualified privilege* to inform us about the activities of the famous. In the landmark case *New York Times v. Sullivan*, 376 U.S. 254 (1964), the U.S. Supreme Court qualified this privilege by requiring that, in order to hold a defendant liable for defaming public officials, a plaintiff had to prove the defendant published the alleged defamatory material with *actual malice* (i.e., "with knowledge that it was false or with reckless disregard of whether it was false or not"). Three years later in *Curtis Publishing Co. v. Butts*, 388 U.S. 153 (1967), the Supreme Court extended the requirements of *Sullivan* to public figures seeking damages for defamation.

LIABILITY OF ONLINE AND INTERNET SERVICE PROVIDERS FOR DEFAMATION

For purposes of establishing liability for publishing defamation, one of the most significant and litigated issues has been the determination of whether online service providers (OSP) and Internet service providers (ISP) (hereafter called service providers) are common carriers, distributors, or publishers of the transmitted material.

Generally, courts have held that a *common carrier* (telephone or telegraph company) of published or transmitted material has virtually no control over the content of what is communicated over their service. Consequently, they are not liable for defamation. In *Lunney v. Prodigy*, 1999 N.Y. LEXIS 3746 (1999) the court held that Prodigy, an ISP, was merely a conduit and not a publisher of profane and threatening messages posted on its bulletin board in Lunney's (a minor teenager) name by an imposter, and therefore was no more responsible for the messages than a telephone company.

Similarly, a *distributor* of published material such as a news vendor or bookstore does not exercise the degree of control over content necessary to establish liability for defamation. See *Smith v. California*, 361 U.S. 147 (1959) where the proprietor of a bookstore was convicted of possessing an obscene book in his store without knowledge of its contents. The Court reversed his conviction, holding that the freedom of expression and press guarantees of the First Amendment prohibits the prosecution of a distributor of an obscene book unless there is proof of "knowledge of the contents of the book."

In contrast, *publishers* of a book, newspaper, or television or radio broadcast can be liable for defamation because they exercise a sufficient degree of editorial control over what they publish. Therefore, it should follow that if a service provider or bulletin board operator controls the content of a publication or has knowledge of its contents, it can be liable if what is published over the service is defamatory.

Two cases dealing with the issue of control over content should be considered as background for the next section that discusses immunity for liability in defamation for OSPs and ISPs. In *Cubby, Inc. v. CompuServe, Inc.*, 776 F. Supp. 135 (S.D. N.Y. 1991) the defendant provided an "electronic" library service containing interest forums upon which daily newspapers were available to subscribers and users and over which the defendant exerted no control or knowledge regarding what was published. In his suit for defamation against the defendant, the plaintiff alleged that on one of these newspapers, *Rumorville,* defamatory statements were published about him. The court found that because the defendant had no control or knowledge of the contents of the publication, it was merely a distributor and could not be held liable as a publisher. An opposite conclusion was reached by the court in *Stratton Oakmont v. PRODIGY Services Company,* 1995 N.Y. Misc. LEXIS 229 (1995), where the defendant owned and operated *Money Talk,* a widely read financial bulletin board upon which members posted messages regarding stocks and other financial information and upon which allegedly defamatory statements were published about the plaintiff. In his suit for defamation against the defendant, the court found that since the defendant employed an agent and software-screening programs for monitoring purposes, it considered the defendant, unlike CompuServe, a publisher rather than a distributor and liable for the defamatory messages.

IMMUNITY FOR SERVICE PROVIDERS FOR OFFENSIVE MATERIAL

Recall our discussion of the Communications Decency Act (CDA) in Chapter 10. There we saw certain provisions of the CDA declared unconstitutional. The CDA legislation manifests intent by Congress to eliminate the potential liability of service providers and users for defamation whether they qualify as distributors under *Cubby* or as publishers under *Stratton.* Congress was concerned with the decision in *Stratton* contemplating that the liability as described would be a disincentive to service providers and others to develop technologies that would result in blocking and filtering devices and, ideally, in user control over what information is published and received by individuals, families, and others. **Section 230 of the Communications Decency Act** of 1996 [CDA 47 U.S.C. § 230(C)(1)] was not only a reflection of that concern but also served to overrule the decision in *Stratton.*

Specifically, § 230 provides that "no provider or user of an interactive computer service shall be treated as a publisher or speaker of any information provided by another information content provider." Further, § 230 eliminates potential civil liability where a provider or user takes a good faith voluntary action to restrict access to or availability of material that the provider or user considers obscene, harassing, or otherwise objectionable, whether or not the material is constitutionally protected. The effect of these provisions is to protect a service provider (e.g., PRODIGY) from being classified as a publisher, particularly in cases where it attempts to exercise even a modicum of control over content.

The following case involves the applicability of § 230 of the CDA to a case involving a plaintiff who is the victim of abusive and defamatory statements attributed to him by an anonymous user of a bulletin board operated by America Online. The issues focus on the conflict between state and federal law and the effective "retroactive" date of the CDA.

Zeran v. America Online, Inc.
129 F.2d 327 (4th Cir. 1997)

Facts

On April 25, 1995, an unidentified person posted a message on an AOL bulletin board advertising "Naughty Oklahoma T-Shirts" featuring offensive and tasteless slogans related to the 1995 bombing of the Alfred P. Murrah Federal Building in Oklahoma City. Those interested in purchasing these shirts were instructed to call Zeran at his home telephone number in the state of Washington. Zeran knew nothing of this posting previously and did not sell shirts from his home.

As a result of this anonymously perpetrated act, Zeran received a high volume of calls at his home, composed primarily of angry and derogatory messages and death threats. On the same day, Zeran contacted AOL and informed it of the posting. AOL assured him that the posting would be removed, but as a matter of policy, AOL would not post a retraction.

The next day, another anonymous message was posted advertising similar shirts with new tasteless slogans, instructing interested parties to call Zeran at home. The angry, threatening calls to Zeran intensified. Over the next few days, an unknown person continued to post related messages and advertised additional items for sale, including bumper stickers and key chains, complete with tasteless slogans. By April 30, Zeran was receiving an abusive telephone call approximately every two minutes. During this time, AOL assured Zeran that the account from which these messages were posted would soon be closed. Zeran reported this activity to the Seattle FBI office.

Meanwhile, an Oklahoma City radio station, KRXO, related the posting to its audience and urged listeners to telephone Zeran as a sign of protest. By May 14, after an Oklahoma City newspaper exposed the postings as a hoax, and after KRXO apologized on air, the number of calls to Zeran subsided to fifteen per day.

Zeran brought this state action against AOL, asserting that AOL unreasonably delayed in removing defamatory messages from its bulletin board service, refused to post retractions, and failed to screen for similar postings thereafter. In essence, Zeran seeks to hold AOL liable in negligence for allowing defamatory speech initiated by a third party to be posted on its bulletin boards. He asserts that as a distributor, AOL is liable for the distribution of material it knew or should have known was of a defamatory character. In its answer, AOL raises § 230 of the CDA as an affirmative defense, arguing it preempts any state common law cause of action Zeran may have against AOL. Zeran counters by arguing that § 230 of the CDA could not be retroactively applied so as to bar his claim against AOL for acts that occurred prior to the effective date of § 230, February 8, 1996. Zeran brought suit in federal district court in Oklahoma. The suit was transferred to a Virginia federal district court, where the court found for AOL. The court agreed with AOL that the federal CDA, enacted prior to Zeran's suit, bars Zeran's state law claims. Zeran filed this appeal to the circuit court.

Judicial Opinion *(Chief Judge Wilkinson)*

One of the many means by which individuals access the Internet is through an interactive computer service. These services . . . allow their subscribers to access information communicated and stored only on each computer service's individual proprietary network. AOL is just such an interactive computer service. Zeran seeks to hold AOL liable for [the state law claim of] defamatory speech initiated by a third party. [Communications Decency Act of 1996 (CDA)] Section 230 entered this litigation as an affirmative defense pled by AOL. The company claimed that Congress immunized interactive computer service providers from claims based on information posted by a third party.

The relevant portion of § 230 states, "No provider or user of an interactive computer service shall be treated as the publisher or speaker of any information provided by another information content provider." By its plain language, § 230 creates a federal immunity to any cause of action that would make service providers liable for information originating with a third-party user of the service. Specifically, § 230 precludes courts from entertaining claims that would place a computer service provider in a publisher's role. Thus, lawsuits seeking to hold a service provider liable for its exercise of a publisher's traditional editorial functions—such as deciding whether to publish, withdraw, postpone or alter content—are barred.

The purpose of this statutory immunity is not difficult to discern. Congress recognized the threat that tort-based lawsuits pose to freedom of speech in the new and burgeoning Internet medium. The imposition of tort liability . . . represent [s] . . . simply another form of intrusive government regulation of speech. Section 230 was enacted, in part, to maintain the robust nature of Internet communication and . . . keep government interference in the medium to a minimum.

None of this means, of course, that the original party who posts defamatory messages would escape accountability. While Congress acted to keep government regulation of the Internet to a minimum, it also found it to be policy of the United States 'to ensure vigorous enforcement of federal criminal laws to deter and punish trafficking in obscenity, stalking, and harassment by means of computer.' Congress made a policy choice, however, not to deter harmful online speech through the separate route of imposing tort liability on companies that serve as intermediaries for other parties' potentially injurious messages.

Another important purpose of § 230 was to encourage service providers to self-regulate the dissemination of offensive material over their services. Section 230 represents the approach of Congress to a problem of national and international dimension. Congress' desire to promote unfettered speech on the Internet must supercede conflicting [state] common law causes of action. Section 230 . . . continues: '[no] cause of action may be brought and no liability may be imposed under any State or local law that is inconsistent with this section.'

The CDA became effective on February 8, 1996. Zeran did not file his complaint until April 23, 1996. Zeran contends that even if § 230 does bar the type of claim he brings here, it cannot be applied retroactively to bar an action arising from AOL's alleged misconduct prior to the CDA's enactment. We disagree. Section 230 applies by its plain terms to complaints brought after the CDA became effective. Here, Zeran did not file his complaint until over two months after § 230's immunity became effective.

Here, Congress's command is explicitly stated. Its exercise of its commerce power is clear and [so Zeran's claims are barred].

For the foregoing reasons, we affirm the judgment of the district court.

AFFIRMED.

Case Questions

1. How can the court justify *not* holding AOL liable, given the fact that even though Zeran informed them, on more than one occasion, of the tasteless messages, they still allowed them to continue to be posted?

2. Do you believe a retraction would have eliminated the harm suffered by Zeran? If so, should they be held liable for failing to post one?

3. What ethical issues are raised by Congress's grant of immunity to service providers under § 230 of the CDA?

[*Note:* In a subsequent action brought by Zeran against KRXO in 2000 for defamation, invasion of privacy and intentional infliction of emotional distress resulting from broadcasting Zeran's phone number, the court dismissed the case for lack of proof. *Zeran v. Diamond Broadcasting, Inc.*, 203 F.3d 714 (10th Cir. 2000)].

In light of the immunity given to service providers under § 230, unless it is revoked or modified, success in libel suits against service providers will likely occur only where a plaintiff can establish that the service provider exhibited some degree of editorial control over content. Such was the attempt in the following case dealing with a libel lawsuit brought by an assistant to then President Clinton against both the author of the alleged defamatory publication and the service provider that made it available online, § 230 notwithstanding.

Sidney Blumenthal v. Matt Drudge and America Online, Inc. (AOL)
992 F. Supp. 44 (D.D.C. April 22, 1998)

Facts

The defendant, Matt Drudge, is the author of an electronic gossip column called the *Drudge Report,* focusing on gossip from Hollywood and Washington, D.C. In late May or early June, Drudge entered into an agreement with AOL, the terms of which would make the report available to all members of AOL's service. Under the agreement, Drudge was to create, edit, update, and "otherwise manage" the content of the report, and AOL could "remove content that AOL reasonably determined violated AOL's standard of service." Subsequent to the agreement, AOL issued a press release describing the kind of material Drudge would provide in the report—gossip and rumor—and urged potential subscribers to sign on to AOL in order to get the report.

The plaintiff, Blumenthal, began working on August 11, 1997, at the White House as an assistant to President Clinton. On the day before in his report, Drudge falsely accuses Blumenthal of having a spousal abuse past that was effectively covered up. These allegedly defamatory remarks were made available to AOL subscribers. The plaintiff seeks to hold AOL liable along with Drudge, suggesting AOL had a role in writing or editing the material in the report. He also argues that Section 230 of the CDA does not provide immunity to AOL because Drudge was not an anonymous person who sent a message over the Internet through AOL, but was a person with whom AOL had a contract that contemplated more than a passive role for AOL. In the contract, AOL reserved the right to remove, or direct [Drudge] to remove, any content that violated AOL's terms of service. AOL moved for summary judgment, raising as a defense the immunity provision under § 230 of the Communications Decency Act of 1996.

Judicial Opinion *(District Judge Friedman)*

The near instantaneous possibilities for the dissemination of information by millions of different information providers around the world to those with access to computers and thus to the Internet have created ever-increasing opportunities for the exchange of information and ideas in "cyberspace." This information revolution has also presented unprecedented challenges relating to the rights to privacy and reputational rights of individuals, to the control of obscene and pornographic materials, and to competition among journalists and news organizations for instant news, rumors and other information that is communicated and so quickly that it is often unchecked and unverified. Needless to say, the legal rules that will govern this new medium are just beginning to take shape.

In February of 1996, Congress made an effort to deal with some of these challenges in enacting the Communications Decency Act of 1996. While various options were open to the Congress, it chose to "promote the continued development of the Internet and other interactive computer services and other interactive media" and "to preserve the vibrant and competitive free market" for such services, largely unfettered by federal or state regulation. Whether wisely or not, it made the legislative judgment to effectively immunize providers of interactive computer services from civil liability in tort with respect to material disseminated by them but created by others. In recognition of the speed with which information may be disseminated and the near impossibility of regulating information content, Congress decided not to treat providers of interactive computer services like other information providers such as newspapers, magazines, or television and radio stations, all of which may be held liable for publishing or distributing obscene or defamatory material written or prepared by others. While Congress could have a different policy choice, it opted not to hold interactive computer service providers liable for their failure to edit, withhold or restrict access to offensive material disseminated through their medium.

Plaintiffs make the additional argument, however, that Section 230 does not provide immunity to AOL in this case because Drudge was not just an anonymous person who sent a message over the Internet through AOL. He is a person with whom AOL contracted . . .

and whom AOL promoted as a reason to subscribe to AOL. Furthermore, the license agreement between AOL and Drudge by its terms contemplates more than a passive role for AOL. AOL reserves the "right to remove, or direct [Drudge] to remove, any content which . . . violates AOL's then-standard Terms of Service . . ."

AOL has made Matt Drudge instantly accessible to members who crave "instant gossip and news breaks." Why is this different, Blumenthal suggests, from AOL advertising and promoting a new purveyor of child pornography or other offensive material? Why should AOL be permitted to tout someone as a gossip columnist or rumormonger who will make such rumors and gossip "instantly accessible" to AOL subscribers, and then claim immunity when that person, as might be anticipated, defames another?

If it were writing on a clean slate, this Court would agree with Plaintiffs. AOL has certain editorial rights with respect to the content provided by Drudge and disseminated by AOL, including the right to require changes in content and to remove it. Yet it takes no responsibility for any damage he may cause. Because it has the right to exercise editorial control over those with whom it contracts and whose words it disseminates, it would seem only fair to hold AOL to the liability standards applied to a publisher or, at least, like a book store owner or library, to the liability standards applied to a distributor. But Congress has made a different policy by providing immunity even where the interactive service provider has an active, even aggressive role in making available content prepared by others. Congress has conferred immunity as an incentive to Internet service providers to self-police . . . even where the self-policing is unsuccessful or not even attempted.

Any attempt to distinguish between "publisher" liability and notice-based "distributor" liability and to argue that Section 230 was only intended to immunize the former would be unavailing. Congress made no distinction . . . in providing immunity from liability.

http://

- You can view the *Drudge Report* at **http://www.drudgereport.com**

While it appears to this Court that AOL has taken advantage of all the benefits conferred by Congress in the Communications Decency Act, and then some . . . the statutory language is clear: AOL is immune from suit, and the Court therefore must GRANT its MOTION FOR SUMMARY JUDGMENT.

Case Questions

1. Do you think there was enough evidence under the terms of the contract between Drudge and AOL to establish that AOL be considered a "content provider" and, therefore, liable as a co-author?

2. What suggestions would you offer to help service providers self-police in order to prevent offensive material from being posted? What if the attempts fail? Do you think Congress will reconsider the impact of Section 230?

3. In enacting Section 230, it appears Congress was more concerned with keeping the Internet "free" than with deterring or preventing injury to reputation. How can this be justified ethically?

This site is no longer accessible, but the Drudge Report may be found at http://www.drudgereport.com.

MATT DRUDGE
Information Center

It Wasn't Just Drudge
By Dick Morris
May 8, 2001

Clinton Aide Settles With Matt Drudge
The New York Times
May 4, 2001

After Years of Coverage: Big Media Silent Case
Drudge Report
May 4, 2001

Andrew Sullivan's Take
AndrewSullivan.com
May 4, 2001

Source: Matt Drudge Information Center, *http://www.cspc.org/drudge/mdinfo.htm*. Reprinted with permission.

In the aftermath of *Drudge, Cubby* and *Zeran,* what is the status of the immunity granted under § 230? Congress's original intent in passing it was to keep free speech alive on the Internet by not holding ISPs liable for the speech of others even if it was harmful. Although many courts continue to follow the precedents established in these cases, some have recently qualified Congress's intent by taking a closer look at the issue of responsibility for content control.

In *Carafano v. Metrosplash.com, Inc.,* Case No. CV 01-0018 DT (C.D. Cal. 2002), the plaintiff was an actress (stage name Chase Masterson) who has appeared on the television show *Star Trek: Deep Space Nine* as "Leeta the Debo Girl." The defendant operated an online matchmaking or dating service. It created member profiles by having them answer a questionnaire that it designed along with having them furnish photos. Although it did not monitor the content of the answers to the questionnaires, it reviewed the photos to make sure they complied with defendant's standards.

Several false statements were posted on the defendant's Web site concerning the plaintiff's sexual activities and practices. She sued for defamation (also invasion of privacy), claiming the defendant was responsible for the statements. The defendant claimed immunity under § 230 as a provider of "interactive computer services." The court disagreed, reasoning that, notwithstanding the fact the defendant did not review or control *content* of the questionnaire, the degree of control exerted in creating the questionnaire and reviewing the photos qualified it as an *information content* provider or publisher and not merely a provider of "interactive computer services."

(*Note:* Even though the defendant was responsible for the content, the court failed to find merit in the plaintiff's other claims of defamation and invasion of privacy because of her status as a celebrity and her inability to prove actual malice by the defendant in publishing the statements. Thus, the court granted summary judgment for the defendant.)

ANONYMOUS SPEECH AND DEFAMATION

Ever since the founding fathers anonymously published the *Federalist Papers,* the right to speak anonymously has been protected. Courts have echoed that fact in cases such as *McIntyre v. Ohio Elections Commission*, 514 U.S. 334, (1995), where the U.S. Supreme Court declared unconstitutional an Ohio statute that prohibited distribution of unsigned political campaign literature. Of course, this right is not absolute and, as we saw in the *Playboy* case in Chapter 10, "Obscenity," the government can regulate protected speech only if it establishes a compelling state interest to do so, and even then, it must use the least restrictive method to do so.

In cyberspace with its unlimited audience, anonymous defamatory speech including that directed at individuals and employers in chat rooms and on bulletin boards has the potential for creating great harm and damage. Plaintiffs suing for defamation have sought to determine the identity of anonymous defendant users by attempting to discover their identity via a subpoena to the service provider. Many of the defamation suits involving this issue are referred to as "John Doe" cases, and, although no federal appeals court or the Supreme Court have yet ruled on this issue, the number of these cases continue to rise, making such a ruling inevitable.

One such recent case, although unrelated to defamation, should be mentioned as it could provide a precedent for the courts deciding defamation cases involving requests for subpoenas to ISPs to determine the identity of anonymous users accused of defamation. In *Recording Industry Association of America (RIAA) v. Verizon Internet Services, Inc.,* 2003 U.S. Dist. LEXIS 681 (D.C.C., January 21, 2003), RIAA served Verizon with a subpoena to discover the identity of one of its subscribers who allegedly had downloaded six hundred songs in one day. The DMCA (Digital Millennium Copyright Act discussed in Chapter 4) allowed such subpoenas in copyright infringement cases, but Verizon refused to honor it. However, the court ordered Verizon to do so, deciding a copyright owner's rights outweighed the First Amendment rights of one who infringes those rights. More significantly, the court reaffirmed the precedent that First Amendment protection as it relates to anonymous speech does not extend to copyright infringement. Could this rationale be applied to cases involving First Amendment issues and anonymous defamatory speech? The answer will depend on the fate of Verizon in the federal appellate courts.

Those courts that have addressed the issue have attempted to balance the freedom to speak anonymously with the right to determine the identity of one who has used that freedom to engage in harmful speech or other illegal activity. In reaching a determination whether to grant a plaintiff's request for a subpoena, many courts will require evidence that the plaintiff satisfy the following conditions:

1. Post a notice of the subpoena addressed to the defendant ("John Doe") on the relevant message board.
2. Provide the court with the content of the alleged defamatory statements.
3. Establish a prima facie case of defamation exists against the defendant.
4. Once the above are satisfied, then the court must determine if the defendant's First Amendment right of anonymous free speech is outweighed by the plaintiff's need to determine the identity of the anonymous defendant.

The above were established in *Dendrite International Inc., v. John Doe No. 3*, 775 A., 2d 756 (N.J. Super, 2001), where the court applied them to a request for a subpoena to identify an anonymous user who had allegedly posted defamatory statements on Yahoo! about the plaintiff's financial status and accounting practices. Even though Dendrite was able to prove all of the statements posted were false, it was unable to prove that the defendant's statements caused losses in the value of Dendrite's stock. Therefore, Dendrite failed to satisfy the requirement that it suffered harm and the court denied the request for the subpoena. In *Immunomedics, Inc., v. Doe*, 342 N.J. Super. 160 (2001), the case was less about defamation but more about an employee who allegedly breached an agreement of confidentiality not to disclose information learned about the company by posting messages on Yahoo! containing proprietary and confidential information about the plaintiff. The court allowed the request for the subpoena stating: "Although anonymous speech on the Internet is protected, there must be an avenue for redress for those who are wronged. Individuals choosing to harm another or violate an agreement through speech on the Internet cannot hope to shield their identity and avoid punishment through invocation of the First Amendment."

SLAPP Suits

SLAPP is an acronym for Strategic Lawsuits Against Public Participation. Over nineteen states have anti-SLAPP laws that address the constitutional issues posed by such suits. Corporations, government officials, and others generally bring **SLAPP defamation suits** against individuals who disagree with their opinions or positions on matters of public interest. Many of these suits have no basis in fact and usually result in being dismissed. The suits are intended to chill First Amendment free speech and the freedom to petition the government. In any event, a plaintiff must spend money to defend against a SLAPP suit, and this fact can deter others from speaking out. Some of these cases have begun to find their way into cyberspace where Web sites and newsgroups have become the medium for expressing criticisms or allegations of wrongdoing against government officials or bodies and corporations.

http://

- For examples of state anti-SLAPP laws and other related information, see the California Anti-SLAPP Project: **http://www.casp.net/ menstate.html**

A recent Massachusetts case, *McDonald v. Paton*, No. 01- P. 323 (Mass. App. Ct., Feb. 3, 2003), is one of the first cases to apply an anti-SLAPP law to cyberspace. In this case, the defendant operated an interactive town forum Web site, a kind of "technological version of a meeting of citizens on the Town Green," where town residents could post their opinions about town affairs and governance. The plaintiff was a town selectman and candidate (a public figure) for reelection who was referred to in a local newspaper as a "Gestapo agent." Subsequently, the defendant posted a definition of "nazi" on her Web site that associated that term with the plaintiff. The plaintiff lost his bid for reelection and brought a SLAPP suit for libel against the defendant. The defendant sought to dismiss the action under the Massachusetts anti-SLAPP statute, but the trial court denied the motion, reasoning the statute did not apply to libel cases because it did not create an absolute privilege in what was posted on the site and the plaintiff might be able to prove the defendant published with actual malice.

The Massachusetts Appeals Court disagreed, reversed the decision, and granted the motion to dismiss holding that the statute indeed did apply to defamation cases because they were the most popular brought under the statute. Further, the court stated the plaintiff was unable to prove that the statements posted were factual or defamatory and that he suffered any damages.

INTERNATIONAL REGULATION OF ONLINE DEFAMATION

The Internet's ever-expanding reach creates great opportunities for communication and information exchange. This reach also increases opportunities for spreading maliciously false statements about another person or company. With a single mouse click, a user can send false information about another person or company around the world. The following section examines key issues related to the regulation of cyber-defamation.

International Efforts to Regulate Cyber-Defamation

Many nations besides the United States are developing their own legal initiatives to regulate cyber-defamation. The following nations typify these efforts around the globe.

United Kingdom. The UK has a pro-plaintiff approach to defamation that directly contradicts U.S. defamation law in many respects. For example, in the UK the burden is on the defendant to prove the statement he made was true, contrary to U.S. law where the plaintiff must show in a defamation action that the defendant's statement was false. Also, unlike U.S. law, a UK publisher of defamatory material is liable for such material regardless of whether or not the publisher had notice the published content was defamatory. Finally, UK defamation law does not require a public figure to show "actual malice" in order to prove defamation. Naturally, if a plaintiff has a choice between a UK and a U.S. forum, inevitably that plaintiff will choose the UK. This could create a rush of forum shopping by cyber-plaintiffs to that country.

The UK's most important law on defamation is the **Defamation Act of 1996**, enacted on July 4 of that year. This act allows a defendant to use as a defense that he or she took reasonable care in publishing the statement and was not aware and had no reason to believe the publication would be defamatory. Section 2 of the act enhances and simplifies how a defendant can make an "offer of amends" regarding a false statement. The defendant can make an offer to publish a suitable correction, issue an apology, and take reasonable steps to minimize any damage done by the statement. The offer of amends must be in writing. If the plaintiff accepts the offer, he or she may not bring or continue defamation proceedings against the defendant that made the publication. However, the plaintiff is entitled to enforce the offer to make amends as necessary.

Australia. The Australian courts are also exercising an expansive reach in online defamation cases. In *Gutnick v. Dow Jones*, 2001 VSC (Victorian Supreme Court) 305, (2001), Joseph Gutnick, an Australian mining magnate, sued news wire service Dow Jones Company (DJC). Gutnick claimed that Dow Jones defamed him when he was allegedly accused of money laundering in an Internet version of an article published online by the *Wall Street Journal,* DJC's flagship publication. The article supposedly portrayed Gutnick as a "con artist."

Gutnick filed suit in Australia, and the Australian lower court found that an Australian citizen may sue a U.S. company in Australia for allegedly defamatory remarks online. The court agreed with Gutnick and concluded that online articles have a global reach and are justly reviewable by Australian courts. The court specifically rejected DJC's argument that the article was published in New York and intended only for a U.S. audience. The court stated that DJC could have limited its online publications only to U.S. readers. DJC unsuccessfully contended that the proper jurisdiction was New Jersey, where the article was printed, not where the article was downloaded. The Australian High Court has heard the appeal and commentators believe the court will probably uphold the lower court's decision.

Internet Service Providers and International Acts of Defamation

Internet service providers (ISPs) have been uniquely vulnerable to defamation-related lawsuits from around the globe. As we discussed earlier, ISPs do not create defamatory statements but merely act as a conduit for the statements of subscribers. Some national courts liken the ISP to a newspaper publisher that is liable for defamation because it has actually "published" the defamatory material. A more effective analogy for an ISP would not be a newspaper publisher, but a mere newsstand. A newsstand is a mere transmitter of the material, and, recall, that under U.S. law would only be liable for defamation if it knew or should have known of the defamation.

Nevertheless, nations around the world are targeting ISPs as responsible for the material posted by their subscribers. Although the individual online defamer may be difficult or impossible to find, ISPs are a significant and easy target for international prosecution. Further, where individual users may have no international assets so as to be virtually judgment proof, ISPs with an international reach are vulnerable to fines, business disruption, and even criminal penalties in the nations in which they do business.

Fortunately for ISPs, many nations are starting to provide defenses by mere transmitters of defamatory statements that are similar to those provided by § 230 of the CDA. In the UK, the government curtailed ISP liability under the previously discussed Defamation Act of 1996. Section 1(1) of the act allows an ISP to avoid liability if the ISP (1) is not the author or publisher of the defamatory statement; (2) "took reasonable care in relation to its publication," and (3) "did not know, and had no reason to believe, that what [the ISP] did caused or contributed to the publication of a defamatory statement." The act also states that an entity is not the author or publisher if it is merely a provider of an electronic medium.

Japan appears to take a lenient approach to cyber-defamation. The Japanese Electronic Network Consortium and the Ministry of International Trade and Industry (MITI) have developed a series of guidelines that promote "public order and good morals" on the Internet. These guidelines state that a user should never post a defamatory statement online.

Nevertheless, the Japanese courts have faced their share of cyber-defamation disputes. In September 2001, the Japanese High Court examined the question of ISP liability in Japan. The plaintiff, a subscriber of the defendant ISP Niftyserve, participated in a forum discussion administrated and monitored by Niftyserve. After another participant posted defamatory antifeminist messages directed at the plaintiff, the plaintiff sued the participant and Niftyserve. The district court concluded that the systems administrator was not liable for failing to promptly delete the message. On appeal, the High Court reversed the decision, holding that a systems administrator is obligated to delete defamatory messages if the targeted person has no other remedy and countermeasures are ineffective.

http://

• To read further about Japan's Internet policies, see **http://www. ascusc.org/jcmc/vol2/issue2/ mashima.html**

Singapore represents the other end of the legal spectrum. There, ISPs are liable for content placed on the Internet. ISPs must register with the **Singapore Broadcasting Authority** (SBA). If the SBA requests cyber-records, the ISP must comply and turn them over. Also, if the SBA directs it to do so, an ISP must remove material detrimental to the public interest.

As these examples reveal, ISP liability varies widely from nation to nation. ISPs must take significant care to protect themselves by investigating the national laws where the ISP does business in order to avoid a flood of defamation lawsuits.

Defamation and the International Choice of Law

When a national court faces the claim of international defamation, the court must select which law to apply: its own, the foreign law where the defamation occurred, or some other national law. The following case highlights a discussion of a plaintiff's efforts to convince a U.S. court to apply English libel law for a message sent on the Internet.

Ellis v. Time
1997 WL 863267, 26 Media L. Rep. 1225 (D.D.C. 1997)

Facts

Richard Ellis, a professional photojournalist, is suing Time, Inc. (*Time*) for libel under American and English law and for intentional interference with business relations. Ellis claims that he was libeled by statements in a *Time* magazine editorial and in an e-mail message to *Time* editorial staff, and that *Time* caused him to be fired from his job. Ellis stated that *Time* published a series of photographs showing child prostitution in Russia that Ellis believed were fake. *Time*'s managing editor responded with a letter to its staff, stating in part, "My problem was never with [Ellis] raising the issue; any journalist who finds or suspects corrupt journalism has the duty to raise it. But Ellis never contacted us with his suspicions, and his attempt to get the pimp to change his story for the promise of money from *Time* is one of the tawdrier events I've witnessed in my years in journalism." Ellis filed defamation actions against *Time* in both U.S. and UK courts.

Judicial Opinion *(District Judge Johnson)*

In addition to his American libel law claims, plaintiff urges the Court to apply English libel law based on the publication in Britain of the allegedly defamatory statements. Unlike American libel law, English libel law places the burden of proof on the defendant to prove that its statements were true. See *McFarlane v. Sheridan Square Press*, 91 F.3d at 1512 (recognizing the different burdens of proof for libel in England and the United States). English law presumes that defamatory words are false and the plaintiff need do no more than prove that defamatory words have been published of him by the defendant; it is for the defendant to prove that the words are true, if he can. As a result, the libel defendant would be held liable for statements the defendant honestly believed to be true and published without any negligence. . . . In addition, English libel law does not require a plaintiff to prove that the libel defendant acted with malice. . . . Even a bona fide belief that the words are true does not constitute a defense. Thus, in dramatic contrast to American law, English law makes libel a strict liability offense.

The Court finds that applying English libel standards would violate the First Amendment's protection of free speech. To ensure the free exchange of ideas, a libel plaintiff must bear the burden of showing that the speech at issue is false. To do otherwise would only result in a deterrence of speech which the Constitution makes free. . . . [In addition,] "application of Indian defamation law or other foreign defamation laws at odds with the [F]irst [A]mendment could have a tremendous chilling effect." 719 F.Supp. at 677.

United States courts must apply rules of law consistent with the Constitution, regardless of where the alleged wrong occurs. Principles of international comity do not dictate otherwise: it is the choice, not the duty, of the United States to acknowledge the laws of another nation. When it is contrary to its policy or prejudicial to its interests, the United States must not apply foreign law. *Hilton v. Guyot,* 159 U.S. 113, 16 S.Ct. 139, 40 L.Ed. 95 (1895).

This Court will not apply English libel law and will grant judgment to defendant on Count three of the complaint.

Case Questions

1. How would the application of UK law in this case infringe on the U.S. Constitution?
2. Why would Ellis insist on applying UK law in this case? What advantages would it provide him?
3. What should *Time* have done in order to prevent this lawsuit from happening?

Summary

The tort of defamation occurs when a person speaks or writes an unprivileged false statement about another's reputation or business that results in damages either actual or presumed. It takes one of two forms. If oral, it is called *slander*; if written, it is called *libel*. Defamation published online is considered libel, not slander. The damages arise because the reputation of the plaintiff is diminished in the eyes of the community. The community may be relatively small, as in the case of a nonfamous or private individual, or it can be vast and without boundaries, as in the case of a public official or figure. The defenses of truth, absolute privilege, and qualified privilege may be available to a defendant in a defamation suit.

If the plaintiff is a private, nonfamous person, the plaintiff may, depending on the applicable state law, have to prove the defendant was negligent in determining whether the statements were true or not. A plaintiff qualifying as a public official or figure will have to prove the defendant was motivated by actual malice, a reckless disregard as to the truth or falsity of the statements made. Prior to the passage of § 230 of the Communications Decency Act (CDA) of 1996, online and Internet service providers could face liability for defamatory materials posted on the services if, as a *publisher,* they exercised control of the contents of the material, or as a *distributor,* they knew or should have known the contents of the material were defamatory.

In an attempt to allow service providers to develop technology that could prevent the publication of online defamation and other objectionable material, and to foster self-regulation, Congress enacted § 230 of the CDA. This section immunizes service providers from liability for defamation where a third party not under the service provider's employ furnished the published material. Immunity also extends where a service provider attempts to restrict access to or availability of material considered to be defamatory or objectionable.

There is a growing number of cases involving online anonymous defamatory speech that have required courts to balance free speech and press rights under the First Amendment with the rights of an individual or a business to determine the identity of and pursue remedies against those who defame them, albeit anonymously. Notwithstanding the fact that the First Amendment and anti-SLAPP laws protect a citizen's freedom to criticize government individuals or a business, SLAPP suits will continue to be brought mostly as a means to deter public comment.

Online defamation is also an international issue. The UK has been widely seen as a pro-plaintiff nation for defamation claims. Other nations are willing to assert jurisdiction over defamation claims made in cyberspace that relate to citizens of that nation. ISPs are particularly vulnerable to defamation claims because they are seen as the gateway for most defamatory statements. It may require many years, if ever, before nations gather and establish a unified policy toward defamatory materials online. Global issues associated with online defamation involve issues of conflict of laws, forum selection, and enforcement of judgments.

Key Terms

flaming, *345*

defamation, *345*

slander, *345*

libel, *345*

slander per se, *346*

absolute privilege, *347*

qualified privilege, *347*

Section 230 of the Communications Decency Act, *349*

SLAPP defamation suits, *357*

Defamation Act of 1996, *359*

Singapore Broadcasting Authority (SBA), *360*

Manager's Checklist

√ As with privacy and obscenity, employers should establish a company policy regarding the sending and publishing of defamatory e-mail messages.

√ Remind employees that they should not assume others cannot access their private e-mail messages even where such is not the intent of the employee. Remember that one speaks or publishes at his or her own peril.

√ Monitor employee e-mails to ensure they do not contain defamatory material that could lead to liability for the employer (as well as the employee).

√ Make sure that if you make statements of fact online about your competition or its goods or services, they do not contain defamatory material.

√ If a defamatory message has been published on company e-mail online, remove it and issue a retraction or apology as soon as possible.

√ If you are a service provider, engage the services of an independent contractor who will assume complete responsibility for controlling and monitoring the contents of all publications to be put online.

√ Remember that in most cases of defamation, speaking or writing the "truth" is an absolute defense.

√ Educate employees about the risks and potential liability for themselves, the company, and others for publishing defamatory messages on bulletin boards, in chat rooms, or in e-mails.

√ Include warnings in employee computer usage and monitoring policies that defamatory speech will not be tolerated.

√ Online businesses will be responsible for the statements placed on their Web site around the globe. Be sure a statement is true and complete before posting it online.

√ The general trend in developed nations is to limit the liability of ISPs for defamatory statements posted by their users. However, ISPs should still have an aggressive antidefamation policy and remove such material whenever it is found.

√ **Ethical Considerations**

While some believe that limiting anonymous speech in cyberspace would better protect society from attacks on reputation, others maintain that to do so would stifle the free exchange of ideas even if some were objectionable. Which view would be better for society?

Case Problems

1. The plaintiff of Pennsylvania operates an offshore betting Web site incorporated in and operating out of Jamaica. The defendant of New York operates Canadian and Australian Web sites on which sports and gambling information is posted. On one of his sites, the defendant posts an article about the plaintiff in which he accuses him of having a "dark past" that includes "two murders." The plaintiff wishes to sue the defendant for defamation in a federal district court for Pennsylvania. What will he have to prove in order for the court to have personal jurisdiction over the defendant? Will he be successful? [*Sports Betting, Inc., v. Tostigan*, 2002 WL 461592 (E.D. Pa. 2002)]

2. Defendant calls the plaintiff a "liar" in a public online forum. The plaintiff sues the defendant, alleging in his complaint that the posting constituted a personal attack that could damage his reputation because it was archived on the Internet. The defendant responds by stating that she and the plaintiff were engaging in a "flame war" where people regularly exchange insults during heated discussions. How should the court decide? [*McCarthy v. McCahan*, Superior Court, San Francisco, March 31, 1998]

3. Schneider is the author of several books on how to save taxes and protect assets. Amazon sells books online and lets users of its Web site post book

reviews about the books it sells. Amazon has guidelines for such reviews and has the right to remove reviews from its Web site. Ten anonymous reviews highly critical of Schneider's books are posted. Schneider's employee informs Amazon of the reviews and it promises but fails to remove them. Schneider seeks to hold Amazon liable for publishing the reviews. Amazon claims immunity under § 230 of the CDA. What was the result? [*Schneider v. Amazon.com, Inc.*, 31 P. 3d 37 (Wash. Ct. App. 2001)]

4. Plaintiff, Ben Ezra, Weinstein and Company, filed a suit against the defendant, America Online (AOL), for allegedly publishing false and defamatory information regarding the value of its stock. It appears that the value of the plaintiff's stock was inaccurately reported on AOL's interactive computer service called "Quotes and Portfolios." All of the stock information that alleged to be erroneous was provided by two separate companies, ComStock and Townsend. Evidence is presented indicating that AOL communicated often with these companies each time there was an error and attempted to have the errors corrected. Plaintiff claims AOL should not enjoy the immunity granted to service providers by § 230 of the CDA. Instead, they should be considered "an information content provider" because they "knowingly and repeatedly" published incorrect information causing damage to the plaintiff. Is AOL entitled to the immunity granted under § 230 of the CDA? [*Ben Ezra, Weinstein and Company, Inc. v. America Online, Inc.* No. Civ. 97-LH/LFG (D. N. M., Mar. 1, 1999)], aff'd. 206 F.3d 980 (10th Cir., Mar. 14, 2000, cert. denied, 531 U.S. 824, Oct. 2, 2000)]

5. Plaintiffs are doctors who operate a Web site called Quackwatch that exposes health-related fraud and medical quackery. The defendant is an advocate of alternative medicine who maintains and operates an Internet discussion group, alt.support.breast-implant, to which she has posted more than eight thousand messages since the middle of 1999. A number of alleged defamatory statements posted by the defendant and others ("John Does") accused the plaintiffs of being "quacks," "arrogant," and "bullies who tried to extort the defendant." The defendant also re-posted on her site a message she received from Usenet newsgroups accusing one of the plaintiffs of "stalking women." The plaintiffs sue for defamation. The defendants claim the statements were criticism related to matters of public concern and should be protected as free speech. They seek a motion to dismiss the suit under the state's anti-SLAPP law. What was the result? Would the defendant be liable for defamation as a result of the re-posted message? [*Barrett v. Clark*, 2001 WL 881259 (Cal. Super. Ct. 2001)]

6. An anonymous user posted a message containing obscene and defamatory content through an ISP. The target of the message, Dr. Laurence Godfrey, sued Demon Internet, Inc., an ISP in England, under the UK Defamation Act of 1996. Godfrey claimed the ISP should be responsible for the defamatory

messages posted through its servers. What was the result? [*Godfrey v. Demon Internet Ltd.*, 1999 E.M.L.R. 542, 149 NLJ 609 (Mar. 26, 1999)]

Additional Readings

- Dwyer, Henry. "Online Rumors Can Be Damaging and Hard to Quell." *Mass. High Tech, The Journal of New England Technology* 19:53 (January 6, 2002).

- Fifer, Samuel, and Sachs, Michael. "The Price of International Free Speech: Nations Deal with Defamation on the Internet." *DePaul-LCA Journal of Art and Entertainment Law* 1 (1997): 8.

- Kaplan, Carl S. "French Decision Prompts Questions About Free Speech and Cyberspace." *New York Times* (February 11, 2002).

INTERNET AND INFORMATION SECURITY

The protection of information is one of the most valuable assets of an organization, and is critical to the operation of a . . . business. An increasing number of businesses rely on information technology for storing, processing and communicating information. Information security provides a sound foundation for business success by safeguarding financial and customer records, and business strategies. It serves to protect against threats and vulnerabilities and to ensure business continuity.

—*"FBI, SBA and Commerce Department Form Alliance," News Release on the Alliance to Promote Information Technology Security for America's Small Businesses, June 12, 2002* (http://www.nipc.gov)

LEARNING OBJECTIVES

After you have read this chapter, you should be able to:

1. Explain the goals of information security in businesses.
2. Describe the various methods for achieving security.
3. Explain how cryptography works.
4. Explain how steganography works.
5. Understand the bases for legal challenges to cryptography.
6. Understand the privacy and law enforcement implications when securing data.
7. Describe how the government attempts to regulate information security products
8. Understand how information security has application to many other areas, such as privacy, digital rights management, and e-commerce.
9. Discuss efforts to harmonize international law related to network and information security.
10. Understand various national and international laws relating to encryption and cryptography systems.

http://

- Additional material relevant to this chapter may be found at the Bentley College CyberLaw Center Web site (**http://ecampus.bentley. edu/dept/cyberlaw**) under Social Issues—Internet and Information Security.

INTRODUCTION

We have transformed our economy into one in which information is as valuable an asset as physical assets. This information age has been made possible by the Internet. As individuals and businesses have migrated to the Internet, the urgent need for security of both information and information technology has rapidly gained momentum. This is due to the reality that although strengths are gained by this interconnectedness, the vulnerabilities of computer systems and information are greatly increased as well. The industry of computer and information security is thriving, as ever more transactions are conducted over the Internet. This chapter discusses the legal and ethical environment of Internet and information security. These legal challenges to information security involve the First, Fourth, and Fifth Amendments, and they impact as well the evolving right of privacy.

THE CHALLENGES OF INTERNET AND INFORMATION SECURITY

The U.S. Computer Emergency Response Team (CERT) estimates that in 2001 there were 530 million Internet users, and that number should reach 1 billion by 2005. The number of Internet host computers—those that store information and relay communications—presently numbers 200 million. Domain names, as well as World Wide Web sites, have increased astronomically. This emergence of computer technologies has created new ways to access information, even such information not intended to be accessed. For example, even as early as 1995 the Pentagon reported suffering 250,000 attacks on its computers; 65 percent of those represented attempts to gain entry to its network. In 1999, Microsoft had to shut down service for its 40 million Hotmail users after it was tipped off about a security vulnerability that left every account freely accessible. In 2002, new computer viruses are rising at a rate of a thousand per month. The viruses are increasingly hearty, virulent, and destructive. Moreover, many are created and unleashed by teens and/or originate offshore, both of which create special challenges for businesses and, ultimately, law enforcement. And with the ability to communicate anonymously, this further complicates the situation. Despite legislative efforts to address many computer offenses, the global interconnection of computers overwhelms any individual business or country's efforts to completely secure computers and networks. Such an immense problem as Internet and information security is not lost on the general population and is usually the principal impediment cited for *not* conducting more transactions over the Internet.

The security of systems, network, information, and information technology is a goal for every network user. The efforts to secure information and transactions is an outgrowth of the law and values of privacy, in which there has developed a body of law protecting individuals from unauthorized access into certain confidential matters.

Information security is broadly defined as the ability to control access to computers, networks, hardware, software, and data. It includes the ability to protect computers and systems from intentional or accidental disclosure, modification, or destruction of proprietary systems or information. It also protects computers and systems from being used as instruments for malicious or illegal activities. The challenge, of course, is how to ensure usability, privacy, and security of protected proprietary information when it is being sent/transmitted by way of the Internet, which is a public network. The problem of information security has come to the forefront of e-business concerns, and for good reason. A 1999 survey confirmed that companies conducting e-business are 57 percent more likely to experience a leak of proprietary information than are brick-and-mortar businesses and 24 percent more likely to experience a hacking-related breach. These complications are directly related to the changes that have occurred in our communications systems. For example, business conducted 150 years ago was conducted in person or by letter. After the telephone was introduced, this became another usual method of conducting business. Telephone calls, like letters, could be intercepted by third parties, but there was still an acceptable level of security. With the advent of wireless communications and public networks, however, the ability to secure communications by ensuring their privacy and integrity is seriously compromised today.

In this era, persons conducting business with each other may not even know what the other person looks or sounds like—these are details from a bygone era. Now individuals are simply relying on perhaps passwords or e-mail addresses as confirmation that the transaction took place and was valid. This is indeed a world away from the time when business was conducted face to face and consummated by a handshake. Now the Internet has developed into the medium of choice for a myriad of complex transactions and communications. This migration of commerce to the Internet surely was not foreseen by the original architects of the Internet. Developed a generation ago as a way to facilitate communications between academic researchers, there was no consideration given to information security matters. This open and public architecture of the Internet, while creating perhaps the greatest public forum and democratizing force in history, is not at all well suited to the communication of private or proprietary information. In fact, the Internet has been characterized as one big party line. The Internet is certainly not security driven. Consequently, an industry whose mission is to find ways to keep information secure has been created to patch security measures onto the very public Internet. The size and magnitude of security issues will rise dramatically in this decade. So will the legal challenges to business and government and individual efforts to control information as well as to access it.

http://▶

- **http://www.cert.org** is a federally funded center for Internet security research.
- **http://www.nipc.gov** is home to the government's national computer and network infrastructure protection center.

THE GOALS OF INTERNET AND INFORMATION SECURITY

Hackers, crackers, snackers, computer forensics, Internet filtering, malicious mobile code, macros and viruses, worms, logic bombs (all forms of malware), plus computer voyeurism, eavesdropping, theft, tampering, forgery, interception—these are fast becoming the subject of government scrutiny and regulation (see Figure 12.4; refer also to Chapter 13 for a more complete discussion of Internet crimes). The interconnectedness and openness of systems worldwide to the Internet poses unprecedented security and privacy challenges our current legal system generally is not well equipped to handle. Because we are tied together by the Internet, we are vulnerable to the same security breaches. Moreover, this issue is exacerbated by two factors: (1) the users' relatively low level of competence/experience in computer and Internet technology; and (2) the fact that the vast majority of the users work with the same Microsoft hardware and software, which increases the transfer speed of malware. Such a proposition demands coordinated security regulations as well as cooperation at the international, federal, and state levels.

As with a home, security breaches occur because there are points of entry. Even though steps are taken to secure these points, they are still not 100 percent safe from intrusion. It is theoretically possible to make a 100 percent secure entry point, but if this scenario features an overload of security devices, it probably would not be usable. Like much else, there are trade-offs between ease of use, privacy, and security. And so it is with information security and the Internet. The Internet was developed with free and open communications, rather than security, as its goal. Yet as business has migrated to the Internet, security measures are, out of necessity, being patched onto the system, but with imperfect results. For if the Internet was to be made 100 percent secure, communications would slow to an unacceptable pace; therefore the Internet functions today with a relative level of security, in which the values of speed and usability have taken precedence over the value of security. Experts continually marvel that the Internet is not brought to its knees more often. The security problem inherent in protecting information on the Internet will never abate if the structure of the system remains the same. It is an open architecture system, with intense commercial pressures to get products to market, where the vast majority of users are generally novices. The software systems being created are typically *buggy*. Hardware, as well as software in many instances, is built on the fly and shipped half formed, in beta-test mode, where customers become free software testers.

It is important at the outset to understand that no means of communications is totally secure, and there are some levels of risk to all of our communications. With this in mind, the goals of information security are to control communications to ensure the following:

- Confidentiality
- Authenticity
- Integrity of *each* electronic communication but accomplished within an environment that also features system usability

First, confidentiality, or privacy, of communications and data must be assured in order to maintain the value of the content and the system itself. Second, verifying the authenticity of users is critical, for otherwise the information and system has no value. Authentication has three possible components: something you know, something you have, or something you are. Finally, maintaining integrity of the data is crucial and ensures that the information is what it is supposed to be. For if these criteria are not met, there is no security and the risk of loss of proprietary information is unacceptably high. The business environment, however, is changing faster than the security industry—and still even faster than the legal environment. To remain competitive, companies need to do business electronically with remote partners, vendors, employees, consultants, and clients. With all of these users accessing the business from different points of entry, especially business partners, it is nearly impossible to determine where one company ends and the next begins. The more virtual a business becomes, the greater its chances of responding to market demands and succeeding competitively. The risk, of course, is that a virtual business will be dangerously insecure.

The goals of confidentiality, authenticity, and integrity of communications from "end to end"—that is, among users, Internets, intranets, extranets, and ISPs—must be balanced with the reality of usability. People must be able to use a system and data efficiently and not be overly burdened with layers upon layers of computer security protections. Security thus must be balanced with usability.

Securing the Internet for business and personal use without sacrificing efficiency and usability is a major aspect of the computer security discussed here. But there is another, more public, issue involved—that of government security. Considered government's most basic role, law enforcement, military, and intelligence-gathering functions rely on access to data and communications. A central problem, though, is that with everybody having access to information security products, most communications are becoming so secure as to render them impenetrable.

Thus highly secure programs and information used for illegitimate purposes thwart the rule of law and ultimately undermine the utility and desirability of the public Internet network. The reach of governmental entities into areas of computer surveillance and security such as encryption is an important and divisive subject in the field of computer and information security. The public aspects of computer security implicate constitutional rights, and there currently exists a conflict of opinion on these issues.

More complex personal and business uses of the Internet will grow only to the extent that usability and security are reasonably assured, but this level of security possibly impedes security and law enforcement functions of governments. It is therefore an understatement to say that the computer and information security industry faces enormous challenges.

Methods and Legal Challenges to Ensuring Enterprise and Communications Security

A vast and increasingly sophisticated computer security industry has developed for businesses in response to the critical need to secure electronic data and systems. Its goals are to protect computers, systems, and data from viruses, eavesdropping, hacking, theft, tampering, forgery, and interception. These needs are particularly important to the extent that the information is, for example, financial (such as credit card numbers), privileged (such as between attorneys and clients), or otherwise proprietary (such as business communications about products that are being developed).

And although there might be security at the client level, it cannot be presumed at the system level. The risks of security breaches are even greater as the public Internet network evolves into the standard mode for business communications. Figure 12.1 lists the top ten security products. Two major categories, or bands, of security have evolved: firewall systems and commercial security systems.

Firewalls. Firewall security systems could be compared to the medieval security plan of a moat. The moat served to guard the inside of the building, allowing entry only

**FIGURE 12.1   The Top Ten Security Products in 1999
                 (beginning with the most popular)**

1. Firewalls

2. Access Controls

3. Client/Server Security

4. LAN/WAN Security

5. Web Security

6. Disaster Recovery

7. Network/Communications Security

8. E-mail Security

9. Encryption

10. Mainframe Security

to authorized individuals through selected gateways. A **firewall** is a system or group of systems that enforces an access control policy between two networks to either block or to permit access. It protects against unauthorized and unauthenticated log-ins and at the same time permits authorized log-ins. Additionally, firewalls have logging and audit features to further ensure security. Firewalls allow for creation of private intranets and networks known as *virtual private networks* (VPNs). In a typical scenario, companies use intranets to post information that only networked employees or partners may access.

Although such a system is not effective against *internal* security threats, it does effectively secure the system from unauthorized *external* threats to entry and access. Although there is not yet any litigation involving firewalls, it is foreseeable where the vulnerabilities are. A defective firewall system, like any other product, is a liability problem for the manufacturers, vendors, and users.

http://

- For more on firewalls, see **http://www.cs.purdue.edu/coast/firewalls**

Those who enter a computer system protected by a firewall may be liable for this unauthorized entry under both state and federal law. In fact, state and federal lawmakers have been continually amending and updating laws to encompass liability for computers acts. The evolving state of laws is discussed later in this chapter. Firewalls are invaluable at protecting a network of computers from outside intrusions, but to the extent that the security breach is from within the organization, they offer no security.

Transactional Security Systems

A firewall can be compared to a moat, and a commercial security scheme could be compared to a truck going through checkpoints at every stage of its journey—from loading, to its driver, the route, to the destination point, and finally, to unloading. A firewall could be considered security of the building itself, and transactional security systems could be considered securing checkpoints along the route while traveling to and from the building—it is analogous to a chain of security. Currently a myriad of commercial security systems are being developed, tested, and marketed, all of which attempt to secure data and information transmitted between businesses, intermediaries, and clients. The goal of transactional security systems is to protect the integrity of the data as it is being transmitted through managing the identities of all parties, as well as authenticating them. First we discuss the principal modes of ensuring commercial computer security. Major emphasis in this chapter is on cryptography and the legal issues it has created.

Password Protection/Script-Based Single Sign-On (SSO). Password protection is probably the primary form of security we recognize. It is reflected in the ubiquitous name and password requests that appear in the workplace and in e-commerce transactions. This method for managing identity information and authenticating users is generally considered easy, but does not offer a high level of security. Moreover, in practice it is a time-consuming security measure due to the phenomenon of forgotten names and/ or passwords. This form of information security is easy to breach and results in impediments to productivity as well as profits.

Certificate Authorities (CAs) and Digital Certificates (DCs). There is another security method for managing identities and authenticating users. **Certificate authorities (CAs)** are trusted third-party organizations that issue and manage security credentials. CAs are responsible for guaranteeing that the individuals or businesses granted the **digital certificates (DCs)** are in fact who they say they are. They validate identity as well as authority. Clearly CAs are critical to the success of e-commerce. CAs are currently centralized by industry and have a wide range of applications, such as e-mail, browsers, and VPNs. CAs issue the DCs, also known as electronic credentials, or digital IDs. DCs permit the electronic identification of users to each other. They act as a digital ID or passport, and only those who can authenticate their identities over the Internet may access the secure data. Moreover, attribute certificates can be created within DCs, and so even authenticated users are limited to certain data. As an example, the payroll manager may be authorized through his or her digital certificate to check on which benefits employees selected for deduction purposes, but the attribute certificate would not allow access to other aspects of that employee's profile such as job performance history.

Biometrics. **Biometrics** is a security method designed to authenticate users by employing technologies that capture immutable human characteristics, again to secure the identification and authentication of users. Commercially available biometrics products at this time include face, iris, retina, voice, or signature, fingerprint, hand geometry, and vein. (Other features currently being investigated are brain waves and eye movements.) Biometric technology has long been used in law enforcement and most recently has been introduced by government agencies to process and verify welfare recipients. For example, biometrics technology creates a record of a person's physical

►http://

- **http://www.itaa.org/infosec** is home to an information security industry group and **http://www.securitypanel.org** is an Internet security portal site.
- **http://www.biometrics.org** is a biometrics consortium site and **http://www.icsalabs.com** is a commercial site offering managed security services.

characteristics, and only that person possessing those exact traits may conduct the transaction. Clearly this technology is superior to a password-based system, for example, but there are risks. And because authentication technology requires users to do more and reveal more, privacy concerns are heightened. There is a story that circulates—about a mugger, who came upon a person using an ATM that featured fingerprint ID technology—so the mugger simply chopped off the victim's finger to authenticate the transaction and access the money. (In reality, though, biometrics technology is too sophisticated for this to happen.) Since the 9/11 terrorist action, interest in biometrics as well as other authentication technologies has soared. Dozens of airports are testing face-scanning technology that checks images against databases of suspects. Malls and other retailers are the next likely tier of buyers for these technologies.

Other Ways to Secure Transactions. There are several other methods to secure transactions. These include tokens, smart cards, holography, processor serial numbers, time-stamping digital signatures, and electronic signatures.

Security Tokens (also known as* digipasses).*** **Security tokens** are another means to authenticate users and secure transactions. These usually augment common passwords by generating a random code number unique to each transaction. Available to interface with either software or hardware, the latter application has recently gained momentum because it supports PKI (discussed next). Taking advantage of the universal serial bus (USB) port, a token the size of a house key is inserted. The computer reads the token that is embedded with passwords and certificates. It is thus a handheld password generator.

Smart Cards. **Smart cards** are similar to tokens but have the added feature of portability—they store digital credentials and can store and retrieve data. For example, employees with smart cards may access the same secure data from offsite computers as they can from computers at the workplace. Smart cards are physically similar to credit cards and contain embedded processors and operating systems. Smart cards are featured in more than 30 million cellular telephones to handle security information. Other possible applications include use in credit cards, bank cards, and as electronic purses.

Holography. Security **holography** products are in high demand at this time. Holographic images can be embossed or incorporated into a photopolymer process. They can be apparent or they may be hidden (such as with the use of infrared ink). Current applications include use on credit cards, ID badges, videocassettes, and CDs. These are usually in the form of hot-stamped foil rainbow-colored wrappers. Tampering with these can immediately expose trademark infringements, product piracy, and counterfeit or gray-market goods.

Processor Serial Numbers in Every CPU. Using **processor serial numbers** as a security element enhances control of information. For example, current serial number technology in which information is embedded into each computer's processing chip has the potential to provide digital signing, time stamping, and secure archiving, along with the feature of *nonrepudiation*. This feature ensures that parties to a contract or communication cannot later deny the authenticity of their signature or that they are the sender of a message or document.

This technology is being hailed by industry as a much-needed authentication element, especially in the many instances when simple passwords offer insufficient security.

http:// ◄

- **http://www.scia.org**
- **http://www.securityholograms.com** is a commercial site that promotes security holograms and **http://www. psynch.com/security/tokens.html** is a commercial site that promotes security tokens to authenticate network services.

Public Key Infrastructure (PKI). **Public key infrastructure (PKI)** represents the integration of software, cryptography, and other services, including CAs that enables the enterprise to achieve optimal systemwide Internet and information security. PKI is the most secure system to date—that is, considering we are patching onto the open architecture of the Internet a series of security measures. With the combination of cryptography and digital certificates, data is secured in four important ways:

- Authentication: that a verified individual (rather than an impersonator) sent the message
- Integrity: that a certain message was sent by the verified individual—unaltered along the way
- Cryptography: the encrypted message serves as a digital signature for the message, and it may be decrypted only by the intended recipient
- Token verification/biometrics/smart cards: these replace name/password log-ons and are an easier more secure option

Although layers of security are desirable and an effective way to control risk, there is an equally critical need for usability as well as interoperability between systems and users. PKI extends business systems securely so clients, partners, and suppliers can function without problems of system incompatibility. Its potential uses include managing privacy, confidentiality, access control, and proof of transmission.

http:// ◄

- A few helpful Web sites on PKI include **http://samsara.law.cwru. edu/comp_law/jvd/** and **http://pki-page.org/**

Cryptography. The previous discussion of Internet and information security mainly dealt with authentication security. This discussion of **cryptography** necessarily focuses on the confidentiality aspect of security. Cryptography has been in use for at least 2,500 years. It does not hide the presence of data, but rather renders it incoherent, or unreadable, until the intended reader deciphers it. Cryptography is a system of coding and then decoding the message.

The first step in cryptography is the **encryption** of the data. An encryption program acts to take the data, known as *plaintext*, and by using a mathematical algorithm, it codes/scrambles the data into a different format known as *ciphertext*. The data only become readable to those possessing the means of **decryption** that will decode the ciphertext—through use of a key that solves the encryption algorithm—back to readable plaintext.

It is important to understand the historical military applications of cryptography, in order to grasp the complexities of the present legal environment of encryption regulation. Cryptography was used to guard classified military information, and for example, it played an important role in the communication of messages by the Axis forces during World War II. Through their Enigma machine, the Allies' "Ultra" Project team managed to decrypt/break enemy code and thereby gain access to their classified information. Cryptography had no civil or commercial applications, and until 1996 it was classified as munitions, under jurisdiction of the State Department's Office of Defense Trade Controls. Because of this history, the U.S. government alone controlled cryptography.

The government monopoly over encryption worked on a single key system (also known as private key or symmetric encryption) in which the same key was used to encrypt, as well as decrypt, communications. Commercial applications of cryptography began in the 1980s due to two factors: computers and the Internet. The former represents the digitization of content, and the latter represents the transfer of content. Responding to this broader use of cryptography, then president Clinton, through Executive Order 13026 (61 Federal Register 58767, 1996), transferred jurisdiction of nonmilitary commercial cryptographic products to the Commerce Department.

This private key cryptography system became much less workable to the extent that a myriad of decentralized nongovernment commercial entities began using cryptography as the core of their information security strategy. The demand for encryption is clearly great. Current uses include professional, commercial, and consumer markets that need secure communications about private, sensitive information between perhaps anonymous individuals—such as online credit card purchases or securing loans.

In 1976, cryptographers Whitfield Duffie (now an engineer at Sun Microsystems) and Martin Hellman invented the theory that it is possible for someone to announce the precise method of coding a message while at the same time retaining a secret private key for decoding it. In 1977, three mathematicians at MIT (Ronald Rivest, Adi Shamir, and Leonard Adleman) patented their RSA Algorithm, turning the Diffie-Hellman concept into a practical application: the public asymmetrical two-key encryption system in use today. The sender and receiver of information do not share the same key, but rather, the parties use their own keys that are mathematically related, but not discoverable to each other. Public key encryption systems work particularly well for the millions of anonymous commercial users.

Encryption and decryption have improved in practice and have become extremely strong, or secure. This is done by increasing the complexity and thus the key length through the introduction of more bits. At this time, the recommended key length is 1,024 bits. Any keys shorter than that are vulnerable to hacking and other attacks.

►http://

- See **http://www.nsa.gov/museum/tour.html**, the national Cryptologic Museum's site.
- The National Institute of Standards and Technology's Computer Security Resource Center is responsible for developing a uniform encryption standard. See **http://csrc.nist.gov/encryption/aes/**
- **http://www.rsasecurity.com/** is a commercial e-security site.

Cryptography makes it possible to control access points and authorization of end users, transfer users, control the timing and length of access to data, track users, and vary the level of security within documents. This outstanding level of control through cryptography is all the more remarkable when you consider the information is posted on a publicly accessible Web site, yet is off limits except to intended users (see Figure 12.2).

http://

- For a try at decoding a message, see **http://www.archives.gov/ digital_classroom/lessons/ zimmermann_telegram/decoding_ activity.html**

A number of legal issues have developed out of the commercial uses of cryptography. Most importantly, the question of whether cryptography is speech or mere computer source code implicates First Amendment rights. The second and related question is how much power the government has to regulate the export of cryptography software. Third, there is a heated controversy over Fourth Amendment rights of privacy and law enforcement regarding the issue of surveillance, as well as government efforts to access decryption/decoding keys.

Finally, government cryptography regulations implicate individuals' Fifth Amendment rights. The legal and ethical environment of cryptography is dynamic, and presently there is no consensus on these important issues.

First Amendment

Is cryptography speech? The importance of this question lies in the fact that speech or expression enjoys **First Amendment** protections from undue government regulation. If cryptography is considered speech or expression, the Constitution guarantees that the government may not unduly control the speech. To complicate things more,

---

FIGURE 12.2   Creating a Secure Message Using Public Key Cryptography

---

First: Sender defines message to be sent.

Second: Sender's software uses an algorithm (known as a *hash function*) to create a digital "freeze frame" of the message. This transformed message is known as a *hash result,* or a message digest.

Third: Sender's software combines the hash result with the sender's private key. This key creates a digital signature unique to that message and key.

Fourth: Sender transmits the message and digital signature over the Internet.

Fifth: Recipient's software receives the message and applies the same hash function as above to the message. This produces a new hash result from the message. This result is compared to the hash result contained within the digital signature. If the two results are identical, the message has not been tampered with.

Sixth: Recipient uses the public key to verify that sender's digital signature was created with the corresponding private key. This confirms that the sender is authentic and the message originated from there.

---

different types of speech merit different levels of First Amendment protection (recall the discussion from Chapter 10, "Obscenity"). In cryptography cases, the essential points being alleged by individuals in possession of cryptography programs are that these programs are protected speech and they are regulated in ways that violate these individuals' First Amendment rights.

The following case highlights one of the commercial applications of cryptography as a way to control use of DVDs. It considers the level of First Amendment protection appropriate for cryptography programs.

Universal City Studios, Inc., Paramount Pictures, Metro-Goldwyn-Mayer, Tristar Pictures, Columbia Pictures, Time Warner Entertainment, Disney Enterprises, Twentieth Century Fox v. Corley
273 F.3d 429 (2nd Cir. 2001 3-Judge Panel Decision)
(as amended January 2002)
Petition for en banc *review filed January 14, 2002*

Facts

CSS

Plaintiffs, eight major U.S. motion picture studios, distribute many of their copyrighted motion pictures for home use on digital versatile disks (DVDs), which contain digital copies of their films. For decades, studios made movies available in analog format. Digital formatting of films became possible with the development of the MPEG-4 technology. The studios were reluctant to use digital format until they first created adequate safeguards against piracy of their copyrighted films. Members of the electronic and computer industries created the Content Scrambling System (CSS) in 1996 (incidentally protected as a trade secret). It is an encryption scheme that employs an algorithm configured by a set of keys to encrypt/ scramble the audio and video contents of DVDs. The contents are decrypted and thus rendered readable by (1) a set of "player keys" contained in compliant DVD players, and (2) a decryption algorithm. A DVD player can display the film but does not give users the ability to use the copy function of the computer to copy the film or to manipulate the digital contents of the DVD. The studios developed a licensing strategy for distributing the technology to manufacturers of DVD players—they were charged a fee and given the player keys and necessary information. In return, they were obliged to keep the player keys confidential. The studios began releasing DVDs in 1997. In 1998, the studios secured added protection against DVD piracy when Congress passed the DMCA, which prohibits the development or use of technology designed to circumvent technological protection measures—such as CSS. But the judge stated that the record is unclear how CSS protects against the *copying* of DVDs—as contrasted with the *playing* of DVDs, on unlicensed players.

DeCSS

In September 1999, Jon Johansen, a Norwegian teenager, along with two other unidentified individuals he met on the Internet, reverse-engineered a licensed DVD player designed to operate on the Microsoft operating system and culled from it the player keys and other information necessary to decrypt CSS. The record suggests that Johansen was trying to develop a DVD player operable on Linux, an alternative system that did not support any licensed DVD players at that time. In order to accomplish this, Johansen wrote a decryption program executable on Microsoft's operating system, called DeCSS. If a users runs DeCSS with a DVD in the disk drive, DeCSS will automatically decrypt the DVD's CSS protection, allowing the user to copy the DVD's files and place them on the user's hard drive. The quality of the decrypted film is identical to that of the original. Additionally, the file can be compressed with compression software, such as the DivX program, available for free on the Internet. Thereafter, the compressed file can easily be copied onto a DVD—or transferred over the Internet. Johansen posted the executable object code (the "1s and 0s")—but not the source code (computer languages, such as BASIC, C, etc.) for DeCSS on his Web site.

The DMCA

The act contains three provisions targeted at the circumvention of technological protections. The second, 1201(a)(2), is at issue in this case. It focuses on those who traffic in measures that control *access* to a protected work. It provides,

> No person shall manufacture, import, offer to the public, provide, or otherwise traffic in any technology, product, service, device . . . that—

> (A) is primarily designed or produced for the purpose of circumventing a technological measure that effectively controls access to a work;

> (B) has only limited commercially significant purpose or use other then to circumvent; or

> (C) is marketed by that person . . . for use in circumventing.

The Defendants

In November 1999, Defendant Corley wrote and placed on his Web site *http://www. 2600.com*, an article about DeCSS. 2600.com covers issues of interest to hackers and vulnerabilities of computer security systems. At the end of the article, Corley posted copies of the object and source code of DeCSS. 2600.com was only one of hundreds of sites that began posting the DeCSS program, or mirrors of it. Plaintiffs sought an injunction against defendants, alleging they violated the DMCA. The trial court ruled in favor of plaintiffs and granted their request for a permanent injunction forbidding defendants from posting, linking, or otherwise trafficking in DeCSS. The court concluded that computer code like DeCSS is speech that is protected/covered by the First Amendment—but that because the DMCA is targeting the *functional* aspect of that speech, it is content neutral, and intermediate scrutiny applies. The court found that the DMCA survives this scrutiny. Defendants appealed.

Judicial Opinion *(Judge Newman)*

This appeal raises significant First Amendment issues concerning one aspect of computer technology—encryption to protect materials in digital form from unauthorized access. These issues . . . are whether computer code is speech, whether computer programs are speech, the scope of First Amendment protection for computer code, and the scope of First Amendment protection for decryption code. We then consider the Appellants' challenge to the injunction's provisions concerning posting and linking. [The court found computer code and computer programs, because they convey information, are considered "speech" within the meaning of the First Amendment. The court next considers the scope of protection for this speech.]

Content-based restrictions [on speech] are permissible only if they serve compelling state interests and do so by the least restrictive means available. A content-neutral restriction is permissible if it serves a substantial governmental interest, the interest is unrelated to the suppression of free expression, and the regulation is narrowly tailored, which in this context requires . . . that the means chosen do not burden substantially more speech than is necessary to further the government's legitimate interests. [Appellants argue that code is pure speech deserving the most stringent protection and] that code is no different, for First Amendment purposes, than blueprints . . . or recipes. We disagree. Unlike a blueprint or a recipe, which cannot yield any functional result without human comprehension of its content, human decision-making, and human action, computer code can instantly cause a computer to accomplish tasks and instantly render the results throughout the world. The only human action required . . . can be as limited and instantaneous as a single click of a mouse. These realities . . . require a First Amendment analysis that treats code as combining nonspeech and speech elements. [DeCSS is a function, yet it is also a form of communication.] Here, dissemination itself carries very substantial risk of imminent harm. The functionality of computer code properly affects the scope of its First Amendment protection.

[Therefore the Court applies the intermediate scrutiny test to each of the posting and linking challenges for evaluating whether to uphold the challenged burden on speech. That test is usually in the form of this analysis: does the burden on speech serve a substantial government interest, and the means chosen do not burden substantially more speech than is necessary to further the government's legitimate interests?]

Posting

The initial issue is whether the posting prohibition is content-neutral, since . . . this classification determines the applicable constitutional standard. The Appellant's argument [that the DMCA targets their expression] fails to recognize that the posting prohibition . . . is content-neutral *i.e.*, without reference to the content of the regulated speech. As a content-neutral regulation with an incidental effect on a speech component, the regulation must serve a substantial governmental interest, the incidental restriction on speech must not burden substantially more speech than is necessary to further that interest. The Government's interest in preventing unauthorized access to encrypted copyrighted material is unquestionably substantial and the regulation of DeCSS by the posting prohibition plainly serves that interest. Moreover, that interest is unrelated to the suppression of free expression.

Linking

In applying the DMCA to linking, [the trial court judge] recognized, as he had with DeCSS code, that a hyperlink has both a speech and a non-speech component. It conveys information, the Internet address of the linked web page, and has the functional capacity to bring the content of the linked web page. [This court agreed that] the DMCA, as applied to the Defendants' linking, served substantial governmental interests and was unrelated to the suppression of free expression. This reality obliges courts considering First Amendment claims in the context of the pending case to choose between two unattractive alternatives: either tolerate some impairment of communication in order to permit Congress to prohibit decryption that may lawfully be prevented, or tolerate some decryption in order to avoid some impairment of communication.

[The District Court's] judgment is affirmed.

Case Questions

1. What is the practical effect of finding that cryptography is a form of speech? expression, just as demonstrations are a form of speech?

2. Do you personally think the three-judge panel of the Second Circuit was correct in applying an intermediate-level scrutiny analysis to this case?

3. What are the effects of this decision for other individuals as well as Web site operators?

The DMCA is an extremely powerful far-reaching legislative initiative that effectively blocks a quite a lot of speech/expression—under the guise of protecting industry's technical protection measures. DMCA measures effectively erase fair use rights and, in fact, criminalize circumvention measures in some instances. The government has filed charges in the first criminal case brought under this statute, in the *United States v. Sklyarov and Elcomsoft* case. (Refer to Chapter 13, "Internet and Computer Crime," for further discussion of this case.)

The speech aspect of cryptography has special implications for the nonprofit academic community, which is a true laboratory for this endeavor. Cryptographic research and information is routinely posted on Web sites for others to critique and comment on, and perhaps to decode as a way of testing its merits. There is a difference of opinion on whether or to what extent the government will regulate this type of speech. In one recent case, a professor accepted the challenge of decrypting the music industry's cryptography program designed to lock up music. Yet he perceived that if he posted his findings on USENIX, he would be prosecuted under the DMCA. Ultimately a New Jersey court dismissed the case. See *http://www.eff.org/IP/DMCA/ Felten_v_RIAA/*.

Regulating the Export of Cryptography Products

The second major legal issue involving cryptography, regulating the export of cryptography products, is directly related to the First Amendment discussion. Recalling cryptography's historic military and Cold War applications, there has been an exaggerated effort on the part of the U.S. government to maintain control of this technology. So-called dual-use commodities such as encryption have been subject to the same controls as weapons. The U.S. Department of Commerce regulates the export of commercial encryption products. It has the authority to grant licenses to export encryption products as well as issue exemptions to its rules. Posting encryption source or object code (on a Web site or even to a newsgroup) is considered an export and thus subject to Commerce's regulations. Even to the extent this is for academic, non-commercial purposes, some restrictions apply. Commerce's licensing program asks— before the fact—what cryptography product is being exported/posted/linked. Then it decides whether to grant or deny the license. Because cryptography possesses elements of speech/expression, this prelicensing policy has the potential, therefore, to act as a prior restraint on speech. Prior restraints on speech are presumptively invalid.

The following two cases, *Junger v. Daley* and *Bernstein v. Department of Commerce*, highlight the problems inherent in attempting to regulate encryption products in the Internet and information age.

Junger v. Daley
209 F.3d 481 (6th Cir. 2000)

Facts

Plaintiff Peter Junger is a law professor at Case Western Reserve University Law School. Junger maintains Web sites containing course materials and other topics. He wishes to post on his Web site various encryption programs he has written. Junger applied for a Commerce Department determination whether his postings were subject to government regulation.

The Export Regulations (in 1998) control the export of certain software. This covers the downloading or causing the downloading of controlled encryption source code and object code to locations outside the United States. The regulations detail procedures to obtain government approval for exporting items on its Control List. Should Commerce approve the application, a license is issued.

Commerce determined that some of Junger's postings of encryption data were subject to regulation, and so Junger filed suit in court claiming the government's control and the review process of encryption software violated rights protected by the First Amendment. He alleged that the licensing requirements work a prior restraint on his First Amendment rights of free speech. Junger filed this appeal to make a facial challenge to the Regulations on First Amendment grounds, seeking declaratory and injunctive relief that would permit him to engage in the unrestricted distribution of encryption software through his Web site.

The district court granted summary judgment in favor of the government, holding that encryption source code is not protected under the First Amendment, that the Regulations are permissible content-neutral regulations, and that they are not subject to facial challenge on prior restraint grounds. Junger appealed this decision.

Judicial Opinion *(Judge Martin)*

The issue of whether or not the First Amendment protects encryption source code is a difficult one because source code has both an expressive feature and a functional feature. The United States does not dispute that it is possible to use encryption source code to represent and convey information and ideas about cryptography and that encryption source code can be used . . . for such informational purposes. [However] the district court concluded that the functional characteristics of source code overshadow its simultaneously expressive nature. The fact that a medium of expression has a functional capacity should not preclude constitutional protection. Rather, the appropriate consideration of the medium's functional capacity is in the analysis of permitted government regulation.

The Supreme Court has explained that all ideas having even the slightest redeeming social importance, including those concerning the advancement of truth, science, morality, and arts, have the full protection of the First Amendment. The Supreme Court has [also] recognized First Amendment protection for symbolic conduct, such as draft-card burning, that has both functional and expressive features. Though unquestionably expressive . . . a musical score cannot be read by the majority of the public, but can be used as a means of communication among musicians. Likewise, computer source code, though unintelligible to many, is the preferred method of communication among computer programmers.

Because computer source code is an expressive means for the exchange of information and ideas about computer programming, we hold that it is protected by the First Amendment. The functional capabilities of source code, and particularly those of encryption source code, should be considered when analyzing the governmental interest in regulating the exchange of this form of speech. Under intermediate scrutiny, the regulation of speech is valid, in part, if it furthers an important or substantial governmental interest. In [the] *Turner Broadcasting System v. FCC* [case], the Supreme Court noted that although an asserted governmental interest may be important, when the government defends restrictions on speech it must do more than simply posit the existence of the disease sought to be cured. The government must demonstrate that the recited harms are real, not merely conjectural, and that the regulation will in fact alleviate these harms in a direct and material way. We recognize that national security interests can outweigh the interests of protected speech and require the regulation of speech. In the present case, the record does not resolve whether the exercise of presidential power in furtherance of national security interests should overrule the interests in allowing the free exchange of encryption source code.

Before any level of judicial scrutiny can be applied to the Regulations, Junger must be in a position to bring a facial challenge to these regulations. In light of the recent amendments to the Export Administration Regulations, the district court should examine the new regulations to determine if Junger can bring a facial challenge.

For the foregoing reasons, we REVERSE the district court and REMAND the case to the district court for consideration of Junger's constitutional challenge to the amended regulations.

Case Questions

1. What is the practical significance of Judge Martin's finding that encryption source code is a form of speech?

2. How could Professor Junger possibly amend his encryption software so as to make it pure speech, deserving of the most exacting judicial scrutiny?

3. What are the values that the First Amendment seeks to protect? Are they implicated in this case?

Bernstein v. U.S. Department of Commerce, Complaint filed in the U.S. District Court for the Northern District of California *No. 95-00582 MHP, January 7, 2002*

Facts

Bernstein is challenging the Export Administration Regulations, 15 C.F.R. 743 et seq. (EARs) that govern, *inter alia*, the export of encryption items from the United States. Bernstein is a professor in the Department of Mathematics, Statistics and Computer Science at the University of Illinois and teaches courses in math and computer science. His current research interests are in computational number theory, cryptography, and computer security, and he has been awarded research grants in these fields. Pursuant to this work, Bernstein communicates with other researchers about his ideas, lectures on these topics, and publishes his work. The work is published on the Internet as well as in journals and books.

In recognition of the commercial uses of cryptography, the government transferred jurisdiction of cryptography software and products to the U.S. Department of Commerce. Commerce issued new regulations (EARs) controlling most encryption items. Commerce continually modifies EAR provisions, but they still regulate in the same way. Commerce maintains licensing requirements for the export of most cryptographic software. This includes posting as well as linking because they are the functional equivalent, in many instances, of exporting. For example, Commerce requires a license for export of cryptographic software performing any other function other than authentication or digital signatures. License requests are reviewed on a case-by-case basis by the Bureau of Export Administration (BXA) in conjunction with other agencies to ensure that decisions are consistent with U.S. security and foreign policy interests. Exceptions to the licensing requirements exist for "mere teaching or discussion of information about cryptography" and for the export of *printed* materials about cryptography.

In 2002, Bernstein filed the most current suit, and although he acknowledges that Commerce's regulatory scheme as amended greatly reduces the possibility his speech may be subject to prior restraint, he alleges the regulations still bar him from fully participating in academic, scientific, and professional activities. For example, the regulations continue to demand a prior review of content and to demand, without a warrant, copies of private correspondence that includes encryption source code. He contends that the EARs violate the First, Fourth, and Fifth Amendment rights. This case has spanned 7 plus years thus far. Earlier decisions have been favorable for Bernstein. For example, the District Court held that source code is speech. [*Bernstein v. Department of State*, 922 F. Supp. 1436 (N.D. Cal. 1996)]. Later, it held that the regulations were arbitrary and acted as an unconstitutional prior restraint in violation of the First Amendment [945 F. Supp. 1279 (N.D. Cal. 1996)]. Still later, the court issued an injunction against the enforcement of the EARs. [974 F. Supp. 1311 (N.D. Cal. 1997)]. On appeal, the Ninth Circuit held that the EARs worked as an unconstitutional prior restraint in violation of the First Amendment because they were essentially a prepublication licensing scheme that burdened content, specifically scientific expression. The Court then immediately withdrew its own opinion in May 1999.

Judicial Opinion

You be the judge in this case. How would you decide the outcome of this challenge to the EARs in the context of Bernstein's academic and professional work?

Clearly, U.S. cryptography policy is in flux at this time. It attempts to regulate while maintaining a strict law enforcement posture, yet also be aware of the safeguards of our constitutional rights. Government cryptography policy attempts to balance four concerns: national security, public safety, privacy, and commerce. Countering these claims, however, are assertions from law enforcement personnel that it must have some control over encryption products in order to effectively address crimes such as drug trafficking and terrorism. Strong encryption of data by individuals makes wiretapping and interception of such data virtually impossible for law enforcement officials. The policy attempts to allow industry to compete effectively while protecting national defense, security, and law enforcement interests. Yet these regulations, software developers assert, place domestic companies at a severe global competitive disadvantage, because no other country has such a restrictive export policy on cryptographic software and products as the United States. Consequently, this has created an incentive for U.S. companies to set up separate businesses overseas for the express purpose of avoiding U.S. encryption export controls.

Steganography. One final method of Internet and information security bears mention, the field of steganography. Similar to cryptography because it involves the process of hiding content, steganography may accomplish even more. **Steganography** is the process of hiding messages within a text or graphic. With the use of steganography, it is not apparent at all that there is a message. In commercial applications, steganography is used in the form of digital watermarks. In fact, *Wired News* and *USA Today* have reported that Osama bin Laden used steganography to hide maps as well as post instructions using the text and images of sports pages, pornography sites, and chat rooms.

Although our focus here for the most part is on the legal environment of business in cyberspace, and more particularly in this chapter on the business challenges with Internet and information security, it is important to briefly mention *government* challenges in maintaining Internet and information security.

Fourth Amendment

Internet and information security is not only a business function, it is now, since the 9/11 terrorist action, a major concern of federal, state, and local governments. Beyond the core of this chapter addressing business information security issues, it is relevant to examine Internet and information security as it impacts Americans as citizens. The question is how the government should respond to the

http://

- To access documents from the *Bernstein* case as well as media reports, see **http://www.eff.org/ Privacy/ITAR_export/Bernstein_case/**
- For a complete overview of U.S. export and licensing regulations, see **http://www.bxa.doc.gov/ Encryption/Default.htm**

http://

- **http://www.outguess.org/** is a site dedicated to the outguess steganographic tool.
- **http://www.stegoarchive.com/** is a site dedicated to watermarking and steganography tools.
- **http://www.digimarc.com** is a commercial site that offers digital watermarking technology services.

increase in both threats and actual incidents of cyberterrorism. How do we balance individuals' constitutional rights, such as those provided by the Fourth and Fifth Amendments, with the national security vulnerabilities that are all too real at this time?

The following excerpt is from the withdrawn Ninth Circuit *Bernstein* opinion, but the Court's observations are particularly relevant to the next section addressing Fourth and Fifth Amendment issues with regard to cryptography, privacy, and security.

> We note that the government's efforts to regulate and control the spread of knowledge relating to encryption may implicate more than the First Amendment rights of cryptographers. In this increasingly electronic age, we are all required in our everyday lives to rely on modern technology to communicate with one another. This reliance on electronic communication, however, has brought with it a dramatic diminution in our ability to communicate privately. Cellular phones are subject to monitoring, e-mail is easily intercepted, and transactions over the Internet are often less than secure. Something as commonplace as furnishing our credit card number, Social Security number, or bank account number puts each of us at risk. Moreover, when we employ electronic methods of communication, we often leave electronic "fingerprints" behind, fingerprints that can be traced back to us. Whether we are surveilled by our government, by criminals, or by our neighbors, it is fair to say that never has our ability to shield our affairs from prying eyes been at such a low ebb. The availability and use of secure encryption may offer an opportunity to reclaim some portion of the privacy we have lost. Government efforts to control encryption thus may well implicate not only the First Amendment rights of cryptographers intent on pushing the boundaries of their science, but also the constitutional rights of each of us as potential recipients of encryption's bounty. Viewed from this perspective, the government's efforts to retard progress in cryptography may implicate the Fourth Amendment, as well as the right to speak anonymously, the right against compelled speech [a Fifth Amendment right], and the right to informational privacy. While we leave for another day the resolution of these difficult issues, it is important to point out that Bernstein's is a suit not merely concerning a small group of scientists laboring in an esoteric field, but also touches on the public interest broadly defined.

The **Fourth Amendment** acts as a limit on the government's power to conduct illegal searches and seizures. It is one of a combination of constitutional provisions that guard against abuses by law enforcement and, ultimately, against the formation of a *de facto* police state. (Recall, too, the discussion from Chapter 9, "Privacy.") The Fourth Amendment provides "The right of the people to be secure in their persons, houses, papers, and effects, against unreasonable searches and seizures, shall not be violated, and no warrants shall issue, but upon probable cause, supported by oath or affirmation, and particularly describing the place to be searched, and the persons or things to be seized." Under the Fourth Amendment, citizens enjoy a "reasonable expectation of privacy." The Supreme Court enunciated this standard in *Katz v. United States* (discussed in Chapter 9, "Privacy"). In general, a search without a warrant violates citizens' expectations of privacy and constitutes an unreasonable search and seizure, and any evidence collected from such a search is inadmissible in court. The Court heard this Fourth Amendment case, and it was called on to reconcile this constitutional right as it is challenged by the advent of high-tech surveillance techniques.

Kyllo v. United States
533 U.S. 27 (2001)

Facts

In 1991, Agent William Elliott of the U.S. Department of the Interior came to suspect that marijuana was being grown in the home belonging to Danny Kyllo, part of a triplex in Florence, Oregon. Indoor marijuana growth typically requires high-intensity lamps. In order to determine whether the amount of heat was emanating from Kyllo's home was consistent with the use of such lamps, at 3.20 A.M. on January 16, 1992, Agents Elliott and Dan Haas used an Agema Thermovision 210 thermal imager to scan the triplex. Thermal imagers detect infrared radiation, which virtually all objects emit but that is not visible to the naked eye. The imager converts radiation into images based on relative warmth—black is cool, white is hot, and shades of gray connote relative differences.

The scan of Kyllo's home took only a few minutes and was performed from the passenger seat of Agent Elliott's vehicle across the street from the front of the house and also from the street in back of the house. The scan showed that the roof over the garage and the side wall of petitioner's home were relatively hot compared to the rest of the home and substantially warmer than neighboring homes in the triplex. Agent Elliott concluded that petitioner was using halide lights to grow marijuana in his house, which indeed he was.

The federal magistrate issued the requested search warrant based on informants' tips, utility bills, and the thermal imaging. The warrant authorized a search of Kyllo's home. The agents found more than a hundred marijuana plants. Kyllo was indicted, and he moved to suppress the evidence seized from this search. The trial court denied Kyllo's motion, finding that the Agema 210 "is a non-intrusive device which emits no rays or beams and shows just a crude visual image, [and] did not show any people or activity within the walls of the structure, and no intimate details of the home were observed." The court of appeals affirmed the district court's decision. The Supreme Court granted certiorari.

Judicial Opinion *(Justice Scalia)*

This case presents the question whether the use of a thermal-imaging device aimed at a private home from a public street to detect relative amounts of heat within the home constitutes a "search" within the meaning of the Fourth Amendment. The Fourth Amendment provides that "[t]he right of the people to be secure in their persons, houses, papers, and effects, against unreasonable searches and seizures, shall not be violated." At the very core of the Fourth Amendment stands the "right of a man to retreat into his own home and there be free from unreasonable governmental intrusion." With very few exceptions, the question whether a warrantless search of a home is reasonable and hence constitutional must be answered no. On the other hand, the antecedent question of whether or not a Fourth Amendment "search" has occurred is not so simple under our precedent. [In *Katz*, this Court considered] eavesdropping by means of an electronic listening device placed on the outside of a telephone booth—a location not within the catalog ("persons, houses, papers, and effects") that the Fourth Amendment protects against unreasonable searches. We held that the Fourth Amendment nonetheless protected Katz from the warrantless eavesdropping because he "justifiably relied" upon the privacy of the telephone booth. We have subsequently applied this principle to hold that a Fourth Amendment search does *not* occur—even when the explicitly protected location of a *house* is concerned—unless the individual manifested a subjective expectation of privacy in the object of the challenged search, and society [is] willing to recognize that expectation as "reasonable." [Accordingly, we have also held] that aerial surveillance of private homes and surrounding areas does not constitute a search. [W]e noted [in these cases] it [was] important that this [was] not an area immediately adjacent to a private home, where privacy expectations are most heightened.

The present case involves officers on a public street engaged in more than naked-eye surveillance of a home. We have previously reserved judgment as to how much technological enhancement of ordinary perception from such a vantage point, if any, is too much. It would be foolish to contend that the degree of privacy secured to citizens by the Fourth Amendment has been entirely unaffected by the advance of technology. The question we confront today is what limits there are upon this power of technology to shrink the realm of guaranteed privacy. [T]here is a ready criterion, with roots deep in the common law, of the minimal expectation of privacy that *exists*, and that is acknowledged to be *reasonable*. To withdraw protection of this minimum expectation would be to permit police technology to erode the privacy guaranteed by the Fourth Amendment. We think that obtaining by sense-enhancing technology any information regarding the interior of the home that could not otherwise have been obtained without physical intrusion into a constitutionally protected area, constitutes a search—at least where the technology in question is not in general public use. This assures preservation of that degree of privacy against government that existed when the Fourth Amendment was adopted.

On the basis of this criterion, the information obtained by the thermal imager in this case was the product of a search. Where, as here, the Government uses a device that is not in general public use, to explore details of the home that would previously have been unknowable without physical intrusion, the surveillance is a "search" as is presumptively unreasonable without a warrant. Since we hold the Thermovision imaging to have been an unlawful search, it will remain for the District Court to determine whether, without the evidence it provided, the search warrant issued in this case was supported by probable cause—and if not, whether there is any other basis for supporting admission of the evidence that the search pursuant to the warrant produced.

The judgment of the Court of Appeals is reversed; the case is remanded for further proceedings consistent with this opinion.

IT IS SO ORDERED.

———————————————————

Justice Stevens, with whom the Chief Justice, Justice O'Connor, and Justice Kennedy join, *dissenting*.

There is, in my judgment, a distinction of constitutional magnitude between "through-the-wall" surveillance that gives the observer or listener direct access to information in a private area, on the one hand, and the thought processes used to draw inferences from information in the public domain, on the other hand. The Court has crafted a rule that purports to deal with direct observations of the inside of the home, but the case before us merely involves indirect deductions from "off-the-wall" surveillance, that is, observations of the exterior of the home. Those observations were made with a fairly primitive thermal imager that gathered data exposed on the outside of petitioner's home but did not invade any constitutionally protected interest in privacy. Although the Court is properly and commendably concerned about the threats to privacy that may flow from advances in the technology available to the law enforcement profession, it has unfortunately failed to heed the tried and true counsel of judicial restraint. Instead of concentrating on the rather mundane issue that is actually presented . . . the Court had endeavored to craft an all-encompassing rule for the future. It would be far wiser to give legislators an unimpeded opportunity to grapple with these emerging issues rather than to shackle them with prematurely devised constitutional constraints.

I respectfully dissent.

Case Questions

1. What bearing does the dissent have on the outcome of this case?
2. What other surveillance technologies are likewise on a collision course with the Fourth Amendment?
3. After this opinion, how is law enforcement supposed to do its job in cases that need surveillance?

Computer and Internet technology—and events such as 9/11—directly challenge the law to adapt to new realities and practices. Scholars query the meaning of our evolving "reasonable expectation of privacy" standard against a backdrop of the Internet and our apparent demand for increased surveillance. Do we even have a reasonable expectation of privacy anymore, due to the advent of the Internet, Social Security numbers, tax filings, and other centralized recordkeeping activities? This is in stark contrast to the concept of privacy conceived of by the Constitution's framers. A body of developing case law suggests that citizens may, in the future, have a lesser expectation of privacy—only for "intimate details." As evidenced by this split of opinion in the *Kyllo* case, courts face a significant burden to protect citizens' rights of privacy as technology, specifically surveillance capabilities, enhances the government's ability to conduct searches and seizures.

Yet these concerns must be considered in conjunction with the current security climate, post 9/11. The interest in national security is so great that there is now a Department of Homeland Security (directed by Tom Ridge) *and* chief of federal cyber-security (Richard Clarke). Officials warn that our nation stands vulnerable to an electronic Pearl Harbor—which could be, by way of example, a coordinated action to bring down systems like telecom, transportation, or power grids. Not only do businesses need to secure their information, the government faces an even more daunting task. We next consider recent government actions in the name of Internet and information security that impact our Fourth Amendment rights, activities made possible by the Internet and our telecommunications infrastructure.

The USA Patriot Act. Congress quickly passed the **USA Patriot Act** in October 2001, just weeks after the 9/11 terrorist action. It strengthens and features many changes in law enforcement (many say at the expense of our constitutional rights, as well as the power of our judicial branch), but our discussion is limited to how the law impacts Internet and information security. We discuss two main provisions here.

First, the act changes communications privacy law. It gives officials greater authority to track and intercept communications. Communications privacy laws feature a three-tier system, created for the "dual purpose of protecting the confidentiality of private telephone, face-to-face, and computer communications while enabling authorities to identify and intercept criminal communications." We cite a few examples of the changes effected by the USA Patriot Act relating to information security, provisions that will surely be challenged in court.

> *Then:* (before the USA Patriot Act was passed): The laws prohibit the interception of live communications, but a warrant for surveillance is allowed as a last resort for serious criminal cases.
> *Now:* (since the USA Patriot Act was passed): The act permits law enforcement to intercept communications to and from a trespasser within a system (with system owner's permission). (Note the absence of any warrant as required by the Fourth Amendment.)

> *Then:* The laws prohibit the interception of stored communications, but a warrant is allowed for *any* criminal investigation (easier to obtain a warrant—without the extraordinary review required for live communications).
> *Now:* The act permits nationwide execution of court orders for access to stored communications, and it treats stored voice mail like stored e-mail (rather than like telephone conversations).

> *Then:* The laws permit use of trap and trace devices and pen registers (like caller ID) that identify the source and destination of calls made to and from a *particular* telephone. Surveillance orders are allowed based on the law enforcement's certification alone and do not require a finding of a court.
> *Now:* The act permits *nationwide* pen register and trap and trace orders for electronic communications, such as e-mail. (This acts as sort of a roving warrant, not attached to a particular telephone as before.)

http://

- See **http://www.epic.org/privacy/ terrorism/hr3162.html** (for the text of the act).

Second, the act changes surveillance law. Before this act, for example, information such as that gleaned through data mining had to be related to an ongoing investigation. Now, data mining is allowed—as the basis for generating suspicion that would cause them to *begin* an investigation. The practical effect of these provisions is to separate information gathering from suspicion of criminal conduct.

Thus, under the act, law enforcement is allowed to conduct what is known as a fishing expedition. Theoretically, law enforcement could gather information on us related to anything we surf or shop online for. For example, they could monitor us and see every copyright-protected song we download for free. These measures most assuredly increase the amount and types of data that law enforcement is able to gather on each of us.

- For just one analysis of the effect of the USA Patriot Act, see **http://www.eff.org/Privacy/ Surveillance/Terrorism_militias/ 20011031_eff_usa_patriot_analysis. html**

Additionally, the act also creates a number of new crimes; creates two types of forfeiture procedures; makes it more difficult for aliens to enter the United States; makes it easier to detain or deport aliens; mandates disclosures from financial institutions on "suspicious" transactions (refer to Chapter 8, "Online Securities Offerings and Transactions"); and it increases penalties for acts of terrorism. Two other current surveillance technologies are deserving of mention because they are so intricately tied to law enforcement efforts.

Carnivore/DCS-1000. Beyond the USA Patriot Act, and even before that act was passed, the Department of Justice's national security branch, the FBI, created a computer system, called **Carnivore/DCS-1000**, to read and analyze packets of data sent to or received by suspects in criminal investigations (see discussion in Chapter 9, "Privacy"). The

- **http://www.fbi.gov/hq/lab/carnivore/ carnlrgmap.html** offers a diagram of the Carnivore search program.

FBI has installed this collection device onto ISP servers. The unprecedented availability and possibility of collecting data is a boon to law enforcement in this era of high-tech criminal activity. Yet Carnivore overcollects data as it mines these data packets; it is equally important to ensure our liberties are protected and that our constitutional guarantees are not eviscerated.

http://www.fbi.gov/hq/lab/carnivore/carnlrgmap.htm

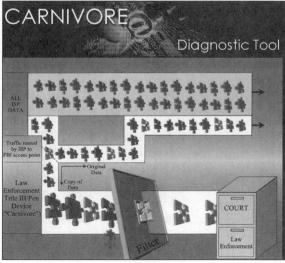

- http://www.fbi.gov/hq/lab/carnivore/
  carnivore.htm is an FBI information
  site on the Carnivore program.
- http://www.stopcarnivore.org/ is a
  public interest site dedicated to
  developing solutions to social
  problems.

Key Logger Systems/Magic Lantern. **Key logger system/ Magic Lantern** is keystroke recording software, and it secretly records *all* computer activity. The FBI began using this software—in a program known as Operation Magic Lantern, but you will not find any data about it on their Web site.

The following case is the first decision involving the government's use of the key logger system, and it must decide whether the system violates the defendants' Fourth Amendment rights and whether it acts to intercept a live communication in violation of the Electronic Communications Privacy Act (ECPA).

United States v. Scarfo
180 F. Supp. 2d 572 (D. N.J. 2001)

Facts

Pursuant to federal search warrants, the FBI entered the business office of Nicodemo Scarfo and Frank Paolercio. The FBI searched their office, Merchant Services, for evidence of an illegal gambling and loan-sharking operation. During their search, the FBI came across a personal computer and attempted to access various files. They were unable to gain entry to an encrypted file name "Factors."

Suspecting the Factors file contained evidence of the illegal operations, the FBI returned later to Merchant Services, and, pursuant to two search warrants, installed what is known as a key logger system (KLS) on the computer in order to decipher the password that would allow entry to the encrypted file. The KLS records the keystrokes an individual enters on a computer's keyboard. The government utilized the KLS in order to "catch" Scarfo's password to the encrypted file while he was entering it onto his keyboard. Scarfo's personal computer features a modem for communication over telephone lines and he possesses an AOL account. The FBI successfully obtained the password to the Factors file and retrieved what is alleged to be incriminating evidence.

A federal grand jury returned a three-count indictment against the defendants charging them with gambling and loan-sharking. Scarfo filed two motions. The first motion was for discovery, requesting the United States to explain how it obtained his password. The second motion was to suppress the evidence recovered from his computer. Finally, he asserts that KLS intercepted a wire communication in violation of the Electronic Communications Privacy Act (ECPA).

The trial court expressed serious concerns over whether the government violated the wiretap statute in utilizing the KLS. Specifically, it was concerned whether the KLS was operating at the *same* time Scarfo was communicating via modem over telephone lines, thereby unlawfully intercepting live wire communications without having applied for a wiretap pursuant to the ECPA. The court ordered the United States to file with the court a report explaining fully the KLS technology and how it functions. The United States responded that the requested information is classified and has national security implications, as governed by the Classified Information Procedures Act. Instead, the government wished to only release an unclassified summary of the KLS. The court agreed, finding that the KLS is properly classified information and a full release of information impacted national security. Accordingly, as to the first motion, the court denied the defendants' request for complete discovery/disclosure of the classified information, but it granted their motion insofar as they are entitled to receive the summary.

Judicial Opinion *(Judge Politan)*

This case presents an interesting issue of first impression dealing with the ever-present tension between individual privacy and liberty rights and law enforcement's use of new and advanced technology to vigorously investigate criminal activity. [This abstract addresses two of the four challenges brought by Scarfo.]

[The Fourth Amendment]

Typically, the proponent of a motion to suppress bears the burden of establishing that his Fourth Amendment rights were violated. The Fourth Amendment states that "no Warrants shall issue, but upon probable cause, supported by Oath or affirmation, and particularly describing the place to be searched, and the persons or things to be seized." The Fourth Amendment requires a certain modicum of particularity in the language of the warrant with respect to the area and items to be searched and/or seized. The particularity requirement exists so that law enforcement officers are constrained from undertaking a boundless and exploratory rummaging through one's personal property.

From a review of the two Court Orders authorizing the searches along with the accompanying Affidavits, it is clear that the Court Orders suffers from no constitutional infirmity with respect to particularity. The [warrant] Judge . . . found probable cause existed. The Order further stated that there was "probable cause to believe that Nicodemo Scarfo's computer, located in the TARGET LOCATION, is being used to store business records of Scarfo's illegal . . . operation, and that the above mentioned records have been encrypted." [The] Order permitted law enforcement officers to "install and leave behind software . . . which will monitor the inputted data . . . so the FBI can capture the password necessary to decrypt computer files." On its face, the Order is very comprehensive and lists the items, including the evidence in the encrypted file, to be seized with more than sufficient specificity. Accordingly . . . the motion to suppress is denied.

IV. Whether the KLS Intercepted Wire Communications

The principal mystery surrounding this case was whether the KLS intercepted a [live as opposed to stored] wire communication in violation of the [ECPA] by recording keystrokes made over a telephone or cable line while the modem operated.

Scarfo's computer contained an encryption program called Pretty Good Privacy (PGP), which is used to encrypt . . . files so that decrypting . . . files requires use of the appropriate passphrase. FBI engineers configured the KLS to avoid intercepting electronic communications typed on the keyboard and simultaneously transmitted real time. To do this, the

FBI designed the component "so that each keystroke was evaluated individually." Hence, when the modem was operating, the KLS did not record keystrokes. Since Scarfo's computer possessed no other means of communicating with another computer save for the modem . . . the KLS did not intercept any wire communications. Accordingly, the Defendants' motion to suppress evidence for violation of [the ECPA] is denied.

In this day and age, it appears that on a daily basis we are overwhelmed with new and exciting technologically-advanced gadgetry. Indeed, the amazing capabilities bestowed upon us by science are at times mind-boggling. As a result, we must be ever vigilant against the evisceration of Constitutional rights at the hands of modern technology. Yet, at the same time, it is likewise true that modern-day criminals have also embraced technological advances and used them to further their felonious purposes. Each day, advanced computer technologies and the increased accessibility to the Internet means criminal behavior is becoming more sophisticated and complex. This includes the ability to find new ways to commit old crimes, as well as new crimes beyond the comprehension of courts. As a result of this surge in so-called cybercrime, law enforcement's ability to vigorously pursue such rogues cannot be hindered where all Constitutional limitations are scrupulously observed.

Case Questions

1. Do you think it was even proper for the warrant judge to issue the order permitting the installation of the KLS? In other words, is the KLS qualitatively different from the pen register system that logs telephone numbers dialed from a certain telephone? Does the KLS reveal more information than a pen register does?
2. Are there any other defenses that Scarfo's lawyers should have attempted in an effort to suppress the evidence obtained from the search?
3. Do you think the government's rules for obtaining warrants can keep up with the crimes being committed?

FIGURE 12.3   **Results of the Fourth Annual Computer Crime and Security Survey of Financial Institutions, U.S. Companies, and Government Agencies**

- 26% reported theft of proprietary information
- 30% reported system penetration (increased for the third consecutive year—1997 to 1999)
- 55% reported unauthorized access by employees (also increased for the third consecutive year)
- 57% reported Internet connection as the source of security breach (up from 37% in 1996)

Source: Computer Security Institute and the FBI

This alarming loss of privacy is a pervasive side effect of the information age where it is theoretically possible to collect data on everyone and everything. For example, Microsoft's 5.0 Internet Explorer automatically sent information to Web sites that users bookmarked. Recall that the Fourth Amendment protects our reasonable expectation of privacy. The question becomes, If this is the way transactions are conducted, is any expectation of privacy reasonable? Do we even have an expectation of privacy anymore; and if so, how are we to articulate it?

http://

- **http:/www.cdt.org** is a public interest site that focuses on free expression and global communications technology.
- For more on these topics, see the following sites: **http://www.fbi. gov**, **www.usdoj.gov**, and **http://www. epic.org**

Fifth Amendment

One of the functions of the **Fifth Amendment** is to protect citizens from being compelled by the government to testify against themselves—known as the right against self-incrimination. This is a familiar feature of criminal legal proceedings and, in practice, it allows defendants to choose whether to take the stand and defend themselves. The burden of proving guilt rests solely with the prosecution.

The Fifth Amendment affords other protections, too—for example, the guarantee that no one will "be deprived of . . . property, without due process of law." Another issue raised in encryption export licensing cases is due process, both procedural and substantive. Under a procedural due process inquiry, courts ask whether a government decision denying a benefit violates the citizens' Fifth Amendment rights to a procedurally fair hearing and decision. Thus a government decision that is deemed arbitrary, capricious, unreasonable, and irrational is held to deny individuals' rights to due process. This appears difficult to prove in encryption export licensing challenges, however, because government safety and security interests would appear to outweigh allegations of unreasonable, arbitrary, or capricious decision making. Finally, there are substantive due process claims involved in encryption export cases. Under a substantive due process inquiry, courts ask whether the challenged substantive law itself is flawed. Courts closely scrutinize the effect of laws concerning important matters such as life or liberty. However, in such cases as encryption, where no fundamental right is at stake, courts will be more deferential to the laws that Congress enacted.

The following case resolves a Fifth Amendment substantive due process challenge to the encryption regulations. It also illustrates the difficulties inherent for individuals and businesses to prevail in these cases.

Karn v. Department of State
925 F. Supp. 1 (D.D.C. 1996)

Facts

Philip Karn submitted a commodity jurisdiction request to export the book *Applied Cryptography* by Bruce Schneier. The book provided information on cryptographic techniques and algorithms, among other things. This license to export was granted. Later, Karn applied for an export license for a diskette containing the same source code that was printed in the book itself.

Reasoning that the diskette was designated as a defense article, the government denied this license request. Karn challenged this denial as violating his First and Fifth amendment rights.

[Because there was already a discussion of First Amendment challenges, this excerpted opinion focuses on the Fifth Amendment challenge. Incidentally, Karn lost his First Amendment claim.]

Judicial Opinion *(Judge Richey)*

[P]laintiff asserts . . . that the defendant's actions violated his right to substantive due process as guaranteed by the Fifth Amendment. The substantive due process provided in the Fifth Amendment, absent the assertion of a fundamental right [such as one's life or liberty], merely requires a reasonable fit between governmental purpose and the means chosen to advance that purpose. Under this deferential standard of review applied in substantive due process challenges to economic legislation, there is no need for mathematical precision in the fit between justification and means. Given this "extremely limited scope of permissible judicial inquiry," the plaintiff's due process claim lacks any merit. The government clearly has an interest in preventing the proliferation of cryptographic software to foreign powers, and the regulation of the export of the cryptographic software is a rational means of achieving that goal. The Court will not substitute its policy judgment for that of the President.

Likewise, the regulation of the plaintiff's diskette as cryptographic software is rational, even when considered in conjunction with the defendants' decision not to subject the book Applied Cryptography to the [licensing denial]. [T]he book contains no machine-readable media, while the diskette is precisely that. Although . . . the book could be placed on machine readable media . . . plaintiff concedes that using the source code in [the book] *Applied Cryptography* to encode material takes greater effort and time than using the Karn diskette. Accordingly, treating the book and diskette differently is not in violation of the plaintiff substantive due process rights.

Conclusion

For the reasons discussed above, the defendant is entitled to summary judgment on the plaintiff's . . . Fifth Amendment claim.

Case Questions

1. Explain the practical effect of Judge Richey's decision.
2. Do you think there was a rational basis for his decision?
3. Given the result in this decision, what advice would you offer Karn on his next export licensing application? Discuss whether your advice would be based on expediency and/or ethical behavior.

FIGURE 12.4   **Most Frequent Security Breaches (from most to least common)**

1. Viruses

2. Employee access abuse

3. Unauthorized access by intruders

4. Theft and destruction of computer resources

5. Leak of proprietary information and trade secrets

6. Theft and destruction of data

7. Access abuse by employees who exceeded their right of access

8. Hacking of telecommunications equipment

The interconnected nature of the Internet multiplies, as well as blurs, liability in which victims are remote through connected parties, and nearly everyone is a defendant. To prevail on a claim, however, there needs to be legal evidence of a break-in or breach, which may typically be found through an audit. Breaches of security may be a civil or criminal offense, or both. Computer security becomes further complicated because it is a global problem. Purely state or federal solutions are inadequate to deal with a problem that has no geographic borders, so an international strategy is best suited for Internet and information security.

INTERNATIONAL ASPECTS OF INTERNET AND INFORMATION SECURITY

Global Network and Information Security

In June 2001, the European Commission published "Network and Information Security: Proposal for a European Policy Approach," acknowledging that the Internet's global connectivity has the unintended result of promoting remote attacks. The commission suggests solutions including educating the public about network security issues, promoting standardization and certification, improving the legal framework, and enhancing international cooperation. Although no binding regulations are embedded in the document, its publication represents an important step toward improving network security. Private interests have supported many of the proposals, giving the document added legitimacy and increasing the document's ability to be used as a springboard for future binding proposals.

Council Framework Decision on Attacks Against Information Systems. On April 19, 2002, the European Commission proposed the **Council Framework Decision on Attacks Against Information Systems** to address attacks on information systems. This framework is meant to contribute

http://

- For a sample commentary on the Network and Information Security document by a private interest group, see **http://www.icrt.org/pos_papers/011209_EC.pdf**

toward efforts against organized crime and terrorism through judicial cooperation. Member states must comply with this framework by December 31, 2003.

The framework decision attempts to harmonize national laws dealing with network and information security issues. Specifically, the framework criminalizes two broad classes of conduct: illegal access and illegal interference. Article 3 states that member states must establish "illegal access" provisions that, at a minimum, prohibit any unauthorized access that is (1) against any part of an information system which has protection measures in place, or (2) done with the intent to cause damage, or (3) done with the intent to result in an economic benefit for the perpetrator. Article 3 states that just the attempt in and of itself to gain unauthorized access is actionable.

Article 4 criminalizes illegal interference. The framework decision defines the term *illegal interference* to include "serious hindering or interruption" of an information system, denial of service attacks, damage or deterioration of computer data, and virus attacks. Each member state is left to themselves to determine the meaning of the phrase "serious hindering or interruption," under its own laws.

Article 5 requires member states to criminalize the aiding, abetting, or attempt of Article 4 and Article 5 offenses. Member states must also have sufficient punitive measures in place to punish offenders. These may include fines or imprisonment.

http://

- To review the framework decision, see **http://europa.eu.int/eur-lex/en/ com/pdf/2002/com2002_0173en01. pdf**

The framework also addresses jurisdictional questions. A member state will have jurisdiction over the offense (1) where the offense is committed in whole or in part on its territory, irrespective of the status or nationality of the person involved, or (2) where the offender is a national of that member state and the act affects individuals or groups of that state, or (3) where the offense is committed for the benefit of a legal person established in the territory of that member state. If the offense falls within the jurisdiction of multiple nations, the nations shall cooperate in order to decide which shall prosecute the offenders. The framework recommends that nations aim to centralize proceedings in a single member state.

Encryption and Cryptography Systems

Governments are grappling with the legal issues arising from the easy availability of strong encryption software. Cryptography, once the creation and work of governments, is now available to anyone in the private sector. Although such a shift may be characterized as the loss of a key governmental power, it has significant benefits for the commercial use of the Internet. As noted in the EU publication *Ensuring Security and Trust in Electronic Commerce,* cryptographic techniques are considered essential tools for establishing security and trust in open networks. That security and trust, in turn, facilitates online commerce and information exchange. The following sections highlight the various initiatives undertaken to develop an overarching legal framework in managing transactional security systems and encryption.

Cryptography and Liberty Survey. Every year, the Electronic Privacy Information Center (EPIC) publishes a survey titled, *Cryptography and Liberty: An International Survey of*

Encryption Policy. This survey examines global treatment of cryptography by various nations. The survey focuses on restrictions to use of cryptography and how such restrictions may infringe on privacy rights and civil liberties. The survey rates as "green" any nation that imposes few controls on encryption or promotes a policy that allows for unhindered use of cryptography. "Yellow" nations have significant domestic controls on cryptography. "Red" nations have executed sweeping regulations on cryptography controls, including regulations addressing domestic use.

The survey rates most nations in the world. For example, Finland is rated a "green" by EPIC. According to EPIC, Finland announced a cryptography policy on January 5, 1999, stating that, "[i]n Finland, the use of strong encryption should not be restricted by legislation or international agreements." Germany is also "green" because it neither prohibits encryption technology nor significantly restricts the export of cryptographic products. India is rated "yellow/red" because of, among other things, its Information Technology Act. This act requires all Internet service providers to monitor all traffic passing through their services and make the traffic available to the government for security reasons. Tunisia is rated "red." Telecommunications providers in Tunisia must receive authorization to encrypt communications and must deposit encryption keys with the Tunisian government. The United States, long the leader in efforts to limit the dissemination of encryption technology, has loosened its restrictions over time, thus receiving a "yellow/green" designation for the first time in 2000. For example, the U.S. government has relaxed export controls of encryption produces and no longer prohibits imports of cryptography into the United States.

http://

- The Electronic Privacy Information Center (EPIC) hosts a cryptography page. See **http://www.epic.org**

Organization for Economic Cooperation and Development (OECD) Guidelines. The OECD is an international organization of thirty industrial market-economy nations that examines issues involving economic, social, and governance challenges of a globalized economy. Members include Japan, Korea, Australia, Mexico, the United States, and most nations of Europe. On March 27, 1997, the OECD issued guidelines addressing cryptography. These guidelines were updated in a document titled, *OECD Guidelines for the Security of Information Systems and Networks: Towards a Culture of Security*, which was adopted by the OECD Council on July 25, 2002. These guidelines list nine principles that the OECD recommends should be followed by all nations regarding cryptography.

1. Awareness: Participants should be aware of the need for security of information systems and networks and what they can do to enhance security.
2. Responsibility: All participants are responsible for the security of information systems and networks.
3. Response: Participants should act in a timely and cooperative manner to prevent, detect, and respond to security incidents.
4. Ethics: Participants should respect the legitimate interests of others.
5. Democracy: The security of information systems should be compatible with essential values of a democratic society.

6. Risk assessment: Participants should conduct risk assessments.

7. Security design and implementation: Participants should incorporate security as an essential element of information systems and networks.

8. Security management: Participants should adopt a comprehensive approach to security management.

9. Reassessment: Participants should review and reassess the security of information systems and networks and make appropriate modifications to security policies, practices, measures, and procedures.

These guidelines are a product of a consensus between OECD governments and non-governmental representatives such as informational technology experts and businesses users of encryption. Although not binding, these principles have apparently been influential among policymakers. For example, a U.S. representative welcomed the guidelines, noting that they "call for new ways of thinking and behaving when using information systems," and hailing them as "a milestone marking a new international understanding of the need to safeguard the information systems upon which we increasingly depend for our way of life."

The Wassenaar Arrangement. On December 2–3, 1998, thirty-three nations signed the **Wassenaar Arrangement**, which prohibits the export of dual-use goods capable of military and civilian applications to certain nations such as Iran, Iraq, Libya, Syria, Serbia, and others. The arrangement agreed in principle "to limit the exports of strong encryption products." In 1999, the signatories diluted this principle and agreed to deregulate exports of selected encryption technologies. This reflects the trend in many developed nations toward the deregulation of encryption technologies as a whole.

Other Countries' Policies. In additional to international efforts, nations are establishing domestic regulations that address encryption technologies. The following examples highlight the differing approaches to regulation encryption around the globe.

United Kingdom The United Kingdom does not have specific rules limiting the importation of encryption products. Both individuals and companies are free to use desired encryption products. However, the UK enacted the *Regulation of Investigatory Powers Act 2000* (RIPA) on October 5, 2000. If law enforcement has obtained encrypted information, RIPA allows authorities to serve a disclosure notice on any person having an encryption key to the information. The individual who receives the disclosure notice must disclose the keys or decrypt the text that the authorities have previously obtained.

China China has placed significant restrictions on encryption technology. Initially, all foreign and Chinese companies or individuals using encryption technology had to register with the government before doing so. After aggressive lobbying efforts by U.S. trade officials and other entities, China relaxed these restrictions. Mobile phones, e-mail systems, and a host of other technologies are now exempt from the registration rule. However, significant restrictions remain. For example, Chinese regulations still define encryption technology as a "state secret." This permits Chinese government to specially regulate and control cryptography measures. As long as these regulations are in effect, they create the potential for invasive supervision by government authorities.

Japan The Japanese government views cryptography as a "central enabling technology for digital commerce." Japan places no domestic restrictions on the private use of cryptography in Japan. Also, Japan does not restrict importation of cryptographic equipment. Commercial interests that are supportive of cryptography play a major role in influencing encryption policy. However, Japan does enforce controls on cryptography exportation pursuant to the Wassenaar Arrangement, limiting exports that have dual military and commercial uses to selected nations. In addition, Japan's Ministry of International Trade and Industry (MITI) may impose selected restrictions on cryptography exportation. For example, in March 2000, MITI prohibited Sony Corporation from exporting its new Playstation 2 game machine because it contained strong encryption. Although the export controls were eventually eased, MITI's action indicates that the Japanese government may take such unilateral action against a product in the future.

Summary

Internet and information security will become a top priority of businesses as well as governments over the next few years. The concerns of security will always remain the same; however, the means of assuring it will constantly change and evolve. It is important to recognize the trade-offs between information security—usability—and privacy, and to evaluate each method of security for its impact on these values. The tensions between cryptography, privacy, security, and law enforcement will be the subject of much public and congressional debate. Constitutional protections for encryption will be debated in courtrooms. The government clearly has a role in this process: it has the ability to regulate the marketplace of security technologies. It also has the fundamental responsibility to protect both privacy and security. The scope of legal responsibility for security and breaches thereof will evolve through case law. International law and international negotiation will play a significant role in developing information security agreements on a global scale within the legal framework as outlined in this chapter. Nations are also considering whether to regulate software encryption. Laws very widely on the issue, but nations seem to be following a general trend toward deregulation. In any event, the stakes are extremely high in these issues; businesses and governments have a keen interest in their outcome.

Key Terms

firewall, *372*
certificate authorities (CAs), *373*
digital certificates (DCs), *373*
biometrics, *373*
security tokens, *374*
smart cards, *374*
holography, *374*
processor serial numbers, *374*
public key infrastructure (PKI), *375*

cryptography, *375*
encryption, *375*
decryption, *375*
First Amendment, *377*
steganography, *385*
Fourth Amendment, *386*
USA Patriot Act, *390*
Carnivore/DCS-1000, *391*
Key logger system/Magic Lantern, *392*
Fifth Amendment, *395*

Council Framework Decision on Attacks Against Information Systems, *397*
Cryptography and Liberty Survey, *398*
Organization for Economic Cooperation and Development (OECD) Guidelines, *399*
Wassenaar Arrangement, *400*

Manager's Checklist

√ Businesses should engage the assistance of information security experts when any new business application is adopted.

√ Businesses should conduct internal audits and additionally hire an outside auditor to monitor all electronic transactions.

√ In conjunction with security experts, businesses should evaluate how to provide the best security for electronic transactions while maintaining efficient, private, and usable systems.

√ Businesses must proceed with extreme caution in the use, sale, posting, or linking of cryptographic programs because their use and export remains highly regulated by the U.S. government.

√ With regard to cryptographic programs, speech rights are implicated.

√ Countries are beginning to establish international frameworks regulating network and information security that criminalize unauthorized access and destruction of data.

√ Countries regulate encryption software in dramatically different ways according to national and cultural interests. Managers must ensure that encryption software used internationally complies with national and international laws.

√ **Ethical Considerations**

Managers must consider many complex ethics issues, including:

- How the maintenance of enterprise and network security may compromise privacy

- How government information security measures may impact business's security measures

- The complex and ever-changing declaration and government licensing requirements for cryptography export products

Case Problems

1. The author of the virus CIH, also known as Chernobyl "space-filler" virus, caused damage to an extremely high number of computers. It wiped out data on disk drives or made it impossible for programs to start up. It activated on the twenty-sixth day of each month, the date of the Chernobyl nuclear accident. What happened to Mr. Chen Ing-hau? (Note that this is a real, not a hypothetical case. Refer to news reports.)

2. Philip Zimmermann wrote a free software program called Pretty Good Privacy (PGP), which permits computer users to encrypt files for secure transmission.

He posted PGP on the Internet as freeware, and it was copied and circulated internationally. What was the result? (This too, is a real case. Refer to news reports.)

3. Two Dutch teenagers used a number of ruses to obtain information about Nvidia products. Nvidia is based in California. Nvidia chips are used in Microsoft's Xbox games. They impersonated Microsoft employees (who were entitled to technical data about the products); they obtained improper access to Nvidia's machines and secured blueprints and information for products as well as other corporate information. They published this information on Web sites frequented by gaming enthusiasts. What was the result? (Refer to news reports.)

4. Charles Booher posted a 168-bit software encryption program on the Internet. Of course, an export license is required before it is disseminated globally, but Booher did not apply for one beforehand. What was the result? (Refer to news reports.)

5. Mykotronx, Inc., a company based in Maryland, produces encryption units. They are used the by U.S. government and its allies to transmit secret information by telephone or fax. Sale of these units must be approved by the National Security Agency. Messrs. Hsu and Yang sought to buy the units as representatives of a Singapore company. Although notified that they needed a license before exporting them, Hsu tried to discuss ways to repackage the units and disguise their ultimate destination. What was the result? (Refer to news reports.)

6. Homeland Security's director (Tom Ridge) and the secretary of transportation (Norman Mineta) proposed a "trusted traveler" card—basically a smart card used by airline travelers allowing them to bypass the long security lines and other measures now in place to address transportation security. Yet the head of the new Transportation Security Administration (John Magaw) worries the card might not be smart enough to thwart terrorist activities. What are the concerns, and what was the result? (Refer to news reports.)

7. The Justice Department proposed (in June 2002) new regulations requiring tens of thousands of Muslim and Middle Eastern visa holders to register with the government and be fingerprinted. Violators could be fined, refused reentry, or possibly deported. The officials commented, "this initiative is designed for individuals from countries who pose the highest risk to our security." Again there is a split within the Bush administration. What was the result? (Refer to news reports.)

8. Mykotronix, a private defense contractor, manufacturers KIV-7HS encryption devices used to encode classified government communications. Eugene Hsu called the company, asked about the technology, and requested pricing information. Company executives reported this call to customs agents. Hsu then

made a deal for the devices with undercover agents posing as company employees. Hsu then attempted to export them outside the United States. What are the concerns, and what was the result? (Refer to news reports.)

9. The Web site *http://www.password-crackers.com* is dedicated to revealing information about cryptography weaknesses and password recovery. This Web site discusses weakness of various systems and provides tips on how to crack specific software. Would this Web site legal if hosted in the United States? China? United Kingdom? Russia? What international regulations should be developed to regulate sites such as this, if any?

Additional Readings

- Allen, Julia H. *The CERT Guide to System and Network Security Practices*. Boston: Addison-Wesley, 2001.

- *Information Security*. This is the official publication of the International Computer Security Association (*http://www.infosecuritymag.com/*).

- Madse, Wayne, et al. "Cryptography and Liberty: An International Survey of Encryption Policy." *John Marshall Journal of Computer & Information Law* 16 (1998): 475.

- Schiffman, Mike. *Hacker's Challenge*. New York: Osborne/McGraw-Hill, 2001.

- Schneier, Bruce. *Applied Cryptography*, 2nd edition. New York: Wiley, 1996.

- Wingfield, Thomas C. *The Law of Information Conflict: National Security Law in Cyberspace*. Falls Church, VA: Aegis Research Corp., 2000.

INTERNET AND COMPUTER CRIME

Many crimes that are not specifically related to computers can be substantially facilitated by the use of computers. The easy access of cyberspace can provide a low-cost high-connectivity way for criminals to reach victims.

—http://www.usdoj.gov, cybercrime page

The Internet is a perfect vehicle for locating potential victims and provides a measure of anonymity for the fraudster.

—http://www.fbi.gov, *press release, April 23, 2001*

LEARNING OBJECTIVES

After you have read this chapter, you should be able to:

1. Understand how the Internet has changed and even enhanced the possibilities for criminal conduct.
2. Explain the elements of a crime.
3. Understand the various ways of committing an Internet crime, such as hacking, cracking, spoofing, sending e-mail bombs, viruses, and worms.
4. Explain what a computer crime is, such as software piracy, gambling, and cyberstalking.
5. Explain the various ways computers are used in the commission of crimes.
6. Understand the various laws under which computer crimes may be prosecuted.
7. Explain the difference in effect for communications in which the sender is anonymous and those in which the sender's identity is known.
8. Describe how businesses or law enforcement can protect the critical infrastructure.
9. Understand recent developments related to international cybercrime initiatives.
10. Discuss international efforts of mutual assistance and cooperation that help combat cybercrime.

http://

- Additional material relevant to this chapter may be found at the Bentley College CyberLaw Center Web site (**http://ecampus.bentley. edu/dept/cyberlaw**) under Social Issues—Cybercrime.

INTRODUCTION

The migration of commercial and government applications to computers and the Internet has caused a corresponding shift from the commission of crimes, traditionally focused on stealing physical assets, to the commission of crimes in cyberspace.

Cybercrime has only recently begun to receive the attention this massive problem warrants. The shift of crime to intangibles and the crimes committed by anonymous or pseudonymous individuals has a staggering impact on society, both socially and economically. This chapter details the crimes made possible by breaching information and computer security systems protocols. It describes the current legal environment of Internet, network, and computer crime.

THE NATURE OF COMPUTER CRIME

Consider this scenario: Morris, a computer science graduate student, created a computer program to demonstrate the inadequacies of Internet security by exploiting security defects. He released a *worm* designed to spread but at the same time draw little attention to itself. He discovered, though, that it replicated and infected machines at a much faster rate than anticipated. Many computers crashed as a result. He later sent an e-mail message instructing programmers how to kill the worm and prevent reinfection, but this message could not get through because the network was too clogged. This negatively affected 6,200 computers at universities, military sites, and medical research facilities. The costs of repair exceeded $98 million. A court found Morris guilty and sentenced him. Moreover, all of this occurred in 1988—many computer generations ago, at a time when there were comparatively few computers and users. The damages are exponentially increased in this new millennium in which the many more users and network applications bring with them a high potential for a greater variety of crime.

Consider another set of scenarios, all hypothetical:

- One person meets with another for the express purpose of selling her a fake investment. The investor likes the plan, turns over her money, and the salesperson runs off with the proceeds.
- One person makes hundreds of telephone calls to sell that same investment. Some people like it and turn over their money, and the salesperson runs off with the proceeds.
- One person places an advertisement in a financial publication to sell shares of this same investment. Thousands of people read this ad; many of them invest; and the salesperson runs off with the proceeds.
- One person, with a laptop and a modem, logs on to the Internet and does a mass mailing of the investment deal to millions of people, a far greater number than could ever be efficiently reached by postal mailing. Millions read this, thousands of them invest; and the salesperson runs off with the proceeds.

The lessons here have not been lost on criminals or on law enforcement efforts. The means of committing crimes are now cheap and ubiquitous. A computer with an Internet connection is all that is needed. Moreover, the number of potential victims is, in theory, limited by only one factor—the number of users connected to the Internet. It is clearly more efficient to perpetrate crime in cyberspace than in the physical world.

Computer crimes are made possible by the combination of computers, digitized content, and telecommunications bandwidth. The power to send data over communications equipment has transformed our society completely. This capacity to send data, however, does not operate in a perfect world. An analogy might be that ever since the first lock was invented, criminals have been trying to pick the locks. And so it is in the information age. Even as data is being sent, criminals may be trying to steal or manipulate it, use it as ransom, spy on it, or copy it.

In fact, the FBI thinks that computer criminals, anonymous individuals operating in a virtual world, will be the next significant wave of crime perpetrators. It is helpful to add some numbers to the discussion as a way of explaining the depth and breadth of the problem facing both governments and businesses. Just in one month, June 2002, the Department of Justice handled a number of cases, ranging from trafficking in counterfeit Microsoft software, stealing trade secrets from a Harvard biology lab, malicious spamming, selling fake Derek Jeter and Nomar Garciaparra sports memorabilia on eBay, credit card scams, to selling prescription drugs online. Half of Visa International, Inc.'s transactions from online sales were disputed or full-fledged frauds. In 1999, federal agents investigated a credit card billing scam. One man alone engineered $45 million of charges in hundreds of thousands of fraudulent transactions. More than 25 percent of all Fortune 500 corporations have been victimized by computer crime.

> **http://**
> - For articles and shows dealing with cybercrime issues, see **http://www.techtv.com**
> - Visit the National Infrastructure Protection Center at **http://www.nipc.gov**
> - For a sense of the magnitude of cybercrime, visit **http://www.securitystats.com**
> - CERT reports on computer and Internet incidents. Its site is found at **http://www.cert.org**

Regarding viruses, before 1999 there was just one level 9 alert per year. The Computer Emergency Response Team (CERT) rates Internet security breaches on a scale of 1 to 10. For example, the Melissa/Love Bug virus was a Level 9 alert—it was the fastest-growing virus in history, forcing the shutdown of servers around the world. (Melissa's creator, David L. Smith, pleaded guilty to computer theft and sending a damaging computer program. Both sides agreed the damages exceeded $80 million. For the federal charge, the court sentenced Smith to two years in prison and a $5,000 fine.) This occurred back in 1999; computer viruses and worms are even heartier and more malicious now. Such scenarios show no signs of abating, either. Business and government systems have migrated to the Internet and become dependent on it, which as we mentioned in Chapter 11 is structured to be an open and user-friendly platform.

These have been the selling points; product security features have not been. Security and crime remain afterthoughts. Consequently, there has not been a lot of discussion, or awareness, of risks, threats, data recovery programs, forensic discovery efforts, contingency plans, and so forth. And as more novices connect to the Internet, there becomes an overall declining expertise of users. These represent ever-greater vulnerabilities; comprehensive solutions do not yet exist.

What Are Computer and Internet Crimes?

Computer crimes may just be high-tech variations of conventional crimes and consist of traditional crimes committed with the help of computers, such as the distribution of child pornography. Other crimes are solely the product of the phenomenon of the Internet. Examples of this include the interception and rerouting of millions of Web users from their intended path (the domain name registration service InterNIC) to a personal Web site, Alter-NIC. Another example is the manipulation of a telephone switch by contestants to ensure their call would be the winning telephone call. [*United States v. Petersen,* 98 F.3d 502 (9th Cir. 1996)].

Computer Crime. **Computer crime** has been broadly defined as any illegal act that involves a computer, its systems, or its applications. It is any intentional act associated in any way with computers where a victim suffered or could have suffered a loss and a perpetrator made or could have made a gain. The U.S. Department of Justice defines computer crime as any illegal act for which knowledge of computer technology is essential either for its perpetration, investigation, or prosecution.

➤ http://

- For a sense of the types of cyber attacks, visit **http://www.attrition.org**
- Some general Web sites on Internet crime include **http://www.fbi.gov** and **http://cybercrime.gov**
- Cybercrime Conference Proceedings may be found at **http://www.cybercrime2002.com/**

Computer crimes are generally those illegal acts that existed *before* computers and the Internet but are now perpetrated with the aid of computers and usually the Internet. Examples include gambling, extortion, fraud, pyramid schemes, and so forth. This lack of precision in definitions is mainly due to the swift emergence of computers with telecommunications abilities. Prior to the Internet and computer networks, the number and variety of computer crimes were extremely limited. Such crimes usually consisted of illegal acts such as computer trespass and data manipulation or destruction.

Internet Crime. **Internet crime** is related to computer crime, but more specifically it relates to those illegal acts specifically made possible by the emergence of the Internet. These include hacking, cracking, spoofing, virus writing, creating worms, logic bombs, distributed denial of service attacks, and so forth.

The Impact on Law Enforcement

In any event, prior to the Internet, crimes were defined and classified in terms of their relationship to physical objects. Most importantly, the ability to damage or trespass or steal computers or data was determined by physical constraints. Criminals could damage or take away only what was on that computer.

The Internet has changed much of this, of course. It was not possible to commit this latter class of crimes prior to the Internet, and so the criminal laws are continually updated to address these novel criminal offenses. This shift away from the tangible corporeal environment to the information economy made possible by the Internet and telecommunications capabilities is an enormous challenge for business, government, and law enforcement. The lack of boundaries and physical constraints, combined both with the speed in which these transactions take place and the magnitude of harm, have changed many of the traditional paradigms of criminal law.

Defining what is a computer or Internet crime becomes further complicated by the fact that such illegal acts are subject to different laws—those at the state level, the federal level, and any applicable foreign countries. In fact, multiple prosecutions are possible for various offenses arising out of the same illegal act.

Common to the enforcement and prosecution for all crimes covered by federal and state criminal statutes are two required elements. First, the government must prove a *criminal act (actus reus)*. This element presents challenges to effective law enforcement, because oftentimes there may not even be a law making that act a crime. Congress has to make the act a crime *before* perpetrators may be charged with a criminal act. As criminals create new schemes, it is up to law enforcement to alert Congress to pass appropriate legislation. As an example of this lag, under the old criminal copyright infringement laws, the perpetrator must have profited from the illegal scheme. Recognizing that many crimes are committed on the Internet with no profit motive or profit taking at all, Congress amended the copyright laws to make certain types of copyright infringement a crime, even where the perpetrator does not personally make a financial gain from the illegal act.

Second, the government must prove a *criminal intent (mens rea)*. (Both elements must exist and be proven "beyond a reasonable doubt.") The second required element—criminal intent—is also an issue in the realm of Internet prosecutions. For example, there have been a number of network break-ins. The catch, though, is that the criminal intent element is not clear. In many of these cases, hackers gain entry just because they can or for a more altruistic reason—to demonstrate to the network staff where the security vulnerabilities lie. These may not add up to the requisite level of criminal intent that is required for charging individuals with committing a crime. Legislators get around the intent element by writing "strict liability" statutes, which makes the act a crime *regardless* of the perpetrator's intent.

Another recent case is an example of how confounding criminal intent is for purposes of prosecuting cybercrime. The charges stem from a government sting operation involving Patrick Naughton, one of the creators of Java programming. A federal agent posed as a thirteen-year-old in conversations with Naughton in an Internet chat room. Naughton represented that he had possession of child pornography and wished to meet "her." Naughton traveled across state lines to meet with this supposed thirteen-year-old girl, and agents arrested Naughton. He was convicted of the possession of child pornography, but the jury deadlocked, along gender lines, on two other counts—soliciting sex with a minor over the Internet and interstate travel to have sex with a minor. The novel aspect of this case is the argument by Naughton's lawyers to the jury that he lacked the requisite mental state (*mens rea*) to commit a crime. Instead, the defense asserted that Naughton was merely participating in an Internet sex fantasy and engaged in fantasy role playing. Naughton testified that probably millions of people are carrying out similar fantasies on the Internet, and they have no intention of actually following through on them. Female jurors believed the prosecution's version; the male jurors believed Naughton's assertion that he was merely playing out a fantasy.

This text mainly addresses cybercrime from the federal perspective. Federal laws are applicable in every U.S. jurisdiction. Bear in mind that even though this chapter discusses

http://

- To understand the statutes Naughton is accused of violating, see **http://www4.law.cornell.edu/ uscode/18/plch117.html**
- The FTC has authority over civil infractions of the law; its site is found at **http://www.ftc.gov**

the federal legal response to criminal acts, there is a body of law addressing other offenses—*civil* infractions, for less serious acts. For example, a copyright infringement may be minor and so only a civil matter, remedied through fines, reimbursement, and so forth. (Refer to Chapter 4, "Copyrights.") Generally, civil actions are brought by either private individual parties or by a government agency, typically the Federal Trade Commission (FTC). One last point: each state has a criminal code, and so even though an act might not be a federal criminal offense, it may be a state crime.

The E-Commerce Risks

The threat of information/data loss due to computer and Internet crime is ever present for businesses. These first-party losses include physical damage; security breaches by insiders as well as outsiders; destruction or theft of information such as intellectual property assets as well as operational data; and lost revenue, time, and opportunity costs associated with such disruptions. Perpetrators accomplish this by accessing computers and networks without authorization or with authorization they have *exceeded*. (Note how information and Internet security measures could limit these losses.) Moreover, these losses carry over to third-party client/vendor/supplier relationships due to the high level of connectivity between such partners.

In just one example, as a result of so much online credit card and shipping fraud, a number of e-retailers have cut back on sales to certain foreign countries. One of these e-retailers—buy.com—has stopped shipping to all but twenty-five foreign countries. This has reduced overall sales because they no longer operate in some large markets (Bob Tedeschi, "E-Tailers Wary of Credit Card Fraud," July 15, 2002, *http://www. nytimes.com/technology/*).

The next section discusses how Internet and computer crimes are classified. Additionally, we cite recent cases to give you a sense of the computer and Internet crime that exists today in our networked environment.

THE ROLE OF COMPUTERS IN CRIME: CRIMES AND PERPETRATORS

The advent of networked computers has created unprecedented opportunities for the anonymous perpetration of crimes. In fact, law enforcement experts say the two most difficult problems they encounter are (1) establishing jurisdiction over alleged perpetrators, and (2) establishing the identities of the alleged perpetrators. First we discuss how computers are used in crime. Then we describe the sorts of crimes actually committed with computers.

How Computers Are Used in the Commission of Crimes

Computers as the Target of Crime. In this respect, the computer itself is the subject of the crime. Perpetrators use computers to obtain information or to interfere or damage operating systems or programs. Perpetrators access operations and systems through *trapdoors* that exist for the bona fide reason of correcting faulty situations. As discussed in Chapter 11, any entry point is potentially exploitable for criminal purposes. For example, perpetrators may illegally take on the role of a systems manager (identity fraud) and access virtually everything in the system or network. Possible criminal offenses resulting from this activity include sabotage of any data such as hospital, government, or business records; theft of customer lists, intellectual property, or intelligence reports; vandalism of Web sites; and the introduction of computer viruses.

Computers as a Tool in the Commission of a Crime. Computers can be used to facilitate crimes. For example, by introducing new programming instructions or manipulating computers' legitimate functions for illegal purposes, perpetrators exploit computers for the commission of crimes. This category includes the transmission of child or other pornography; fraudulent use of ATM or wire transfers; fraud in any e-commerce transaction; fraudulent electronic billing scams; and even murder (in one case, the suspect allegedly changed medication and dosage information about a patient into the hospital's computer system).

Computers as Incidental to a Crime. The use of a computer is not absolutely necessary to the commission of this class of crime. These consist of traditional crimes, such as money laundering, bookmaking, and drug dealing. Computers are used in these crimes for recordkeeping purposes. (Recall the *Scarfo* case from Chapter 11.) These are still considered computer crimes because perpetrators rely on them in their illegal operations.

CRIMES BEING COMMITTED IN TODAY'S NETWORKED ENVIRONMENT

> A place inhabited by thieves, con men, perverts, child molesters, road agents, malcontents and miscreants. No, this is not the old west or the slums of the inner city, this is the Internet of the 21st Century. (*http://www.techPolice.com*, citing California Department of Justice special agent, Fred Adler)

Although many of these crimes might sound familiar to you, the fact that they are being committed by or with computers and usually over the Internet has significant ramifications, because computers are inevitably highly accurate and efficient. And it is extremely difficult to identify alleged perpetrators and prosecute computer crimes. This section categorizes the cybercrimes that are most prevalent today, classified according to who, or what, is harmed by the illegal acts. Of course, in many instances there is an overlap among crimes and criminal charges. Because the vast majority of cases are resolved prior to trial either through plea agreements or settlements, many of the reports of these cases are available only as news stories rather than in the form of court decisions.

http://

- The Computer Security Institute and the FBI issued a joint report and survey on cybercrime, available at **http://www.gocsi.com/ press/20020407.html**
- The FBI's Internet Fraud Complaint Center is found at **http://www. ifccfbi.gov**
- The *U.S. Attorneys' Bulletin*, May 2001, details Internet fraud. See **http://www.usdoj.gov/criminal/ cybercrime/usamay2001_1.htm**

Crimes Against Persons or Businesses

Fraud. **Fraud** is the act of knowingly making material false representations that victims rely on. In the realm of the Internet, these mainly concern online fraud in four categories:

1. Retail sales (misleading customers, counterfeit goods or services, nondeliverable goods)
2. Auction sales (due to shill bidding, shill feedback)
3. Financial opportunities ("pump-and-dump," and its opposite, the "cyber-smear"; also: Ponzi, pyramid, "work-at-home" schemes—recall the *Abacus* case)
4. Payment cards (credit and debit cards). This last category, of course, overlaps with the first three. This is the main fraud that supports criminals in their perpetration of additional crimes on the Internet such as identity theft. The U.S. Secret Service estimates that $500 million a year is lost by consumers who have credit card and calling card numbers stolen from online databases.

Identity Theft. This is a subgroup of fraud, but we single it out because it is the leading consumer fraud complaint in 2001, exceeding the next leading category—auction fraud—by a factor of four. **Identity theft** is the hijacking of someone else's identity information, such as their personal number on their social security card, driver's license, work ID, or credit cards. Moreover, this information is available online through e-mail extractor programs, from commercial services such as Equifax, Experian and Lexis/Nexis, or even through shoulder surfing, mailbox theft, and dumpster diving. Hackers may penetrate corporate databases to download this information. In one recent case, an Algerian man faces federal identity theft charges for allegedly stealing the identities of twenty-one members of a health club. He copied this information from their membership cards. He is linked with the terrorists from the 9/11 action. After stealing identity data, it is possible to steal just about anything. As with fraud, identity theft is committed to facilitate other crimes. The following case is an identity theft case, and although the theft occurs without use of the Internet (there is not yet a decided Internet identity fraud case), this opinion offers an excellent example of the ramifications of identity theft.

United States v. Sample
213 F.3d 1029 (8th Cir. 2000)

Facts

From 1995 to 1997, Julianne Sample engaged in an elaborate financial fraud and identity theft scheme. Sample perpetrated her scheme by procuring personal information about her roommates, casual acquaintances, visitors, and individuals she met through other friends. Sample also worked in tandem with her boyfriend, Thomas Melton. Melton, a former employee of Builders Square, often forwarded personal information obtained from his customers to Sample. Once Sample purloined this information from her unsuspecting victims, she began the process of stealing their identities. Sample used the personal information to open various bank accounts, secure credit cards, and even establish false driver's licenses in the names of her victims. Sample then utilized the credit cards to make multiple purchases in her victims' names. She also wrote checks and withdrew money from her fraudulent bank accounts. In one instance, Sample, posting as Keri Shirk, visited a regional health center, and there she altered Shirk's medical records and obtained a prescription in Shirk's name.

Sample pleaded guilty in a state court to one count of forgery and two counts of felony theft and was sentenced to serve eighteen months in prison. While in state prison, the U.S. Secret Service interviewed Sample, and then she admitted to orchestrating an extensive identity takeover scheme and stealing thousands from her victims. Sample "guesstimated" that she either caused or intended to cause her victims to lose a combined amount in excess of $70,000. Following this interview, a federal grand jury indicted Sample for one count of credit card fraud. Sample agreed to plead guilty to the charge. The government agreed that the total amount of actual and intended loss fell between $40,000 and $70,000. The parties acknowledged in the agreement, however, that the federal district court retained discretion with regard to all sentencing decisions.

Prior to Sample's sentencing hearing, the U.S. Probation Office prepared a Pre-Sentence Investigation Report (PSIR). The PSIR concluded that, contrary to Sample's plea agreement, the actual and intended loss fell between $70,000 and $120,000. The PSIR also stated that an upward departure from the federally mandated sentencing guideline range prescribed in the U.S. Sentencing Guidelines Manual *might* be warranted based on the factors delineated therein.

The federal district court sentenced Sample and held that an upward departure was warranted in this case. It based this departure decision on the degree of psychological harm that Sample inflicted on her victims. It then sentenced Sample to thirty months in prison. Sample appeals her sentence to this court.

Judicial Opinion *(Judge Hansen)*

Sample argues that the district court erred when it decided to upwardly depart in this case. Sample challenges [both] the decision to impose an upward departure as well as the reasonableness of the extent of the departure. We review . . . under a[n] abuse of discretion standard [this is comparable to rational basis scrutiny]. We note that a departure is appropriate only in extraordinary cases where there exists an 'aggravating or mitigating circumstance of a kind, or to a degree, *not* adequately taken into consideration by the . . . guidelines. [Thus] the district court may depart, provided that the applicable Guideline does not already take the factor into account. [Specifically] the Guidelines encourage an upward departure whenever the amount of loss fails to capture the harmfulness and seriousness of the conduct. [This occurs] when the conduct causes reasonably foreseeable physical or psychological harm, or severe emotional distress, to the victim of the crime.

In this case, the record is replete with evidence that Sample caused her victims to suffer severe emotional trauma. Two of Sample's victims, Shirk and Paula Jensen, testified at Sample's sentencing hearing regarding the degree of disruption and turmoil wrought upon their lives as a result of Sample's deceptions.

Jensen testified as follows:

Once I learned of this crime committed against me, I was terrified to be alone, fearful that someone may steal my children, frightened that someone may be following me, afraid to write a check, horrified that someone was out there destroying my good name and credit, and there wasn't anything I could do about it. . . . Try to imagine the time and frustration and the endless hours spent on the phone and going in person to places in an effort to prove my real identity. All the time I was being treated like a criminal. No one believed me. . . .

I cannot even begin to explain the embarrassment and the humiliation that I feel when I'm rejected [sic] credit or when stores refuse to accept my checks because of the criminal actions of Ms. Sample. Try to imagine how demoralizing it is to be treated like a criminal for a crime committed against you. Emotionally, it's very degrading.

Probably the most serious and traumatic situation involved me almost being arrested after a minor traffic accident because warrants listed under my social security number came up because I'm an alias of her. I now have to carry this legal statement with me at all times to prove my real identity. . . .

The anger, fear, and anxiety that this has caused is going to leave me scarred forever. It will never be over for me. I have a difficult time trusting people because now, of course, I'm suspicious of what someone is going to do to me. The time I've had to spend towards getting this mess straightened out has taken me away from my children. I'll never be able to get that back.

I've had two missed days off [sic] work trying to get different problems straightened out, and the frustration of the many phone calls that I've had to deal with while I've been at work that relate to this case has been overwhelming and distracting. I'm an elementary school teacher, and it has been extremely difficult for me to deal with these phone calls and then immediately step back into my classroom emotionally ready to meet the educational needs of my students.

Shirk offered similar testimony.

Based upon our review of the record, we conclude that more than enough evidence exists for the district court to find that Sample caused her victims to suffer severe emotional distress and trauma. While Sample may not have been able to apprehend the precise effects of the harm caused by her actions, she undoubtedly could foresee the level of personal upheaval likely to result from an identity theft scheme. Sample's identity theft . . . exhibits a degree of callousness sufficient to justify a nine-month upward departure.

For the reasons stated above, we affirm the judgment of the district court.

Case Questions

1. Identify the types of identity information that are the most valuable and visit some Web sites and see if you can find such information for sale. Which identity information is the easiest to obtain?

2. Based on your knowledge of security practices, name some ways in which we could better secure our identity information.

3. Do you think the court was justified in its upward departure from the sentencing guidelines? Is there a better, more effective way to punish Sample?

The problems associated with the crime of identity theft are further compounded by issues relating to various statutes of limitations. Statutes of limitation exist in order to ensure that claims are brought in a timely manner. The Supreme Court recently heard an identity theft case. In *TRW, Inc. v. Andrews*, 534 U.S. 19 (2001), a receptionist in a doctor's office copied Andrews's data, moved to Las Vegas, and opened accounts in Andrews's name. Andrews discovered this a few years later when she requested a copy of her credit report and realized what had happened. Yet Andrews is barred from suing the credit agency because she brought her action more than two years later, too late according to the relevant statute of limitations. The Supreme Court rejected a broad interpretation that the statute should run only when the victim *learns* of the wrongdoing, and instead it upheld the rule that the statute begins running on the date of the wrongdoing.

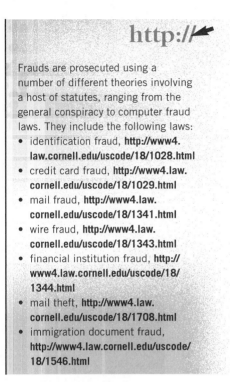

Frauds are prosecuted using a number of different theories involving a host of statutes, ranging from the general conspiracy to computer fraud laws. They include the following laws:

- identification fraud, **http://www4. law.cornell.edu/uscode/18/1028.html**
- credit card fraud, **http://www4.law. cornell.edu/uscode/18/1029.html**
- mail fraud, **http://www4.law. cornell.edu/uscode/18/1341.html**
- wire fraud, **http://www4.law. cornell.edu/uscode/18/1343.html**
- financial institution fraud, **http://www4.law.cornell.edu/uscode/18/1344.html**
- mail theft, **http://www4.law. cornell.edu/uscode/18/1708.html**
- immigration document fraud, **http://www4.law.cornell.edu/uscode/18/1546.html**

Gambling. Largely conducted offshore due to restrictive U.S. laws, Nevada has become the first state to approve **Internet gambling**, which reportedly reaps $6 billion a year in revenues. New Jersey may follow Nevada's lead. Interstate gambling using the Internet is illegal unless (1) it is legal in every state impacted in the communications; and (2) adults only are participating. It is difficult to verify such information, especially when it is self-reported, and so law enforcement is virtually ineffectual in this field. (Also, Recall the *SG* case from Chapter 7.)

President Bush is currently urging Congress to pass a bill to regulate Internet gambling. Under the current regulatory environment, the federal government has traditionally deferred to states in regulating gambling activities. To the extent organized crime took hold of gambling, Congress passed a statute dealing in part with this issue.

Spamming. **Spamming** (discussed in Chapter 9, "Privacy") may be fraudulent and may, or may not, be a crime. A number of fraud laws may be invoked. (There is just one federal law specifically targeting spam, and it is limited to fraudulent *telephone* solicitations. For marketers, the Internet offers incredible efficiencies. But it is an unwelcome nuisance for recipients. The Federal Trade Commission (FTC), although not empowered to stop spam, has the power to enforce laws prohibiting fraudulent or deceptive

http://

- One assistant U.S. attorney calls identity theft the crime of the new millennium and reports on recent criminal activity in this area. See **http://www.usdoj.gov/criminal/ cybercrime/usamarch2001_3.htm** and the Identity Theft Act, **http:// www4.law.cornell.edu/uscode/18/ 1028.html**, particularly Subsection (a)(7). This act criminalizes fraud in the connection with the unlawful theft and misuse of personally identifying data (such as licenses, biometric data) and provides for fines and/or imprisonment for up to fifteen years.
- The transmission of wagering information law can be found at **http://www4.law.cornell.edu/uscode/ 18/1084.html**, which makes it a crime to use a wire communication facility to transmit bets or wagers, or information therefrom. Penalties include a fine and/or imprisonment for up to two years.
- Internet gun sales are covered by existing laws, specifically the Gun Control Act, **http://www4.law. cornell.edu/uscode/18/922.html**
- Internet drug sales are governed, for the most part, by the Controlled Substances Act, regulating online pharmacies and other sites that offer or dispense controlled substances: **http://www4.law. cornell.edu/uscode/21/829.html** and **http://www4.law.cornell.edu/ uscode/21/841.html** Penalties are complicated, and terms are extremely harsh.
- Internet alcohol sales are governed by the Webb-Kenyon Act prohibiting the shipment of alcohol into a state in violation of state law. See **http://www4.law.cornell. edu/uscode/27/122.html**

marketing practices. Moreover, states such as Virginia (where AOL is headquartered) are increasingly taking the initiative and outlawing spam because there is no federal law. In a recent case, a state court judge agreed with the state of Washington's arguments, and it upheld a federal Commerce Clause challenge to that state's antispam legislation. Therefore, it is now illegal to spam into Washington.

Sale of Controlled Items. Nonprescriptive and prescriptive drugs (such as Viagra and Cipro), firearms, explosives, cigarettes, alcohol, and even IDs and visas may be found for sale on the Internet. Many of these sites ask for user information, but this ends up as *self*-identifying information— generated by the users—and is not very reliable. This area of law is very unsettled at this time. For example, a federal judge rejected the state of New York's ban in Internet cigarette sales as violative of the federal Commerce Clause. (Notice the difference in outcome with the Washington spam case.) There is some thought about using the mail and wire fraud statutes for prosecuting such cases. It is also unclear whether these activities should be classified as civil or criminal.

Pornography/Obscenity. **Pornography** that involves children, or is obscene, is a crime. This involves the transmission or sale of such images. Studies show that pedophiles are turning to Internet chat rooms to solicit children for illegal acts or even just to gain their confidence and elicit information from them. In a recent case, for example, as a result of its Operation Candyman, the FBI arrested a child pornography ring consisting of more than a hundred people nationwide. Twenty-seven of those admitted to having molested more than forty children. They are charged with possession, production, and/or distribution of child pornography. Moreover, there were nearly four thousand members of this group site. In one case, defendants were convicted for operating an electronic bulletin board that posted pictures from sexually explicit magazines [*United States v. Thomas,* 74 F.3d 701 (6th Cir. 1996)].

Congress has repeatedly attempted to regulate obscenity on the Internet, especially as it impacts children. (Refer to Chapter 10, "Obscenity.") There are essentially two impediments to regulating Internet obscenity or child pornography. First is the First Amendment issue. Due to the impact on speech and expression of such statutes, courts closely scrutinize these laws, and such a review is nearly always fatal for the statute. Second, the Internet is inherently difficult to regulate because the historic paradigm of obscenity regulation has been the geographically based rule of the prevailing local community standard. The Internet is anything but local; there is no such community on the Internet, and so the paradigm has proved inapplicable.

In this next case, the Supreme Court is asked to decide a question for the Internet age: whether pornography involving *virtual* images of children should be considered illegal, the same as pornography involving real children. (This opinion also resolved a split among those circuit courts to have considered this contentious issue. Moreover, the justices of the Supreme Court were badly split on this case.)

Ashcroft v. Free Speech Coalition
535 U.S. 234 (2002)

Facts

The Free Speech Coalition (FSC) is a trade association of businesses involved in the production and distribution of "adult-oriented materials." Appellants also include Bold Type, Inc., publisher of a book espousing the ideals of nudism; Jim Gingerich, a New York artist whose paintings include large-scale nudes; and Ron Raffaelli, a professional photographer whose works include nude and erotic photographs.

In 1996, members of Congress passed the **Child Pornography Prevention Act (CPPA)** in an effort to combat the use of computer technology to produce pornography using computer-generated images that look like real children. The new law sought to stifle the use of technology for illicit purposes. In the past, Congress had always acted to prevent harm to *real* children involved in the production of child pornography. Congress shifted the paradigm from the illegality of child pornography that involved the use of real children in its creation to now forbid a "visual depiction" that "is, or appears to be, of a minor engaging in sexually explicit conduct." The premise of the CPPA is the asserted impact of such images on the children who may view them. The law is also based on the notion that child pornography—real as well as virtual—increases the incidence of illegal activities involving real children, such as crimes generated by child molesters and pedophiles. The CPPA makes criminal the generation of images of fictitious children engaged in imaginary but explicit sexual conduct.

The CPPA defines child pornography as "any visual depiction, including any photograph, film, video, picture, or computer or computer-generated image or picture, whether made or produced by electronic, mechanical, or other means, of sexually explicit conduct." At issue in this appeal are the definitions contained in Subsections (B) and (D) of 18 U.S.C. Section 2256(8). This section bans sexually explicit depictions that appear to be minors. It bans visual depictions that are "advertised, promoted, presented, described or distributed in such a manner that conveys that impression" that they contain sexually explicit depictions of minors. (This challenge essentially surrounds FSC's contention that the two phrases "appear to be minors" and "conveys the impression" are so vague and overbroad that they do not meet the requirements of the First Amendment.)

The district court rejected FSC's claims and upheld the statute. The Ninth Circuit noted that this appeal "presents a conflict between one of society's most cherished rights—freedom of expression—and one of the government's most profound obligations—the protection of minors." It ultimately reversed the decision, however, concluding that the CPPA's prohibitions on speech were overbroad and thus unconstitutional. (Four other courts of appeals upheld the CPPA in the face of similar challenges.) The Supreme Court granted certiorari to resolve the split among the circuit courts.

Judicial Opinion *(Justice Kennedy)*

We consider in this case whether the Child Pornography Prevention Act . . . abridges the freedom of speech. The principal question to be resolved, then, is whether the CPPA is constitutional where it proscribes a significant universe of speech that is neither obscene under *Miller* nor child pornography under *Ferber*.

Before [this statute] Congress defined child pornography as the type of depictions at issue in *Ferber*, images made using actual minors. The CPPA retains that prohibition . . . and adds three other prohibited categories of speech. The prohibition on 'any visual depiction' does not depend at all on how the image is produced. The section captures a range of depictions, sometimes called 'virtual child pornography.' These images do not involve, let alone harm, any children in the production process; but Congress decided the materials threaten children in other, less direct, ways.

Under *Miller* . . . the Government must prove that the work, taken as a whole, appeals to the prurient interest, is patently offensive in light of community standards, and lacks serious literary, artistic, political, or scientific value. The CPPA, however, extends to images that appear to depict a minor engaging in sexually explicit activity without regard to the *Miller* requirements. Any depiction of sexually explicit activity, no matter how it is presented, is proscribed. The CPPA applies to a picture in a psychology manual, as well as a movie depicting the horrors of sexual abuse. The CPPA prohibits speech despite its serious literary, artistic, political, or scientific value. Both themes—teenage sexual activity and the sexual abuse of children—have inspired countless literary works. William Shakespeare created the most famous pair of teenage lovers. Contemporary movies pursue similar themes. Last year's Academy Awards featured the movie, 'Traffic.' The film portrays a teenager . . . which in the end leads her to a filthy room to trade sex for drugs.

As a general principle, the First Amendment bars the government from dictating what we see or read or speak or hear. The freedom of speech has its limits; it does not embrace certain categories of speech, including defamation, incitement, obscenity, and pornography produced with real children. None of the[se] [categories] includes the speech prohibited by the CPPA. The CPPAs penalties are indeed severe. A first offender may be imprisoned for 15 years. A repeat offender faces a prison sentence of not less than 5 years and not more than 30 years in prison. [T]his case provides a textbook example of why we permit facial challenges to statutes that burden expression. With these severe penalties in force, few legitimate movie producers or book publishers, or few other speakers in any capacity, would risk distributing images in or near the uncertain reach of this law.

The government may not suppress lawful speech as the means to suppress unlawful speech. In these cases, the defendant can demonstrate no [real] children were harmed in producing the images. In sum, section 2256 covers materials beyond the categories recognized in *Ferber* and *Miller*, and the reasons the Government offers in support of limiting the freedom of speech have no justification. The provision abridges the freedom to engage in a substantial amount of lawful speech. For this reason, it is overbroad and unconstitutional.

The judgment of the Court of Appeals is affirmed.

IT IS SO ORDERED.

Case Questions

1. What is Congress's next best strategy to regulate (if it still desires to) computer-generated child pornography?
2. What do you think of the protections for this activity under the First Amendment, as a majority of the Supreme Court interprets it?
3. What are the implications for businesses based on this decision?

The **Child Online Protection Act (COPA)** is found at *http://www4.law.cornell. edu/uscode/47/231.html*. This statute applies strictly commercial transmissions of material that is "harmful to minors," and to define what it harmful, it draws on the *Miller* community test. What is a community in our global network becomes the key question, for which there is not yet an answer. This is another way the Internet impacts our traditional historical legal paradigms. The *Miller* standard does not translate well to the global community. This case, too, reached the Supreme Court in the 2001–2002 term. Again, the Court was divided. It vacated an earlier decision and remanded the case back to the Third Circuit, and asked it to decide whether COPA is unconstitutional in contravention of the First Amendment [*Ashcroft v. American Civil Liberties Union*, 122 S. Ct. 1700, 2002 U.S. LEXIS 3421 (May 13, 2002)]. In the meantime, COPA is not in effect. Refer back to Chapter 10, "Obscenity."

http://

- The CPPA discussed in this case is found at **http://www4.law.cornell. edu/uscode/18/2252A.html** The general obscenity statutes are found at **http://www4.law.cornell.edu/uscode/ 18/pch71.html** These statutes outlaw the interstate or foreign transportation for commercial purposes of any lewd, lascivious book or any other matter of indecent or immoral character. Violations may result in up to five years of imprisonment and/or fines.

Stalking and Harassment. **Stalking** and **harassment** consists of terrorizing people over the Internet and includes communications of taunts, profanity, or demands. In one case, an employee sent up to fifty e-mails a day to a supervisor for the purpose of harassing him. This person was charged with telecommunications harassment. In two other cases, the stalkers first committed identity theft and then assumed the women's identities in cyberspace. Through newsgroup messages, the stalkers posted ads inviting strangers to the women's home. The messages included extremely detailed information about the women's schedules, telephone and address information, and social plans. In another case, the perpetrator located in Kansas City terrorized a group of youngsters in Massachusetts he did not know. He convinced them he was ready to carry out a murderous rampage. Massachusetts did not at the time have a law criminalizing this act. In another instance, a perpetrator paid $45 to docusearch.com for the Social Security number of a woman he was obsessed with; he later purchased the name of her employer—and then tracked her down and murdered her. This last example is a hybrid action of stalking and hate. Antiabortion extremists have begun a strategy of filming patients and their abortion clinic providers; uploading these images onto the Web, and possibly inciting violence.

Hate Crimes. These are typically the communication of threatening hate-filled messages attacking people simply based on their traits of race, color, sex, religion, ethnicity, or sexual orientation. Note that First Amendment concerns are raised in these cases. In one recent case, a college student pleaded guilty to sending derogatory e-mails to a number of people who had Hispanic-sounding last names. Prosecuting these cases at the federal level is hampered by the lack of a law that directly addresses Internet hate crimes. The main statute prosecutors charge with is a law enacted during the 1960s U.S. civil rights movement. The statute makes it a crime to intimidate individuals into not exercising their federally protected rights. It does not recognize as actionable those crimes against women or those based on the victim's sexual orientation or disability. As with spam, state hate crime legislation is more comprehensive than federal legislation.

Murder and Death Threats. Again, note First Amendment concerns here associated with **murder and death threats**. Internet death threats have been sent to a number of public figures because of what they have said or for their associations. Former president Clinton has been subject to threats, as have a myriad of teachers, classmates, and co-workers. In another case, a college student wrote a short story and posted it to a publicly available Internet newsgroup. It graphically described the torture, rape, and murder of a woman who was named after one of the student's classmates. Officials charged him in a criminal prosecution for transmitting threats via e-mail to injure or kidnap another. The court had

http://

- For an example of such a site that may promote/incite violence, visit **http://www.christiangallery.com/atrocity/** The text of the Domestic Violence and Stalking Act may be found at **http://www4.law.cornell.edu/uscode/18/2261A.html** Penalties include fines, and/or up to life imprisonment if the stalking results in death to the victim.
- Hate Crimes are prosecuted under the federal civil rights statutes, found at **http://www4.law.cornell.edu/uscode/18/245.html** and **http://www4.law.cornell.edu/uscode/18/247.html** Penalties include fines, and/or up to life imprisonment. Moreover, the death penalty may be invoked where a death results. Women are afforded additional protection under the Violence Against Women Act: **http://www4.law.cornell.edu/uscode/42/13981.html** For an example of a state statute, see California Penal Code sections 1170.75 and 666.7, where that state considers hate crimes an aggravating factor (and thus more serious crime) and provides sentencing enhancements for hate crimes.

to decide whether the threat was true and imminent (and thus outside the protection of the First Amendment) or whether it was merely a discussion of desires, and thus protected speech within the First Amendment. What do you think [*United States v. Baker*, 890 F. Supp. 1375 (E.D. Mich. 1995)]?

Crimes Against Property

http://

Physical Property. These crimes are covered for the most part by the Computer Fraud and Abuse Act. Because this is the main statute for addressing computer and Internet crime, we detail this law before we discuss the various crimes it addresses. We also present two important cases interpreting this law.

- These crimes are prosecuted under the extortion and threats statute found at **http://www4.law.cornell.edu/uscode/18/875.html** The penalties include a fine and/or up to twenty years' imprisonment.
- To read the entire CFAA, visit **http://www4.law.cornell.edu/uscode/18/1030.html**

Computer Fraud and Abuse Act (CFAA), 18 U.S.C. § 1030. The **Computer Fraud and Abuse Act** is the first law to treat computer-related crimes as distinct federal offenses.

This act made it unnecessary to amend individually nearly every federal law to include offenses committed with the use of computers. Significantly, this act protects all computers connected to the Internet and all computer activities, whether they occur locally or nationally.

The CFAA has three goals: to protect the

1. *confidentiality* of the data/communications.
2. *integrity* of the data/communications.
3. *availability* of the data/communications

Pursuant to these goals, the CFAA prohibits using computers to commit any of the following seven crimes:

- knowingly commit espionage by accessing information without authorization or exceeding authorized access
- access other information without authorization or exceeding authorized access
- access any nonpublic government computer
- access any computer with an intent to commit fraud
- knowingly or intentionally damage a computer
- knowingly traffic in passwords
- threaten to cause damage to a computer with the intent to extort money or other things of value

The following case, briefly mentioned at the beginning of this chapter, is presented now as an example of a prosecution under the CFAA. This incident is considered one of the earliest significant events to bring the problem of cybercrime to the attention of the public and law enforcement officials.

United States v. Morris
928 F.2d 504 (2nd Cir.), cert. denied, 502 U.S. 817 (1991)

Facts

Refer to pages 406–407 for a recitation of the facts.

Morris was found guilty of violating 18 U.S.C. § 1030(a)(5)(a) following a jury trial. He was sentenced to three years of probation, 400 hours of community service, and fined $10,050. Morris appealed the trial court's decision to the circuit court.

Judicial Opinion *(Judge Newman)*

Section 1030(a)(5)(A) [of the CFAA] penalizes the conduct of an individual who intentionally accesses a federal interest computer [a government computer] without authorization. Morris contends that his conduct constituted, at most, 'exceeding authorized access' rather than the 'unauthorized access' that the subsection punishes. Morris argues that there was insufficient evidence to convict him of 'unauthorized access.' Morris was authorized to use computers at Cornell, Harvard, and Berkeley, all of which were on INTERNET. As a result, Morris was authorized to communicate with other computers on the network to send electronic mail (SEND MAIL), and to find out certain information about the users of other computers (finger demon). The question is whether Morris's transmission of his worm constituted exceeding authorized access or accessing without authorization.

The evidence permitted the jury to conclude that Morris's use of SEND MAIL and finger demon features constituted access without authorization. While a case might arise where the use of SEND MAIL or finger demon falls within a nebulous area in which the line between accessing without authorization and exceeding authorized access may not be clear, Morris's conduct here falls well within the area of unauthorized access. Morris did not use either of those features in any way related to their intended function. He did not send or read mail nor discover information about other users; instead he found holes in both programs that permitted him a special and unauthorized access route into other computers.

Although the evidence may have shown that defendant's initial insertion of the worm simply exceeded his authorized access, the evidence also demonstrated that the worm was designed to spread to other computers at which he had no account and no authority, express or implied, to unleash the worm program.

Accordingly, the evidence did support the jury's conclusion that defendant accessed without authority as opposed to merely exceeding the scope of his authority.

For the foregoing reasons, the judgment of the District Court is AFFIRMED.

Case Questions

1. What was the critical reason for the court deciding that Morris's actions violated the law?

2. Do you think the necessary element of criminal intent by Morris was present in this case?

3. Was it ethical of Morris to test his program on the Internet without first sending notice of the test?

This next case, prosecuted under Section 1030(a)(4) of the CFAA, shows how courts read the statutes to distinguish what is, and is not, a crime. This case is also briefly mentioned in the context of wire fraud, which we discuss later.

United States v. Czubinski
106 F.3d 1069 (1st Cir. 1997)

Facts

Richard Czubinski was employed by the Boston office of the Taxpayer Services Division of the IRS. To perform his official duties, Czubinski routinely accessed information from one of the IRS's computer systems. Using his valid password and certain search codes, he was able to retrieve income tax information regarding virtually any taxpayer in the United States. IRS rules plainly state that employees with passwords and access codes are not permitted to access files on its systems outside of the course of their official duties. Czubinski carried out numerous unauthorized searches of IRS files and knowingly disregarded IRS rules. Forensic audit trails establish that Czubinski accessed information regarding the tax return of individuals involved with the David Duke campaign when he was a presidential candidate; the joint tax return of an assistant district attorney (he had been prosecuting Czubinski's father); the tax return of Boston city counselor Jim Kelly's campaign committee (Kelly had defeated Czubinski in an election); the tax return of a woman Czubinski had dated a few times; and so on. There was no evidence that he disclosed or sold this information to any third parties. Following a jury trial, Czubinski was convicted on four counts of computer fraud. Czubinski appealed his conviction.

Judicial Opinion *(Judge Torruella)*

We have never before addressed section 1030(a)(4). Czubinski unquestionably exceeded authorized access to a Federal interest computer. On appeal he argues that he did not obtain "anything of value." We agree, finding that his searches of taxpayer return information did not satisfy the statutory requirement that he obtain "anything of value." The value of information is relative to one's needs and objectives; here, the government had to show that the information was valuable to Czubinski in light of a fraudulent scheme. The government failed, however, to prove that Czubinski intended anything more than to satisfy idle curiosity.

The plain language of section 1030(a)(4) emphasizes that more than mere unauthorized use is required: the 'thing obtained' may not merely be the unauthorized use. It is the showing of some additional end—to which the unauthorized access is a means—that is lacking here. The evidence did not show that Czubinski's end was anything more than to satisfy his curiosity by viewing information about friends, acquaintances, and political rivals. No evidence suggests that he printed out, recorded, or used the information he browsed. No rational jury could conclude beyond a reasonable doubt that Czubinski intended to use or disclose that information, and merely viewing information cannot be deemed the same as obtaining something of value for the purposes of this statute.

The legislative history further supports our reading of the term "anything of value." [Accordingly] we find that Czubinski has not obtained valuable information in furtherance of a fraudulent scheme for the purposes of section 1030(a)(4).

Conclusion

The defendant's conviction is thus REVERSED on all counts.

Case Questions

1. Are there other possible strategies to take to address Czubinski's actions?
2. Should this law be amended to cover such actions as Czubinski's?
3. Could Czubinski's actions be justified under any circumstances?

The following are the typical physical property crimes committed and prosecuted under the CFAA.

Hacking. **Hacking** into Web sites, also called *owning* the site, is currently of epidemic proportions. Although security experts learn system vulnerabilities from hackers that post details of security holes they have uncovered (a practice known as *full disclosure*), there are still costs associated with these break-ins. With regard to whether to charge hackers for committing crimes, the *intent* of the perpetrators—whether they possessed a criminal intent at the time of the act—is a major issue. Many of these hackers have quasi-political agendas. There are sites devoted to advising users about hacking. See, for example, *http://www.2600.com*.

Cracking. **Cracking** is a name given to malicious (i.e., criminal) hacking. The most infamous of these was Kevin Mitnick, who was arrested and held without bail based on a $300 million estimate of the damage he caused. He copied proprietary software from computers owned by cellular telephone manufacturers.

➤http://

- For more information on this case, see **http://www.kevinmitnick.com**

Mitnick subsequently pleaded guilty and was sentenced to forty-six months of detention. Cases of cracking are legion. This is the criminal act that leads to the commission of other crimes. For example, hackers/crackers recently broke into *USA Today*'s Web site and defaced it. They replaced the real news stories with fake news stories that lampooned newsmakers and religions and also said that Israel was under attack. The stories were falsely credited to the Associated Press service.

Malware. This represents the acts made possible after the hacking/cracking. Perpetrators are thereby able to insert malware into servers, systems, and databases. **Malware** is a class of harmful software that includes virus writing, transmission of worms, logic/time bomb/trojan horse, sniffer programs, denial of service attacks, data manipulation, Web spoofing, and Web site defacements. To the extent these are perpetrated by anonymous individuals who can mask their IP addresses, or are using someone else's identity, or are offshore, prosecuting such cases is nearly impossible.

Virus Writing. Programs that have the ability to self-replicate and attach themselves to a host/another program and send itself to another system are called **virus writing**. For example, the Melissa virus caused computers to send e-mails with an attachment containing the virus to the first fifty addresses in the users' e-mail address book. If users opened the attachment in certain word processing programs, the virus infected that machine and its e-mail address book, and the virus began to replicate—going to this next group of addresses, and so forth.

Worm. Worms are similar to viruses. A **worm** replicates independently without needing a host and sends itself to other systems. One recent worm, named Goner, looks for and deletes a number of programs, including Internet security programs, and launches software that may later be used by hackers to launch further attacks.

Logic Bomb/E-mail Bomb. A **logic bomb** is a destructive action triggered at some specific date or time.

Trojan Horse. **Trojan horse** is a program with a hidden destructive functionality. It masquerades as legitimate software.

Password Sniffer. Almost every password **sniffer program** is a trojan horse, and this is one of the most popular forms of attacks used by hackers. This is due to the Internet's open architecture and the networks' "broadcast technology" whereby every message can be read by every computer on that network. Sniffers usually capture the first few hundred bytes of all telnet, ftp, and rlogin sessions and thereby obtain users' passwords.

Denial of Service Attacks. Also known as distributed **denial of service attacks**, these are characterized by acts that prevent legitimate users of a service from using that service. This could be in the form of flooding a network with traffic and disrupting connections or services. In May 2001, the White House site (*http://www.whitehouse.gov*) was hit by its third denial of service attack that month. A seventeen-year-old hacker recently jammed the sites of Amazon, Yahoo, Dell, eBay, and CNN.

Data Manipulation. The crime of **data manipulation** involves corrupting existing information. It could consist of manipulation of work products, grades, or research, for example.

Web Spoofing. **Spoofing** is a con game. It allows attackers to create a "shadow copy" of the entire World Wide Web on users' computers. When users access the Internet, the source IP address is forged, and they are actually being funneled through the attackers' computers, thereby allowing attackers to monitor all of the users' activities, passwords, or account numbers.

Web Site Defacements. **Web site defacement** is the act of gaining access to the Web server (which is often accomplished by identity theft) and corrupting content on the site's pages. Many times the defacers are motivated by political or social reasons. Again, there is a thin line between protected expression and crime. There was a marked increase in site defacements after the 9/11 terrorist action. Federal officials recently charged a fifteen-year-old boy with breaking into at least three NASA computer systems and altering their Web sites—to show images related to the hacking group Electronic Souls.

Crimes Against Intellectual Property

Copyright, trademark, and economic espionage laws have been amended over time to criminalize acts that previously were just civil infractions. As the U.S. economy relies to an ever-greater degree on digital content, intellectual property may comprise the most valuable assets of a business. **Software piracy** is perhaps the poster act of cybercrime; it is essentially the face of cybercrime at this time. Cases are legion here as well. Software that is pirated may be programs, songs, films—any copyright-protected digital content. To the extent that bandwidth has increased, it is possible to put even more complex (and valuable) copyright-protected content in digital format.

➤http://

- To see a chart of all recent federal criminal intellectual property cases, visit **http://www.cybercrime. gov/ipcases.htm** The criminal laws are found at **http://www4.law. cornell.edu/uscode/18/2319.html** and **http://www4.law.cornell.edu/ uscode/18/2319A.html** It is illegal to reproduce or distribute (during any 180-day period) over ten copies of one or more copyright-protected work having a total retail value in excess of $2,500. Penalties include a fine and up to five years imprisonment. Second and subsequent offenses bring up to ten years' imprisonment. These criminal provisions apply, even if there is no financial gain to perpetrators.
- For more information on the DrinkOrDie case, see **http://www. cybercrime.gov/sankusSent.htm**

Copyright Offenses. Copyright protection is granted to any creative work, and the holder has certain rights, including rights over reproduction and distribution. Because copyright protection laws clearly burden speech and expression, the doctrine of fair use allows a certain amount of unauthorized copying (refer to Chapter 4). However, when copyright-protected software contains a license agreement (which is virtually always—see Chapter 6, "Online Contracting"), the restrictions on use are even more stringent. In recognition of the serious concerns that piracy raises, in terms of cost and product control, recently Vivendi Universal S.A. created a new position to deal with software piracy: senior vice president of anti-piracy.

The next case is an example of how the law is chasing the crime. In 1997, after intense software industry lobbying, Congress made "recreational piracy" a criminal offense. (Previously it was just a civil offense, punishable by a fine.) The **No Electronic Theft Act** makes it a crime, punishable by up to three years in jail, to swap more than $2,500 in software. (After this case concluded, the FBI in December 2001 arrested members of the DrinkOrDie group. It consisted of a global network; members included students at many U.S. universities; its content included films, software programs, and music.)

United States v. Rothberg
2001 U.S. Dist. LEXIS 21119 (N.D. Ill. December 20, 2001); & 2002 U.S. Dist. LEXIS 1569 (N.D. Ill. February 1, 2002)

Facts

An international coalition of individuals formed an underground group known as Pirates with Attitude (PWA). It operated a number of file transfer protocol (FTP) web sites; the longest lasting one was called Sentinel. FTP sites are configured for the transfer of software files. PWA maintained a library of pirated software and it was accessible only to authorized users entering through known IP addresses. PWA allowed members to download thousands of copyright-protected software programs for free. PWA stored the software on a hidden Internet site, located at the University of Sherbrooke in Quebec, Canada, without the university's knowledge or authorization. Intel employees who were among the defendants assembled the hardware and shipped it, at Intel's expense, to site operators in Canada where it was installed and configured. This was done without Intel's knowledge or consent.

PWA members communicated with each other in real time on private Internet relay chat channels. Leading members met to vote on inviting new members to join, as well as promoting existing members to more senior positions. The group was organized into leaders and members, with each assigned a specific role. For example, some defendants supplied computer hardware to PWA, "suppliers" funneled programs to PWA, "couriers" transferred software to PWA, "crackers' stripped away the copy protection code that often is embedded in commercially released software, "packagers" tested and prepared programs for release, and others maintained the FTP sites. During the course of Sentinel's operation, tens of thousands of copyright-protected programs were available for downloading from the site and included operating systems and utilities as well as applications, games, and MP3 files. Through a confidential informant, the FBI gained access to Sentinel and traced the server to the university, leading to the arrest of PWA members.

The United States charged the defendants with (1) criminal copyright infringement under the No Electronic Theft Act (NET Act), and (2) conspiracy to commit this crime. Under the NET Act, swapping more than $2,500 in software, regardless of the circumstances, is punishable by up to three years in prison. Additionally, conspiracy to infringe a copyright is punishable by up to five years in prison and a $250,000 fine, or, as an alternative, the court may impose a fine totaling twice the gross gain to any defendant, or twice the gross loss to any victim, whichever is greater. Restitution is mandatory. Thirteen of the defendants pleaded guilty in the case. Another defendant opted for trial and was convicted of conspiracy and sentenced to two years in prison. The remaining defendants are fugitives and believed to be outside of the United States. At the time of the seizure, an FBI specialist produced a list of five thousand programs still on Sentinel. Based on this, the United States estimated the retail value of the programs at $1.1 million.

But later, as the United States was preparing for the trial of the one defendant, a different FBI specialist conducted further analysis of Sentinel and determined that 54,671 programs had been uploaded to the site, and therefore the value of the programs, for restitution and sentencing purposes, should be set at $10 million plus. This is the matter before the court.

Judicial Opinion *(Judge Kennelly)*

Certain defendants have jointly moved to preclude the government from arguing for any valuation in excess of $1.1 million, claiming that this violates their plea agreements.

The defendants argue that the proper valuation is zero, and they have challenged the accuracy and reliability of the government's $10+ million figure on various grounds. As a threshold matter . . . the defendants who pled guilty have challenged the government's right to assert the new, higher loss figure, claiming that when they pled guilty, they had an understanding that the loss figure would not exceed the $1.1 million figure the government was then advocating. A plea agreement is a contract. When a defendant's guilty plea rests in any significant degree on a promise or agreement of the prosecutor, so that it can be said to be a part of the inducement or consideration, such promise must be fulfilled. The simple fact, however, is that the government made no promise . . . not to advocate a higher valuation figure greater than $1.1 million. The plea agreement says that the government's claim is the that value of the infringing items was '*in excess* of $1 million.' 'In excess' does not mean 'slightly in excess.' Moreover, the plea agreements each contained an acknowledgment by the defendant and defense counsel that 'the above calculations are preliminary in nature and are based on facts known to the government as of the time of the Plea Agreement.' [The court therefore denied defendants' motions to resolve the perceived ambiguities in the Plea Agreement, but it did allow defendants to withdraw their guilty pleas if they wished to do so.]

[The court next considered how to count and then to value, for restitution and sentencing purposes, the pirated software.] The government does not contend, however, that all 54,671 uploads were actually functioning version of computer programs. The only reasonable alternative available to the Court is to use as the base for the value calculation the number of functioning programs that remained on the Sentinel site at the time of the seizure. There were 5,046 separate directories . . . [and] when these were filtered . . . 3,947 [of them contained programs]. The FBI tested 71 [of these] and found that . . . 94% of them functioned in the same manner as the retail version[s]. [Therefore] we will base our value determination on that figure: 94% of 3,747, or 3,710 programs.

The next issue is the determination of the value of the 3,710 infringing items. The government . . . derived an average . . . retail . . . price of $384 per program. Defendants argue that because PWA did not sell the infringing software, the value for [Sentencing] Guidelines purposes is zero. The Court disagrees. First of all, the Guideline . . . requires us to determine the retail *value*. [T]he fact that PWA did not charge a fee does not mean that the fully functioning software that it distributed was worthless. [Furthermore] to become a member of the group . . . an individual had to contribute something of value, either services (such as providing 'cracking') . . . or goods [such as hardware]. . . . These facts are more than sufficient to show that the pirated software had value.

The question, however, is what the value is. We cannot simply adopt the retail price of the legitimate software without considering other factors. In this case [however] we lack any solid evidence of the value . . . other than the retail price of the genuine articles. Defendants have offered evidence garnered from reports of other cases in which counterfeit software was sold on the black market. But . . . black market pricing is not always a proper surrogate for actual value. In this case the programs were fully-functioning versions . . . and they were . . . made available for mass distribution by PWA. The only significant differences between PWA's programs and the genuine articles were the unavailability of a manual, technical support, and a warranty.

The law is clear that when there is an absence of other reliable evidence concerning the value of the infringing item . . . the Court may adopt the retail price of the genuine item as the value of the infringing item. For these reasons, the Court will use the $384 average price determined by the government . . . as the average price for the full set of the infringing items. We therefore find that the value of the infringing items for purposes of [the Sentencing] Guideline . . . is $1,424,640.

Case Questions

1. A number of scholars think the No Electronic Theft Act is an extreme reaction to recreational piracy and the punishment does not fit the crime. What do you think?
2. How could manufacturers deal with the piracy problem on their own, rather than invoking the help of Congress to make a new law?
3. Is there any ethical justification at all for these criminal investigations and prosecutions—that are time consuming and expensive and where the software industry has not provided hard numbers on the costs of recreational piracy?

Software piracy made the headlines following the 2002 Grammy Awards where the president of the National Academy of Recording Arts and Sciences delivered a speech about unauthorized trading of songs on the Internet. He admitted he hired three people to break the No Electronic Theft Act, and he showed clips of what they downloaded during the ceremony. The software and entertainment industries initially focused on shutting down file-sharing sites in an effort to stem piracy, but they have just begun to turn their attention to the actual software pirates—individuals using the services.

Copyright Management Offenses. Under the **Digital Millennium Copyright Act (DMCA)**, it is a crime to traffic in devices primarily designed for the purpose of circumventing technological protection measures (antipiracy devices). This statute targets those who willfully and for purposes of commercial advantage or private financial gain engage in circumvention. Again, Congress passed this act after intense industry lobbying and in an effort to conform with international IP laws. Of note, the United States is pursuing its first criminal indictment under the DMCA against ElcomSoft, a Russian company, alleged to have made a device, called the Advanced Books E-Processor, that circumvents the access controls for Adobe's e-books software. In May 2002, the United States denied ElcomSoft's motion to dismiss the case for lack

►http://

- For more up-to-date information on this case, visit **http://www.eff.org** and click on ElcomSoft/Skylarov. Also, the Department of Justice's reports may be found at **http://www. cybercrime.gov/sklyarovAgree.htm**
- To read the full text of the DMCA, visit **http://www4.law.cornell.edu/ uscode/17/ch12.html** For the first offense, penalties include up to $500,000 in fines and up to five years' imprisonment. Second and all subsequent offenses provide for penalties of up to $1 million in fines and up to ten years' imprisonment.
- One trade group concerned with counterfeit software is the Software and Information Industries Association. See **http://www.siia.net**
- To read the text of the criminal trademark provisions, visit **http://www4.law.cornell.edu/uscode/ 18/2318.html** and **http://www4.law. cornell.edu/uscode/18/2320.html** Penalties include fines, forfeiture and destruction of the goods; and up to five years' imprisonment. Under Section 2320, it is a crime to intentionally traffic in goods or services knowing the marks are counterfeit. Penalties include fines of up to $2 million and up to ten years' imprisonment.

of jurisdiction, and so the case will proceed. One of Elcom-Soft's employees, Dmitri Skylarov, spoke about this product at a DefCon convention, which was the act that triggered this prosecution.

In another recent instance—with a different outcome—an MIT graduate student found a way to circumvent Microsoft's Xbox security system. He posted his report on a publicly accessible site, noting that hackers could exploit a flaw in the system to identify individual players from their game machines. He will not be charged for violating the DMCA. Under the DMCA, it is not a crime to decrypt antipiracy devices for the purpose of conducting research and other scholarly work (recall the *Corley* case from Chapter 11, in which a civil suit was brought for violations of the DMCA.)

Trademark Offenses. It is a crime to knowingly traffic in counterfeit labels, copies, or programs (including documentation or packaging). This encompasses music labels, computer programs, computer program documentation or packaging, and films. Counterfeiting cases typically involve both criminal **trademark infringement** and copyright infringement. In a recent case, U.S. Customs agents in California seized counterfeit goods valued at $100 million, including about $60 million of fake Microsoft products. (Pirated copies of Windows XP showed up in some Asian countries before Microsoft officially launched the product there.) In another instance, companies were found to knowingly be using unlicensed software, also punishable as a crime.

In one criminal trademark infringement case, a firm distributed computer memory boards in counterfeit IBM boxes. The company purchased memory chips and modules that were not manufactured by IBM and packaged them in counterfeit IBM boxes. Because the products appeared to be IBMs, the defendants were able to resell them at a premium price. In a plea agreement, the company agreed to a $2.2 million fine and will repay IBM $1.1 million.

Economic Espionage/Netspionage and Trade Secret Theft Offenses. The main statute in the **Economic Espionage Act (EEA)** criminalizes the theft or misappropriation of trade secrets by computer or other means. The first section specifically addresses the theft of trade secrets/economic espionage with the intent to benefit a foreign government or entity. It defines a trade secret broadly to include any proprietary information that is *reasonably* protected from public disclosure. This is one of the most stark instances of how cybercrime reduces competitiveness. Competitors, and even employees, steal information about products, development, marketing, and sales. Whether gaining an edge on a competitor, profits, and/or work rage are the motives, companies are increasingly aware of the value of digital content, which is so at risk in networked systems. In one recent case, the FBI arrested Lucent software engineers and accused them of conspiring to steal a technology called PathStar in order to sell it in China to Datang Telecom. In another case, Akamai Technologies sued rival software maker Speedera Networks to prevent Speedera from using data Akamai protected as a trade secret.

Commercial Extortion. These are cases in which **extortion**, or blackmail demands, are made in return for something of value. In one recent case, a still-unknown intruder gained access to all of the databases of Internet retailer CD Universe and demanded $100,000. After CD Universe refused this demand, the intruder posted some of the credit card files. The extortionist is believed to be in Eastern Europe, beyond the reach of U.S. law enforcement officials.

Money Laundering. **Money laundering** has been made easier to commit based on the development of new technologies such as Internet banking and smart cards, even while the technology for monitoring of these transactions has not kept pace. For even though financial institutions are able to track fund flows and their origin and destination points, they have not developed systems to identify and authenticate controlling parties. The **USA Patriot Act** mandated more stringent reporting requirements following the 9/11 terrorist action, such as the production of Suspicious Activity Reports, discussed in Chapter 8, "Online Securities Offerings and Transactions."

Trespass, Vandalism, Theft of Hardware. Laptop theft and other computer theft is a well-known and documented problem.

Hardware Weapons. **Hardware weapons** include high-energy radio frequency (**HERF**) weapons. These are radio transmitters that send a concentrated signal at a target to put it out of commission. Also, there are electromagnetic pulse (**EMP**) weapons that destroy or disable electronics of all computers and communications systems in a large area.

Other Federal Laws Invoked in Internet and Computer Crime Prosecutions

Computer and related crimes may be charged under a number of other statutes besides the CFAA. And although there may additionally be civil remedies for computer violations, this next section discusses general federal criminal statutes that complement federal enforcement of specific cybercrimes. Additionally the conspiracy statute is included because it is commonly alleged in many complaints.

http://

- To read the Economic Espionage Act, visit **http://www4.law. cornell.edu/uscode/18/plch90.html** Offenses result in up to fifteen years of imprisonment and/or fines up to $10 million, as well as forfeiture of the property or proceeds thereof. An impediment to the effectiveness of the EEA, however, is the possible reluctance of companies to cooperate with the government because of the risk of being forced to disclose sensitive data in discovery.
- To read the extortion laws, visit **http://www4.law.cornell.edu/uscode/ 18/plch95.html**

Electronic Communications Privacy Act (ECPA). The **Electronic Communications Privacy Act**, discussed in Chapter 9, essentially broadens privacy protections for computer users by expanding its definitions of communications as those affecting interstate and foreign commerce. This act otherwise updates existing laws prohibiting the interception of live as well as stored wire or electronic communications. The ECPA criminalizes this interception when the communication is obtained, altered, or rendered inaccessible to authorized users.

Violations of the ECPA may result in imprisonment for up to two years and/or a fine. The ECPA also includes the Federal Wiretap Act, found at Section 2511. This section criminalizes the intentional interception or use of any intercepted wire, oral, or electronic communication. Fines are up to $5,000. This section is increasingly used in cybercrime cases as communications are migrating from the wired to the wireless environment.

http://

- The live wiretap statute is found at **http://www4.law.cornell.edu/uscode/18/plch119.html** The stored electronic communications statute is found at **http://www4.law.cornell.edu/uscode/18/plch121.html**
- To read the EFTA, visit **http://www4.law.cornell.edu/uscode/15/1693n.html**
- To read the statutes, visit **http://www4.law.cornell.edu/uscode/18/plch63.html**

Electronic Funds Transfer Act (EFTA). The **Electronic Funds Transfer Act** (EFTA) criminalizes the giving of false or inaccurate or insufficient information. It also outlaws any transactions involving counterfeit, stolen, fictitious, or other debit instruments. Debit instruments include cards, codes, and so on, that are used to initiate an EFT. Penalties include up to ten years' imprisonment or up to $10,000 in fines.

Mail and Wire Fraud Statutes. **Mail and wire fraud statutes** have wide-ranging application to computer and Internet crime. Under these acts, it is illegal to use the mails, interstate, or foreign communications to devise fraudulent schemes for obtaining money or property. These statutes, although not primarily regarded as cybercrime statutes, have application to many of the prosecutions for cybercrime. These statutes outlaw any computer-aided or enabled theft. Penalties include fines up to $1 million and/or imprisonment for up to thirty years. Wire fraud charges were brought against the defendant in the _United States v. Czubinski,_ case. The court found, however, that neither of the two elements of wire fraud, (1) the knowing and willing participation in a scheme to defraud and (2) the use of interstate wire communications in furtherance of the scheme, were established beyond a reasonable doubt, because there was no underlying scheme to defraud.

Racketeer-Influenced and Corrupt Organization Statutes (RICO). Officials often charge defendants with racketeering in concert with other crimes they have committed, such as fraud, extortion, bribery, dealing in obscene matter, and so forth. The RICO statutes are invoked when there is evidence of an overall scheme, conspiracy, pattern of racketeering and criminal activity. The statute makes it a crime to receive income from such schemes. Violations are punishable by fines, up to twenty years of imprisonment, and forfeiture of property.

National Stolen Property Act. The **National Stolen Property Act** prohibits the transport or transmission in interstate or foreign commerce of any tangible goods over $5,000 in value, knowing these goods have been stolen or taken by fraud. This act was amended to include intellectual property as well. Sentences for violations of this act include fines and/or imprisonment for up to ten years.

Conspiracy. Usually most prosecutions involve a conspiracy, and so a general conspiracy charge is a very common complement to any criminal indictment (see, for example, the indictment in the ElcomSoft case).

Crimes Against Government or Government Functions

In many cases, perpetrators have underlying philosophical or political motivations for their actions. These crimes used to be committed by rogue states; now they are committed by stateless rogues. Armed with information technologies and weapons, criminals can damage critical infrastructures consisting of telecommunications, medical institutions, and utilities as well as government functions. The U.S. government's Internet network is the same open one we use; for certain functions, it is important for the government to move to a closed network system. One that has been talked about is the govnet system.

http://

- To read the RICO statutes, see **http://www4.law.cornell.edu/uscode/18/plch96.html**
- To read the text of the statute, see **http://www4.law.cornell.edu/uscode/18/plch113.html**
- To read the text of the conspiracy statute, see **http://www.law.cornell.edu/uscode/18/371.html**
- For a demonstration page of the proposed govnet site, see **http://158.72.28.38/govnet/govnet.formdemo.govfront_page**

Threats/Extortion Leading to Shutdown of Essential Services. The potentially paralyzing effect of disruptions and shutdowns now has the attention of legislators. For example, the Legion of Doom hacking group gained the ability to alter, disrupt, or shut down local telephone service. In another incident, 40 percent of a patient's records were destroyed at a major medical center. In another incident, a teenager gained access to an airport's traffic control system and left it without telephone or data service. Hackers/crackers routinely vandalize government Web sites and deface or otherwise destroy them. The incidents continue without abatement.

Espionage. **Espionage** involves the act of spying on government entities or officials. In one case, a hacker in Germany was being paid by the KGB to learn U.S. military secrets. In another case, it is alleged a Los Alamos nuclear scientist used his computer to pass massive amounts of top-secret weapons data to China.

Terrorism. This could be physical **terrorism** or attacks on the Internet, in the form of undermining or disabling entire countries, without ever firing a shot. In one such attack, a foreign hacker worked with two young U.S. citizens, and they successfully mounted cyber-attacks against Pentagon systems, a nuclear weapons research lab, and other targets. Cyberterrorism could also involve nonphysical acts such as extortion and blackmail.

Cyberterrorism/Cyberwarfare. In a different generation, the tools of warfare and terrorism belonged to nations. They consisted of physical machines of destruction: guns,

- To read the terrorism statutes, visit
http://www4.law.cornell.edu/uscode/
18/pIch113B.html

tanks, missiles, and so forth. In today's environment, the tools of warfare belong to anyone with a laptop and an Internet connection. The Center for Strategic and International Studies reports, "America's most wanted transnational terrorist, Osama bin Laden, uses laptops with satellite uplinks and heavily encrypted messages to liaise across national borders with his global underground network. There is no shortage of terrorist recipes on the Internet, step-by-step cookbooks for hackers and crackers . . . and cyberterrorists" (*http://www.csis.org/pubs/cyberfor.html*).

Intentional attacks against U.S. critical infrastructure and systems have already begun. The 9/11 terrorist action caused massive dislocation and failure of telecommunications and transportation systems, in addition to the mortal damage. Security is no longer just physical machines of warfare protecting us; rather now, it is defined by the complementary use of weapons of information warfare.

The USA Patriot Act, discussed in part in Chapter 11, represents Congress's attempt to shore up national security as well as to fight the crime of terrorism. The act expands the authorization for surveillance, searches, and data mining activities. It authorizes a number of activities that were once considered in violation of our constitutional rights. For example, the act authorizes the FBI to check the library reading records of terrorist suspects. Even as the law authorizes such checks, it makes it a crime for librarians to reveal the same information. The FBI still needs a warrant to do this search, but it no longer needs to establish probable cause, just that it has reason to suspect the person is involved with a terrorist or a terrorist plot. (Recall too, the discussion from Chapter 11 regarding expanded availability of taps on live and stored communications, use of pen register and trap and trace devices, data mining, Web surfing—in addition to law enforcement's Carnivore and key logger systems).

The USA Patriot Act impacts crime fighting in other important ways. The racketeering statute, known as RICO, will be used more now that it can be used in crimes for which there is no monetary gain. The Treasury Department requires businesses to file a suspicious activity report on any person who spends $10,000 or more in cash. Treasury also targeted money laundering through financial institutions (see Chapter 11). It makes watchdogs of ordinary businesses.

The act broadens the scope of records that law enforcement may subpoena from electronics communications services. It creates single jurisdiction search warrants for investigations of terrorism that have nationwide, rather than local, effects.

Once suspects are apprehended, the act makes important changes to these procedures. The Department of Justice put into effect a rule giving the government authority to monitor communications between people in federal custody and their lawyers if the attorney general deems it reasonably necessary in order to deter further acts of violence or terrorism. Attorney-client confidentiality privilege does not exist here. Hundreds of people were detained and arrested after 9/11, yet their status was not resolved in a timely fashion. Finally, suspected terrorists are to be tried before secretive military tribunals rather than through public civilian courts. The USA Patriot Act has not yet been challenged in court, and so it remains to be seen whether these stepped-up security and crime-fighting measures violate U.S. constitutional rights.

http://◄

- For the text of the USA Patriot Act, see **http://www.epic.org/privacy/ terrorism/hr3162.html** Also see the government site: **http://www. ncix.gov**

CORPORATE FORENSICS AND THE IMPACT OF THE INTERNET: GATHERING AND PRESERVING EVIDENCE

Technology and crime go hand in hand at this time. Commentators believe that many of these crimes have to do with the perceived anonymity of the Internet. It has been said that the ability to act anonymously in large groups brings out the worst in humans.

The Internet has brought this issue to the forefront of cybercrime management. For example, an employee of an Oregon company was recently accused of stealing equipment from his office. He immediately denied the charges and started covering his tracks, first by deleting incriminating e-mails and filed documents. When he learned his computer was to be subpoenaed, he installed "scrubbing" software designed to wipe clean the computer's hard drive.

When this perceived anonymity is coupled with tools such as encryption and scrubbing software to further ensure this identity cover, it becomes nearly impossible to prosecute these crimes. The identity of the perpetrator may not be known, and the evidence may be destroyed.

Historically in the United States, a great deal of value has been placed on an individual's privacy from government intrusion (as recognized in the Fourth Amendment) and, more generally, on an individual's right to privacy (embodied in such judicial decisions as recognizing the right to be left alone, including the right to marry without regard to race, and the right to control procreation, etc.). This has also been the subject of some legislation. The interest in being anonymous and the software that makes this feasible is an outgrowth of these values. In direct tension to and contrast with this is society's demand for accountability—for individuals to be responsible for their actions—and for perpetrators to be made known and accountable for their conduct. The effect of the Internet on these basic societal values cannot be overstated.

Anonymous communications have great value in some instances, such as for corporate whistle-blowers. There are many Web sites offering tools for anonymous communications. However, such a mode of communication incidentally benefits criminals who are able to avoid detection and arrest through the use of encryption and other programs. It is possible to reconcile anonymity and accountability in a compromise environment of confidentiality. Users could remain anonymous, but there would be a third party—an escrow-key holder (who may, in the future, be your ISP or the government)—who could, under agreed-upon circumstances (such as under a court order) reveal the user's identity. Law enforcement officials would naturally wish to be third-party escrow-key holders. The holders of such keys, though, hold a valuable asset, which tempts abuse. The government's role in the investigation and prosecution of cybercrime is most basically to prove that a crime was committed and the person charged is guilty of that crime. There is a question of whether law enforcement efforts are equal to the challenges of cybercrime.

In order to prove the crime, evidence must be submitted to the court. The process of gathering this evidence is done at the investigation phase. The government might wish to issue a **subpoena**, an affirmative order by a court to produce specific records or to appear as a witness in court. Failure to comply with it renders the individual in contempt of court. In one recent case, federal officials were investigating a hacker who broke into computers at the *New York Times*. MSNBC broadcast a story about the hacking attack. And so the investigators sent a subpoena to MSNBC demanding reporters' notes, e-mail, and other information. MSNBC challenged the power of the attorney who requested it; and it was resolved in favor of MSNBC, because such subpoenas must be approved either by the U.S. attorney general personally or his deputy—and this one was not. In another recent case, the New York state attorney general subpoenaed Internet payment provider PayPal, Inc. He requested online gambling payment records because the gambling was possibly in contravention of state law.

Finally, New York's attorney general is involved in another criminal investigation in which he is gathering evidence through issuance of subpoenas. One securities analyst for Salomon Smith Barney failed to disclose to investors that he was also making stock-purchasing recommendations. The attorney general uncovered a series of e-mail exchanges, which he characterizes as the "smoking gun" in this case. It is important to be aware of the potential for abuse in the process and be wary of requests for unjustified or unsubstantiated subpoenas. Subpoena-issuing guidelines act as a protection of fundamental liberties.

➤**http://**

- For an example of anonymizer software, visit **http://www.anonymizer.com**
- To read the statutory law on searches and seizures, visit **http://www4.law.cornell.edu/uscode/18/plch109.html**

Also in an investigation officials may wish to search a certain location. (Recall the *Scarfo* and *Kyllo* cases.) Searches and seizures are governed by the Fourth Amendment. Under the Fourth Amendment, the government is prohibited from conducting a search or seizure unless it is done pursuant to a search warrant. These warrants must be "narrowly drawn," stating with particularity the items to be searched or seized. Should these rules not be observed, evidence from the defective search may not be inadmissible in court. For example, in one recent case, the government's search of an attorney's home office was challenged as overbroad, as not sufficiently particular. The warrant authorized seizure of "all computers . . . storage devices . . . software systems." It did not limit the search to the home office or list the specific crimes for which the equipment was sought. The court agreed with the defendant that his Fourth Amendment rights had been violated (but ultimately ruled the evidence did not have to be excluded because the search team acted in good faith—one of the exceptions to the rule) [*United States v. Hunter*, 13 F. Supp. 2d 574 (D. Vt. 1998)].

The Department of Justice has issued guidelines for searching and seizing computers, and in particular there is discussion of ways in which searching computers is different from searching desks, filing cabinets, or automobiles. These guidelines also address seizing hardware as well as information, how to handle networks and bulletin board services, how to draft warrants, how to preserve evidence, and so on.

This detection and prosecution of cybercrime is aided in great part by recent developments in information security. In fact, within the professions of information security, law enforcement, and even accounting, there have emerged *cybersleuths,* computer forensics experts who specialize in electronic discovery through examination of deleted files, disks, Zip disks, backup tapes, and hard drives. This also involves reconstructing communications and data that are on systems or transmitted through ISPs. The forensic examination process starts with making a duplicate image of the storage media under scrutiny and then conducting a complete search for specific words, files, or documents. In fact, an entire department at Deloitte & Touche LLP is devoted to finding hackers, virus writers, and cyberspies. In one recent case, Deloitte & Touche was asked by a company to examine the financial records of another company it had recently purchased. Its concerns were confirmed after D&T revived all computer data the acquired company thought it had erased. The deal was subsequently restructured.

In cases where a crime is suspected, the information is handed over to law enforcement authorities. When this information is transferred from person to person before being offered to the court as evidence, these transfers must comply with the legal doctrine of *chain of custody,* in which it must be shown the evidence presented is exactly what was taken from the crime scene. This becomes complicated by the fact that such evidence is easily altered, and, if this is so, the evidence may not be admissible. The gathering and preservation of computer evidence is indeed fraught with difficulties. A final word about the application of constitutional rights to Internet crime: the First and Fourth Amendments have been discussed in their relation to government action and criminal prosecutions. The Fifth Amendment is also a powerful safeguard against possible arbitrary government authority. In a criminal prosecution, the Fifth Amendment provides citizens with a number of important rights, such as the right to due process (the laws must be constitutional and procedures must be fair) and the right against self-incrimination (defendants may not be compelled to testify against themselves). These were discussed in more detail in Chapter 11. The government must bring forward its case, proving *beyond a reasonable doubt* that the defendant was the one who committed the act; that the act is a crime under the law; and that each element of the crime is present. This burden of proof is extremely demanding, and this acts as just another check in safeguarding our constitutional rights.

INTERNATIONAL ASPECTS OF INTERNET CRIME

The Internet has become a powerful forum for engaging in illegal activities, especially because in this era there is a greater probability of not being prosecuted for an international cybercrime than for other classes of crime. Businesses are deeply concerned about the problem. As Dean O'Hare, chairman and CEO of Chubb Corporation, stated at a meeting of business executives,

> Business transactions would be impeded or cease, complicating our economic recovery and sending our global stock markets into a tailspin. We must not allow this to happen. [Business and government leaders] need to better understand the enormous threat we face and take measures to secure cyberspace.

Pricewaterhouse Coopers estimates that cybercrime costs business more than $1.5 trillon worldwide in a single year. Boundaries are of no consequence to Internet crime. Previously, if a crime was committed and if the police thought the alleged perpetrator was fleeing the country with the goods, law enforcement details were dispatched to all exit points in the country. Road, airport, and train station details checking passports are quaint anachronisms in the information age. There are no borders, passports, or checkpoints on the Internet. It is one global universe online, and consequently domestic laws become inadequate to deal with the complexity of international Internet crime. We must coordinate laws, information and intelligence gathering, and enforcement schemes.

During the 1990s, nations made some progress on developing international Internet cybercrime initiatives. For example, the United States pledged to cooperate with the leaders of the seven other leading industrialized nations: England, France, Germany, Italy, Russia, Japan, Canada, altogether known as the Group of Eight (G-8). The Council of Europe introduced recommendations relating to problems of criminal procedural law connected with information technology. Moreover, the Organization for Economic Cooperation and Development (OECD) issued guidelines for the security of information systems. The OECD recommends that its member countries engage in an international collaboration to develop compatible practices and procedures, including mutual investigative assistance.

Finally, nongovernmental organizations (NGOs) have spoken about cybercrime issues. For example, the International Federation of the Phonographic Industry is coordinating a worldwide effort to remove illegal MP3 music files from the Internet. The following initiatives represent some of the most recent significant developments in the global effort to prevent and prosecute crimes in cyberspace.

Council of Europe Convention on Cybercrime

The Council of Europe, representing forty-three states, including all European Union members, established a forum in 1949 to address topics of human rights, democracy, and the rule of law in Europe. Since the late 1980s, the council has been working to address the growing international concern over threats posed by hacking and other computer-related crimes. After publishing a series of studies and inviting other nations (including the United States, Canada, Japan, and South Africa) to participate, in 2001 it approved a key initiative called the **Council of Europe Convention on Cybercrime**. Twenty-nine nations, including the United States, signed the Convention. The Convention is now open for signature by other nations. Once the Convention is ratified (thus far by five countries), it becomes binding law in the ratifying counties. The United States signed the Convention, but it awaits ratification by the Senate.

Criminalization of Illegal Acts. The agreement encompasses both traditional crimes that have found a new venue through the Internet as well as new crimes that now exist as a result of the Internet. The Convention requires each signatory nation to criminalize a number of activities relating to the confidentiality of computer data, the integrity of computer systems, computer fraud, computer forgery, and child pornography. The agreement also criminalizes copyright infringement consistent with other copyright conventions.

http://

- To review a copy of the Convention on Cybercrime, see **http://conventions.coe.int/treaty/EN/projets/FinalCybercrime.htm**

The Council of Europe is also planning to draft a protocol addressing racist and xenophobic offenses committed through computer systems. The council defines such racist and xenophobic propaganda as "any written material, any image, or any other representation of thoughts or theories, which advocates, promotes or incites hatred, discrimination or violence, against any individual or group of individuals, based on race, colour, descent or national or ethnic origin, as well as religion if used as a pretext for any of these factors." Article 3 of the Protocol draft requires criminalization of the distribution of racist or xenophobic materials via a computer system. Article 4 of the Protocol draft prohibits threatening a person with the commission of a serious criminal offense through a computer system based on the race or nationality of that person. Although this protocol is undoubtedly being favorably reviewed in many countries, consider how such a protocol will fare in the United States, with its heritage of freedom of speech as embodied in the First Amendment.

Mutual Assistance and Facilitation of Cybercrime Investigations. The Convention establishes rules for facilitating cooperative investigations of cybercrime. Signatories agree to help one another "to the widest extent possible" in criminal investigations or proceedings. Although cross-border searches are still restricted, law enforcement agents from member nations may collect computer-based evidence from one another. The Convention also establishes a "24/7 Network" whereby each signatory will have a point of contact available to ensure immediate assistance in coordinating criminal investigations or proceedings.

The Convention establishes procedures to facilitate criminal investigation. The Convention requires that nations shall enact laws facilitating the expeditious preservation of computer data and computer traffic data, including real-time data collection. Procedural rules must also be enacted by member states that provide conditions and safeguards to access of this data.

European Commission Communication on Computer-Related Crime

In January 2001, the European Commission released a **Communication on Computer-Related Crime**. The communication discusses the importance of a coordinated policy effort to combat computer-related crime. Several initiatives have developed as a result of the communication, which are described next.

- To visit the EU Forum on Cybercrime, see **http:// cybercrime-forum.cec.eu.int**

EU Forum on Cybercrime. The European Commission established an online **Forum on Cybercrime**. The Web site provides a platform for discussion and cooperation between law enforcement agencies, ISPs, telecommunications operators, civil liberties organizations, computer representatives, data protection authorities, and other interested groups. The Web site provides links to EU initiatives and legislation related to cybercrime and hosts forums on data retention, security, and other issues.

Other International Cybercrime Initiatives. Other initiatives are being developed on a global scale to control international cybercrime. For example, in 2001, the EU's European Council agreed to establish a European-wide arrest warrant that applies to all cybercrime offenses. This initiative allows the judiciary of any member state to issue an arrest warrant for offenses punishable for over a year or when the perpetrator has been sentenced to custody for over four months. When an arrest is conducted on the basis of this warrant, the person in custody must be handed over to the member state issuing the warrant within three months. The agreement effectively abolishes formal extradition procedures between EU states for various offenses, including cybercrimes.

Successful International Cooperation Combating Cybercrime: The Bloomberg Example

International cooperation in stopping cybercrime has resulted in the discovery and prosecution of a number of complex Internet fraud and virus attacks. The international sting described next, the attempted cyberextortion of Michael Bloomberg, highlights the benefits of coordinated international cyber-enforcement efforts.

Cyberextortion of Michael Bloomberg. Michael Bloomberg is the owner of Bloomberg, L.P., a successful global information services and media company, in addition to serving as the mayor of New York City. On March 24, 2000, the Bloomberg corporate office received an email message from an anonymous hacker calling himself Alex. "Alex" claimed he had detailed knowledge of the company's computer system. Alex asked for compensation for discovering the security breach.

Bloomberg contacted the Federal Bureau of Investigation (FBI) for help. He followed the FBI's direction and communicated with Alex, agreeing to deposit $200,000 in a European bank in exchange for Alex's promise to disclose how he broke into the computer system and assistance in rectifying the problem. Alex and Bloomberg agreed to meet in London to "negotiate" an agreement. After Bloomberg agreed to pay Alex's travel expenses, the FBI traced the money to a bank in Latvia and found that Alex lived in Kazakhstan.

The FBI contacted Scotland Yard and the Kazakh Special Services and developed an international sting. Bloomberg and two Scotland Yard agents, posing as an executive and a translator, met Alex and his associate. After the meeting, the pair was arrested.

They were charged with one count of interfering with commerce by using extortion, one count of extortion of a corporation using threatening communications, and one count of unauthorized computer intrusion.

Barry Mawn, an assistant director with the FBI, commented on the case:

> The investigation and these charges should dispel the notion that using a computer to commit criminal acts literally a world away from one's victim provides a zone of safety from law enforcement scrutiny. In fact, the growth of computer related crime in recent years has resulted closer cooperation among law enforcement agencies around the world. This investigation demonstrates the cooperation of both American business entities and our international law enforcement partners to address 21st century crime.

The Future of International Cooperation. Clearly, international cooperation is essential to address the unique law enforcement challenges the Internet presents. Countries must each develop harmonious laws to combat cybercrime, for crime will migrate to the country with the weakest enforcement efforts. Second, treaties addressing the maintenance and sharing of information are critically important. Mutual assistance is necessary for law enforcement to have any effect. Third, there must be extradition treaties between nations that provide for the expeditious transfer of suspects and evidence. International Internet and computer crime has a growth potential like no other type of crime. It will flourish until agreements between countries are enacted regarding extradition, evidence gathering, and preservation. This pressure for international cooperation among countries in an effort to combat cybercrime may even yield other unexpected dividends.

Summary

Internet and network computer crime are the unfortunate results of crime migrating to the places where the assets are. Computers are used in different ways to commit crimes, ranging from fraud to espionage to terrorism. Some individuals are committing crimes even with no intent to profit from their actions.

Federal, state, and international laws are constantly created or amended in an effort to keep up with the new and creative crimes being committed. To compound all of this, the Web is largely a private sector enterprise. However, no matter how many laws Congress or the states pass, the most effective anticrime strategy is one of self-protection—a strategy of securing one's own digital assets. Individuals, businesses, and governments must be vigilant in their efforts to secure information, computers, and networks against criminal activities. Governments are also attempting international initiatives to suppress cybercrime. Nations are becoming increasingly cooperative in sharing information and assisting in the prosecution of international cybercriminals. The government's need to address cyberterrorism on both a national and a international level is of urgent importance at this time, yet questions about its tactics persist. Is the price of collective security our civil liberties?

Key Terms

computer crime, *408*

Internet crime, *408*

fraud, *412*

identity theft, *412*

Internet gambling, *415*

spamming, *415*

pornography, *416*

Child Pornography Prevention Act (CPPA), *417*

Child Online Protection Act (COPA), *419*

stalking, *419*

harassment, *419*

hate crimes, *420*

murder and death threats, *420*

Computer Fraud and Abuse Act, *421*

hacking, *424*

cracking, *424*

malware, *425*

virus writing, *425*

worm, *425*

logic bomb, *425*

trojan horse, *425*

sniffer program, *425*

denial of service attacks, *425*

data manipulation, *425*

spoofing, *426*

Web site defacement, *426*

software piracy, *426*

No Electronic Theft Act, *426*

Digital Millennium Copyright Act (DMCA), *429*

trademark infringement, *430*

Economic Espionage Act (EEA), *430*

extortion, *431*

money laundering, *431*

USA Patriot Act, *431*

hardware weapons: HERF and EMP, *431*

Electronic Communications Privacy Act (ECPA), *432*

Electronic Funds Transfer Act, *432*

mail and wire fraud statutes, *432*

National Stolen Property Act, *433*

espionage, *433*

terrorism, *433*

subpoena, *436*

Council of Europe Convention on Cybercrime, *438*

EU Communication on Computer-Related Crime, *439*

EU Forum on Cybercrime, *440*

Manager's Checklist

√ Internal and external audits should be conducted on a regular basis.

√ Office policies should be developed addressing all forms of computer use, including explanations and examples of what constitutes appropriate use—and misuse.

√ It is important to keep abreast of changes in the law. This is a particularly changeable time for Internet and computer legislation.

√ Businesses must be prepared to work with law enforcement agents because most of the cybercrime is currently internal and external economic espionage.

√ Businesses must take appropriate precautions regarding the protection of proprietary or trade secret information and for the personnel responsible for its management.

√ Businesses must protect against both international and national crime. Companies concerned about Internet crime should become more active in developing a dialogue with law enforcement on international cybercrime initiatives.

√ A general trend toward harmonization exists in the criminalization of cybercrimes. Western nations presently are harmonizing international resources for law enforcement. This trend must continue to other nations.

√ Businesses of any size must be aware their computer systems are vulnerable to international cybercrimes.

√ Ethical Considerations

Managers must consider many complex ethics issues, including:

- How the government might use private businesses in the pursuit of suspects
- How private companies might be liable for crimes such as identity theft, committed by employees using workplace computers
- How to monitor employee activity given the competing interests of employee privacy and employer liability

Case Problems

1. Defendant used various false names and questionable documents to trade and attempt to trade stocks through E*TRADE, an electronic brokerage firm. He opened his first account using a laptop and a personal check he knew would bounce. He then opened accounts with five other online brokerage firms by mailing them fraudulent checks from his E*TRADE accounts. He hoped his share purchases would rise and thus "cover" the bad checks. What was the result?

2. Defendant worked for and owned stock options in PairGain technologies. He posted on Yahoo! a fabricated Bloomberg (financial) report that purported to reveal a buyout of PairGain by another firm. This fake report drove up the price of PairGain stock to record levels. What was the result?

3. A bank employee who was fired later entered the bank's computer systems using her old password and logged into the bank's mainframe. The former employee contends she just called up several computer files and logged off. The government asserts she changed several of the files and deleted others. What was the result? [*United States v. Sablan*, 92 F.3d 865 (9th Cir. 1996)]

4. Defendant selected names from the telephone book and then hacked into TRW, a consumer credit reporting agency. He then ordered fraudulent credit cards and made charges on these cards. What was the result? [*United States v. Petersen*, 98 F.3d 502 (9th Cir. 1996)]

5. Steve Jackson Games operated an electronic bulletin board system and offered customers the ability to send and receive private e-mail. This e-mail was stored temporarily on the BBS hard drive until customers retrieved their mail. Suspecting illegal activities, the Secret Service applied for a search warrant and conducted a search. They seized a computer used to operate the BBS containing mail that was not yet retrieved by subscribers. Is this an unlawful intercept under the Federal Wiretap Act? [*Steve Jackson Games, Inc. v. United States Secret Service*, 36 F.3d 457 (5th Cir. 1994)]

6. NDS Group extracted code from TV smart cards made by Canal Plus Group and transmitted in a digital file. The code was then published on the Web so anyone could produce a counterfeit smart card. What laws were used in

prosecuting this case? [Bruce Orwall, "Vivendi's Canal Plus Alleges NDS Helped Steal Digital-TV Broadcasts," March 12, 2002, *http://www.wsj.com*, and click on Internet and online]

7. The government seized over ten thousand packaged computer towers imported from Taiwan and brought to California. The towers bear certification marks registered to United Laboratories. The government charged the defendants with criminal trademark offenses. The defendants contend that the laws apply only to counterfeit *trademarks* and not to *certification marks*. Which side prevails? [*United States v. 10,510 Packaged Computer Towers*, 152 F. Supp. 2d 1189 (N.D. Cal. 2001)]

8. Computer Associates filed suit against rival Quest Software accusing Quest and four employees of stealing the software code that the four developed while working for Islandia, a Computer Associates subsidiary. What two offenses will Computer Associates allege? [Reuters, "Computer Associates Files Suit Against Quest Software," July 9, 2002, *http://www.nytimes.com*, and click on the Technology Page]

9. On May 3, 2000, a computer virus now known as "Love Bug" crippled millions of computers worldwide. Investigators found the virus originated from Remel Ramones, a reclusive bank employee who lived in a ramshackle Manila apartment. U.S. investigators faced a number of legal problems. Delays occurred in obtaining a Filipino search warrant, allowing the apartment's residents to dispose of their personal computers. No criminal law at the time criminalized computer vandalism in the Philippines. The arrest warrant instead stated that Ramones was arrested for computer and bank fraud. Soon after, the Filipino government dismissed the case against Ramones. What problems does this example highlight? What international initiatives could have facilitated the arrest and prosecution of Ramones?

Additional Readings

- Boni, William C., and Kovacich, Gerald L. *I-Way Robbery: Crime on the Internet*. Boston: Butterworth-Heinemann, 1999.

- Green, Rebecca Jacobson. "Computer Crimes." *American Criminal Law Review* 39 (2002): 273.

- Meinel, Carolyn. "Code Red for the Web." *Scientific American* (October 2001): 42.

- Power, Richard. "2002 CSI/FBI Computer Crime and Security Survey." *Computer Security, Issues and Trends* 8:1 (Spring 2002) (*http://www.gocsi.com*).

Appendix A

The Constitution of the United States

Preamble

We the People of the United States, in Order to form a more perfect Union, establish Justice, insure domestic Tranquility, provide for the common defence, promote the general Welfare, and secure the Blessings of Liberty to ourselves and our Posterity, do ordain and establish this Constitution for the United States of America.

Article I

Section 1

All legislative Powers herein granted shall be vested in a Congress of the United States, which shall consist of a Senate and House of Representatives.

Section 2

The House of Representatives shall be composed of Members chosen every second Year by the People of the several States, and the Electors in each State shall have the Qualifications requisite for Electors of the most numerous Branch of the State Legislature.

No Person shall be a Representative who shall not have attained to the Age of twenty five Years, and been seven Years a Citizen of the United States, and who shall not, when elected, be an Inhabitant of that State in which he shall be chosen.

Representatives and direct Taxes shall be apportioned among the several States which may be included within this Union, according to their respective Numbers, which shall be determined by adding to the whole Number of free Persons, including those bound to Service for a Term of Years, and excluding Indians not taxed, three fifths of all other Persons. The actual Enumeration shall be made within three Years after the first Meeting of the Congress of the United States, and within every subsequent Term of ten Years, in such Manner as they shall by Law direct. The Number of Representatives shall not exceed one for every thirty Thousand, but each State shall have at Least one Representative; and until such enumeration shall be made, the State of New Hampshire shall be entitled to chuse three, Massachusetts eight, Rhode Island and Providence Plantations one, Connecticut five, New York six, New Jersey four, Pennsylvania eight, Delaware one, Maryland six, Virginia ten, North Carolina five, South Carolina five, and Georgia three.

When vacancies happen in the Representation from any State, the Executive Authority thereof shall issue Writs of Election to fill such Vacancies.

The House of Representatives shall chuse their Speaker and other Officers; and shall have the sole Power of Impeachment.

Section 3

The Senate of the United States shall be composed of two Senators from each State, chosen by the Legislature thereof, for six Years; and each Senator shall have one Vote.

Immediately after they shall be assembled in Consequence of the first Election, they shall be divided as equally as may be into three Classes. The Seats of the Senators of the first Class shall be vacated at the Expiration of the second Year, of the second Class at the Expiration of the fourth Year, and of the third Class at the Expiration of the sixth Year, so that one third may be chosen every second Year; and if Vacancies happen by Resignation, or otherwise, during the Recess of the Legislature of any State, the Executive thereof may make temporary Appointments until the next Meeting of the Legislature, which shall then fill such Vacancies.

No Person shall be a Senator who shall not have attained to the Age of thirty Years, and been nine Years a Citizen of the United States, and who shall not, when elected, be an Inhabitant of that State for which he shall be chosen.

The Vice President of the United States shall be President of the Senate, but shall have no Vote, unless they be equally divided.

The Senate shall chuse their other Officers, and also a President pro tempore, in the Absence of the Vice President, or when he shall exercise the Office of President of the United States.

The Senate shall have the sole Power to try all Impeachments. When sitting for that Purpose, they shall be on Oath or Affirmation. When the President of the United States is tried, the Chief Justice shall preside: And no Person shall be convicted without the Concurrence of two thirds of the Members present.

Judgment in Cases of Impeachment shall not extend further than to removal from Office, and disqualification to hold and enjoy any Office of honor, Trust, or Profit under the United States: but the Party convicted shall nevertheless be liable and subject to Indictment, Trial, Judgment, and Punishment, according to Law.

Section 4

The Times, Places and Manner of holding Elections for Senators and Representatives, shall be prescribed in each State by the Legislature thereof; but the Congress may at any time by Law make or alter such Regulations, except as to the Places of chusing Senators.

The Congress shall assemble at least once in every Year, and such Meeting shall be on the first Monday in December, unless they shall by Law appoint a different Day.

Section 5

Each House shall be the Judge of the Elections, Returns, and Qualifications of its own Members, and a Majority of each shall constitute a Quorum to do Business; but a smaller Number may adjourn from day to day, and may be authorized to compel the Attendance of absent Members, in such Manner, and under such Penalties as each House may provide.

Each House may determine the Rules of its Proceedings, punish its Members for disorderly Behavior, and, with the Concurrence of two thirds, expel a Member.

Each House shall keep a Journal of its Proceedings, and from time to time publish the same, excepting such Parts as may in their Judgment require Secrecy; and the Yeas and Nays of the Members of either House on any question shall, at the Desire of one fifth of those Present, be entered on the Journal.

Neither House, during the Session of Congress, shall, without the Consent of the other, adjourn for more than three days, nor to any other Place than that in which the two Houses shall be sitting.

Section 6

The Senators and Representatives shall receive a Compensation for their Services, to be ascertained by Law, and paid out of the Treasury of the United States. They shall in all Cases, except Treason, Felony and Breach of the Peace, be privileged from Arrest during their Attendance at the Session of their respective Houses, and in going to and returning from the same; and for any Speech or Debate in either House, they shall not be questioned in any other Place.

No Senator or Representative shall, during the Time for which he was elected, be appointed to any civil Office under the Authority of the United States, which shall have been created, or the Emoluments whereof shall have been increased during such time; and no Person holding any Office under the United States, shall be a Member of either House during his Continuance in Office.

Section 7

All Bills for raising Revenue shall originate in the House of Representatives; but the Senate may propose or concur with Amendments as on other Bills.

Every Bill which shall have passed the House of Representatives and the Senate, shall, before it become a Law, be presented to the President of the United States; If he approve he shall sign it, but if not he shall return it, with his Objections to the House in which it shall have originated, who shall enter the Objections at large on their Journal, and proceed to reconsider it. If after such Reconsideration two thirds of that House shall agree to pass the Bill, it shall be sent together with the Objections, to the other House, by which it shall likewise be reconsidered, and if approved by two thirds of that House, it shall become a Law. But in all such Cases the Votes of both Houses shall be determined by Yeas and Nays, and the Names of the Persons voting for and against the Bill shall be entered on the Journal of each House respectively. If any Bill shall not be returned by the President within ten Days (Sundays excepted) after it shall have been presented to him, the Same shall be a Law, in like Manner as if he had signed it, unless the Congress by their Adjournment prevent its Return in which Case it shall not be a Law.

Every Order, Resolution, or Vote, to which the Concurrence of the Senate and House of Representatives may be necessary (except on a question of Adjournment) shall be presented to the President of the United States; and before the Same shall take Effect, shall be approved by him, or being disapproved by him, shall be repassed by two thirds of the Senate and House of Representatives, according to the Rules and Limitations prescribed in the Case of a Bill.

Section 8

The Congress shall have Power To lay and collect Taxes, Duties, Imposts and Excises, to pay the Debts and provide for the common Defence and general Welfare of the United States; but all Duties, Imposts and Excises shall be uniform throughout the United States;

To borrow Money on the credit of the United States;

To regulate Commerce with foreign Nations, and among the several States, and with the Indian Tribes;

To establish an uniform Rule of Naturalization, and uniform Laws on the subject of Bankruptcies throughout the United States;

To coin Money, regulate the Value thereof, and of foreign Coin, and fix the Standard of Weights and Measures;

To provide for the Punishment of counterfeiting the Securities and current Coin of the United States;

To establish Post Offices and post Roads;

To promote the Progress of Science and useful Arts, by securing for limited Times to Authors and Inventors the exclusive Right to their respective Writings and Discoveries;

To constitute Tribunals inferior to the supreme Court;

To define and punish Piracies and Felonies committed on the high Seas, and Offenses against the Law of Nations;

To declare War, grant Letters of Marque and Reprisal, and make Rules concerning Captures on Land and Water;

To raise and support Armies, but no Appropriation of Money to that Use shall be for a longer Term than two Years;

To provide and maintain a Navy;

To make Rules for the Government and Regulation of the land and naval Forces;

To provide for calling forth the Militia to execute the Laws of the Union, suppress Insurrections and repel Invasions;

To provide for organizing, arming, and disciplining, the Militia, and for governing such Part of them as may be employed in the Service of the United States, reserving to the States respectively, the Appointment of the Officers, and the Authority of training the Militia according to the discipline prescribed by Congress;

To exercise exclusive Legislation in all Cases whatsoever, over such District (not exceeding ten Miles square) as may, by Cession of particular States, and the Acceptance of Congress, become the Seat of the Government of the United States, and to exercise like Authority over all Places purchased by the Consent of the Legislature of the State in which the Same shall be, for the Erection of Forts, Magazines, Arsenals, dock-Yards, and other needful Buildings;—And

To make all Laws which shall be necessary and proper for carrying into Execution the foregoing Powers, and all other Powers vested by this Constitution in the Government of the United States, or in any Department or Officer thereof.

Section 9

The Migration or Importation of such Persons as any of the States now existing shall think proper to admit, shall not be prohibited by the Congress prior to the Year one thousand eight hundred and eight, but a Tax or duty may be imposed on such Importation, not exceeding ten dollars for each Person.

The privilege of the Writ of Habeas Corpus shall not be suspended, unless when in Cases of Rebellion or Invasion the public Safety may require it.

No Bill of Attainder or ex post facto Law shall be passed.

No Capitation, or other direct, Tax shall be laid, unless in Proportion to the Census or Enumeration herein before directed to be taken.

No Tax or Duty shall be laid on Articles exported from any State.

No Preference shall be given by any Regulation of Commerce or Revenue to the Ports of one State over those of another: nor shall Vessels bound to, or from, one State be obliged to enter, clear, or pay Duties in another.

No Money shall be drawn from the Treasury, but in Consequence of Appropriations made by Law; and a regular Statement and Account of the Receipts and Expenditures of all public Money shall be published from time to time.

No Title of Nobility shall be granted by the United States: And no Person holding any Office of Profit or Trust under them, shall, without the Consent of the Congress, accept of any present, Emolument, Office, or Title, of any kind whatever, from any King, Prince, or foreign State.

Section 10

No State shall enter into any Treaty, Alliance, or Confederation; grant Letters of Marque and Reprisal; coin Money; emit Bills of Credit; make any Thing but gold and silver Coin a Tender in Payment of Debts; pass any Bill of Attainder, ex post facto Law, or Law impairing the Obligation of Contracts, or grant any Title of Nobility.

No State shall, without the Consent of the Congress, lay any Imposts or Duties on Imports or Exports, except what may be absolutely necessary for executing its inspection Laws: and the net Produce of all Duties and Imposts, laid by any State on

Imports or Exports, shall be for the Use of the Treasury of the United States; and all such Laws shall be subject to the Revision and Controul of the Congress.

No State shall, without the Consent of Congress, lay any Duty of Tonnage, keep Troops, or Ships of War in time of Peace, enter into any Agreement or Compact with another State, or with a foreign Power, or engage in War, unless actually invaded, or in such imminent Danger as will not admit of delay.

Article II

Section 1

The executive Power shall be vested in a President of the United States of America. He shall hold his Office during the Term of four Years, and, together with the Vice President, chosen for the same Term, be elected, as follows:

Each State shall appoint, in such Manner as the Legislature thereof may direct, a Number of Electors, equal to the whole Number of Senators and Representatives to which the State may be entitled in the Congress; but no Senator or Representative, or Person holding an Office of Trust or Profit under the United States, shall be appointed an Elector.

The Electors shall meet in their respective States, and vote by Ballot for two Persons, of whom one at least shall not be an Inhabitant of the same State with themselves. And they shall make a List of all the Persons voted for, and of the Number of Votes for each; which List they shall sign and certify, and transmit sealed to the Seat of the Government of the United States, directed to the President of the Senate. The President of the Senate shall, in the Presence of the Senate and House of Representatives, open all the Certificates, and the Votes shall then be counted. The Person having the greatest Number of Votes shall be the President, if such Number be a Majority of the whole Number of Electors appointed; and if there be more than one who have such Majority, and have an equal Number of Votes, then the House of Representatives shall immediately chuse by Ballot one of them for President; and if no Person have a Majority, then from the five highest on the List the said House shall in like Manner chuse the President. But in chusing the President, the Votes shall be taken by States, the Representation from each State having one Vote; A quorum for this Purpose shall consist of a Member or Members from two thirds of the States, and a Majority of all the States shall be necessary to a Choice. In every Case, after the Choice of the President, the Person having the greater Number of Votes of the Electors shall be the Vice President. But if there should remain two or more who have equal Votes, the Senate shall chuse from them by Ballot the Vice President.

The Congress may determine the Time of chusing the Electors, and the Day on which they shall give their Votes; which Day shall be the same throughout the United States.

No person except a natural born Citizen, or a Citizen of the United States, at the time of the Adoption of this Constitution, shall be eligible to the Office of President;

neither shall any Person be eligible to that Office who shall not have attained to the Age of thirty five Years, and been fourteen Years a Resident within the United States.

In Case of the Removal of the President from Office, or of his Death, Resignation or Inability to discharge the Powers and Duties of the said Office, the same shall devolve on the Vice President, and the Congress may by Law provide for the Case of Removal, Death, Resignation or Inability, both of the President and Vice President, declaring what Officer shall then act as President, and such Officer shall act accordingly, until the Disability be removed, or a President shall be elected.

The President shall, at stated Times, receive for his Services, a Compensation, which shall neither be increased nor diminished during the Period for which he shall have been elected, and he shall not receive within that Period any other Emolument from the United States, or any of them.

Before he enter on the Execution of his Office, he shall take the following Oath or Affirmation: "I do solemnly swear (or affirm) that I will faithfully execute the Office of President of the United States, and will to the best of my Ability, preserve, protect and defend the Constitution of the United States."

Section 2

The President shall be Commander in Chief of the Army and Navy of the United States, and of the Militia of the several States, when called into the actual Service of the United States; he may require the Opinion, in writing, of the principal Officer in each of the executive Departments, upon any Subject relating to the Duties of their respective Offices, and he shall have Power to grant Reprieves and Pardons for Offenses against the United States, except in Cases of Impeachment.

He shall have Power, by and with the Advice and Consent of the Senate to make Treaties, provided two thirds of the Senators present concur; and he shall nominate, and by and with the Advice and Consent of the Senate, shall appoint Ambassadors, other public Ministers and Consuls, Judges of the supreme Court, and all other Officers of the United States, whose Appointments are not herein otherwise provided for, and which shall be established by Law; but the Congress may by Law vest the Appointment of such inferior Officers, as they think proper, in the President alone, in the Courts of Law, or in the Heads of Departments.

The President shall have Power to fill up all Vacancies that may happen during the Recess of the Senate, by granting Commissions which shall expire at the End of their next Session.

Section 3

He shall from time to time give to the Congress Information of the State of the Union, and recommend to their Consideration such Measures as he shall judge necessary and expedient; he may, on extraordinary Occasions, convene both Houses, or either of them, and in Case of Disagreement between them, with Respect to the Time of Adjournment, he may adjourn them to such Time as he shall think proper; he shall receive Ambassadors and other public Ministers; he shall take Care that the Laws be faithfully executed, and shall Commission all the Officers of the United States.

Section 4

The President, Vice President and all civil Officers of the United States, shall be removed from Office on Impeachment for, and Conviction of, Treason, Bribery, or other high Crimes and Misdemeanors.

Article III

Section 1

The judicial Power of the United States, shall be vested in one supreme Court, and in such inferior Courts as the Congress may from time to time ordain and establish. The Judges, both of the supreme and inferior Courts, shall hold their Offices during good Behaviour, and shall, at stated Times, receive for their Services a Compensation, which shall not be diminished during their Continuance in Office.

Section 2

The judicial Power shall extend to all Cases, in Law and Equity, arising under this Constitution, the Laws of the United States, and Treaties made, or which shall be made, under their Authority;—to all Cases affecting Ambassadors, other public Ministers and Consuls;—to all Cases of admiralty and maritime Jurisdiction;—to Controversies to which the United States shall be a Party;—to Controversies between two or more States;—between a State and Citizens of another State;—between Citizens of different States;—between Citizens of the same State claiming Lands under Grants of different States, and between a State, or the Citizens thereof, and foreign States, Citizens or Subjects.

In all Cases affecting Ambassadors, other public Ministers and Consuls, and those in which a State shall be a Party, the supreme Court shall have original Jurisdiction. In all the other Cases before mentioned, the supreme Court shall have appellate Jurisdiction, both as to Law and Fact, with such Exceptions, and under such Regulations as the Congress shall make.

The Trial of all Crimes, except in Cases of Impeachment, shall be by Jury; and such Trial shall be held in the State where the said Crimes shall have been committed; but when not committed within any State, the Trial shall be at such Place or Places as the Congress may by Law have directed.

Section 3

Treason against the United States, shall consist only in levying War against them, or, in adhering to their Enemies, giving them Aid and Comfort. No Person shall be convicted of Treason unless on the Testimony of two Witnesses to the same overt Act, or on Confession in open Court.

The Congress shall have Power to declare the Punishment of Treason, but no Attainder of Treason shall work Corruption of Blood, or Forfeiture except during the Life of the Person attainted.

Article IV

Section 1

Full Faith and Credit shall be given in each State to the public Acts, Records, and judicial Proceedings of every other State. And the Congress may by general Laws prescribe the Manner in which such Acts, Records and Proceedings shall be proved, and the Effect thereof.

Section 2

The Citizens of each State shall be entitled to all Privileges and Immunities of Citizens in the several States.

A Person charged in any State with Treason, Felony, or other Crime, who shall flee from Justice, and be found in another State, shall on Demand of the executive Authority of the State from which he fled, be delivered up, to be removed to the State having Jurisdiction of the Crime.

No Person held to Service or Labour in one State, under the Laws thereof, escaping into another, shall, in Consequence of any Law or Regulation therein, be discharged from such Service or Labour, but shall be delivered up on Claim of the Party to whom such Service or Labour may be due.

Section 3

New States may be admitted by the Congress into this Union; but no new State shall be formed or erected within the Jurisdiction of any other State; nor any State be formed by the Junction of two or more States, or Parts of States, without the Consent of the Legislatures of the States concerned as well as of the Congress.

The Congress shall have Power to dispose of and make all needful Rules and Regulations respecting the Territory or other Property belonging to the United States; and nothing in this Constitution shall be so construed as to Prejudice any Claims of the United States, or of any particular State.

Section 4

The United States shall guarantee to every State in this Union a Republican Form of Government, and shall protect each of them against Invasion; and on Application of the Legislature, or of the Executive (when the Legislature cannot be convened) against domestic Violence.

Article V

The Congress, whenever two thirds of both Houses shall deem it necessary, shall propose Amendments to this Constitution, or, on the Application of the Legislatures of two thirds of the several States, shall call a Convention for proposing Amendments, which, in either Case, shall be valid to all Intents and Purposes, as part of this Constitution, when ratified by the Legislatures of three fourths of the several States, or by Conventions in three fourths thereof, as the one or the other Mode of Ratification may be proposed by the Congress; Provided that no Amendment which may be made prior to the Year One thousand eight hundred and eight shall in any Manner affect the first and fourth Clauses in the Ninth Section of the first Article; and that no State, without its Consent, shall be deprived of its equal Suffrage in the Senate.

Article VI

All Debts contracted and Engagements entered into, before the Adoption of this Constitution shall be as valid against the United States under this Constitution, as under the Confederation.

This Constitution, and the Laws of the United States which shall be made in Pursuance thereof; and all Treaties made, or which shall be made, under the Authority of the United States, shall be the supreme Law of the Land; and the Judges in every State shall be bound thereby, any Thing in the Constitution or Laws of any State to the Contrary notwithstanding.

The Senators and Representatives before mentioned, and the Members of the several State Legislatures, and all executive and judicial Officers, both of the United States and of the several States, shall be bound by Oath or Affirmation, to support this Constitution; but no religious Test shall ever be required as a Qualification to any Office or public Trust under the United States.

Article VII

The Ratification of the Conventions of nine States shall be sufficient for the Establishment of this Constitution between the States so ratifying the Same.

Amendment I [1791]

Congress shall make no law respecting an establishment of religion, or prohibiting the free exercise thereof; or abridging the freedom of speech, or of the press; or the right of the people peaceably to assembly, and to petition the Government for a redress of grievances.

Amendment II [1791]

A well regulated Militia, being necessary to the security of a free State, the right of the people to keep and bear Arms, shall not be infringed.

Amendment III [1791]

No Soldier shall, in time of peace be quartered in any house, without the consent of the Owner, nor in time of war, but in a manner to be prescribed by law.

Amendment IV [1791]

The right of the people to be secure in their persons, houses, papers, and effects, against unreasonable searches and seizures, shall not be violated, and no Warrants shall issue, but upon probable cause, supported by Oath or affirmation, and particularly describing the place to be searched, and the persons or things to be seized.

Amendment V [1791]

No person shall be held to answer for a capital, or otherwise infamous crime, unless on a presentment or indictment of a Grand Jury, except in cases arising in the land or naval forces, or in the Militia, when in actual service in time of War or public danger; nor shall any person be subject for the same offence to be twice put in jeopardy of life or limb; nor shall be compelled in any criminal case to be a witness against himself, nor be deprived of life, liberty, or property, without due process of law; nor shall private property be taken for public use, without just compensation.

Amendment VI [1791]

In all criminal prosecutions, the accused shall enjoy the right to a speedy and public trial, by an impartial jury of the State and district wherein the crime shall have been committed, which district shall have been previously ascertained by law, and to be informed of the nature and cause of the accusation; to be confronted with the witnesses against him; to have compulsory process for obtaining witnesses in his favor, and to have the Assistance of Counsel for his defence.

Amendment VII [1791]

In Suits at common law, where the value in controversy shall exceed twenty dollars, the right of trial by jury shall be preserved, and no fact tried by jury, shall be otherwise re-examined in any Court of the United States, than according to the rules of the common law.

Amendment VIII [1791]

Excessive bail shall not be required, nor excessive fines imposed, nor cruel and unusual punishments inflicted.

Amendment IX [1791]

The enumeration in the Constitution, of certain rights, shall not be construed to deny or disparage others retained by the people.

Amendment X [1791]

The powers not delegated to the United States by the Constitution, nor prohibited by it to the States, are reserved to the States respectively, or to the people.

Amendment XI [1798]

The Judicial power of the United States shall not be construed to extend to any suit in law or equity, commenced or prosecuted against one of the United States by Citizens of another State, or by Citizens or Subjects of any Foreign State.

Amendment XII [1804]

The Electors shall meet in their respective states, and vote by ballot for President and Vice-President, one of whom, at least, shall not be an inhabitant of the same state with themselves; they shall name in their ballots the person voted for as President, and in distinct ballots the person voted for as Vice-President, and they shall make distinct lists of all persons voted for as President, and of all persons voted for as Vice-President, and of the number of votes for each, which lists they shall sign and certify, and transmit sealed to the seat of the government of the United States, directed to the President of the Senate;—The President of the Senate shall, in the presence of the Senate and House of Representatives, open all the certificates and the votes shall then be counted;—The person having the greatest number of votes for President, shall be the President, if such number be a majority of the whole number of Electors appointed; and if no person have such majority, then from the persons having the highest numbers not exceeding three on the list of those voted for as President, the House of Representatives shall choose immediately, by ballot, the President. But in choosing the President, the votes shall be taken by states, the representation from each state having one vote; a quorum for this purpose shall consist of a member or members from two-thirds of the states, and a majority of all states shall be necessary to a choice. And if the House of Representatives shall not choose a President whenever the right of choice shall devolve upon them, before the fourth day of March next following, then the Vice-President shall act as President, as in the case of the death or other constitutional disability of the President.—The person having the greatest number of votes as Vice-President, shall be the Vice-

President, if such number be a majority of the whole number of Electors appointed, and if no person have a majority, then from the two highest numbers on the list, the Senate shall choose the Vice-President; a quorum for the purpose shall consist of two-thirds of the whole number of Senators, and a majority of the whole number shall be necessary to a choice. But no person constitutionally ineligible to the office of President shall be eligible to that of Vice-President of the United States.

Amendment XIII [1865]

Section 1

Neither slavery nor involuntary servitude, except as a punishment for crime whereof the party shall have been duly convicted, shall exist within the United States, or any place subject to their jurisdiction.

Section 2

Congress shall have power to enforce this article by appropriate legislation.

Amendment XIV [1868]

Section 1

All persons born or naturalized in the United States, and subject to the jurisdiction thereof, are citizens of the United States and of the State wherein they reside. No State shall make or enforce any law which shall abridge the privileges or immunities of citizens of the United States; nor shall any State deprive any person of life, liberty, or property, without due process of law; nor deny to any person within its jurisdiction the equal protection of the laws.

Section 2

Representatives shall be apportioned among the several States according to their respective numbers, counting the whole number of persons in each State, excluding Indians not taxed. But when the right to vote at any election for the choice of electors for President and Vice President of the United States, Representatives in Congress, the Executive and Judicial officers of a State, or the members of the Legislature thereof, is denied to any of the male inhabitants of such State, being twenty-one years of age, and citizens of the United States, or in any way abridged, except for participation in rebellion, or other crime, the basis of representation therein shall be reduced in the proportion which the number of such male citizens shall bear to the whole number of male citizens twenty-one years of age in such State.

Section 3

No person shall be a Senator or Representative in Congress, or elector of President and Vice President, or hold any office, civil or military, under the United States, or under any State, who having previously taken an oath, as a member of Congress, or as an officer of the United States, or as a member of any State legislature, or as an executive or judicial officer of any State, to support the Constitution of the United States, shall have engaged in insurrection or rebellion against the same, or given aid or comfort to the enemies thereof. But Congress may by a vote of two-thirds of each House, remove such disability.

Section 4

The validity of the public debt of the United States, authorized by law, including debts incurred for payment of pensions and bounties for services in suppressing insurrection or rebellion, shall not be questioned. But neither the United States nor any State shall assume or pay any debt or obligation incurred in aid of insurrection or rebellion against the United States, or any claim for the loss or emancipation of any slave; but all such debts, obligations and claims shall be held illegal and void.

Section 5

The Congress shall have power to enforce, by appropriate legislation, the provisions of this article.

Amendment XV [1870]

Section 1

The right of citizens of the United States to vote shall not be denied or abridged by the United States or by any State on account of race, color, or previous condition of servitude.

Section 2

The Congress shall have power to enforce this article by appropriate legislation.

Amendment XVI [1913]

The Congress shall have power to lay and collect taxes on incomes, from whatever source derived, without apportionment among the several States, and without regard to any census or enumeration.

Amendment XVII [1913]

Section 1

The Senate of the United States shall be composed of two Senators from each State, elected by the people thereof, for six years; and each Senator shall have one vote. The electors in each State shall have the qualifications requisite for electors of the most numerous branch of the State legislatures.

Section 2

When vacancies happen in the representation of any State in the Senate, the executive authority of such State shall issue writs of election to fill such vacancies: *Provided*, That the legislature of any State may empower the executive thereof to make temporary appointments until the people fill the vacancies by election as the legislature may direct.

Section 3

This amendment shall not be so construed as to affect the election or term of any Senator chosen before it becomes valid as part of the Constitution.

Amendment XVIII [1919]

Section 1

After one year from the ratification of this article the manufacture, sale, or transportation of intoxicating liquors within, the importation thereof into, or the exportation thereof from the United States and all territory subject to the jurisdiction thereof for beverage purposes is hereby prohibited.

Section 2

The Congress and the several States shall have concurrent power to enforce this article by appropriate legislation.

Section 3

This article shall be inoperative unless it shall have been ratified as an amendment to the Constitution by the legislatures of the several States, as provided in the Constitution, within seven years from the date of the submission hereof to the States by the Congress.

Amendment XIX [1920]

Section 1

The right of citizens of the United States to vote shall not be denied or abridged by the United States or by any State on account of sex.

Section 2

Congress shall have power to enforce this article by appropriate legislation.

Amendment XX [1933]

Section 1

The terms of the President and Vice President shall end at noon on the 20th day of January, and the terms of Senators and Representatives at noon on the 3d day of

January, of the years in which such terms would have ended if this article had not been ratified; and the terms of their successors shall then begin.

Section 2

The Congress shall assemble at least once in every year, and such meeting shall begin at noon on the 3d day of January, unless they shall by law appoint a different day.

Section 3

If, at the time fixed for the beginning of the term of the President, the President elect shall have died, the Vice President elect shall become President. If the President shall not have been chosen before the time fixed for the beginning of his term, or if the President elect shall have failed to qualify, then the Vice President elect shall act as President until a President shall have qualified; and the Congress may by law provide for the case wherein neither a President elect nor a Vice President elect shall have qualified, declaring who shall then act as President, or the manner in which one who is to act shall be selected, and such person shall act accordingly until a President or Vice President shall have qualified.

Section 4

The Congress may by law provide for the case of the death of any of the persons from whom the House of Representatives may choose a President whenever the right of choice shall have devolved upon them, and for the case of the death of any of the persons from whom the Senate may choose a Vice President whenever the right of choice shall have devolved upon them.

Section 5

Sections 1 and 2 shall take effect on the 15th day of October following the ratification of this article.

Section 6

This article shall be inoperative unless it shall have been ratified as an amendment to the Constitution by the legislatures of three-fourths of the several States within seven years from the date of its submission.

Amendment XXI [1933]

Section 1

The eighteenth article of amendment to the Constitution of the United States is hereby repealed.

Section 2

The transportation or importation into any State, Territory, or possession of the United States for delivery or use therein of intoxicating liquors, in violation of the laws thereof, is hereby prohibited.

Section 3

This article shall be inoperative unless it shall have been ratified as an amendment to the Constitution by conventions in the several States, as provided in the Constitution, within seven years from the date of the submission hereof to the States by the Congress.

Amendment XXII [1951]

Section 1

No person shall be elected to the office of the President more than twice, and no person who has held the office of President, or acted as President, for more than two years of a term to which some other person was elected President shall be elected to the office of President more than once. But this Article shall not apply to any person holding the office of President when this Article was proposed by the Congress, and shall not prevent any person who may be holding the office of President, or acting as President, during the term within which this Article becomes operative from holding the office of President or acting as President during the remainder of such term.

Section 2

This article shall be inoperative unless it shall have been ratified as an amendment to the Constitution by the legislatures of three-fourths of the several States within seven years from the date of its submission to the States by the Congress.

Amendment XXIII [1961]

Section 1

The District constituting the seat of Government of the United States shall appoint in such manner as the Congress may direct:

A number of electors of President and Vice President equal to the whole number of Senators and Representatives in Congress to which the District would be entitled if it were a State, but in no event more than the least populous state; they shall be in addition to those appointed by the states, but they shall be considered, for the purposes of the election of President and Vice President, to be electors appointed by a state; and they shall meet in the District and perform such duties as provided by the twelfth article of amendment.

Section 2

The Congress shall have power to enforce this article by appropriate legislation.

Amendment XXIV [1964]

Section 1

The right of citizens of the United States to vote in any primary or other election for President or Vice President, for electors for President or Vice President, or for

Senator or Representative in Congress, shall not be denied or abridged by the United States, or any State by reason of failure to pay any poll tax or other tax.

Section 2

The Congress shall have power to enforce this article by appropriate legislation.

Amendment XXV [1967]

Section 1

In case of the removal of the President from office or of his death or resignation, the Vice President shall become President.

Section 2

Whenever there is a vacancy in the office of the Vice President, the President shall nominate a Vice President who shall take office upon confirmation by a majority vote of both Houses of Congress.

Section 3

Whenever the President transmits to the President pro tempore of the Senate and the Speaker of the House of Representatives his written declaration that he is unable to discharge the powers and duties of his office, and until he transmits to them a written declaration to the contrary, such powers and duties shall be discharged by the Vice President as Acting President.

Section 4

Whenever the Vice President and a majority of either the principal officers of the executive departments or of such other body as Congress may by law provide, transmit to the President pro tempore of the Senate and the Speaker of the House of Representatives their written declaration that the President is unable to discharge the powers and duties of his office, the Vice President shall immediately assume the powers and duties of the office as Acting President.

Thereafter, when the President transmits to the President pro tempore of the Senate and the Speaker of the House of Representatives his written declaration that no inability exists, he shall resume the powers and duties of his office unless the Vice President and a majority of either the principal officers of the executive department or of such other body as Congress may by law provide, transmit within four days to the President pro tempore of the Senate and the Speaker of the House of Representatives their written declaration that the President is unable to discharge the powers and duties of his office. Thereupon Congress shall decide the issue, assembling within forty-eight hours for that purpose if not in session. If the Congress, within twenty-one days after receipt of the latter written declaration, or, if Congress is not in session, within twenty-one days after Congress is required to assemble, determines by two-thirds vote of both Houses that the President is unable to discharge the powers and duties of his office, the Vice President shall continue to discharge the same as Acting President; otherwise, the President shall resume the powers and duties of his office.

Amendment XXVI [1971]

Section 1

The right of citizens of the United States, who are eighteen years of age or older, to vote shall not be denied or abridged by the United States or by any State on account of age.

Section 2

The Congress shall have power to enforce this article by appropriate legislation.

Amendment XXVII [1992]

No law, varying the compensation for the services of the Senators and Representatives, shall take effect, until an election of Representatives shall have intervened.

Appendix B

Digital Millennium Copyright Act of 1998

http://www.dfc.org/dfc1/Active_Issues/graphic/DMCA_index.html

Section 1. Short Title

This Act may be cited as the "Digital Millennium Copyright Act."

Sec. 2. Table of Contents

Title V—Protection of Certain Original Designs

Appendix C

Excerpts from the Anticybersquatting Consumer Protection Act of 1999

http://www.eff.org/Infrastructure/DNS_control/s1255_1999_bill.html

S. 1255 To protect consumers and promote electronic commerce by amending certain trademark infringement, dilution, and counterfeiting laws, and for other purposes.

Section 1. Short Title

This Act may be cited as the "Anticybersquatting Consumer Protection Act."

Sec. 2. Findings

Congress finds that the unauthorized registration or use of trademarks as Internet domain names or other identifiers of online locations (commonly known as 'cyber-squatting')—

(1) results in consumer fraud and public confusion as to the true source or sponsorship of products and services;

(2) impairs electronic commerce, which is important to the economy of the United States; and

(3) deprives owners of trademarks of substantial revenues and consumer goodwill.

Sec. 3. Trademark Remedies

(a) RECOVERY FOR VIOLATION OF RIGHTS- Section 35 of the Act entitled 'An Act to provide for the registration and protection of trade-marks used in commerce, to carry out the provisions of certain international conventions, and for other purposes,' approved July 5, 1946, (commonly referred to as the 'Trademark Act of 1946') (15 U.S.C. 1117) is amended by adding at the end the following:

'(d)(1) In this subsection, the term 'Internet' has the meaning given that term in section 230(f)(1) of the Communications Act of 1934 (47 U.S.C. 230(f)(1)).

'(2)(A) In a case involving the registration or use of an identifier described in subparagraph (B), the plaintiff may elect, at any time before final judgment is rendered by the trial court, to recover, instead of actual damages and profits under subsection (a)—

'(i) an award of statutory damages in the amount of—

'(I) not less than $1,000 or more than $100,000 per trademark per identifier, as the court considers just; or

'(II) if the court finds that the registration or use of the registered trademark as an identifier was willful, not less than $3,000 or more than $300,000 per trademark per identifier, as the court considers just; and

'(ii) full costs and reasonable attorney's fees.

'(B) An identifier referred to in subparagraph (A) is an Internet domain name or other identifier of an online location that is—

'(i) the trademark of a person or entity other than the person or entity registering or using the identifier; or

'(ii) sufficiently similar to a trademark of a person or entity other than the person or entity registering or using the identifier as to be likely to—

'(I) cause confusion or mistake;

'(II) deceive; or

'(III) cause dilution of the distinctive quality of a famous trademark'.

(b) REMEDIES FOR DILUTION OF FAMOUS MARKS- Section 43(c)(2) of the Act entitled 'An Act to provide for the registration and protection of trade-marks used in commerce, to carry out the provisions of certain international conventions, and for other purposes', approved July 5, 1946, (commonly referred to as the 'Trademark Act of 1946') (15 U.S.C. 1125(c)(2)) is amended by striking '35(a)' and inserting '35 (a) and (d)'.

Sec. 4. Criminal Use of Counterfeit Trademark

(a) IN GENERAL- Section 2320(a) of title 18, United States Code, is amended—

(1) by inserting '(1)' after '(a)';

(2) by striking 'section that occurs' and inserting 'paragraph that occurs'; and

(3) by adding at the end the following:

'(2)(A) In this paragraph, the term 'Internet' has the meaning given that term in section 230(f)(1) of the Communications Act of 1934 (47 U.S.C. 230(f)(1)).

'(B)(i) Except as provided in clause (ii), whoever knowingly and fraudulently or in bad faith registers or uses an identifier described in subparagraph (C) shall be guilty of a Class B misdemeanor.

'(ii) In the case of an offense by a person under this paragraph that occurs after that person is convicted of another offense under this section, that person shall be guilty of a Class E felony.

'(C) An identifier referred to in subparagraph (B) is an Internet domain name or other identifier of an online location that is—

'(i) the trademark of a person or entity other than the person or entity registering or using the identifier; or

'(ii) sufficiently similar to a trademark of a person or entity other than the person or entity registering or using the identifier as to be likely to—

'(I) cause confusion or mistake;

'(II) deceive; or

'(III) cause dilution of the distinctive quality of a famous trademark.

'(D)(i) For the purposes of a prosecution under this paragraph, if all of the conditions described in clause (ii) apply to the registration or use of an identifier described in subparagraph (C) by a defendant, those conditions shall constitute prima facie evidence that the registration or use was fraudulent or in bad faith.

'(ii) The conditions referred to in clause (i) are as follows:

'(I) The defendant registered or used an identifier described in subparagraph (C)—

'(aa) with intent to cause confusion or mistake, deceive, or cause dilution of the distinctive quality of a famous trademark; or

'(bb) with the intention of diverting consumers from the domain or other online location of the person or entity who is the owner of a trademark described in subparagraph (C) to the domain or other online location of the defendant.

'(II) The defendant—

'(aa) provided false information in the defendant's application to register the identifier; or

'(bb) offered to transfer the registration of the identifier to the trademark owner or another person or entity in consideration for any thing of value.

'(III) The identifier is not—

'(aa) the defendant's legal first name or surname; or

'(bb) a trademark of the defendant used in legitimate commerce before the earlier of the first use of the registered trademark referred to in subparagraph (C) or the effective date of the registration of that trademark.

'(iii) The application of this subparagraph shall not be exclusive. Nothing in this subparagraph may be construed to limit the applicability of subparagraph (B).'

(b) Sentencing Guidelines

(1) IN GENERAL- Pursuant to the authority granted to the United States Sentencing Commission under section 994(p) of title 28, United States Code, the United States Sentencing Commission shall—

(A) review the Federal sentencing guidelines for crimes against intellectual property (including offenses under section 2320 of title 18, United States Code); and

(B) promulgate such amendments to the Federal Sentencing Guidelines as are necessary to ensure that the applicable sentence for a defendant convicted of a crime against intellectual property is sufficiently stringent to deter such a crime.

(2) FACTORS FOR CONSIDERATION- In carrying out this subsection, the United States Sentencing Commission shall—

(A) take into account the findings under section 2; and

(B) ensure that the amendments promulgated under paragraph (1)(B) adequately provide for sentencing for crimes described in paragraph (2) of section 2320(a) of title 18, United States Code, as added by subsection (a).

Sec. 5. Limitation of Liability

Section 39 of the Act entitled 'An Act to provide for the registration and protection of trademarks used in commerce, to carry out the provisions of certain international conventions, and for other purposes,' approved July 5, 1946, (commonly referred to as the 'Trademark Act of 1946') (15 U.S.C. 1121) is amended by adding at the end the following:

'(c)(1) In this subsection, the term 'Internet' has the meaning given that term in section 230(f)(1) of the Communications Act of 1934 (47 U.S.C. 230(f)(1)).

'(2)(A) An Internet service provider, domain name registrar, or registry described in subparagraph (B) shall not be liable for monetary relief to any person for a removal or transfer described in that subparagraph, without regard to whether the domain name or other identifier is ultimately determined to be infringing or dilutive.

'(B) An Internet service provider, domain name registrar, or registry referred to in subparagraph (A) is a provider, registrar, or registry that, upon receipt of a written notice from the owner of a trademark registered in the Patent and Trademark Office, removes from domain name service (DNS) service or registration, or transfers to the trademark owner, an Internet domain name or other identifier of an online location alleged to be infringing or dilutive, in compliance with—

'(i) a court order; or

'(ii) the reasonable implementation of a policy prohibiting the unauthorized registration or use of another's registered trademark as an Internet domain name or other identifier of an online location.'

Appendix D

Uniform Domain Name Dispute Resolution Policy (the "Policy")

http://www.icann.org/udrp/udrp.htm

Approved by ICANN: October 24, 1999

1. **Purpose.**

   This Uniform Domain Name Dispute Resolution Policy (the "Policy") has been adopted by the Internet Corporation for Assigned Names and Numbers ("ICANN"), is incorporated by reference into your Registration Agreement, and sets forth the terms and conditions in connection with a dispute between you and any party other than us (the registrar) over the registration and use of an Internet domain name registered by you. Proceedings under Paragraph 4 of this Policy will be conducted according to the Rules for Uniform Domain Name Dispute Resolution Policy (the "Rules of Procedure") and the selected administrative-dispute-resolution service provider's supplemental rules.

2. **Your Representations.**

   By applying to register a domain name, or by asking us to maintain or renew a domain name registration, you hereby represent and warrant to us that

   a. the statements that you made in your Registration Agreement are complete and accurate;

   b. to your knowledge, the registration of the domain name will not infringe upon or otherwise violate the rights of any third party;

   c. you are not registering the domain name for an unlawful purpose; and

   d. you will not knowingly use the domain name in violation of any applicable laws or regulations.

   It is your responsibility to determine whether your domain name registration infringes or violates someone else's rights.

3. **Cancellations, Transfers, and Changes.**

   We will cancel, transfer or otherwise make changes to domain name registrations under the following circumstances:

   a. subject to the provisions of Paragraph 8, our receipt of written or appropriate electronic instructions from you or your authorized agent to take such action;

   b. our receipt of an order from a court or arbitral tribunal, in each case of competent jurisdiction, requiring such action; and/or

   c. our receipt of a decision of an Administrative Panel requiring such action in any administrative proceeding to which you were a party and which was conducted under this Policy or a later version of this Policy adopted by ICANN. (See Paragraph 4(i) and (k) below.)

We may also cancel, transfer or otherwise make changes to a domain name registration in accordance with the terms of your Registration Agreement or other legal requirements.

4. **Mandatory Administrative Proceeding.**

This Paragraph sets forth the type of disputes for which you are required to submit to a mandatory administrative proceeding. These proceedings will be conducted before one of the administrative-dispute-resolution service providers listed under Providers.

a. Applicable Disputes. You are required to submit to a mandatory administrative proceeding in the event that a third party (a "complainant") asserts to the applicable Provider, in compliance with the Rules of Procedure, that

i. your domain name is identical or confusingly similar to a trademark or service mark in which the complainant has rights; and

ii. you have no rights or legitimate interests in respect of the domain name; and

iii. your domain name has been registered and is being used in bad faith.

In the administrative proceeding, the complainant must prove that each of these three elements are present.

b. Evidence of Registration and Use in Bad Faith. For the purposes of Paragraph 4(a)(iii), the following circumstances, in particular but without limitation, if found by the Panel to be present, shall be evidence of the registration and use of a domain name in bad faith:

i. circumstances indicating that you have registered or you have acquired the domain name primarily for the purpose of selling, renting, or otherwise transferring the domain name registration to the complainant who is the owner of the trademark or service mark or to a competitor of that complainant, for valuable consideration in excess of your documented out-of-pocket costs directly related to the domain name; or

ii. you have registered the domain name in order to prevent the owner of the trademark or service mark from reflecting the mark in a corresponding domain name, provided that you have engaged in a pattern of such conduct; or

iii. you have registered the domain name primarily for the purpose of disrupting the business of a competitor; or

iv. by using the domain name, you have intentionally attempted to attract, for commercial gain, Internet users to your web site or other on-line location, by creating a likelihood of confusion with the complainant's mark as to the source, sponsorship, affiliation, or endorsement of your web site or location or of a product or service on your web site or location.

c. How to Demonstrate Your Rights to and Legitimate Interests in the Domain Name in Responding to a Complaint. When you receive a complaint, you should refer to Paragraph 5 of the Rules of Procedure in determining how your response should be prepared. Any of the following circumstances, in particular but without limitation, if found by the Panel to be proved based on its evaluation of all evidence presented, shall demonstrate your rights or legitimate interests to the domain name for purposes of Paragraph 4(a)(ii):

i. before any notice to you of the dispute, your use of, or demonstrable preparations to use, the domain name or a name corresponding to the domain name in connection with a bona fide offering of goods or services; or

ii. you (as an individual, business, or other organization) have been commonly known by the domain name, even if you have acquired no trademark or service mark rights; or

iii. you are making a legitimate noncommercial or fair use of the domain name, without intent for commercial gain to misleadingly divert consumers or to tarnish the trademark or service mark at issue.

d. Selection of Provider. The complainant shall select the Provider from among those approved by ICANN by submitting the complaint to that Provider. The selected Provider will administer the proceeding, except in cases of consolidation as described in Paragraph 4(f).

e. Initiation of Proceeding and Process and Appointment of Administrative Panel. The Rules of Procedure state the process for initiating and conducting a proceeding and for appointing the panel that will decide the dispute (the "Administrative Panel").

f. Consolidation. In the event of multiple disputes between you and a complainant, either you or the complainant may petition to consolidate the disputes before a single Administrative Panel. This petition shall be made to the first Administrative Panel appointed to hear a pending dispute between the parties. This Administrative Panel may consolidate before it any or all such disputes in its sole discretion, provided that the disputes being consolidated are governed by this Policy or a later version of this Policy adopted by ICANN.

g. Fees. All fees charged by a Provider in connection with any dispute before an Administrative Panel pursuant to this Policy shall be paid by the complainant, except in cases where you elect to expand the Administrative Panel from one to three panelists as provided in Paragraph 5(b)(iv) of the Rules of Procedure, in which case all fees will be split evenly by you and the complainant.

h. Our Involvement in Administrative Proceedings. We do not, and will not, participate in the administration or conduct of any proceeding before an Administrative Panel. In addition, we will not be liable as a result of any decisions rendered by the Administrative Panel.

i. Remedies. The remedies available to a complainant pursuant to any proceeding before an Administrative Panel shall be limited to requiring the cancellation of your domain name or the transfer of your domain name registration to the complainant.

j. Notification and Publication. The Provider shall notify us of any decision made by an Administrative Panel with respect to a domain name you have registered with us. All decisions under this Policy will be published in full over the Internet, except when an Administrative Panel determines in an exceptional case to redact portions of its decision.

k. Availability of Court Proceedings. The mandatory administrative proceeding requirements set forth in Paragraph 4 shall not prevent either you or the complainant from submitting the dispute to a court of competent jurisdiction for independent resolution before such mandatory administrative proceeding is commenced or after such proceeding is concluded. If an Administrative Panel decides that your domain name registration should be canceled or transferred, we will wait ten (10) business days (as observed in the location of our principal office) after we are informed by the applicable Provider of the Administrative Panel's decision before implementing that decision. We will then implement the decision unless we have received from you during that ten (10) business-day period official documentation (such as a copy of a complaint, file-stamped by the clerk of the court) that you have commenced a lawsuit against the complainant in a jurisdiction to which the complainant has submitted under Paragraph 3(b)(xiii) of the Rules of Procedure. (In general, that jurisdiction is either the location of our principal office or of your address as shown in our Whois database. See Paragraphs 1 and 3(b)(xiii) of the Rules of Procedure for details.) If we receive such documentation within the ten (10) business-day period, we will not implement the Administrative Panel's decision, and we will take no further action, until we receive

    i. evidence satisfactory to us of a resolution between the parties;

    ii. evidence satisfactory to us that your lawsuit has been dismissed or withdrawn; or

    iii. a copy of an order from such court dismissing your lawsuit or ordering that you do not have the right to continue to use your domain name.

5. **All Other Disputes and Litigation.**

All other disputes between you and any party other than us regarding your domain name registration that are not brought pursuant to the mandatory administrative proceeding provisions of Paragraph 4 shall be resolved between you and such other party through any court, arbitration or other proceeding that may be available.

6. **Our Involvement in Disputes.**

We will not participate in any way in any dispute between you and any party other than us regarding the registration and use of your domain name. You shall not name us as a party or otherwise include us in any such proceeding. In the event that we are named as a party in any such proceeding, we reserve the right to raise any and all defenses deemed appropriate, and to take any other action necessary to defend ourselves.

7. **Maintaining the Status Quo.**

We will not cancel, transfer, activate, deactivate, or otherwise change the status of any domain name registration under this Policy except as provided in Paragraph 3 above.

8. **Transfers During a Dispute.**

    a. Transfers of a Domain Name to a New Holder. You may not transfer your domain name registration to another holder

        i. during a pending administrative proceeding brought pursuant to Paragraph 4 or for a period of fifteen (15) business days (as observed in the location of our principal place of business) after such proceeding is concluded; or

        ii. during a pending court proceeding or arbitration commenced regarding your domain name unless the party to whom the domain name registration is being transferred agrees, in writing, to be bound by the decision of the court or arbitrator.

We reserve the right to cancel any transfer of a domain name registration to another holder that is made in violation of this subparagraph.

b. Changing Registrars. You may not transfer your domain name registration to another registrar during a pending administrative proceeding brought pursuant to Paragraph 4 or for a period of fifteen (15) business days (as observed in the location of our principal place of business) after such proceeding is concluded. You may transfer administration of your domain name registration to another registrar during a pending court action or arbitration, provided that the domain name you have registered with us shall continue to be subject to the proceedings commenced against you in accordance with the terms of this Policy. In the event that you transfer a domain name registration to us during the pendency of a court action or arbitration, such dispute shall remain subject to the domain name dispute policy of the registrar from which the domain name registration was transferred.

9. **Policy Modifications.**

We reserve the right to modify this Policy at any time with the permission of ICANN. We will post our revised Policy for at least thirty (30) calendar days before it becomes effective. Unless this Policy has already been invoked by the submission of a complaint to a Provider, in which event the version of the Policy in effect at the time it was invoked will apply to you until the dispute is over, all such changes will be binding upon you with respect to any domain name registration dispute, whether the dispute arose before, on or after the effective date of our change. In the event that you object to a change in this Policy, your sole remedy is to cancel your domain name registration with us, provided that you will not be entitled to a refund of any fees you paid to us. The revised Policy will apply to you until you cancel your domain name registration.

Additional information regarding the Uniform Domain Name Dispute Resolution Policy & Rules may be found at *http://www.icann.org/udrp/udrp.htm.*

Appendix E

Federal Trademark Dilution Act

http://www4.law.cornell.edu/uscode/15/ch22.html

United States Code TITLE 15, CHAPTER 22, SUBCHAPTER III

(c) Remedies for dilution of famous marks

(1) The owner of a famous mark shall be entitled, subject to the principles of equity and upon such terms as the court deems reasonable, to an injunction against another person's commercial use in commerce of a mark or trade name, if such use begins after the mark has become famous and causes dilution of the distinctive quality of the mark, and to obtain such other relief as is provided in this subsection. In determining whether a mark is distinctive and famous, a court may consider factors such as, but not limited to—

(A) the degree of inherent or acquired distinctiveness of the mark;

(B) the duration and extent of use of the mark in connection with the goods or services with which the mark is used;

(C) the duration and extent of advertising and publicity of the mark;

(D) the geographical extent of the trading area in which the mark is used;

(E) the channels of trade for the goods or services with which the mark is used;

(F) the degree of recognition of the mark in the trading areas and channels of trade used by the mark's owner and the person against whom the injunction is sought;

(G) the nature and extent of use of the same or similar marks by third parties; and

(H) whether the mark was registered under the Act of March 3, 1881, or the Act of February 20, 1905, or on the principal register.

(2) In an action brought under this subsection, the owner of the famous mark shall be entitled only to injunctive relief unless the person against whom the injunction is sought willfully intended to trade on the owner's reputation or to cause dilution of the famous mark. If such willful intent is proven, the owner of the famous mark shall also be entitled to the remedies set forth in sections 1117(a) and 1118 of this title, subject to the discretion of the court and the principles of equity.

(3) The ownership by a person of a valid registration under the Act of March 3, 1881, or the Act of February 20, 1905, or on the principal register shall be a complete bar to an action against that person, with respect to that mark, that is brought by another person under the common law or a statute of a State and that seeks to prevent dilution of the distinctiveness of a mark, label, or form of advertisement.

(4) The following shall not be actionable under this section:

(A) Fair use of a famous mark by another person in comparative commercial advertising or promotion to identify the competing goods or services of the owner of the famous mark.

(B) Noncommercial use of a mark.

(C) All forms of news reporting and news commentary.

Appendix F

Uniform Commercial Code, Article 2–Sales

For full text, see *http://www.law.cornell.edu/ucc/2/overview.html*

Part 1. Short Title, General Construction and Subject Matter

§ 2-101. Short Title.
§ 2-102. Scope; Certain Security and Other Transactions Excluded From This Article.
§ 2-103. Definitions and Index of Definitions.
§ 2-104. Definitions: "Merchant"; "Between Merchants"; "Financing Agency."
§ 2-105. Definitions: Transferability; "Goods"; "Future" Goods; "Lot"; "Commercial Unit."
§ 2-106. Definitions: "Contract"; "Agreement"; "Contract for sale"; "Sale"; "Present sale"; "Conforming" to Contract; "Termination"; "Cancellation."
§ 2-107. Goods to Be Severed From Realty: Recording.

Part 2. Form, Formation and Readjustment of Contract

§ 2-201. Formal Requirements; Statute of Frauds.
§ 2-202. Final Written Expression: Parol or Extrinsic Evidence.
§ 2-203. Seals Inoperative.
§ 2-204. Formation in General.
§ 2-205. Firm Offers.
§ 2-206. Offer and Acceptance in Formation of Contract.
§ 2-207. Additional Terms in Acceptance or Confirmation.
§ 2-208. Course of Performance or Practical Construction.
§ 2-209. Modification, Rescission, and Waiver.
§ 2-210. Delegation of Performance; Assignment of Rights.

Part 3. General Obligation and Construction of Contract

§ 2-301. General Obligations of Parties.
§ 2-302. Unconscionable Contract or Clause.
§ 2-303. Allocation or Division of Risks.
§ 2-304. Price Payable in Money, Goods, Realty, or Otherwise.
§ 2-305. Open Price Term.
§ 2-306. Output, Requirements and Exclusive Dealings.
§ 2-307. Delivery in Single Lot or Several Lots.
§ 2-308. Absence of Specified Place for Delivery.
§ 2-309. Absence of Specific Time Provisions; Notice of Termination.

Part 4. Title, Creditors and Good Faith Purchasers

Part 5. Performance

Part 6. Breach, Repudiation and Excuse

Part 7. Remedies

Appendix G

Securities Laws

For the complete Securities Act of 1933 and the Securities Exchange Act of 1934 compilations, refer to this site: *http://www.sec.gov/about/laws.shtml*

Securities Act of 1933

Securities Exchange Act of 1934

Section 20A—Liability to Contemporaneous Traders for Insider Trading
Section 21—Investigations and Actions
Section 21A—Civil Penalties for Insider Trading
Section 21B—Civil Remedies In Administrative Proceedings
Section 21C—Cease-and-Desist Proceedings
Section 21D—Private Securities Litigation
Section 21E—Application of Safe Harbor for Forward-Looking Statements
Section 22—Hearings by Commission
Section 23—Rules, Regulations, and Orders; Annual Reports
Section 24—Public Availability of Information
Section 25—Court Review of Orders and Rules
Section 26—Unlawful Representations
Section 27—Jurisdiction of Offenses and Suits
Section 27A—Special Provision Relating to Statute of Limitations on Private Causes of Action
Section 28—Effect on Existing Law
Section 29—Validity of Contracts
Section 30—Foreign Securities Exchanges
Section 30A—Prohibited Foreign Trade Practices by Issuers
Section 31—Transaction Fees
Section 32—Penalties
Section 33—Separability
Section 34—Effective Date
Section 35—Authorization of Appropriations
Section 35A—Requirements for the EDGAR System
Section 36—General Exemptive Authority

Appendix H

Patent Act

For the complete patent statutory compilation, refer to this site: *http://www4.law.cornell.edu/uscode/35/*

PART I—Patent And Trademark Office

PART II—Patentability Of Inventions And Grant Of Patents

PART III—Patents And Protection Of Patent Rights

PART IV—Patent Cooperation Treaty

Appendix I

Gramm-Leach-Bliley Act of 1999 (GLB) (Financial Services Modernization Act)

http://www.ftc.gov/privacy/glbact/glbsub1.htm

TITLE V—Privacy

15 USC, Subchapter I - Sec. 6801-6809
Disclosure of Nonpublic Personal Information
Privacy Obligation Policy—It is the policy of the Congress that each financial institution has an affirmative and continuing obligation to respect the privacy of its customers and to protect the security and confidentiality of those customers' nonpublic personal information.
Sec. 6801. Protection of nonpublic personal information.
Sec. 6802. Obligations with respect to disclosures of personal information.
Sec. 6803. Disclosure of institution privacy policy.
Sec. 6804. Rulemaking.
Sec. 6805. Enforcement.
Sec. 6806. Relation to other provisions.
Sec. 6807. Relation to State laws.
Sec. 6808. Study of information sharing among financial affiliates.
Sec. 6809. Definitions.
15 USC, Subchapter II, Sec. 6821-6827
(*http://www.ftc.gov/privacy/glbact/glbsub2.htm*)
Fraudulent Access to Financial Information
Sec. 6821. Privacy protection for customer information of financial institutions.
Sec. 6822. Administrative enforcement.
Sec. 6823. Criminal penalty.
Sec. 6824. Relation to State laws.
Sec. 6825. Agency guidance.
Sec. 6826. Reports
(a) Report to the Congress.
Sec. 6827. Definitions.

Appendix J

Health Insurance Portability and Accountability Act (HIPAA) of 1996, Pub. L. 104-191

http://www.hhs.gov/ocr/part1.pdf and/or *http://www.hhs.gov/ocr/hipaa/*

To amend the Internal Revenue Code of 1986 to improve portability and continuity of health insurance coverage in the group and individual markets, to combat waste, fraud, and abuse in health insurance and health care delivery, to promote the use of medical savings accounts, to improve access to long-term care services and coverage, to simplify the administration of health insurance, and for other purposes.
Standards for Privacy of Individually Identifiable Health Information
45 CFR, Parts 160 and 164

Appendix K

Children's Online Privacy Protection Act of 1998

http://www4.law.cornell.edu/uscode/15/ch91.html#PC91

United States Code TITLE 15, CHAPTER 91

Sec. 6501. Definitions

In this chapter:

(1) Child
The term "child" means an individual under the age of 13.

Sec. 6502. Regulation of unfair and deceptive acts and practices in connection with collection and use of personal information from and about children on the Internet

(a) Acts prohibited
(1) In general
It is unlawful for an operator of a website or online service directed to children, or any operator that has actual knowledge that it is collecting personal information from a child, to collect personal information from a child in a manner that violates the regulations prescribed under subsection (b) of this section.

(2) Disclosure to parent protected
Notwithstanding paragraph (1), neither an operator of such a website or online service nor the operator's agent shall be held to be liable under any Federal or State law for any disclosure made in good faith and following reasonable procedures in responding to a request for disclosure of personal information under subsection (b)(1)(B)(iii) of this section to the parent of a child.

(b) Regulations
(1) In general
Not later than 1 year after October 21, 1998, the Commission shall promulgate under section 553 of title 5 regulations that—

(A) require the operator of any website or online service directed to children that collects personal information from children or the operator of a website or online service that has actual knowledge that it is collecting personal information from a child—

(i) to provide notice on the website of what information is collected from children by the operator, how the operator uses such information, and the operator's disclosure practices for such information; and

(ii) to obtain verifiable parental consent for the collection, use, or disclosure of personal information from children;

(B) require the operator to provide, upon request of a parent under this subparagraph whose child has provided personal information to that website or online service, upon proper identification of that parent, to such parent—

(i) a description of the specific types of personal information collected from the child by that operator;

(ii) the opportunity at any time to refuse to permit the operator's further use or maintenance in retrievable form, or future online collection, of personal information from that child; and

(iii) notwithstanding any other provision of law, a means that is reasonable under the circumstances for the parent to obtain any personal information collected from that child;

(C) prohibit conditioning a child's participation in a game, the offering of a prize, or another activity on the child disclosing more personal information than is reasonably necessary to participate in such activity; and

(D) require the operator of such a website or online service to establish and maintain reasonable procedures to protect the confidentiality, security, and integrity of personal information collected from children.

(2) When consent not required

The regulations shall provide that verifiable parental consent under paragraph (1)(A)(ii) is not required in the case of—

(A) online contact information collected from a child that is used only to respond directly on a one-time basis to a specific request from the child and is not used to recontact the child and is not maintained in retrievable form by the operator;

(B) a request for the name or online contact information of a parent or child that is used for the sole purpose of obtaining parental consent or providing notice under this section and where such information is not maintained in retrievable form by the operator if parental consent is not obtained after a reasonable time;

(C) online contact information collected from a child that is used only to respond more than once directly to a specific request from the child and is not used to recontact the child beyond the scope of that request—

(i) if, before any additional response after the initial response to the child, the operator uses reasonable efforts to provide a parent notice of the online contact information collected from the child, the purposes for which it is to be used, and an opportunity for the parent to request that the operator make no further use of the information and that it not be maintained in retrievable form; or

(ii) without notice to the parent in such circumstances as the Commission may determine are appropriate, taking into consideration the benefits to the child of access to information and services, and risks to the security and privacy of the child, in regulations promulgated under this subsection;

(D) the name of the child and online contact information (to the extent reasonably necessary to protect the safety of a child participant on the site)—

(i) used only for the purpose of protecting such safety;

(ii) not used to recontact the child or for any other purpose; and

(iii) not disclosed on the site, if the operator uses reasonable efforts to provide a parent notice of the name and online contact information collected from the child, the purposes for which it is to be used, and an opportunity for the parent to request that the operator make no further use of the information and that it not be maintained in retrievable form; or

(E) the collection, use, or dissemination of such information by the operator of such a website or online service necessary—

(i) to protect the security or integrity of its website;

(ii) to take precautions against liability;

(iii) to respond to judicial process; or

(iv) to the extent permitted under other provisions of law, to provide information to law enforcement agencies or for an investigation on a matter related to public safety.

Appendix L

Electronic Communications Privacy Act of 1986

http://www4.law.cornell.edu/uscode/18/pIch119.html

US CODE TITLE 18, PART I, CHAPTER 119

Sec. 2510. Definitions

As used in this chapter—

(1) "wire communication" means any aural transfer made in whole or in part through the use of facilities for the transmission of communications by the aid of wire, cable, or other like connection between the point of origin and the point of reception (including the use of such connection in a switching station) furnished or operated by any person engaged in providing or operating such facilities for the transmission of interstate or foreign communications or communications affecting interstate or foreign commerce and such term includes any electronic storage of such communication;

(2) "oral communication" means any oral communication uttered by a person exhibiting an expectation that such communication is not subject to interception under circumstances justifying such expectation, but such term does not include any electronic communication;

(3) "State" means any State of the United States, the District of Columbia, the Commonwealth of Puerto Rico, and any territory or possession of the United States;

(4) "intercept" means the aural or other acquisition of the contents of any wire, electronic, or oral communication through the use of any electronic, mechanical, or other device.

(5) "electronic, mechanical, or other device" means any device or apparatus which can be sued to intercept a wire, oral, or electronic communication other than—

   (a) any telephone or telegraph instrument, equipment or facility, or any component thereof,

      (i) furnished to the subscriber or user by a provider of wire or electronic communication service in the ordinary course of its business and being used by the subscriber or user in the ordinary course of its business or furnished by such subscriber or user for connection to the facilities of such service and used in the ordinary course of its business; or

      (ii) being used by a provider of wire or electronic communication service in the ordinary course of its business, or by an investigative or law enforcement officer in the ordinary course of his duties;

(b) a hearing aid or similar device being used to correct subnormal hearing to not better than normal;

(6) "person" means any employee, or agent of the United States or any State or political subdivision thereof, and any individual, partnership, association, joint stock company, trust, or corporation;

(7) "Investigative or law enforcement officer" means any officer of the United States or of a State or political subdivision thereof, who is empowered by law to conduct investigations of or to make arrests for offenses enumerated in this chapter, and any attorney authorized by law to prosecute or participate in the prosecution of such offenses;

* * * * * * * * * * * * * *

(12) "electronic communication" means any transfer of signs, signals, writing, images, sounds, data, or intelligence of any nature transmitted in whole or in part by a wire, radio, electromagnetic, photoelectronic or photooptical system that affects interstate or foreign commerce, but does not include—

(A) the radio portion of a cordless telephone communication that is transmitted between the cordless telephone handset and the base unit;

(B) any wire or oral communication;

(C) any communication made through a tone-only paging device;

(D) any communication from a tracking device (as defined in section 3117 of this title); or

(13) "user" means any person or entity who-

(A) uses an electronic communication service; and

(B) is duly authorized by the provider of such service to engage in such use;

(14) "electronic communication system" means any wire, radio, electromagnetic, photooptical or photoelectronic facilities for the transmission of electronic communications, and any computer facilities or related electronic equipment for the electronic storage of such communications;

(15) "electronic communication service" means any service which provides to users thereof the ability to send or receive wire or electronic communications;

(16) "readily accessible to the general public" means, with respect to a radio communication, that such communication is not   -

(A) scrambled or encrypted;

(B) transmitted using modulation techniques whose essential parameters have been withheld from the public with the intention of preserving the privacy of such communication;

(C) carried on a subcarrier or other signal subsidiary to a radio transmission;

(D) transmitted over a communication system provided by a common carrier, unless the communication is a tone only paging system communication;

(E) transmitted on frequencies allocated under part 25, subpart D, E, or F of part 74, or part 94 of the Rules of the Federal Communications commission, unless, in the case of a communication transmitted on a frequency allocated under part 74 that is not exclusively allocated to broadcast auxiliary services, the communication is a two-way voice communication by radio;

(17) "electronic storage" means

(A) any temporary intermediate storage of a wire or electronic communication incidental to the electronic transmission thereof; and

(B) any storage of such communication by an electronic communication service for purposes of backup protection of such communication;

* * * * * * * * * * * * * * *

Sec. 2511. Interception and disclosure of wire, oral, or electronic communications prohibited

(1) Except as otherwise specifically provided in this chapter any person who—

(a) intentionally intercepts, endeavors to intercept, or procures any other person to intercept or endeavor to intercept, any wire, oral, or electronic communication;

(b) intentionally uses, endeavors to use, or procures any other person to use or endeavor to use any electronic, mechanical, or other device to intercept any oral communication when—

(i) such device is affixed to, or otherwise transmits a signal through, a wire, cable, or other like connection used in wire communication; or

(ii) such device transmits communications by radio, or interferes with the transmission of such communication; or

(iii) such person knows, or has reason to know, that such device or any component thereof has been sent through the mail or transported in interstate or foreign commerce; or

(iv) such use or endeavor to use (A) takes place on the premises of any business or other commercial establishment the operations of which affect interstate or foreign commerce; or (B) obtains or is for the purpose of obtaining information relating to the operations of any business or other commercial establishment the operations of which affect interstate or foreign commerce; or

(v) such person acts in the District of Columbia, the Commonwealth of Puerto Rico, or any territory or possession of the United States;

(c) intentionally discloses, or endeavors to disclose, to any other person the contents of any wire, oral, or electronic communication, knowing or having reason to know that the information was obtained through the interception of a wire, oral, or electronic communication in violation of this subsection; or

(d) intentionally uses, or endeavors to use, the contents of any wire, oral, or electronic communication, knowing or having reason to know that the information was obtained through the interception of a wire, oral, or electronic communication in violation of this subsection; shall be punished as provided in subsection (4) or shall be subject to suit as provided in subsection (5).

(2)(a)

(i) It shall not be unlawful under this chapter for an operator of a switchboard, or an officer, employee, or agent of a provider of a wire or electronic communication service, whose facilities are used in the transmission of a wire communication, to intercept, disclose, or use that communication in the normal course of his employment while engaged in any activity which is a necessary incident to the rendition of his service or to the protection of the rights or property of the provider of that service, except that a provider of wire communication service to the public shall not utilize service observing or random monitoring except for mechanical or service quality control checks.

* * * * * * * * * * * * * *

(3)(a) Except as provided in paragraph (b) of this subsection, a person or entity providing an electronic communication service to the public shall not intentionally divulge the contents of any communication (other than one to such person or entity, or an agent thereof) while in transmission on that service to any person or entity other than an addressee or intended recipient of such communication or an agent of such addressee or intended recipient.

(b) A person or entity providing electronic communication service to the public may divulge the contents of any such communication—

(i) as otherwise authorized in section 2511(2)(a) or 2517 of this title;

(ii) with the lawful consent of the originator or any addressee or intended recipient of such communication;

(iii) to a person employed or authorized, or whose facilities are used, to forward such communication to its destination; or

(iv) which were inadvertently obtained by the service provider and which appear to pertain to the commission of a crime, if such divulgence is made to a law enforcement agency.

(4)(a) Except as provided in paragraph (b) of this subsection or in subsection (5), whoever violates subsection (1) of this section shall be fined under this title or imprisoned not more than five years, or both.

Sec. 2515. Prohibition of use as evidence of intercepted wire or oral communications
http://www4.law.cornell.edu/uscode/18/2515.html

Sec. 2516. Authorization for interception of wire, oral, or electronic Communications
http://www4.law.cornell.edu/uscode/18/2516.html

Sec. 2517. Authorization for disclosure and use of intercepted wire, oral, or electronic communications
http://www4.law.cornell.edu/uscode/18/2517.html

Sec. 2518. Procedure for interception of wire, oral, or electronic communications
http://www4.law.cornell.edu/uscode/18/2518.html

* * * * * * * * * * * * * *

CHAPTER 121. STORED WIRE AND ELECTRONIC COMMUNICATIONS AND TRANSACTIONAL RECORDS ACCESS
Sec. 2701. Unlawful access to stored communications

(a) Offense. Except as provided in subsection (c) of this section whoever—

(1) intentionally accesses without authorization a facility through which an electronic communication service is provided; or

(2) intentionally exceeds an authorization to access that facility; and thereby obtains, alters, or prevents authorized access to a wire or electronic communication while it is in electronic storage in such system shall be punished as provided in subsection (b) of this section.

(b) Punishment. The punishment for an offense under subsection (a) of this section is—

(1) if the offense is committed for purposes of commercial advantage, malicious destruction or damage, or private commercial gain—

(A) a fine of not more than $ 250,000 or imprisonment for not more than one year, or both, in the case of a first offense under this subparagraph; and (B) a fine under this title or imprisonment for not more than two years, or both, for any subsequent offense under this subparagraph; and

(2) a fine of not more than $ 5,000 or imprisonment for not more than six months, or both, in any other case.

(c) Exceptions. Subsection (a) of this section does not apply with respect to conduct authorized—

(1) by the person or entity providing a wire or electronic communications service;

(2) by a user of that service with respect to a communication of or intended for that user; or

(3) in section 2703, 2704 or 2518 of this title.

Sec. 2702. Disclosure of contents

(a) Prohibitions. Except as provided in subsection (b)—

(1) a person or entity providing an electronic communication service to the public shall not knowingly divulge to any person or entity the contents of a communication while in electronic storage by that service; and

(2) a person or entity providing remote computing service to the public shall not knowingly divulge to any person or entity the contents of any communication which is carried or maintained on that service—

(A) on behalf of, and received by means of electronic transmission from (or created by means of computer processing of communications received by means of electronic transmission from), a subscriber or customer of such service; and

(B) solely for the purpose of providing storage or computer processing services to such subscriber or customer, if the provider is not authorized to access the contents of any such communications for purposes of providing any services other than storage or computer processing.

(b) Exceptions. A person or entity may divulge the contents of a communication—

(1) to an addressee or intended recipient of such communication or an agent of such addressee or intended recipient;

(2) as otherwise authorized in section 2517, 2511(2)(a), or 2703 of this title;

(3) with the lawful consent of the originator or an addressee or intended recipient of such communication, or the subscriber in the case of remote computing service;

(4) to a person employed or authorized or whose facilities are used to forward such communication to its destination;

(5) as may be necessarily incident to the rendition of the service or to the protection of the rights or property of the provider of that service; or

(6) to a law enforcement agency, if such contents—

(A) were inadvertently obtained by the service provider; and (B) appear to pertain to the commission of a crime.

Appendix M

Child Pornography Prevention Act of 1996

http://www4.law.cornell.edu/uscode/18/2251.html

United States Code TITLE 18, PART I, CHAPTER 110

Sec. 2251. Sexual exploitation of children and other abuse of children

(a) Any person who employs, uses, persuades, induces, entices, or coerces any minor to engage in, or who has a minor assist any other person to engage in, or who transports any minor in interstate or foreign commerce, or in any Territory or Possession of the United States, with the intent that such minor engage in, any sexually explicit conduct for the purpose of producing any visual depiction of such conduct, shall be punished as provided under subsection (d), if such person knows or has reason to know that such visual depiction will be transported in interstate or foreign commerce or mailed, if that visual depiction was produced using materials that have been mailed, shipped, or transported in interstate or foreign commerce by any means, including by computer, or if such visual depiction has actually been transported in interstate or foreign commerce or mailed.

(b) Any parent, legal guardian, or person having custody or control of a minor who knowingly permits such minor to engage in, or to assist any other person to engage in, sexually explicit conduct for the purpose of producing any visual depiction of such conduct shall be punished as provided under subsection (d) of this section, if such parent, legal guardian, or person knows or has reason to know that such visual depiction will be transported in interstate or foreign commerce or mailed, if that visual depiction was produced using materials that have been mailed, shipped, or transported in interstate or foreign commerce by any means, including by computer, or if such visual depiction has actually been transported in interstate or foreign commerce or mailed.

(c) (1) Any person who, in a circumstance described in paragraph (2), knowingly makes, prints, or publishes, or causes to be made, printed, or published, any notice or advertisement seeking or offering—

(A) to receive, exchange, buy, produce, display, distribute, or reproduce, any visual depiction, if the production of such visual depiction involves the use of a minor engaging in sexually explicit conduct and such visual depiction is of such conduct; or

(B) participation in any act of sexually explicit conduct by or with any minor for the purpose of producing a visual depiction of such conduct; shall be punished as provided under subsection (d).

(2) The circumstance referred to in paragraph (1) is that—

(A) such person knows or has reason to know that such notice or advertisement will be transported in interstate or foreign commerce by any means including by computer or mailed; or

(B) such notice or advertisement is transported in interstate or foreign commerce by any means including by computer or mailed.

(d) Any individual who violates, or attempts or conspires to violate, this section shall be fined under this title or imprisoned not less than 10 years nor more than 20 years, and [1] both, but if such person has one prior conviction under this chapter, chapter 109A, or chapter 117, or under the laws of any State relating to the sexual exploitation of children, such person shall be fined under this title and imprisoned for not less than 15 years nor more than 30 years, but if such person has 2 or more prior convictions under this chapter, chapter 109A, or chapter 117, or under the laws of any State relating to the sexual exploitation of children, such person shall be fined under this title and imprisoned not less than 30 years nor more than life. Any organization that violates, or attempts or conspires to violate, this section shall be fined under this title. Whoever, in the course of an offense under this section, engages in conduct that results in the death of a person, shall be punished by death or imprisoned for any term of years or for life.

Appendix N

Communications Decency Act of 1996

http://www4.law.cornell.edu/uscode/47/230.html

United States Code TITLE 47, CHAPTER 5, SUBCHAPTER II

Sec. 230. Protection for private blocking and screening of offensive material

  (c) Protection for ''Good Samaritan'' blocking and screening of offensive material
    (1) Treatment of publisher or speaker
        No provider or user of an interactive computer service shall be treated as the publisher or speaker of any information provided by another information content provider.
    (2) Civil liability
        No provider or user of an interactive computer service shall be held liable on account of—
(A) any action voluntarily taken in good faith to restrict access to or availability of material that the provider or user considers to be obscene, lewd, lascivious, filthy, excessively violent, harassing, or otherwise objectionable, whether or not such material is constitutionally protected; or
(B) any action taken to enable or make available to information content providers or others the technical means to restrict access to material described in paragraph (1). [1] (A).''
  (d) Obligations of interactive computer service
    A provider of interactive computer service shall, at the time of entering an agreement with a customer for the provision of interactive computer service and in a manner deemed appropriate by the provider, notify such customer that parental control protections (such as computer hardware, software, or filtering services) are commercially available that may assist the customer in limiting access to material that is harmful to minors. Such notice shall identify, or provide the customer with access to information identifying, current providers of such protections.

Appendix O

Uniting and Strengthening America by Providing Tools Required to Intercept and Obstruct Terrorism Act of 2001 (USA PATRIOT Act)—H. R. 3162

AN ACT

To deter and punish terrorist acts in the United States and around the world, to enhance law enforcement investigatory tools, and for other purposes.
http://www.epic.org/privacy/terrorism/hr3162.html

Section 1. Short Title and Table of Contents.

(a)SHORT TITLE—This Act may be cited as the 'Uniting and Strengthening America by Providing Appropriate Tools Required to Intercept and Obstruct Terrorism (USA PATRIOT ACT) Act of 2001'. (b) TABLE OF CONTENTS- The table of contents for this Act is as follows:

Title II—Enhanced Surveillance Procedures

Sec. 216. Modification of authorities relating to use of pen registers and trap and trace devices.

Sec. 217. Interception of computer trespasser communications.

Sec. 218. Foreign intelligence information.

Sec. 222. Assistance to law enforcement agencies.

Sec. 223. Civil liability for certain unauthorized disclosures.

Sec. 224. Sunset.

Sec. 225. Immunity for compliance with FISA wiretap.

Appendix P

UNCITRAL Model Law on Electronic Commerce

http://www.uncitral.org/english/texts/electcom/ml-ec.htm

[Original: Arabic, Chinese, English, French, Russian, Spanish]

Part one. Electronic commerce in general

CHAPTER I. GENERAL PROVISIONS

Article 1. Sphere of application*

This Law** applies to any kind of information in the form of a data message used in the context*** of commercial**** activities.

* The Commission suggests the following text for States that might wish to limit the applicability of this Law to international data messages:

"This Law applies to a data message as defined in paragraph (1) of article 2 where the data message relates to international commerce."

** This Law does not override any rule of law intended for the protection of consumers.

*** The Commission suggests the following text for States that might wish to extend the applicability of this Law: "This Law applies to any kind of information in the form of a data message, except in the following situations: [. . .]."

**** The term "commercial" should be given a wide interpretation so as to cover matters arising from all relationships of a commercial nature, whether contractual or not. Relationships of a commercial nature include, but are not limited to, the following transactions: any trade transaction for the supply or exchange of goods or services; distribution agreement; commercial representation or agency; factoring; leasing; construction of works; consulting; engineering; licensing; investment; financing; banking; insurance; exploitation agreement or concession; joint venture and other forms of industrial or business cooperation; carriage of goods or passengers by air, sea, rail or road.

Article 2. Definitions
For the purposes of this Law:

(a) "Data message" means information generated, sent, received or stored by electronic, optical or similar means including, but not limited to, electronic data interchange (EDI), electronic mail, telegram, telex or telecopy;

(b) "Electronic data interchange (EDI)" means the electronic transfer from computer to computer of information using an agreed standard to structure the information;

(c) "Originator" of a data message means a person by whom, or on whose behalf, the data message purports to have been sent or generated prior to storage, if any, but it does not include a person acting as an intermediary with respect to that data message;

(d) "Addressee" of a data message means a person who is intended by the originator to receive the data message, but does not include a person acting as an intermediary with respect to that data message;

(e) "Intermediary," with respect to a particular data message, means a person who, on behalf of another person, sends, receives or stores that data message or provides other services with respect to that data message;

(f) "Information system" means a system for generating, sending, receiving, storing or otherwise processing data messages.

Article 3. Interpretation

(1) In the interpretation of this Law, regard is to be had to its international origin and to the need to promote uniformity in its application and the observance of good faith. (2) Questions concerning matters governed by this Law which are not expressly settled in it are to be settled in conformity with the general principles on which this Law is based.

Article 4. Variation by agreement

CHAPTER II. APPLICATION OF LEGAL REQUIREMENTS TO DATA MESSAGES

Article 5. Legal recognition of data messages

Information shall not be denied legal effect, validity or enforceability solely on the grounds that it is in the form of a data message.

Article 5 bis. Incorporation by reference

Information shall not be denied legal effect, validity or enforceability solely on the grounds that it is not contained in the data message purporting to give rise to such legal effect, but is merely referred to in that data message.

Article 6. Writing

Article 7. Signature

Article 8. Original

Article 9. Admissibility and evidential weight of data messages

(1) In any legal proceedings, nothing in the application of the rules of evidence shall apply so as to deny the admissibility of a data message in evidence:

(a) on the sole ground that it is a data message; or,

(b) if it is the best evidence that the person adducing it could reasonably be expected to obtain, on the grounds that it is not in its original form.

(2) Information in the form of a data message shall be given due evidential weight. In assessing the evidential weight of a data message, regard shall be had to the reliability of the manner in which the data message was generated, stored or communicated, to the reliability of the manner in which the integrity of the information was maintained, to the manner in which its originator was identified, and to any other relevant factor.

Article 10. Retention of data messages

CHAPTER III. COMMUNICATION OF DATA MESSAGES

Article 11. Formation and validity of contracts

(1) In the context of contract formation, unless otherwise agreed by the parties, an offer and the acceptance of an offer may be expressed by means of data messages. Where a data message is used in the formation of a contract, that contract shall not be denied validity or enforceability on the sole ground that a data message was used for that purpose.
(2) The provisions of this article do not apply to the following: [. . .].

Article 12. Recognition by parties of data messages

(1) As between the originator and the addressee of a data message, a declaration of will or other statement shall not be denied legal effect, validity or enforceability solely on the grounds that it is in the form of a data message.
(2) The provisions of this article do not apply to the following: [. . .].

Article 13. Attribution of data messages
(1) A data message is that of the originator if it was sent by the originator itself.
(2) As between the originator and the addressee, a data message is deemed to be that of the originator if it was sent:
   (a) by a person who had the authority to act on behalf of the originator in respect of that data message; or
   (b) by an information system programmed by, or on behalf of, the originator to operate automatically.
(3) As between the originator and the addressee, an addressee is entitled to regard a data message as being that of the originator, and to act on that assumption, if:
   (a) in order to ascertain whether the data message was that of the originator, the addressee properly applied a procedure previously agreed to by the originator for that purpose; or
   (b) the data message as received by the addressee resulted from the actions of a person whose relationship with the originator or with any agent of the originator enabled that person to gain access to a method used by the originator to identify data messages as its own.
(4) Paragraph (3) does not apply:
   (a) as of the time when the addressee has both received notice from the originator that the data message is not that of the originator, and had reasonable time to act accordingly; or

(b) in a case within paragraph (3)(b), at any time when the addressee knew or should have known, had it exercised reasonable care or used any agreed procedure, that the data message was not that of the originator.

(5) Where a data message is that of the originator or is deemed to be that of the originator, or the addressee is entitled to act on that assumption, then, as between the originator and the addressee, the addressee is entitled to regard the data message as received as being what the originator intended to send, and to act on that assumption. The addressee is not so entitled when it knew or should have known, had it exercised reasonable care or used any agreed procedure, that the transmission resulted in any error in the data message as received.

(6) The addressee is entitled to regard each data message received as a separate data message and to act on that assumption, except to the extent that it duplicates another data message and the addressee knew or should have known, had it exercised reasonable care or used any agreed procedure, that the data message was a duplicate.

Article 14. Acknowledgement of receipt

Article 15. Time and place of dispatch and receipt of data messages

Part two. Electronic commerce in specific areas

CHAPTER I. CARRIAGE OF GOODS

Article 16. Actions related to contracts of carriage of goods

Without derogating from the provisions of part one of this Law, this chapter applies to any action in connection with, or in pursuance of, a contract of carriage of goods, including but not limited to:
  (a) (i) furnishing the marks, number, quantity or weight of goods;
      (ii) stating or declaring the nature or value of goods;
      (iii) issuing a receipt for goods;
      (iv) confirming that goods have been loaded;
  (b) (i) notifying a person of terms and conditions of the contract;
      (ii) giving instructions to a carrier;
  (c) (i) claiming delivery of goods;
      (ii) authorizing release of goods;
      (iii) giving notice of loss of, or damage to, goods;
  (d) giving any other notice or statement in connection with the performance of the contract;
  (e) undertaking to deliver goods to a named person or a person authorized to claim delivery;
  (f) granting, acquiring, renouncing, surrendering, transferring or negotiating rights in goods;
  (g) acquiring or transferring rights and obligations under the contract.

Article 17. Transport documents

Appendix Q

Cybercrime Laws

For the complete cybercrime statutory compilation, refer to this site: *http://www. cybercrime.gov*

Homeland Security Act of 2002

- Text of Section 225
- Amendments and Redline Showing Changes Resulting from Section 896 of the 2002 Homeland Security Act and Section 225 of the 2002 cyber Security Enhancement Act
- Text of the USA PATRIOT Act (via Thomas)
- Field Guidance on New Authorities that Relate to Computer Crime and Electronic Evidence Enacted in the USA Patriot Act of 2001
- Redline Version of USA PATRIOT Act

Federal Criminal Code Related to Computer Crime

- 18 U.S.C. § 1029. Fraud and Related Activity in Connection with Access Devices
- 18 U.S.C. § 1030. Fraud and Related Activity in Connection with Computers
- 18 U.S.C. § 1362. Communication Lines, Stations, or Systems
- 18 U.S.C. § 2510 et seq. Wire and Electronic Communications Interception and Interception of Oral Communications
- 18 U.S.C. § 2701 et seq. Stored Wire and Electronic Communications and Transactional Records Access

Federal Statutes Protecting Intellectual Property Rights

The following is a list of criminal statutes that protect intellectual property rights.

Copyright Offenses

17 U.S.C. 506
18 U.S.C. 2319
18 U.S.C. 2318

Copyright Felony Act Legislative History

Copyright Management Offenses—Digital Millennium Copyright Act (DMCA)

17 U.S.C. 1201
17 U.S.C. 1202

17 U.S.C. 1203
17 U.S.C. 1204
17 U.S.C. 1205

Bootlegging Offenses

18 U.S.C. 2319A

Trademark Offenses

18 U.S.C. 2320

Trade Secret Offenses

18 U.S.C. 1831
18 U.S.C. 1832
18 U.S.C. 1833
18 U.S.C. 1834
18 U.S.C. 1835
18 U.S.C. 1836
18 U.S.C. 1837
18 U.S.C. 1838
18 U.S.C. 1839

Offenses Relating to the Integrity of IP Systems

17 U.S.C. 506(c-d)
17 U.S.C. 506(e)
18 U.S.C. 497
35 U.S.C. 292

Offenses Relating to the Misuse of Dissemination Systems

18 U.S.C. 1341
18 U.S.C. 1343
18 U.S.C. 2512
47 U.S.C. 553
47 U.S.C. 605

Glossary

A

Absolute privilege Defense to a suit in defamation granted to those involved in legislative or judicial proceedings.

Act of State Doctrine Doctrine that one government will not judge the legality of acts of another government committed within the latter's territory.

Adhesion contract A contract that is unilateral and non-negotiable. It is legal as long as it is "reasonable and fair."

Advisory Commission on Electronic Commerce A commission established by the Internet tax freedom act to study the implications of taxing e-commerce.

Agreement on Trade-Related Aspects of Intellectual Property Rights (TRIPS) International agreement (one of the World Trade Organizations's multilateral agreements) that establishes a comprehensive set of rights and obligations governing international trade in intellectual property.

American Inventors Protection Act Amended scattered sections of the Patent Act that are intended to strengthen inventor's rights in relation to other later inventors and patent promotion companies. It also strengthens third parties' right to examine and comment on patent applications.

Anticybersquatting Consumer Protection Act (ACPA) Protects registered trademark holders from online cyber-piracy (registering as domain names another person or company's trademark).

Assignment of contractual rights The voluntary transfer of a contracting party's rights to a third person.

B

Biometrics Security technology designed to authenticate users by capturing human characteristics.

Blue Sky laws Any state laws relating to the regulation of securities.

Business Extension Rule The ECPA section that requires a plaintiff to prove the defendant used a devise capable of intercepting an electronic communication. It exempts from liability any devise furnished to the subscriber or used by a service provider in the ordinary course of business.

Business methods patent Considered to include any process involving data processing, calculations, conversions, and so on, used for business operations and management.

C

Cable Communications Protection Act (CCPA) of 1984 Deals with the privacy rights a subscriber to cable television should expect regarding personal data that the cable television operator gathers.

Cache Temporary storage space on the hard drive.

California Limited Offering Exemption Similar to Reg D offerings, it is limited to businesses organized under California law.

Carnivore/DCS-1000 Computer system that the FBI has installed onto ISPs' servers, in order to read and analyze packets of data sent to or received by suspects in criminal investigations.

Certificate authorities (CAs) They issue and manage digital certificates and are centralized by industry with a wide range of applications, such as e-mail, browsers, and VPNs.

Child Online Protection Act (COPA) of 1998 Expanded the provisions of the Child Pornography Protection Act to include online transmissions by service providers and e-commerce site providers.

Child Pornography Protection Act (CPPA) of 1996 Prohibits and criminalizes trafficking in child pornography.

Choice of law clause Clause in a contract that designates the law that will govern any contractual dispute.

Click-wrap license A license that appears on a computer screen when software is first being installed; and which the purchaser must accept before the installation will proceed.

Code of Liberalization of Capital Movements Established in 1961, the code requires signatory nations to progressively abolish their restrictions on the movement of capital in their country.

Commerce clause For tax purposes, the clause means that a tax must be fairly apportioned, it cannot discriminate, and it must be fairly related to the services provided by the state. The business must have a substantial nexus with the taxing state.

Communications Decency Act (CDA) of 1996 Makes it a crime for anyone to knowingly transport obscene material for sale or distribution either in foreign or interstate commerce or through the use of an interactive computer service. Parts of it have been declared unconstitutional.

Computer crime Broadly defined as any illegal act that involves a computer, its systems, or its applications.

Computer Fraud and Abuse Act (CFAA) of 1986 The preeminent statute used in prosecuting the range of computer crimes.

Consenting adults defense Defense against an obscenity charge; in most cases, people are entitled to First Amendment and privacy protection for actions involving consenting adults in the privacy of their home.

Consideration The main reason for a person to enter a contract; a legal obligation assumed or a legal right surrendered.

Contemporary community standards As part of the first prong of the three-prong Miller test, these are the standards that a local community holds with regard to its tolerance of obscenity.

Contributory infringement The tort of contributing to the direct infringement of another by a party who knew of the direct infringement and could have taken simple measures to prevent further damages.

Convention on Insider Trading Cooperative agreement developed by the Council of Europe allowing agencies in one country to request assistance from other countries' agencies about securities-related enforcement issues.

Cookies Small text files that a server can store on the user's machine to track the user's Web-viewing habits.

Copyright Infringement Act This act prohibits the reproduction or distribution of protected works even if there is no profit derived from such efforts.

Council of Europe Convention on Cybercrime International agreement that promotes cooperation and standardization among nations regarding crimes committed in cyberspace.

Cracking This is the name given to intentional, malicious hacking, and is a crime.

Cyberporn Obscene material transmitted over the Internet or through e-mail.

Cyberspace Term originally used by William Gibson in his 1982 novel Neuromancer. The totality of all the world's computers, represented as a visual virtual three dimensional domain in which a user may move and act with the consequences in the real world.

D

Data Encryption Standard (DES) The U.S. government's data security standard for cryptography.

Data manipulation This is the crime of changing or erasing existing information.

Decryption The second step in cryptography, whereby ciphertext is decoded and thus translated back into readable text.

Defamation Oral or written false statements that wrongfully harm a person's reputation.

Delegation of duties The transfer of a contracting party's obligations to a third person.

Denial of service attacks Overloading a server to keep others from gaining access.

Derivative work A work based on one or more preexisting copyrighted works.

Digital certificates (DCs) Digital ID or passport, so that only those who can authenticate their identities may access the secure data.

Digital Millennium Copyright Act (DMCA) Makes it a crime to traffic in devices that are primarily designed for the purpose of circumventing technological protection measures (antipiracy devices). It targets those who willfully, and for purposes of commercial advantage or private financial gain, engage in circumvention.

Direct infringement Action that violates a copyright owner's exclusive statutory rights with or without a specific intent to infringe.

Direct Public Offering (DPO) See Internet securities offerings.

Doctrine of Equivalents Judicial construct that permits a finding of patent infringement—even when the claims are not literally infringed, where the challenged invention is so similar to the patented invention.

Domain name A business address on the Internet.

Domain name system (DNS) a text name matched to the Internet protocol that makes it easier for users to access sites.

Due process clause A constitutional requirement for personal jurisdiction based on two criteria: the non-resident e-business has sufficient minimum contacts in the forum state where the case is being tried, and jurisdiction in that court will not offend traditional notions of fair play and justice.

E

EC Communication on Computer-Related Crime States the importance of a coordinated policy effort to combat computer-related crime and has resulted in the formation of a number of initiatives.

E-commerce General term that encompasses any commercial transaction involving the exchange of goods, services, or information over the Internet.

Economic Espionage Act (EEA) Federal act providing for civil and criminal penalties for the misuse, misappropriation, or theft of information protected as a trade secret.

EDI Trading Partner Agreement Agreement written on paper and signed by trading partners to validate electronic transactions with the intent of making them as enforceable as paper contracts.

Electronic Communications Privacy Act (ECPA) of 1986 This act outlaws the unauthorized interception, access, and disclosure of wire or electronic communications.

Electronic Data Interchange (EDI) Transfer of electronic data between companies.

Electronic Funds Transfer Act (EFTA) This act outlaws the giving of inaccurate or insufficient information in an EFT, or transactions involving counterfeit, stolen, or fictitious debit instruments.

Electronic roadshow A management presentation to qualified investors following delivery of prospectuses. Content is limited to materials in the prospectus but it is (usually) good publicity.

Encryption The first step in cryptography, whereby plaintex data is encoded by use of a mathematical algorithm to create cipher text stored in a different format known as ciphertext.

E-Sign Act giving electronic signatures and contracts the same validity as traditional handwritten and copy signatures.

Espionage Involves the act of spying or monitoring, and includes the theft or misappropriation of secrets by computer or other means.

EU Forum on Cybercrime Online forum available to various interest groups to discuss cybercrime regarding data retention, security, and other issues.

European Union (EU) Intergovernmental organization of European states that strives for freedom, justice, and economic progress for its members as well as an economic and monetary union.

European Union's Directive on Privacy Protection Requires the fifteen member states of the EU to adopt legislation that seeks to protect the fundamental rights and freedoms of an individual, particularly the right to privacy as it relates to the processing and collection of personal data.

Exclusive statutory rights Rights of copyright owner to reproduce and distribute works, prepare derivative works based on the work, and perform and publicly display the copyright work.

Extortion This involves a ransom demand (blackmail) in exchange for something of value, usually directed at a business or government.

Extranet Access of the company intranet by a limited number of customers, suppliers, or business partners.

F

Fair Credit Reporting Act (FCRA) of 1970 Ensures that the credit reports furnished by consumer credit reporting agencies are accurate, impartial, and respect privacy.

Fair use doctrine Statutory limitation on exclusive rights of a copyright owner, allowing for free speech, use of material and is subject to guidelines.

Fifth Amendment Amendment to the U.S. Constitution providing that no person shall be compelled in any criminal case to be a witness against himself.

File transfer protocol (FTP) System that moves files from one computer to another.

Firewall A computer between the networked computers and the network, that secures this system from unauthorized access.

First sale doctrine Limits the copyright owner's exclusive right to distribute publicly a copy of the work when the copyright material was lawfully acquired by another.

Fixed creative work One that is sufficiently permanent to permit it to be perceived, reproduced, or otherwise communicated for a period of more than transitory duration.

Forum the court or locale wherein causes are judicially tried.

Forum non conveniens Doctrine that a court will decline to hear a dispute when it can be better or more conveniently heard in a foreign forum.

Forum selection clause A provision in a contract that designates the forum where disputes will be settled.

Fourth Amendment Amendment to the U.S. Constitution providing that the people have the right to be protected against unreasonable searches and seizures conducted by the government.

Fraud An illegal act involving deception of identity or purposes, in order to gain something of value.

G

Gambling Discussed here in a criminal context involving participation either in a jurisdiction where it is illegal; or with an underage person; or one who has diminished capacity.

Good Samaritan defense A defense against the Communications Decency Act protecting an online service provider or user of an interactive computer service from civil liability as a publisher or speaker of any information provided by another content provider.

Government interest test A test that directs a court if it must determine the laws that apply to a dispute, to apply the laws of the country that has the most interest in determining the countries that have a legitimate interest in the outcome of the dispute.

H

Hacking The process of gaining access to computers or sites where no access was intended—this may be a crime in some jurisdictions.

Harassment The communication of taunts, profanity, or demands.

Hardware weapons These include radio frequency or electromagnetic pulse weapons that knock out a system's electronic equipment.

Hate crimes Discussed here in a criminal context as the communication of threatening, hate-filled messages attacking people based on their traits of national origin, race, color, sex, religion, ethnicity, or sexual orientation.

Holography An authentification technology involving the use of images incorporated into a photopolymer process.

Hypertext markup language (HTML) Platform-independent language that makes the Internet accessible on any type of computer.

I

Identity theft Occurs when personal identifiable information (PII) such as an account number or Social Security number is stolen and used to obtain financial services.

In personam jurisdiction The power of a court or other government agency to determine the rights of natural and judicial persons appearing before it.

In rem jurisdiction The power of a court or other government agency to determine the ownership rights of persons with respect to particular property located within the territory of the forum.

Independent derivation The same secret was developed independently by another party and acts as a defense to trade secret misappropriation claims.

Inevitable disclosure Presumes a trade secret will be inevitably exposed, and so the business may sue to prevent the employee from going to work for a competitor.

Infringement Act of using part of all of the claims that make up another's invention—without their knowledge or assent, and without compensation.

Inherently distinctive trademarks Suggestive, arbitrary, and fanciful trademarks.

Interactive Web site A Web site that actively seeks business from customers.

Intergovernmental organization (IGO) An organization set up by two or more countries to carry out activities of common interest to them.

International Organization of Securities Commissions (IOSCO) International organization that promotes information exchange between member nations and promotes standards to maintain just and efficient markets.

Internet Corporation for Assigned Names and Numbers (ICANN) A nonprofit public-benefit nongovernment organization with an international board of directors. Its mission is to create new top-level domain names. Selected by the U.S. government to manage the domain name system.

Internet protocol (IP) a unique computer address that consists of four series of three numbers allowing communication between computers.

Internet securities offerings (ISOs) This refers to any equity offering done via the Internet.

Internet service provider (ISP) Company that connects users to the Internet.

Internet Tax Freedom Act (ITFA) of 1998 Act that prevents federal, state, and local governments from imposing any new taxes on the Internet for three years. Some existing taxes were grandfathered in.

Intranet Use of the Internet within an organization.

Intrastate offering exemption Helps finance local business by waiving requirements on securities offerings.

Intrusion upon Seclusion One of four types of common law torts for the invasion of privacy; defined as intentionally intruding on the solitude or private affairs of another person.

J

Java Universal computer language run by a program built into browsers.

Jurisdiction The authority of a court or other government agency to hear and resolve a dispute.

K

Key logger system/Magic Lantern Keystroke recording software that may, among other features, read users' passwords as they enter them and has the ability to secretly record all computer activity.

L

Liability insurance policy Insurance policy purchased to provide insurance protection against liability to third persons for covered losses.

Libel Written or published defamation.

Literary, artistic, political, and socially redeemable value The third prong in the three-prong Miller test; material that has redeemable or socially acceptable value is not considered obscene.

Logic bombs Programs that remain essentially undetected until they detonate, set off by the onset of an event or a date.

Long-arm statue State law that allows courts to claim personal jurisdiction over a nonresident defendant whose principal business is outside the state.

M

Mail and wire fraud statutes These statutes make it a crime to use the mails, interstate, or foreign communications to fraudulently obtain money or property.

Malware Any harmful software or hardware, including viruses, worms, logic bombs, and so on.

Market maintenance theory When vendors' state activities are significantly associated with the taxpayers' ability to establish and maintain market in the state for its sales.

Mass-market license A provision in a license that allows consumer purchasers to return software if the terms of the license are unacceptable.

Minimum contacts Legal measure of a nonresident defendant's purposeful use of the benefits of a state's economic market.

Mirror image rule Rule that a contractual offer will not be accepted, and a contract will not be formed, unless the terms of the acceptance adhere exactly to the terms of the offer.

Misappropriation Acquisition of a trade secret by one who knows or has reason to know the trade secret was acquired by improper means or wrongful disclosure of a trade secret to another without consent.

Misappropriation of a Person's Name or Likeness Causing Injury to Reputation One of four types of common law torts for the invasion of privacy; defined as use of the name or picture of a living person for commercial purposes without that person's consent.

Money laundering The act of flowing funds through various financial institutions so

that the original source of the funds cannot be determined.

Most significant relationship test Test that directs a court, if it must determine the laws that apply to a dispute, to apply the laws of the country that has the most real and significant "contacts" with the parties and their transactions.

Motion to dismiss A legal maneuver to have a case dismissed because of lack of personal jurisdiction. The case may be then tried before the appropriate court that has jurisdiction.

N

Nationality principle of jurisdiction Doctrine that a court has criminal jurisdiction if the victim is a national of the forum state.

Netiquette An unofficial attempt at self-regulation by businesses engaged in cyberspace; a kind of ethical code that requires courtesy online and respect for bandwidth capacity.

Network Solutions, Inc. (NSI) A private company that, until recently, held a monopoly on second-level domain name registration.

Nexus Physical connection with the taxing state where the customer is located.

Nexus attribution For state tax purposes can occur by having agents who are sales representatives, employees, or individual contractors working on sales on behalf of a company in another state.

Ninth Amendment Amendment to the U.S. Constitution providing that the rights not enumerated or expressed in the Constitution are retained by the people.

No-Action Letter SEC method of responding to company's inquiry and that it will not take enforcement action on the matter.

No Electronic Theft Act (NET Act) of 1997 Amending the Copyright Infringement Act establishing that there is infringement, even without economic gain to the user, when the copyrighted material has a total retail value of more than $2,500.

Noncompetition agreement Prohibits parties from competing with the business for a period of time and within a certain geographic area.

Nondisclosure agreement Prohibits parties from disclosing confidential information.

Nongovernmental organization (NGO) An international organization whose members are persons other than countries.

Nonsolicitation agreement Prohibits parties from attempting to lure away employees who may have knowledge or access to trade secrets.

North American Free Trade Agreement (NAFTA) International agreement that regulates and promotes trade between the United States, Canada, and Mexico.

North American Securities Administrators Association (NASAA) Organization of state securities agencies that oversee securities regulation and investor protection.

O

Off-Shore offerings Offers for sale of securities that are made outside of the U.S. to non-U.S. persons.

Organization for Economic Cooperation and Development (OECD) International organization promoting international cooperation in the areas of economic and social governance.

P

Packet Bundle of data traveling on the Internet.

Paris Convention Treaty that defines intellectual property rights and allows a signatory nation to submit a patent application in another nation.

Parol evidence rule Rule that parties to a complete and final written contract cannot introduce evidence in court of prior or contemporaneous agreements to to contradict the meaning of the contract.

Passive personality principle of jurisdiction Jurisdiction based on the nationality or national character of the person injured by the offense.

Passive Web site A Web site that transmits information only and doesn't solicit business.

Patent Government grant of an exclusive property right for a novel useful invention for up to twenty years.

Patent Act The main regulatory law, setting forth the conditions and requirements for securing a patent, as well as outlining causes of actions and remedies for patent infringement

Patent Cooperation Treaty (PCT) Treaty among 100 countries that provides for a centralized registration program. This acts to simplify and reduce costs associated with obtaining international patent protection, as well as facilitate public access to technical information relating to inventions.

Patently offensive The second prong of the three-prong Miller test; material that is obviously offensive in its exhibition of sexual activity.

Physical presence test Elements that can determine for tax purposes whether a company is subject to state tax jurisdiction.

Pornography Any depictions of persons that are obscene.

Pretexting Results when personal financial information such as a bank account number is fraudulently or falsely

obtained by contacting the victim's bank or financial institution under the pretext of being or impersonating the actual customer.

Principal Register Publication of the PTO that lists registered trademarks.

Prior art Evidence that part or all of the invention was already in public circulation or use up to a year prior to filing for a patent. It renders the invention unpatentable.

Privacy Act of 1994 Establishes requirements that must be satisfied before government agencies or departments can disclose records and documents in its possession that contain personal information about individuals.

Privacy Protection Act (PPA) of 1980 Applies to law enforcement agencies and allows Fourth Amendment protection against unreasonable searches and seizures of work product materials used to disseminate some form of public communication, or affecting interstate commerce.

Private key Encryption of messages using a key known only to the communicating parties.

Private placement offering exemptions Simplifies capital raising process for businesses. Offerings are available only to certain investors.

Processor serial number An authentification technology wherein a unique number is embedded in every central processing unit of computers.

Prospectus SEC-mandated statement delivered to each investor, and it details financial conditions and business the company is engaged in.

Protection of Children from Sexual Predators Act of 1998 This act expands liability to those who attempt to use the Internet for purposes of child pornog-

raphy; commercial pornographers are specifically targeted.

Protective principle Doctrine that a court has criminal jurisdiction if the victim is a national of the forum state.

Prurient interest The first prong of the three-prong Miller test; prurient material has a "tendency to excite lustful thoughts."

Public Disclosure of Private Facts Causing Injury to Reputation One of four types of common law torts for the invasion of privacy; defined as revealing highly personal facts or information about another, leading to damage to their reputation.

Public key infrastructure (PKI) Encryption and associated technologies in the issuance and management of digital credentials to provide multi-layered security.

Public performance Performance of a copyrighted work in a place open to the public or where a substantial number of people outside a normal circle of family and social acquaintances are gathered.

Publicly Placing Another in a False Light One of four types of common law torts for the invasion of privacy; defined as falsely connecting a person to an immoral, illegal, or embarrassing situation resulting in damage to their reputation.

Q

Qualified privilege Defense to a suit in defamation usually granted to statements made in good faith to others who have a legitimate interest in the information contained in the statement. Examples include employer references and recommendations.

R

Reg A offerings Streamlined procedures of registered offerings for small business.

Reg D offerings Investment offerings exempt from federal registered offerings requirements for small business including rules 504, 505, and 506.

Reg S Exemption Securities offers and sales that occur *outside* the United States do not fall within Section 5 of the act, and thus they are exempted from Securities Act registration requirements.

Requirements of a Contract Five requirements must be satisfied in order for a contract to be entered into properly: mutual assent, consideration, capacity, legality, and form.

Restatement Second of the Law of Contract Summary of common law contract rules.

Reverse engineering A lawful activity under trade secret law that acts as a defense to trade secret misappropriation claims.

Rule 504 A Reg D exemption allowing businesses to raise up to $1 million in 12 months.

Rule 505 A Reg D exemption allowing businesses to raise up to $5 million in 12 months.

Rule 506 A Reg D exemption allowing businesses to raise up to $5 million without time restrictions.

S

Sales tax Tax paid by consumer and collected by the merchant at point of purchase on tangible personal property.

Scienter (Latin for "knowledge") Refers to the requirement that defendant knew an act would result in a wrong.

Secondary meaning A characteristic that permits a general word to acquire distinctiveness that makes it registrable as a trademark.

Section 230 of the Communications Decency Act Provides that an Internet service provider would not be treated as publishers or distributors, and would thus not be held liable for defamation posted by the service provider.

Secure Electronic Transactions (SETs) Industry standards of cryptography governing commercial transactions.

Securities Act of 1933 Law passed by Congress in response to the stock market crash of 1929 that set regulations for trading in securities.

Securities Act of 1934 (Exchange Act) Regulates accounting and recordkeeping of domestic companies registered with the SEC.

Securities and Exchange Commission (SEC) Government agency that regulates securities trading and administers U.S. securities laws.

Security An interest in a business; this can take many forms, but should include an investment in a common enterprise with a reasonable expectation of profit derived from the work of others.

Security tokens Also called digipasses; another means to authenticate users.

Service mark Words, phrases, logos, or other graphic symbols that promote services and are also granted legal protection.

Shrink-wrap license Terms of a contractual license that are not available for review until after the product is opened and the shrink-wrap packaging is removed.

Signature A person's name, initials, or symbol, used by that person to authenticate a writing.

Slander Oral defamation.

Slander per se Categories of oral defamation in which damages to reputation are presumed to exist.

Small Corporate Offering Registration An exemption (called seed capital exemption) usually involved with companies in the early stages of product or service development.

Smart cards Similar to tokens, they have the added feature of portability; users may access data even at offsite computers.

Software piracy This is the act of duplicating and distributing copyright-protected materials without authorization from or payment to the copyright owner.

Sonny Bono Copyright Term Extension Act A 1998 act that extended the term of copyright protection from 70 years to 90 years after the author's death.

Spamming Sending unsolicited bulk e-mail advertisements.

Spoofing Setting up sites to look like other sites.

Stalking The act of shadowing or menacing a person.

Statutory damages Payment entitled by plaintiff in lieu of actual damages.

Steganography Process of hiding messages *within* text or graphics.

Subpoena Affirmative order by a court to produce specific records or to appear as a witness in court.

Supplemental Register Publication of the PTO that provides constructive notice of ownership to companies in all fifty states that you are using a trademark not yet registrable.

Suspicious Activity Reports (SARs) Per USA Patriot Act requirements, mutual funds and other financial services companies must file Suspicious Activity Reports (SARs) with the Treasury Department whenever the conduct of clients or even potential clients indicates possible money laundering activities. Suspicious activities are loosely defined in the act.

T

Telephone Consumer Protection Act (TCPA) of 1991 Extends privacy rights to several aspects of telephone marketing activities.

Territoriality principle Doctrine that a court has criminal jurisdiction if an offense is committed within the forum state.

Terrorism The act of undermining or disabling systems, and may involve extortion or blackmail.

Third party beneficiary A person who benefits from a contract without being a party to it.

Trade dress A colored design or shape associated with a product.

Trade-Related Aspects of Intellectual Property Rights (TRIPS) International agreement that reaffirms earlier intellectual property treaties such as the Paris Convention; it requires signatories to afford equal intellectual property protection to nationals of signatory nations.

Trade secret Any secret information owned or developed by a business that gives it a competitive advantage.

Trademark A word, name, or device or any combination thereof, including a sound, used by any person to identify and distinguish goods from those of others.

Trespass The act of breaking into computers or networks either without authorization or in excess of one's authorization.

Trojan horses Programs that have the ability to hide and replicate themselves.

U

UCITA Set of commercial rules designed to regulate transactions of computer information and licensing of software.

UETA Set of commercial rules supporting the validity of electronic contracts as a viable medium for forming agreements.

UNCISG Key international framework addressing international goods commerce that is similar to the uniform commercial code.

UNCITRAL Internationally agreed on model standard for developing a coherent global regulatory system in electronic commerce.

Unconscionable contract Agreement that is so outrageously unfair to one party that a court refuses to enforce it in a court of law.

Uniform Commercial Code (UCC) Uniform set of state laws adopted by all fifty states governing contracts involving goods, leases, and other transactions.

Uniform Foreign Money-Judgments Recognition Act Provides that a foreign judgment is generally recognizable except, for example, in cases of fraud, violations of public policy, or conflict with another judgment.

Uniform resource locator (URL) The name of a file stored on a Web server.

Uniform Trade Secrets Act Virtually identical to the Economic Espionage Act in its definition of a trade secret, this model law has been adopted by approximately forty-one states.

United States Patent & Trademark Office (USPTO) Government-sponsored registrar and rule-making agency for patents.

Universality principle Doctrine that a court has criminal jurisdiction if the forum state has the defendant in custody.

USA Patriot Act Statute passed just after the 9/11 terrorist action providing for enhanced law enforcement and surveillance capabilities.

Use tax Tax paid by consumer on tangible goods purchased out of state for use within a taxing state.

V

Vesting of rights doctrine Doctrine that direct a court, if it must determine the laws that apply to a dispute, to apply the laws of the country where the parties' rights become legally effective.

Vicarious infringement Occurs when a company receives direct financial benefit from the infringement by another and had the right and ability to supervise the infringement activity.

Video Privacy Protection Act (VPPA) of 1988 Expands the CCPA to prohibit the use and disclosure of personal information about the videocassettes and related products an individual rents or buys.

Virus writing The act of writing programs that have the ability to attach themselves to other programs in other computers and thereby replicate themselves.

W

Warranty Assurance in a contract that a product will satisfy certain standards.

Wassenaar Arrangement International agreement that prohibits the export of dual-use goods such as encryption, which are capable of military and civilian applications, to terrorist nations including Iran, Iraq, Libya, Syria, and Sudan.

World Intellectual Property Organization (WIPO) International organization dedicated to the promotion of human creativity and the protection of intellectual property.

Worm A program designed to infiltrate systems and destroy data.

Index